To Monica
from
David E. Brown

BRINGING BACK THE GAME

ARIZONA WILDLIFE MANAGEMENT | 1912–1962

3/24/2013

Other titles in the Arizona Wildlife History Series,
available from the Arizona Game and Fish Department:

Man and Wildlife in Arizona: The American Exploration Period, 1824–1865

Arizona Wildlife: The Territorial Years, 1863–1912

BRINGING BACK THE GAME

ARIZONA WILDLIFE MANAGEMENT | 1912–1962

By David E. Brown

With contributions from Bud Bassett, Bill Broyles, Neil Carmony, Jim Heffelfinger, Larry Riley, Harley Shaw, Bill Silvey, Roger Sorensen, and Paul Webb

Arizona Game and Fish Department
Phoenix, Arizona

Published by
Arizona Game and Fish Department
5000 W. Carefree Highway, Phoenix, Arizona 85086
www.azgfd.gov

Text: David E. Brown, with contributions from Bud Bassett, Bill Broyles, Neil Carmony, Jim Heffelfinger, Larry Riley, Harley Shaw, Bill Silvey, Roger Sorensen, and Paul Webb

Book Editor: Julie Hammonds

Designer: Kurt Krause, Krause Creative
Cover Design: Kurt Krause, Krause Creative, and Susan Geer, Spiral Creative Services
Front and back cover photos are from the Arizona Game and Fish Department's files.

ISBN: 978-0-9175-6-3560

Library of Congress Control Number: 2012943461

FIRST EDITION DECEMBER 2012
21 20 19 18 17 16 15 14 13 12 1 2 3 4 5 6 7 8 9 10

Printed in the United States of America

CONTENTS

IV. Wildlife Management's Happy Times, 1954–62

V. Arizona in 1962: Wildlife and Landscape Summary

Appendices

Not printed: A supplemental document containing laws related to wildlife in Arizona from statehood in 1912 through 1962 is available on the Arizona Game and Fish Department's website, www.azgfd.gov. Search for the "Bringing Back the Game: State Fish and Game Laws, 1912–1962" document.

FOREWORD

When I was studying wildlife science at Arizona State University in the mid-1970s, I took a summer job at the Arizona Game and Fish Department, and met Dave Brown. My job was banding doves along the Gila River near Arlington. Dave was the small game supervisor at the time, and so he was my first supervisor at the department.

More than a decade earlier, a department reorganization had turned the traditional Arizona game ranger into a newly minted "wildlife manager." Dave had come aboard in the second group of these college-educated officer-biologists. They were expected to take on a variety of duties in their districts, from game surveys and creel counts to law enforcement patrols. These wildlife managers essentially represented the department at the local level throughout Arizona—and still do.

Dave was a law enforcement officer and a wildlife scientist from the early 1960s to the late 1980s, the decades just following the ones covered in this book. After moving into the Game Branch, he worked with wildlife managers and regional office supervisors all over the state. So, he came to personally know many of the characters mentioned in these pages, and heard stories of many more. Who could have guessed that the Dave Brown we knew back then, the officer and biologist who rose to lead the Game Branch, would also become a talented historian?

When it came time to write this book, nobody was better positioned to document how the state's wildlife management evolved during the first 50 years after statehood than Dave. He didn't just dig through old records after the fact: He drew on memories of the people involved, and recalled their efforts to implement many of the policies and programs put in place during those first five decades of state history.

The young state of Arizona's wildlife management programs were not developed in isolation. During the formative years described in this book, Arizona's programs influenced, and were influenced by, people and events of national significance. One of the people most profoundly affected by Arizona was Aldo Leopold, later known as "the father of modern wildlife management." Leopold spent time in Arizona at the start of his career, but those days on the Apache National Forest and his later visits to address the state's fledgling game protective associations made an indelible impression. Arizona strongly influenced Leopold's thinking and writings—including *A Sand County Almanac.*

As Arizona was developing its wildlife management programs, our nation's wildlife conservation system was evolving to become what we call the North American Model of Wildlife Conservation—widely regarded as the most successful system of wildlife conservation on the globe. The North American Model states that wildlife is held in the public trust and managed to provide opportunities for all . . . hunters, anglers, wildlife watchers, and wildlife enthusiasts. This book documents 50 years of continuous effort to manage wildlife by those tenets.

The model also says hunters and anglers fund wildlife conservation: They have done so in Arizona since 1913, when the first hunting and fishing licenses were sold for 50 cents apiece. According to the North American Model, we rely on science as the basis for wildlife policy. Well, the University of Arizona first teamed up with the US Biological Survey and other government entities to study wildlife in the 1920s. Our knowledge of species, habitats, populations, and trends has continued to grow by leaps and bounds, as have our partnerships with other agencies, state and federal.

When I became director of the Arizona Game and Fish Department in 2008, I said the department's success in fulfilling its public trust mission on behalf of Arizonans depended on four pillars:

1. The quality of our workforce;
2. The quality of our knowledge and the competency of our processes;
3. The public's passion for wildlife; and
4. The Commission system.

Read this book, and you will see the establishment and evolution of those four pillars over time. You'll read about real people: Game rangers and wildlife biologists who applied what they knew to the realities they saw on the ground, learned from past mistakes, and tried new methods for enhancing game and fish populations.

Published to honor the state's centennial year, this is the third in a series of books about Arizona's wildlife management history. The series now covers almost 150 years, spanning from 1824 to 1962, a remarkable achievement. In absorbing detail, *Bringing Back the Game* recounts stories of Arizona's wildlife management during the crucial half-century after statehood. Although the details may be unique to Arizona, the book's themes will resonate with readers throughout the West. *Bringing Back the Game* makes a major contribution to what we know about wildlife management history; plus, it's a really good read. A humble, heartfelt thanks goes to Dave Brown for providing us this personal view of wildlife management history in Arizona.

–Larry Voyles, Director
Arizona Game and Fish Department
Phoenix, Arizona
June 19, 2012

PREFACE

Bringing Back the Game is the third in a series of books on the history of Arizona's wildlife. Published by the Arizona Game and Fish Department, the agency responsible for managing the state's wildlife, the series began with Goode P. Davis's *Man and Wildlife in Arizona: The American Exploration Period, 1824–1865.* Edited by Neil Carmony and me, Davis's book uses firsthand accounts from Anglo-American explorers to describe wildlife and landscape conditions in Arizona when the state was relatively pristine and inhabited mostly by Native Americans and a few Mexicans. An important historical reference, *Man and Wildlife in Arizona* has been reprinted three times since it first appeared in 1982.

Following the same format, and using quotes from publications and newspapers of the day, *Arizona Wildlife: The Territorial Years, 1863–1912* begins where Davis's book leaves off. It documents early attempts to inventory the territory's flora and fauna and describes the horrific decline in many Arizona species and habitats during the frontier period. Yet, attendant with this destruction were the seeds of recovery and the beginnings of attitudes and regulations that would allow for the great wildlife diversity we enjoy today.

In this third volume, we relate how the state's sportsmen helped resurrect game species from their nadir to a condition bordering on superabundance. We see the US Forest Service preserve the most important big game habitats and watch as a fledgling Arizona Game and Fish Department advances from a small, politically driven bureaucracy involved primarily in information and education to a professional agency engaged in law enforcement, wildlife management, wildlife research, and land and lake management.

Many people contributed their knowledge and writing talents to this book. Neil Carmony, Joseph Monfeli, and Melanie Tluczek shared their expertise pertaining to the history of the Arizona Game Protective Association and its relationship with the Arizona Game and Fish Department. Other contributors lending their extensive knowledge to the project were Harley G. Shaw (mountain lions and landscape history), Bill Broyles (federal refuge history), and Jim Heffelfinger (deer and elk management). Ray Kohls (law enforcement), Larry Riley (fisheries), and Paul M. Webb (game transplants) provided essential information on various programs important to the department's history.

An essential resource in the preparation of *Bringing Back the Game* were the minutes of the Arizona Game and Fish Commission, which reflect the progression of game management actions from 1929 through 1962 and the history of the agency this commission administrated. Information about wildlife laws and regulations before and after the watershed year of 1929 was gleaned from the Ross-Blakley Law Library at the Sandra Day O'Connor College of Law at Arizona State University, and from the helpful staff at Arizona State Library, Archives and Public Records.

If you ever wondered how Arizona's system of game and fish management came about, this is the book for you!

–David E. Brown

ACKNOWLEDGMENTS

Bringing Back the Game is the product of a large cadre of cooperators. Primary to its initiation were Arizona Game and Fish Department Director **Larry Voyles**, Assistant Director **Gary Hovatter**, and Publications Unit Supervisor **Bob Miles**. Their sense of history prompted this cooperative effort between the department and Arizona State Library, Archives and Public Records.

This book can be said to have begun in 1961, when I first started working for the department. Occupying several regional and game management positions, I was fortunate to have such supervisors as **Don Smith, Ted Knipe, Paul M. Webb, John Russo**, and **Tom Barnes,** who instilled in me a sense of the department's history while sharing their own experiences and perspectives on the time before my arrival.

As I began working on this book, other like-minded department employees, both active and retired, who greatly contributed to its historical value include **George Andrejko, Tom Britt, John Carr, Richard Glinski, Ray Kohls, Jeff McMichael, Larry Riley**, and **Harley Shaw**. Kohls was especially helpful, and his excellent detective work was instrumental in running down key biographical information on many historical figures. Other current and former department employees who materially enhanced this book, either by providing interviews or facilitating access to historical records, include **Randy Babb, Cecelia Carpenter, Cindy David, Steve Gallizioli, Amber Munig, Mike Rabe, Heidi Rayment, Melissa Swain, Wendell Swank,** and **Brian Wakeling.**

Kimberly Kreuzer at the Arizona Wildlife Federation was helpful in reviewing information about the Arizona Game Protective Association. The cooperation of **Melanie Sturgeon** of the Arizona State Library, Archives and Public Records was equally important, and the enthusiastic assistance of her staff assured the project's success. Especially helpful were Arizona History Librarian **Ellen Greene,** Archivist and Photograph Collections Curator **Wendi Goen**, Archivist **Libby Coyner,** and Map Reference Librarian **Julie Hoff**. Also essential was the wholehearted cooperation of **Linda Reib, Nancy Sawyer,** and State Capitol Archivist **Marian Shepherd** of the Arizona Memory Project.

The state's historical societies provided outstanding support. I am especially grateful to **Alexandria Caster, Jill McCleary,** and **Katherine Reeve,** of the Arizona Historical Society and Arizona History Museum in Tucson; **Ashley Smith, Rebekah Tabah,** and **Peter Welsh,** also of the Arizona Historical Society; **Cyndi Eisenberger** of the Gila Bend Historical Society and Museum; **Carol Brooks** of the Arizona Historical Society/Yuma; and the Casa Grande Valley Historical Society and Museum.

Other important material was gleaned from the Cline Library at Northern Arizona University and the Arizona State University Libraries, Department of Archives and Special Collections. Particular thanks go to **Erika B. Castaño** and **Charles Wommack,** University of Arizona Libraries Special Collections; **Jess Vogelsang,** Cline Library; and **Chris Kollen,** University of Arizona Libraries Map Collection.

Several people and institutions donated the use of photographs or supplied other needed information. Individual contributors included **Mara E. Weisenberger,** US Fish and

Wildlife Service; **Mark Heitlinger,** Santa Rita Experimental Range; **John Alcock,** Arizona State University; **Jeff Kida,** *Arizona Highways;* **Donna Colletta,** *Arizona Republic;* **Mike Pallesen,** Arizona Agricultural Statistics Service; **Steve Manheimer,** Arizona Agricultural Statistics Service, USDA-NASS Arizona Field Office; **Mikele Painter** and **Richa Wilson,** US Forest Service, Region 4; **Catherine Baudoin,** Maxwell Museum of Anthropology; and **Margaret Hangan,** the Kaibab National Forest's heritage and tribal relations program manager.

Other people who contributed in meaningful ways to the preparation of this book include **Warner** and **Wendy Glenn, Kelly Glenn Kimbro, Lois Goodwin, David Rasmussen, Leon Shumway, Eldon "Buck" Buckner, Rhonda Appel,** and **Charles J.** and **Georgia Biller.**

Critical to the book's realization was **Julie Hammonds,** whose sage advice throughout the editing process made each chapter relevant and readable. Without her, and the diligent efforts of the contributors—**Bud Bassett, Bill Broyles, Neil Carmony, Jim Heffelfinger, Larry Riley, Harley Shaw, Bill Silvey, Roger Sorensen,** and **Paul Webb**—the completion of this project would have been impossible.

–David E. Brown

INTRODUCTION

Much has been made of the "North American Model," a collective phrase used to describe how America's sportsmen initiated a game and fish conservation movement that evolved into the most successful wildlife management program in the world. Financed and led by ammunition and firearm companies, this movement composed largely of sportsmen succeeded in passing legislation that outlawed subsistence hunting and the commercial use of game and fish, established closed seasons and bag limits, funded wildlife restoration measures through the sale of licenses and firearms, supported predator-control programs, created game refuges, and most important, provided the political and legal framework that enabled state and federal game and fish agencies to restore and manage the country's wildlife resources (Mahoney 2007; Watt 2007).

The nation having been profligate in destroying its natural resources during its first century, it was nothing short of miraculous that in the late 1800s, a reformed citizenry embraced a nationwide game protection movement led by sportsmen bent on preserving their principal form of recreation. What is perhaps even more remarkable is that the leaders of this movement were persuasive enough to change a whole society's "take what you can" attitude to one that restricted consumption of game and fish species for use at a later time. It takes a great leap of faith to forgo present opportunity for future dividends. The societies of few other nations have been so inclined, and it was only through the Protestant ethic of delayed gratification that the "model" succeeded in restoring America's wildlife—Arizona's included.

That such a movement was even possible was due to a remarkable few individuals who pointed the way—men like George Bird Grinnell, John Muir, William T. Hornaday, and John Burnham, later the founder of the American Game Protective Association. But as important as these founders were, their contributions pale into mere supporting roles when compared to the contributions of President Theodore Roosevelt and his colleagues in the Boone and Crockett Club. It was T. R.'s executive actions that boldly created the national forests and a system of national monuments and game preserves—land withdrawals in which Arizona played a prominent role. For this reason alone, Arizona had a leg up when compared to most other states.

But the "Baby State" was woefully behind its predecessors when it came to a sportsmen-led political effort. Although a wildlife conservation movement in the Southwest was well underway at the time of statehood, this was based in New Mexico, not Arizona. A serendipitous juxtaposition of naturalists and personalities allowed New Mexico to take the lead in both biological enquiry[1] and public participation in wildlife protection. Thanks to an early cadre of conservation giants such as Aldo Leopold, Miles Buford, J. Stokley Ligon, and Elliot Barker, the "Land of Enchantment" possessed a sportsmen's political apparatus that was 10 to 20 years ahead of Arizona's. It was Aldo Leopold's Forest Service–sponsored travels from New Mexico to Arizona, and his preaching to Arizona's

[1] Authoritative works on New Mexico's mammals (V. Bailey 1931), birds (F. M. Bailey 1928), game animals and habitats (Ligon 1927), and fishes (Koster 1957) all preceded comparative contributions by Arizona authorities by 20 years or more.

game and gun clubs, that solidified the will to follow New Mexico's lead and form an Arizona Game Protective Association. Only then were Arizona conservation leaders able to organize the state's sportsmen into a political force capable of promulgating game and fish legislation and seeing to it that wildlife laws were enforced.

It is today difficult to realize the important role of sportsmen (women were not yet much involved in outdoor legislation) in the nation's and states' conservation movements. One has to remember that hunting and fishing were then not only the most important forms of outdoor recreation, these activities were the only outdoor recreation. There was no golf, no recreational boating, no ATVs, and few organized sporting events. Hiking, camping, and horseback riding were viewed as daily necessities rather than recreation or exercise. Birdwatching and other non-consumptive wildlife enjoyment were practiced by only a relative few, and most of these people were specimen and egg collectors, more to be regulated against than heeded as conservationists.

When the state initiated efforts to manage its own wildlife in 1913, the Arizona State Legislature authorized the hiring of a State Game Warden at a salary of $1,200 per annum and gave him $1,000 in traveling expenses. Another $1,500 was allocated to hire an office deputy and to field deputy wardens; an additional special appropriation of $500 was to promulgate, publish, and distribute the game laws. Operational revenues were to be derived from a hunting and fishing license that cost 50 cents. Much of the money went to trapping and translocating quail and purchasing Chinese ring-necked pheasants and other exotic game birds. There was no open season on elk, mountain sheep, antelope, Montezuma quail, or blue grouse. Fish management was focused on importing exotic game fish, building hatcheries, and providing large catches. No one cared about native fishes, if indeed their presence was even recognized.

When State Game Warden George M. Willard filed his first report to the governor in 1914, his biggest concern was the lawlessness and carelessness of Arizona hunters. Willard bemoaned the loss of wild turkeys, deer, antelope, and mountain sheep from much of Arizona, and feared the state's 15,000 to 20,000 hunters, now that they had automobiles, would soon exterminate what few big game animals remained on the national forests. The only abundant game was the ubiquitous Gambel's quail. Even doves were deemed in need of added protection because they were being hunted during the breeding season. So deplorable was the game situation in his opinion that he intended to recommend a closed season on all the varieties of big game the following year. To compensate the Game and Fish Fund for the loss in revenue attendant with these closed seasons, he recommended increasing the cost of a license to one dollar.

Arizona's game and fish faced many stumbling blocks in the first 50 years of statehood, natural as well as man-made. In their attempts to improve game and fish conditions, there was much infighting between sportsmen, the governor, the legislature, and certain coalitions, both within the general public and within the government. Gradually, through various laws and the courts, the respective jurisdictions required to manage wildlife were worked out. In general, the states would retain management authority over big and small game, while the US Fish and Wildlife Service would have legal authority over most bird species and migratory bird refuges. Authority over predators and rodents was more divided, the state relinquishing its management responsibilities over these species in exchange for federal assistance. With the exception of migratory birds and nuisance wildlife, federal agencies would manage habitat and not wildlife. The Biological Survey, dominant in the field of predatory and noxious animal control, eventually would be much reduced, and the management of wildlife on federal lands would become a policy of cooperation rather than a series of programs based on responsibility.

The Arizona Game and Fish Department blossomed from a staff of 11 persons in 1916 to a department employing 180 men and women in 1962—an increase of more than 1500% and more than three times the percent change in the state's exploding population. Along the way, sportsmen convinced a general electorate that a commission-led agency at the state level was the best way to manage Arizona's game and fish species.

In Arizona's first 50 years of statehood, most wildlife species, especially the game animals, responded beyond the restoration hopes of even the most enthusiastic conservationist. A half-century of progress verified the optimism of Arizona's pioneer sportsmen, despite the increase in the state's human population to 1.3 million by 1960. The loss of wildlife species was effectively staunched, with relatively few species lost after 1912. Most of those were considered pests or unwanted predators (e.g., the river otter, black-tailed prairie dog, gray wolf, and grizzly bear). By 1962, most people considered the disappearance of these animals acceptable if not inevitable alongside the absence of the Colorado River salmon and other big river fishes.

In 1962, deer numbers and harvests were at all-time highs, as were the numbers of pronghorn, doves, and quail. Elk were increasing in numbers and expanding their range until this species would rival deer as Arizona's premier game animal. Mountain sheep were again being hunted and certain small game species once totally protected—Mearns' quail, blue grouse, and band-tailed pigeons—were again being proposed as huntable game. Fishing had become a popular sport that rapidly expanded with the construction of a half-dozen major reservoirs and more to come. The Arizona Game Protective Association, now the Arizona Wildlife Federation, was then at its apogee of members and influence—it was commonly stated that no commissioner could be appointed without the AGPA's endorsement. Arizona was enjoying what hunters and fishermen knew as the "happy years." How this came about makes a story well worth reading.

–David E. Brown

SECTION I

GAME AS A SPORTSMAN'S RESPONSIBILITY

1912–28

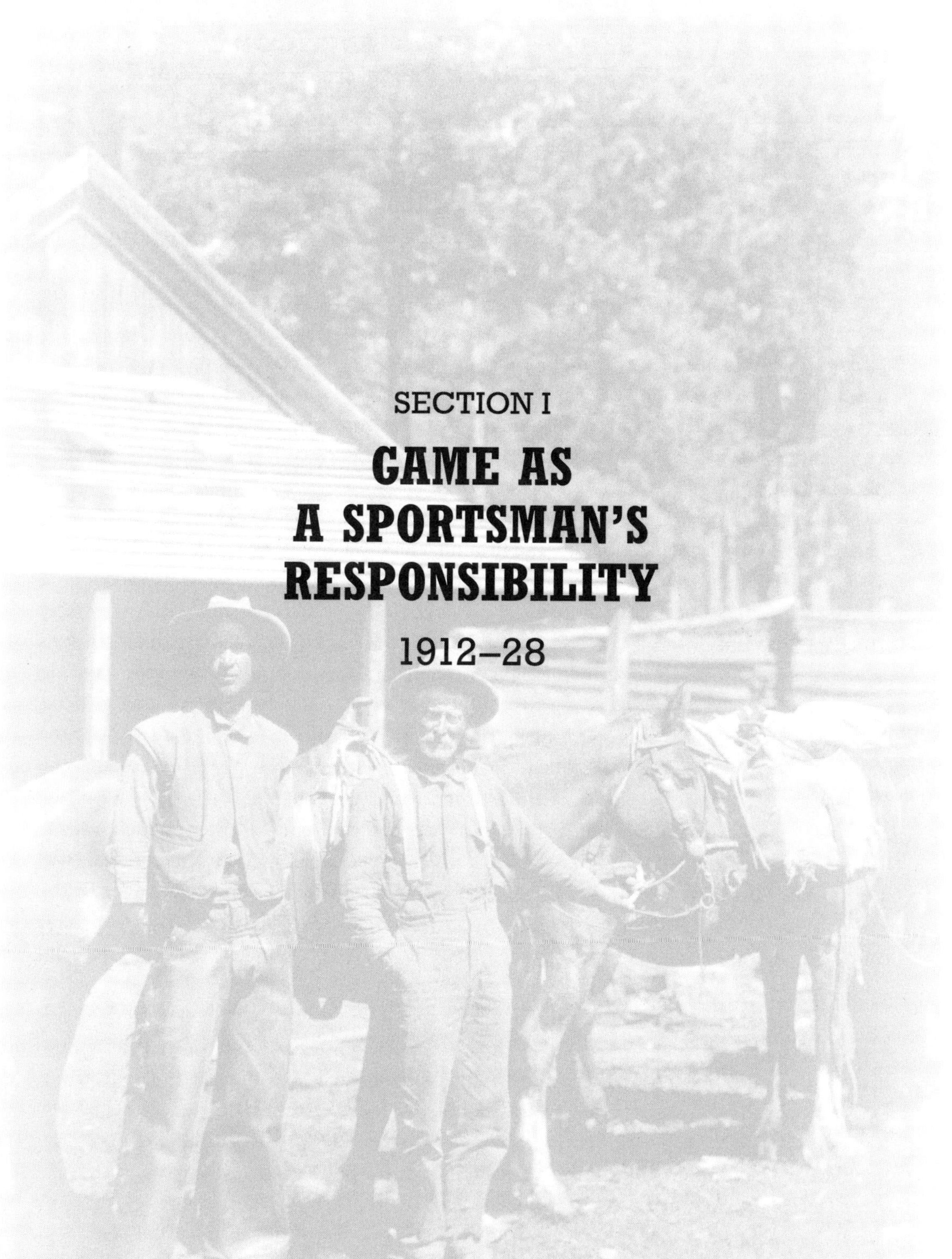

A NEW STATE, A NEW GAME CODE, AND A NEW GAME AND FISH DEPARTMENT

David E. Brown and Neil B. Carmony

Arizona, the last conterminous state to enter the Union and known as "The Baby State," was a latecomer to America's wildlife conservation movement. Wildlife preservation in the United States was still a largely eastern-state concept that had originated with such national figures as President Theodore Roosevelt, George Bird Grinnell, William T. Hornaday, and other members of the Boone and Crockett Club.

Hence, Arizonans generally were unaware or uncaring when it came to the conservation movement's major schism regarding hunting. Some, such as Hornaday, saw hunters as the cause for the lack of game and wanted hunting banned or greatly curtailed. Others, originally few in number, considered hunters and their desire to foster their sport as a solution to the lack of game.

One organization taking the latter approach was the American Game Protective Association, which was formed in 1911 and headquartered in New York under the leadership of John B. Burnham. Organized and financed by small-arms manufacturers such as the Winchester Repeating Arms company, the association realized that the paucity of game attendant with the closing of the American frontier was bad for business. Unless attitudes changed, and protective measures were taken, there simply would be no need for sporting arms or ammunition. Burnham and his followers therefore set about organizing affiliate associations peopled by hunters wanting more game to hunt. By 1912, this fervor and a support for more protective game laws had seeped westward into New Mexico and the office of the US Forest Service's Southwestern District in Albuquerque.

Unlike New Mexico, which had strong game protection association proponents at the time of statehood, Arizona's wildlife lacked a strong voice speaking on its behalf. This was unfortunate, as the state's landscapes and game populations had suffered greatly with the advent of settlement. Although it would be an overstatement to describe Arizona's habitat conditions in 1912 as ruined, the wildlife situation was dire. The need to curtail hunting was not yet widely recognized, and a frontier mentality prevailed.

Mining, farming, homesteading, and livestock-raising were what interested Arizonans and their government. Even though commercial hunters were no longer providing game for restaurants and markets, subsistence hunting by homesteaders and other rural residents remained commonplace. Sportsmen's clubs were mostly shooting clubs, and few hunters could be described as conservationists (Brown 2009). Moreover, the increasing popularity of the automobile and a mounting fervor for new roads now threatened to take armed citizens into every corner of the backcountry.

Photos taken at the time attest to the concern that much of the state had been devastated by grazing and drought (Brown 1900; Turner et al. 2003). Writing about wildlife conditions in the Southwest at the time of statehood, J. Stokley Ligon (1927) described the habitat situation as "poverty stricken." He believed game numbers in Arizona and New Mexico were then so low, and the habitat so compromised, that game populations

Scouting for game in an automobile, ca. 1914. Early Arizonans feared that automobile travel would allow hunters to get into the same "backcountry" reached by horseback, but in far less time and with no need to feed and water the horse. (Arizona Historical Society Museum at Papago Park)

could only recover if diseases were controlled, predators killed, forest fires suppressed, and range abuses curtailed. He and his colleague Aldo Leopold, a Forest Service recreation specialist in Albuquerque, preached that not only were such corrective measures necessary to bring back the game, legislation must be enacted to establish game refuges, reduce bag limits, close seasons, and fund the propagation of game and fish stock. As for the habitat, he reasoned that the greatest enemy of wildlife was not the man with the gun but domestic animals grazing yearlong on the open range—a situation aggravated by an overabundance of cattle brought on by an improved market during World War I. Only on the national forests were there any expectations for recovery of wildlife populations, and only then if corrective measures were taken and enforced by legal action.

There were good reasons to hope for improved conditions. Mule deer and turkeys were still present in reasonable numbers in central Arizona's national forests, as were white-tailed deer in the southeastern quarter of the state. Wildlife was faring well in such areas as on Fort Huachuca and the Apache Indian reservations. Not only had forest rangers and guards been successful in maintaining some semblance of ecological health on the national forests, there were still remote areas in the western deserts and north of the Grand Canyon where the distance to water had thwarted efforts to transform the land. Also, a new class of citizen conservationists was developing: salesmen, newspaper editors, and small businessmen, who, together with miners and certain ranchers, desired better hunting and fishing opportunities. They were willing to devote the time needed to bring about the change in public attitudes that would produce these results.

The problem was how to instill a belief, in those who considered hunting as a source of recreation, that more hunt regulations and game protection would bring future benefits. The principal enemy of wildlife, it was often stated, was not the sport hunter but the "game hog" who killed game with no thought to tomorrow. Sharing this concern were many of the large ranchers, who wanted better regulations and fewer people on their rangelands. It was therefore natural that sportsmen and cattlemen would become allies in the cause of wildlife protection, in contrast to the small landholder or "nester," who not only subsisted on game, but whose more closely tended stock denied wildlife essential feed and cover.

The State of Arizona's First Game Code

A first step on the way to game recovery was thought to be better laws and more regulations—a task that belonged to the new state legislators, as a referendum in 1912 had negated the territorial game code in anticipation that the new Arizona State Legislature would create a state game code. It was anticipated that a new code would include regulations to better protect game animals and create a department of fish and game to carry out the legislature's directives regarding the destruction of predators and the establishment of game refuges or preserves (Brown 2009).

Creating a new state game code was not easy. Four bills were introduced in the Arizona State Senate before one was passed on to the House of Representatives to be sent to a committee, where it was amended on May 16, 1912. Then, when the amended bill was returned for reconciliation, a motion was made to postpone the bill indefinitely. That motion failing, the bill was again amended, shortening the September 1–January 1 deer season to October 1–December 1.

The senate version of a reconciled HB127 was then sent to Gov. George W. P. Hunt, who vetoed it on the basis that there was no fee for a general hunting and fishing license and therefore no means of financing a game and fish fund other than through legislative appropriations and the payment of fines. Recommending a one-dollar fee for a general hunting and fishing license, the governor also objected to the lack of protection for roadrunners and great horned owls. Also coming in for the governor's displeasure was the bill's lack of a closed season on bobwhite, grouse, and pheasants, as he considered bobwhite "rare" and grouse and pheasants beneficial.

Jokes regarding the lack of protection for "hoot owls" aside, and there were many, Hunt's veto left the state without a game and fish code. The regular session of the legislature having ended, the legislators were forced to draft a new version of the game code in a special session—one that would be acceptable to the governor. Senator George H. Chase of Greenlee County, the primary author of the original bill, therefore drafted a revised version (SB42), which passed the senate 18–0. Then, after a week's debate in the house and an amendment to change the deer season to October 1 to December 15, the bill was approved by a vote of 28–4. The governor signed the bill on June 15, 1912 and the measure became Chapter 82 of the Session Laws of the First Special Session. Arizona had now been without a game code for four months, the referendum of 1912 having repealed the territorial game code.

Disagreement over the validity of SB42 was now invoked against Chapter 82, as it was claimed the 1912 referendum was not a valid election. The governor also now objected to the legislation that he had just signed, on the basis that the new game code did not outlaw the selling of game and did not properly compensate the office of a State Game Warden.

Hunt also wanted the 50-cent resident hunting and fishing license available to all settlers regardless of their time spent in Arizona.

Hence, as of March 1913, more than a year after statehood, Arizona's game and fish code was still in a state of flux. Objections to the contrary, the Arizona Supreme Court ruled that the referendum was indeed valid, that SB42 had been properly authorized, and that a 50-cent license would now be required for Arizona residents to take game and fish (Brown 2009).

The First State Game Wardens

Although Arizona's admission to statehood had been greeted with great optimism, and a game code had finally been crafted, many hunters and fishermen continued to be unsatisfied with both the game situation and the legislation regulating the taking of fish and game. The native elk had disappeared and the recent stocking of elk from Yellowstone had been accomplished mostly through donations and the work of volunteers. Bighorn and pronghorn numbers had so declined that these species were no longer legally hunted, and deer numbers were considered in need of improvement almost everywhere. Turkeys in southern Arizona had virtually disappeared, and most serious wildlife observers considered the laws protecting game animals inadequate. Bears and javelina had no protection, and the only game species deemed in adequate supply were doves and Gambel's quail. Even so, the regulations on these species were bemoaned as too liberal—both doves and quail being managed more as agricultural pests than as game birds. Although such "rare" birds as grouse, fool's quail, and bobwhite were protected along with roadrunners and songbirds, regulations pertaining to waterfowl, shorebirds, and band-tailed pigeons had yet to be adequately formulated.

Frank Rogers, Arizona's first State Game Warden. Rogers was in office for only a few months before dying of pneumonia in a Los Angeles hospital. (Arizona State Library, Archives and Public Records, History and Archives Division, #01-2938)

In accordance with the provisions of the referendum and new game code, Governor Hunt retired the three fish and game commissioners he had appointed on May 10, 1912 (A. W. Snyder, Charles M. Bledsoe, and T. T. Cull) and appointed Frank W. Rogers State Game Warden on January 28, 1913. (For a complete list of State Game Wardens and Game and Fish Department Directors, see Appendix A.) Rogers, a Verde Valley aviculturist and farmer, was a strong believer in game preservation through wildlife education. Having only the most meager of funds to launch a game and fish department, Rogers was provided a special $50 travel appropriation to "supervise" the unloading of elk destined to arrive in February—a task he shared with his first deputy warden, N. C. Bledsoe of Winslow.

George M. Willard (right) with Gov. George Hunt (center), May 20, 1918. Appointed by Hunt, Willard was Arizona's first State Game Warden of consequence. (Arizona State Library, Archives and Public Records, History and Archives Division, #01-3186)

Realizing it would take time to collect enough funds to field Rogers's goal of having a deputy warden in each county, Hunt recommended that Forest Service rangers be deputized as state wardens—a practice that had been in use in both Arizona and New Mexico territories.

Rogers's efforts to fund and field a game and fish department were cut short by his death from bronchial pneumonia in a Los Angeles hospital after only a few months in office. In his stead, Governor Hunt appointed George MacDonald Willard to be State Game Warden on June 11, 1913. Willard would serve intermittently in this capacity until 1926 and was thus, for all practical purposes, Arizona's first State Game Warden, an office equivalent to today's director of the Arizona Game and Fish Department.

On first examination, Willard appears to have been an odd choice for State Game Warden. Born in Sacramento, California, Willard had come to Arizona's Verde Valley in 1885, where his family took up mining and prospecting. Young Willard worked at the mine in Jerome. Possessing only three or four years of formal education, Willard was self-schooled before he homesteaded a ranch near Cottonwood about 1890. Neither a hunter nor a fisherman, he pursued hobbies such as landscape photography and writing poetry. He was nonetheless much interested in wildlife, especially birds. Never one to take a position contrary to his benefactor, Governor Hunt, Willard comes across as a loyal civil servant and a firm believer in wildlife education (Willard Profile 1916).

In a published report to Governor Hunt (nearly all of his departmental correspondence was to the governor), Willard (1914) noted that when the Arizona Game and Fish

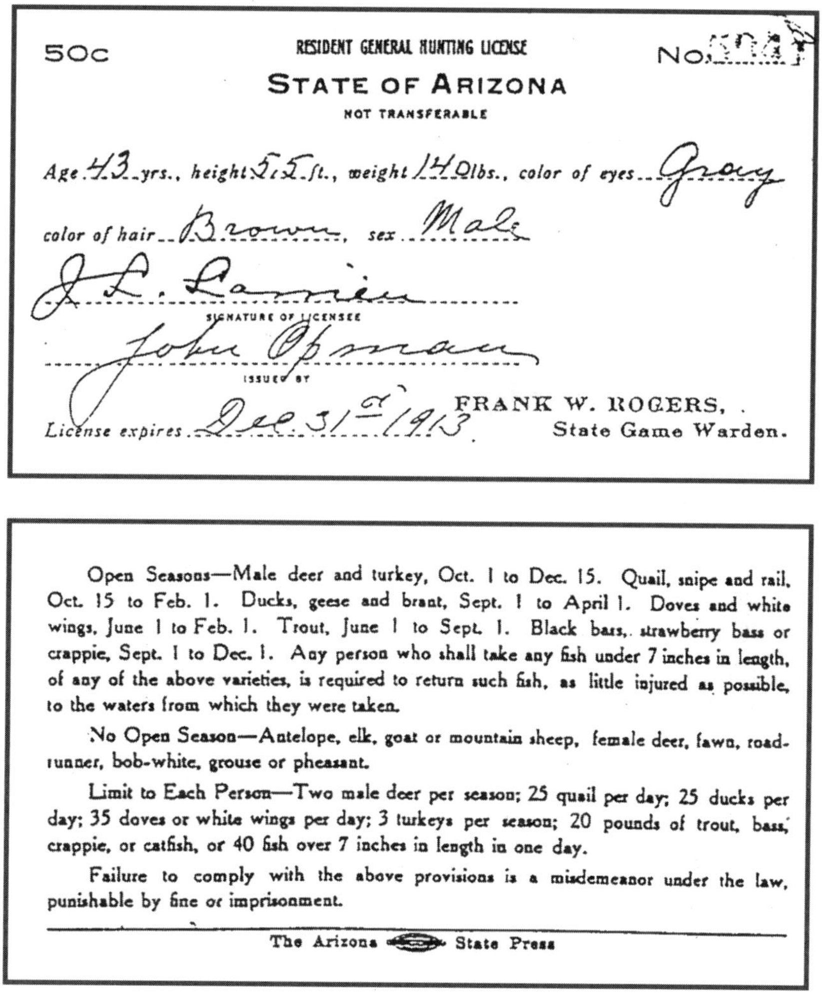

50c RESIDENT GENERAL HUNTING LICENSE No.

STATE OF ARIZONA

NOT TRANSFERABLE

Age 43 yrs., height 5'5 ft., weight 140 lbs., color of eyes Gray

color of hair Brown, sex Male

SIGNATURE OF LICENSEE

ISSUED BY

License expires Dec 31st 1913 FRANK W. ROGERS, State Game Warden.

Open Seasons—Male deer and turkey, Oct. 1 to Dec. 15. Quail, snipe and rail, Oct. 15 to Feb. 1. Ducks, geese and brant, Sept. 1 to April 1. Doves and white wings, June 1 to Feb. 1. Trout, June 1 to Sept. 1. Black bass, strawberry bass or crappie, Sept. 1 to Dec. 1. Any person who shall take any fish under 7 inches in length, of any of the above varieties, is required to return such fish, as little injured as possible, to the waters from which they were taken.

No Open Season—Antelope, elk, goat or mountain sheep, female deer, fawn, road-runner, bob-white, grouse or pheasant.

Limit to Each Person—Two male deer per season; 25 quail per day; 25 ducks per day; 35 doves or white wings per day; 3 turkeys per season; 20 pounds of trout, bass, crappie, or catfish, or 40 fish over 7 inches in length in one day.

Failure to comply with the above provisions is a misdemeanor under the law, punishable by fine or imprisonment.

The Arizona State Press

Early hunting license showing seasons and regulations on back of license. (AGFD files)

Department was created in 1913, the legislature appropriated only $1,200 per annum for a warden and an office deputy, with another $1,000 allocated for traveling expenses. An initial operating fund of $500 was also appropriated, with the provision that half of the fines collected for game and fish violations would go to the local justice of the peace. The justice of the peace would then turn half of the money over to the state treasurer to be deposited in the Game and Fish Fund, the remaining half of the fine going to the arresting person or deputy, if not a salaried peace officer. If these funds, fines, and license revenues proved inadequate to meet the salary of the State Game Warden, the remainder would be supplemented by an appropriation from the state treasury. Once in office, the State Game Warden was also given the ability to issue wildlife collecting and holding permits, including permits for the raising of game species for propagation purposes.

The State Game Warden was authorized to appoint or relieve deputy wardens in every county of the state, each to enforce the law in their respective county and to receive

State Game Warden George Willard (kneeling at center) and his staff of deputies in 1916. Dwight Pettis (wearing hat) was Willard's right-hand man. The woman is May Belle Craig, office manager and Arizona's first female deputy warden. (Arizona State Library, Archives and Public Records, History and Archives Division)

half of the monies from any fines imposed. Each deputy was required to put up a $500 bond, after which he would be authorized a three-dollar travel allowance per diem, to be paid semi-monthly on receipt of a voucher. The deputies were subject to being fined themselves if found not to uphold and prosecute the game laws.

Clearly, the office of the State Game Warden was designed to be an instrument of the governor acting within the laws passed by the legislature. As such, his principal mission was to sell licenses and enforce the game code—the latter a nearly impossible job without the help of Forest Service rangers and guards. Other duties included the procurement of fish and game birds for stocking, and the posting and patrolling of any game refuges or preserves that might be authorized by the legislature or Forest Service. There was simply no money for surveys or inventories. Education was to be stressed over enforcement.

Most of the special fund of $500 appropriated by the legislature for special projects in 1914 had been spent on importing game birds, which were turned over to private farmers to raise. Willard, a bird fancier himself, recommended the state purchase a game farm in the near future. The elk release south of Winslow had cost virtually nothing, the Benevolent and Protective Order of Elks having borne the $2,125 cost of the transplant. Willard noted that an April 1914 survey had shown at least 53 elk present in the Chevelon country—a hopeful sign and one that encouraged him to second Governor Hunt's suggestion for an elk transplant to the Graham Mountains near Safford.

Activities in 1914 included the trapping and translocation of 25- to 30-dozen quail in response to complaints from farmers—a situation Willard commented on as unusual, in that this was one game species that was plentiful. "Turtle doves" and white-winged doves, while common, were deemed priority species in need of protection, as four months of the open season occurred during the birds' breeding season. Willard's chief concern was the misuse of firearms by careless and lawless hunters in the Salt River Valley who were endangering landowners and themselves. Due to the lack of funds and manpower, Willard admitted doing little to enforce the recently promulgated game laws.

Willard bemoaned the loss of wild turkeys, deer, antelope, and mountain sheep from much of Arizona and feared the 20,000 or so licensed hunters would soon exterminate the remaining big game due to the advent of the automobile. He compared Arizona unfavorably to Eastern states such as New York where game populations had recovered, and thought the situation so dire in Arizona that he recommended a closed season in 1915 on all varieties of big game species. To make up for the loss in revenue caused by the resulting drop in license sales, he suggested the fee for a general license be increased from 50 cents to one dollar, noting that the only big game remaining in Arizona was on the national forests and Indian reservations. Small game hunting would thus provide the necessary revenue.

On a more positive note, Willard had begun hiring deputy wardens as early as 1913, beginning with two ex–Arizona Rangers, Reuben L. McNeill[1] and O. F. Hicks (the Arizona Rangers were disbanded in 1909). The work of the new hires proved progressively satisfactory, and Willard was able to state that more convictions of game-law violators had occurred in the last six months than in the previous history of the state. Their action had in turn resulted in an increase in assistance from the civil authorities and more cooperation from the state's 100 or so Forest Service rangers. The Indian Service also had been helpful in ordering the Indians to obey the state game laws and confine their activities to the reservations. By the end of 1914, Willard had accrued a balance of $7,000 in the Game and Fish Fund, with about $1,500 of this amount intended for a train-car load of elk for a release in the Graham Mountains (Willard 1914).

A "protectionist" in his wildlife management approach, Willard appears to have been a conscientious and capable administrator. By the spring of 1916, the Arizona Game and Fish Department contained 11 employees—Willard, nine deputies, and his "chief deputy," May Belle Craig. Another particularly valuable deputy was Dwight Ernest Pettis of Phoenix, who served as warden at large for the entire state and taught an early version of an environmental education course. Much of Pettis's time was spent visiting schools and putting on programs in which he distributed free copies of the game laws, gave out posters, and distributed copies of Farmers' Bulletin No. 692, a US Biological Survey publication emphasizing the value of most birds to agriculture and other human endeavors. Hicks and Craig did similar work in southeastern Arizona and in Phoenix. The highlight of Willard's first term as State Game Warden was Arizona's First Annual Bird Day, held May 4, 1916 (Shaw 2009).

Willard, like much of the public, expressed dissatisfaction with the state's game and fish code. No refuges had been created and the federal government was taking on the

[1]During Reuben L. McNeill's long tenure as a department employee, his name appears in various spellings, including Rube Neal, Rube Neill, and Ruben Neill, as well as Reuben L. McNeill.

Advertisement of a popular Phoenix sporting goods store touting the shooting of white-winged doves for sport prior to September 1. (Phoenix Evening Gazette, *1925; Arizona State Library, Archives and Public Records, History and Archives Division)*

task of conducting predator control, most of which was being done to benefit livestock interests rather than for game protection. The Game and Fish Fund was woefully small, and Arizona had neither a fish hatchery nor a bird farm. Any proposed changes in a species' protected status or desire to create a game refuge had to wait until the legislature met—which was every other year. Worse yet, the legislature was too often reluctant to make any changes in the game code objected to by economic interests, including sporting goods stores as well as farmers. To otherwise modify the state game code required an initiative bypassing the legislature, and that required a strong game protective association similar to the one organized in New Mexico in 1913.

It was largely for this reason that an evangelizing Aldo Leopold arrived in Springerville, Arizona, from Albuquerque in 1916 to help organize local game protective associations. After forming a local association in his first home station with the Forest Service in Springerville, he went on to promote associations in Flagstaff, Payson, and Tucson. One of the first projects undertaken by Leopold and his converts was to update Arizona's game laws, viewed as woefully inadequate by nearly everyone, including Governor Hunt. Arizona's game protective association members viewed the existing code as not only out of date, but too liberal.[2] Unable to interest legislators in revising the code, the sportsmen

[2]Nonhunters often don't realize how conservative many sport hunters once were regarding the length of hunting seasons and the size of bag limits.

circulated initiative petitions and managed to place a measure amending Arizona's game laws on the November 1916 general election ballot.

The 1916 initiative passed narrowly, shortening Arizona's deer season from two and one-half months to one month and reducing the bag limit from two bucks per year to one; the turkey season was likewise shortened and the annual bag limit decreased from three birds to two. The quail season was shortened and the bag limit reduced from 25 birds per day to 20. Most important, the price of a resident hunting and fishing license was increased from 50 cents to $1.25, thereby increasing the money available to the State Game Warden and allowing him to send more deputy wardens into the field to enforce the laws. Only an estimated 18,000 licenses had been sold in 1916, which, at 50 cents apiece, provided only $8,690.50 over and above the legislature's appropriation for the salaries of Willard and his chief deputy. Now, for the first time, money would be available to hire a sufficient number of deputies, build a fish hatchery, propagate game birds, and possibly even trap predators.

New Governor, New State Game Warden

The gubernatorial election of 1916 had been hotly contested. When the ballots were counted, Hunt appeared to have lost the governor's race to the Republican candidate, Tom Campbell, by less than 50 votes. Recounts took much longer then than now; Campbell assumed office, leaving Hunt to wage his re-election campaign in the courts. As was his prerogative, Campbell replaced State Game Warden Willard with Joseph V. Prochaska—a former postmaster from Miami, Arizona—who was described in *Who's Who in Arizona in 1913* as a "natural born hustler and booster." Prochaska's initial term was short-lived, as a recount returned Hunt and Willard to office in 1918.

The patronage system in place during Hunt's terms in office is illustrated by the appointment of Mary Platten, Arizona's first female deputy warden to serve in the field. She wrote Hunt in January 1918, requesting a position as deputy warden and declaring she was willing to serve without pay. Her request was forwarded to Willard, who hired her at full pay for a full-time job (*Coconino Sun*, February 1, 1918). However, in November 1918, Hunt decided not to stand for re-election and Campbell was elected governor. When he took office in 1919 and again named Prochaska State Game Warden, Platten (along with all the other appointed deputy wardens) was out of a job.

Prochaska was more of a "hands-on" State Game Warden than Willard. He prosecuted many of the court cases personally and supervised the distribution of fish from the US Fish Commission. The legislature by now having established a number of large game preserves on national forests, Prochaska (1921) took it upon himself to post most of the refuges, covering 24,647 miles by car, 1,847 miles by rail, and 200 miles on horseback during his administration.

Prochaska was also a hunter who, unlike his predecessor, took an active role when it came to predator control. Predator-control expenditures for the state in 1919 were $14,252.17 versus $12,129.80 spent by the federal government. Pleased with the result, Prochaska recommended that 25% of the Game and Fish Fund be used in the future for the destruction of predators, provided that a like amount from the general fund was

Joseph V. Prochaska, who served as State Game Warden during the years when Republican Tom Campbell was governor (1917, 1921, 1922). (Arizona State Library, Archives and Public Records, History and Archives Division, #97-7807)

used for the payment of bounties approved by a committee composed of the Livestock Sanitary Board, the chairman of the Sheep Commission, and the State Game Warden (Prochaska 1921).

Noting that he really only assumed charge of the department in January 1919, Prochaska was proud of his accomplishments. He organized a field force of new deputies and embarked on a series of lectures before civic bodies, parent teacher associations, councils of Boy Scouts, and students, all the time striving to increase wildlife awareness and open lines of communication between the department and the public through bird study programs and newspaper publicity. In this respect his administration continued Willard's wildlife education program, and he actively encouraged his deputies to engage in field trips and projects with scout troops.

Also, like Willard, Prochaska was a strong advocate of game and fish propagation as well as conservation, spending most of the department budget between 1919 and 1921, distributing fish from federal hatcheries and initiating construction of a state fish hatchery on the South Fork of the Little Colorado River. A favorite project was his "Museum of Arizona Animals, Birds and Fish," an exhibit of mounted specimens housed in the basement of the Capitol. The specimens had been collected by Prochaska and his deputies and prepared by Deputy Warden Charles Evans. Also on the department's inventory were 241 mounted specimens out on loan to various schools and used for nature study.

Prochaska was also heavily involved with the state's elk herd. He reported spending seven weeks in the field surveying elk numbers, running down complaints of poaching by residents of Flagstaff and Winslow, and assessing crop damage complaints from "nesters." Although he "disproved" that any serious damage was being done by elk, he thought the elk herd, which he then estimated to number about 500, needed to be broken up. The legislature had approved a depredation complaint in 1915, and any more such actions could easily strip the Game and Fish Fund of its meager resources.

He therefore scheduled a 50-bull permit elk hunt to take place in October 1919, but canceled the season due to heavy rains in August and September. The wet weather did little to discourage participation by deer and turkey hunters, and their activities in October were thought to scatter the elk, which had formerly all wintered around Chevelon Butte. As a result of the hunters' actions, Prochaska determined that the elk were now dispersed as far west as Anderson Mesa, as far east as Pinedale, and as far south as Tonto

Basin. He therefore recommended that an elk hunt of 50–100 permits be held every other year. Such was not to be, the legislature deeming otherwise.

In a report covering the years 1917, 1919, 1920, and 1921, Prochaska (1922) emphasized that his tenure had been one of preserving and protecting the state's game and fish resources, stocking game birds and fish, encouraging bird study in schools, and training boy scouts in nature study. He complained of the difficulty of getting convictions during "these times" (there was an economic depression and livestock glut after World War I) and recommended the abolishment of the entire game code passed in 1916. He nonetheless believed Arizona had more game and fish in 1922 than in 1916—a statement that was probably true, as the years 1916–1922 had generally been above average in rainfall.

His accounting shows a significant increase in revenue after 1916 and a relatively stable income for the department during his tenure:

- 1917: (Prochaska) $18,361.94
- 1918: (Willard) $18,201.85
- 1919: (Prochaska) $22,096.83
- 1920: (Prochaska) $23,447.39
- 1921: (Prochaska) $22,457.31
- 1922: (est.) $25,000.00

When Hunt returned from serving as ambassador to Siam (now Thailand) and was again re-elected in November 1922, Prochaska resigned, along with most of his deputies. On January 6, 1923, Deputy Warden E. C. Castleberry assumed the office of State Game Warden. Castleberry was replaced on February 15 by C. E. Golding, who in turn was replaced when Hunt reappointed Willard on June 14, 1923. Neither Castleberry nor Golding was in office long enough to preside over any significant changes in policy. A protectionist by nature, Willard was not about to ask the legislature to liberalize any hunting season, much less recommend an elk hunt as Prochaska had done; at least, not without Hunt's blessings.

State Game Warden Willard Returns

Willard was the only Arizona delegate to the December 1923 Antelope Conference in Washington, D. C., where he had little to report or recommend (Nelson 1925). Nor was Willard apparently involved in the federal government's transplant of pronghorn fawns to Hermit Basin within Grand Canyon National Park the succeeding year—the only location then available where pronghorn could be released and protected. That the National Park was the only public land area in Arizona closed to both hunting and grazing apparently offset any concerns as to the small area of suitable habitat.

Money was tight. In 1924, the legislature appropriated, in addition to Willard's salary, $1,800 for office deputy Luella M. Roberts, $1,200 each for two field deputies, and $3,200 for part-time deputies. Willard's small field force was bolstered by a cadre of voluntary deputies who were paid only one-half of the fines collected from the violators brought to court. That there was no shortage of volunteers is attested to by the number of deputy wardens enrolled from each county: 8 in Apache, 29 in Cochise, 21 in Coconino, 5 in Greenlee, 16 in Gila, 4 in Graham, 48 in Maricopa, 3 in Mohave, 6 in Navajo, 8 in Pima, 12 in Pinal, 6 in Santa Cruz, 25 in Yavapai, and 20 in Yuma.

Although some of these deputies never arrested anyone, the mere fact these warden volunteers were out there had to have been somewhat of a deterrent to the "game hogs" they were supposed to bring to justice. Such a volunteer force came with a number of problems, not the least of which was the difficulty of a deputy warden or local sheriff obtaining sufficient evidence to make an arrest or issue a citation that would hold up in court.

Willard was not a voluminous writer, but his relatively few communiqués (nearly all to Governor Hunt) were well written. His response to the Forest Service's increasing concern regarding the billowing deer herd on the Kaibab was first expressed in a letter to Hunt on October 19, 1923.[3] In a later letter to Hunt on June 12, 1925, Willard uncharacteristically boasted that hatchery superintendent John E. Griffith had successfully delivered a half-million rainbow trout fingerlings from the new South Fork hatchery near Springerville to 14 different locations—some including such distant streams as Weber, Horton, and Oak creeks. This feat was made possible only by the extraordinary efforts of deputies Pettis, Greer, and McAlister, who, to deliver the last of the fish to Oak Creek Canyon, went 24½ hours without stopping.[4] Willard proudly reported that the losses were less than 1/10 of one percent, compared to previous losses of 10%–50% when the US Bureau of Fisheries brought trout to Arizona from federal hatcheries.

Willard considered such a huge contribution from the state's hatchery on the South Fork of the Little Colorado River to be a cause for celebration, even though the hatchery was begun in 1922 under the guidance of State Game Warden Prochaska. That Arizona finally had its own hatchery up and running was regarded as a momentous event and represented a longtime goal of the state's sportsmen. Nor was Willard stingy in his kudos, also crediting the invaluable assistance of volunteers with the Flagstaff and Verde Valley game protective associations, a $200 contribution from the Yavapai County Board of Supervisors, the United Verde Copper Company, Flagstaff Lumber Company, and a one-ton Ford truck provided by the Arizona Highway Department. Upon delivery, the young fish were either packed in to remote springs and streams by Forest Service rangers or placed in specially constructed "rearing ponds" to be watched over by deputies and volunteers until the monsoon, and danger of flooding, had passed.

Most of Willard's remaining years in office were spent responding to the various disputes arising out of the Kaibab deer controversy. In an undated letter to Hunt, Willard expressed his "legal opinion" regarding the "Status of the Kaibab Deer Herd." In it, he blamed the controversy on a jurisdictional dispute between the two federal agencies

---

[3] Willard's realization that the enforcement of the game laws depended on the public, prompted this slogan on the department's stationary: "You will help protect the game if you will report violations to this office."

[4] Deputies as of June 12, 1925, included D. E. Pettis (Phoenix), Jack W. Fuss (Flagstaff), R. W. Betts (Williams), W. W. Freeman (Snowflake), R. E. McAlister (Jerome), C. C. Cleveland (Espiro), W. O. Hamblin (Eager), and C. N. Greer (El Capitan). Luella M. Roberts was office deputy. The slogan on the stationary that year was "If you are a friend of Arizona you are not a friend of the Colorado Pact ..."

(Forest Service and National Park Service) and the failure of the federal government to recognize that the deer belonged to the state of Arizona as a matter of property rights. By seemingly overlooking and ignoring the state's sole right to issue deer hunting licenses—and, before 1912, the territory's claim to the deer on and off Grand Cañon Game Preserve—the two federal agencies had provoked a regrettable legal crisis.

Willard died of complications from pneumonia on April 5, 1926 at age 64, leaving his wife to publish two albums of his poetry posthumously. Although no expert on wildlife or game matters, Willard was a well-intentioned and loyal appointee and a conscientious protector of wildlife.

Pettis Becomes State Game Warden

Willard's longtime deputy and loyal colleague, Dwight Pettis, was appointed State Game Warden on April 15, 1926. A sincere wildlife conservationist, Pettis was also the first State Game Warden to have a formal education, as he had gone to normal school and taught for 2½ years before coming to Arizona. Honest and conscientious, he loved wild game even though he himself was not a hunter. His principal hobby was photographing Arizona's flora and fauna.

State Game Warden Dwight E. Pettis, once Willard's chief deputy, succeeded to the office in 1927. (Arizona State Library, Archives and Public Records, History and Archives Division, #01-1464)

The father of five children, Pettis devoted much of his energies to educating schoolchildren on the values of wildlife, a program he started when Willard hired him in 1913. His presentations were accompanied by talks in which he distributed Audubon Society leaflets and "Liberty Bell Bird Club" buttons. When distributing his leaflets at schools or at fairs, he frequently made presentations using bird, fish, and big game posters as props. He also had a slide show, and showed a wildlife protection film prepared by E. E. Kunselman of *Pathe News.* During these and other events, he distributed printed copies of the regulations, which also appeared on the backs of hunting and fishing licenses. Pettis was, in effect, Arizona's first wildlife information and education specialist.

Well traveled and more wildlife-aware than most of his deputy wardens, Pettis (1928) recognized early on that deer herds were becoming stressed in refuge areas other than the Kaibab, particularly white-tailed deer in the Grahams and Catalinas. He recognized, despite the wet winter of 1927, that the Kaibab situation remained a management crisis and realized his department should have more discretionary powers when it came to regulating deer numbers, hinting even at the possibility of issuing doe hunting permits. Although he considered mourning doves to be as plentiful as 10 years earlier, he thought that the federal law allowing white-winged doves to be shot before September 1 was causing this species to diminish rapidly. Invoking the slogan, "Remember the Passenger Pigeon," he decried the slaughter of these birds in the mesquite thickets where they nested. Like the sportsmen he worked with, Pettis thought the 1916 game law outdated and the state in need of more refuges. He wanted more federal protection for migratory shorebirds and waterfowl due to habitat losses and excessive shooting.

Even though Pettis does not appear to have been a hunter, he was a strong supporter of the Arizona Game Protective Association, working with its affiliates on such projects as fish planting, game bird stocking, and introducing elk to new habitats in the White Mountains (Pettis 1928). Especially interested in elk, Pettis estimated that the Chevelon elk herd had increased to between 750 and 1,000 head, while noting that not more than 50 of these animals roamed the Mescal Mountains and that the elk in the Graham Mountains had disappeared. He nonetheless continued to recommend a transplant of elk to the Chiricahua Mountains, despite having some reservations about the amount of habitat available there. He was a staunch supporter of wildlife propagation, farming out turkeys and pheasants to both organizations and individuals. Like Willard before him, he shipped quail to various areas in and out of state, while recommending the establishment of a quail refuge three miles west of Congress Junction to provide a reliable source for future transplants.

Pettis wanted a more specific bag limit on trout and desired regulations to protect birds and animals around springs and other water sources. Fishing also would be prohibited within a certain distance of dams if he had his way, and it would be illegal to waste fish or game meat. He recommended closed seasons on black bears, tree squirrels, and "wild hogs," wanting these animals to be hunted during the open deer season with bag limits of one javelina and one bear. Realizing that the state game refuges authorized by the legislature were too large, difficult to administer, and unpopular, he urged formation of a "game refuge committee" to recommend which refuges were needed and which should be decreased in size or retired. He also wanted all fish hatcheries and game and fur farms licensed and supervised by the department.

Pettis considered Arizona's antelope situation to have improved, especially in recent years, due to the animals having adapted to timbered areas, but thought there was no "need" for an antelope season at present—an overpopulation then being considered necessary to open a hunting season. The state having purchased 98 bison in December 1927—the remnants of Uncle Jimmy Owens's herd—hunters were allowed to take seven of the oldest animals. The feat was facilitated by a new bridge across the Colorado River at Lees Ferry. Pettis was also instrumental in negotiating the use of a Forest Service allotment south of the Kane Ranch that was supposed to be permanent pasture for 250 head. On this basis, he scheduled another 10 animals for harvest in 1928.

Many of Pettis's recommendations came to pass, including the replacement or removal of Prochaska's museum specimens in the Capitol building, which had suffered from a lack of protection and special housing. Pettis was also an advocate for a zoo of native animals to be housed at Papago Park, noting that a deer park operated by H. G. Bush in Mesa was a major attraction with its eleven species of deer, four bison, two elk, and two antelope. Most importantly, he recommended a varied license structure having different classes of licenses and different fees for different activities. For example, as fur prices then were high, he suggested the adoption of a $2.50 trapping license in lieu of the $1.25 resident general license for the taking of furbearing animals.

In summation, Pettis's (1928) report of his time as State Game Warden represents an accelerated extension of Willard's tenure; his greatest accomplishments were increased fish production, an elk transplant, and making the buffalo ranch a permanent acquisition. Surprisingly, despite his time in office encompassing some of the most contentious aspects of the Kaibab deer controversy, he barely mentions either the state's involvement or its lack of involvement in the dispute. This issue, he, like Willard before him, apparently left largely to Governor Hunt.

Working Toward a New Game Code

Although the state's sportsmen had been elated by the success of their 1916 initiative establishing a new game code, within a few years they were working for its repeal. Game conditions continued to be viewed as cause for concern, and a number of new and innovative programs were being proposed to allow game populations to recover. But with the cooperation of legislators required for any change in the status quo, any attempt to foster a new approach was difficult to implement. Conservationists wanted quick action in response to changing game conditions, but were continually stymied by regulations that were locked in place by the state legislature. A more flexible form of game administration had to be devised.

In 1921, after much political wrangling, Leopold and the New Mexico Game Protective Association persuaded that state's legislature to give an unpaid commission, appointed by the governor, the authority to establish game regulations having the force of law. The commission had the power to set hunting seasons and bag limits, establish state wildlife refuges, and direct the activities of the State Game Warden and his deputies. Such a commission could meet at any time and act quickly in case of a wildlife crisis. A commission also could devote its full attention to game and fish matters and shield the game department from undue political influence—as remained the case in Arizona, where the State Game Warden served at the pleasure of the governor. This situation led to rumors that State Game Wardens granted special permits and other favors to friends of the governor.

There was some basis to these rumors, in Arizona's case. Influential persons could obtain special permits for game-farm turkeys and pheasants as well as take wildlife out of season, while landowners were issued hunt permits to take doves out of season. For example, in 1921 Golding advised white-winged dove hunters they could hunt these birds out of season with a special permit:

> With reference to the white wings, please be advised that this department will not open the season at this time. However, the law provides that farmers may protect their property from the depredations of birds and animals, and we are also in receipt of an opinion that the farmer may give permission to others to shoot on his land.

> However a written permit is necessary for the reason that the hunter might be picked up by a game warden and it might be some trouble for him to prove where he obtained his birds. But where he is in possession of a written permit the game warden will not bother him. (Pettis to E. H. Dressing, published in the *Yuma Daily Sun*, June 10, 1923)

Members of the Arizona Game Protective Association, which had been organized in 1923, desperately wanted a game commission similar to New Mexico's for their state. But they were stymied by the rigid nature of the initiative they had earlier so strongly supported. In Arizona, a law or initiative enacted by a direct vote of the people can be changed or repealed only by another direct vote. The Arizona Constitution reads: "The veto power of the Governor, or the power of the Legislature, to repeal or amend, shall not extend to initiative or referendum measures approved by a majority vote of the qualified electors."

Thus, the state legislature could not tinker with the 1916 game code, nor could a commission, if one were established. Before a new game code and commission could be instituted, the 1916 initiative would have to be repealed at the ballot box. But requests by Arizona Game Protective Association affiliates and their allies to place a referendum on the ballot in 1924 fell on deaf ears, as did another attempt at a referendum in 1926.

Three major events occurred in November 1928 that would shape the future of Arizona's wildlife management program like no single month's actions before or since. A referendum abolishing the 1916 game code and new legislation establishing an Arizona Game and Fish Commission would be passed by the electorate and approved by the legislature. Governor Hunt would be voted temporarily out of office. And, the US Supreme Court would rule in favor of the federal government in a legal dispute between the Forest Service and the state of Arizona over which agency had the right to conduct deer hunts on the Kaibab.

Pettis was a strong advocate of the 1928 referendum, even though he knew the provisions of the new game code would likely result in his losing the job of State Game Warden.[5] Another of his legacies was his careful record keeping, which provided a benchmark by which to measure the changes to come during the next administration. His balance sheets for 1926 and 1927 show license revenues of $41,014.68 and $57,473.38 respectively, and expenses of $42,349.00 and $59,717.43 with cash-on-hand balances of $18,748.84 and $16,504.79—the balance presumably made up by fines and legislative appropriations. The biggest expenses were paying the salaries of the deputies, building and supervising two fish hatcheries, running the Phoenix office, and operating the game farm in Phoenix, along with $10,397.44 for purchasing bison and $11,078.07 for elk.

---

[5] This indeed came to pass. A professional public servant, Pettis went back to being a deputy warden under Robert L. Bayless, who was the first State Game Warden appointed by the first Arizona Game and Fish Commission.

ARIZONA'S FIRST CONSERVATION PRIORITY: PROTECTING BENEFICIAL BIRDS

David E. Brown

Gov. George Hunt and those he appointed to the office of State Game Warden were more interested in songbirds than game birds—an attitude that caused some sportsmen to derisively term them "bird lovers" and worse. Nonetheless, fostering a fascination and appreciation of birds was a major motivational factor for many wildlife conservationists at the turn of the century, as exemplified by collectors of Arm & Hammer bird cards and other bird-lore memorabilia.

An appreciation of the value of birds was also reflected in the new state game code, which prohibited the killing of songbirds and the collecting of all bird eggs. Although hawks, owls, and other predatory or "harmful" birds were not protected, the "chaparral cock" was included in the list of protected species at the governor's insistence despite the bird's reputation as a killer of baby quail. Hunt failed in his effort to have great horned owls protected—his attempt to protect "hoot owls" causing some derision in the Arizona State Legislature.

Nevertheless, such regulations were quite progressive for a frontier state, as was the law accommodating the custom of Hispanic Arizonans to keep mockingbirds, thrashers, and other songbirds in cages.[1] Also progressive for the time was requiring bird and egg collectors to obtain a permit from the State Game Warden justifying their activities, whether their collecting was done as a hobby or for scientific purposes.

The first annual Arizona Bird Day was held in 1916 by the order of Gov. George Hunt. A booklet accompanied the festivities. (Courtesy of Ed Parry)

As befitted the governor's interest in birds, much of State Game Warden George Willard's and his deputy Dwight Pettis's time was spent visiting schools and putting on bird awareness programs. They distributed free copies of the game laws along with Farmers' Bulletin No. 692, a US Biological Survey publication emphasizing the value of most birds to agriculture and other human pursuits. O. F. Hicks and May Belle Craig were deputies who did similar work in southeastern Arizona and in Phoenix. The highlight of Willard's first term as State Game Warden was undoubtedly Arizona's First Annual Bird Day, a celebration held May 4, 1916, by official order of Governor Hunt and dedicated to the memory of John James Audubon (Shaw 2009).

Willard, in a "Bird Day" booklet accompanying Hunt's proclamation, congratulated the teachers who had assisted in making their pupils more aware of the economic and social value of birds and profiled the educational work accomplished

[1] Sportsmen and early wildlife conservationists were generally disdainful of Hispanic culture when it came to wildlife, and none of the game wardens or their deputies possessed Spanish surnames; despite interest in both hunting and predator control within the Hispanic community, few if any department personnel, predator-control agents, or sportsmen club officers were "Latinos." (see also Brown 2009)

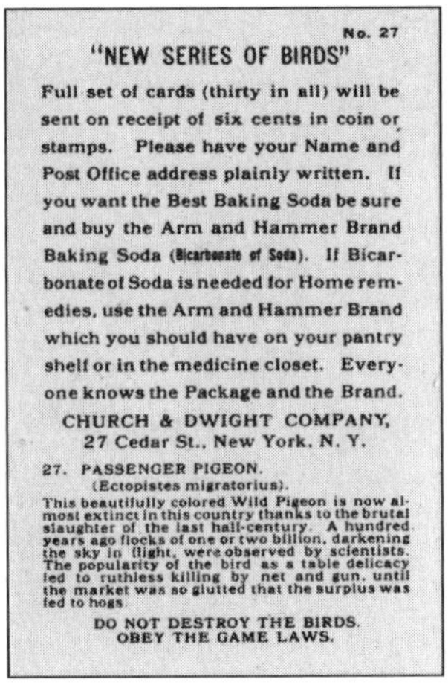
No. 27
"NEW SERIES OF BIRDS"

Full set of cards (thirty in all) will be sent on receipt of six cents in coin or stamps. Please have your Name and Post Office address plainly written. If you want the Best Baking Soda be sure and buy the Arm and Hammer Brand Baking Soda (Bicarbonate of Soda). If Bicarbonate of Soda is needed for Home remedies, use the Arm and Hammer Brand which you should have on your pantry shelf or in the medicine closet. Everyone knows the Package and the Brand.

CHURCH & DWIGHT COMPANY,
27 Cedar St., New York, N. Y.

27. PASSENGER PIGEON.
(Ectopistes migratorius).

This beautifully colored Wild Pigeon is now almost extinct in this country thanks to the brutal slaughter of the last half-century. A hundred years ago flocks of one or two billion, darkening the sky in flight, were observed by scientists. The popularity of the bird as a table delicacy led to ruthless killing by net and gun, until the market was so glutted that the surplus was fed to hogs.

DO NOT DESTROY THE BIRDS.
OBEY THE GAME LAWS.

Bird card packaged with Arm & Hammer baking soda at the time of statehood. This particular card portrays a passenger pigeon, which was then nearly extinct. Collecting cards, posters, and other depictions of birds was a popular pastime. The cards were used to teach people how beneficial birds could be. (Note text from back of card, above right.)

by deputies Pettis and Hicks. Also included in this publication, the Arizona Game and Fish Department's first, are photographs of Willard and his deputies, paragraphs from the game code, a summary of federal bird laws pertaining to Arizona, a rationale for protecting songbirds by Willard, a justification for protecting the roadrunner by Pettis, and poetry praising birds.

The main thrust of the booklet, however, was to celebrate essays, artwork, and photographs featuring Arizona animals sent in by grammar- and high-school students in a "Wild Life Conservation Contest" held by the Game and Fish Department for exhibit in its tent at the State Fair in November 1915. Although the first prize for writing went to Phoenix High School's Alfred E. Wilson for his essay on Arizona (Gambel's) quail, the contest emphasized the preservation of game and nongame species alike.

Farmers were not as enamored of birds as the governor's office was, particularly when it came to grain-eating species, including such game birds as the Gambel's quail, white-winged dove, and mourning dove. The prevailing attitude toward these species was that these birds were too numerous in certain agricultural areas and should be reduced in numbers as agricultural pests. For this reason, the legislature was reluctant to shorten the June 1–February 1 dove season—an open season that was unpopular with Willard (1914) and his warden force, as it not only provided large bag limits, it permitted shooting to take place when white-winged and mourning doves were nesting and raising young. Although Willard was sympathetic to the doves' plight, the numbers of birds then feeding in southern Arizona's grain-laden agricultural fields was huge and the reluctance of farmers and hunters to restrict the shooting of the state's most common game birds was beyond the department's ability to change.

As a result of these depredation claims, department personnel began trapping Gambel's quail and either releasing them in non-farming areas or trading them for game bird stock. Migratory birds, including waterfowl and such game birds as the white-winged

PROCLAMATION OF BIRD DAY

Executive Department
State of Arizona

With the advancement of the civilized races of the world toward their ultimate destiny, man grows constantly more mindful of his kinship with nature and more humane in his feeling toward every creature which has life. In all humanitarian work, it has been found that kindness and consideration for dumb animals and birds is closely linked with morality in the abstract.

From a more utilitarian viewpoint, it is universally recognized that birds enhance the pleasantness of human existence and, by destroying harmful insects, render an appreciable service to agriculture.

In view of the foregoing, it is fitting that the public should adopt practical measures for the preservation of song birds and for inculcating in growing generations a wholesome recognition of the service which they render mankind.

NOW, THEREFORE, I, George W. P. Hunt, Governor of Arizona, in pursuance of my official duty, do hereby proclaim and set apart, Thursday, May 4th, 1916, as Bird Day, and do earnestly urge the statewide observance of the day by appropriate instructional exercises in all the schools of the State.

IN WITNESS WHEREOF, I have hereunto set my hand and caused the Great Seal of the State of Arizona to be affixed.

Done at Phoenix, the Capital, this 20th day of April, A. D. 1916.

GEORGE W. P. HUNT
Governor of Arizona

Attest:

SIDNEY P. OSBORN
Secretary of State

DEDICATION

To the memory of John James Audubon, the first and foremost student of birds and their ways, who, having understood them, became their warmest friend and champion; whose lifelong labor in his chosen field of investigation enriched the world with a stock of knowledge, this little book is reverently

Dedicated
by the
Arizona State Game Department

Arizona's First Annual Bird Day celebration was held May 4, 1916, by official order of Gov. George Hunt and dedicated to the memory of John James Audubon, as shown in this re-creation based on the original proclamation in the "Bird Day" booklet. (AGFD files)

dove and mourning dove, were soon to become a more complex issue. When Arizona was admitted into the Union on February 14, 1912, the state was granted management authority for all game birds, including all species of waterfowl, shorebirds, cranes, rails, doves, and band-tailed pigeons, as well as songbirds and raptors. This situation changed with passage of the Migratory Bird Treaty Act of 1918—federal legislation verifying the Migratory Bird Treaty of 1916 and making migratory bird regulations a federal responsibility that superseded state law should a conflict occur.

As in other states, migratory bird hunting was a mainstay of Arizona's wildlife heritage. That this was so, especially in regard to doves and waterfowl, is indicated by newspaper articles prior to statehood, including this piece in a Tucson daily:

> Duck shooting along the Cienega below the Empire ranch [Pantano Ciénega], at Buenos Ayres on the lake of Pedro Aguirre [Aguirre Lake], and on the big Casa Grande reservoir [Picacho Reservoir] is the fascination of the nimrods. Cold nights have brought in the ducks and sport will be good. Even on the Allison canal and other irrigating ditches around Tucson, many ducks are found. The most successful hunters are those on the shooting ground as early as 4:30 or 5:00 o'clock in the morning. (*Arizona Daily Star*, November 3, 1903)

Market hunting was not an important factor regulating migratory bird numbers in Arizona, as it was in other states. Sporadic migration patterns and lack of waterfowl concentrations near large settlements relegated commercial shooting to a minor role, with hunters concentrated mainly along the Salt River near Phoenix and Tempe, along the lower Gila and Colorado rivers near Yuma, and at such places as Tavasci Marsh along the Verde River. Hunting for waterfowl in Arizona Territory was mostly for personal recreation and subsistence, the federal Lacey Act of 1900 having largely extinguished the sale of plumage from colony-nesting birds taken along the lower Colorado River (Brown 2009).

Just the same, the market-hunting lobby and the issue of not wanting to protect migratory birds for someone else to shoot prevented meaningful protective measures until statehood, when it became apparent federal legislation was needed to ensure a perpetual supply of ducks and doves. Federal laws seeking to manage game species were widely considered to be unconstitutional, however. In 1911, the American Game Protection Association in New York made a national migratory bird protection bill a primary objective (Brown 1985a). Having few market hunters and no tradition of spring shooting, Arizona passed its own law in 1912 establishing a statewide duck, goose, brant, and coot season from October 15 through January 31 for 1912–13 with a 25-bird bag limit. Doves, particularly white-winged doves, were more problematic, and the season set by the legislature on this species and mourning doves opened June 1 and continued to February 1, with a bag limit on both species of 35 birds per day.

The same year Arizona became a state, three bills were introduced in Congress to protect migratory birds. One of these, the Weeks-McLean Law, was attached as a rider to the agricultural appropriations bill and signed unknowingly in 1913 by outgoing President William Howard Taft. This bill outlawed the spring shooting of migratory game birds, greatly restricted commercial hunting, and established the secretary of agriculture's right to fix closed seasons for selected species.

The legislature made no move to change the law, and season and bag limits remained intact until the sportsmen-backed initiative of 1916 shortened the dove season to July 15 to December 31 and reduced the bag limit from 35 to 25 doves in the aggregate—thus bringing Arizona into compliance with the soon-to-be-passed federal Migratory Bird Treaty Act of 1918. This same initiative also reduced the length of the waterfowl season to October 15 to January 1 and set a 25-bird duck and goose bag limit.

A more active game manager than Willard, State Game Warden Joe Prochaska (1921) purchased quantities of wild rice, wild celery, and wild millet seed in August 1919 for planting in Stoneman Lake, Kinnikinick Lake, Lake Mary, Mormon Lake, Howard Lake, Rogers Lake, and the oxbow marshes along the Verde, Salt, and Gila rivers. Pleased with the response to his efforts, Prochaska recommended $1,500 be allocated for future purchases—a recommendation apparently ignored by his successors.

Under the terms of the Migratory Bird Treaty Act, the Biological Survey was given authority to close the seasons on swans, wood ducks, cranes, curlews, godwits, upland plovers, and all of the smaller shorebirds as of September 1, 1918. Band-tailed pigeons were also protected, no doubt due to the lesson of the passenger pigeon, which was firmly etched in the mind of American conservationists (neither Arizona nor the Biological Survey would recognize band-tailed pigeons as game birds until 1932). The act, while hailed by wildlife conservationists, was still widely held to be unconstitutional and vulnerable to challenge in the courts. As a result, it was largely ignored in some states, including much of Arizona (Trefethen 1961).

Arizona adopted the regulatory framework for the waterfowl seasons specified in the Migratory Bird Treaty (October 16, 1917 to January 31, 1918) but reduced the allowable bag of 25 ducks per day to a daily limit of 20, as was a state's prerogative. Arizona's July 15 opening of dove season, contained within its 1916 initiative, was now outside the federal government's September 1 guideline closing the season on all migratory birds. Although many state officials, including Governor Hunt (who hunted waterfowl), continued to consider the management of wildlife a state responsibility, Arizona had already conceded the management of predators and noxious rodents to the Department of Agriculture. Moreover, Arizona, unlike some other states, did little to contest the federal framework except in the case of white-winged doves. Regulations concerning this latter species therefore caused some consternation when federal authority over migratory birds was sustained by the US Supreme Court *(Missouri v. Holland).*

For its part, the federal government had only withdrawn one migratory bird refuge in Arizona, the area below the high-water mark on the shoreline of massive Roosevelt Lake on the Tonto National Forest. This national wildlife refuge, the Salt River Bird Reservation, had been withdrawn in 1909 by executive order of President Theodore Roosevelt in anticipation of Roosevelt Dam's completion in 1910. No refuge personnel or feeding areas had been provided, and the Salt River Bird Reservation was merely a body of water and shoreline closed to hunting.

Another area investigated for possible status as a federal migratory bird refuge, probably under the direction of the Biological Survey's Wells W. Cooke, was Marsh Lake (now Big Lake) on the Apache National Forest. Although federal biologist Edward A. Goldman (1926a) reported seven species of waterfowl nesting at Marsh Lake and saw a long-billed curlew there during his summer survey in 1915, none of the White Mountain lakes was made a national wildlife refuge at that time, national forest status apparently being deemed protection enough. Other areas in Arizona would be investigated as national wildlife refuges for migratory birds, but not until the 1930s.

Although Governor Hunt and his wardens were firm believers in states' rights, they refrained from making a major issue out of the more restrictive seasons and bag limits contained within the federal framework, the courts having ruled that mourning doves were migratory game birds and subject to a closed season prior to September 1 (California Fish and Game Department 1923). White-winged doves were another issue, and Arizonans would continue to contest any attempt to delay the opening of the whitewing season until September 1, due to the bird's early migration habits and the knowledge that many of these birds left the state prior to this date.

White-winged doves were indeed a problem species. Gilman (1911) described the status of this bird in the then-great San Xavier mesquite thicket south of Tucson immediately prior to statehood:

> They come in such great numbers that the wheat fields suffer and loss is considerable. . . . At present there is no closed season and the beautiful birds may be shot whenever present. There was an attempt recently made to have them protected, but such a howl went up from the ranchers that nothing was done.

Even though hunt regulations after 1916 continued to call for opening the dove season on or after July 15, special dispensation for agricultural areas allowed June hunting to continue past 1918 and into the 1920s. Some, including writer Jack O'Connor (1939), thought a decline in whitewings reported during World War I was caused by a shift to the raising of cotton instead of grain, an argument that continues to be used to explain whitewing population changes to the present day. Alexander Wetmore (1920), who studied white-winged doves in June 1919 in Arlington Valley, where large tracts of mesquite bottomlands bordered a patchwork of new grain farms, was of a different opinion:

> It has been common practice for many years for sportsmen to hunt white-winged doves during the months of June and July when the birds were ranging over the cultivated fields. Though this has been done under the guise of protecting crops it has been carried on in the main simply for sport, as the majority of the doves killed are shot in stubble fields from which the grain has been removed, or when in flight to or from the colonies in localities where they may be doing no damage. Occasionally men and boys even invaded the nesting colonies and slipped about among the low mesquites potting the male birds or shooting the females as sat on their nests containing eggs and young. Others, waiting until the squabs were nearly grown, knocked the young doves

Aerial view of the Gila River in the vicinity of Powers Butte near the junction of the Hassayampa River in 1941. Harboring numerous sloughs and populated by native riparian vegetation, such sites were important waterfowl resting and wintering areas, in addition to being havens for nesting doves, quail, and other species. (AGFD files)

> from their nests with poles and gathered them in sacks for table use. Such harrying during the season when the birds are breeding can not be considered legitimate and can lead only to the decimation of the species. The mortality among young from the killing of their parents is tremendous.

Wetmore (1920) went on to predict that the large colonies of white-winged doves along the lower Gila would soon disappear because of the rapid expansion of irrigation projects and the steady cutting and clearing of the mesquite forests. As for the department's sentiments, State Game Warden Willard had a "remember the passenger pigeon" heading on his department stationery.

Although the white-winged dove was in no real danger of extirpation, the hunt pressure on colonial populations could be severe. Shoots at sites where the birds concentrated attracted hunters from far and wide, and Arizona's sporting-goods dealers openly advertised the good gunning to be had. Some shoots did result in excessive bags, even by Arizona standards. The governor's file in the state archives contains a letter by a J. F. Brown, dated March 29, 1927, bitterly complaining about his party of nine millionaire sportsmen from Los Angeles being cited by a deputy warden after hunting whitewings on the Gila Indian Reservation near Sacaton. This party of railroad magnates and Hollywood personalities (including Hal Roach, the director of the *Our Gang* comedies) had hunted on the reservation before and had a reputation for excessive behavior and taking large bags of birds. In this case, their bag of 382 whitewings was within the limit for the number of days involved, and the citation issued in Casa Grande was for not having nonresident state licenses in addition to their Indian permits. Both State Game Warden Pettis and Governor Hunt backed up their man, and several of the Californians sent letters of apology when it was explained that the law required hunters to have a valid Arizona license to possess wildlife when within the state.

Some today question the reports of 70-foot-tall mesquites, but such giants did indeed occur, as attested to by this specimen. It was photographed at the junction of Sycamore Creek and the Verde River on the Fort McDowell Indian Reservation in 1978. The man in the portrait, Dr. Charles H. Lowe, is 6 feet, 6 inches tall. (David E. Brown)

Such prodigious whitewing shoots became less common as the 1920s progressed. In a later investigation, federal biologist Johnson Neff (1940a, 1940b) reported that the large colonies of whitewings formerly present at Arlington, Sacaton, and other locations along the Gila and Santa Cruz rivers "disappeared" in the 1920s and that it was "the nearly unanimous opinion of Arizona's deputy game wardens that the whitewings have been decreasing every year."

It was also about this time that Picacho Reservoir, south of Coolidge, became a mecca as a hunting locale for migratory birds. The original reservoir dated back to 1886, when a consortium of farmers formed a cooperative to divert water from the Gila River to irrigate the saltbush- and mesquite-covered plains south of Florence. To allocate and store the river's waters, they employed mule teams and *fresno* scrapers to construct an earthen canal and two reservoirs adjacent to McClellan Wash. The main impoundment, originally known as the Florence or Casa Grande Reservoir, would eventually become known as "Picacho Lake" due to the prominent peak and pass located a dozen miles to the south. Within a few years of its genesis, this earthen reservoir was not only storing water, it was attracting doves and waterfowl like no other place in southern Arizona.

In an effort to irrigate more acreage, Congress was petitioned to expand the facilities through the newly created Reclamation Service. With help from Senator Carl Hayden, funding was appropriated and an additional Florence-Casa Grande Canal was initiated in 1912, the year Arizona became a state. Construction was delayed by World War I, so the expansion was not completed until 1922. Then, except for periodic repairs and minor modifications by the irrigation district, the reservoir remained essentially unchanged through the mid-1920s.

These years were the heyday of the *Represito* (Little Reservoir) Gun Club. A shoot at Picacho Lake was a rich man's avocation, with the sports coming mostly from Tucson, Mesa, and Florence and paying $100 for a membership, plus hefty yearly dues of $50. Membership entitled use of one of the club's boat docks, a choice of from 20 to 40 boats, and occupancy of a bunkhouse leased from the Florence Irrigation District. The shooting was good, with 20-bird limits being taken regularly (Brown 2004).

Then, after the federal government completed Coolidge Dam upstream from the Ashurst-Hayden diversion dam in 1929, a new but still earthen Florence-Casa Grande Canal was constructed. By 1933, the old Florence Irrigation District had been dissolved, the upper reservoir abandoned, and Picacho Reservoir incorporated into the newly formed San Carlos Irrigation Project, where its primary function was to store and settle the silt-laden waters coming down the San Pedro River below Coolidge Dam. With a bigger canal system, more water was now available and more land was planted in cotton and other crops. Local farming communities such as La Palma, Valley Farms, Coolidge, and Eloy attained some measure of prosperity. Picacho Reservoir received national attention when sportswriter Charlie Gilham published an article about the fabulous duck hunting to be had there in *Outdoor Life* titled "Ducks in the Desert."

Although whitewings and waterfowl received most of the attention, mourning doves continued to be the most numerous game bird in Arizona. So numerous and commonplace was this species that little was done to manage it other than shooting—a situation that would continue until the 1950s, and even then most of the emphasis would be on its more exotic and vulnerable white-winged cousin. Band-tailed pigeons, or "blue-rocks" as they were more commonly known, while recognized as a game bird in the Migratory Bird Treaty Act, were regarded as too few and too vulnerable to hunt, and thus retained their protected status despite the bird's sporting qualities and attractiveness as a game species. The season on bandtails remained closed in Arizona until the 1930s, when the Arizona Game and Fish Commission began issuing permits to take depredating pigeons between May 15 and July 31. Shorebirds and other migratory game birds were considered of little consequence in Arizona.

By 1927, Arizona was in general compliance with federal guidelines when it came to migratory bird seasons. The new game code that took effect in 1929 contained a waterfowl season that was set to open October 16 and continue through January 31, with a daily bag limit of 15 ducks and 2 geese. The 1929 season on mourning doves opened September 1 and closed December 15, with a bag limit of 20 doves. The whitewing season continued to open July 15 and run through August 31, in defiance of the Migratory Bird Treaty Act. In accordance with federal guidelines, the new commission authorized a season on plovers, curlews, snipe, yellowlegs, and coots that opened October 16 and ran through November 30, even though these birds provided little hunting opportunity in Arizona.

On March 18, 1929, the newly formed commission assumed the authority of issuing collecting permits for birds alive or dead. Bird species not protected were limited to

English sparrows, crows, hawks, great horned owls, kingfishers, magpies and jays, and roadrunners—the lack of closed seasons on the owl and the roadrunner representing a snub of the recently, though temporarily, removed Governor Hunt. Shooting hours established for migratory birds were set at one-half hour before sunrise to sunset—a federal time frame that remains in effect to this day.

Neither the Arizona Game and Fish Commission nor the Biological Survey authorized much in the way of field work on migratory birds in Arizona through the 1930s. Money and personnel were in short supply, and little could be done in any event. In 1930, the commission approved matching funds to assist the Arizona Game Protective Association in planting duck foods, and the following year, despite some differences of opinion, the association requested the commission to have the department's migratory-bird season dates and bag limits (other than for doves) conform to federal regulations. Although the commission acknowledged the association's recommendation that the mourning dove season in northern Arizona open on August 15, the commission did not challenge the federal season framework, which opened dove seasons September 1.

In 1932, the commission adopted the recommendation of a special committee of the Arizona State Senate to support an early form of the Pittman-Robertson Act called the "penny a shell" excise tax, then in Congress. This bill, if passed by Congress, would use the tax money so raised solely for waterfowl and waterfowl habitat. Although this particular bill failed, both the Biological Survey and the commission agreed to a change in the federal waterfowl regulations authorizing a noon opening of a split waterfowl season that divided the state into northern and southern zones. As always, the commission preserved its prerogative to reduce but not increase the 12-duck limit permitted by the federal framework.

Depredation complaints involving band-tailed pigeons feeding in cherry orchards and on other crops became an increasing problem after 1930, with disgruntled fruit-tree growers in Camp Creek, Oak Creek, and other localities asking the governor and commission to relieve them from these "raids." So persistent did these complaints become that in 1932, the federal government acquiesced to a 15-day season with a 10-bird bag limit for Arizona and New Mexico. In response, Arizona's commission opened a season on band-tailed pigeons with a 10-bird bag limit from December 1–15, 1934—a time when all but a few wintering pigeons had left the state. Complaints during the late summer and early fall months therefore continued, and special depredation permits were soon being issued to the extent that there was almost no closed season on the species (Fitzhugh 1970). After experimental seasons were opened in October, November, and December, a more realistic season opening was finally authorized for September 16, 1940. Although a study by the Biological Survey showed pigeons to be increasing in the Western states during the 1930s and 1940s (J. A. Neff 1947), populations of these birds abruptly dropped off in the late 1940s for unknown reasons. Given a decline in both pigeons and pigeon depredation complaints, the season was again closed in 1951 and not reopened again until 1966.

By the mid-1930s, the commission was complying with federal regulations when it came to all migratory birds. On January 17, 1934, the commission not only supported

New York (Komatke) Thicket as it appeared in July 1941 (top) and July 1972. Groundwater pumping and upstream flow diversions resulted in the death of most of the big mesquites. 1941 photo by Lee Arnold, Arizona Game and Fish Department. (From Brown and Bosman 1983, reproduced with permission)

the concept of the federal government's acquiring waterfowl refuges within the state, it endorsed the federal duck stamp bill then before Congress. Given an impetus to manage waterfowl, the commission directed State Game Warden Shelby L. "Lefty" Lewis to draw up plans for a Big Lake Game Refuge one-half mile in from the high-water mark of Big (Marsh) Lake and close the refuge to fishing during the waterfowl nesting season.

In 1935, the state and federal governments were in general agreement when it came to migratory bird regulations. The state limited shooting hours to 7 a.m.–4 p.m., which was more restrictive than the federal regulations, and no live decoys or baiting were allowed. Shotguns were required to hold a maximum of three shot-shells and a $1 duck stamp was required of all waterfowl hunters over age 16. There was no open season on swans, Ross' geese, ruddy ducks, buffleheads, or wood ducks. A bag limit of 10 ducks and 4 geese was established, along with limits of 25 sora rails, 15 coots, and 15 snipe per day. A dove season of September 9 through January 5 was authorized, with a bag limit of 20 mourning doves per day or in possession.

On a local level, the commission restricted waterfowl shooting at Picacho Reservoir to Wednesdays and Sundays within one-half mile of the water's edge—the result of a request by the Tucson Game Protective Association, an action that was rescinded in 1938.

Other migratory bird actions undertaken by the commission consisted of issuing a special permit to a citrus farmer at Higley to kill woodpeckers in 1937, and the authorization of a refuge at the newly completed Apache Lake on the Salt River in 1938. More important, the commission approved a federal program designed to benefit waterfowl below Boulder Dam—one that would result in the creation of Havasu and Imperial national wildlife refuges. On July 15, 1940, it entered into agreements with the US Fish and Wildlife Service and Forest Service to jointly administer an Apache Migratory Waterfowl Refuge in the White Mountains and a Bill Williams Wildlife Management Unit on the Tusayan National Forest—areas used by nesting waterfowl in those years having sufficient winter runoff.

In 1936, the Migratory Bird Treaty was amended to include Mexico and its migratory birds. To restore white-winged dove populations, Arizona's commission postponed the opening of the season to August 5 in 1937 and imposed a bag limit of 15 birds. The best flights were now restricted to New York (Komatke) Thicket and other sites on the Gila Indian Reservation, and the more remote lands along the Gila River between Arlington and Yuma. The flights out of San Xavier Thicket had by now been reduced to numbers thought to be below the area's nesting potential.

Johnson Neff (1940a, 1940b), a federal biologist hired by the Biological Survey to work on white-winged doves, considered the harvests of 1937, 1938, and 1939 to have been excessive, and the birds more sparse than before. Hunt pressure was deemed excessive even in such remote localities as Agua Caliente and Texas Hill, and Neff estimated that 75% of the 20,000 birds present in New York Thicket in 1937 had been killed. He considered the drought year of 1939 as another disaster. Meanwhile, mesquite cutting and clearing was taking a heavy toll on the dove's nesting habitats. State Federal-Aid biologists E. R. Tinkham (1941) and Lee Arnold (1943) described the San Xavier thicket as only "a one time great nesting colony for whitewings" and no longer capable of supporting the large colony of "thirty years ago."

In 1940, the commission recommended postponing the opening of the whitewing season to August 16, and in 1941 the Fish and Wildlife Service recommended setting the season back to September 1, as this species had been severely depleted during the previous five years. The commission reluctantly agreed, and closed the season with the understanding that Neff would continue his study in cooperation with department biologists who were also studying the effects of predation on the bird's nesting success. The September 1 opening was later approved, and a bag limit of 15 whitewings and/or mourning doves was set, with only 15 mourning doves permitted after September 15.

Whether because of the added protection of nesting birds, an increase in nesting habitat due to the proliferation of exotic saltcedar, an increase in cultivated grain farming, or a combination of all these factors, whitewing numbers again increased. A statewide survey of whitewing colonies after World War II showed good numbers of birds again present along the lower Colorado, Gila, and Santa Cruz rivers, and by 1948, whitewing nesting success and shooting were again considered "good" (Pulich 1948; Lawson 1949b; Shaw 1961). New York Thicket was then still in generally good condition, and plans were made to preserve a hundred-acre remnant of the mesquite forest at San Xavier that still contained 70-foot trees (Pulich 1948).

As for Picacho Reservoir, it had become increasingly apparent during the dry years of the 1930s that the Gila River's waters had been over-allocated; the reservoir was now often dry or nearly so. But these dry years only made the wet years more productive when they came. Picacho's periodic drying and flooding regime nurtured robust aquatic plant growth and the surrounding mesquites grew to generous proportions.

With the coming of another series of wet years beginning in 1941, large flocks of migrating ducks and geese again began visiting the reservoir, which now also hosted increasingly huge numbers of white-winged doves, mourning doves, Gambel's quail, and cottontail rabbits. Interest in the reservoir as a wildlife area was rekindled. The Arizona Game and Fish Commission entertained proposals to make Picacho Reservoir a wildlife refuge and otherwise manage this water body for outdoor recreation, including fishing.

But by the early 1950s, the San Pedro's silt-laden waters had reduced Picacho's storage capacity from 18,000 acre-feet of water to less than 2,000. And even though the reservoir's embankments were raised and strengthened to create a newer, larger water body, the silt accumulation continued. Over the next 20 years, the inflow channel from the Florence-Casa Grande Canal required constant dredging to keep delivering water to the "lake" until the reservoir's capacity was again down to only 5,000 acre-feet. Just the same, the lake continued to attract great flights of both nesting and migratory birds, and its woody environs supported large numbers of resident wildlife—nongame birds as well as bullfrogs and such aquatic game as black bass, carp, and catfish—all of which would enter the lake via the canal and be harvested en masse when the reservoir went dry, as it periodically did.

Foremost among man's developments to benefit waterfowl and other migratory birds during the 1930s and 1940s were stock ponds, also referred to as *repressos*, *charcos*, or "tanks." These impoundments consist of earthen dams built to capture small-drainage runoff. Used as a watering source for livestock since the Mexicans first operated cattle ranches in southern Arizona, these *repressos* greatly increased in numbers in the 1930s with passage of the Soil Conservation and Domestic Allotment Act, the Agricultural Adjustment or "Triple A" Act, and other Depression-era measures subsidizing their construction. Additional tanks continued to be built through the 1940s and 1950s, reaching a crescendo about 1956 (Jody Latimer, Arizona State Land Department, pers. comm., 2008). The surface area of water impounded ranged from a fraction of an acre up to as many as 50 surface acres. Turbid and subject to great fluctuations in water levels, these small, eutrophic impoundments constituted a great boon to migratory waterfowl as resting sites, regardless of their drawbacks (concentrating livestock at these water sites encouraged soil erosion) (McAuliffe 1998).

After World War II, Arizona hired Warren Pulich as an ornithologist, a position that morphed into waterfowl biologist (Arizona Game and Fish Commission 1948). Nesting studies, a banding program, and winter waterfowl surveys followed, and with waterfowl biologists such as Pulich (1947, 1949) and later Wes Fleming, waterfowl coordination between the state and the Fish and Wildlife Service improved. The result was that season regulations and other framework issues were worked out prior to commission meetings and publication in the Federal Register.

After 1940, Federal-Aid monies made possible the development and management of state waterfowl management areas such as Mittry Lake, Arlington, Robbins Butte, and Cibola (Fleming 1959), which augmented the new federal refuges along the lower Colorado River. Less long-lasting was the designation of the 640-acre Bumstead and 480-acre Ramsey-Heaslet state migratory waterfowl refuges in 1949. Both were private farm ponds in Maricopa County. Neither appears to have been open to the public, and the refuge designation was more a means of protecting private property from trespass than a management tool for waterfowl.

Even less advantageous to waterfowl were increased fishing revenues derived from Dingell-Johnson monies, as the increased emphasis on fishing opportunity after 1950 resulted in such waterfowl areas as Big, Ashurst, and Kinnikinick lakes being improved for fishing, at the expense of nesting waterfowl (AGFD 1955a, 1955b; Brown 1985a).

Waterfowl regulations reflected the fact that most ducks and geese shot in Arizona were migrating from farther north. As a result, season dates and bag limits were tailored to provide maximum hunting opportunity and take advantage of periodic surpluses in certain species, while protecting those deemed more scarce or vulnerable, such as wood ducks, hooded mergansers, redheads, and canvasbacks. Peripheral nesting species in Arizona, such as Mexican ducks and black-bellied whistling ducks, were ignored (Brown 1985a).

Mourning dove seasons and bag limits had also become standardized by 1950, and in cooperation with the federal government, Arizona became a leading state in dove management. A banding program for mourning doves was initiated in 1951, and call-count surveys began the following year. In 1953, hunt information collected through the use of check stations and wing boxes showed that dove-hunt success in Arizona was twice that of any other state and that more Arizona hunters shot more doves than any other game (Gallizioli 1953a). A 10-bird bag limit on mourning doves with a continuous 40-day season beginning September 1 remained in effect until 1956, when regulations were liberalized to allow a 15-bird bag limit and a 50-day split season. Although the bag limit was again reduced to 10 the following year, the split season remained in effect, allowing the shooting of locally raised doves in September and migrant birds from more northern states in November and December.

Recognizing the continued importance of the white-winged dove as a game bird, the department began systematically collecting hunt data on this species in 1951, and an annual banding program was initiated for whitewings in 1953 (Gallizioli 1953a, 1954a). Although a large percentage of the birds were migrating before the hunting season opened, hunt success during the first week of September was generally good and populations were considered to be still increasing. The 1954 season was the best in years, and Gallizioli (1954a) described one opening-day flight as containing "a minimum of 10,000 whitewings. . . . Flock followed flock in what appeared to be an endless stream. Limit bags were taken in from 15 to 30 minutes even by mediocre shooters." In some years and in some localities, the whitewings persisted for one to three weeks after the opening of the season.

A statewide call-count survey for white-winged doves was begun on an annual basis in 1957, and check stations, band recovery, and hunt questionnaires monitored the birds' status. Flight counts by department biologist Harley Shaw between Maricopa and Gila Bend in August 1957, 1958, and 1959 estimated as many as 60,000 birds flying southward (Harley Shaw, retired from Arizona Game and Fish Department, pers. comm., 2010). In 1957, the 25-bird bag limit was reinstated. Ten years later, a greatly increased cadre of hunters reported harvesting three-quarters of a million whitewings—an all-time record.

Things were changing, however, and not for the better. Groundwater pumping, land clearing, and other incursions were beginning to take a toll. By the 1960s, the whitewings' prime nesting habitats along the Colorado, Gila, and Santa Cruz rivers and their tributaries were being degraded, not only by farmland expansion, but by a series of flood-control and water-salvage projects planned by the US Bureau of Reclamation, Army Corps of Engineers, US Geological Survey, and Maricopa Flood Control District. Despite numerous whitewing nesting studies showing the value of these riverine thickets, many prime nesting areas were destined to be compromised, if not destroyed (Stair 1958; Shaw and Jett 1960; Carr 1960; Wigal 1973). Worse, groundwater pumping with diesel engines was now added to a growing list of factors (including channelization and fire) that were destroying colonial nesting sites.

By the mid-1960s, the great mesquite forests at San Xavier, Komatke, and along the lower Colorado and Gila rivers were all but gone. To make matters worse for the doves, cotton was now rapidly replacing wheat, milo-maize, and safflower as Arizona's primary summer agricultural crop. Although the white-winged dove would remain one of Arizona's most ubiquitous birds, its uniquely important value as a tourist-attracting target was coming to a close (Brown 1989).

Songbirds, as well as eagles and other raptors, continued to receive increased protection through the 1920s, 1930s, and 1940s. In 1935, the Game and Fish Commission directed State Game Warden Lewis to tighten up on scientific collecting permits and not to issue more than two such permits per protected species. The golden eagle, formerly considered to be a predator of lambs and pronghorn fawns, received federal protection in 1962, when amendments to the Bald Eagle Protection Act of 1940 made killing either species a federal offense. The Animal Damage Control unit of the US Fish and Wildlife Service, however, continued to kill golden eagles in sheep-raising areas through the 1970s.

Protection for most bird species was enhanced in 1972, when amendments to the Migratory Bird Treaty Act of 1918 afforded legal protection to all native birds in Arizona save crows. With the crusade against predatory animals waning, federal and state laws now protected great horned owls and such previously unprotected accipiters as the goshawk, Cooper's hawk, and sharp-shinned hawk, leaving only exotic nuisances such as house sparrows and starlings unprotected.

Some species, including shorebirds, did not fare as well as other migratory species in the half-century after statehood. Although protected by closed seasons, Arizona's shorebirds were severely impacted by drainage projects and other marshland reclamation programs, coupled with inappropriate grazing and other land uses. As a consequence, upland species such as long-billed curlews and upland plovers, while defined as game, had not been subject to hunting since the 1920s. There had also been no open season on rails, and the Yuma clapper rail, a race of king rail once thought to be endemic to the lower Colorado River, was so rarely encountered that it would be placed on the original endangered species list. Still other migratory game birds such as coots and gallinules, while numerous and subject to an open season, have remained generally ignored from both a recreational and a management perspective.

Sandhill cranes, although they had formerly nested in Arizona, attracted little attention until after 1962. The relatively few sandhills wintering in Arizona at that time were mostly confined to the Colorado River Indian Reservation along the lower Colorado River, where approximately 210 birds were censused in 1961 (Phillips, Marshall, and Monson 1964). These birds and a small flock wintering between Arlington and Gila Bend were then the only cranes visiting Arizona. This condition would change remarkably for the better with the short-stopping of cranes from the Rocky Mountains and other northern populations in Sulphur Springs Valley after 1970 (Brown and Perkins 1981)—a subject that will have to wait until the next book on Arizona's wildlife history is written.

STATE REFUGES ARE THE FIRST STEP TO GAME RECOVERY

David E. Brown

When Aldo Leopold addressed Flagstaff's sportsmen at the Empress Theater in October 1916, his message was simple and direct. Arizona's game animals were on the ropes and only the state's sportsmen could rectify the situation. The solution was for every sportsman to join a game protective association and demand a more responsive game and fish department and more restrictive game laws.

That any big game animals remained at all was only due to the protection provided by the national forests Leopold represented, and like the other leading conservationists of the time, he preached that the way to game recovery was through a process by which:

1. Sportsmen would demand further protection for game and fish, do away with game hogs, and see to it that game laws were rigidly and impartially enforced.
2. An unrelenting war would be waged on predatory animals, thereby allowing depleted game populations a chance to recover.
3. A series of game refuges or preserves would protect desirable wildlife species from hunting, thereby allowing game to attain carrying capacity and surplus animals to expand onto adjacent lands open to hunting.

These recommendations were not new. William Hornaday had recently published two books on these very concepts, particularly emphasizing the need for hunting closures. John Burnham, with the backing of arms and ammunition manufacturers, had been advocating a combination of these same methods through the American Game Protective Association since 1911.

The New Mexico Game Protective Association was promoting a game protection program along these lines in Arizona's sister state. Similar concepts were also the cornerstone of the Boone and Crockett Club and were promulgated by the organization's founders. America's foremost conservationist, President Theodore Roosevelt, had implemented these principles when he established Grand Cañon Game Preserve by executive order in 1906, thereby curtailing hunting throughout most of the Kaibab Plateau.

Gov. George Hunt and his appointed State Game Wardens were also strong believers in game preserves. Hunt went so far as to recommend that the first Arizona State Legislature create a game refuge out of the Camp Grant Military Reservation, which had recently been ceded to the state by the federal government. Frank Rogers, Arizona's first State Game Warden, expressed his desire for a state game refuge in the area where elk had been released in Cabin Draw as early as 1913.

As a result, Arizona's legislature proposed HB32, which if passed, would have established a huge game preserve on the Coconino and Sitgreaves national forests. This bill was strongly opposed by the state's cattlemen, who requested that any legislator who was a member of the Benevolent and Protective Order of Elks be declared ineligible to vote on this piece of legislation due to a conflict of interest. The Elks had been the primary sponsor of the elk transplant the refuge was designed to benefit. The cattlemen need not have worried. The bill, which would have emphasized elk over cattle, was indefinitely postponed in a resounding vote by the entire Arizona State House of Representatives. Similarly, a bill introduced by a Pima County legislator to create a game preserve out of Camp Grant and most of the adjacent Crook National Forest was defeated when it was pointed out that prohibiting hunting in such an expansive amount of real estate would deny people in the Gila Valley a place to hunt deer.

Clearly, establishing a system of state refuges in Arizona would not be easy. And even if such a system were created, a small and impoverished game and fish department would be hard-pressed to properly post and patrol a system of refuges. It was all State Game Warden George Willard could do in 1914 to recruit wardens to enforce the game laws and sell wildlife conservation to Arizona's schoolchildren.

Also, unlike eastern New Mexico, which was the model for many of Arizona's conservation programs, Arizona contained few large blocks of private ranchland that cooperators would consent to transform into hunting preserves. As in western New Mexico, Arizona's national forests were the only option for withdrawing refuges of sufficient size to restock Arizona's game herds. Moreover, US Forest Service rangers were mandated and willing to undertake the task of patrolling game preserves, should the state provide the authority and political cover. Forest Service supervisors, looking for allies in a politically contentious West, were eager to enlist and accommodate sportsmen in a crusade to establish the national forests as America's game country.

Refuges, or the concept of refuges, also were popular with the non-hunting public. Ranchers saw refuges as a means of reducing trespass, and homesteaders liked having exclusive use of surrounding lands. Game wardens and forest rangers alike looked upon refuges as tools to assist them in the execution of their duties. Most important, nearly everyone agreed with the logic that refuges would be an effective means to game restoration. Only commercial hunters, poachers, rustlers, and disenfranchised Indians were considered to be opposed to refuges.

In the years immediately after statehood, the legislature was responsible for all laws and regulations pertaining to game and fish matters. The problem was that Arizona's legislature met in regular session only every other year and in special sessions as needed. Although a majority of the state's citizens considered the advantages of establishing state refuges on national forests as obvious, getting legislators to sponsor refuge bills during the next regular session required a certain amount of lobbying. And even when such sponsors were found, it might be two years or more before such legislation could be enacted.

Leopold and his allies among the sportsmen and stockmen, firm believers in refuges, would soon see the results of their fervor. In February and March 1917, Arizona's third legislature passed acts establishing a Mount Graham State Game Preserve, a Huachuca State Game Preserve, a Pinal Mountains State Game Preserve, and a Blue Range State Game Preserve. With the more conservative Governor Hunt temporarily out of office, Gov. Tom Campbell immediately signed all four bills, which directed that the refuges, all of which were almost entirely on national forest land, be supervised by his State Game Warden. The legislative session that followed, the state's fourth, established the Catalina Mountains portion of the Coronado National Forest as a game preserve in July 1919, under the same conditions as those prescribed by the third legislature.

All five refuges were huge in extent, encompassing almost entire mountain ranges and comprising hundreds of thousands of acres. Although the refuges were closed to the taking of game animals, the laws specifically stated that, "nothing in this Act should be construed to interfere with the grazing of livestock or the taking of predators and other obnoxious animals." Anyone found guilty of hunting or taking game species within the refuge was to be fined not less than $50 or more than $250, or imprisoned in the county jail for a period of not less than three months or more than one year.

Game refuges may have been more popular with sportsmen and the legislature than with the Game and Fish Department's wardens, who had to post and patrol those areas so designated. Neither State Game Warden Willard nor his temporary successor, Joe Prochaska, made much mention of refuges in their reports to governors Hunt and Campbell, other than Prochaska's stating that he personally posted and policed all of the refuges in existence in 1921. The hoped-for strategy of allowing surplus game to expand out of protected breeding preserves to repopulate the surrounding countryside would now be tested. Moreover, additional refuges were in the works.

In 1923, the legislature set aside the remotest portions of the Coconino and Tusayan (Kaibab) national forests west of Sycamore Canyon in a Coconino-Yavapai State Game Preserve. This was done at the behest of the newly formed Arizona Game Protective Association, urged on by its president, Thomas E. McCullough of Flagstaff. As with the other refuges established by the legislature, only the hunting and trapping of deer, antelope, turkeys, and other game animals were prohibited, and the act specifically stated that the grazing of livestock and other legitimate uses of the national forests would continue.

In 1927, State Game Warden Dwight Pettis reported that deer on most of the refuges were doing well and that populations of whitetails in the Graham and Catalina mountain preserves were approaching the "thickness" of deer on the by-now infamous Grand Cañon (North Kaibab) Game Preserve. The large size of the existing refuges was also being recognized as a management problem, and Pettis suggested a committee be formed to recommend changes in game preserve boundaries. While noting the difficulties inherent in having only the state legislature able to adjust refuge boundaries or open refuges to hunting, Pettis also suggested creating smaller refuges close to urban centers. He recommended, for example, establishing a quail refuge in the Congress Junction vicinity, that area then being needed as a reliable source of quail for transplants. That same year, the legislature modified the boundaries of the Blue Range Game Preserve downward, withdrawing that portion between the Arizona-New Mexico border and the Blue and San Francisco rivers. Local businessmen were complaining that some preserves were just too large, and local sportsmen wanted more area open to hunting.

When the new game code of 1928 went into effect, and game and fish matters were put under the direction of a three-man commission, the state had seven refuges compris-

Old refuge sign in Bear Canyon marking the southern boundary of the Williams Game Refuge. Many such signs were never picked up and persisted for years after a refuge had been decommissioned. The fine print at the bottom of the sign states: "The Area Behind This Sign is Set Apart as a Refuge for Game Animals and Birds. Help Make Arizona's Hunting Better by the Refuge System Instead of a Closed Season." Photo by Michael L. Rice. (Courtesy of Tom Britt)

ing 1,732,120 acres, including the 700,000-acre federal refuge on the north Kaibab. Given authority to create and adjust refuge boundaries, the Arizona Game and Fish Commission took action to grandfather in all of the legislature's refuges as one of its first actions, on April 6, 1929. The ability to create more refuges and adjust others were what many sportsmen-conservationists had been waiting for, and the first commission immediately created five new refuges near Flagstaff, including Mormon Lake, Munds Park, and San Francisco Mountain near where Commissioner McCullough resided.

The remainder of 1929 saw six more state refuges established in Yavapai County, including Pine Mountain and Mingus Mountain. Other actions reduced the size of the legislature's Mount Graham, Catalina Mountain, and Huachuca Mountain refuges and created the first refuge primarily for quail (Wickenburg State Game Refuge along the Hassayampa River). Additional refuges were established, one primarily for elk (Cabin Draw), and another large preserve in the Pinal Mountains. State Game Warden Robert Bayless also recommended that the commission support the Tucson Mountain Game Protective Association's request for a Tucson Mountain Game Refuge, provided that Pima County take over the refuge's management as a county park. All in all, the commission added 23 more refuges that year, including the Santa Rita Refuge, where the University of Arizona intended to do a quail study. Species specifically "protected" in preserves now included both species of deer, elk, antelope, and mountain sheep (Catalina Mountain) as well as turkey—a featured species of many of the refuges.

Arizona's 29 game refuges encompassed nearly a million and a half acres. Bayless considered range conditions in most of the refuges to be good despite the fact that none were closed to grazing. Exceptions were the Munds Park and Pine Mountain preserves, where some overuse by livestock was noted. Although the commission was now favoring smaller refuges, and considered the Coconino-Yavapai refuge to be larger than required, both the commission and the department approved of the arrangement by which the Forest Service was in charge of the range and the department managed the game. Commissioners and most of the general public also liked having areas where game could be seen easily. Hence, refuges remained popular as a game-conservation measure, as did seasonal closures for both game and fish species. The commission closed Oak Creek to fishing upstream from the Sedona Bridge to its headwaters, and the entire area south of the Gila River was closed to the hunting of mule deer.

In the meantime, Forest Service officials were becoming concerned that the state's game recovery program might be succeeding too well. Based on reports from rangers, ranchers, range technicians, and some sportsmen, deer and other big game animals appeared to be exceeding the carrying capacity of their ranges. To "get at the facts," a multidisciplinary team of investigators was formed, which would spend the better part of April 1931 inspecting five "problem areas." Three of these areas—the Santa Catalina Mountain portion of the Coronado National Forest, the Coconino-Yavapai Refuge on the Tusayan National Forest, and the Blue Range on the Crook National Forest—were all or partially contained within game preserves established by the legislature. The two other areas, Hay Lake on the Coconino National Forest and the Cabin Draw-Chevelon area of the Sitgreaves National Forest, involved mostly antelope and elk and had been created by the Forest Service and Game and Fish Commission, respectively. The Forest Service's fear was that irreparable harm might be done to the recovery ability of the national forest's rangelands, as browse conditions were beginning to look similar to what was then taking place on the game preserve portion of the north Kaibab.

The survey team comprised representatives of the US Biological Survey (Edward Goldman), University of Arizona (Andrew A. Nichol), Arizona Game and Fish Commission (Les B. Hart), Arizona Game and Fish Department (Kenner C. Kartchner), and local officials representing the Forest Service, Arizona Cattlegrowers Association, and Arizona Woolgrowers Association. Although all of the inspectors agreed that game numbers were high and that browse plants were locally damaged, the committee was less than unanimous as to what to do about the situation. The state's commission and department representatives, gratified to be faced with the problem of too many deer, wanted to take a "go slow" approach, pointing out that some of the damage being done appeared to be due to cattle. In separate reports, Goldman and Nichol blamed the problem on too many game animals and called for opening the three refuges to deer hunting and initiating antelope and elk hunts in the other two areas. Goldman and Nichol both stressed the need to reduce rather than merely check the game populations, even recommending a doe season on a portion of the Santa Catalina Mountain Refuge. Both biologists also suggested that mountain lion control be reduced in heavily browsed areas not used by livestock.

The refuge concept was now more popular than ever, so the idea of opening these areas to hunting seemed counterintuitive to a public that desired more game outside the preserves. And, was not the problem of too many deer, antelope, and elk in those areas where the species were protected prima facie evidence of the success of the refuge system? Although the commission considered some of the refuges too large, and agreed that some areas might contain too many deer, it was pointed out that limited portions of problem refuges could be opened to the hunting of only those species requiring control. The Arizona Game Protective Association and the commissioners they supported agreed that future refuges would be smaller but more numerous.

The 1930s saw an almost frantic effort to reduce, relocate, adjust, and redefine—but mostly establish—a dizzying array of state refuges as commissioners, affiliates of the Arizona Game Protective Association, forest rangers, and department personnel recommended pet areas for inclusion in the state refuge system. Although some of the new refuges, such as Trumbull Mountain, Harquahala Mountain, Boulder Canyon, House Rock Valley, Wallapi, and Tucson Mountain, encompassed 40,000 acres or more, some quail refuges contained acreages ranging from less than 100 to 6,000 acres. Some refuges were open for the hunting of certain species and closed for others. For example, portions of Pinal Mountain State Game Refuge were opened to quail hunting in 1931, while the Blue Range and Coconino-Williams state game refuges were opened in 1933 to deer hunting but not turkey hunting. Seasonal closures for both game and fish species also remained popular. Apache County was closed to quail hunting to protect transplanted birds, and the entire state was closed to javelina hunting in 1932 in an attempt to increase the species' numbers.

A serious problem, particularly with the larger refuges, was the difficulty of posting and patrolling any changes in the areas closed to hunting. A 1931 law governing the signing of refuges required that refuges and any other lands closed to the possession of firearms be posted at least at quarter-mile intervals. The one-foot-square signs used black lettering on yellow background. These difficulties, coupled with increasing game populations, caused an increasing number of critics to question the wisdom of keeping some of the larger refuges closed to hunting. In 1936, the commission abolished the 248,280-acre Blue and Rincon refuges, marking the first year that more acreage was removed from protected status than added. At the June 1938 commission meeting, the need for a more comprehensive refuge policy was discussed at length. By 1939, there were 76 game refuges in the state, not counting national parks and monuments.

Refuges continued to be popular through the 1940s, even though steps were now being taken to restrict their size and control their proliferation. Outside assistance in patrolling the preserves was actively sought, and the Chiricahua and Huachuca game refuges were reinstated only with the promised cooperation of the Coronado National Forest and the Bisbee Game Protective Association. A citizen request for a game refuge in Yuma County was denied, as was the Forest Service's proposal for a huge federal refuge

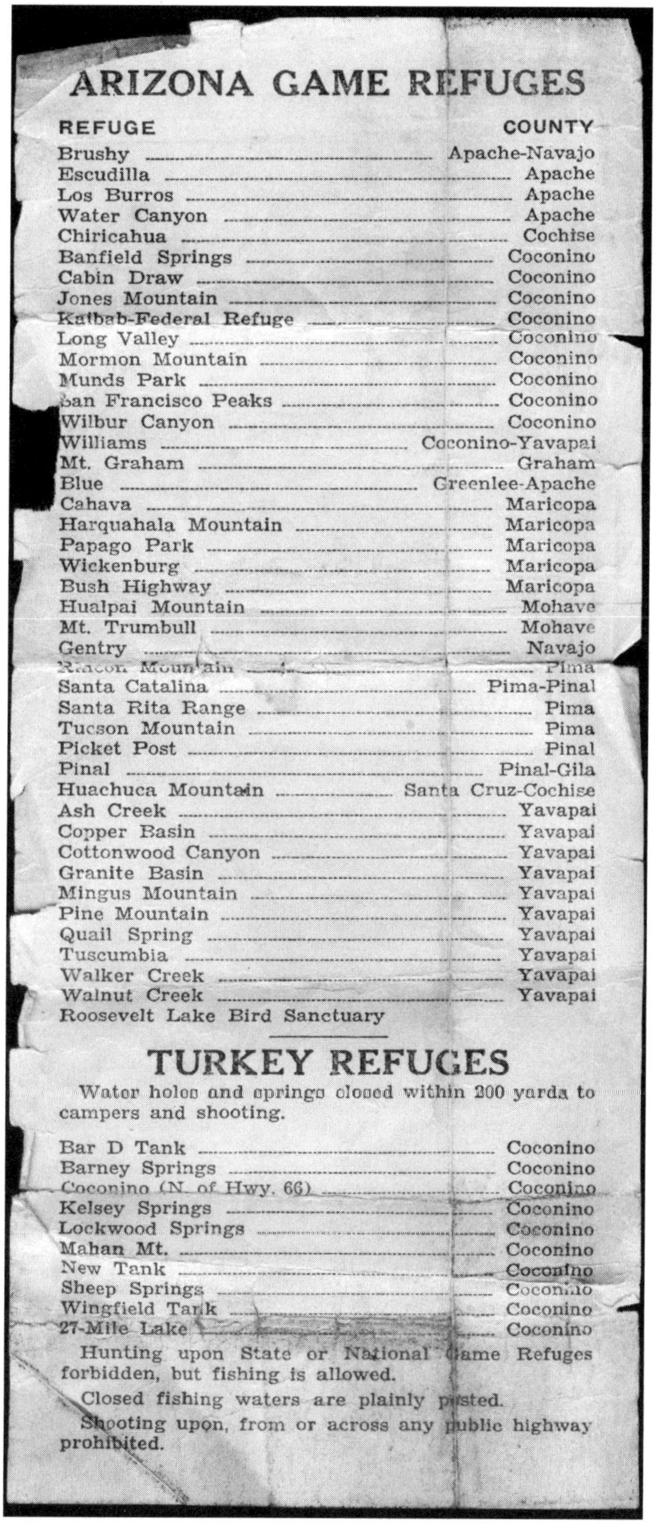

ARIZONA GAME REFUGES

REFUGE	COUNTY
Brushy	Apache-Navajo
Escudilla	Apache
Los Burros	Apache
Water Canyon	Apache
Chiricahua	Cochise
Banfield Springs	Coconino
Cabin Draw	Coconino
Jones Mountain	Coconino
Kaibab-Federal Refuge	Coconino
Long Valley	Coconino
Mormon Mountain	Coconino
Munds Park	Coconino
San Francisco Peaks	Coconino
Wilbur Canyon	Coconino
Williams	Coconino-Yavapai
Mt. Graham	Graham
Blue	Greenlee-Apache
Cahava	Maricopa
Harquahala Mountain	Maricopa
Papago Park	Maricopa
Wickenburg	Maricopa
Bush Highway	Maricopa
Hualpai Mountain	Mohave
Mt. Trumbull	Mohave
Gentry	Navajo
Rincon Mountain	Pima
Santa Catalina	Pima-Pinal
Santa Rita Range	Pima
Tucson Mountain	Pima
Picket Post	Pinal
Pinal	Pinal-Gila
Huachuca Mountain	Santa Cruz-Cochise
Ash Creek	Yavapai
Copper Basin	Yavapai
Cottonwood Canyon	Yavapai
Granite Basin	Yavapai
Mingus Mountain	Yavapai
Pine Mountain	Yavapai
Quail Spring	Yavapai
Tuscumbia	Yavapai
Walker Creek	Yavapai
Walnut Creek	Yavapai
Roosevelt Lake Bird Sanctuary	

TURKEY REFUGES

Water holes and springs closed within 200 yards to campers and shooting.

Bar D Tank	Coconino
Barney Springs	Coconino
Coconino (N. of Hwy. 66)	Coconino
Kelsey Springs	Coconino
Lockwood Springs	Coconino
Mahan Mt.	Coconino
New Tank	Coconino
Sheep Springs	Coconino
Wingfield Tank	Coconino
27-Mile Lake	Coconino

Hunting upon State or National Game Refuges forbidden, but fishing is allowed.

Closed fishing waters are plainly posted.

Shooting upon, from or across any public highway prohibited.

A list of refuges took up a full column in the 1933 hunt regulations. (AGFD files)

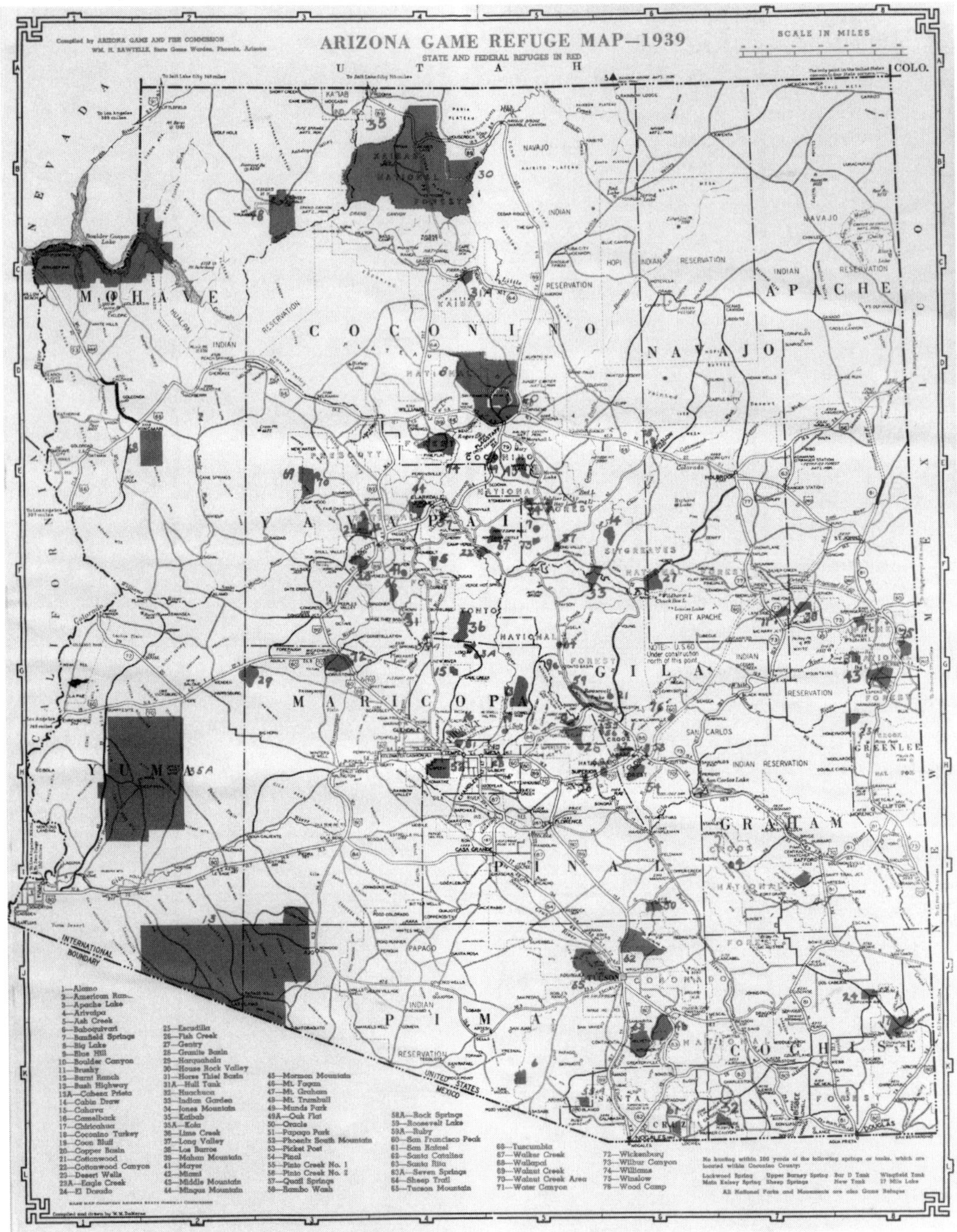

Arizona game refuge map, 1939. Seventy-six refuges are listed. (AGFD files)

encompassing from 30 to 60 square miles at the junction of the Coconino, Sitgreaves, Tonto, and Crook national forests.

Refuge proponents and opponents continued to make themselves heard, and the commission took under advisement a request by the Yavapai County Cattlegrowers to abolish the Pine Mountain Game Refuge. Objections to refuges—other than not being able to hunt within their boundaries—included complaints regarding restrictions against carrying firearms and livestock having to compete with too many game animals. A resolution by the Florence and Superior game protective associations for a series of new refuges in Pinal County (including one to protect a small band of antelope south of Florence Junction) was denied. Principally as a matter of state's rights, the commission had also objected to a federal proposal in January 1939 for national game refuges in Yuma and in Pima County (the Kofa and Cabeza Prieta national game ranges) pending further negotiations between the US Department of the Interior's Division of Grazing and the Biological Survey.

Permitted uses within the refuges were also becoming more flexible. Permittees were no longer given permission to post state lands as refuges, and new regulations allowed the automatic posting of lands within half a mile of a dwelling or water, negating the need to establish a refuge to protect individual watering sites. In 1938, the commission also rescinded the need for special permits to hunt predatory animals on state refuges with and without the use of dogs. In 1939, Roosevelt Lake National Wildlife Refuge was opened to public fishing. In May of that year, the closed season on mule deer, bear, and turkeys south of the Gila River was rescinded, and the following day all trout waters previously closed to fishing were opened. Refuges remained an integral part of game conservation strategy, however. As a result, the commission established several new refuges in 1939 and adjusted the boundaries of several others. But, as a sign of things to come, proposals for a number of other refuges were denied.

The state's game refuge system was again discussed at length during the December 14, 1939, commission meeting, and it was decided that either the State Game Warden or someone hired through the Pittman-Robertson Act should evaluate the preserves and recommend needed revisions. Although no one was hired to evaluate the refuges per se, deputy wardens and biologists began making evaluations based on whether or not the refuges were accomplishing their purpose. Like some forest rangers, some department personnel continued to be pro-refuge, while others were more critical, or at least more circumspect, regarding their accomplishments. In 1941, the state laid claim to 81 refuges—an all-time high.

On March 17, 1942, the Ruby State Game Refuge was abolished along with three others, as surveys had shown that the purpose of the refuges had not been accomplished. In the former case, an introduction of masked bobwhite had failed and the refuge was no longer needed. Two more refuges were abolished in July 1942 and the South Mountain Park and Baboquivari state refuges were reduced in size. Refuges continued to be popular within both the commission and the department, though, and that same year a new 15,400-acre Tortolita-Owlhead Game Refuge was established on the recommendations of department biologist Ted Knipe and Deputy Warden William P. "Blue" Tharp. This action, in turn, was followed by the abolishment of the Catalina Mountain Game Refuge due to the objections of outspoken outdoor writer Jack O'Connor, who opposed hunt closures when it could be shown that refuge status no longer served a management purpose—in this case, allowing a bighorn sheep population to increase.

With the improvement of game populations after World War II, support for game refuges waned. In November 1945, the commission ordered a review of all refuges. Some preserves, such as Aravaipa State Game Refuge, were abolished, while others had their boundaries modified (e.g., Granite Basin).

Nonetheless, other refuges continued to be acquired. On June 16, 1948, on the advice of department director Thomas L. Kimball, the commission approved a Paradise Valley Game Refuge, which centered around a newly developed water catchment for quail.

Opening refuges formerly closed to hunting also posed problems. The Tortolita-Owlhead refuge, opened to deer hunting in 1952, generated considerable comment from hunters who thought the deer herd there had been terribly "mauled" by excessive hunting pressure. Refuge proposals by the public could also prove difficult to quell, even though some of the proposals were designed to protect property and waters more than game. Two refuge proposals that were entertained but never finalized involved suggestions by the California Fish and Game Department for *buro* deer and tule elk refuges along the Colorado River, the former in the Cibola area and the latter in Topock Marsh.

After much negotiation, the US Army transferred Fort Huachuca to the state of Arizona on June 16, 1947. Both the facilities and the reservation were turned over to the Arizona Game and Fish Department and the area made into the Huachuca Game Refuge. Such a designation was now modified to better fit the department's needs, and when pronghorn and bison were translocated to the refuge, the reservation was designated as the Charles T. Vorhies Game Habitat Research Project. Refuges established merely as sanctuaries to protect game were now considered obsolete. Perhaps to emphasize this point, Director Kimball made no mention of either the refuges or the refuge program in his biennial report to the commission for 1949–51.

During the 1950s it became standard practice to abolish, reduce, or otherwise revise refuges at the June season-setting commission meetings. In 1952, the Gabrielson Report recommended no change in the department's "sound system" of abolishing refuges that have accomplished their objective. As stated by Wendell Swank in his book, *The Mule Deer in the Arizona Chaparral*, the problem by then was how to harvest more deer and other game, not protect animals from hunting. As a result, most refuges had been either abolished or redesignated as wildlife areas beginning in 1950. The Three Bar, for example, was designated a wildlife area, to be used for wildlife research and management purposes, including hunting. Then, at the June 1957 commission meeting, the department's chief of game management, Larry Powell, recommended the abolishment of the six remaining refuges save May Memorial, Luna Lake, and Papago Park. The commission agreed, and directed that all refuges be abolished exactly one year later.

When I joined the Arizona Game and Fish Department in 1961, the only wildlife refuges remaining were May Memorial in the Chiricahua Mountains, Luna Lake near

Springerville, and Tucson Mountain Wildlife Area west of Tucson. This latter refuge had been abolished in April 1958, but given a reprieve due to the concern of residents that an open deer season would pose a danger to the homeowners. Wendell Swank, on becoming director, vowed to remove even these last vestiges but was prevented from doing so by Commissioner C. J. "Jack" Mantle, who agreed with his Tucson constituents in wanting refuge status to continue. The dilemma was solved by making the Tucson Mountain Wildlife Area open only to archery hunting. May Memorial Refuge had been bequeathed to the department with the caveat that it would remain an inviolate refuge in perpetuity. With the conversion of Luna Lake to a wildlife area, Arizona's refuge program was at an end.

Today, with many game species below par, some sportsmen question whether the refuge system should be reinstated as a means to bring back the game. Alas, such simplistic solutions are no longer possible, if they ever were. Although the refuges were correctly regarded as a means of habitat preservation, being off-limits to hunters is not in itself sufficient to increase game numbers. Nor does sport hunting necessarily reduce game numbers or keep animals from increasing. This was made abundantly clear in the 1950s, when deer numbers increased both on and off the refuges to the point that overbrowsing became a range management problem nearly statewide.

Similarly, when game numbers declined in the late 1960s and early 1970s, national parks and other refuges, real and de facto, felt the same impacts as areas open to hunting. Game populations on the Three Bar Wildlife Area, as well as on Saguaro, Grand Canyon, and other national parks, followed the same general population trends on and off these de facto refuges.

Whether because of climatic reasons, lack of predator control, or other variables, merely closing an area to hunting does not often result in an increase in game populations. Nor has it been found that game populations increase adjacent to refuges and preserves. Long-term game abundance or scarcity depends on habitat quality and fluctuates in response to weather and other variables rather than properly regulated hunting (Heffelfinger 2006).

THE QUEST FOR HATCHERIES AND BETTER FISHING

Bud Bassett, David E. Brown, Bill Silvey, Larry Riley, and Roger Sorensen

The challenge for Arizona's sport fishery managers has always been about the same. Arizona is an arid place, perhaps more so in the early years. The problem has been getting the "mostest out of the leastest": increasing the fishing potential in a dry state. There have been a few proven strategies to increase that potential, some of which were good ideas and others with which people would argue.

In general, people made the best decisions they could with the information and tools available. When it came down to adding fishing potential to meet a growing demand, they knew they had several options: add new kinds of fish (nonnative) to those already here; add new lakes and reservoirs where people could fish; produce and stock fish to meet the demands of the public; and explore using Arizona's native fishes as a resource. From the 1880s through the early 1960s, the state's fishery managers would practice them all.

As early as 1881, residents of the territory were concerned about the availability of fish and fishing. In 1881, the Arizona Territorial Fish Commission was formed (Brown 2009). It was made up of three commissioners appointed by the governor. Their interests were both for sport and for sustenance. They would be renamed the Territorial Fish and Game Commission in 1891, but in the beginning much of their attention was focused on securing fish for planting in Arizona.

A lot of that focus was on getting the new fish from Europe, the carp, for stocking in Arizona's waters. While Commissioner J. H. Taggert, business manager for the commission, expressed frustration at the inability to get carp successfully to northern Arizona, his counterpart Commissioner Richard Rule bragged about his success introducing them in southern Arizona. Taggert suggested an appropriation of $5,000 would be appropriate to construct a hatchery in Arizona for rearing carp, and maybe to secure some shad for the Colorado River.

By 1897, the Territorial Commission had grown to 15 members: three commissioners and 12 "assistant commissioners." Most of these "wardens" worked without pay. To raise money for the commission, the Territorial Legislature authorized a $10 nonresident license. Seven years later a resident license would be added at the cost of 50 cents.

Neither fishing nor fish hatcheries are mentioned in State Game Warden George Willard's 1914 report on conditions impacting Arizona's wildlife, and one is left with the impression that fishing issues were a minor concern in the Arizona Game and Fish Department during most of Gov. George Hunt's administration. Outside of its efforts to prevent game hogs from overfishing the state's trout waters and using "Giant Powder" or other illegal fishing methods, and its reports on stream pollution and misappropriation, the state's early involvement with fishes was mostly to encourage the US Bureau of Fisheries to stock Roosevelt Lake and other Arizona waters with game fish.

In truth, Willard's department had neither the money nor the facilities to do much in the way of fish management. Fishing regulations were rudimentary. They consisted of a June 1–September 1 trout season, and a September 1–December 1 season on black bass and crappie. Fish less than seven inches long were not to be kept.

Fish and fish hatcheries remained very much on the mind of Arizona's sportsmen, and the public was adamant in its demand for both "better hunting *and* fishing." Although the state's warm-water fishing opportunities were limited, Roosevelt Lake then being the only major reservoir, a plentiful supply of trout waters existed in the high country. The problem was that the more accessible of these cold-water streams, such as Sedona's Oak Creek, were inadequate to meet the demands of fishermen, especially since some of the best trout waters were tied up on the Fort Apache Indian Reservation. As a result, rural businesses and politicians pressed both the Arizona State Legislature and the department for a hatchery that would provide an abundant and continuous trout fishery independent of stockings by the federal government.

Willard's temporary successor, Joe Prochaska, exhibited more interest in fish and fish stocking than his predecessor and kept track of the numbers and kinds of fishes the Bureau of Fisheries stocked during his time in office. In those days, prior to 1923, the state was totally dependent on a few federal and private hatcheries for both adult fish and fry. Department personnel supervised the stockings and participated in the plantings, taking fingerling-sized fish of several species from Roosevelt, Lakeside, Mormon, and Stoneman lakes and releasing them in suitable-appearing waters throughout Arizona.

Fish stockings conducted during Prochaska's tenure included such warm-water species as largemouth bass (22,570), catfish (7,700, species undisclosed), yellow perch (1,425), crappie (900, species undisclosed), and sunfish (900, species undisclosed). Trout releases consisted of 132,000 "black-spotted mountain trout"[1] released in 45 locations and 78,000 rainbows released at 20 locations. The logistics involved with these transplants were formidable. Most of the trout shipments from federal hatcheries arrived at the railroad station in Holbrook in late August and had to be translocated quickly to remote streams by deputy wardens and volunteer sportsmen. As a general rule, the native "mountain trout" appear to have enjoyed better release sites, many of the rainbow trout being released in warmer waters such as in the Salt River at Tempe, at Horseshoe Bend, and above Roosevelt Lake (Prochaska 1921). No attempt was made to assess the status of resident trout prior to the releases, and whatever individual strains of trout were originally present in these streams were compromised by 1922.

Prochaska (1921) thought most of Arizona's streams and warm-water lakes had adequate populations of stocked fish. He thought the greatest need was for Arizona to have its own fish hatchery, if for no other reason than to have a place to house the trout fry received from the federal government until they could be transplanted at a more propitious time. Although sympathetic legislators had introduced appropriation bills to build a

[1] It would be interesting to know the sources and fates of these "native trout," which were released in numerous locations throughout the state including, in addition to the White Mountains, Bright Angel Creek in the Grand Canyon, Eagle Creek, Blue River, Oak Creek, the East Verde, Sabino Creek in the Catalina Mountains, and Turkey Creek in the Chiricahua Mountains.

The South Fork Hatchery on the south fork of the Little Colorado River, shortly after completion. (AGFD files)

hatchery in Arizona, some allocating as much as $30,000 for the purpose, these measures failed to pass. Prochaska thought these bills failed because the estimated construction costs had been too high.

Taking it upon himself to visit private hatcheries near Salt Lake City, Utah, and with the support of Springerville businessmen, Prochaska estimated that a trout hatchery could be built on the south fork of the Little Colorado River for $10,000. Even this amount would be difficult to raise without a special appropriation. Little money was coming into the department due to the low cost of hunting and fishing licenses, the shortage of game, and the restrictive seasons then in place.

To finance the hatchery, Prochaska proposed that 25% of the Game and Fish Fund be set aside for construction costs, with the expectation that increased fishing-license sales would pay the operating costs. An additional incentive for beginning the South Fork Hatchery in 1922 was an understanding with the Indian agent for the Fort Apache Indian Reservation that the government would stock the reservation with trout purchased from South Fork and that fishermen on the reservation would buy state fishing licenses.

Begun during Prochaska's administration, the South Fork Hatchery was troubled from the beginning. The arrangement with the Indian Service fell through, and construction was temporarily halted when Governor Hunt returned to office in 1922. A return to the status quo was not popular with either Arizona's fishermen or White Mountain residents, however, and on January 22, 1923, the Apache County Farm Bureau sent a letter to state Senator Mulford Winsor complaining that the county's trout streams had been "fished out" even in areas away from surfaced roads. The Farm Bureau wanted the hatchery completed as a financial investment in Arizona and considered the department's paying a watchman $3 a day to watch over a nonproductive property an unnecessary expense. It wanted a fish culturist sent out immediately to take charge and finish the hatchery.

Construction resumed and South Fork Hatchery was completed in 1923. Facilities included an enclosed hatchery house, along with about 70 hatching troughs, some rearing ponds and a residence (Bassett, Silvey, and Sorensen 1998). The initial crew consisted of one winter and two summer employees under the supervision of John E. Griffith. Deputy Warden John N. House, who had formerly been in charge of South Fork, added to the hatchery's controversy when he wrote Governor Hunt on May 23, 1923, complaining that the hatchery was poorly located and built more to benefit the Becker family than to distribute fish throughout the White Mountains. Whatever the reason for the location, House pointed out that the hatchery's accessibility was limited, and the supply of water insufficient (House to Hunt, May 23, 1923, Fish and Game, Box 2A, Folder 7. Arizona State Library, Archives and Public Records).

Having the Little Colorado River as a water source did constitute a problem. When 200,000 rainbow trout and 150,000 cutthroat trout eggs arrived from the Plymouth Rock Hatchery in Massachusetts in 1924, all were lost the succeeding winter when the water remained unexpectedly cold for a prolonged period. Although better success was achieved in following years, the river's frigid water proved to be a chronic problem, as temperatures were not only extremely cold during winter months but subject to extreme temperature fluctuations and too warm for raising trout in summer.

Nonetheless, South Fork Hatchery managed to limp along through the 1920s into the early 1930s, producing more than a million fry and fingerling trout during its better years. As of 1928, the number of fingerling trout stocked from South Fork Hatchery included 208,500 rainbows planted in the Little Colorado River drainage; 81,000 in Black River; 114,000 in White River; and 166,000 elsewhere. Another 22,000 cutthroat trout were split between Bennie and Hall creeks in the White Mountains (Pettis 1928).

Thelma McMichael and a largemouth black bass taken at Roosevelt Lake, ca. 1929. Largemouth black bass and bluegill were the most popular and commonly stocked fishes in Arizona's warm-water reservoirs. The bass could attain great size in new impoundments in only a few years. (Courtesy of Jeff McMichael)

A Phoenix party enjoying the results of an excursion to the El Golfo area below the mouth of the Colorado River, ca. 1925. The large fish is a tortuava; the others are sea bass. (Herb and Dorothy McLaughlin Collection, Arizona State University Libraries, #CP MCL 97885)

In the meantime, the demand for a state-run trout hatchery intensified, not only from chambers of commerce and local recreation businesses, but from sportsmen belonging to trout-country affiliates within the Arizona Game Protective Association, which had been formed in 1923. As a result of pressures from the Flagstaff and Verde Valley sportsmen's clubs, a small hatchery dwelling and two small square rearing ponds[2] were built at Sterling Springs at the head of Oak Creek in 1925. Sportsmen obtained water rights for this venture, originally known as Oak Creek Ponds, from the Santa Fe Railroad. Producing mostly fry, the facilities were upgraded in 1930, after which 150,000 trout were received and raised there each year. Then, in 1938, a washout ended the hatchery's role as a major rearing station.

Pressures from Springerville resulted in the department's acquiring a spring-fed hatchery at Squirrel Springs on Bennie Creek in 1926. A tributary of the Little Colorado River near Greer, Squirrel Springs was designed to serve as a model for future hatcheries, according to hatchery supervisors Griffith and F. A. Bengard. Using spring water at a relative constant temperature rather than stream water, Squirrel Springs Hatchery consisted of a hatchery shelter, a residence for the lone caretaker, and a few dirt rearing ponds. The spring's flow was limited, however, and Bengard later recommended that both the Squirrel Springs and South Fork properties be sold and another hatchery be constructed or purchased elsewhere. Nonetheless, trout production continued at Squirrel Springs until 1934, when both this hatchery and South Fork were officially retired.

Another locality demanding a hatchery in the 1920s was Payson and nearby communities below the Mogollon Rim in Gila County. In response, the department developed Horton Creek near Kohl's Ranch in 1928. Producing only fry, this facility consisted of a hatchery building and several nursery troughs. Fluctuating summer water flows kept pro-

---

[2] Ponds in which small fish are held and fed for later transport and release.

duction down at this station, with a high of only some 750,000 trout being planted in 1929. The site was abandoned when the hatchery building slipped into Horton Creek in 1932.

Despite the state's now having a hatchery program, Arizona continued to rely on the Bureau of Fisheries for both warm-water and cold-water fishes. In his final report to Governor Hunt, State Game Warden Dwight Pettis (1928) mentioned three shipments of fish received and paid for by the Bureau of Fisheries between 1925 and 1928. Most of these plantings were of warm-water species (the state did not yet have a warm-water hatchery), and included bass, "sun-perch," and catfish released in Roosevelt Lake in November 1925, along with an additional 278,000 "pond fishes" (black bass, catfish, sunfish, and yellow perch) planted in 1926 by deputies, sportsmen volunteers, and boy scouts. Another plant included a carload of largemouth bass released in Mormon Lake, which was then considered a nearly permanent body of water.

Cold-water species from federal hatcheries included 67,000 trout planted in the Salt River below Roosevelt Lake in the summer of 1926 with assistance from the Gila County Game Protective Association, which helped finance the stocking. Another 1,630,000 trout, mostly rainbows, were planted at several locations in the White Mountains in 1927, along with 20,000 "black-spotted" native trout. Channel catfish, also purchased in June 1927, were released in a pond 18 miles northwest of Tucson. Other recommended plants in northern and southern Arizona were denied by the US Fish Commission due to a backlog of commitments, including stocking San Carlos Lake, the irrigation reservoir behind Coolidge Dam scheduled for completion in 1928.

An interesting aside is mention of two small shipments of Louisiana bullfrogs in 1926 and 1927, both of which were released along the Salt River near Phoenix with the promise of several thousand more as soon as funding permitted (Pettis 1928). Meanwhile the department was making plans for a warm-water hatchery of its own at Papago Park between Phoenix and Tempe. The need for such a hatchery was no doubt fueled by two new hydroelectric reservoirs constructed by the Salt River Project below Roosevelt Dam—Canyon Lake (950 surface acres), completed in 1925, and Apache Lake (2,600 surface acres), completed in 1927. Even more promising was Lake Pleasant, an irrigation reservoir on the Agua Fria River, which was dedicated in 1927.

Despite these improvements, Arizona was not yet a major fishing destination, and the more adventurous anglers continued to travel to other states or the Gulf of California for their fishing vacation. So intense was the desire for additional hatcheries for both trout and warm-water fishes that another, larger fish hatchery became a major campaign slogan. The Arizona Game Protective Association and affiliates, pushing to repeal the 1916 game code, had promised a game and fish commission that would be more responsive to demands for more trout and better fishing. Indeed, "better hunting *and* fishing" was destined to become not only the motto for the association but for the department itself. Hatcheries and more fish was a promise the new Arizona Game and Fish Commission would keep.

GAME BIRDS AND GAME FARMS

David E. Brown

All early Arizona wildlife observers—sportsmen, birdwatchers, and wardens—agreed that the state had an abundance of native game birds and that populations of Gambel's quail, white-winged doves, and mourning doves were such that these species could be nearly as much nuisance as sport. Yet, as was also the case with Arizona's native trout, the natural abundance and resilience of native animals could not compensate for what might be achieved through the acquisition of a "better stock" of game and fish. The desire for larger and more prolific game birds was secondary only to the demand for a steady supply of game fish in the minds of the state's sportsmen. Game farms and fish hatcheries were therefore top priorities for a fledgling game and fish department.

It was probably for these reasons that Gov. George Hunt selected Frank Rogers to be Arizona's first State Game Warden on January 28, 1913. Rogers, an aviculturist who had been associated with the New York Zoological Gardens before moving to Arizona's Verde Valley, had attracted attention at the 1912 Arizona State Fair for his exotic bird exhibit.

As soon as Rogers returned from his first assignment overseeing the elk transplant south of Winslow, he set to work ordering pheasants and other fowl from Oregon breeders for release in Arizona. But after only a few months in office, Rogers died. Hunt replaced Rogers with another Verde Valley resident, George Willard, a bird lover who shared Rogers's penchant for exotic game birds and other wildlife.

One of State Game Warden Willard's first acts on taking office on June 11, 1914, was to use the $500 special appropriation the Arizona State Legislature had provided the Game and Fish Fund to determine the adaptability of the "Chinese Pheasant and other imported game birds to the food and climate conditions of Arizona." There then being no game farm or other state facility in which to raise exotic birds, pheasants and other game birds were purchased from game breeders and apportioned out to organizations and individuals to raise and release.

Once the initial funds were exhausted, plans were made to trap from 25- to 30-dozen Gambel's quail for release at several places along the lower Colorado River in Arizona and for use as trade for other game birds. How many and what kind of birds were obtained is unknown, but the University of Arizona bird collection contains a ring-necked pheasant that was one member of a dozen pairs slated for release in the fields near Tucson in 1915. Two mountain quail were also shipped to Arizona at about the same time from Oregon's state game farm.

Encouraged by the popularity of his program and the success of pheasants elsewhere in the United States, Willard (1914) recommended that the Game and Fish Fund be provided an additional appropriation to either lease or purchase a suitable tract of land for a state game farm for the propagation of ring-necked pheasants and other game birds. But even though acquiring a game farm constituted a priority secondary only to acquiring a fish hatchery, money was lacking for either.

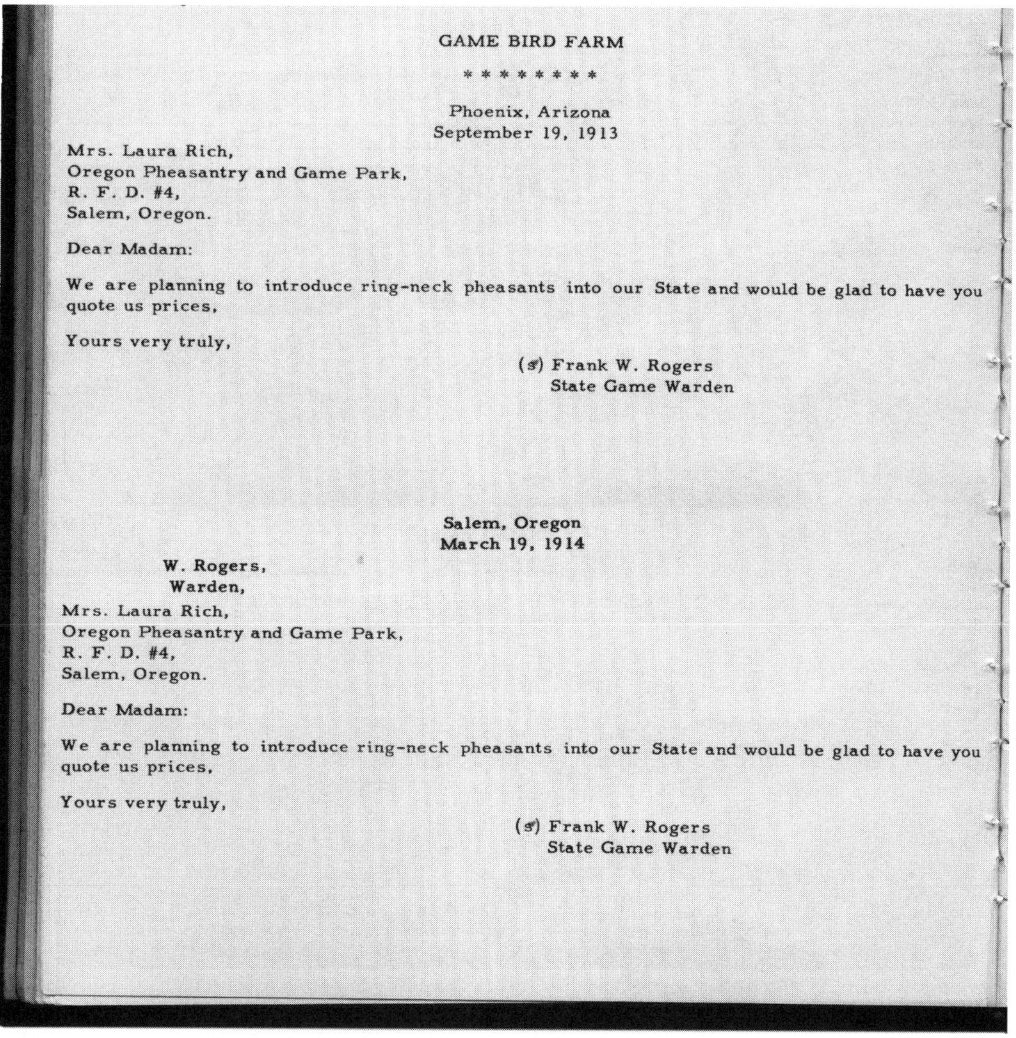

GAME BIRD FARM

* * * * * * * *

Phoenix, Arizona
September 19, 1913

Mrs. Laura Rich,
Oregon Pheasantry and Game Park,
R. F. D. #4,
Salem, Oregon.

Dear Madam:

We are planning to introduce ring-neck pheasants into our State and would be glad to have you quote us prices,

Yours very truly,

(s) Frank W. Rogers
State Game Warden

Salem, Oregon
March 19, 1914

W. Rogers,
Warden,

Mrs. Laura Rich,
Oregon Pheasantry and Game Park,
R. F. D. #4,
Salem, Oregon.

Dear Madam:

We are planning to introduce ring-neck pheasants into our State and would be glad to have you quote us prices,

Yours very truly,

(s) Frank W. Rogers
State Game Warden

State Game Warden Frank Rogers's letter to the Oregon Pheasantry and Game Park, and their reply, were reprinted in the 1947–49 Biennial Report of the Arizona Game and Fish Commission. (AGFD files)

Some imported birds did well in captivity, and the demand for additional stockings continued. The result was that a number of gun clubs, bird fanciers, and youth groups continued to release locally raised pheasants in the Salt River Valley and elsewhere in Arizona through 1919. Unfortunately, lack of experience, and the haphazard release procedures involved, resulted in the success of the pheasant stockings being inconclusive (Lawson 1940a).

Wild turkeys and their eggs were also farmed out. A December 1918 letter in the Arizona Game Protective Association files states, "Pettis [a deputy warden under Willard] started yesterday for the Graham mountains with a bunch of wild turkeys to be liberated there. We put 18 turkeys on the Huachuca Reserve about three months ago and we thought we had better liberate the remainder of the bunch before we left the job and

The Arizona Game and Fish Department was transplanting wild turkeys as early as 1918. (AGFD files)

take no chances on them decorating the dinner table of Joe [Prochaska] and his friends, as we suspect was the end of most of the stuff we turned over to them before." Joe Prochaska had become the interim State Game Warden after the contested election of 1916.

Prochaska (1921), who was again appointed State Game Warden from January 1919 through the end of 1922, was also an advocate of game-bird stocking. A more seasoned outdoorsman than Willard, Prochaska recognized the value of wild stock over pen-reared birds. He trapped 81 turkeys in the White Mountains during the fall of 1919 and spring of 1920 for distribution in the Catalina (18), Hualapai (21), Pinal (11), Chiricahua (16), and Camp Wood (15) mountains—all of which he deemed a success, other than the transplant to the Catalinas (Prochaska 1921).

At that time, farmers were complaining of quail eating sprouting seeds and unharvested grain. Quail suspected of such depredations continued to be trapped in the Salt River Valley and other farming areas. These birds were either sent to other areas in Arizona, including native habitats near Wheatfields and Oracle, or traded out of state. One of these exchanges resulted in the state's obtaining helmeted guinea fowl that had been trapped in Puerto Rico by a Kansas game-bird breeder. Other trades brought pheasants for Boy Scout troops to raise and release in the state's agricultural areas.

After the re-election of Governor Hunt in 1922 and a couple of interim State Game Warden appointments, during which game farms were licensed by the department for a fee of $10, Willard was again appointed State Game Warden on June 14, 1923. The next year, the state leased a game farm between Seventh and Eighth Streets on East McDowell Road near Hunt's Phoenix residence (Tom McCullough, Arizona Game and Fish Commission, pers. comm.). Here, and at a succeeding state game farm north of Phoenix on North Glendale Avenue, game farm supervisors carried on experiments in the raising of turkeys, quail, pheasants, chukar, and Hungarian partridge, with the result that a lot of birds and eggs were distributed, and an untold number of birds released into the wild. For his part, on July 13, 1925, Willard sent letters to cooperators in Prescott, Sentinel, Mesa, Winslow, and Phoenix, requesting that they report on the success of their pheasant transplants. Responses ranged from unknown to "quite satisfactory."

When Willard died in 1926, he was replaced by one of his most stalwart deputies, Dwight Pettis. Pettis (1928) continued the program of distributing ring-necked pheasants and their eggs to interested parties, even though he concluded that his program "had done very little good as has the distribution of 144 eggs." Although some pheasants were seen up to seven years after release, he rated their eventual status "unknown." Similar results were also reported for a dozen Hungarian partridge that, once obtained, had been kept at the game farm until the peak of the nesting season had passed. Only one bird had nested, laying but three eggs, and only adult birds were later observed after the remaining partridges were liberated in a Salt River Valley alfalfa field.

Pettis (1928) considered, and then rejected, a proposal to import chachalacas, deeming the birds too noisy and aggressive. Instead, he continued to trap depredating Gambel's quail, shipping 200 out of state in 1926 and 1927 and moving countless others within the state. He also provided 26 parties, including several Boy Scout troops, with 211 game-farm turkeys and 281 eggs to raise. He released 142 young turkeys in nine locations, including the Graham (38), Pinal (15), and other mountain ranges where wild-trapped birds had previously been released. This practice may have been devastating to any wild birds present, as Pettis (1928) noted what appeared to be a "poultry disease" in his captive birds. Moreover, the financial costs of these releases had been substantial, given the scarcity of money in the Game and Fish Fund at the time. In 1926, the costs for raising pheasants and turkeys were tallied at $1,720.95, including $1,035 for the game farm superintendent's salary. In 1927, the cost was even higher—$397.44 for operating costs and $1,500 for the superintendent.

Later, in the imbroglio over the sportsmen-sponsored referendum establishing a Game and Fish Commission, which Hunt opposed, the game farm was used as a weapon against the governor's administration. Tom McCullough, a leading advocate of the referendum and then one of the first commissioners, would later accuse the governor and the State Game Warden of distributing game farm turkeys and pheasants as political favors (Gallizioli 2012). There was undoubtedly some truth to the accusation. When Gov. John Phillips appointed Robert Bayless State Game Warden on January 22, 1929, Bayless found in the wastebasket receipts from the game farm showing who received pheasants and turkeys and how many. Immediately prior to Thanksgiving, and immediately before Christmas, a number of turkeys and several trios of pheasants had been distributed as political favors in 1928.

In 1929, the newly formed Arizona Game and Fish Commission ordered Bayless to draft rules regulating game farms. The commission would now issue game-farm permits only to qualifying game and fish breeders. Bayless, when distributing the West Glendale game farm's birds and eggs, would retain one-half of the birds and eggs produced. On January 1, 1930, the receiving parties, including affiliates of the Arizona Game Protective

Association, would report the disposition of the birds and eggs received. Breeders not in compliance with their license requirements would be fined from $25 to $50.

Game farms continued to be problematic. On March 26, 1931, the Arizona Game and Fish Commission found it necessary to rewrite an agreement with a game-farm operator in Santa Cruz County. As the Depression intensified, with the Arizona Game and Fish Department in turmoil and the state in financial crisis, the commission ordered the state game farm discontinued on July 7, 1933. The stock was to be distributed to licensed breeders, and removable property would be stored at the State Fair Grounds. Private farms continued to raise birds for the state, but the charge for a permit dropped from $10 to $5 the following year.

Game-bird stocking was a permissible activity under the terms of the Pittman-Robertson Act, and when Federal-Aid monies became available in 1939, a project was designed to find out why pheasants in most of Arizona had failed to sustain themselves. As a result, one of the first Federal-Aid projects approved was an investigation of potential introduction sites and a systematic evaluation of releases of birds obtained from Arizona game breeders and the Ligon Game Farm in New Mexico. Included in this evaluation were 12 locations where pheasants had been liberated between 1939 and 1942 (Lawson 1940b; Arrington 1942a). A similar program involving the release of chukars was discontinued in 1941 until such time as more adaptable stock or more suitable release areas for this species could be located.

Despite pre-release screening procedures, predator control, and some encouraging early reports in the more promising sites, pheasants refused to take hold in most of Arizona (Gambrell 1941). By the end of the Federal-Aid release program in 1942, the outlook was rated as good only in the vicinities of Buckeye, Safford-Thatcher, and Camp Verde, with the birds considered established only in the northern farming areas of Richville, Springerville, Snowflake, and Fredonia. Releases in the populous and extensively farmed areas—Phoenix, Mesa, Casa Grande, and Tucson—were recommended to be discontinued barring more conducive farming practices or new information. Lawson (1940a) suspected, correctly, that low humidity might be contributing to reproductive failure in the Salt River Valley and other desert locales, despite reports of numerous pheasants from private releases being present at Gillespie Farms near Gila Bend.

On June 29, 1946, Director Herbert L. Reid announced to the Arizona Game Protective Association that the department's Louis L. "Buzz" Lawson was converting the Safford National Wildlife Refuge (the former Cluff Ranch) to a game farm for the raising of pheasants, chukars, and mountain quail on an "experimental" basis. The farm and its artesian wells, which had been assumed by the federal government from the Cluff family for nonpayment of taxes, had been transferred to the department after a series of negotiations. On his return from military service in April 1946, Lawson traveled to game farms in New Mexico and Kansas to see how these operations worked. Cautious as to the feasibility of stocking exotic game birds, Lawson thought the farm might prove its worth. Sportsmen were invited to come to the Game and Fish Commission meeting and comment. The commission agreed with the sportsmen that a game farm was a desirable

Chukar were among the game birds raised on game farms and released starting in the mid-1920s. (AGFD files)

operation, and Les N. Kelly of Pima was hired in October 1948 at $200 a month as farm supervisor (Carr 1994).

It was soon decided that pheasants released in southern Arizona were a losing proposition due to the lack of humidity. Instead, almost 10,000 chukars from the Cluff Ranch Game Farm were released at 29 locations between 1946 and 1949 (Brown 1989). The object was to release 200 or more birds at each release site—a well-watered canyon in an area of open junipers and/or oaks with good grass and weed cover. Most of the chukar release locations selected were between 4,000 and 7,000 feet elevation (Lawson 1949a). The fewer mountain quail releases were between the upper range of Gambel's quail and below 9,000 feet. Alas, few of the releases showed much promise of sustaining a population of either species. In 1949, at Lawson's recommendation, the department discontinued its game-farm operations after an expenditure of $43,073.90. The facilities were converted to a residence for a biologist and then made into a regional office.

Follow-up investigations in 1950 and 1951 showed chukars still holding on in the Graham and Catalina mountains, near Saint Johns, at Raymond Ranch, along the Little Colorado River from Springerville to below Lyman Reservoir, on the OW Ranch (where several broods had reportedly been raised), in upper Sycamore Canyon, in Lime Creek, in the Phoenix and White Tank mountains, in upper Cataract Canyon and along Kanab Creek. None of these localities had what was deemed a huntable population, and Lawson (1951) recommended against additional releases of game-farm stock. Future stockings of chukars and other exotic game birds, a few of which were successful, originated with either wild-trapped birds or birds obtained from game farms other than the Arizona Game and Fish Department's.

FIGHTING ANIMAL ENEMIES BECOMES A FEDERAL RESPONSIBILITY

David E. Brown

When Arizona became a state, populations of wild ungulates were at their nadir. The state's rangelands were depleted due to overstocking of cattle and sheep along with a series of droughts. The big predators—wolves, mountain lions, and to a lesser extent grizzlies—had switched to feeding on livestock, rather than following their natural prey into oblivion. The high reproductive rate of wolves and the cryptic nature of lions allowed these animals to maintain a sizeable, if not growing, presence, despite being hunted by bounty hunters, ranchmen, and trappers.

Stockmen argued that livestock husbandry could not be an economic success as long as wolves and other predators decimated their herds, and lobbied for government intervention to solve the "problem" (Brown 1983, 1985b, 2009). Although hunters pretty much agreed that wolves, mountain lions, and coyotes had to be reduced or eliminated for game populations to recover, it was the ranchmen who hired most of the bounty hunters and convinced the US Forest Service to hire "forest guards" (forest rangers specifically assigned to the tasks of trapping big predators while guarding the national forests from fire, illegal logging, and open-range grazing).

Roots of Federal Predator Control

Whatever the desire of its citizens, Arizona had no enabling legislation authorizing the State Game Warden or any other state government agency to perform predator control. As a result, most of the predator killing was done by Forest Service guards and freelance bounty hunters—local men well versed in the art of trapping.

In addition to the sale of the pelt, the primary motivation for hunting predators was a territorial law establishing bounties, which had been carried over to statehood on May 20, 1912. This act prescribed that the county board of supervisors *shall* pay $10 for *lobos* (wolves) and mountain lions taken within their county; other bounties were discretionary, stating that the county *may* pay $2 for coyotes, $1 for bobcats or wildcats, 25 cents for raccoons, and a nickel each for prairie dogs, gophers, and jackrabbits, provided that the hides were presented for inspection in their entirety (both ears in the case of jackrabbits). After an affidavit was signed stating that the animals were taken by the presenter in the county making payment, the hides were marked but not mutilated (to retain their commercial value).

The amounts paid out only hint at the relative damage alleged as being done by the malefactors. Wolves were odious to Western ranchers, who thought it particularly unfair for the national forests to collect grazing fees without providing any protection from these and the other predators found on the lands they administered. Agreeing with this argument, and wanting to build a political constituency for the Department of Agriculture, the US Biological Survey was all too eager to take on the role as the nation's wildlife control agency.

Jesse Ellison, owner of the Nail Ranch below the Mogollon Rim, with recently taken grizzlies and black bears. Homesteaders and ranchers were heavily involved with predator control for recreational and economic reasons and took far more big predators than did the PARC. (Arizona Historical Society/Tucson, #53899, Folder 1, PC 040)

Vernon Bailey, staff biologist for the Biological Survey, had written a bulletin in 1907 describing the problem with wolves, titled *Wolves in Relation to Stock, Game and the National Forest Reserves.* This publication, accompanied by another, *Directions for the Destruction of Wolves and Coyotes,* described existing conditions and provided a prescription for relief.

> The enormous losses suffered by stockmen of the western cattle ranges and the destruction of game on forest reserves, game preserves, and in national parks through the depredations of wolves have led to special investigations by the Biological Survey in cooperation with the Forest Service, to ascertain the best methods for destroying these pests. The results appear in the present report, which includes also field notes on the distribution, abundance, and breeding habits of wolves.
>
> The chief object of the report is to put in the hands of every hunter, trapper, forest ranger, and ranchman directions for trapping, poisoning, and hunting wolves and finding the dens of young. (Bailey 1907)

Needing a constituency to retain the national forests in federal ownership, the Forest Service became an eager proponent of predator control. Nor was the Forest Service's effort limited to producing bulletins. Bailey (1908) reported that in one year Forest Service personnel removed 127 wolves from Arizona's national forests—a number that government hunters would never surpass in the war against predators that was to follow.

Bounties, although popular among the public, presented problems and were inefficiently applied, whether paid by the rancher or the county. Professional hunters were

January catch of one wolf and coyotes by US Forest Service hunter T. B. Bledsol (lower right) on the Kaibab National Forest, ca. 1914. (Arizona Historical Foundation, Will C. Barnes Collection)

naturally most eager to hunt or trap in those areas where predators were abundant and bounties generous. Should their efforts have the desired results, and predator numbers be reduced, interest and funding would wane. Bounties were also prone to abuse, with hunters seeking out the areas where the most animals were available, even if it meant bringing in hides from Mexico or out of state. Thus, once a notorious stock-killer was taken, or a population of a particular predator reduced in numbers, the tendency was to move on until another stock-killer showed up or the predator population recouped its losses.

Variations in fur prices could also frustrate attempts at predator control, as interest fell off in years and months when fur prices were low or not at their prime. Identification of animals turned in for bounty could also be a problem, and fraud was thought to be common—so much so that Bailey (1909) published a key to help bounty payers differentiate between the scalps and hides of wolves, coyotes, feral dogs, and other animals submitted for payment.

Pleased to have ranchmen as political supporters, the administrators of the Southwest's national forests eagerly joined into cooperative agreements with the states of New Mexico and Arizona to hire forest guards to enforce the laws and remove predatory animals. Wolves and mountain lions were the primary targets, but stockmen also lobbied for the taking of "big bears," i.e., grizzlies and stock-killing black bears. Again, it was reasoned that federal assistance was only fair, as the national forests harbored most of the black bears and nearly all the grizzlies.

Many sportsmen were of like mind with ranchmen when it came to predator control, especially bounties. They needed little urging to join the livestock interests in wanting the federal government to kill the predators that were also killing what game remained. Although forest guards were doing their job in controlling wolves and mountain lions, they had other duties to perform and were not always able to respond with the commitment desired. What was needed, in the minds of the anti-predator forces, was a control program that would concentrate on removing not only predators, but other "noxious animals." Ranchers and forest rangers alike strove to reduce or eliminate prairie dogs, porcupines, and other "varmints" competing with livestock for forage or otherwise damaging the economies of the rural West. The Biological Survey was eager to accomplish this task, provided sufficient appropriations could be found and enough competent hunters hired.

In 1914, J. Stokley Ligon was mapping and poisoning prairie-dog towns near Springerville for Gustav Becker and other ranchers who wanted these animals eliminated. An ardent "conservationist," Ligon had recently taken up the cause against predators and noxious animals—a cause in which he was joined by a young forest ranger named Aldo Leopold (Shaw 2011). The two men stumped Arizona and New Mexico, lecturing ranchers, sportsmen's organizations, and anyone who would listen, on the need for better game laws, more game refuges, and government predator-control. Both men believed predator control was an essential component of game management, and that the agency best able to do the job was the Biological Survey—a federal bureau already in place and charged with eliminating nuisance wildlife (Robinson 2005).

The lobbying efforts were successful. On June 30, 1914, Congress made the Biological Survey responsible for experiments and demonstrations in destroying wolves, prairie dogs, and other animals injurious to agriculture and animal husbandry. A sum of $125,000 was appropriated for fiscal year 1914–15 and 300 hunters hired to carry out the mission throughout the West. Now was the time, Ligon and Leopold harangued the sportsmen, to throw all their support behind the Biological Survey and insist that the job be finished to the last wolf and lion, lest these "vermin" regain the range (Brown and Carmony 1990). By the close of fiscal year 1916, Western rangelands had been organized into control districts under competent supervisors with a cadre of professional hunters. The inspector for the New Mexico-Arizona district was none other than Stokley Ligon.

The PARC Wastes No Time

Ligon wasted no time in getting his district's Predatory Animal and Rodent Control branch organized and functioning, hiring his first trapper in September 1915. Most of the remainder of the year he spent experimenting with predator trappers and lion hunters—some of whom were irresponsible and did more harm than good. Even worse, some achieved poor catch records. Only half the men hired were deemed worth keeping. By June 1916, Ligon had whittled his force down to 24 men, having tried out 332.

A hunter and trapper himself, Ligon used the $20,000 appropriated for the New Mexico-Arizona district to hire hunters with a reputation, including about a dozen well-known "wolfers." Some of the best of these were former bounty hunters, men such as Jack Hays, Eddie Ligon, and E. E. "Eddy" Anderson of Douglas, Arizona, with Anderson assigned to work the border country of southeast Arizona and southwest New Mexico. All agreed wolves would be the primary target, as this was the species causing the greatest damage.

New Mexico was emphasized over Arizona, due to this state's better wolf habitat and bigger wolf problems. Arizona was not ignored, however. That year, Eddie Ligon claimed the PARC's first wolves in Arizona in the Cherry-Mingus Mountain region and in the rugged Fossil Creek area. During its first short year of operation, PARC's hunters only took 33 adult wolves and 36 pups and fetuses in the district through the use of traps, poison, and denning[1] (Ligon 1916). Things were just getting started.

Ligon (1916) outlined a battle plan for the following year, again emphasizing the need to take wolves:

> While we have not carried on the wolf work so extensively in Arizona as we have in the state of New Mexico, we have done some good service in Arizona and it is with pleasure that I state that it is my . . . estimate that there are not more than 70 adult gray wolves in the State of New Mexico at the present time, and perhaps that same number in Arizona.[2]

Ligon hated professional bounty hunters almost as much as the wolves themselves, as these men not only competed with his government hunters, they tried to undermine the work of his government men with the county boards of supervisors, sheep herders, and small cattle outfits, leaving him to work mostly with the Forest Service and the larger cattle ranches. Like other early-day predator-control inspectors, Ligon sold his program on the basis of continued performance and quality control, and he deeply resented sheep herders and their dogs for purloining government-obtained carcasses and setting off and stealing traps on the government's inventory. His own employees could also be a problem, and he constantly harangued them about not turning in hides for inspection and failing to send in the skulls of porcupines and other catches to the National Museum as requested.

Ligon was especially conscious of the need to demonstrate cost effectiveness. He calculated the cost of the 3,201 days worked by his 33 hunters as $8,476.66 during fiscal year 1915–16. This cost was more than offset by the damage purportedly done by the 69 wolves claimed (3 of which he took himself), not to mention the 6 lions, 358 coyotes, 103 bobcats, 27 porcupines,[3] 11 eagles, 7 bears, 94 fox, 50 skunks, and 21 badgers taken that year (Ligon 1916).

Fiscal year 1916–17 saw the PARC expand its efforts in Arizona, particularly in regard to wolf work, which was not only the agency's top priority, but also required the most expertise and dedication. By now, many of the best bounty hunters in the Southwest were working for PARC, including the legendary Ben V. Lilly. The salaried government hunt-

---

[1] Digging out and killing pups in the den.

[2] With only a few wolves killed in Arizona by PARC hunters, most of the wolves had to have been taken by Forest Service guards, bounty hunters, and fur trappers.

[3] The Forest Service considered porcupines a major source of damage to young ponderosa pine trees and wanted them killed whenever possible. Although Biological Survey biologists such as Mark E. Musgrave and Walter P. Taylor recognized that this overabundance of porcupines was probably due to lion-control, they reasoned that killing porcupines was less costly than the losses that would be incurred from letting up on lions (Brown and Babb 2009).

The Predatory Animal and Rodent Control branch of the Biological Survey counted coyotes among the animal enemies to be reduced. In fiscal year 1915–16, 358 coyotes were reported taken by PARC hunters. (AGFD files)

ers were gaining the respect of the ranchers due to their ability to remain on the range until the job was done.

Most important, larger kills were now being reported. Ligon (1917) predicted wolves would soon be eliminated from both Arizona and New Mexico, where some 40 hunters were now working at a cost of $14,718.92 (of which $4,009.33 was spent in Arizona). The year's take in Arizona was 13 wolves, 14 lions, 1 jaguar, 5 bears, 200 coyotes, 41 bobcats, 45 foxes, 22 skunks, 2 raccoons, 18 badgers, and 41 porcupines. There was also progress on the political front. The Arizona State Legislature passed an act in 1917 authorizing counties to assess a property tax, with the monies to be used in cooperation with the Biological Survey to destroy prairie dogs and other noxious rodents.

One species, the grizzly, was already on its way out. C. Hart Merriam (1922), using information supplied by Ligon and other Biological Survey staff, listed grizzlies as extant in Arizona only in the White Mountains region, the rugged wilderness area south of Bill Williams Mountain, two locations below the Mogollon Rim, and in the Catalina and Rincon mountains. These estimates were too generous and already outdated. The last grizzly below the Mogollon Rim in Gila County had been killed in 1915 and grizzlies west of the White Mountains and south of the Gila River were fast disappearing (Brown 1985b). Even the more common black bear was by now reduced in both numbers and distribution, as stockmen and PARC agents considered all bears to be stock-killers at some time or another (Ligon 1917).

All the animals mentioned in Ligon's 1917 report from Arizona appear to have been taken through the use of traps and dogs, but PARC hunters in New Mexico were using poison baits and other "predacides" against wolves, and a poisoning campaign was being planned for the coming winter in Arizona. While in common use by ranchmen and bounty hunters, poison had not yet been emphasized as a government control-method in Arizona, due to the objections of houndsmen and fur trappers whose lion dogs were susceptible to the poisons then in use. Strychnine and other poisons would prove to be indiscriminate killers, removing not just the target animals but other species with which they shared habitat.

Ligon and the PARC were uncertain about the effectiveness of using poisons on lions and other animals, as the natural history and behaviors of several target species were still unknown.[4] The taxonomy of some species was as yet uncertain, and the Biological Survey requested that the skulls and hides of certain animals taken by PARC agents be turned in for shipment to Washington and the National Museum for scientific description.

Arizona Gets Involved

In the first years of statehood, Arizona remained relatively uninvolved in predator and rodent control issues, relegating even the payment of bounties to the counties. That the state was leaving control efforts up to the federal government was surprising, given the political strength of the livestock industry and Hunt's strong belief in states' rights when it came to wildlife matters. Whether the reason for the laissez-faire attitude was mostly philosophical or financial is unknown, but neither State Game Warden George Willard nor his fledging department engaged in either type of control. This would soon change.

When America entered World War I in 1917, an increased demand for beef caused a rise in cattle prices. Ligon and his stock-raising constituency were quick to use the war to intensify their battle against predators. Any and all cattle losses meant dollars taken away from the war effort, and exaggerated claims of the damage wreaked by predatory animals were repeated in speeches throughout the Southwest. Ligon and the PARC used large dollar figures for estimated losses to justify increasingly greater appropriations to fund their efforts, and although game proponents such as Aldo Leopold may not have agreed with the statistics, they supported greater expenditures to hunt down predators. More control was obviously needed, and killing predators and rodents cost money—money needed to field personnel and outfit them with traps and poison. With the economics based on an "estimated" basis rather than a more objective cost-benefit analysis, it was hoped that what Congress and the state legislatures did not provide in the way of appropriations, state and livestock cooperators would.

In 1917, the legislature authorized counties to levy a tax of ½ mil (1/20 of a cent) on all real personal property for a prairie-dog fund to be used solely for destroying noxious rodents. Once a county tax was levied, that county would hire agents to distribute poisons to cooperating ranchers and farmers, who would coordinate their work with state and federal officials. The program would be activated once 100 landowners had petitioned

[4] Lilly, for example, told Ligon (1917) that mountain lions could raise two litters of young per year and Musgrave reported seeing porcupines mating in the "missionary position." (Taylor 1935a)

to participate. Only landowners in counties not paying a bounty on the animals to be poisoned were eligible. This legislation became moot when the legislature appropriated $25,000 on June 18, 1918, for the destruction of both predators and rodents on the condition that Congress appropriate a like amount to the PARC.

PARC's Influence Grows

The war year of 1917–18 was important to the PARC in Arizona. Although Ligon (1918) complained of the difficulty of hiring and retaining competent men during wartime, and continued to stress the problem of some ranchmen's favoring bounty hunters over his PARC personnel, he was increasingly satisfied with the progress being made in the numbers of animals destroyed. His district's take for the year included 111 wolves (30 in Arizona), 42 lions, 6 bears, 1,310 coyotes, 215 bobcats, 192 foxes, 97 skunks, 13 raccoons, 72 porcupines, 85 badgers, 2 peccaries, 2 wild dogs, and 2 black-footed ferrets—the Biological Survey's totem animal (Ligon 1918). Ligon considered the wolf in Arizona to now be so reduced in numbers as to cause no serious financial losses. He thought that much progress had also been made in controlling lions and "big bears" despite there being only three good houndsmen still working in Arizona (Lilly, J. Ramsey Patterson, and T. T. Loveless).

Ligon now sought to incorporate two major changes in his district's operations. First, the New Mexico-Arizona district would support the parent agency's new program of using methods other than trapping to kill coyotes—now the number one cause of financial loss. Second, the district would conduct research studies to better determine the amount of damage being done by the smaller species.

Given his new directives, Ligon wanted the PARC to be divided into a field inspection branch that would do the actual control work, and a scientific research branch that would determine how to best alleviate losses to domestic stock. Interestingly, his plans made no mention of the Arizona Game and Fish Department or the need for predator control for game-management purposes. That his was an effective political strategy was made clear when the legislature voted to make Arizona a "Survey Cooperator" through the participation of both the state's cattlegrowers and woolgrowers associations.

Although bears and lions remained problem animals in certain areas, the wolf was now considered eliminated. Ligon thought coyote control to be the biggest challenge facing the PARC in Arizona. This challenge required a poison campaign, as soon as some hurried experiments were conducted in poisoning coyotes and bobcats in New Mexico and on certain sheep ranges northwest of Phoenix. Ligon (1918) therefore set about making plans for a major coyote-poisoning campaign in northern Arizona during the winter of 1918–19. Assured of good cooperation from the Forest Service and Arizona's ranching community, Ligon directed PARC agent Mark E. Musgrave to embark on a winter campaign.

Ligon (1918) was concerned that the public might pressure his men against killing bears and fur-bearing animals, as these species were deemed to have value. He therefore cautioned against the political consequences if the PARC failed to pursue bears:

> As the wolves and lions are killed out in certain districts, much light is thrown on the case against bears as predatory animals. Guilt is now being placed on them, where in years gone by it was generally supposed that bear did little killing of domestic stock. They are becoming more destructive to cattle in recent years. The dry seasons have probably added to their killing, since the shortage of feed has created a demand for range everywhere, even in the highest and most heavily forested regions—the home of the big bears—thus throwing the helpless stock into the very haunts of the animals.
>
> In Arizona quite a lot of killing has been reported from the White Mountains and Blue Range, and the southern part of the State and in the central portion south of Williams. . . . We are working after these cattle-killers and expect to have the guilty animals destroyed by the end of the year.
>
> To fail to listen to the requests from ranchmen for protection against bears would have a serious weakening effect on our organization. Destructive animals of whatever species, should be controlled. There is no danger of bears being eliminated so long as we have our parks and wild northern woods. Even our reluctance in killing the smaller bears creates discord between our methods and the interest of the ranchmen.

Ligon was an astute observer. He knew bear depredations were increasing because there were now more livestock on the range and thus a more intense use of forage. Green grass and other herbaceous plants were important spring foods for bears coming out of hibernation—a food supply in increasingly short supply due to heavy livestock grazing. That more cattle and sheep were now on the range necessitated the bears' turning to livestock as a source of spring protein in lieu of the depleted amount of grass (Brown 1985b).

During fiscal year 1918–19, New Mexico and Arizona were split into separate PARC districts. Musgrave was appointed inspector in Arizona and Ligon remained New Mexico inspector. Musgrave was one of Ligon's field men and, like other early PARC administrators such as Stanley Young and Ligon himself, familiar with field conditions. Musgrave was also astute when it came to public relations, fostering working relationships with stockmen, sportsmen, politicians, and even Governor Hunt himself. A speaker at every sportsmen's and stockmen's convention, Musgrave spoke and wrote articles about the "enemy animals" he sought to eliminate and represented himself as a federal game expert—an exalted position in those days of untrained wildlife biologists, and a role secondary only to that given to the Biological Survey's chief, Dr. Edward W. Nelson and its senior biologist, Edward Goldman.

Musgrave, moreover, was an effective and demanding supervisor, keeping his 10–20 or more field men both informed and in line with monthly newsletters. These newsletters kept tabs on the catches of his men and encouraged competition by listing those achieving kills worth 15 points or more on an "honor roll." Those not making the list for more than a few months were "let go" and replaced by new men. Getting on the monthly honor roll

Stokley Ligon (smaller man on right) and two of his hunters, Ben Lilly (left) and Jack Thompson (center) in 1920. Ligon prided himself on getting the best and most notorious hunters for the PARC. (US Biological Survey, courtesy of J. E. Hawley)

was not that difficult, as a single wolf or lion was worth 15 points, killing a bear earned 10 points, and coyotes and bobcats were each worth one point. Foxes were worth half a point, and the value of feral dogs varied on the location and the amount of damage being done. By the mid-1920s, Musgrave's newsletters also sported the letterhead, "Remember our slogan, 'Bring them in regardless of how'" in reference to the PARC's desire to get hunters to wean themselves off traps and dogs and turn to strychnine and other poisons.

Given the widespread belief that predators were holding down game numbers, it is somewhat surprising that predator control was not even mentioned in State Game Warden Willard's (1914) report to Governor Hunt describing game conditions at the time of statehood. There is no evidence Willard and his deputies ever recommended predator control or supported a predator-control program. Nor does Willard mention a need to support the federal government in its attempts at conducting predator control for stockmen. One is left with the impression that both Willard and Hunt were content to let the stockmen and the legislature handle the predator issue while the department concentrated on its public education program to encourage wildlife appreciation and enforce the game laws. Thus, both men appear to have been willing to let the federal government usurp states' rights when it came to the issue of controlling "bad animals," despite the demand by sportsmen that something be done to bring back the game. This acceptance of federal responsibility for varmints would cease, if only temporarily, with the election of 1918.

Arizona Becomes More Active

The election for governor in November 1918 was close and contested. The declared winner, Tom Campbell, replaced Willard with Joe Prochaska—a "hands-on" State Game Warden with a vested interest in predator control in that he was a professional predator hunter himself. Prochaska immediately instituted a "statewide trapping campaign" against predatory animals using paid volunteers—a program facilitated on March 19, 1919, when a bill requiring trappers to have a state trapping license became law without the governor's signature.

Prochaska's (1921) campaign in 1919 consisted of paying 217 licensed fur trappers $150 a month, with the provision that each trapper would turn over to the state the hides of the animals taken. If the trapper brought in pelts worth more money in the fur market than his salary, the trapper received the excess amount. Fur prices being high in 1919, none of the trappers failed to make his $150 minimum, each earning from $165 to $242 a month with a total take of 21 wolves, 12 lions, 9 bears, 1,310 coyotes, 714 bobcats, 414 foxes, 809 skunks, 32 badgers, and 21 raccoons.[5] Coyote pelts were then bringing in $10 apiece and bobcats $6, while wolves were worth $7.50 with a $10 bounty, skunks were worth $5.50, foxes $4.50, badgers $4.50, and raccoons $3.50. Lions were turned in for bounty or sold for their trophy value.

Fur prices were so good that the next year, 1920, saw the number of participating licensed trappers increase to 632. The average trapper earned around $200 a month, a very good living during the economic depression following World War I.

Although only 267 trapping licenses were sold in 1921, the fur market having fallen, Prochaska was able to resume and expand his anti-predator campaign with the purchase of a pair of lion hounds. With Stelza Tillman, he took eight lions on the elk range south of Winslow on the Sitgreaves National Forest. Lions were apparently also numerous in the Galiuro Mountains that year, as Deputy Warden Owsley A. Reneer of Thatcher took 21 of these cats in that range. All in all, the take by Prochaska and his deputies that year included 16 wolves, 40 lions, 692 coyotes, 65 bobcats, 53 foxes, and 21 bears.

These numbers allowed Prochaska to make a favorable comparison between the state's effort that year and the federal government's take of 26 wolves, 16 lions, 408 coyotes, 27 bobcats, 89 foxes, and 7 bears. Prochaska was also able to point out that even though it had cost $2,123 more to field the state's trappers than the federal government's PARC agents, his trappers had contributed $3,000 to the Game and Fish Fund through their purchase of trapper's licenses. All in all, Prochaska calculated that predator control was a profitable enterprise for the state, in that it only cost about $100 for every wolf, lion, and bear taken—an amount much less than the damage that these animals would do if left unchecked. The comparison was moot—Hunt was re-elected in 1922, putting an end to the state's predator-control effort for the time being.

---

[5] Small game and poultry were then considered to be as seriously impacted by predators as livestock and big game.

Gaining Control Amid Shifting Conditions

There was by now some nascent opposition to the federal program, none yet substantial. Fur trappers objected to the federal government's use of poisons and the take of valuable pelts. Houndsmen were also prone to consider bears as big game animals; sportsmen would hire houndsmen for their services to engage in some sport while attempting to obtain a bear rug. Ligon (1919), with his nose ever to the wind, appeared to change his stance on bears while wanting his agency to do the management:

> The smaller bears need protection the same as deer and turkey, leaving the matter of control of individuals in the hands of Government forces that will operate under permit or agreement.

Musgrave's (1919) forces also let up on bears, if only temporarily; only four bears were reported taken by PARC forces in Arizona during fiscal year 1918–19, as the Biological Survey increasingly turned to poisons as a means of destroying coyotes and prairie dogs. Initial results appeared promising, despite the new tools' requiring greater preparation and supervision. Prairie dogs were successfully eliminated from Cochise County by 1921 and coyote populations had been lowered through the use of strychnine (Musgrave 1920, 1921; Hoffmeister 1984). Bears, in hibernation when most of the poison was applied, were relatively immune to this type of control, necessitating the trailing, trapping, and shooting of 18 bears[6] by the PARC in fiscal year 1920–21. Musgrave (1921) explained why:

> Owing to the extreme dry condition of the ranges in Arizona this year bear have done more damage than they have ever done before and we have found it necessary to kill them off. Along the Blue Range and around the head of Friscoe and Blue River they have been exceptionally bad, and Mr. Charles Miller was detailed to the work of killing off the most destructive of them. He has succeeded in getting six adult bear in the last two months.

Ligon and Musgrave's lobbying efforts were also paying off. On June 8, 1919, the legislature appropriated $25,000 for predator and rodent control, to be spent under the supervision of the Biological Survey. In 1919, the legislature passed emergency legislation making Arizona a partner with the Biological Survey and appropriated $50,000 for fiscal years 1919 and 1920, to be matched and distributed to the Survey through the Arizona Livestock Sanitary Board (for predators) and the University of Arizona Extension Service (for rodents and jackrabbits). Pelts from animals taken would continue to be auctioned by the Survey, and in 1921, the bounty law in Arizona was revised to make all county bounty payments discretionary. That year too, with Cochise County declared to be prairie-dog free, the PARC launched an intensive cooperative program with the Agricultural Extension Service, ranchers, and farmers to target Graham County as the next theatre of operations to be declared free of black-tailed prairie dogs.

---

[6] Some of these may have been grizzlies—the species is not given.

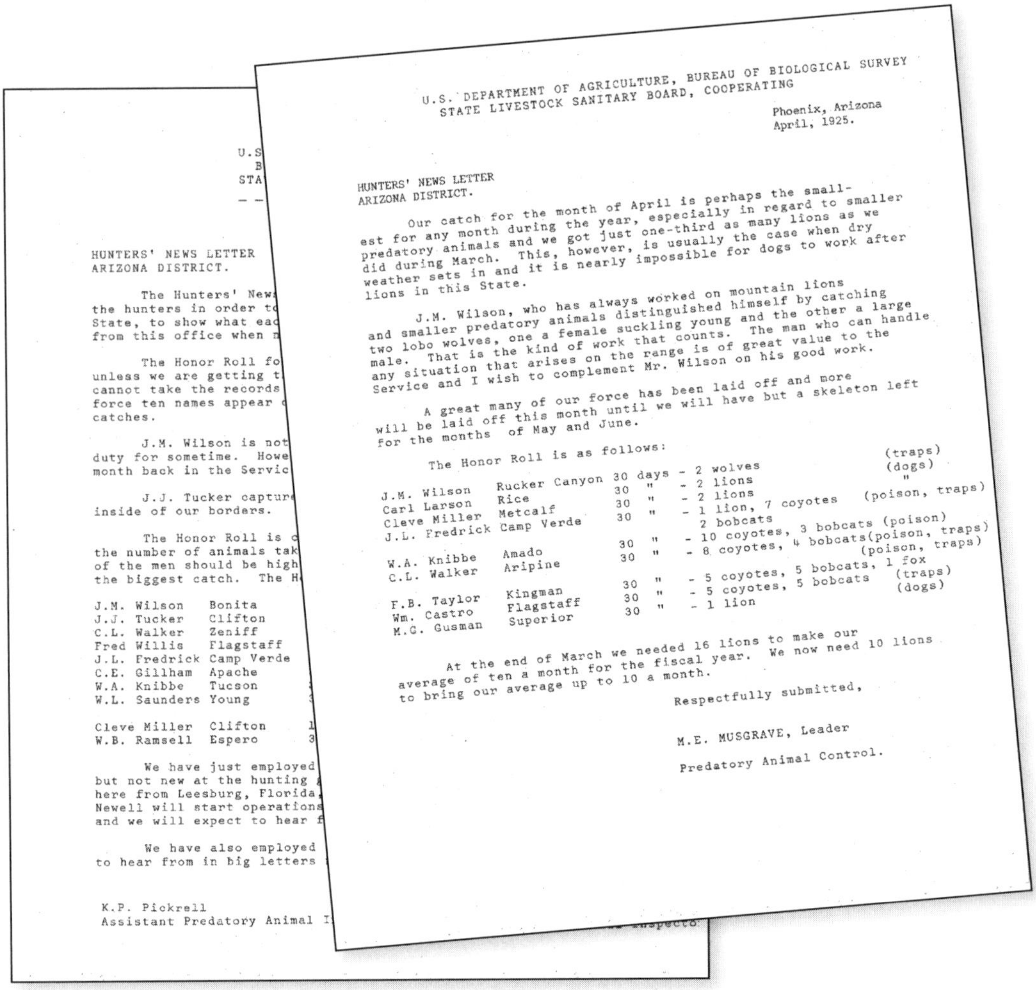
U.S

B

STA

HUNTERS' NEWS LETTER
ARIZONA DISTRICT.

The Hunters' New
the hunters in order t
State, to show what ea
from this office when

The Honor Roll fo
unless we are getting t
cannot take the records
force ten names appear
catches.

J.M. Wilson is not
duty for sometime. Howe
month back in the Servic

J.J. Tucker captur
inside of our borders.

The Honor Roll is
the number of animals tak
of the men should be high
the biggest catch. The H

J.M. Wilson	Bonita
J.J. Tucker	Clifton
C.L. Walker	Zeniff
Fred Willis	Flagstaff
J.L. Fredrick	Camp Verde
C.E. Gillham	Apache
W.A. Knibbe	Tucson
W.L. Saunders	Young
Cleve Miller	Clifton
W.B. Ramsell	Espero

We have just employed
but not new at the hunting
here from Leesburg, Florida,
Newell will start operations
and we will expect to hear

We have also employed
to hear from in big letters

K.P. Pickrell
Assistant Predatory Animal I

U.S. DEPARTMENT OF AGRICULTURE, BUREAU OF BIOLOGICAL SURVEY
STATE LIVESTOCK SANITARY BOARD, COOPERATING

Phoenix, Arizona
April, 1925.

HUNTERS' NEWS LETTER
ARIZONA DISTRICT.

Our catch for the month of April is perhaps the smallest for any month during the year, especially in regard to smaller predatory animals and we got just one-third as many lions as we did during March. This, however, is usually the case when dry weather sets in and it is nearly impossible for dogs to work after lions in this State.

J.M. Wilson, who has always worked on mountain lions and smaller predatory animals distinguished himself by catching two lobo wolves, one a female suckling young and the other a large male. That is the kind of work that counts. The man who can handle any situation that arises on the range is of great value to the Service and I wish to complement Mr. Wilson on his good work.

A great many of our force has been laid off and more will be laid off this month until we will have but a skeleton left for the months of May and June.

The Honor Roll is as follows:

J.M. Wilson	Rucker Canyon	30 days	- 2 wolves	(traps)
Carl Larson	Rice	30 "	- 2 lions	(dogs)
Cleve Miller	Metcalf	30 "	- 2 lions	"
J.L. Fredrick	Camp Verde	30 "	- 1 lion, 7 coyotes 2 bobcats	(poison, traps)
			- 10 coyotes, 3 bobcats	(poison)
W.A. Knibbe	Amado	30 "	- 8 coyotes, 4 bobcats	(poison, traps)
C.L. Walker	Aripine	30 "		(poison, traps)
F.B. Taylor	Kingman	30 "	- 5 coyotes, 5 bobcats, 1 fox	(traps)
Wm. Castro	Flagstaff	30 "	- 5 coyotes, 5 bobcats	(dogs)
M.G. Gusman	Superior	30 "	- 1 lion	

At the end of March we needed 16 lions to make our average of ten a month for the fiscal year. We now need 10 lions to bring our average up to 10 a month.

Respectfully submitted,

M.E. MUSGRAVE, Leader

Predatory Animal Control.

Two examples of Musgrave's monthly newsletters, which were sent out to his predator-control personnel in Arizona. Thirty was the expected number of work days per month, and men not making the honor roll were soon dropped. (AGFD files)

What followed was a time of government austerity. In the country's postwar recession, Arizona's cotton boom collapsed. On March 18, 1921, the legislature halved the state's annual appropriation to PARC to $25,000 for fiscal years 1922 and 1923. This resulted in the legislature's having to allocate a special appropriation to pay PARC's claim for monies already spent in the state and not covered by $12,576 in matching funds. These amounts were substantial: This same legislature only appropriated $19,430 for the Game and Fish Fund for fiscal year 1922, an amount that had to cover salaries, hatchery construction, and all other game and fish activities.

Fearing other cuts might be proposed during the postwar recession, Musgrave asked ranchers to state their losses in writing as a means to justify future appropriations. Four hundred and forty-five stockmen and farmers reported $378,151 in livestock losses, with a 2%–10% loss in their calf, colt, and lamb crops attributed to predators. Using the 2% figure, Musgrave calculated the annual loss in Arizona from predatory animals at more

Mark Musgrave and five mountain lions taken by PARC personnel, ca. 1923. At least two of the cats appear to be juveniles. Some of the takes by early PARC hunters were impressive, with several men killing more than 100 lions during their career with the US Biological Survey. (US Biological Survey)

than $1.5 million, with similar losses from rodents and lagomorphs based on "widely accepted" estimates (Musgrave 1919, 1920, 1921).

In May 1922, PARC hunter Ramsey Patterson and his friend Jimmy Norman killed the last grizzly west of the White Mountains—an old male in the Bear Canyon-Government Canyon area of the Sycamore-Yavapai Game Refuge (Brown 1985b).

Thirty bears were taken by PARC hunters and their state cooperators in New Mexico and Arizona in 1922–23 (Brown 1985b). Musgrave's (1923) newsletters to his field men, while attesting to the agency's desire to downplay bears, continued to include them as PARC targets along with wolves and lions, provided his hunters made sure any bears taken were indeed stock-killers—a fine point that was often ignored. Bears continued to be worth 10 points toward the 15 points required to get on the "honor roll"–only five points fewer than the 15 points earned for a wolf or lion. Ten points earned was an important incentive, as government hunters who did not produce were dropped from the rolls—pronto.

Musgrave had vigorously carried out the wolf campaign since starting his tenure in 1919, when he made a special effort to kill wolves, hybrids, and a pack of wild dogs ranging along the Arizona-New Mexico border. Musgrave's (1919) opinion was that "wolves are not numerous in this State, but are scattered over a very large area, and there are a great many individuals that cover a big range and are very shy." To eliminate these resident individuals, he initiated a wolf-trapping program that concentrated on the watersheds of the Black River, Eagle Creek, and Bonita Creek in the White Mountains and along Blue River. This program, while time-consuming, was eventually successful, and by 1925 his men were working to remove the last wolves on the Apache Indian reservations. For his part, Ligon (1919) still believed the wolves in Arizona and New Mexico were no longer a serious menace, but added that "trapping the remaining wolves is going to be a long, drawn out process."

Musgrave's (1919) men reported taking eight wolves in the White Mountains that year, with another 15 along the Arizona-Sonora border. "When operations stopped in May, there were few or no wolves left on this side of the border," PARC personnel having claimed more than 60 of these animals in fiscal year 1919–20—an all-time record. Clearly, predator numbers were as difficult to arrive at then as now. But the pressure was on. Another 58 wolves were reported taken in Arizona during the next two years, some of them with strychnine (Musgrave 1921, 1922).

Again, Musgrave pushed his men to expand their use of poison. Some of his hunters, particularly the houndsmen, remained reluctant to use this tool, not only for fear their dogs might be killed, but because such kills could not always be retrieved for credit—an important incentive instilled by Musgrave himself. Just the same, some 13 million acres of Arizona grazing land were treated with poison in fiscal year 1922–23. Of the 37 wolves reported taken by PARC hunters that year, 14 were described as being killed with poison (Musgrave 1923). Stockmen reported finding another six to eight wolf carcasses on their ranges, presumably the result of poison; there were undoubtedly others, and this does not include the coyotes, foxes, porcupines, prairie dogs, and other animals killed in this manner.

That Musgrave was making progress was borne out in 1924, when the number of wolves taken in Arizona fell to 22 adults and seven pups—most of them south of the Mogollon Rim and along the border. Declarations were again made that the time of resident wolves in Arizona was at an end when the only lobos reported by PARC hunters the next year were 31 unverified "wolves" claimed by agent Charles E. Gillham (Musgrave 1925). Ranchers reported only three additional wolves taken across the state in 1925, and hopes again ran high that the wolf had been eliminated from Arizona. But then, after a lull in 1925 and 1926, another 16 wolves were reported taken in Arizona by PARC hunters and cooperators (Brown 1983). Although 14 of these animals were close enough to the Mexico or New Mexico borders to be considered transients, the locations of the other two indicated that a few wolves were still present on the Apache reservations and centered in the vicinity of Black River.

In January 1926, Musgrave had 16 hunters afield who took 19 lions (all with dogs), 2 wolves, and 105 coyotes (93 with poison). His goal was for his men to collectively take 10 lions a month or 120 a year, and he threatened to let go those who were below average in performance.

By 1928, Musgrave was able to list only five wolves among the toll of 1,643 major predators taken by his hunters and cooperators. Nonetheless, these numbers represented only a fraction of the actual toll, in that more than 10 million acres of Arizona's grazing lands were treated that year with poison (probably strychnine). The best news for the PARC inspector was that no claims were made of wolves killing livestock and only seven wolves were thought to have entered Arizona during the year, five of which had been destroyed (Musgrave 1928).

Lions were also now regarded as being under control: Musgrave's goal of having his houndsmen kill 10 lions a month was paying off. Indeed, some of his houndsmen, such as Albert F. Jones, M. G. Gusman, and Ramsey Patterson, had attained prodigious records, each taking hundreds of lions. The PARC's agents now hoped to concentrate on experiments to eliminate the more persistent predators and rodents through the use of new predacides and new poisoning techniques (Robinson 2005).

Bears remained a thorny problem. Though the PARC was claiming a more relaxed stock-killer policy and the Forest Service thought bear populations were increasing, Musgrave's (1924) hunters took a record number of bears in 1924—some with poison. Such killing was increasingly unpopular with sportsmen, who favored the sport hunting of bears using professional guides—a pastime encouraged by PARC administrators, but viewed with ambivalence by some of Musgrave's agents and disregarded by stockmen:

> Bear are increasing in the State of Arizona. There are perhaps three times as many here now on the range as there were in 1918. Consequently it is becoming necessary for us to pay more attention to the stock-killing bear. In one place near Blue River and about forty miles north of Clifton stockmen located five bear in a canyon and found that they had been slaughtering stock. Cleve Miller was notified and cleaned up the entire bunch on one day. (Musgrave 1924)

Bears posed other problems. Both Musgrave and Ligon (1924) considered poison an indispensable tool for killing predators as well as rodents, and reported that "poison has come to stay." The principal poison at that time was strychnine, rolled in tissue and sandwiched between pork fat strips or in tallow. Carcasses of animals that had died of natural causes made the best poison stations. Designed to take coyotes, bait stations were not selective, and often bait was taken by any carnivorous or omnivorous animal that came along, be it a coyote or otter.

Not only was the PARC setting out poison bait stations, but "approximately 155,000 poison baits were being distributed to cooperators free of charge" (Ligon 1924). That more bears and other non-target species were not killed was only due to the reluctance of certain Forest Service administrators to condone poisoning on their forests and the objections of the PARC's houndsmen, who were prevented from working lions and bears in poison-treated areas. This was a real concern, as a well-trained dog could be worth from $100 to $500, and several dogs had been killed by poison. Not only could the PARC no longer induce lion hunters to hunt treated rangelands or country adjacent to where baits had been placed, some of the best houndsmen were leaving the Biological Survey altogether.

Transition to Rodent Control

In 1924, the Forest Service resumed the practice of keeping estimates of big game species numbers on each national forest. Although most game species were thought to be increasing, Forest Service rangers estimated only 27 grizzlies in Arizona. These figures were merely educated guesses, not based on any census techniques other than stock-killing complaints and speculation. It was also about this time that district inspectors asked PARC hunters what was going on with various game and predator populations. These data, while considered useful to the Biological Survey and passed on to the state, were nothing but opinions and had little relation to how many game animals and "big bears"[7] were present on and off the national forests.

What is known is that 16 bears were reported taken in Arizona by the PARC and its cooperators during fiscal year 1924–25 and 10 the following year (Musgrave 1925, 1926). Bears were gaining public support as game animals, as demonstrated in January 1927 by an editorial in the first issue of *Arizona Wild Life*, published by the Arizona Game Protective Association. This article stated that, contrary to government reports,[8] bears in Arizona had become scarce, and it urged that legislation be enacted for a closed season and bag limit—at least on black and "brown" bears. Throughout that year and into 1928, additional articles objected to the widespread use of poison by government agents due to the loss of hunting dogs and the destruction of valuable wildlife species. How many otters, ferrets, and other furbearers were poisoned was not even speculated on, much less documented.

Always quick to react to changes in the political wind, Musgrave (1927) was "glad to report . . . these animals [bears] are increasing on our ranges." As for the more predatory grizzlies, the Forest Service dropped its estimate of this species in Arizona to 10. Musgrave (1928) thought the number to be even less, stating, "To the best of our knowledge there is one large grizzly left in the state. This animal ranges from the New Mexico line around Blue, Arizona, over to the White Mountains south and east of McNary."

Pressure to manage bears rather than kill them increased in 1928, when the electorate voted in Arizona's new game code protecting all bears as game animals with a fall hunting season and a bag limit of one bear. Following New Mexico's example, the Arizona legislation also allowed the Game and Fish Commission to issue a permit for the killing of any bear that was destroying livestock or found within a certain distance of human habitation and threatening life or property. No blanket permits were to be issued; each incident was to be evaluated on its individual merits.

> It was only necessary for us to take six bear in the State of Arizona during the fiscal year. . . . The fact that a great many thousands of head of cattle and sheep have been permanently removed from the range, giving vegetation a better chance to grow, will give more food for the bear and make him less of a

[7] The PARC reports are cagey in that they rarely report grizzlies taken *per se*, but instead consider "big bears" as stock-killers, i.e., grizzlies and the larger black bears. And even then not all grizzlies taken are reported.

[8] Both Musgrave (1927) and several national forests were reporting an increase in black and brown (cinnamon phase) bears. In truth, neither Musgrave nor anyone else knew the true status of either species of bear in Arizona.

Mark E. Musgrave with reportedly the largest black bear taken in Arizona. Musgrave was two-faced about the taking of bears, telling sportsmen that PARC men only went after "big bears" known to be stock-killers while encouraging PARC personnel to take whatever animals stockmen wanted killed. (US Biological Survey, courtesy of Bob Housholder)

> predatory animal. This past year the state legislature put the bear on the protected list in Arizona. However, we are given permission by the State Game Commission to kill any bear that are destroying livestock. (Musgrave 1929)

Only one wolf was claimed taken by the PARC in 1928, though 43 were submitted for bounty by other trappers (Musgrave 1929). Reports of wolves continued, and several hunters were assigned to investigate specific incidents involving wolves. Musgrave personally visited Guadalupe Canyon in the Peloncillo Mountains east of Douglas where a wolf had been reported as coming in from Mexico. A hunter, Albert S. Field, was assigned to set traps in every pass in the Peloncillos and leave them set until the wolf was caught—which it finally was. Later, Field caught a second wolf that got away, leaving two toes in the trap. And although livestock losses from wolves were reported as "negligible," PARC hunters took 1,800 lions, bears, coyotes, bobcats, and other "major predators" that year (Musgrave 1929).

Musgrave had much to show for his efforts when he passed the reins of PARC's Arizona district on to Donald A. Gilchrist in 1929. Although it was true that the battle for appropriations was not always won, and there were some setbacks (the legislature had cut the state's annual contribution to the Biological Survey in 1925 to $15,000 a year), a number of victories against his animal enemies could be justifiably claimed.[9]

Wolves and grizzlies had been eliminated from the state for all practical purposes. Several jaguars had been taken, and the "Mexican leopard" was no longer a resident animal if it indeed ever had been (Brown and Lopéz-Gonzaléz 2001). Mountain lions and black bears were thought to have been much reduced and their numbers manageable. The war against coyotes was proceeding apace, and much progress had been made in the battle against rodents and other noxious animals. This was especially so in the case of the prairie dog, which had been touted as "cleared" from 1,659,203 acres. In 1928–29 alone, nine federal agents, four state employees,[10] and 4,068 private cooperators had distributed 102,961 pounds of poison grain and 2,390 pounds of carbon disulphide (used as a gas) to kill:

- 67,898 prairie dogs on 331,524 acres,
- 1,677 ground squirrels on 15,396 acres,
- 7,992 gophers on 104,179 acres,
- 14,328 jackrabbits on 80,878 acres,
- 360 porcupines on 1,120 acres,
- 372 mice on 2,286 acres,
- 360 rats on 870 acres,
- 303 cotton rats on 4,513 acres,
- 9,565 kangaroo rats on 102,030 acres, and
- 66 packrats on 1,085 acres.

Federal funds expended were $20,685.68, as opposed to $14,999.53 for the state and $77,753 contributed from private operators (Gilchrist 1929).

By 1929, prairie dogs had become the species most despised. The war against the black-tailed prairie dog was essentially over in Arizona, with Cochise, Graham, Santa Cruz, and Greenlee counties declared prairie-dog free. The PARC was not the only government agency attempting to eliminate these animals. As it did with porcupines, the Forest Service contributed money to the prairie-dog eradication program on a cost-share basis, with the emphasis on Zuni prairie dogs (*Cynomys gunnisoni*) in the Apache, Coconino, and Tusayan national forests. Previous efforts on the Apache had left this national forest nearly prairie-dog free, although it was considered doubtful these animals could ever be totally eliminated.

---

[9]Even small game species were then thought to be controlled primarily by predators, and animals were classified as either beneficial (i.e., game animals and songbirds) or predatory/noxious (e.g., coyotes and jackrabbits). For example, a March 21, 1924, article by Will C. Barnes reports that Kaibab squirrels appear to be declining and a war is being waged against the hawks and other predators that are claimed to take them. That fluctuations in the populations of tassel-eared squirrels were controlled by climatic factors (snow depth) was not then appreciated (Brown 1984a).

[10]These were not employees of the Arizona Game and Fish Department, but people hired through the state's agriculture department.

Wolves and Lions Reported Taken by PARC Hunters in Arizona, 1918–62

Year	PARC Lions	PARC Wolves
1918	?	27
1919	42	26
1920	79	64
1921	52	37
1922	54	58
1923	77	37
1924	77	22
1925	127	31
1926	93	18
1927	112	16
1928	108	5
1929	145	43
1930	146	14
1931	174	3
1932	86	8
1933	80	4
1934	68	3
1935	129	7
1936	94	5
1937	79	5
1938	55	3
1939	63	8
1940	78	6
1941	54	1
1942	66	8
1943	71	5
1944	73	6
1945	60	5
1946	35	4
1947	46	3
1948	190	4
1949	185	1
1950	212	0
1951	181	2
1952	198	2
1953	200	0
1954	201	0
1955	230	0
1956	189	0
1957	266	0
1958	264	3
1959	243	0
1960	215	3
1961	242	1
1962	231	0

Note: Numbers include bountied wolves and lions after 1947.

The remaining dogs were to be gassed with carbon bisulphide, even though the only sure removal strategy developed on the Coconino had been the laborious process of pre-baiting the areas around dry-farmed parks with steamed oats and then killing the dogs with oats and grain treated with thallium poison. Even then, some shooting was necessary, as the animals became poison-shy after their numbers had been reduced from eight dogs per acre to one dog for every four acres. That year, 1929, Mohave County was also declared prairie-dog free due to the assistance of cooperative ranchers and the Hualapai Indian Reservation agency (Gilchrist 1929).

Many cooperators were now more involved with rodent control than predator control. Ranchers supplied horses and other amenities to the agents as they attempted to increase the carrying capacity of their farms and ranges. To sell their program, PARC agents constructed demonstration plots with prairie-dog exclosures, illustrating the effectiveness of prairie-dog control in producing more grass. Gopher control was also proving popular. Gilchrist could brag that more than 2,000 cooperators were engaged in gopher control in every county of the state, with a major effort in Maricopa County's citrus groves and along its 600 miles of canals.

It was no accident that future district inspectors such as Ben Foster and Everett M. Mercer were rodent-control specialists rather than predatory-animal agents. Not that the days of government predator-control were over in some ways the war against predators had only begun.

THE KAIBAB DEER CONTROVERSY

David E. Brown

"The Terrible Lesson of the Kaibab"[1] has been told several times, and has often been used to make the point that human protection and predator control caused an overabundance of deer, resulting in an ecological and political disaster (Hall 1925; Rasmussen 1941; Leopold, Sowls, and Spencer 1947; Russo 1964).

In truth, this, the first recorded deer irruption, was not the result of a simple cause-and-effect relationship, but a complex phenomenon that remains imperfectly understood (Caughley 1970; Young 2002). There have been other deer irruptions with and without predator control, and deer numbers have declined to low levels despite legal protection.

Nor has all of the story been told in regards to the state's role, which while initially minor, eventually resulted in a precedent-setting decision by the US Supreme Court. This was the only Supreme Court ruling to arise out of an Arizona wildlife lawsuit. The resulting actions had a major impact on deer management in Arizona and the West for 60 years. Hence, a re-examination of some of the particulars appears in order.

From Game Preserve to National Park

Large, remote, and geographically isolated, the 700,000-acre Grand Cañon National Game Preserve and its environs atop the Kaibab Plateau in northern Arizona has a unique natural and social history. Established in 1906 at the suggestion of President Theodore Roosevelt, the game preserve area lies at about 6,500 to 9,200 feet elevation and supports a variety of cold temperate and subalpine biotic communities, including desertscrub, grassland, chaparral, and conifer forest. This uniquely attractive 1,462-square-mile refuge, encompassing the Kaibab Plateau and adjacent mule deer winter range, has been intensively studied and described by several investigators.[2]

The effects of the preserve's geology on what has come to be known as the north Kaibab mule deer herd are especially important, as the Precambrian limestone of the plateau has resulted in the area possessing virtually no live streams, few springs, and scant permanent water (Dutton 1882; Rasmussen 1941). The relatively few natural water bodies present, such as Jacob and Greenland lakes, are shallow, sediment-filled depressions or "sinkholes" that are more seasonal than permanent. Groundwater is generally unreachable to windmills.

The plateau's high elevation, persistent snow cover, and lack of permanent water have caused the Kaibab's celebrated deer herd to be almost entirely migratory. Because of the plateau's isolation and paucity of water, no permanent populations of elk, bear, or turkey were native to the Kaibab.

---

[1]The printed origin of this often-repeated phrase goes back to at least Trefethen, J. B., "The Terrible Lesson of the Kaibab," *National Wildlife*, June–July 1967.

[2]These include Dutton (1882), Hall (1925), Mann and Locke (1931), Rasmussen (1941), Russo (1964), and others.

Use of the Kaibab Plateau or "Buckskin Mountain" by Native Americans was also seasonal, at least since Anasazi times (J. W. Powell 1925). The principal Native American visitors, the Kaibabits, a tribe of Paiutes, came to the Kaibab in the fall to hunt deer and rabbits, and later, to trade with Navajos. Neither of these Indian tribes resided on the plateau permanently, and their buckskin take was estimated to have been no more than about 800 deer a year (Rasmussen 1941). Native American use declined rapidly after Mormon pioneers arrived in the 1850s and 1860s, and by the time John Wesley Powell visited the plateau with Harvey C. Demotte in the summer of 1872, the number of Indians was much reduced. Deer numbers were then described as "plentiful" (Dellenbaugh 1908).

Much more influential on the deer and other resources on the Kaibab Plateau were the impacts of livestock companies such as the Grand Canyon Cattle Company that came to the area from Utah after 1870. These impacts were particularly severe when the number of livestock pastured on the plateau was said to have increased from about 2,000 cattle in 1885–86 to some 20,000 cattle and 200,000 sheep in 1887–88 (Mann and Locke 1931). Given the limited markets available in such a remote area, these numbers may have been exaggerated, but it is known that local ranchers continued to graze livestock on the plateau in reduced numbers until President Benjamin Harrison created the Grand Cañon Forest Reserve in 1893 (Rasmussen 1941).

By the time President Theodore Roosevelt included the plateau in the Grand Cañon National Game Preserve in 1906, no large commercial livestock companies remained active in the area. The government's grazing permits were mostly issued to Mormon ranchers living in southern Utah or on the "Arizona Strip"—the remote part of Arizona north of the Colorado River.

Harsh winters and undependable water sources meant few homesteaders and ranchers settled on the Kaibab Plateau proper. This relatively light use, coupled with the limestone substrate and lack of permanent streams, tended to limit soil surface erosion and arroyo cutting on the plateau compared to lower elevations. Although a sawmill was in operation at Big Spring as early as 1871, and several mines had been worked at various times, few access roads had been constructed prior to the plateau's designation as a game preserve (Mann and Locke 1931). As a result, little commercial logging had occurred by the time the overlapping Kaibab National Forest of 706,000 acres was established on July 21, 1908 (see map, page 85).

Roosevelt had visited the Grand Canyon in 1903 and was mightily impressed by the scenery and the area's potential as game country. Thus, when Senator Reed Smoot of Utah introduced legislation paving the way for executive proclamations, it was only natural that Roosevelt would think of the North Rim of the canyon as a big game preserve, in that the area was already well known for its mule deer. Roosevelt may have also been influenced by his friend Charles Jesse "Buffalo" Jones, who had a permit from the secretary of agriculture to operate a game ranch on the plateau, where he intended to feature bison and elk and raise "cattalo" (hybrid bison and Galloway cattle). Indeed, Roosevelt was so impressed with the concept of game preserves that at one time he entertained the idea of making game preserves out of all of the national forests (T. Roosevelt 1908).

Roosevelt's proclamation by no means marked the end of his interest in the Kaibab. In 1913, he arranged a lion hunt there with Jones's partner, James "Uncle Jimmy" Owens (T. Roosevelt 1913). Jones had moved on to other enterprises, leaving Owens to tend to the plateau and its bison (elk were never introduced to the Kaibab). Indeed, Owens was the preserve's appointed game warden and predator hunter between 1906 and 1918, during which time he hunted lions for bounty. He also guided sport hunters, including author Zane Grey in 1908 (Grey 1924a) and movie actor Rex Beach in 1917 (Beach 1917–18).

Owens claimed to have taken 503 lions during his 18-year career on the Kaibab (1906–23) or 28 lions a year.[3] This claim, while often discounted as an exaggeration, appears more reasonable when it is remembered that these early takes also included kittens and fetuses. In truth, this figure is undoubtedly more reliable than the estimates of livestock, deer, and predator numbers made during the early history of the Kaibab. And although there are no records of organized predator-control work taking place on the Kaibab prior to 1922 by the Predator and Rodent Control branch of the US Biological Survey, forest guards and bounty hunters took an unknown but significant number of mountain lions in addition to wolves and coyotes between 1906 and 1922 (Brown 1983).

Adding to the Kaibab Plateau's increasingly complex land status was the creation of a National Park Service in 1916 and Grand Canyon National Park on February 26, 1919. The inclusion of 300,000 acres of the North Rim portion of the preserve in a national park meant that a policy of deer preservation rather than management would forevermore prevail on the southern third of the Kaibab deer herd's summer range.

Deer Numbers Rise

Almost immediately upon the park's establishment, Park Service Director Stephen Mather began ballyhooing the new national park as a tourist attraction that possessed incredible scenery and untold numbers of deer (Young 2002). Expanding from a tourist camp established on the North Rim in 1917, the national park was soon accessed by a road extending the length of the plateau, which would bring into view hundreds of deer in DeMotte and V. T. "parks" (meadows). Not content with these scenic possibilities, Mather conspired to enlarge the park's boundaries northward so that even more deer would be available for viewing purposes.

US Forest Service ranger J. C. Roak (1920, *in* Young 2002) first observed a rapidly increasing population of deer in 1918. Concerned about overbrowsing, the forest examiner in charge of game and fish, S. B. Locke, conducted a range investigation of the deer's west-side winter range in April 1920. As reported, Locke and the other Forest Service rangers found significant damage being done to the deer's browse plants. Although range conditions varied from site to site, and the deer were judged to be in "excellent condition," their numbers were such that Locke thought Roak's estimate of 15,000 to 20,000 animals (10 to 14 deer per square mile) for the Kaibab Plateau might be too conservative (Roak

---

[3]This figure is from a February 11, 1924, article by J. W. Strode in *Know Your State* (Strode 1924). The interview was repeated in the *Silver Belt* newspaper. Other sources, e.g., Rasmussen 1941, place the number at "nearly 600." Like Jones's lion tallies, these figures probably include kittens and even fetuses (Brown 2009).

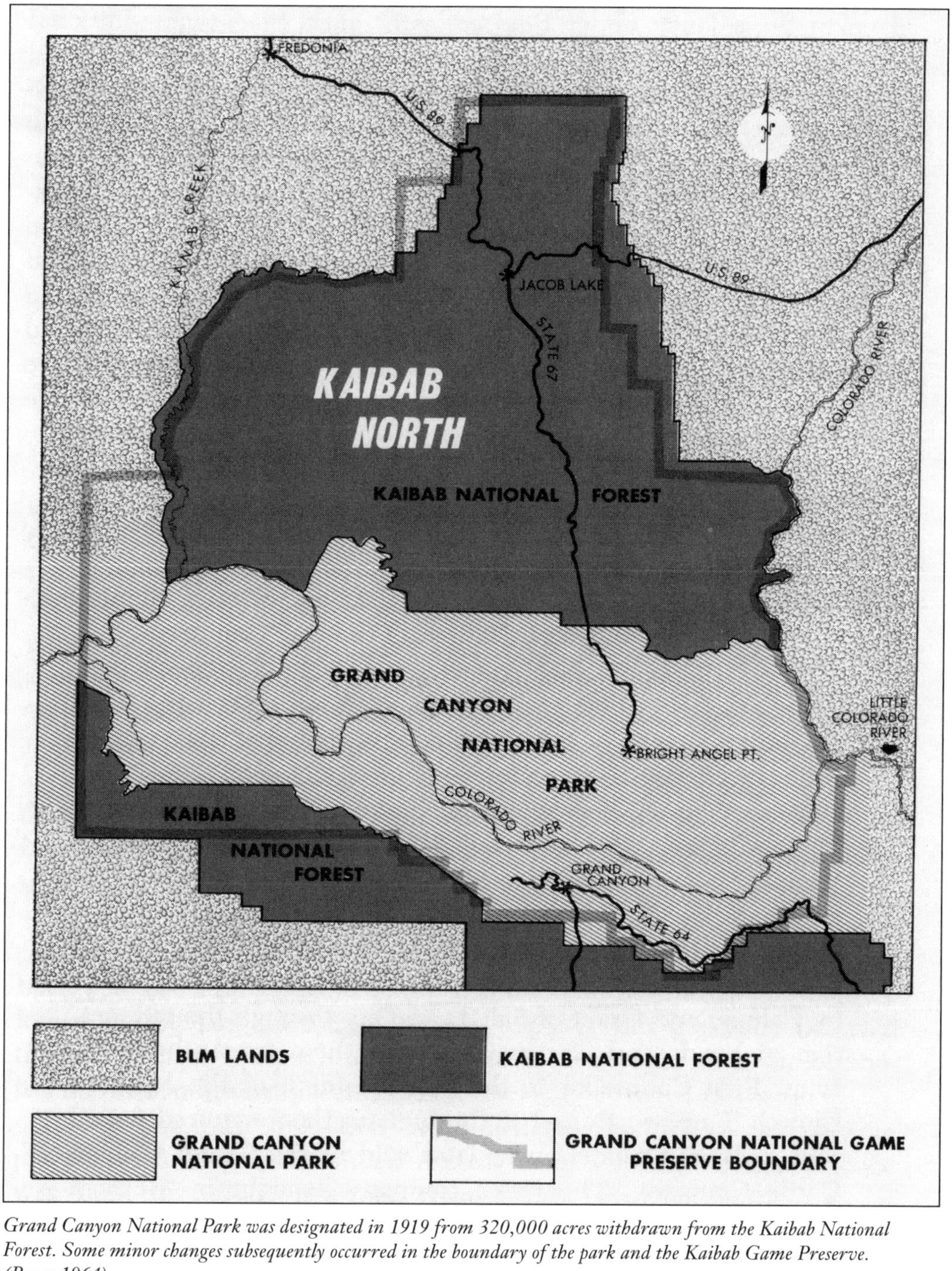

Grand Canyon National Park was designated in 1919 from 320,000 acres withdrawn from the Kaibab National Forest. Some minor changes subsequently occurred in the boundary of the park and the Kaibab Game Preserve. (Russo 1964)

"Uncle Jimmy" Owens and his pack train at Jacob Lake. On the left is Benj. Wilmot, a cattleman. Owens, on the right, a guide and hunter, was known as the "cougar killer" of the Kaibab. 1918 photo by E. S. Shipp. (US Forest Service, Southwestern Region, Kaibab National Forest)

1920). A table at the end of this chapter shows what is known about deer numbers in this area from 1912 through 1962.

Locke recommended no change in management policy, and strongly advised against an open hunting season due to the ease of killing what he thought to be large numbers of naïve deer. Roak, the local ranger, wanted a plan of action, but Locke thought more surveys should be conducted before a management plan could be formulated. In the meantime, Owens's take of 67 lions during the previous five years was regarded as sufficient only to keep the deer's numbers in check, as the forest rangers thought the large numbers of lions taken merely reflected the large numbers of deer available. Locke, for one, believed that there had not been any real increase in deer since 1917. Predator control was therefore now recommended to be instituted on a more formal basis, as the deer were not starving, and a reduction in lion numbers would allow the deer to increase and occupy additional areas. Because most of the browse damage was on points leading down to the winter range, Locke recommended that the rangers break up these concentrations on horseback, thereby forcing the deer into vacant or lightly occupied areas (Mann and Locke 1931; Young 2002).

In 1920, the Forest Service wanted to continue managing the Kaibab for multiple use as per its mandate. Mindful of its ranching constituency, the Forest Service hoped for increased numbers of both deer and livestock and recommended that the US Biological Survey consider instituting predator control both in and outside the new national park. This the Biological Survey agreed to do, and in the fall of 1920, lion hunters from the district office in Ogden, Utah, under the supervision of George E. Holman, were sent to the Kaibab National Forest. The recommended increase in livestock did not sit well with Mather and the Park Service, who wanted both livestock and predators removed from the Park. Determined to promote the Kaibab's deer herd as an attraction, the Park Service planned to make room for more deer by removing livestock from the national park's dusty, overgrazed meadows, which were no longer of much use to cattle anyway. It was thought that any problem arising from too many deer would solve itself (Young 2002).

The Issue of Deer Control

The issue of deer control on the Kaibab National Forest was controversial from the beginning. By 1921, Forest Service inspectors were reporting deer-caused damage to trees, and it was becoming obvious deer numbers would have to be reduced if more rangeland were to be available to livestock. Predator control was by now well underway, with two of Holman's houndsmen having taken 23 lions north of Grand Canyon National Park during the winter of 1920–21 (Young 2002). Nonetheless, Forest Service personnel continued to regard the lion presence as a formidable control on deer numbers and resisted suggestions by the Biological Survey to remove some deer by hunting, as they judged the range adequate to support more deer if the animals were better distributed. Unsure what to do, grazing supervisor Locke decided that a professional survey by outside range and game experts was called for—the first of many that would take place on the Kaibab and other national forests during the 1920s (Russo 1964).

The problem was that there were then no game experts, and no agency had ever encountered the problem of too many deer. The Arizona Game and Fish Department had no professional expertise. State Game Wardens such as George Willard and Dwight Pettis learned on the job, as did Forest Service specialists such as Aldo Leopold in New Mexico. But even if such expertise were available, the state's deputy wardens were spread way too thin, with only one warden per county, while Leopold was involved with Forest Service problems in Albuquerque. The only outdoorsmen in the Southwest with wide experience in wildlife range conditions were with the Biological Survey. The Southwest "expert," Stokley Ligon, was busy organizing and administrating the PARC. Former Biological Survey Supervisor C. Hart Merriam was long gone, and the survey's present supervisor, Dr. Edward Nelson, was more than 65 years old and close to retirement. The best choices available within the Biological Survey to lead a team of wildlife investigators were Merriam's protégé, Vernon Bailey, and Nelson's chief assistant and troubleshooter, senior biologist Edward Goldman (Brown 2009).

In September 1922, Nelson sent Goldman to conduct a coordinated investigation of conditions on the Kaibab Plateau with Locke and other Forest Service personnel. After a two-week survey of the plateau, both Goldman and Locke (1922) expressed concern with the condition of the range as well as the abundance and condition of the deer. They estimated at least 20,000 deer as being "everywhere abundant" and exhibiting a robust reproductive success with high fawn:doe ratios. They also concluded that the capacity for cattle had been reached and recommended immediate cattle reductions due to the paucity of available grass. Goldman and Locke (1922) cautioned that deer reductions might be

Tour bus at Jacob Lake Inn. Tourists were lured to the Kaibab to view herds of deer as well as the area's scenic wonders. No date. Photographer unknown. (US Forest Service, Southwestern Region, Kaibab National Forest)

needed in the near future, as this species had reached its carrying capacity—the first government officials to suggest such an action. Goldman considered the situation to be critical, as did some of the Forest Service rangers. They also continued to recommend predator control "if future studies deemed warranted."

By November 1922, the Forest Service and Biological Survey had prepared a "plan of management" that had been reviewed by such notable experts as Leopold in Albuquerque and Chief Forester William B. Greely in Washington. In this report Goldman recommended the removal of 2,000 deer (10%), noting that the Forest Service needed to inform the Arizona Game and Fish Department of its intentions. Any such action by the Forest Service posed a problem, as would soon be made clear by State Game Warden Willard. The Arizona game code required out-of-state hunters to pay $20 for a big game permit, a cost that would discourage participation by Utah residents and other out-of-state hunters and hinder the desired reduction. Equally or more important, any change in the state's hunt season or bag limit would require repealing the 1916 law. Also, for political reasons, both federal services recommended that the Biological Survey increase its pressure on lions and coyotes—a recommendation designed to appeal to sportsmen and ranchers. Such a recommendation in the face of too many deer, while less popular with the National Park Service, would also be open to challenge by some out-of-state critics, namely such academics such as Joseph Dixon and Dr. Joseph Grinnell (Young 2002).

During the summer of 1923, Nelson himself visited the Kaibab, and in October State Game Warden Willard toured the plateau and observed the situation firsthand. On October 19, Willard wrote a six-page letter to Gov. George Hunt describing a trip to the Kaibab with two of his deputies (Willard to Hunt 1923). Willard informed Hunt that they had left Springerville for the Kaibab on October 4 to confer with Nelson and representatives of the Forest Service regarding what should be done to check the overstocking and overgrazing of Grand Cañon National Game Preserve, which was said to have reached the "danger point." In Fredonia, the three wardens met Kaibab Forest Service Supervisor

McPeters, grazing supervisor Locke, and a ranger named Evans, who, in a day's drive around the national forest's upper elevations, showed the three men more deer than Willard had seen in all of Arizona in nearly six years as State Game Warden.

The second day, Willard and Pettis went to Big Springs Ranger Station, an intermediate range location, with Locke and the local ranger, Benjamin Swapp. Here the men took a 15-mile horseback ride through pine forest and oak brush (*Quercus gambelii*), where they counted 177–190 deer. Willard reported deer trails that looked like domestic sheep pastures and commented on the overbrowsed appearance of deerbrush (*Ceanothus integerrimus*) and oak brush, expressing particular concern about the high-lined aspen trees and the fact that this most attractive of forest trees was no longer producing seedlings. Although he expressed concern there was no aspen foliage within the reach of deer, he believed the oaks and deerbrush were in less dire condition, despite these plants being more valuable to the deer's needs.

The Forest Service rangers told Willard the deer population was estimated at 20,000 animals, with the next spring's fawn crop forecasted to add another 5,000 to 8,000 deer to the herd. Willard agreed that the danger point to the deer's welfare either had been reached or was about to be reached. He was informed that the government (Forest Service) was about to take measures to hold the deer in check. Harvests of up to 2,000 deer a year were being planned. To reduce negative publicity, it was explained, hunts would be concentrated in areas where deer were congested, to help spread the animals out and away from sites likely to be visited by tourists. A major selling point was that the state would share in any revenues derived from the hunt after administrative costs were deducted.

Willard stated he was in favor of the plan, as the federal government would bear the entire cost of carrying out the work while sharing with the state any proceeds derived from hunting permits over and above administrative costs. In his closing statements, he told Hunt he regretfully agreed with the Forest Service plan, but that to make a cooperative effort possible, the legislature would have to provide the necessary changes in the state game code.

Making Plans

In the fall of 1923, Governor Hunt decided to see the Kaibab deer herd and situation for himself—a decision that prompted Nelson to write the governor a letter expressing his pleasure at Hunt's upcoming trip and anticipating the governor's delight at seeing the concentrations of deer in the parks, which would not be open to hunting (Nelson to Hunt, October 1, 1923, Governor's Files, Arizona State Library, Archives and Public Records). Hunt's guides would be Locke and R. H. Rutledge. The forest rangers told Hunt there were now 5,685 head of cattle and horses on the Kaibab and 3,660 head of sheep, in addition to the 25,000 deer. Rutledge explained the forage problems involved and the inability of the deer to find adequate forage off of the plateau. He hoped the governor would understand the foresters' concern after seeing the situation firsthand, and realize that the Forest Service would have to either supervise a permit deer hunt or have government hunters reduce the deer herd. (Rutledge to Hunt, October 1, 1923 memo, Governor's Files, Arizona State Library, Archives and Public Records).

Although Willard agreed that a deer problem existed and was sympathetic to the Forest Service's plans, his approval of a hunt was with no small regret. Willard maintained that the state's licensing laws posed a problem, as the Kaibab was difficult to reach for Arizonans and most hunters would likely come from Utah, California, or some other state. Getting enough hunters, resident or nonresident, to meet the Forest Service's desired harvest goals within the current game laws would be difficult. Moreover, he anticipated that neither the Arizona State Legislature nor the governor would want a deer hunt that would turn the Kaibab into a commercial game factory.

The three federal agencies (the Forest Service, the Biological Survey, and the National Park Service) and the state, each aware of the burgeoning deer herd, were unsure what to do, given the need to maintain what they viewed as their mandates and prerogatives. The biggest player was of course the Forest Service; in particular, the Kaibab National Forest and Regional Forester Rutledge, whose range and timber resources were in jeopardy. The Forest Service also had the most men on the ground, conducting range evaluations and viewing the problem firsthand. Intent on protecting "their" aspens and other browse plants, the rangers and their supervisors were the most inclined to "do something" and viewed reducing the deer population through shooting as the best if not only option (Goldman 1925a, 1926b).

The Biological Survey's main participant was Goldman, who, as the spokesman for the agency with the most wildlife expertise, sought to give an unbiased scientific assessment of the deer situation and come up with a solution. Goldman and Mark Musgrave, the Arizona supervisor for the survey's Predator and Rodent Control branch, were also keen on maintaining the survey's good relationship with its ranching constituency and the state of Arizona. Although Goldman supported reducing the deer herd by hunting, the Biological Survey was loathe to forgo what it viewed as its predator-control mandate (Young 2002). Did it not make more sense for humans to benefit from the surplus deer rather than mountain lions? After all, it was the government's protection of the deer herd from both humans and predators that had made the increase in deer possible. Why should lions be the beneficiaries of this action, and why let up on predators that eventually would have to be removed anyway?

The National Park Service, represented at the national level by the charismatic Mather, and soon to be joined at the local level by Supervisor Miner R. Tillotson, was mostly interested in securing as much of the Kaibab's scenery and deer as possible within Grand Canyon National Park. Moreover, the Park Service was increasingly moving against a policy of reducing either deer or predator numbers—in essence wanting a "let nature find its own balance" approach (Young 2002).

The state, with its disinterested legislature and impoverished game and fish department, would have as its principal delegate its strong-willed governor. Hunt was dead set against shooting what he considered tame, easy-to-kill deer, whose only crime was to be too plentiful. The governor was not about to agree to any plan that killed more deer than was absolutely necessary, and he was adamant that the state's game laws must be followed. The newly organized Arizona Game Protective Association, while composed primarily of sportsmen and naturally prone to accept a hunting solution, was nonetheless also protective of the state's deer and sympathetic with their governor.

People viewed the Kaibab controversy in different ways, and there are numerous opinions within the various reports, letters, and summaries describing the situation in the early 1920s. One thing is clear: There was no shortage of ideas, interpretations, and suggestions for what to do. The uniquely novel issue of what to do with too many deer was debated by bureaucrats, biologists, ranchers, hunters, conservationists, preservationists, and states'-rights advocates. Most commentators, including Charles McCormick (1924), a Fredonia-area rancher, favored nonlethal solutions, such as adjusting the national park's borders, that would give the park most of the forested deer range and keep most of the rangelands within the national forest (Young 2002). Others were more sanguine. One experienced naturalist, George Shiras III (1924), after conducting an independent inspection of the Kaibab in September 1923, was appalled at the deplorable condition of some of the deer he saw and opined that from 30,000 to 40,000 deer were on the verge of starving to death.

Hoping to find some sort of consensus, a committee was formed in January 1924. Guided by Forest Examiner Locke, Goldman, and R. T. Evans (US Geological Survey), the committee was led by members of the Boone and Crockett Club (Heyward Cutting), the American Game Protective Association (John Burnham), the American National Livestock Breeders Association (T. W. Tomlinson), and T. Gilbert Pearson, who represented the National Association of Audubon Societies and the National Parks Association. To get the facts, the committee conducted a 10-day investigation of the Kaibab to determine how best to improve the forage and reduce the deer herd. State Game Warden Willard did not attend, probably because Governor Hunt was intent on making his own tour on the plateau, something he or Willard did at least three times during the controversy (Governor's Files 1923–33; Russo 1964; Young 2002).

The committee saw plenty of deer in poor flesh and reported the worst range conditions the members had ever seen (Cutting et al. 1924). Dwarf buckbrush (*Ceanothus fendleri*) and snowberry (*Symphoricarpos oreophilus*) plants were particularly hard hit and no longer deemed capable of supporting the number of deer desired. But even though some dead deer were found, the committee found a number of areas that appeared to have escaped the deer's heavy presence. Many of the participants nonetheless agreed with Shiras that the Forest Service estimate of 20,000 deer plus 6,000 fawns was too conservative and thought that the number was closer to 50,000 (Rasmussen later thought the number might be closer to 100,000).[4] Although the committee did not recommend a figure as to the number of deer they thought the Kaibab could reasonably support, the consensus was that deer numbers should be reduced 50% through trapping and transplanting and "some shooting."

---

[4]If so, the density of deer on the Kaibab summer and winter range combined would have been about 68 deer per square mile. The density on the winter range alone would therefore have been enormous, exceeding the maximum density of ca. 98 deer per square mile in an artificial deer enclosure on the Arizona Game and Fish Department's Three Bar Wildlife Area in 2006—a density so great that the fence was taken down for humanitarian reasons.

The first central hunting camp. This camp was at Slide Reservoir. 1924 photo by S. B. Locke. (US Forest Service, Southwestern Region, Kaibab National Forest)

Dealing With the Deer Irruption

The first serious drought in more than 20 years now occurred, and Shiras's predictions were borne out. Kaibab ranger Swapp estimated a 60% loss in the deer herd during the harsh winter of 1924–25 (Young 2002). Not only were deer now dying in record numbers, but the range was continuing to deteriorate.

The Forest Service was desperate to relieve the pressure on the Kaibab's forests and rangelands and agreed to embark on a deer-shooting and deer-trapping program. On September 19, 1924, acting Forester E. A. Sherman, noting that Hunt and Willard had inspected conditions firsthand, advised Hunt of the Forest Service's responsibilities as per Congress and the need for the state to cooperate with the findings of the committee and include the Kaibab in the deer season scheduled to open October 1, 1924. Hunt increasingly opposed solving the problem by shooting deer, however, even writing an article opposing such a "slaughter" (Governor's Files, Arizona State Library, Archives and Public Records).

Weary of dickering, and acting on the advice of the government's solicitor, the Forest Service announced the Kaibab National Forest would issue three deer permits to each hunter who paid a special $5 government fee to participate in a deer-hunting season that would open at noon, November 8, 1924—a hunt outside of the framework established by state law.

In response, Governor Hunt had State Game Warden Willard send Jack Fuss, deputy warden for Coconino County, to stop the hunt on the Kaibab. Although arrests were threatened, and apparently some made by the Coconino County sheriff, no deer were confiscated, the season being terminated by sending the hunters home and locking the gate to the winter range (Fuss 1999). Most of the hunters were from Fredonia and southern Utah and not easily prosecuted by Arizona officers in any event. A flurry of telegrams followed between Hunt, local law enforcement officers, and the governor of Utah, with the outcome resulting in a "gentleman's agreement." The Forest Service would open another season on November 15, this one an eight-day hunt that was more in line with Arizona's statutes. The state would receive $1.25 of the $5 fee paid by hunters wanting to hunt on the Kaibab (Fuss 1999).

The hunt was unpopular among some members of the newly formed Arizona Game Protective Association, as well as with the hunting public (Several letters to Governor Hunt, Governor's Files 1923–33, Record Group 1, Subgroup 8, Box 3, Arizona State Library, Archives and Public Records). Only 270 hunters from 18 states participated in the hunt, taking 675 deer or 2.5 animals per hunter (Russo 1964). Arizona deputies were directed to arrest any hunters who took deer off the federal preserve without a state hunting license. Although only a few hundred deer were killed and no one was arrested by the department, the hunt caused a major break between the Forest Service and the state—a rift that continued through to 1925, when deer hunters without state licenses were again subject to arrest despite their killing deer on federal land. Nor was the east side of the Kaibab open to hunting, that part of the deer range being reserved for another deer-reduction strategy.

In a parallel effort to reduce the number of deer on the Kaibab, a part-time rancher named George McCormick, Charles's brother, proposed driving the deer off the Kaibab Plateau and through the Grand Canyon to the South Rim. A persuasive promoter, McCormick was supported not only by several of his friends in Flagstaff, including certain members of the Arizona Game Protective Association, but by Governor Hunt, who thought the bizarre proposal both practical and possible. The Forest Service was skeptical of the deer drive's success, and the Park Service was hostile to the idea, but both agencies acquiesced to the drive to appease the state and the public sentiment stirred up by McCormick (Young 2002).

The intent of this deer drive on the east range was to deliver not less than 3,000 nor more than 8,000 deer to the South Rim, where the animals would be delivered into state custody for $2.50 each. Once on the South Rim, the deer were supposed to be herded to four areas in Coconino County having deer populations that were less dense than desired (Letter from George McCormick to Hunt, October 17, 1924, Governor's Files, Arizona State Library, Archives and Public Records).

Although State Game Warden Willard had serious reservations about the proposal, he was either unable or unwilling to confront Hunt on the issue and agreed to give it a try. He sent Deputy Warden Fuss (1999) to accompany McCormick and a number of volunteers on a hazardous "trail" across the Grand Canyon in December with 27 horses and a mule, there then being no bridge across the Colorado River.

In the meantime, Willard, Chief Deputy Pettis, and Deputy Warden C. N. Greer arrived on the east range, joining McCormick and leaving Forest Supervisor Locke to administer the final days of the deer hunt on the Kaibab's west side (December 11, 1924, article, Arizona State Library, Archives and Public Records). Winter was now setting in and snow flurries were already falling, a factor the now 62-year-old Willard hoped would bode well for the success of the drive (Willard to Hunt, December 11, 1924, Arizona Game and Fish folder, Arizona State Library, Archives and Public Records).

On the basis of his endorsements and persuasive nature, McCormick had enticed cameramen working for David "D. W." Griffith to make a film, scripted by author Zane Grey, recording the drive to cross the preserve (Carmony 2002). In an interesting aside, McCormick's brother, Charles, who lived in Fredonia, wrote a letter to Hunt tattling that Willard approved of unrestricted hunting on the Kaibab (McCormick to Hunt, November 6, 1924, Arizona State Library, Archives and Public Records). Charles McCormick, like others, also worried that the Navajos would kill any deer released on the South Rim.

Whatever his abilities as a salesman, George McCormick had no real knowledge of the country, and he proved to be a poor organizer. The plan was a "ridiculous" waste of time, money, and horseflesh from the beginning[5] (Fuss 1999). Just the same, on December 16, during the onset of a snowstorm, more than 100 horsemen and Navajo Indians attempted to herd the deer down South Canyon to Saddle Canyon, and then down Nankoweep Canyon into the Grand Canyon and across the Colorado River to the Tanner Trail. Needless to say, the drive was an abject failure. The horsemen arrived at Saddle Canyon with no deer in front of them but thousands behind them (Grey 1924b; Mann and Locke 1931; Russo 1964; Fuss 1999; Carmony 2003). Willard telegraphed Hunt: "Drive Off Hunting On. No Deer No Pictures."

Standoff, Then Compromise

E. Raymond Hall, then a graduate student working for the Biological Survey, conducted a mule deer life-history study on the Kaibab commencing on June 7, 1925. After spending 13 days with Goldman and Forest Service officials making a general survey of conditions on the plateau, he spent another 41 days studying and collecting 15 mule deer. A careful observer, Hall not only reported on the deer's behavior and natural history but made a number of astute observations regarding the deer's summer range (Hall 1925). He estimated the number of deer then present at about 25,000 animals, a guess based on as much information as previous estimates had been. Hall also noted that deer numbers and herd composition were strongly influenced by topography and water distribution in addition to forage availability. Does, particularly those with fawns, were not randomly distributed, but were strongly associated with the presence of water and certain topographical features.

Hall considered forage availability to be the primary control of not only the deer's distribution but also their numbers, describing such high-quality forage plants as wild pea (*Lathyrus* spp.) as practically extirpated and dwarf buckbrush as having been killed over large areas. Cliffrose (*Cowania mexicana*)—the major winter forage—was described as not supplying a third of the browse it normally could. Another important browse, snowberry, was considered to be reduced nearly to the same degree as the buckbrush. Hall reported

[5]At least two packhorses fell to their death when McCormick's party attempted to cross the Grand Canyon on a little-used trail during the winter weather (Fuss 1999).

The persuasive George McCormick enticed cameramen working for D. W. Griffith to film the "Great Kaibab Deer Drive" from the Kaibab Plateau to the Grand Canyon's South Rim. Of course, the plan to drive deer was an abject failure. (Arizona Historical Society/Flagstaff, Jack Fuss Photo Collection at Northern Arizona University, Cline Library, #AHSND.PH.467-111)

that no aspen regeneration had been seen for at least five years. Worst of all, secondary plants such as junipers were now being heavily grazed. The deer were even feeding on conifers. For the first time, deer damage was noted on ponderosa pine (*Pinus ponderosa*)—the plateau's prime timber tree.

Many of the deer Hall saw were emaciated and lame, even though large, robust bucks were also seen—a phenomenon he attributed to the larger animals' ability to reach more nutritious forage. He also reported many deer dying during the winter of 1924–25, with a disproportionate number of yearlings being found dead on the winter range. On the winter range, where forage conditions were as bad as, if not worse than, those on the summer range, he thought the deer were especially hard-pressed due to the added burden of having to compete with cattle. Although the deer he observed on the summer range were also starving, Hall noted few predators or predator kills that were not attributable to coyotes. He also found fawns to be conspicuously underrepresented compared to reports in previous years, observing a ratio of only one fawn for every 3½ adult deer or a fawn:doe ratio of 29 fawns per 100 does. Hall (1925), who would go on to become one of America's premier mammalogists, attributed the overabundance of deer to the effective control of predators, a situation he thought in need of correction—an opinion not necessarily shared by his employer, the Biological Survey (Goldman 1925b; Hall 1930).

Although 1924 and 1925 had been dry, and the winter of 1924–25 more harsh than usual, the *Forest Service Game Report* for 1925 reported the condition of the deer to be much improved. This apparent anomaly was due to early and copious summer rains, which had transformed Pleasant Valley and V. T. Park from "dust bowls" prior to the survey period to lush meadows, while the adjacent pine forests supported a profusion of mushrooms. Nonetheless, fewer deer were observed than previously, and 75% of the yearlings or previous year's fawns were thought to have died (Goldman 1925b). Cattle, an increasingly minor component on the Kaibab National Forest, were also reported to be in

Deer browse. Lower branches of cliffrose or buckbrush fed on by deer in South Canyon. 1924 photo by S. B. Locke. (US Forest Service, Southwestern Region, Kaibab National Forest)

excess of carrying capacity, and predators appeared less common despite the PARC's not having done any control work for two years (Goldman 1925a).

Meanwhile, the standoff between the Forest Service and the state of Arizona continued, exacerbated now by the ambitions of Grand Canyon National Park. Returning from a series of wildlife conferences, Willard and Pettis stopped to visit the Kaibab. They were dismayed to learn Mather was attempting to have all of the plateau 26 miles back from the rim of the Grand Canyon included in the national park, thus making half of the plateau's commercial timber, grazing, and deer herd unavailable for consumptive use (Willard to Hunt, September 18, 1924, Governor's Files, Box 3, Arizona State Library, Archives and Public Records).

Considering the Forest Service's plans the lesser of two evils, the state went along with a hunt in 1925 in which 366 permits or agreements were issued to hunters from 10 states. Only 392 deer were taken, with another 40 condemned as unfit for consumption despite the biggest buck's weighing 213 pounds. The hunt results in 1926 were also judged inadequate: 86 hunters from 14 states took 584 deer, not counting those condemned as unfit to eat (see table, page 100). The bottom line was that sport hunting under the restrictions imposed by the state was less effective in reducing deer numbers than natural losses (Locke 1930).[6]

[6]Dwight Pettis, in a June 1929 article in *Arizona Wild Life*, gave the Arizona Game and Fish Department's point of view, stating that George Willard had agreed to allow nonresident hunters and a three-deer bag limit of any sex deer for the 1924 deer season, and that it was the Coconino County Sheriff who arrested Utah hunters, not Willard. The state's role in succeeding hunts was also confused by Governor Hunt's overruling Willard in 1926, 1927, and 1928, with the governor insisting that the provisions of the 1916 game law be carried out.

In a December 27, 1926, game report, the Kaibab National Forest stated, "[A]s near as we are able to judge the total number [of deer] remains at 30,000, not including this year's fawns." The following year, the Forest Service's estimate dropped to 28,000, with 4,000 deer reported dead: 1,900 from starvation, 982 from hunting, and 1,000 due to predators. Neither sport hunting, translocations, nor fawn removal programs were effectively curtailing the number of deer. Deer were still succumbing to starvation, and in the minds of the Forest Service rangers, continued to threaten the very forest itself.

As a result, the Forest Service filed for an injunction in federal district court seeking to prohibit the state from enforcing its game code, with the federal government arguing it had the right to protect its forage resources from the state's deer (Young 2002). On June 24, 1927, after the Forest Service obtained a favorable ruling, Hunt and now State Game Warden Pettis appealed the district court's ruling (Mann 1929 *in* Young 2002). Seeing itself with no other choice, the Forest Service then took its case to the US Supreme Court and won. The Forest Service's mandate to protect the nation's vegetation trumped the state's right to protect its citizens' deer.

Forest Service technicians estimated a deer population of 20,000–25,000 deer during the summer of 1927—a significant if questionable decline from the 30,000 estimated the previous December. Fearful that the state would argue that the problem was being solved and that the Kaibab was "running out of deer," the Forest Service intensified its browse measurements and bolstered its position by having Goldman, Bailey, and other biologists conduct additional studies (Locke 1930; Goldman 1932). Not wanting to push the court's rulings further than necessary, federal solicitors advised the Forest Service to go slow and cooperate with the state insofar as possible. Interagency agreement was preferable to confrontation (Russo 1964).

In an attempt at compromise, the Forest Service surrendered 46,000 acres of the Kaibab National Forest to the Park Service, thus allowing Supervisor Tillotson and his agency to protect more deer from hunting on Grand Canyon National Park. In the fall of 1927, the remaining forest was open to deer hunting, with 1,001 hunters from 13 states taking 907 deer. That year also saw the resumption of predator control outside the national park with the Biological Survey's PARC personnel taking 4 lions, 111 bobcats, and 403 coyotes. This was also about the time that the last wolves were removed from the Kaibab (Brown 1983).

The die-off of deer during the winter of 1927–28 was considered appalling, with 87 dead deer found in one location. Even when the 1928 fawn recruitment was considered, the number of deer was thought to have declined by some 3,000 animals, including those lost to starvation, 1,000 or so removed during the 1927 hunt, and another 1,700 that were attributed to predators despite the fact that 44 lions were taken that year.

The use of range inspections and browse transect surveys now greatly expanded. These surveys continued to show that the key browse plants remained in critical shape, with many cliffrose plants being killed. "Deer-lines," areas of stripped vegetation within the reach of deer, were seen even on such low-quality forage plants as junipers. Deer numbers were thought to still be too high for browse plants to survive, much less recover (Russo 1964; Young 2002).

In 1928, another 30-day October season resulted in 926 sportsmen from 17 states taking 1,003 deer—with nonresidents again outnumbering residents three to one. In a new twist in the regulations, 33 deer were allowed to be killed for camp use—a practice that would remain in the memory of hunters for years to come. Again, insufficient deer were taken to materially reduce the population and allow the cliffrose and other browse plants to recover.

The 1929 hunt was a repeat of the previous year's, except the number of hunt permits was greatly increased. What was different was that for 10 days in mid-December, the Forest Service took the unprecedented action of supervising the killing of deer by salaried government hunters as per its court-ruled prerogative. The government hunters arrived on December 14, each equipped with a saddle horse and assigned a goal of 15 deer per day. The hunters were also provided a two-man processing team in a buckboard, as well as two packhorses.

Reports vary, but Forest Service records show that 1,124 deer were stacked, racked, and distributed before the killing ceased, most of the animals coming from the west-side winter range, but at least 216 being removed from the east-side game range. The venison was all to go to the Navajo Indians, but there was much spoilage and a significant amount of the meat was condemned as unfit to eat (Russo 1964; Young 2002). All in all, 3,688 mule deer had been removed from the Kaibab by hunting that year, the most to date, a number that caused the state to argue that Kaibab deer were now in danger of becoming scarce (Young 2002).

Reaching Equilibrium

The year 1929 was also important in that the Supreme Court had affirmed the Forest Service's right to protect the Kaibab's forage resources, Hunt had been voted out of office in 1928, a new game code had been approved, and the first Arizona Game and Fish Commission had been appointed. Because of these actions, the Forest Service and Arizona Game and Fish Department were now able to reach a cooperative agreement to "remove the excessive number of deer" by jointly opening certain areas of the Kaibab National Forest to hunting under Arizona game laws and Forest Service regulations (Bayless 1930). Although the deer's primary forage plants were still judged as being too heavily browsed, the winter of 1929–30 was relatively mild, and the 20,000 or so deer thought to be coming onto the summer range in the spring of 1930 were described as being in reasonably good condition (Pettis to Governor Hunt, Governor's Files, 192333, Box 3, Record Group 1, Subgroup 8, 1930. Arizona State Library, Archives and Public Records).

The conditions for the 1930 hunting season were stringent and detailed: two hunting areas were designated, one on the east side and one on the west side, the seasons of which were respectively, October 1–November 30 and October 16–November 30. An unspecified number of hunters were to check in and out at two check stations, where they were required to have an Arizona hunting license and pay a $1.50 "Government Fee." A series of hunting camps, supervised by forest rangers and deputy wardens, would be available in the hunt areas, as would concessionaires providing horses, packers, and meals at $1 each. The bag limit was set at two deer, only one of which could be a buck, and metal tags were to be attached to each deer killed. Later, after the government hunters had finished, more than 5,000 deer had been harvested and the program was terminated (see table, next page). That many deer would not be harvested on the Kaibab for many years to come and the herd was now considered under control. The most serious confrontations among the agencies were now in the past, and mutually agreed deer seasons would continue on through the 1930s.

Many dramas were yet to unfold on the Kaibab, but for the present, some degree of equilibrium had been reached—if not biologically, at least politically. Both deer hunting and predator control would continue, with a lion hunter named Jack Butler removing 150 lions from 1929 to 1931. The expansion desires for Grand Canyon National Park had been appeased for the time being, and a revitalized Arizona Game Protective Association would continue to monitor the recommendations promulgated by both the Forest Service and Game and Fish Department. If nothing else, the Kaibab controversy had demonstrated the need for professional big game investigations and the monitoring of key browse plants. Hunt recommendations would hopefully now be based more on biological data than on political compromise, novel ideas, and new experiments.

D. Irwin Rasmussen (1941), like Hall (1925) and others, attributed the 20% increase per year "boom" in the deer herd from 1906 to the early 1920s to a relaxation of grazing competition from livestock after 1890, the protection from killing by humans, and the removal of natural predators. But although each of these factors may have played a role in the deer's increase, it can also be argued that more than mere cause and effect or lack of management was involved.

For one thing, organized predator control did not seriously get underway until after 1922, by which time the deer herd had reached unmanageable proportions. The numbers of lions taken by Owens between 1906 and 1918, said to be between 500 and 600, or approximately 50 per year, while more than twice the number of lions harvested on the Kaibab in good years today, is not unreasonable, given that Owens hunted yearlong on and off the preserve, and that he counted kittens and fetuses in his take. Nor did he take wolves or other predators.

Owens's efforts, coupled with those of other hunters, probably kept lion numbers in check without making any appreciable reduction in the overall population. Those who hunted lions with Owens during that time—Zane Grey, President Theodore Roosevelt, and Rex Beach—all report finding abundant lions and lion sign. Also allowing deer numbers to increase may have been the removal of wolves, even though PARC agents had not finalized this task until 1926 when deer numbers were already in decline. Grand Canyon National Park's anti–predator-control policy arrived too late and the park was too small in extent to provide a refuge for wolves either on the North or South rims.

Further evidence that lion numbers were not materially reduced on the Kaibab Plateau until after 1924 is Rasmussen's (1941) testimony that both coyotes and porcupines increased during his tenure from June 1929 through December 1931. Rasmussen estimated a density of three to five porcupines per section of forest, the PARC's and Forest Service's agents killing between 150 and 200 porcupines a year during his study. On one occasion, during the summer of 1929, he reported 23 different porcupines being caught in coyote

Estimated Deer, Precipitation, Hunt Information, and Livestock Numbers Reported for North Kaibab, 1906–62

Source: Modified from Russo 1964

Year	Estimated Mule Deer	Ann. Precip. St. George	No. of Hunters	Mule Deer Harvested	Bucks	Antlerless	Deer per 100 Hunters	Permitted Cattle	Permitted Sheep	Notes
1906	4,000	11.08						9,000	20,000	Estimate by Rasmussen (1941)
1907		9.71						8,000	10,000	
1908		10.49						13,750	5,000	
1909		16.75						14,000	7,500	
1910		9.65						14,383	5,000	
1911		8.52						14,471	5,000	
1912		11.92						13,922	5,000	Jimmy Owens active on Kaibab Plateau
1913		8.70						15,210	5,000	Jimmy Owens active on Kaibab Plateau
1914		7.75						10,892	5,000	Jimmy Owens active on Kaibab Plateau
1915		10.00						8,313	5,000	
1916		10.42						8,847	5,000	
1917		7.58						9,625	5,000	
1918		8.74						8,886	5,000	
1919		7.02						10,991	5,145	
1920		11.53						10,095	4,555	
1921		10.03						7,404	4,375	
1922		7.75						7,068	2,664	
1923		6.12						7,106	3,566	
1924	10,0000	4.40	300	683	675		2.25	4,356	3,508	5 lions and 10 wolves removed; first hunt (Mann and Locke 1941)
1925		10.02	266	432	359		98	3,019	1,155	7 lions removed by PARC; light harvest
1926	30,000	7.48	586	615	553		94.5	3,084	2,150	9 wolves and 119 coyotes removed; too few deer removed
1927	28,000	11.43	1,001	907	887		88.6	1,078	2,405	11 lions, 403 coyotes, and 111 bobcats removed
1928		6.06	926	1,003	880		95	1,228	2,405	44 lions, 577 coyotes, and 103 bobcats removed
1929		5.48	2,372	3,688			155.5	2,803	2,405	25 lions, 368 coyotes, and 96 bobcats removed; govt. hunters
1930	20,000–30,000	10.29	2,704	5,033			186	1,904	2,405	15 lions, 255 coyotes, 102 bobcats removed; deer killed by govt. hunters
1931	20,000	11.29	980	965	618	261	89.7	1,762	2,405	Predator control by PARC phased out

(continued . . .)

Estimated Deer, Precipitation, Hunt Information, and Livestock Numbers Reported for North Kaibab, 1906–62

Year	Estimated Mule Deer	Ann. Precip. St. George	No. of Hunters	Mule Deer Harvested	Bucks	Antlerless	Deer per 100 Hunters	Permit-ted Cattle	Permitted Sheep	Notes
1932	14,700	11.97	670	622	406	216	92.8	1,888	2,405	
1933	16,000	6.63	932	859	491	360	91.3	2,160	2,450	
1934	16,500	5.39	1,185	1,035	542	447	83.5	3,936	2,450	
1935	17,000	9.54	922	874	522	320	84.8	4,008	2,405	
1936		9.68	1,564	1,433	857	492	86.2	2,972	1,280	
1937		7.57	1,919	1,456	716	659	71.1	2,555	1,280	
1938	15,000	7.00	1,662	1,395	692	626	79.3	2,126	1,280	
1939		9.60	1,085	715	391	302	64.6	2,137	1,284	
1940	5,000	10.86	851	662	413	249	78	1,620	1,280	
1941		14.38	894	601	409	192	67	2,371	1,276	Predator control reinstated
1942		6.39	645	538	322	216	85.4	2,162	1,280	
1943		9.65	520	393	230	163	75.5	2,554	1,280	
1944		7.05	971	694	415	279	71.4	2,304	1,280	
1945		7.87	704	398	253	145	56.5	3,274	0	
1946		8.50	394	251	251	0	63.7	3,178	0	
1947		5.62	873	618	618	0	70.8	2,947	0	
1948		4.51	1,843	1,153	1,553	0	62.6	2,985	0	
1949		9.04	2,552	1,388	1,388	0	54.4	2771	0	
1950		4.10	4,556	2,858	2,254	0	62.7	3,059	0	
1951		10.67	4,754	2,519	1,905	604	53	2,407	0	
1952		8.15	6,446	4,312	1,770	614	66.9	2,363	0	
1953		3.93	7,166	6,053	2,884	2,542	84.5	2,250	0	
1954		8.97	10,648	8,058	3,973	4,085	75.7	no record	0	Highest harvest on record
1955	11,889	0.10	4,140	2,311	1,004	1,227	55.0	2,336	0	
1956	17,885	3.58	4,321	2,687	1,189	1,498	62.2	2,540	0	
1957	18,092	11.42	5,377	3,239	1,748	1,491	60.2	2,364	0	Bonus 2-deer hunt
1958	20,886	10.55	9,693	5,911	2,273	3,638	59.6	2,908	0	Includes archery kill
1959	16,135	5.90	4,867	3,761	1,411	2,350	55.3	2,672	0	Includes archery kill
1960	12,254	7.03	3,983	1,530	789	745	40.1	2,472	0	Includes 219 archery hunters killing 26 deer
1961	13,681	6.54	2,585	810	296	514	31.6	2,889	0	
1962		4.21	2,586	1,203	666	537	47.4	2,552	0	
Mean		**8.27**								

Notes: For 1907–34, livestock permit numbers do not reflect actual numbers, despite the Forest Service's having obtained management authority in 1907. Numbers were poorly controlled until 1934 due to lack of boundary fences and other reasons (Mann 1941). For 1922–31, feral horses and trespass stock were removed by shooting.

traps on 25 consecutive nights with eight more killed in the same place in 1930. These numbers of porcupines suggest a much-reduced lion population (Brown and Babb 2009), but not one that was in effect until after the deer population decline of 1924–25 and the initiation of predator control by the PARC—the same agency charged with the killing of porcupines.

That livestock grazing and the recovery from grazing played a role is also not open to question, although documentation on just how this came about is unclear and masked by the effects of the large numbers of deer already present after the onset of Forest Service surveys in 1918. Certainly, cattle and sheep numbers, increasingly curtailed by economics and government regulations after 1906 (see table, page 100), had a major influence on the plateau's range conditions, and the killing of 1,310 feral horses by Forest Service agents between 1922 and 1931 was not without some impact.

But Rasmussen, who spent as much time on the Kaibab as anyone other than Forest Service personnel, was in full agreement with that agency's inspectors that both the summer and winter ranges had been mostly depleted by deer rather than livestock. So destitute was the plateau's deer forage that such species as willows (*Salix* spp.) and raspberries (*Rubus* spp.) were almost totally eliminated, while aspen (*Populus tremuloides*) regeneration failed to occur for some 20 years. Rasmussen, who noted that grass was increasing in the plateau's floral composition, attributed most of the vegetation change to deer use, not livestock, stating that he thought climate and weather had little effect on the vegetation during his tenure.

More than one factor was undoubtedly responsible for the deer irruption; my suspicion is that weather played a significant role in the increase in deer on the north Kaibab. Lion removal, while allowing the deer herd to increase unchecked, was only one of two major reasons for the original build-up of the deer population. The second reason was a high level of fawn recruitment due to above- or near-average precipitation occurring nearly every year from 1905 through 1921, with even the driest years of 1914, 1917, and 1919 being within 15% of the long-term mean. Good fawn recruitment and high mule deer population levels are strongly related to consecutive years of high precipitation (Smith and LeCount 1979; Carmony 2003; Heffelfinger 2006). It was not until 1923 and 1924 that drought conditions prevailed and deer numbers plummeted, with few fawns being recruited from 1924 through 1928 (Rasmussen 1941). As for the increase in deer being due solely to the cessation of human harvests, it should be remembered that a similar irruption did not occur on the South Rim of the Grand Canyon until many years later despite total protection of the deer there by the National Park Service after 1919.

ARIZONA'S ELK RESTORATION

David E. Brown and Jim Heffelfinger

In 1893, the Arizona Territorial Legislature imposed a closed season on elk, but this was not soon enough to save the state's native elk from extirpation. Never numerous or widespread, the so-called Merriam's elk[1] had disappeared during the settlement years for reasons that remain imperfectly understood. With reports of Merriam's elk drying up completely by 1910, concerned citizens were eager to participate in any program that would restore this important native game animal.

The story of the first elk reintroduction to Arizona by Dr. Robert N. Looney, a frontier doctor in Prescott, and the state's Elks Lodges in 1913 has been told several times, most accurately in an article edited by Neil Carmony in the January–February 2003 issue of *Arizona Wildlife Views*. After reading an article on trapping and shipping elk in the August 1912 issue of *Outdoor Life* magazine, the young doctor contacted the Boone and Crockett Club, who advised him on the details of translocating animals. Having gained the support of Gov. George Hunt and the Benevolent and Protective Order of Elks, Looney and the Elks secured a permit to transport 80 head of elk from Yellowstone National Park and release them on the Sitgreaves National Forest southeast of Winslow, Arizona.

Arizona members of the Elks provided financial and logistical support. Although Governor Hunt was enthusiastic about the transplant, the state had no money available to finance such a venture. The only department money involved consisted of a special $50 travel stipend to the new State Game Warden, Frank Rogers, to oversee the unloading of the elk at Winslow. This he did, advising Hunt on the success of the transplant by telegram on February 20, 1913.

The Yellowstone elk were captured out of the northern Yellowstone herd near Gardiner, Montana, in February 1913 and shipped by railroad to Winslow, Arizona. Although the permit was for only 80 head, a few additional animals were included, and 86 elk arrived in Winslow (see table, page 109). The elk (14 bulls, 4 adult cows, and 68 heifer yearlings) were unloaded from the rail cars and held in the stockyards. Then they were transported to a holding pen at Cabin Draw in the Chevelon District of the Sitgreaves National Forest in 12 wooden, horse-drawn wagons modified for the task. Olaus Murie (1951) reported in *The Elk of North America* that in 1937 a large bull elk was harvested south of Winslow bearing an ear tag from the 1913 release. If so, this animal would have been at least 25 years of age.

The frequent retelling of that famous first elk translocation obscures the fact that there were other, equally colorful, elk releases in Arizona. Yellowstone's elk continued to overpopulate their winter range, and the federal government maintained its offer to provide surplus animals to any state or responsible party that wanted them. The catch was

[1]The description of *Cervus merriami* was based on two male specimens sent to the US National Museum by Dr. Edward Nelson and described by C. Hart Merriam, a notorious taxonomic "splitter." There is little reason to differentiate the native elk of Arizona and New Mexico from others of the same species in the Rocky Mountains.

Loading elk in cars at Gardiner, Montana in 1913 to be shipped to other states. (Arizona Historical Society/Tucson, Will C. Barnes Collection, #13-5999, PC10, Box 7, Folder 235)

Elk in crates from Yellowstone National Park being unloaded onto wagons at Winslow, Arizona in 1913 before being pulled by horse to their release site in Cabin Draw. These were the first of several loads of Yellowstone elk that became the Arizona elk we enjoy today. (AGFD files)

that the recipients had to provide a suitable release site and pay for the elk's transportation. This could be a problem, as the elk had to be captured and shipped from the winter range by rail car and thus were only available when most states' "elk country" was inaccessible.

One of the provisions prescribed in the Arizona 1912 game code was to restock Arizona's depleted wildlife populations. Free elk were especially attractive, even though stockmen worried about elk competing with livestock for forage, and some sportsmen believed elk would displace the state's struggling populations of deer and antelope. It was therefore not until 1918 that George Willard, who had been appointed to replace Rogers as State Game Warden by Governor Hunt, made arrangements to obtain a second shipment of elk.

The original plan called for transporting 56 elk from Gardiner, Montana, to Clifton, Arizona. Then Deputy Warden Frank Maxwell would herd them to the Blue Range Game Preserve. However, the Montana man assigned to accompany the elk on their train ride pointed out the inadvisability of trying to drive wild elk from Clifton to the Blue, warning that the animals would likely scatter and go into New Mexico.

Realizing the need for a change in plans, Willard wrote Maxwell on March 29, 1918, that his administration "would not survive" a transplant of elk to New Mexico. He then informed his deputy that, since the elk were intended for Maxwell's home district around Nutrioso, north of the Blue Range, and because he was the only man experienced enough to drive them, he was to trail the elk from just east of Globe to the White Mountains—a distance of more than 100 miles as the crow flies. To soften the blow of such an arduous assignment, Willard told Maxwell this was to be his only responsibility throughout the summer, and his allowance for horse hire would be increased to $1.50 per day.

Not all of the elk were destined for the White Mountains. One railroad car of 22 elk was unloaded at Pima (west of Safford), where it was hoped the animals would make their way into the Graham (Pinaleño) Mountains. Whether or not they did is unknown, but less than 10 years later State Game Warden Dwight Pettis reported that none of these elk remained.

The remainder of the shipment, some 34 head, was sent on to Cutter, a railroad siding east of Globe near the present site of the Apache Gold Casino. What happened at Cutter is now mostly legend, but it appears the elk either broke loose or were turned loose. Once released, the animals were determined to go their own way. Instead of being driven north by Maxwell across the Natanes Rim toward the Blue Range, most of the elk headed south toward the Mescal Mountains in the southeast corner of the San Carlos Indian Reservation.

The state's unintended gift to the San Carlos Apaches proved surprisingly persistent. Although a few ponderosa pines are present in the Mescals, most of the "elk habitat" in this range is chaparral brush and grassland. Ten years later, in 1927, the Cutter herd was estimated to number only 50 or less. But then, as livestock waters were developed, elk numbers gradually rose until the population was conservatively estimated to number between 150 and 300. Livestock operators on the reservation thought any elk were too many, and petitioned the Arizona Game and Fish Commission to authorize an any-elk hunt in the fall of 1950. The commission complied and issued 150 permits that, combined with another any-elk hunt of 250 permits the following year, resulted in 258 elk being removed by hunters.

The Cutter herd, as it was popularly called, was further reduced by a series of hunts by tribal members that continued until 1965, after which time the elk were commonly shot on sight. Pat O'Brien, a wildlife manager in Globe who carefully researched the history of the Cutter herd, reported in a 1979 article in *Arizona Wildlife Views* magazine that the elk were then reduced to four small herds totaling about 52 individuals in an area covering 150 square miles. Lacking protected status, the herd's numbers continued to decline. With the possible exception of a few animals holding out in the foothills of the Pinal Mountains, such Mescal Mountains place names as Elk Tank, Elk Spring, and Elk Dam are now only of historic interest.

Transporting Yellowstone National Park elk from the rail siding at Holbrook, Arizona, to the Campbell Blue Creek was a major feat, owing to two feet of fresh snow. The men had to break trail with cars and on foot to make it through the pass two to three miles south of Alpine, Arizona. (AGFD files)

In an attempt to prevent future fiascos, Arizona entered into an agreement in 1919 with the US Biological Survey and US Forest Service stating that no further elk introductions would be made without the consent of all three parties. A series of cooperative elk surveys were also begun that year to determine the extent of Arizona's elk population on the Mogollon Rim and the validity of depredation complaints in and around the Sitgreaves National Forest. Federal biologist Edward Goldman and State Game Warden Joe Prochaska concluded that the state harbored between 300 and 500 head—maybe more—and recommended a limited hunt to scatter the elk, which were then largely confined to the western portions of the Sitgreaves National Forest; the Coconino National Forest east of Blue Ridge Road; and the Tonto National Forest north of Tonto Basin. Wet weather, a lack of manpower, and a change of administration, all conspired to forestall a hunt.

Eight years later, in 1927, an *Arizona Wild Life* article by Apache National Forest Supervisor Kenner Kartchner reported that Arizona's elk numbers had increased to about 800, but that their distribution had changed little. Thus, when State Game Warden Pettis addressed the White Mountains Sportsmen's Association in Springerville that year, and asked the club's members what they thought about an introduction of 60 elk to the Blue Range Refuge, the response was instant approval. The Game and Fish Department would pay the $800 capture and shipping charges, and the elk would be sent by rail to Holbrook, where they would be loaded in trucks chartered to take them to the Blue. Thanks to the diplomatic skills of Pettis and Kartchner, the Blue's cattlemen agreed to the transplant. The White Mountains Sportsmen would foot most of the $250 hauling cost, while the Apache and Greenlee county boards of supervisors each contributed five dollars. The sportsmen would also build the crates and arrange for the trucks.

Although this introduction was more carefully considered than the ones in 1918, there were still problems. For one, the sportsmen thought only yearling elk would be shipped. Accordingly, a holding pasture of alfalfa was leased at Springerville to hold 30 yearlings until spring. These plans had to be dropped when Pettis, who had supervised the shipment from Yellowstone and accompanied the elk, showed up at Holbrook with mostly adult animals. The crates had to be rebuilt, an additional cost funded by the Holbrook Gun Club, and a chore personally undertaken by Pettis and two of his deputies, W. W. Freeman and W. O. Hamblin.

Finally, amid much grumbling from the drivers, 27 elk (all that could be loaded) were trucked from Holbrook to Springerville on February 10, 1927. In addition to a large six-wheeled vehicle, the convoy consisted of two smaller trucks holding six elk each. The remaining elk, some 30 head, were sent on in a rail car to be released near Williams.

The trucks arrived in Springerville about 10 p.m. to considerable fanfare and comment. The weather being freezing and the road treacherous, the men took rooms for the night to ensure a fresh start at 6:30 in the morning. Three elk—a cow, a yearling bull, and a heifer—died during the night from being too crowded, but the rest of the animals survived just fine. Although frozen, the road had been judged passable for at least a mile past Alpine. Excellent time was made until the convoy reached a hill south of Alpine on the Coronado Trail. Here, the trucks encountered two feet of snow, requiring the men to break a trail with their cars and on foot. When a truck slid off the road, a horse team pulled the errant vehicle back on the track. Finally, at 4 p.m., the caravan reached Campbell Blue Creek, where the remaining 22 elk in good condition (16 cows, 2 heifers, 3 yearling bulls, and 1 bull that was two or three years old) were released directly into the wild. Nearly every animal had to be dragged out of the truck with ropes. Given a ton of baled meadow hay and a salt block, the elk were then left in the care of Deputy Warden Hamblin, who would watch over them until spring.

The second carload of elk, intended for Williams, was sent on to Kingman due to the opposition of local stockmen. The elk arrived in Kingman on February 11, and, after being fed and watered, were released in the foothills of the Hualapai Mountains on Admission Day 1927. As with the elk in the Campbell Blue, these animals had to be dragged out of the railroad car, whence they were harried up a ridge to the Hualapai Mountains by horsemen.

When ranchers succeeded in sending the railroad car of elk on to Kingman, Arizona Game Protective Association officers Tom McCullough and Gordon Evans redoubled their determination to get elk reintroduced to the Flagstaff-Williams area. A former Forest Service employee, McCullough was a deft politician who knew the ins and outs of rural politics. With Pettis's assistance, the two men not only obtained the Forest Service's and Biological Survey's agreement to the release, they also convinced the Arizona Cattle-growers Association to go along with an introduction of 60 elk.

Of 63 elk shipped, 55 survived to be unloaded just north of Williams in early 1928. This time the release went smoothly. The railroad to the Grand Canyon passed through reasonable elk habitat, forgoing the need for unloading the elk into crates and transporting them by truck or wagons to a remote holding area. Nor was there a need to drive the animals by horseback. By all accounts everything went well, and the elk drifted southward and westward onto the Coconino-Yavapai Game Preserve. As the herd's numbers increased, so did its distribution, and the elk presently found north, west, and south of Flagstaff probably originated from this transplant. For years afterward, McCullough and Evans regarded this release as one of their and the Arizona Game Protective Association's greatest successes.

The final release was a shipment of 40 elk (four of which died en route) to the Hualapai Reservation in 1963—an introduction first proposed in the early 1930s. A translocation of elk to the Chiricahua Mountains, a popular recommendation when proposed by Governor Hunt and State Game Warden Pettis in the late 1920s, was eventually nixed by succeeding administrations and Coronado National Forest Supervisor Fred Winn due to the lack of wet meadows in that mountain range.

Except for the translocation of 29 elk from Arizona to Kentucky in 2000, these are the only elk translocations into or out of the state in the historical record. Because of the interest and research this topic has received, it is unlikely that any translocations went unrecorded.

These relatively small releases succeeded beyond anyone's expectations. There were only 281 Yellowstone elk known to be released in Arizona between 1913 and 1963, and this source stock has multiplied to well over 24,000 animals. The only introduction to

Historical Arizona Elk Translocations, 1913 to the Present
Source: AGFD and Arizona Game Protective Association

Capture Date	Capture Site	Release Site	Number Captured	Number Mortalities[a]	Number Released[a]	Release Sex[a]
2/1913	Yellowstone National Park (Gardiner, Montana)	Cabin Draw, Chevelon Creek, Sitgreaves NF (GMU 4B)	86	4	82	14M:4F: 64yrlg
1918	Yellowstone National Park	Graham Mountains[b] (GMU 31); El Capitan Mountain, south of Cutter, San Carlos I.R. (GMU 26)	60	4	56 (22) (34)	
2/12/27	Yellowstone National Park	Campbell Blue, south of Alpine (GMU 27); Hualapai Mountains, southeast of Kingman (GMU 16A)	57	5 (5)	52 (22) (30)	(4M:18F)
1928	Yellowstone National Park	Bill Williams Mountain (GMU 8)	63	8	55	
12/22/63	Yellowstone National Park (Slough Creek, Wyoming)	Park Tank, Peach Springs Hualapai I.R. (GMU 14)	40	4F	36	12M:24F

[a]Parentheses ( ) subdivide the total number of elk released into the number released at each specific site in the "release sites" column.

[b]Graham Mountain release unsuccessful.

Note: NF=National Forest; GMU=Game management unit; M=Male; F=Female; yrlg=yearling; I.R.=Indian Reservation

have failed was the attempt to release elk in the Graham Mountains favored by Governor Hunt and State Game Warden Willard in 1918. Today, elk inhabit nearly every forested area in northern Arizona, including the small ponderosa pine forest atop Dean Peak in the Hualapai Mountains. Movements of elk into southeastern Arizona have resulted in a small herd being established north of Willcox. Given the events of 1918, it is ironic that this herd spends some time each year in the Graham Mountains.

As early as 1929, Arizona's elk were thought to have increased to more than 3,000 and a hunt to harvest 1,000 animals was recommended—a hunt that was finally realized in 1935, when 266 bull permits were authorized and 145 elk harvested. Elk have been hunted nearly every year since, with the exception of a few years during World War II. Since then, the state's elk herd has grown substantially, until more than 11,000 elk were harvested in the fall of 1994—80 years after the first release. Today, several game management units annually produce more harvested elk than were originally brought into the state.

Not only do we have quantity, we have quality as well. Arizona is known for its ability to produce trophy bulls. In the latest edition of Boone and Crockett Club's *Records of North American Big Game*, 14 of the 53 largest elk (26%) ever harvested came from Arizona. What accounts for our large-antlered elk in Arizona? Some sportsmen have speculated that our trophies represent an influence of Merriam's elk that somehow survived to the first release in 1913 and then interbred with Yellowstone elk. This genetic influence, they say, is the reason for the large antlers that crown Arizona's bull elk.

Recently, a genetic analysis was conducted to compare today's Arizona elk to see if there was any hint of genetic variations that does not occur in Yellowstone elk. If some

Arizona elk have a very different genetic signature that did not come from Yellowstone, this could be interpreted as evidence that Merriam's elk contributed to the building of Arizona's elk herds. Seven different genetic variants (haplotypes) were found in Arizona's elk, but all were commonly found in Yellowstone elk. The analysis showed that all the Arizona haplotypes are exactly what one would expect from a sample of Yellowstone elk. In other words, there is no evidence to suggest that elk from Arizona are anything but a subsample of elk from Yellowstone.

SECTION II

A ROUGH ROAD TO RECOVERY

1929–39

THE ARIZONA GAME PROTECTIVE ASSOCIATION GETS ITS ACT TOGETHER

David E. Brown, Joseph Monfeli, and Melanie Tluczek

It was no accident that Arizona's first sportsmen's clubs originated in small towns within or close to a national forest. Not only were forest administrators and rangers drawn to conservation issues as part of their duties; helping to organize hunting and fishing clubs was part of the Forest Service mandate in Arizona and New Mexico (USDA Forest Service 1915; Brown and Carmony 1990). Working with cattle ranchers, small-town businessmen, government employees, and, in some areas, miners and other workmen, forest rangers set about forming sportsmen's organizations dedicated to game conservation. The most responsive of these clubs were those adopting the tenets of the American Game Protective Association—an organization sponsored by the firearm and ammunition industry to perpetuate sport hunting and the industry's products (Trefethen 1961).

That these clubs were to become the state's foremost wildlife-conservation organizations was only natural, in that hunting and fishing were virtually the only outdoor recreation pursued in frontier Arizona. Study and appreciation of natural history, while important pastimes for a few academics and professionals, paled into insignificance when compared to hunting and fishing, activities practiced by most citizens in what was then a rural state of villages and small towns. And, although personal opinions might vary as to how to perpetuate game animals and prevent the extinctions that had recently occurred with the passenger pigeon in the East and the bobwhite quail in Arizona, one unifying tenet characterized America's game restoration movement. This concept, an integral component of the Protestant ethic and one promoted by President Theodore Roosevelt, was that sacrifice and delayed gratification would result in improved conditions in the future.

The exact origins of Arizona's game protection movement are murky, but an organizational landmark was when about 35 sportsmen formed a Flagstaff Game Protective Association in 1916 at a meeting attended by Aldo Leopold (Brown and Carmony 1990). As was often true, local interest had been aroused by a planned action, in this case some proposed land exchanges that would fence off public access to certain hunting areas on Forest Service land. So important were these lands to local sportsmen that the association sent a delegation to Washington to press their concerns—apparently with some success. The association's main representative was Tom McCullough, a former recreation officer with the Coconino National Forest. Shortly afterward, other organizational meetings in Tucson, Globe, and Prescott resulted in the formation of other game protective associations.

Local land exchanges did not fuel a state sportsmen's organization, however. The overriding concern of most hunter-conservationists at the time was the need to change the state's game and fish code and department—the former regarded by most sportsmen as a holdover from territorial days and too lenient and ineffective. With the Arizona State Legislature unwilling to act, the Flagstaff Game Protective Association drafted and circulated a new game code, one that soon assumed the form of a statewide initiative to take to the secretary of state and the electorate.

As soon as a new game code was passed in 1916, many sportsmen realized it had been too hastily drawn, and even more protective measures were required to prevent game hogs from decimating wildlife populations. (Courtesy of Bob Housholder)

In 1916, the public voted on and passed this new game code, which had more restrictive regulations and shorter hunting seasons. But almost as soon as the new game code was passed, many sportsmen realized the new regulations had been too hastily drawn, and even more protective measures were required. The problem was that the 1916 game and fish code could not be changed by legislative action because it had been passed as an initiative. What was seen originally as a road map to better hunting and fishing had become an obstacle to needed increases in license fees, more restrictive regulations, and a more responsive game and fish department.

Formation of the AGPA

In 1923, at another meeting in Flagstaff, a statewide Arizona Game Protective Association was formed with McCullough as president—a position to which he would be re-elected for the next two years (see Appendix C). Composed of four affiliates, the AGPA modeled its objectives after those of the New Mexico Game Protective Association:

1. Secure a proper and scientific management of fish, game, and other natural resources in perpetuity;
2. Secure a game and fish commission and department staffed with competent personnel without political obligation or interference; and
3. Educate the public with the principles of sportsmanship and the need for proper resource management.

Not only did the 1916 game and fish code fail to protect certain animals such as beavers—an omission the legislature did rectify—it made no provision for either the legislature or the governor to respond to the deer crisis developing on the Kaibab in the early 1920s. Perhaps the most serious inadequacy was the low price being charged for licenses. With little revenue coming in, and the legislature reluctant to provide supplemental appropriations, the Game and Fish Fund was hard-pressed even to finance the department's law enforcement obligations. Short of funds itself, in 1925 the AGPA did not send a delegate to the Pronghorn Antelope Conference in Washington, D. C.

Additional affiliates were being organized, however, and in 1924, the AGPA asked the legislature to formulate a referendum repealing the game code. It was turned down. Such conflicts provided a good incentive to join the AGPA, and by the end of 1925, 10 AGPA affiliates could boast a total of 891 members. Six sent delegates to the association's annual convention in Prescott. In 1926, 10 "locals" came to the convention at the Santa Rita Hotel in Tucson with delegates from Gila County, Tucson (two affiliates), Bisbee, Verde Valley, Prescott, White Mountains, Flagstaff, and the newly organized Southside (Salt River Valley) association. Another, as yet unchartered, association representing Phoenix was also present. What was more, according to the minutes of the fourth annual convention, most of these associations contained 100 or more members.

The Tucson convention in 1926 was important in several respects. Although the convention's theme stressed the importance of forming new associations and repealing the 1916 game code, association delegates also had other agendas, including resolutions for the propagation of fish and game (Gila County), the control of predators (Gila County), more enforcement of game and fish laws (Southside), additional game refuges (White Mountains, Flagstaff), and regulations prohibiting the taking of undersized fish (Flagstaff).

President Fred L. Benham was unable to attend, but was represented by F. E. A. Kimball, who presented these and other resolutions, including one promoting the restoration of native wildlife as opposed to importing nonnative species. This ban on exotics, while popular with the Tucson and Salt River associations, initiated some debate, resulting in enough opposition from the populous Gila County delegation that it was returned to the committee for later action. Other resolutions passed by the delegates commended Arizona's ranchers for their contributions to the protection of game species and advocated protection for the unique Chiricahua tree squirrel. Another resolution that passed (even though the legislation itself failed) was one supporting Arizona's congressional delegation for getting the Migratory Bird Refuge and Public Shooting Grounds bill through the US Senate.

The principal speaker at the 1926 convention was Stokley Ligon, then a member of the New Mexico Game and Fish Commission. Ligon emphasized that similar problems faced game in Arizona and New Mexico, and advocated New Mexico's game protective association and commission form of game and fish administration as a wildlife conservation model. While stressing overgrazing as the foremost problem faced by game animals, Ligon also reminded delegates that it was the owners of large cattle ranches who were the most helpful when it came to protecting game and that ranchers had helped New Mexico establish between 60 and 70 refuges.

Other actions included the appointment of a publicity committee for passing the "repealer," a referendum on the 1916 game code. Drafted by James A. Diffin and Walter

Taylor, it was the AGPA's number-one project. Mark Musgrave gave a presentation on how predator control was helping game numbers recover, the PARC by now having taken nearly 800 lions and essentially eliminated the wolf in Arizona. Deputy State Game Warden R. E. McAlister reiterated the need for a new game code, as the number of hunters had grown from 18,000 in 1916 to 30,000 in 1925. That the department now had its own fish hatchery in the White Mountains (the South Fork Hatchery on the Little Colorado River) was regarded as a major achievement, prompting the Flagstaff association to transfer the club's trout-rearing ponds at Oak Creek to the department. McCullough was elected president and Taylor was selected secretary.

The composition of the affiliates was highly variable, ranging from the more hunter-driven Tucson Game Protective Association to the more outdoor-oriented Tucson Natural History Society, which contained a number of academics as well as community leaders. Many AGPA leaders depended on the Tucson society to write what they hoped would be a new game and fish code. The society's calendar of meetings for 1924–25 and its list of members, while not typical of other clubs, are therefore of interest, as they provide some insights into the purposes of this important affiliate.

The Tucson Natural History Society roster that year lists 109 members, at least 43 of whom appear to be women, many of them single. Said to be composed of lovers of nature and the great outdoors, the organization encouraged interest in the plant and animal life of southern Arizona and helped in the conservation of "wild life" and preservation of natural resources. The annual membership was $1, a sustaining member paying $5 and a life member $50. Members included such Tucson notables as Byron Cummings and Herbert Drachman, along with professional academics such as Andrew Nichol, Dr. Forrest Shreve, Dr. Charles Vorhies, Dean John Thornber, and Dr. Walter Taylor.

The society supported a 15-point platform that, among other things, stood for vigorous and impartial enforcement of all game, fish, and forest laws; a nonpartisan board of state fish and game commissioners; repeal of the present game laws; the destruction of harmful predatory animals other than furbearers; and an adequate system of game refuges. Principles of good sportsmanship were stressed and game hogs and deer contests opposed.

Lectures were offered monthly, with field trips from October through May. Trips included hikes, horseback rides, and auto tours to such places as the Santa Rita Mountains, Oracle, Sabino Canyon, Colossal Cave, Cochise Stronghold, and Chiricahua National Monument. Vorhies, of the University of Arizona, was the society's president and chair of the executive committee; program committee officers included Taylor, Nichol, Kimball, and W. E. Bryan.

Understanding that legislation was the only way to bring about change, and that this required a major lobbying effort, AGPA's next two annual conventions took place at the Adams Hotel in Phoenix—the capital city's center for political lobbying.

The crucial convention was held September 29, 1928. President Fred Sutter of Phoenix presided over 11 local affiliates and 24 delegates, the association now having 18 affiliates—eight of them less than a year old. Jim Diffin of Bisbee was elected president,

"Game hogs" was a term used both for hunters taking more than the bag limit and for poachers taking game out of season. Finding and arresting violators such as this group camped in the backcountry was extremely difficult, but game hogs were a constant concern among early AGPA members. (Arizona Wildlife Federation)

with Ben Tinker of Tucson vice president for the southern district, Henry Brinkmeyer of Prescott vice president for the central district, and McCullough vice president for the northern district. One more club was added before the end of the year, giving the AGPA a roster of 19 affiliates from such far-flung localities as Superior, Ajo, Seligman, and the Gila and Verde valleys, not to mention metropolitan Tucson, Phoenix, and Flagstaff. The executive board of new officers stressed that it was now or never: An all-out effort was needed to pass the referendum in November, removing the old game code and replacing it with a new one of the AGPA's design.

The AGPA would have a replacement for the 1916 game code ready. A legislation code committee made up of Diffin, Taylor, Les Hart, Dr. E. P. Mathewson, Fred Winn, and A. J. Eager was busy drafting a lengthy and well-considered series of regulations to take to the legislature as soon as the old code was repealed. A key provision of the new code was for the governor to appoint a three-man commission to administer a department that would be free of political influence insofar as possible. To stress the importance of the latter point, the AGPA published a letter written by State Game Warden George Willard to an applicant for a deputy warden's job:

> Yours of August 9th at hand. Glad that you are able to show a clean political slate. I do not care what a man's politics are just so he is a good clean democrat. I have had the opportunity twice in the past of seeing my own good men kicked out simply to make room for Republicans at the pie counter, damned poor ones at that. Therefore I do not intend that the few favors at the disposal of this department shall go to a foe of the administration. And I will further assure you that no matter how high a man assays in democracy or what his political pull he will have to be at least one hundred percent game warden to hold the job and I have no doubt that such a man can be found. (Gallizioli 2012)

Arizona Wild Life and the Referendum

A major accomplishment, one that would help push the referendum over the top and ensure the establishment of a new game code, was the publication of the official AGPA magazine, *Arizona Wild Life*, in October 1928. Coming just in time to alert readers of the need to vote for the referendum, the initial issue was created by an editorial staff composed of Taylor, McCullough, Diffin, Tinker, F. O. Krohn, and Robert H. Presley. Intended to be published as a quarterly in a large black-and-white format similar to the popular magazines of the day, *Arizona Wild Life* presented editorials, natural history articles, and reminiscences about previous game and fish populations. Authors included Taylor, Diffin, McCullough, Winn, and other AGPA notables. Also included in the first issue were reports on game and fish stockings by the department and an essay by State Game Warden Dwight Pettis on the federal politics behind the Kaibab situation. Needless to say, the magazine's slant was to promote the AGPA and its desire to improve game conditions. The motto was "We Stand Behind Every Warden Who Does His Duty."

The 1928 election was a good one for the AGPA. Referendum No. 314 repealing the 1916 game code passed with a plurality of 2,374 votes, losing only in Graham, Greenlee, Maricopa, and Yuma counties. Equally fortunate for the AGPA was the election of John Phillips over Gov. George Hunt—the first time that Hunt had been defeated in a race for governor.

A Brief Time in the Sun

The next two years were heady ones for the AGPA. Governor Phillips, an avid fisherman, turned out to be a good friend of the association, as did the new legislature. The AGPA's new game code was quickly passed and signed into law with only minor revisions. Phillips appointed the first three-man commission (Albert Jones, Phoenix, chair; Les Hart, Tucson; and Tom McCullough, Flagstaff)—a slate wholeheartedly approved by the AGPA. Robert Bayless, an AGPA member with a working knowledge of hunting and fishing issues, was selected as State Game Warden.

Diffin, a school superintendant and an early AGPA organizer, was elected AGPA president in both 1929 and 1930. Not content to rest on their laurels, a committee of executive directors was formed composed of Diffin and several vice presidents[1] who continued to promote the creation of affiliates, confer with the legislature, and work with the governor. The commission even went so far as to pass a regulation giving the governor the first bison permit issued for 1930—a courtesy validated when Bayless guided Phillips to a large bull bison at House Rock.

In addition to lobbying for more refuges and additional appropriations for the Arizona Game and Fish Department, the AGPA executive committee entertained a number of resolutions at its annual conventions, usually held early in the fall. These resolutions, which might be submitted by either the executive committee or one of the affiliate associations, were statements of purpose or intent, and intended to pressure individuals,

---

[1]C. C. Faires of Globe, vice president at large; Kenner Kartchner, vice president at large; Dr. Harold S. Colton, vice president for northern counties; A. J. Eager, vice president of southern counties; C. C. Stewart, vice president of eastern counties; S. A. Spear, vice president of central counties; and Glenn W. Persons, secretary-treasurer.

Arizona Wild Life *and its successors,* Arizona Wild Life and Sportsman *and* Arizona Wildlife Sportsman, *provided an essential communication medium not only for AGPA members but with the wildlife conservation public. Early issues carried a "Conservation Pledge" and, after 1950, the slogan, "Voice of the Arizona Outdoorsman," which it was. (AGFD files; Arizona Wildlife Federation)*

organizations, and governments to take particular actions. For example, three resolutions passed in 1928. They called for the repeal of the 1916 game code, requested a temporary halt to elk introductions as too costly, and expressed support for a bill then in Congress that provided for federal migratory-bird refuges.

Eight resolutions were passed in 1929 and six in 1930. Several took the form of recommendations to the commission and were more or less local in nature, such as wanting to close all streams in the Chiricahua Mountains to fishing until sufficient rehabilitation work had been done, open Fort Huachuca to public hunting, and not have an elk season. Other resolutions were regional in scope, and included closing certain areas north of the Grand Canyon to cattle grazing, establishing a committee to secure a buffalo refuge at House Rock, and supporting a statewide game survey. Another resolution commended the US Biological Survey for not using poison and for not killing bears in the forested regions of the state. Once approved, these resolutions were sent to the Arizona Game and Fish Commission, the chief of the Biological Survey, or whatever agency was germane to the issue being addressed.

In the meantime, the magazine, under the guidance of an editorial board made up of Diffin, McCullough, Taylor, Frank Grubb, and Kenner Kartchner, was proceeding as a quarterly. Sent to members of subscribing affiliates or available at 35 cents a copy, *Arizona Wild Life* was off to an auspicious start and attracting a growing number of advertisers. In addition to items from the editors, contributions included game and fish department news

Gov. John Phillips signs the bill transferring wildlife management authority from the Arizona State Legislature to an Arizona Game and Fish Commission in 1929. State Game Warden Robert Bayless is standing at left. (Arizona Wild Life *magazine, April 1929)*

(including the printing of the new game code in its entirety) and biographies of the new commissioners and State Game Warden. Donald Gilchrist wrote articles featuring the exploits of his Predator and Rodent Control branch of the Biological Survey, including the taking of 146 lions in 1929.

Affiliate news was especially welcome. Both Tucson affiliates and their different constituencies were profiled. Many of the articles and editorials were written by AGPA members, including Taylor, Vorhies, McCullough, Kartchner, and Judge C. C. Faires, who was regarded as an authority on waterfowl. An "Around the Campfire" column encouraged guest editorials. Major topics included the Kaibab deer situation, recognition of the black bear as a game animal, the need for a junior game protective association, and the teaching of game conservation in schools—issues destined to be AGPA concerns for years to come.

TOUGH TIMES FOR A FLEDGLING ARIZONA GAME AND FISH COMMISSION

David E. Brown

There was good reason for Arizona's sportsmen and other citizens to be disgruntled with Arizona's game and fish laws in the 1920s. The 1916 code was difficult to amend, and thus unresponsive to changing conditions.

The only solution acceptable to the Arizona Game Protective Association was for the electorate to repeal the 1916 initiative and pass a new game and fish code. Restoration programs would require funding, and new legislation was needed if the Arizona Game and Fish Department was to build fish hatcheries, import game, and control predators. Increased funding required either a license fee increase or a special appropriation from the legislature.

But the legislature was not about to give a fledging game and fish agency money to squander on wildlife, and Gov. George Hunt let it be known the cost of a license was already high enough ($1.25). Given that 28,000 sportsmen were licensed, an annual game and fish budget of more than $50,000 was considered money enough.

After the electorate failed to repeal the 1916 initiative in the 1926 election, the AGPA doubled its efforts to pass a "repealer" in 1928. To ensure success, the AGPA drafted an improved game code that incorporated the best thinking then available. The new code would provide for a three-man state commission that could adjust the price of a hunting and fishing license and make other changes as needed. Should this new game and fish code be enacted, the Arizona Game and Fish Commission would have sole responsibility for administrating the monies derived from a new set of license fees. These doubled the cost of a general hunting and fishing licenses to $2.50, and established a series of other licenses ranging from $1.25 for a resident fishing license to $35 for a nonresident hunting and fishing license. Furs then being big business, trappers would have to purchase a $3.50 trapper's license.

The AGPA's new game code succeeded in 1928. In the same election, voters chose John Phillips over Gov. George Hunt—the first time Hunt had been defeated in a race for governor. As a parting shot, Hunt signed the referendum the first week of December 1928 while he was still in office, thus repealing the existing game and fish laws without waiting the 30 days for the new game code to take effect when the Ninth Legislature convened in January 1929. So the Eighth Legislature voted to retain the old laws until the new code was submitted, passing the bill with an emergency clause.

With passage of the referendum in the 1928 election, the new game and fish code was ratified on January 22, 1929, transferring wildlife management authority from the legislature to an Arizona Game and Fish Commission. Modeled after a game code drafted by the New Mexico Game Protective Association and enacted into law in that state in 1921, Arizona's new commission form of rule-making was pure genius. Although the governor would appoint the initial State Game Warden and Game and Fish Commission, the commissioners' terms of office were staggered so that future commissioners would be named under different administrations. To further soften the political influence of any one governor, no more than two of the commissioners could be from the same political party and each would have to reside in a different county. Future State Game Wardens—holders of the office that eventually would become director of the Arizona Game and Fish Department—would act as secretaries to the commission and be selected by that body, not by the governor.

The new game code was enacted at a good time. The new governor, Phillips, was a sportsman and friend of the AGPA. Phillips selected three commissioners from a slate offered by the AGPA—Chairman Albert Jones of Phoenix, Les Hart of Tucson, and Tom McCullough of Flagstaff.

First Actions of the New Commission

Robert L. Bayless, Arizona's first Commission-appointed State Game Warden. Unfortunately, Bayless's term in office was cut short when Gov. George Hunt unjustly accused Bayless of malfeasance and nepotism. (AGFD files)

The new commission took its job most seriously. At its first meeting, on April 6, 1929, the commissioners formed a Resolutions Committee and asked the press, the AGPA, and Arizona's civic governments to assist them in their deliberations. Governor Hunt's appointed State Game Warden, Dwight Pettis, was replaced by Robert Bayless, a Salt River Valley citrus farmer. Bayless would receive a salary of $3,600 per year, $1,000 as an operating budget to pay bills of $50 or less, and $200 to build a private office inside the department's office in the State Capitol Building. He was also provided a stenographer at $150 a month and authorized to vet and appoint deputy wardens on a nonsalaried basis.

Other agenda items included arrangements for issuing duplicate licenses and providing for a "pioneer's license" for those who were 70 years or older and had resided in the state for a year. The commission also endorsed a bill then in Congress creating a Saguaro-Papago National Park between Phoenix and Tempe.

The year 1929 saw a flurry of commission meetings, often more than one a month. There was much to do and each commissioner had an agenda. Numerous fishing closures were promulgated and several game refuges established, starting in Coconino County, where AGPA membership was strong. Two new trucks were purchased and 10,000 metal refuge signs ordered.

Although the department continued to hire deputy wardens for two-year terms, the enforcement of the new game and fish laws also depended upon nonsalaried deputies. These were paid the amount of the fine up to $10, with no payment for suspended fines or sentences. A $50 reward was authorized for any citizen providing information leading to

Zane Grey (left) and his son Romer with a bear taken below the Mogollon Rim. Grey was Arizona's foremost adventure writer. The commission's refusal to give him a permit to kill bear out of season caused great acrimony. (Zane Grey Cabin Historical Society and Norman Mead, www.meadpublishing.com)

the conviction of a person killing an antelope or a bighorn sheep; $25 for a deer. Cooperation with federal agencies improved and the commission passed a resolution endorsing work taking place on the Santa Rita Experimental Range. The commission also directed Bayless to work with Arizona's congressional delegation in obtaining a Joint Wildlife Experiment Station for game research.[1]

Some commission meetings were contentious, and one in particular resulted in serious acrimony.

Zane Grey was Arizona's most well-known author and foremost publicist of hunting. A longtime chronicler of outdoor events featuring Arizona landscapes and characters, he liked to vacation at his cabin under the "Tonto Rim" and hunt bears, turkeys, and other game while visiting with his friends and guides, Babe and John Haught. Prior to one of these ventures in 1929, he met Commissioner McCullough in Flagstaff and learned that the new game code provided a closed season on bear during the time of his planned visit.

Thinking his stature made for allowing an exception, Grey requested a special permit to take bear prior to the date of the open season. State Game Wardens had granted exceptions in the past for hunting whitewings. Informed by Bayless that the commission would have to issue such a permit, he appealed for one at an October 29 meeting in Phoenix. When the commission refused to grant his request, and informed him that he would have to purchase a nonresident license when the season was open, Grey took this action as a personal insult. He vowed to leave Arizona and never hunt in the state again—a vow he kept (Kant 2000).

Additional actions taken by the commission during those early years included placing more restrictions on the legal catch lengths of fishes and instigating season closures on turkeys, bears, and mule deer south of the Gila River. The emphasis was on programs. Some of the commission's actions were costly. Bayless was authorized to spend $10,000 for a fish hatchery in Pinetop, and plans were made to construct other hatcheries at Mormon Lake and Indian Gardens. No fewer than seven men were hired to engage in predator-control work.

[1]The designation of such an area did not come to fruition. Instead, the department became an active participant in the projects being conducted on the Forest Service's Santa Rita Experimental Range.

Such expenses required close monitoring. The commission directed Bayless to check license dealer reports and renew only dealerships with businesses that followed instructions and met the department's reporting requirements. The commission also had a CPA audit the books from the time the commission took office through the end of the year, and then directed Bayless to destroy all unused and returned license books for 1929. Sensing trouble, Chairman McCullough directed Bayless to have the Southwest Audit Company audit the books through December 22, 1930, after it became clear that a new governor had been elected.

A Challenge from Governor Hunt

The commission would now face its greatest challenge as a rule-making body. In November 1930, riding in on a Democrat landslide heralded by the Great Depression, Governor Hunt was re-elected to his seventh term. And he did not like what the Arizona Game and Fish Commission and its department had done. To complicate matters further, Commissioner Jones had died in office on the last day of February 1930 and been replaced by John B. Sloane, a Phoenix attorney. Lynn Lockhart of Phoenix had replaced Chairman McCullough, who had only a two-year appointment, in early 1931. Hunt retained Lockhart as not being "part of the problem," and "retired" commissioners Hart and Sloane, accusing them and the State Game Warden of malfeasance.

Governor Hunt had long dominated Arizona politics, having been Arizona's only governor until he was defeated by Phillips in 1928. Flamboyant and strong-willed, Hunt also had definite ideas about wildlife and game management. A strong states' rights advocate, Hunt considered the Migratory Bird Treaty Act an infringement on the states' wildlife management prerogative, even though he was strongly protective of most birds, including such then-unpopular species as roadrunners and great horned owls.

Although he hunted geese and other waterfowl, the governor could also be a protectionist. Not wanting "tame deer" shot, Hunt had almost single-handedly precipitated a crisis between the state and the US Forest Service in 1924, when he opposed hunting deer on the Kaibab even though the animals were destroying the very browse they depended upon. Hunt also had endorsed a scheme to drive deer across the Grand Canyon to restock depleted deer ranges near Flagstaff—a ridiculous venture that made Arizona a national laughingstock. Unabashed, the governor precipitated a lawsuit that resulted in the Supreme Court's limiting a state's right to manage its wildlife when it could be shown that excess numbers of animals were damaging government land.

Although Hunt respected the US Biological Survey—the agency that took on the task of killing predators and rodents—he looked upon the Forest Service and National Park Service as agencies that wanted to usurp the state's lawful rights when it came to game and fish matters. Hunt considered the recent ruling by the Supreme Court giving habitat management control on the Kaibab to the Forest Service wrongheaded, and he thought the commission's cooperation with that agency reprehensible because the federal government threatened the state's game and fish management authority.

Governor Hunt did not like commissions and resented their authority over state agencies because they were removed from his and the legislature's direct control, a situation he made abundantly clear in his address to the legislature in 1931. Not only did he consider the commission form of government "impractical, unresponsive to public opinion, undemocratic, wasteful and inefficient," he disapproved of commissions making and enforcing laws that he considered the purview of the state attorney general. Wanting department heads to be responsible solely to the governor, he recommended that the Game and Fish Commission in particular be abolished as a dismal failure, and that the legislature take immediate action to abolish all commissions.

Ultraconservative when it came to wildlife protection, he considered the status of most species of wildlife to have declined since passage of the 1928 game code.[2] Especially galling to the governor was the transfer of management authority over game and fish species from the legislature and public at large to an agency under the influence of sportsmen who participated in the annual "carnage" then taking place on the Kaibab and elsewhere. That the commission had appointed Bayless to replace Pettis, who had ably served as State Game Warden during Hunt's previous administration, must have also riled him.

Anticipating trouble, the commission had Bayless (1930) prepare a lengthy and detailed report summarizing the commission's many accomplishments—perhaps too many. Acting under the slogan, "Better Hunting and Fishing for Arizona," the commission had organized the department into five major divisions—administration, law, game, fish hatcheries, and education, with a research branch located within the game group. Sixteen deputy wardens were augmented by several "special deputies" who assisted the department on special occasions, along with 1,100 nonsalaried deputies recommended by the AGPA, Forest Service, and the department's regular deputies. The commission also added 23 new refuges to the state refuge system with the intent of protecting quail and every big game species, leaving Mohave County as the only county without a preserve. The commission had developed a "rearing ponds" strategy to raise bigger fish by holding young fish in ponds located close to sites where they would be released as catchables. Construction was begun on another hatchery at Pinetop, with plans drawn up for a bass hatchery at Papago Park.

Other activities, some of which were sure to displease Hunt, included cooperative agreements with the Forest Service to jointly manage and hunt the Kaibab deer herd and translocate Kaibab deer to other parts of northern and central Arizona. Any hunter who arrived on either the east- or west-side camps on the Kaibab was allowed to hunt. Both bucks and does were harvested, with another 275 deer translocated. Pronghorn numbers having increased to at least 4,000 head, traps were being constructed below Anderson Mesa and near Chavez Pass in an effort to determine if these animals could be successfully captured and transplanted.

The governor reacted with a vengeance. On May 25, 1931, Hunt not only charged the commission with malfeasance, he replaced commissioners Sloane and Hart with two

[2] That this was not the case would be made clear in a letter to the governor from his "friend" Mark Musgrave, the Predator and Rodent Control branch supervisor, on August 4, 1932, which included photos of overbrowsed junipers and other plants on the Kaibab, Mogollon Rim, Clear Creek, and Anderson Mesa due to too many deer, elk, and antelope (Musgrave to Governor Hunt, Governor's files, 1923–33, Box 3, Record Group 1, Subgroup 8. Arizona State Library, Archives and Public Records).

Alfred E. Mann at his desk in the Capitol in 1931, where he was custodian before being appointed State Game Warden. Mann's tenure was fortunately short-lived, as he was considered vengeful and incompetent. (Arizona State Library, Archives and Public Records, History and Archives Division, #01-3534)

appointees of his own, Dan W. Francis of Flagstaff and W. A. Julian of Tucson. Julian, a former Tucson mayor, refused to be seated and Lockhart was "elected" chairman. Most damaging of all was the appointment at the next commission meeting of Alfred E. Mann, the custodian of the State Capitol Building, to replace Bayless as State Game Warden. Thus, not only was a new acting secretary to the commission installed—one who knew nothing about wildlife—every commissioner was now a Hunt appointee. To complete the purge, 11 deputy wardens were immediately laid off without pay and three new deputies placed on the payroll. All nonsalaried deputy warden commissions were recalled and their cards and badges rescinded. Ironically, Joe Prochaska, the former State Game Warden appointed by Gov. Tom Campbell, was placed on the payroll as a "range expert." William H. Sawtelle, the son of a prominent superior court judge, was made chief office deputy.

The reasons given for Hunt's charges—the destruction of the 1929 license stubs and other records, the over-expenditure of funds for the Pinetop hatchery, and a $1,700 bookkeeping deficit on June 30, 1931—were largely bogus, and did not hold up in court. Hunt could not abolish the commission form of government outright, because the law had been passed in response to a referendum and approved by the legislature. But he could have the two wayward commissioners subjected to a second trial in the legislature and have his commissioners replace the State Game Warden. Although the legislature also dismissed the charges, Hunt's action was validated in July 1931, when the governor's dismissal of commissioners Sloane and Hart was upheld in Arizona Superior Court. An appeal by Sloane and Hart to the State Supreme Court, while supported by the AGPA, was thwarted when the commissioners withdrew their complaints based on legal advice that the governor was allowed to replace any commissioner whom he could demonstrate as unsuitable. Unable to win in the Arizona Supreme Court, the AGPA president withdrew his support of Sloane and Hart on July 31, 1931.

State Game Warden William C. Joyner at retirement. (Arizona State Library, Archives and Public Records, History and Archives Division)

Little was accomplished during Mann's brief tenure as State Game Warden. His first action was to inspect all of the hatcheries, which he reported to Hunt to be in a filthy condition and incompetently managed (Governor's Files, 1931–32, Arizona State Library, Archives and Public Records). As he knew little about either wildlife or fish husbandry, Mann's admonishments did not result in any major administrative changes by the commission, and he was soon relegated to cost-saving inspections and proposals for uniforms (one reportedly having deputy wardens wear red and blue, like Canadian Mounties).[3]

Ineffective and apparently ignored by Lockhart and the other commissioners, Mann appears to have become somewhat of a pariah. On December 12, 1931, the recently appointed commissioner from Warren, Harry A. Clark, moved that the position of range expert, held by Prochaska, be abolished—a move unanimously supported by the rest of the commission. Two weeks later, Mann informed the commission he would resign as of the next day—a resignation that was immediately and unanimously accepted.

To replace Mann as State Game Warden, the commission appointed William C. Joyner, a former state senator and political supporter of the governor. A purchasing agent with the State Highway Department, Joyner served a term that is best known for completion of the Hunt Bass Hatchery at Papago Park.

A Time of Reconciliation

An attempt by the legislature to pass a referendum on the 1929 game code having failed, the department's political fortune took a turn for the better when Hunt was defeated in the 1932 Democratic primary. On May 12, 1933, commission chairman Lockhart announced that Shelby "Lefty" Lewis, a Flagstaff hotel manager, would succeed Joyner as State Game Warden, Joyner's tenure having expired April 6 with the unexpired term of Bayless. Joyner's secretary also resigned at this time. Joyner was praised for managing the department during difficult circumstances. Lewis, who was appointed for a four-year term, would be off to a fresh start in his management of an agency now having 24 employees.

Lewis's term of office was much less tumultuous than that of his predecessors, and was characterized by frugality and conservative hunting and fishing regulations. The AGPA's influence was an important consideration in his actions. The appointment of Charles

[3]Arizona Wildlife Federation files.

Beach, a rancher from Vail, and other conservative commissioners, made the 1930s a time of reconciliation and consolidation.

The big problem was money, as the Depression had reduced license sales to below 33,000 at a time when the commission was closing game seasons, enacting fishing closures, and creating more game refuges. As a result, a cadre of nonsalaried deputies were reinstated and paid half of the fines collected. Most department personnel saw their pay reduced on February 21, 1933, and a week later, all employees were laid off for an indefinite period, only to be rehired on March 16, 1933.

State Game Warden Shelby "Lefty" Lewis. A former Arlington, Texas, baseball pitcher and Flagstaff hotel manager, Lewis oversaw a cash-strapped Arizona Game and Fish Department through much of the 1930s. (Microfiche copy of Phoenix Evening Gazette *photo from Arizona State Library, Archives and Public Records, History and Archives Division)*

Advances were slow and tenuous. Small pay raises were given to 11 deputies in 1934, but the payment of fines to nonsalaried deputies ceased. And even though the season on javelina remained closed, there was a gradual liberalization of hunting and fishing regulations after 1934, when portions of the larger refuges were open to hunting during the deer season. A month-long quail season with a 12-bird bag limit was authorized at a commission meeting in 1935, when the bag limit on turkeys in Gila County was reduced to one and the tree squirrel season closed indefinitely. More progressive changes occurred when the commission voted to have all migratory bird seasons and bag limits conform to federal regulations, to endorse migratory bird or "duck" stamp legislation, and to open a bull elk season on a permit basis.

Economic difficulties continued to impact the outdoor community. The AGPA discontinued publication of its magazine, *Arizona Wildlife and Sportsman.* In December 1936, the department laid off six special deputies and three other employees. Beset with financial crises, the commission had to be frugal. Income from licenses and buffalo meat came to $98,798.23 in 1936, while only $80,903.85 was disbursed (S. L. Lewis 1936). Only 315 citations were written by 15 full-time deputies and six part-time wardens that year.[4] Lewis, reappointed State Game Warden in May 1937, was forced to lay off still more deputies in July. Although the state's buffalo ranch continued to operate, the game farm on Glendale Avenue was discontinued.

Resigning in ill health, Lewis was replaced by his chief deputy, Sawtelle, who was appointed State Game Warden for a four-year term beginning November 19, 1937. Lewis's

[4]The biggest ticket writers were Reuben McNeill (63), Mervin Smith (45), Jay Klaus (36), and William "Blue" Tharp (34).

(1936) main accomplishments had been maintaining the status quo within a balanced budget while constructing a new hatchery on Tonto Creek, improving the bass hatchery, and establishing 15 new refuges.

Sawtelle's administration resulted in a number of innovations. Negotiations were begun to acquire a new hatchery at Page Springs, and regulations on the taking of trout and other fish species were simplified. An "any elk" season was initiated, old refuges were abolished and new ones created. An open season on javelina was reinstated for February 1939, and archery hunting was made legal for certain hunts. Blanket orders prohibiting the taking of bear, turkey, and mule deer south of the Gila River were rescinded. The status of game refuges received more thought, and a recommendation for a split season on deer heralded the beginning of management by game management unit. A requirement for an 80-cent deer tag, approved in 1939, would result in both a new source of revenue and eventually a sample frame for estimating deer harvests.

The department's difficulties, both financial and professional, took a major turn for the better in 1939, when the legislature voted to accept the federal aid provisions of the Pittman-Robertson Act passed by Congress in 1937—an action unanimously supported by the commission. The department would now receive a three-to-one match from a federal fund derived from a 20% excise tax on firearms and ammunition for every dollar allocated from the Game and Fish Fund. The caveat was that these monies could only be spent for wildlife management and research purposes, including habitat acquisition; no Federal-Aid money could be used for law enforcement or information and education purposes.

This new legislation not only provided an important new source of revenue for the department, it did much to foster the hiring of college-trained biologists and increased the agency's professional capability. Nor was there any delay in the expenditure of these monies. Within a few months of commission approval, Federal-Aid Coordinator Andrew Nichol was directed to conduct a comprehensive five-year investigation of the 10 principal problems then facing Arizona's wildlife. On the downside, the department's use of its funds for Federal-Aid dollars meant reducing its field force to eight deputy wardens on December 31, 1939.

Finances therefore remained a huge problem, and Sawtelle proved to be a poor money manager. Expenses and equipment costs were poorly monitored, and as a consequence, all patrol work had to be curtailed in January 1939 due to a lack of funds. Whether a commission directive the following September, directing all deputies to run trap lines at the close of the hunting seasons in their district, was enacted solely for predator-control purposes or to increase the income of deputy wardens through fur sales is uncertain. It is recorded that commission chairman Charles Beach wanted to engage boy scouts for predator-control efforts while reducing the field force by eight men in January 1940. Still, the following May, Sawtelle hired more trappers. All in all, the reduction in state revenues attendant with the Depression was expressed in a reduction of the field force rather than a drop in expenditures and capital outlay.

The department's relationships with the Forest Service, Biological Survey, and US Grazing Service continued to generally improve during the 1930s, resulting in several signed agreements between these agencies and the commission. There remained several points of disagreement between the state and federal governments, nonetheless. The National Park Service was regarded with suspicion particularly for its continued attempts to increase the size of Grand Canyon National Park on the north Kaibab and for various proposals for new refuges and monuments in western Arizona. The commission initially opposed the creation of what would become the Kofa and Cabeza Prieta national game ranges for fear that these areas would be managed by the National Park Service, as was Organ Pipe Cactus National Monument. This opposition subsided only when the Biological Survey assured the commission it would jointly administer these game ranges with the Grazing Service.

Although Sawtelle had attempted to take the politics out of the department's operations and had instituted a number of innovations—including purchase of Page Springs hatchery—his administration had been dogged by poor bookkeeping. A $5,000 lawsuit, later dismissed, had been filed against Sawtelle by a Greenlee County resident, and there were several other unfortunate incidents during his administration.

One of the most publicized of the latter involved a judge in Prescott, who ordered the execution of a trapper's hound for illegally killing a deer. After Spot's owner had been arrested by Deputy Warden Otto Nicks and convicted of taking a deer out of season, Nicks was directed to have the hound killed by a dogcatcher, as Spot was the instrument of taking. This having been done, the public outcry was almost entirely critical of the judge and the department.

On March 20, 1940, Sawtelle resigned as State Game Warden for the good of the department, and the commission appointed Kenner Kartchner acting State Game Warden. The department's auditor, M. S. Mills, resigned the following month.

The War Years

Kartchner, a 17-year veteran with the Forest Service, was not only knowledgeable about the state's wildlife, he proved to be a capable administrator. The financial status of the department soon improved, and the commission appointed him State Game Warden on August 17, 1940, and promoted Harry Conolly to be his chief deputy. Kartchner put the department on a budget similar to those approved by the legislature for other state agencies and made a number of other administrative improvements.

A former Federal-Aid technician, Kartchner had his administration send out the first game questionnaire in 1941, thereby providing harvest estimates of the various game species that were based on more than the guesses previously promulgated by Forest Service personnel. Arizona's first antelope season since statehood was authorized in 1941, and the following year the department improved the status of this species by purchasing Raymond Ranch east of Anderson Mesa with Federal-Aid money. Other projects initiated during Kartchner's administration included a study of the nesting habits and success of white-winged doves, the first systematic surveys on quail and other game, and monitoring of the harvests of big game species through check stations.

Kenner C. Kartchner (right) in House Rock Valley. After a 17-year career with the Forest Service, Kartchner proved an able administrator of the Game and Fish Department. (Family photo courtesy of Dale Shumway)

Although the war years would bring a time of quiescence to many department activities, a responsible commission and an efficient administration were now in place. Wildlife populations were regarded as generally on the increase, and the AGPA's sportsmen could tout that "when the boys come home there will be plenty of game to greet them." Although a war economy was causing Arizona's human population, both temporary and permanent, to grow at an unprecedented rate, the impacts of these newcomers on wildlife were mitigated by gas rationing and an increase in people leaving the land to work in cities and towns.

There are those today who would favor the replacement of the commission form of game and fish management by a department of natural resources. Those who do should examine the situation in the states that have adopted such a system. Most conservationists and nearly all wildlife biologists agree that even though the commission form of wildlife management is subject to personal biases and influences, wildlife agencies operate more efficiently and with less political interference under a commission form of government than under administrations supervised by governors, legislators, and boards of directors. It is doubtful that a governor or legislature, left to their own volition, would have accepted the terms of the Pittman-Robertson Act, by which they would have surrendered their control of game and fish expenditures. Yet, it was just such a transfer of budgetary control that led to the financial well-being and professional structure of modern game and fish departments.

MORE HATCHERIES AND BETTER FISHING

Bud Bassett, David E. Brown, Bill Silvey, Roger Sorensen, and Larry Riley

When the new Arizona Game and Fish Commission took office in 1929, the state's sportsmen expected more fish hatcheries and more fish to be high on the agenda. It was the sportsmen, after all, who had determined that the commission form of government was the best means of administrating the state's Game and Fish Fund and the Arizona Game and Fish Department. The heading on the stationery of both the commission and the Arizona Game Protective Association—"Better Hunting and Fishing for Arizona"—was no accident.

The sportsmen would not be disappointed. Gov. John Phillips, who appointed the commission's three members, was an avid fisherman.

The commission took its better-fishing mandate seriously. One of its first actions, taken on April 6, 1929, was to close the newly constructed Coolidge (San Carlos) Lake to fishing, believing new fish populations needed protection if they were to increase and prosper. Other early actions, in what would become a spring tradition of setting fishery regulations, included continuing the requirement for a $1 seining permit to capture minnows and charging a $10 permit to allow people to net carp and suckers for food.

As for game fish, it was then believed that both trout and warm-water species were being over-harvested, so regulations were passed closing portions of Oak Creek and Lake Mary to fishing—actions that almost certainly reflected the influences of Commissioner Tom McCullough and the Flagstaff affiliate of the AGPA.

Bag limits on those areas open to fishing remained generous, because at the time, people often travelled some distance to fish and relied on their catch for food. The first commission set a bag limit for trout of 25 fish or 25 pounds, while restricting the daily take on other game species to 30 fish or 25 pounds. The exception was black bass, on which the limit was set at 15 fish or 25 pounds. All game fish less than seven inches long were to be released except for yellow perch, crappie, and catfish, which had no size limit.

Early fishery managers were trying hard to be efficient when it came to planting fish, especially regarding the survival of fry planted in streams. As early as 1932, fishery managers were examining the effectiveness of their stocking procedures and recommending fall plantings of seven- to nine-inch trout in places such as Oak Creek and Tonto Creek.

To improve trout fishing, the commission directed the newly appointed State Game Warden, Robert Bayless, to confer with US Forest Service supervisors on stream conditions and identify those waters suitable for stocking. This action was followed by additional fishing closures—the beginning of a series of openings and closings that would continue on into the 1940s. These were done in the belief that closed seasons were needed to allow fish to increase and reproduce, and that spawning areas were in special need of protection.

String of trout taken in the White Mountains by the McMichael family, ca. 1929. Unlike game animals, fish species were never subjected to the closed seasons and low bag limits that were popular with sportsmen and the Arizona Game and Fish Commission in the 1930s and early 1940s. (Courtesy of Jeff McMichael)

Hence, additional closures and limitations quickly followed, as the commission closed Oak Creek to fishing until June 1, 1930, increased the legal length of largemouth bass in the creel to 10 inches, and closed the East Verde River from Webber Spring to the Pine-Payson road to all fishing. Additional restrictions set a 10-fish limit for Grand Canyon National Park, while other actions closed certain waters in the White Mountains of east-central Arizona and in the Catalina Mountains near Tucson.

Arizona's First Hatcheries

What was really deemed needed was a new hatchery—one that could meet demands for trout fishing through increased fish production. Although the US Fish Commission had opened a fish hatchery in Dexter, New Mexico, in 1931, production was limited by quantity and distance and consisted almost entirely of warm-water game fish. The department's existing hatchery facilities, including the main hatchery on the south fork of the Little Colorado River, had proven inadequate to meet demand, so the commission embarked on a program that would make the 1930s the glory days of hatchery construction.

The site for the showpiece effort had already been selected, and on July 30, 1930, the commission authorized $10,000 for State Game Warden Bayless to build a full-service hatchery at a spring near Pinetop—a site that would later become the department's Region I office. This directive was followed up in November with orders to proceed with additional hatcheries and rearing ponds at Mormon Lake and Indian Gardens, for a total hatchery outlay of $27,000 that would also include the operating costs of the department's existing hatcheries at South Fork, Sterling Springs, Squirrel Springs, and Horton Creek.

Although there was some hassle over the initial bids submitted for the Pinetop and Mormon Lake facilities, acquisition and construction proceeded. On January 8, 1931,

Site for a new catch pond at Pinetop Hatchery, ca. 1937. During the 1930s and 1940s, Pinetop was the "jewel in the crown" of state hatcheries. (AGFD files)

a 15-acre bass hatchery and holding pond was purchased at Double Springs,[1] adjacent to Mormon Lake, along with nine rearing ponds at Squirrel Springs. Another hatchery facility had also been built in 1930 at Indian Gardens near Kohl's Ranch, due to a demand for trout in the Payson area.[2] To transplant the fish, Bayless purchased two trucks, one of them a special fish-hauling truck that could also double for hauling deer.

The Pinetop Hatchery was the "jewel in the crown." Not fully completed until 1932, at a total cost of approximately $20,000, this hatchery began producing trout in 1931 and quickly became the state's major trout producer and rearing facility. Within two years of this hatchery's completion, all trout eggs hatched by the state came from Pinetop, the young fish then being transported to various waters for rearing.

An excellent site with an ample supply of 54-degree water, Pinetop lived up to its promise as a full-service hatchery, complete with 40 concrete and dirt rearing ponds and raceways. Holding space was not a problem, as most of the fish were reared to a maximum of five inches a catchable size trout-release program not yet existing. Up to three million eggs a year were hatched, and when a catchable-size release program did develop, up to 190,000 seven-inch trout a year were raised here. Then in 1954, following a dry period, the water supply at Pinetop failed and the station was closed.

Meanwhile, operations at the South Fork, Squirrel Springs, and Horton Creek hatcheries continued, eventually resulting in the raising and planting of 1,132,269 rainbows from South Fork, 525,208 rainbows from Squirrel Springs, and 304,094 brook trout and 415,374 "black-spotted natives"[3] from Horton. Except for the continued use of a couple

---

[1] Intended originally for the production of bass, Double Springs consisted primarily of a few earthen rearing ponds and never was a major producer of fish. Warm-water fish operations at Double Springs ceased in 1932 with the completion of Hunt Bass Hatchery in Phoenix. Some trout continued to be raised there for local release until 1937, when the hatchery was closed due to inadequate water and the drying up of Mormon Lake.

[2] Consisting of a residence, raceways, and an earthen rearing pond, Indian Gardens closed in 1941 due to declining water supplies from the spring—a common malady with Arizona hatcheries.

[3] Arizona's native trout were then presumed to be cutthroats, as the Little Colorado River is a tributary of the upper Colorado River. These "black-spotted natives" were nonetheless obtained from hatcheries, in Colorado and elsewhere (Martinez 2011).

of small rearing ponds, South Fork, Arizona's original hatchery, was only maintained for another year or so, and closed in 1932 with the completion of the hatchery at Pinetop. Squirrel Springs would have been closed at that time also, but continued to operate for a few more years due to political pressure from residents of Springerville. All told, about $18,000 had been spent on these smaller hatcheries (Bassett, Silvey, and Sorensen 1998).

As for warm-water fish plantings, the commission was still largely dependent on the US Bureau of Fisheries, which in 1930 provided the department and its AGPA and Boy Scout volunteers 27,000 largemouth bass, 750,000 catfish, 10,000 channel catfish, 6,700 yellow perch, 2,000 bream, and 6,000 crappie.

Gov. George Hunt was jealous of his prerogatives, and did not like commission actions that he considered to infringe on or usurp them. He took out his dislike on the fisheries program in general and Pinetop Hatchery in particular, accusing the commission and State Game Warden Bayless of cost overruns and a number of legal infractions attendant with Pinetop's construction and operation. He sent State Game Warden Alfred Mann, (the former Capitol custodian, who knew little or nothing about running a hatchery), on an impromptu hatchery tour. Mann reported the facilities to be in filthy condition and chastised or fired several hatchery workers.

In his report to the governor, Mann blamed hatchery supervisor Albert W. "Dud" Yoder for lack of dedication to the program and fired hatchery biologist Herbert Reid.[4] Although both Yoder and Reid were later absolved of Mann's accusations and reinstated, morale remained low and little was accomplished in the way of game and fish management during the remainder of Hunt's term as governor and Mann's abbreviated administration, with one notable exception—Reid's construction of the department's first warm-water hatchery.

Given Hunt's pique with the commission and department, it is somewhat ironic that the next and most celebrated of the department's hatcheries was named for him—the Hunt Bass Hatchery, constructed in Phoenix's Papago Park. Completed in 1932, the year Hunt was voted out of office, this warm-water hatchery was a monument to the governor, State Game Warden William Joyner, the Salt River Project, the Works Project Administration, the Civilian Conservation Corps, and hatchery supervisor Reid, who saw the hatchery through to completion at nominal cost.

Built with considerable help from the WPA and CCC, the original hatchery consisted of several large rearing ponds, a small raceway, a hatchery house, and various attendant buildings and residences. So successful was this cooperative effort that the commission passed a resolution praising the CCC for its construction projects in Papago Park, singling out the Hunt Bass Hatchery as an example of what could be accomplished when various groups worked together. The AGPA praised Reid not only for completing the hatchery under difficult circumstances, but for his fish-raising skills.

In its heyday in the 1930s, the hatchery's annual production ran a little under 100,000 largemouth bass and a little over 100,000 bluegills, in addition to crappie and other warm-water species. Hunt Bass Hatchery was the source of the fish used to stock many

---

[4] Reid eventually became State Game Warden and Yoder the acting director of the department.

reservoirs constructed in the 1930s, including Saguaro Lake behind Stewart Mountain Dam. Peak production was reached in 1941, when 278,000 largemouth bass were shipped out of Papago Park to various lakes and reservoirs.

A Time of Conservation Management

The 1930s was a time of political turmoil, financial austerity, and conservative fish management for the commission and the department. Fishing restrictions continued to dominate the commission's actions. The department's fisheries program concentrated on protective closures, compensated for by hatchery production. Improvements were nonetheless made to the Pinetop Hatchery and Oak Creek and Indian Gardens rearing ponds (S. L. Lewis 1936).

Enforcement of the fishing regulations was a law enforcement priority; in what may have been the first license revocation, the commission revoked the licenses of two Prescott men on June 1, 1932, for eight months, for dynamiting fish. Later that year the commission closed Canyon Creek to fishing at the request of the owners of OW Ranch—making this stream, in effect, an Arizona fish refuge. Such closures, like the many game refuges then in place, proved popular. Before the end of the decade, additional refuges would be established for a number of waters, including Big Lake, the West Fork of Oak Creek, and (at the Forest Service's request) the heads of Horton and Tonto creeks.

With the exception of the native trouts or "yellow bellies," which, while recognized for their unique characteristics, were thought to be local variants of Rocky Mountain cutthroat trout (*Oncorhynchus clarki*), Arizona's native fishes were esteemed neither as game fish nor table fare.[5] The chubs or "Verde trout" were regarded as "bony," while the suckers were thought to have "soft flesh" and provide poor sport. Both "Verde trout" or "bonytails" and suckers were as likely to be seined as taken by hook and line. (See timeline in Appendix E for the status of Arizona's native fish species from 1912 to 1962.)

The Colorado salmon (*Ptychocheilus lucius*) had been so reduced in numbers by 1934, due to agricultural developments dewatering the Colorado River below the Alamo Canal and the big water habitats along the lower Salt and Gila rivers, that this species was no longer available in numbers sufficient to provide food or sport (Mulch and Gamble 1954, R. R. Miller 1972; Minckley 1973; Mueller and Marsh 2002; Brown 2009).

More closings (and openings) followed, with special regulations being promulgated for specific areas, beginning with San Carlos Lake and Oak Creek and continuing on until nearly every body of water had its own fishing season, bag limit, or other specific rules. The general fishing regulations became increasingly restrictive, as the commission disallowed any fishing in waters containing trout except during the trout season and prohibited trout fishing between 9 p.m. and 4 a.m.

Other rules promulgated in the 1930s but later rescinded or modified included numerous stream closures and re-openings, the establishment of a trout season (4 a.m. May 30 to 9 p.m. September 30, 1934), changes in daily and weekly bag limits, and a Depression-era

---

[5] The reason for stocking rainbow and cutthroat trout was the difficulty of obtaining eggs and fry in the desired quantity, as the state depended on the US Fish Commission to supply most of Arizona's trout eggs, as well as a large number of its fry and fingerlings, before Pinetop Hatchery was completed in 1932. By then, almost all of Arizona's trout waters had been subjected to releases of hatchery-produced rainbows and populated by hybrids (Minckley 1973).

Fishermen with strings of "bonytails" (roundtail chub) along the Salt River or a major canal shortly after the turn of the century. Native fish such as these, while providing much recreation, were never defined as game. Photo by Herb McLaughlin. (McLaughlin Collection, Arizona State University Libraries, #CP MCL 97929)

measure that called for no license or charge to seine carp and suckers for food. Nor were such fish subject to bag limits after May 22, 1933.

Hatcheries remained a major emphasis of the commission and the department despite the poor economy, as these facilities had to bridge any gaps in demand caused by increasingly stringent fishing regulations. Retiring hatcheries proved nearly as difficult as funding and managing existing ones. In 1932, the commission instructed the Theodore Roosevelt Council of the Boy Scouts to remove all materials from the abandoned Horton Creek Hatchery for scout use.[6] In 1935, State Game Warden Shelby Lewis was given permission to sell the South Fork and Squirrel Springs properties due to the lack of water at these facilities. Buyers were apparently scarce though, as the commission later gifted the Squirrel Springs buildings to the Boy Scouts. Even this disposition failed to remove the hatcheries from the department's inventory, and in January 1938 the commission directed State Game Warden William Sawtelle to prepare the paperwork to abandon both the South Fork and Squirrel Springs properties.

Continued lobbying by the AGPA for a federal hatchery in Arizona having been unsuccessful through most of the 1930s, additional efforts for warm-water hatchery production were limited to working with the Salt River Project to improve the water delivery system for the Hunt Bass Hatchery. Supervising and retaining professional hatchery workers posed additional problems, and in 1933 the bass hatchery supervisor at Mormon Lake was let go—a not-uncommon fate of Game and Fish employees in the 1930s.

[6] The hatchery had slid into Horton Creek due to heavy snows and flooding. The scouts were given the hatchery materials for $1. These were used to build a dining hall at their summer camp, Camp Geronimo, on Weber Creek.

Dedication of the Hunt Bass Hatchery. Hatchery supervisor Herbert L. Reid is the man sitting in the center of the photo. (AGFD files)

By the mid-1930s it was increasingly apparent that warm-water fishes were often stunted—a condition attributed to both intra- and inter-specific competition. The removal of "rough fish" (carp, buffalofish,[7] and most native species) was therefore a serious concern, as was the overabundance and size of the smaller species of game fish. As a result, the bag limits on yellow perch and catfish were removed from problem sites such as Lake Pleasant, and by the fall of 1937 the bag limits on "ring" (yellow) perch and "charr" (another name for Verde trout) had been removed entirely. The inappropriate release of bait fish was also now recognized as a problem, and the use of live minnows was prohibited in the Agua Fria drainage above and below Carl Pleasant Dam that same year. Finally, in 1938 a contract was signed with the F. A. Grastet Fish Company of Los Angeles for the removal of "rough fish" from Arizona waters, with another permit being issued in the spring of 1940 for the commercial netting and sale of buffalofish in Roosevelt Lake, with 10% of the proceeds to go to the Game and Fish Fund.

Austerity limitations aside, communities and resort operators below the Mogollon Rim were adamant that the department replace the fish no longer being produced by the defunct hatchery on Horton Creek and the ailing facility at Indian Gardens. Construction therefore started on a 20-trough hatchery at the head of Tonto Creek, with a hatchery building, a caretaker's house, a garage, and outdoor rearing ponds delivering the first fish in 1938 (S. L. Lewis 1936; Bassett, Silvey, and Sorensen 1998).[8]

Here, the water supply was sufficient for the development of an all-around facility, so construction was geared to provide both hatching and rearing facilities. By 1942, Tonto was able to produce some 100,000 "catchable" trout annually, as well as large numbers

---

[7] Fish of the genus *Ictiobus*, principally *I. cyprinellus*. Introduced into Roosevelt Lake in 1918, these and other species of "rough fish" had been introduced into Arizona by the US Bureau of Fisheries (Minckley 1973).

[8] Tonto Creek Hatchery still exists but looks very different today. The hatchery building was constructed by the WPA and is eligible for listing on the national register of historic places.

of fingerlings. Additional pond facilities were completed in 1949, and the hatchery has proved to be a consistent and valuable fish producer through to the present time.

As an example of fish production figures in the 1930s, Lewis (1936), in the decade's only annual report, tallied some 1,261,347 trout and 232,700 warm-water fish planted in 1936, at a cost of less than one cent a trout and 2.8 cents per warm-water species. The biggest bass stockings went to Coolidge, Stewart Mountain, Canyon, and Apache reservoirs, with sizeable stockings also going to Stehr and Peck's lakes. Some 33,500 fingerling bass and a number of bluegill/bream fingerlings were also imported from the federal hatchery at Dexter, New Mexico. Lewis's report broke down the trout stockings as follows:

- Apache National Forest: Some 743,978 trout were planted on this forest, 6,500 of which were catchable size of seven inches or more. Some 27,400 of the smaller trout were "natives," 16,000 of which were planted in Big Lake, along with 303,600 rainbows and 226,000 brook trout.
- Crook National Forest: 48,150 trout were planted on this forest—all catchable natives (cutthroats) save for 6,000 brookies.
- Coconino National Forest: 186,525 trout were planted on this forest, of which 11,000 were greater than seven inches long. This includes 20,050 natives planted in Oak Creek, along with 1,275 brook trout and many rainbows.
- Sitgreaves National Forest: More than 130,800 trout were planted on this forest (600 natives).
- Tonto National Forest: 58,054 trout were planted on the Tonto (28,800 natives). Just 1,704 of the latter were "catchables."
- Fort Apache Indian Reservation: Only 93,800 trout (74,800 natives) were planted on this reservation.

Happier Times

Although the Sawtelle administration (November 21, 1937, to March 20, 1940) attempted to simplify and liberalize fishing regulations, their attempts to do so were often thwarted by local demands and politics. An AGPA representative was now present at every spring commission meeting, and the desires of its local affiliates could not be ignored. Besides, some of the sportsmen's suggestions for temporary closures and restrictions appeared to be based on common sense. Apache Lake and the upper portions of Saguaro Lake were therefore closed to fishing in 1937 to protect bass during the spawning season. Mormon Lake was reopened to fishing with the caveat that trout could only be taken during the trout season, which was set for May 30 through September 20, 1937. Other fishing closures in the upper end of Saguaro Lake and in the Tonto arm of Roosevelt Lake attempted to protect spawning fish from March 1 to May 27.

Stehr Lake, Encanto Lake, and other small bodies of water were also subject to a series of openings and closings based on local concerns. In 1938, the crappie limit on Lake Mary was modified to allow for a daily bag limit of 40 fish per family per day. The limit on channel catfish was standardized at 10 per day or 15 pounds and one fish, each catfish having to be 12 inches or more in length. On the other hand, limits on the legal length

Fishing at Luna Lake, ca. 1938. That year, limits on the legal length of trout in the creel were abolished, and all trout caught had to be retained and included in the bag limit. (AGFD files)

of trout in the creel were abolished, and all trout caught had to be retained and included in the bag limit.

Trout production in 1938 was sufficient for the commission to authorize the department to sell fry trout to private individuals if and when they could be spared. Indeed, private hatcheries had always been an important supplier of fish in Arizona. One of the most important of these was the Arizona Trout Farm at Page Springs near Cornville, which had held a 50-year lease on the springs since 1932. Here, the owner, James Page, maintained four rearing ponds, primarily for the use of Verde Valley residents.

Always in need of new hatchery sites, the commission directed the department in 1938 to purchase the Arizona Trout Company's lease for $7,250, payable at $600 per year. Also acquired in this bargain deal were 16 concrete raceways, 6 concrete ponds, 4 circular and 4 rectangular dirt ponds, a 20-trough egg hatchery and water cooling tower, a feed house, a store house, 2 dwellings, and the services of Dan Purtyman, who was retained to run the hatchery for the department.

Over the next 10 years, Page Springs produced between 30,000 and 50,000 pounds of trout a year, the production varying due mostly to management needs and the success of the pond culture. The hatchery's water temperature—a constant 68 degrees—was at the upper extreme for raising trout, so to lower the water temperatures, the ponds were designed to be 12 to 14 feet deep. Because the amount of labor required to harvest the fish in this deep water was excessive, at one time 18 people were permanently employed there. The springs provided an excellent water source, however. Later on, the ponds were made more shallow, the raceways were modified, and the culture methods were adjusted so that fewer staff were required.

Arizona's fisheries-management program took on a more professional aspect in the spring of 1940 with the appointment of Kenner Kartchner as acting State Game Warden. Kartchner appointed Reid as director of the Fisheries Division, thereby revitalizing both the hatchery and fish-management program.

An astute politician, Kartchner asked the AGPA's advice on several impending actions and sought the organization's help opening Sabino Lake and Desert Shores near Tucson to fishing. Other fishing opportunities were created by dropping the bag limit on catfish and changing the size limit on bass to nine inches. No trout waters were closed during the 1940 trout season and several fishing closures were rescinded. Bag limits on the now-filling Lake Mead were dropped as negotiations for the dual administration of the Colorado River fisheries with Nevada got underway. With Mormon Lake going dry and Roosevelt Lake being drained, Kartchner cleared the way with the AGPA to open the former to all fishing as soon as possible, while directing that the nongame fish in the latter be salvaged and given to the people on relief.

Also in 1940, the commission approved a plan by Reid to form a committee of interested persons to determine what fish species should be restocked in Mormon Lake when it began refilling. They instituted a policy change—locating rearing ponds at the hatcheries rather than in proximity to the release areas—due to poor success with volunteers supervising rearing ponds on the East Verde and at Government Springs near Greer.

The following year, the commission reduced the minimum length of channel catfish in the creel from 12 to 10 inches. Mormon Lake and Lake Mary were opened to year-round fishing for all species regardless of previous closures, and Oak Creek Canyon was again opened to fishing. On the down side, Apache and Roosevelt lakes were closed to all fishing until June 15, 1942, due to being drained and replanted with bass. Discussed but not enacted was a proposal for the hatcheries and all department buildings to be painted ivory white with an olive green roof and trim.

The years going into World War II were generally happy times for the commission's fisheries program. The completion of Boulder Dam in 1935, along with the filling of the other large reservoirs on the lower Colorado, Verde, and Salt rivers, was viewed as a great benefit to both fish and waterfowl. On July 11, 1940, the commission had thanked the Civilian Conservation Corps and Forest Service for rehabilitating Arizona's trout streams and nearly doubling their trout carrying capacity.[9] All seven of the Hunt Bass Hatchery lakes were in full operation, producing enough largemouth bass and bluegills to meet the demands occasioned by the draining and refilling of reservoirs and the ad hoc stocking of smaller impoundments. Other warm-water species, such as crappies and catfish, could be seined elsewhere and transported as needed, and private and federal hatcheries were available to supply fish and eggs when requested. All told, some 606,687 warm-water fishes

---

[9]There is some confusion regarding the role played by the Civilian Conservation Corps in Arizona's wildlife conservation movement. Although the US Army organized some 108 CCC camps in Arizona during the years 1933–1942, the work, with few exceptions, was supervised by federal agencies such as the Forest Service, National Park Service, Soil Erosion Service, and US Biological Survey. Of these, the Forest Service and Soil Conservation Service were the most important, with the Biological Survey primarily supervising the control of porcupines and other rodents. The Arizona Game and Fish Department supervised the construction of the Hunt Bass Hatchery, which was mostly a WPA project. Most CCC projects were designed to slow or halt soil erosion, and consisted of building diversion dams, rock dams, gabions, contour furrows, and stream rehabilitation structures (Seymour 1998; Lamb et al. 2008).

Fisheries director Herbert L. Reid and two deputy wardens, Reuben McNeill and Kearny Moore (left to right), with two channel catfish and a flathead catfish taken on the lower Colorado River in 1943. Importing new species of game fish was a common activity on the lower Colorado River even before statehood. (Arizona Historical Society/Yuma)

were planted in 1941, about half of which were largemouth bass. Warm-water plantings from the Hunt Bass Hatchery in 1942 included 68,999 largemouths (mostly to Canyon Lake), 157,060 bluegills, and 41,700 smallmouth bass, with another 20,150 largemouths received from the US Fish and Wildlife Service.

The trout hatcheries and rearing ponds at Pinetop, Tonto, and Page Springs were operating at full capacity, with 306,083 trout planted on the national forests in 1941 and 1,994,688 in 1942—now mostly rainbows and browns, with a few grayling and brook trout thrown in (Arizona Game and Fish Commission 1942).

There were problems, to be sure. A major change in the trout-stocking policy was necessitated in 1941, when it was found that fry and fingerling trout stocked in streams during the summer months experienced poor overwinter survival (10%–15%). This created a problem in heavily fished streams, as this survival rate for stocked fish could not meet the following summer's demand. A "creel-size" or "catchable" stocking program had to be instituted. In 1942, the concept of "put-and-take" trout fishery management was officially named and adopted by the commission. Other problems with hatchery-raised trout included the high cost of fish food (horsemeat provided by the Maricopa Tallow Works in Tempe), the periodic outbreaks of disease, predation from piscivorous birds and other predators, and losses experienced during planting.

Despite the problems, the early 1940s was a productive time for Arizona's fishermen. A parade of new reservoirs had provided habitats for largemouth bass and bluegill. Catfish were now a popular catch in the big rivers such as the Colorado. The emphasis on stocking catchable warm-water fish declined as fishery managers recognized nature could do a better and less expensive job of stocking and growing fish. By 1947, the Hunt Bass Hatchery was operating on stand-by for use in restocking a lake or pond after it had gone dry, been "renovated," or for some other reason needed a new supply of "brood fish." Meanwhile, the "newer" hatcheries were producing a steady stream of rainbow, brown, and other trouts for high-country lakes. And now, with the taming of the lower Colorado, bigger reservoirs and bigger fish were just a matter of time.

THE GAME DEPARTMENT TAKES UP BUFFALO RANCHING

David E. Brown

After his experiment to cross bison with Galloway cattle failed, Buffalo Jones rounded up what he could of his buffalo in House Rock Valley in 1909 and drove them to the railhead at Lund, Utah, to sell to a buyer in New Mexico (Easton and Brown 1961; Brown 2009).

The remaining buffalo, some 15 to 20 head, belonged to his partner, Uncle Jimmy Owens. Jones left these on the Kaibab Plateau. By then, Owens had been hired as a warden and forest guard for the Grand Cañon National Game Preserve and was spending most of his time hunting mountain lions on the north Kaibab for bounty and for recreational hunting clients, including President Theodore Roosevelt, Zane Grey, and Rex Beach. In no position to be tied down with day-to-day ranching operations, Owens pretty much allowed his little herd of bison to range at will, and the herd had increased to about 50 head or so in 1915 (Brown 2009). The country being generally dry, Owens's buffalo drifted down to the Kaibab's east range, taking up residence in House Rock Valley and watering in South Canyon and at developments maintained by the valley's ranchers.

Left to fend for itself, the herd continued to slowly grow in numbers, with Owens occasionally selling a few animals to local stockmen. Such was the situation in 1923 when Owens, now 73 years old and in failing health, let it be known he wanted out of the buffalo business.

Learning of his offer, Gov. George Hunt and State Game Warden George Willard, both of whom had visited House Rock Valley, thought the state should purchase the 77 or so bison then present. But the Arizona Game and Fish Department had no funds to do so. As a result, Owens sold 18 buffalo to the Grand Canyon Cattle Company. These animals were sent to the company's ranch in Chihuahua, Mexico. Another animal, a "pinto" steer born and castrated in 1917, was sold to a private party (Buffington and Garrettson 1980).

Thus, only 57 bison remained on the Kaibab when the governor had his State Game Warden begin negotiations with Arizona's congressional delegation, the Arizona State Legislature, and the American Bison Society, looking for a way for the state to acquire what came to be known as the House Rock Valley buffalo herd (Strode 1924).

Persistence paid off. Although the legislature failed to appropriate the agreed-upon purchase price of $10,000, Governor Hunt arranged for the state to acquire Owens's buffalo by giving him a down payment and paying him $125 a month out of the Game and Fish Fund; in essence, a two-year installment plan that allowed Owens to retire to his home state of Texas in 1928.

When the final payment for what was supposed to be 100 buffalo, but was now only 98, came due in December 1927, 15 of the oldest bulls were harvested and two cows culled. Each hunter kept 100 pounds of meat from the animal killed, with the remainder going to the state to sell. The exception was one old bull, which was scheduled to go to the state museum at the University of Arizona.

Uncle Jimmy Owens's bison herd in House Rock Valley at the time of purchase by the state of Arizona. Photo by George M. Willard. (From booklet celebrating Arizona's First Annual Bird Day, courtesy of Ed Parry)

In the meantime, Hunt had announced that a public drawing would take place at the 1928 State Fair, during which 15 (actually 10) hunters would be selected to participate in a buffalo shoot, with access to House Rock Valley now being provided via the new bridge across the Colorado River at Lees Ferry (Edmund Seymour of the American Bison Society to Governor Hunt, Governor's Files, Arizona State Library, Archives and Public Records).

Feeding the buffalo was a problem. Although the US Forest Service was to provide a pasture south of the Kane Ranch deemed adequate for 250 head, the animals were often on Grazing Service land leased to others. That year, 14 calves were added to the herd. Two were taken to the Arizona State Fair in Phoenix. Another four buffalo, all young bulls, were shipped to House Rock Valley from South Dakota in crates—the first new blood to augment the herd in its 24-year history.

The succeeding years' shoots, although small and designed to allow the herd to increase, were enormously popular and generated much good press. Arizona was ballyhooed as the only place in the world where a member of the public could hunt buffalo. The new Arizona Game and Fish Commission, which acquired management authority over the department's buffalo herd in 1929, also considered the buffalo a great asset, and authorized hunts for from six to 14 permit-holders nearly every year from 1930 through 1940. By that time, the herd had grown to 250 head.

All of the hunters who showed up to these hunts were successful. The animals were rounded up and held in a pasture prior to the hunt in an "all hands on deck" operation that involved not only J. B. Edwards, the deputy warden from Fredonia, but the State Game Warden and his deputies from throughout the state.

These hunts were all held in January or February, with 20%–40% of the permits going to nonresidents. To apply for a permit, one had to submit the number of one's Class A or Class C (nonresident) license to the office of the State Game Warden. Hunters and

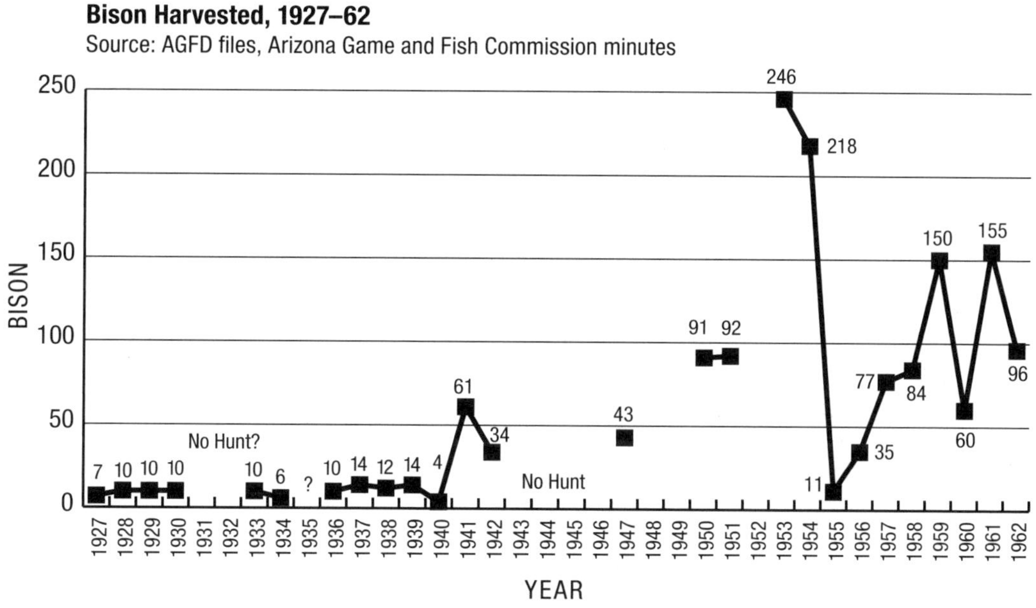

alternates were selected at a public drawing. No fee was charged over and above the cost of the hunting license. Each hunter was allowed to keep the head and hide of his buffalo and 100 pounds or one quarter of the meat. The hunters also chose the buffalo to be killed, with each shooter selecting an animal in the order that he was drawn. The hunts were financed by the sale of buffalo meat. The income provided a substantial portion of the department's meager budget.

In January 1928, the department hired a caretaker—Charles Lewis of Kanab, Utah—whose salary was $25 a month. Prior to that time, and intermittently thereafter, the buffalo were looked after by a man named Anderson or a deputy warden. Although the buffalo were mostly on government grazing land, they had to share the range with livestock, as a request by Arizona's legislature and the Game and Fish Department for the federal government to cede the state a "buffalo range" never materialized due to opposition from stockmen. This was unfortunate, as the situation in some years was nothing short of desperate. Even the water for the animals had to be arranged through the brokerage of John H. Page and Company and purchased from the Grand Canyon Cattle Company.

That all of the hunts in the 1930s were conducted as soon after January 1 as feasible was probably due to the lack of refrigeration, as the hunters might have to process the bison by themselves. Killing buffalo in midwinter could be problematical. On January 27, 1937, the Arizona Game and Fish Commission had to postpone that year's buffalo hunt for an indefinite period due to heavy snow and bad weather.

Some of these hunts proved newsworthy, including the February 1933 hunt in which three women were drawn as alternates, with one of them, Cecile Hough of Phoenix, selected as one of the 10 shooters. Some 500 people watched as nine men and Hough killed their buffalo over a two-day hunt supervised by the top echelon of the department: State Game Warden William Joyner, Deputy State Game Warden William Sawtelle, Chief Field Deputy R. S. Kimball, and Deputy Warden C. B. England. To everyone's

Deputy Warden T. W. Hunt and US Marshall George Mauk with a bull bison taken during the annual buffalo hunt in 1930. Mauk's hunting partner was Gov. John Phillips; at the time, it was customary for the first buffalo permit to go to the governor. Photo by Robert Bayless. (Arizona Wild Life *magazine, June 1930).*

amazement, Hough, who had never before ridden a horse or fired a rifle, killed the first buffalo with a perfect shot from horseback.

Just seeing a buffalo was considered a thrill, and the House Rock herd was a "must see," if unreliable, tourist attraction for visitors to the Kaibab Plateau and southern Utah. Nor was it unusual in those days for "pintos" (animals with light brown or white spots) to show up in the state's herd. Whether these animals were throwbacks to the former crossbreeding effort with Galloway cattle or color mutations in the original bison brought in by Jones was a matter of much debate. Whatever the case, such animals were treasured as historical oddities to be sold rather than regarded as culls to be eliminated. Of the 126 bison tallied in the January 1935 roundup, seven were pintos—all believed to have been sired by one large pinto bull.

On learning this, the commission directed State Game Warden Shelby Lewis to sell the bull and all of the pinto calves if a suitable buyer could be found. Buyers there were, and in January 1940, four buffalo from House Rock were "loaned" to the Toverea Packing Company for display on East Washington Street. Like all such animals, these buffalo remained the property of the state, and when one of the pinto buffalo died at the "Toverea Zoo," the commission directed that its head and horns be given to the University of Arizona and the hide turned over to Ted Sliger of Buckhorn for mounting, with the caveat that the department could purchase it at some future date.

House Rock Valley's buffalo faced a number of obstacles in the 1930s, not the least of which involved a scarcity of feed and water. Although the Forest Service provided an allotment for the state's buffalo, the herd continued to share their government range with cattle owned by stockmen.

The most immediate problem was water. The only waters available to the buffalo were controlled by the cattlemen, who demanded that the commission withdraw its water-right application in South Canyon and pay Page and Company $300 a year for the buffaloes' use of the company's water. Brokering water use arrangements with Page and Company thus became an ongoing task for State Game Warden Joyner and his successors. The situation eventually resulted in a proposal that would limit the state's buffalo herd at Kane Springs to 100 head, with another 100 bison going to Page and Company in lieu of the department's paying the company $200 per month in watering charges. Although this proposal was later rejected, it was mandated that the state's herd would be limited to 200 head.

Range conditions were another persistent problem, and in 1936, State Game Warden Lewis ordered Deputy Warden Edwards to investigate the buffalo situation at House Rock. The herd was reported to be suffering from shortages of feed and water, but Edwards found the herd 15 miles southeast of Kane to be in better condition than at any time since June 1935. Nonetheless, the bison had no home of their own, and the State Game Warden knew the bison either had to have more access to feed and water or be reduced in number. Attempts to secure a federal refuge having failed, on March 11, 1938, the commission directed State Game Warden Sawtelle to draft legislation authorizing the sale of a portion or portions of the buffalo herd and/or to negotiate the exchange of a limited number of buffalo with any interested state or individual having game animals for propagation purposes.

As was the case with so many department conundrums, it was the Pittman-Robertson Act that provided relief for the buffalo ranch. State Game Warden Kenner Kartchner worked with representatives from the Forest Service, the US Grazing Service (precursor to the Bureau of Land Management), and livestock permittees to come up with a grazing plan. The plan considered the amount of forage available for both cattle and bison, while recognizing the department had no water in House Rock Valley outside the one Kaibab Forest allotment.

To resolve this latter problem, Kartchner investigated building a feeder line off a Forest Service pipeline to water the House Rock Valley buffalo herd in South Canyon. Should this pipeline be completed through the use of Federal-Aid dollars, the $200 monthly water charge to Page and Company would cease and the department could maintain its original allotment of 200 head.

The commission voted to harvest 61 buffalo in 1941, thus bringing the House Rock herd down to 200 bison as per Kartchner's agreement. A similar number had been removed the previous year, when commission chairman George Wrench allowed those filming the movie *Western Union* to feed and stampede the buffalo, provided none of the animals was roped or shot. It was also directed at that time that about 50 head of buffalo be located around the "Pools" near the highway, where they might be seen by the traveling public, although just how this was to be accomplished was not spelled out.

Hunt regulations changed in 1940, when it was decided that hunters, after choosing their buffalo in the order drawn, could now purchase one or all of the quarters at 10 cents a pound for front quarters or 12 cents a pound for hindquarters—the first time a fee was charged to the hunter other than the cost of a license. Also, the buffalo would now be dressed and skinned by special butchers hired for the occasion, with half of their charge paid by the department and half paid by the hunters. There was also a requirement, rescinded in 1944, that hunters who drew any special tag, whether for buffalo, antelope, or elk, would be ineligible for future buffalo draws.

In 1941, the commission adopted a policy by which applicants wishing to obtain and display a live buffalo had to furnish a $50 bond for each animal to guarantee its safe return to House Rock. The animal's ownership remained with the state, as did that of any

Billie Pilcher got his buffalo on a hunt at House Rock in 1942. (AGFD files)

offspring produced. The commission also required that each animal "on loan" had to be properly cared for and identified.

Range conditions at House Rock remained a matter of concern even after the wet winter of 1940–41, and in September of that year, the commission announced it was looking for suitable buffalo ranch locations south of the Colorado River, sending requests to all the national forest supervisors to name any locations they deemed suitable. By this time too, the long distance, the periodic forage shortages, and the large administrative costs involved had caused some department constituents to question whether the House Rock operation was more of a liability than a revenue producer.

But even though the commission was considering alternatives to its annual buffalo hunt, Arizona's buffalo herd continued to be favorably viewed by most of the public. Moreover, the new pipeline at House Rock had cost $18,500, and the commission was heavily invested in the buffalo and the ranch headquarters at Kane Ranch now that both had adequate water. Assistance also was seen coming from another quarter. Even as Raymond Ranch below Anderson Mesa was being investigated as a Federal-Aid acquisition for wintering pronghorn, some commission members were considering Raymond as an alternative buffalo ranch.

In 1942, the Arizona Game and Fish Commission authorized the department to purchase the 20,320-acre Raymond Ranch. When Federal-Aid biologist Orville N. "Pop" Arrington (1952) reported that pronghorn did not always winter on Raymond Ranch and those that did were not feeding on the grasses proliferating there after the removal of livestock, it was an easy decision to establish a second bison herd at Raymond Ranch.

Fencing and tanks were built and a well drilled with Pittman-Robertson funds, and the first buffalo were trucked to Raymond Ranch in October 1945. Three bulls and nine cows were also transported to Raymond by truck from Wichita Wildlife Refuge, along with 16 more cows from House Rock. The following spring, 22 young cows and two young bulls were transferred to Raymond Ranch from House Rock Valley to form the nucleus of the department's second herd (Arrington 1952). According to a survey taken by Wayne Lathim, the department now had 238 bison. A buffalo caretaker, who would also serve as a game ranger and predator trapper, was hired for Raymond, but no hunt would be held that year at either ranch.

Meanwhile, at Raymond Ranch, the original nucleus had increased to 146 bison, due to the lack of competition with livestock and several years of adequate precipitation. Indeed, the eastern half of the range was reported to have become well-sodded, with grama grass growing where bare ground and snakeweed had dominated the landscape in 1942. So abundant was this grass in the swales that it could reportedly be baled into hay during the summers of 1947–49 (Arrington 1952).

Pressures for additional range having subsided, the commission passed on an offer for another buffalo ranch in Hualapai Valley, promising instead to start up a herd at Fort Huachuca. Some bison were traded to the state of Sonora, Mexico, however, and 43 animals were taken during a February 1947 hunt. The meat brought in some $3,536 in much-needed revenue. Thirty-one buffalo were scheduled to be killed during a January 1948 hunt, with another 80 bulls to be taken in December 1948. Grazing lease problems at House Rock persisted, and the remaining 239 adult and yearling bison exceeded the allotted number, another attempt to secure a 23,000-acre range for the animals having fallen through.

House Rock experienced another drought in the spring of 1950. Despite a decision in 1946 to limit the carrying capacity of Raymond Ranch to 150 head, necessity now required the transport of a large number of animals from House Rock to Raymond. Once another 166 animals arrived, the Raymond Ranch herd reached 358 head—a number clearly in excess of the carrying capacity of the range. Complicating matters further was a commission ruling that the buffalo ranches must support themselves and that no live buffalo could be sold to anyone.

Range conditions, chronically poor, continued to deteriorate in House Rock Valley. Fortunately, the department had acquired some 35,000 acres of nearly pure grassland in 1947 on what had been Fort Huachuca and was now called the Charles T. Vorhies Research Project Area. Some 166 bison were moved to either Raymond Ranch or Fort Huachuca in July 1950. This left only 86 buffalo at House Rock—approximately the same number of animals present when Owens first offered the herd for sale in 1923.

Unfortunately, the drought continued into the summer of 1950, and the usual rains of July and August did not materialize. Now Raymond Ranch, too, was critically overstocked. The previous winter's precipitation having been negligible, there was little "green-up" and no appreciable grass growth. Another buffalo management crisis was in the making.

Ranch house at Raymond Ranch. According to a 1949 journal entry by Mary Heddings, "The house itself is wonderful. Stone walls, two feet thick—very decorative and good insulation against both heat and cold. . . . The kitchen is . . . large enough for a six-foot table and benches (handmade)." ("Mary's Raymond Ranch" journal, AGFD files)

That fall, another agreement was reached between the Arizona Game and Fish Department, the Forest Service, and the Bureau of Land Management, by which the department relinquished any grazing rights on government land in House Rock Valley in return for a Kaibab National Forest permit for the exclusive use of bison and other game species in the South Canyon[1] and Fence Canyon allotments.

In the way of further improvements, the department now built a headquarters for the buffalo ranch manager on its property in House Rock Valley, again using Federal-Aid funds for the ranch's purchase and construction. Although buffalo hunts were scheduled to take place during the fall of 1950, no hunt was authorized for House Rock due to the small number of bison present, most of the animals having been removed to Raymond Ranch or Fort Huachuca or harvested.

With fences and windmills already in place there, it was a relatively simple operation to translocate 101 buffalo from Raymond Ranch to the Vorhies Research Project Area in October 1950. The following month, hunters harvested another 91 head from the Raymond Ranch herd, supplemented by the removal of another 74 bison in the spring of 1951. So many buffalo were killed in 1950 that not all of the meat could be sold and some

[1]Now known as the "Buffalo Allotment." The Fence Canyon allotment had previously been used as emergency pasture.

quarters spoiled or had to be given away (Gresham 1953). Another seven buffalo were sold to Knott's Berry Farm for a fee of $500 for bulls and $300 for cows. These reductions left only 92 adult bison on Raymond Ranch—a number well below the designated carrying capacity. Even so, range conditions were so poor that 58 of these buffalo were driven to the nine-square-mile Grapevine Forest Service allotment on Anderson Mesa, which had been acquired with the purchase of Raymond Ranch and was maintained as a non-grazed wildlife allotment for pronghorn.

The first buffalo actually had arrived at the Vorhies Research Project Area in May 1949, when 113 bulls, cows, and yearlings were brought in from House Rock. These animals were supplemented by an introduction of three more bulls from House Rock that summer and an infusion of 15 yearling bulls from the National Bison Range near Moise, Montana, in October 1949. After the additional bison arrived from Raymond Ranch in 1950, there were 351 adult bison and 74 calves (425 buffalo) on the Vorhies Research Project Area.

Then, in the spring of 1951, their available range was cut from 20,000 acres to 13,000 acres (Wallmo 1949–51). Worse, the winter of 1950–51 had been dry and drought conditions again prevailed. Excessive grazing was such that denudation and trailing in the washes were imposing serious erosion problems (Wallmo 1951). Although some of these problems might have been solved with better water distribution, a more insurmountable problem was the US Army's decision that year to reactivate Fort Huachuca and have nearly all of the buffalo removed.

In the fall of 1952, there were 96 bison at House Rock, 48 on Raymond Ranch, and 461 on the Vorhies Research Project Area—a total of just over 600 buffalo. And although no hunts were scheduled in 1952 for House Rock or Raymond Ranch, where reduced stocking was having the desired effect, the military's reactivation of Fort Huachuca necessitated the removal of 250 bison by hunters during a season that lasted from January 26

Buffalo roundup at Raymond Ranch in 1950. (AGFD files)

The sign at the entrance to House Rock Buffalo Range, ca. 1962. House Rock reached an all-time high of 305 buffalo in 1959. (AGFD files)

through February 4, 1953. Those animals remaining were harvested or sold the following fall, leaving House Rock and Raymond Ranch as the only wildlife areas containing state-owned buffalo.

Removing Fort Huachuca's buffalo was not easy. To begin with, 15 animals were reported missing in December 1952, with some known to have been poached. This triggered an intensive inventory showing that, of the 550 head supposed to be on the fort in January 1953, only 461 could be located and classified. The 1953 hunt was also a public relations problem: 440 buffalo were held in the corral at one time, with 246 animals scheduled to be killed. Killing such a large number of bison in such a manner warranted criticism in an article in *Life* magazine and meant some unsold meat had to be given to the Boy Scouts. Even then, some buffalo remained, and it took two more hunts and the sale of 20 animals to Mexico before the fort could be declared bison-free in January 1956.

The bloom was now off the rose when it came to the desirability of the buffalo ranches, as far as many people within and outside the Game and Fish Department were concerned. In 1956, the commission seriously considered reducing the state's herd to 100 head and keeping only one buffalo ranch. Nonetheless, the presence of buffalo remained popular with the hunting public and the department had a major financial commitment in the two ranches it owned. Told the buffalo ranches might yet be managed as a self-sustaining enterprise, the commission authorized an increase in the cost of a buffalo permit in 1959 and voted to renew its leases with the State Land Department and Forest Service.

Hunt procedures were slightly modified on all the ranches after 1950, as larger numbers of animals now had to be killed. No longer were the animals rounded up and dispatched on the open range. The hunts were now the responsibility of the department's Law Enforcement Division and supervised by game rangers who, after rounding up the buffalo to be shot, held them in wooden corrals. From eight to 10 animals were released in groups before a like number of shooters, who took their animal in the order in which the hunter was drawn—a situation that persisted until 1972. A $25 permit fee was required of those entering the drawing, in addition to the hunting license requirement. In return, the shooter received the hide, head, and one of the front quarters, along with the ability to purchase one or all of his or her animal's remaining quarters.

Hunts were now scheduled in October, beginning with 21 animals harvested at House Rock in 1953 and nine culls removed from Raymond Ranch that same year. After that time, the ranches were operated in a manner similar to a livestock operation, in which the number of animals retained was determined on the basis of the perceived carrying capacity of the range. Hunts took place at the two ranches in alternate years. Both were expected to be economically self-supporting, with department personnel doing the skinning and processing.

Although buffalo numbers at Raymond Ranch never again attained the high of 358 reached in 1950, House Rock reached an all-time high of 305 buffalo in 1959. Annual surveys in 1962 tallied 239 bison at House Rock and 157 at Raymond Ranch.

In the years that followed, hunts at both buffalo ranches increasingly took on the aspects of an intra-departmental rodeo participated in by department horsemen, skinners, backup shooters, and the permittees themselves (Brown 1984c). The buffalo to be shot continued to be rounded up prior to the season, divided into bull, cow, and yearling categories, and held until the selected animal or group of animals was released to be shot by an intensely watched hunter. These "corral shoots," as they were called, ceased in 1972 when public pressures demanded that the department provide a more sporting-like atmosphere in more natural surroundings.

THE FOREST SERVICE AND GAME DEPARTMENT VIE FOR MANAGEMENT AUTHORITY OVER BIG GAME

David E. Brown

> The big issue is whether or not we are ready to turn our wildlife over to the United States Bureau of Fisheries, United States Bureau of Biological Survey, United States National Park Service and the United States Forest Service. Unless we wake up to our privileges, duties, and responsibilities, the big four will run the whole show before long. (Dwight Pettis, State Game Warden, in *Arizona Wild Life*, June 1929)

As the 1920s drew to a close, the state of Arizona had good reason to be apprehensive that the US Forest Service would take over its big game management responsibilities. Although the states were regarded as having the constitutional authority to regulate the taking of game and other wildlife, it was the national forests that provided most of the habitat for the West's big game animals. And in November 1928, the US Supreme Court had ruled the Forest Service had the right to remove wildlife endangering that habitat.

The Forest Service was the agency that possessed the resources to manage wildlife: It had a cadre of forest rangers in the field, range and game specialists at the district headquarters in Albuquerque, and the appropriations to fund them. Forest guards and forest rangers had been the principal enforcers of the game laws since Congress established the national forests in 1905, and the few wildlife and range experts then available were employed either by the Forest Service or its sister agency, the US Biological Survey.[1] What was more, the Forest Service increasingly regarded game and recreation as forest commodities similar to timber, grass, and other renewable resources (Brown and Carmony 1990). At the district level, Aldo Leopold was even experimenting with methodologies and formulae to survey big game animals and develop harvest objectives for the various forests (Leopold 1920).

The states, Arizona included, had only a few administrators and deputy wardens to manage wildlife and, with game numbers at low levels, little prospects of increased funding. An initiative passed in 1916 precluded Arizona's game department from adjusting big game seasons and bag limits, and all of the state's game refuges were on national forests. Arizona had already ceded responsibility for controlling predators and noxious rodents to the Biological Survey, and was having to adjust to the federal takeover of waterfowl and other migratory birds by the same federal agency.

Recreation, including hunting, was increasingly viewed as a Forest Service commodity, and the Southwest's forest supervisors were having their rangers estimate game numbers and harvests. Now that the Supreme Court had weighed in on the side of the Forest Service to protect deer forage rather than deer, the questions of when and how many animals to remove would be up to range managers rather than game wardens. That

[1] For example, the 1915 Forest Service handbook by Aldo Leopold details survey methods and other management procedures expected of Forest Service rangers.

prescribed numbers of animals *needed* to be harvested was a concept Arizona and the other states were as yet ill-equipped to deal with, as all previous emphasis had been on protecting deer and other big game animals from being killed.

The Forest Service was not the only federal agency striving to expand its area of responsibility. On September 8, 1925, State Game Warden George Willard wrote Gov. George Hunt that Stephen Mather was attempting to enlarge Grand Canyon National Park to take in the most productive portions of the Kaibab National Forest. Not satisfied with a Forest Service proposal to turn over 46,000 acres of the Kaibab National Forest and Game Preserve to the Park Service, Mather wanted no hunting, no grazing, and no predator control to disturb the public's deer-viewing pleasure for 26 miles back from the rim of the Grand Canyon. If Mather were successful, half of the Kaibab Plateau's commercial timber and its most productive summer range would be "off limits" within Grand Canyon National Park.

Recognizing the need to form an alliance against a greater evil, state and Forest Service administrators and leaders of the Arizona Game Protective Association strived to draft a compromise management program that would accomplish the Kaibab National Forest's mandates and comply with state game laws. To do so required repeal of Arizona's 1916 game laws and enactment of a new game code—one that would allow for refuge boundary adjustments, more flexible seasons, and different definitions of what constituted a "legal" deer. To not do so would eliminate the ability to take does and fawns and would force the Forest Service to reduce its deer herds through the use of government hunters.

Fortunately, the Forest Service was then peopled by first-generation administrators who, while dedicated to the resource, were astute and experienced in the political battles of the West and prone to compromise. National forest supervisors also supported Leopold's "More Game Movement" and readily promoted the numbers of game animals within their jurisdiction. To provide a financial justification for Leopold's program, the Coconino National Forest in December 1925 touted population estimates of 1,809 antelope, 19,638 deer (as opposed to 30,000 deer on the Kaibab), 797 elk, a handful of mountain sheep on the San Francisco Peaks, 95 black bear, and 1,233 javelina, for a total estimated value of $1,477,395.

Although no one credited the above-average precipitation of the 1920s as a cause of higher game numbers, preferring to attribute any increase to protection from poachers and lion control, the Forest Service was concerned that several game refuges on the national forests were experiencing game irruptions. As on the Kaibab, Forest Service administrators responded to these irruptions by inviting concerned agencies and individuals to go on inspection trips to the problem area and see the overbrowsing firsthand. Here, on the ground, and with the evidence there to see, the Forest Service would attempt to convince the parties of the problem's severity and discuss possible solutions. Ironically, the rationale for this approach to increase the amount of hunting was based on range conditions rather than game numbers. Deer and other game would be hunted when the *need* arrived, not when sufficient animals were available.

On November 16, 1927, State Game Warden Dwight Pettis wrote Governor Hunt describing the results of such an inspection trip with Deputy Warden F. H. Holladay. Along with Forest Service personnel, the men had just completed a four-day inspection tour of the Graham Mountains Game Preserve, where an abundance of deer sign was noted, along with some heavy browsing on the mountains' south slopes. Salt licks put out by Holladay showed much use, although no cattle permits had been issued in this part of the refuge for the past two years. The investigators did not consider range conditions to be critical, but recommended opening that part of the refuge west of Taylor Pass to deer hunting in an attempt to alleviate the damage being done to the browse.

The problem was that neither the department nor the governor had authority to open the preserve or modify the deer season. Such actions were the prerogative of the Arizona State Legislature. Pettis recommended that in lieu of the legislature's taking action, which was problematical, the state should pass a statute establishing a game refuge committee that would have the authority to act in such cases (Governor's Files, Arizona State Library, Archives and Public Records). Clearly, some sort of legislative action was needed to avoid future confrontations with the Forest Service—confrontations the state would lose, according to the dictates of the upcoming Supreme Court decision.

The need for a game refuge committee became moot with passage of the "repealer" in November 1928 and the establishment of an Arizona Game and Fish Commission that would formulate hunt regulations on an as-needed instead of a political basis. No longer need such decisions be made by uninterested legislators. The new game code had been designed and promoted by an Arizona Game Protective Association that demanded a more responsive game department, and its members insisted on an active State Game Warden and commission—positions that would logically come from the ranks of the AGPA, now that Governor Hunt had been voted out of office. The Arizona Game and Fish Commission would make the important game management decisions, which meant the department would no longer have to merely react to or oppose the recommendations of either the Forest Service or the governor.

The Game and Fish Commission Makes Itself Heard

The new commission wasted no time getting involved with its big game responsibilities. Deer populations were thought to be excessive on several national forests, and in May 1929, the Forest Service instigated a series of inspection trips to follow an investigation of overbrowsing by deer (AGPA 1929). The Arizona portion of the examination began on the Mount Graham Refuge in the Pinaleño Mountains, where white-tailed deer numbers were estimated at 10,000 and deer were inflicting severe damage on aspens, mountain mahogany, and other deer forage plants.

Those present included Forest Supervisor Fred Winn, Forest Service Grazing Inspector Dwight A. Shoemaker, and C. E. Rachford, representing the Forest Service; Mark Musgrave and Walter Taylor for the Biological Survey; and Les Hart of Tucson—the newly appointed chairman of the Arizona Game and Fish Commission. At the end of the survey, the party recommended the refuge be reduced in size and the area open to deer hunting have a bag limit of one buck and one doe, with the goal of removing 2,500

Edward A. Goldman was a senior biologist for the US Biological Survey during most of the first half of the twentieth century. By the 1920s, he was regarded as one of the most knowledgeable naturalists of the day. (Biological Survey Unit, USGS Patuxent Wildlife Research Center)

deer each year. Trapping and transplanting deer was also considered, and if the removal goal had not been met in the fall of 1930, the committee recommended a cessation of lion control in the upper elevations not used by livestock.

This survey was followed by field trips to the Chiricahua and Catalina mountains, on which Winn, Shoemaker, and other Forest Service rangers were accompanied by Musgrave and Edward Goldman of the Biological Survey. Hart was again present, as was Kenner Kartchner, acting as the department's range expert. The party estimated the number of deer in the Chiricahuas, where no refuge had been established, to number only about 2,500 whitetails. No refuges were suggested, but predator control was recommended, as was an introduction of wild turkeys.

Walter Mann, supervisor of the Kaibab National Forest, was instrumental in building a cooperative climate for wildlife management between federal land managers and the state of Arizona. (Courtesy of Rhonda Appel)

By way of contrast, overuse by both deer and cattle was noted in the Catalina Mountains, where 3,500 whitetails were estimated to roam. Here, recommendations were made to reduce the number of deer and revise the boundary of the Santa Catalina Game Reserve. A revised boundary would include only desert bighorn sheep habitat in the area where Deputy Warden Robin Montgomery had reported seeing 93 head in three bands during a January 1927 snowstorm. As in the Grahams, the deer hunt recommendation was for a limit of one buck and one doe per hunter during the 1929 and 1930 seasons. Lion control was to continue unless deer hunters failed to reduce deer numbers. Most important, the parties agreed that the state must assist the Forest Service in maintaining proper cover and forage and cooperate in a coordinated game management plan.

The Kaibab remained the focal point for deer management issues. On July 1, 1929, Gov. John Phillips gave a keynote address at a meeting in Flagstaff that heralded yet another inspection tour of the Kaibab—one that would produce an agreement for alleviating the browse conditions there. Those present included Biological Survey Chief Paul G. Redington; his erstwhile assistants Edward Goldman and Vernon Bailey; Forest Supervisor Walter G. Mann and his staff of rangers; Horace Albright and Superintendant Miner Tillotson from the National Park Service; and the new State Game Warden, Robert Bayless. Also present was a contingent of academics, including University of Arizona President Homer L. Shantz and three wildlife and range professors, Charles Vorhies, John J. Thornber, and William G. McGinnies. Vorhies was also an officeholder in the Tucson Natural History Association, an AGPA affiliate.

Each member of the party had concerns to air: The Park Service wanted more deer trapping and an enlarged Grand Canyon National Park, while Vorhies would debate Goldman and Bailey on the advisability of lion hunting and the use of poisons as a predator-control method. All agreed that more studies were needed but that the browse situation must be rectified. The National Park Service still wanted tourists to be able to see a spectacular number of deer, and opposed the Forest Service and state participants who wanted to alleviate the browse situation through an increase in deer hunting. The conflict was no longer the state vs. the Forest Service, but Arizona and the Forest Service vs. the Park Service.

Deer hunt recommendations and the Kaibab situation were discussed at length during the July 1929 meeting of the Arizona Game and Fish Commission by Commissioners Hart, Albert Jones, and Tom McCullough. At the season-setting meeting the following month, the commission agreed the Kaibab would be open to deer hunting from October 1 to December 15, 1929, to licensed resident and nonresident hunters who had a $1.50 permit from the Forest Service, as per the cooperative agreement between the two agencies. The bag limit was set at two deer, only one of which could be a buck. Only the national forest portion of the Kaibab was open to hunting. All carcasses and hides were to be tagged and inspected by commission representatives in what would be the first check station manned by personnel from the Arizona Game and Fish Department.

Although the commission considered similar deer-season arrangements for the Graham and Catalina mountains, the two-deer bag limit was strongly opposed by AGPA members from Graham County. By way of compromise, the commission voted to open the refuge areas to deer hunting, and by a two-to-one vote, retained the 30-day statewide deer season. Conservative by nature, the commission also closed the mule deer season south of the Gila River in November 1929, and the following March, eliminated bear and turkey seasons in southern Arizona. Another 1929 action made it compulsory for hunters to submit deer and turkey tag returns regarding their success.[2]

That winter, Bayless joined Supervisor Mann and his survey crew on the Kaibab deer counts. The forest rangers were bolstered by the state's cooperative spirit and desire to see the deer herd retained within "carrying capacity"—a concept then being developed by Mann, Leopold, S. B. Locke, and D. Irwin Rasmussen. Mann also endorsed the new game code and had to have been pleased with the agreement that made him the prime deer manager on the Kaibab, an action attributable to Mann's systematic surveys and studies (Young 2002).

The Forest Service also appreciated the commission's opposition to any expansion of Grand Canyon National Park. Also of potential benefit to the Forest Service and its range-management responsibilities were commission actions adjusting and shrinking the size of several refuges and directing Bayless to spend up to $300 for the construction of traps and fences to capture excess numbers of antelope on Anderson Mesa. The work would be supervised by federal biologist Musgrave with the help of the Forest Service. Then, in November 1930, this era of governmental cooperation came to a halt; Governor

---

[2]What the results of these surveys were was never discovered during the course of this investigation.

During the 1930s, when authorities wanted information regarding Arizona's plants and animals they turned to Andrew Nichol for the answers. Nichol was considered the state's foremost natural-history expert on everything from cacti to bighorn sheep. (Arizona Historical Society/Tucson, #AHS4848)

Hunt was re-elected, bringing a temporary end to the state-federal relationship fostered by the Forest Service and AGPA.

The 1930 Kaibab deer hunt had been the most successful yet, with 5,033 deer killed (Russo 1964). Moreover, with the deer-trapping program also showing promise (Heffelfinger and Webb 2010), Supervisor Mann had reason for optimism. Undeterred by the change in state administration, he continued his range studies, orchestrating another joint winter survey in February 1931. The survey comprised not only a large Forest Service staff (including range expert Locke), but also James Brooks and Art Brown of the National Park Service; Rasmussen, Kartchner, and W. D. Judd of the Arizona Game and Fish Department; and George Pratt of the AGPA (Young 2002). The state's range expert was Andrew Nichol, representing the University of Arizona.

Although the group's deer herd estimates varied from Brooks's 20,000 to Mann's 30,000, a cooperative atmosphere prevailed because herd reduction was now taking place, thereby allowing the discussions on range conditions to turn toward livestock management rather than just deer removal.

In June 1931, Regional Forester R. H. Rutledge organized yet another eight-day "show-me" trip to the Kaibab. In addition to including many of the representatives from the previous trip, the American Society of Mammalogists was now represented, making some 28 participants in all. Items for discussion included not only browse conditions and the number of deer, but predator control and range conditions for livestock. Although most of the representatives came away from the survey believing that there were now fewer deer, the only point of universal agreement was a continuing need to cooperate.

In a summary of the June meeting, Grand Canyon National Park Supervisor Tillotson expressed the opinion that the Kaibab had a large but declining deer herd and that the committee of representatives present agreed hunting should continue at or about the same level as in 1930 with the Forest Service in charge—a conclusion acknowledging that even though game belonged to the state, the habitat was the federal government's responsibility. The committee also recommended removing unnecessary cattle from the plateau, but sidestepped the predator-control issue. The two years of increased cooperation between the state and the federal government was much touted, and it was hoped the Kaibab would serve as a game management model to follow elsewhere. All in all, the committee concluded that the vegetation might be improving.

Hunt's intransigence nonetheless continued to threaten the cooperative venture, in that he wanted more deer for both tourists and deer hunters. He insisted on a one-deer bag limit and an end to using government hunters to accomplish harvest goals—thereby threatening another confrontation. Wanting to maintain a spirit of cooperation, Mann agreed to a reduced harvest, despite having the backing of both his supervisors and the committee, who believed a greater harvest was needed than could be achieved under Hunt's limitations. As a result, only 965 deer were killed in 1931 and no predator control was authorized. Although no one reported on the financial aspect, the department could little afford such declines in license sales during such difficult financial times.

Joint Field Trips in Forests of Concern

The Kaibab was not the only national forest of concern. Using the strategy of conducting joint field trips to support its need for deer reductions, the Forest Service had also conducted a round of inspection trips in April 1931 for other national forests in Arizona, finding five areas of concern (Goldman 1931a–c):

- The Santa Catalina Mountains refuge portion of the Coronado National Forest;
- The Coconino-Yavapai Game Refuge on the Tusayan National Forest;
- The Hay Lake antelope range on the Coconino National Forest;
- The elk range on the Sitgreaves National Forest; and
- The Blue Range Game Refuge on the Apache and Crook national forests.

Leading each trip were Goldman, senior biologist with the Biological Survey; Musgrave, Forest Service game specialist; and Shoemaker, Forest Service grazing inspector, along with a retinue of Forest Service supervisors and specialists such as Winn from the Coronado National Forest. Other personnel attending one or more of the inspections included Hart of the Arizona Game and Fish Commission (Catalinas); range expert Kartchner (Catalinas, Sitgreaves, and Blue Range); Nichol for the University of Arizona; and representatives from the Arizona Cattlegrowers Association, Arizona Woolgrowers Association, and Arizona Game Protective Association. A summary of the committee's report showed that:

1. Heavy browsing was occurring in the wooded and forested portions of the Coronado National Forest's Catalina Mountains despite light use by cattle. Although half of the 92,986-acre game refuge had been opened to deer hunting in 1929, it was obvious too many white-tailed deer remained, with especially severe browse damage noted near high-elevation recreation sites. Hart et al. (1931a) recommended deer numbers at higher elevations be checked if not reduced, and the remainder of the refuge be opened to deer hunting, save small areas around recreation sites, habitats occupied by bighorn sheep, and a refuge area near Oracle. Should these measures not succeed in reducing the damage to such important browse plants as aspen, madrone, and mountain mahogany, most committee members recommended a doe season be instituted until a sufficient number of white-tailed deer had been removed.

High-lined junipers on the Coconino National Forest's Anderson Mesa in April 1931. Most of the damaged junipers appear to be invading single-seed juniper (Juniperus monosperma) *and alligator-bark juniper* (Juniperus deppeana). *Photo by Andrew Nichol or Mark Musgrave. (Governor's Files, Arizona State Library, Archives and Public Records, History and Archives Division)*

2. Two days had been spent examining the 133,120-acre Coconino-Yavapai Game Refuge that the Flagstaff Game Protective Association had worked to set aside for deer, turkey, and antelope. Although the grass in some areas showed improvement, overuse of browse plants was general throughout the refuge, with junipers grazed as high as a deer could reach. Cliffrose (*Cowania mexicana*) in particular showed damage. The browsing was so heavy that mast supplies for turkeys were thought to be threatened.

3. The Hay Lake area of Anderson Mesa on the Coconino National Forest was of special interest to Goldman and the Coconino National Forest's supervisor, Edward G. Miller. Here, the committee noted heavy browsing of junipers, rabbitbrush, snakeweed, gooseberry (*Ribes* spp.), antelope-weed (*Eriogonum* spp.), and skunkbush sumac (*Rhus trilobata*). Four pronghorn stomachs had been collected, which showed that antelope did not eat grass but did feed on the junipers or cedars. Not wanting to kill antelope, the committee supported the trapping and translocation program recently initiated.

4. The committee was told elk now ranged over 300,000 acres of the Sitgreaves National Forest and south to the Mogollon Rim. The elk were shown to favor canyon habitats, with heavy use and damage observed on willows, cottonwoods, and dogwoods. Grass in the intervening pine forests was in short supply. Elk were also reportedly invading wet meadows and fields of rye and other small grains on private land. Although a hunt was not specifically recommended, the committee recommended that a limit on elk numbers be considered.

5. The week of April 21–26 was spent evaluating the 749,628-acre Blue Range Preserve. Some 510,000 acres of the preserve remained closed after the rest had been opened to deer hunting in 1928. Forage conditions were variable and the committee found bear sign and sighted a few elk and wild turkey. Most of the refuge, especially the steeper slopes, was occupied by whitetails, with mule deer restricted to more open areas.

Elk damage to alligator-bark juniper and other trees along Clear Creek on the Coconino National Forest in April 1931. The man is believed to be Edward A. Goldman. Photo by Andrew Nichol. (Governor's Files, Arizona State Library, Archives and Public Records, History and Archives Division)

Rangers and agency representatives preparing for a group deer survey and census on the Kaibab in 1924. Group surveys were the method by which the Forest Service sold its game management programs, and were used to get the department to recommend deer hunt seasons designed to protect the national forest's vegetation. (AGFD files)

> Although much of the heavy browse use was due to livestock grazing, most of the present over-cropping was attributed to too many deer, with conspicuous "browse lines" and heavy crop depredations reported along Blue River.

Goldman, a senior biologist with the Biological Survey, filed a separate report than the rest of the committee, in which he recognized the need for more stringent measures. Goldman did not believe white-tailed deer needed refuge protection as a general rule, and thought such designations in southern Arizona's mountain "islands" unnecessary.[3] He wanted instead to open the refuges to deer hunting, with the bag limit in the Catalina Mountains and in the Blue Range to include both bucks and does, even hesitantly recommending that lion control be limited to the protection of livestock in these ranges. Goldman also differed from the committee in his thinking that the Coconino-Yavapai refuge should be opened to the hunting of buck mule deer, with the removal of some doe deer also considered. He did agree that the refuge should remain closed to the taking of turkey and antelope.

The antelope situation at Hay Lake was a surprise to Goldman (1931a–c). The estimated population of 2,500 to 3,500 head then present represented a considerable increase over his estimate of 200 animals, made when he worked in this area in 1913. Goldman considered Anderson Mesa's browse conditions a cause for serious concern, while noting that the heavy use occurred on some junipers and not others. Although he encouraged the trapping and release of wild antelope over bottle-fed babies, Goldman wondered if this species could ever be successfully trapped. He therefore reluctantly recommended that some antelope be killed, knowing such action would be unpopular with the state and the

[3] Hence, Goldman preceded Weldon Heald and others in the use of the "island" term to describe the vegetation of southern Arizona's mountain ranges.

public. Goldman also wanted Arizona's elk herd limited to 1,000 head. He considered the present population, estimated at several thousand, to be too many. He therefore recommended a 10-day fall elk hunt with a bag limit of one bull and one cow elk, provided the hunt were carefully monitored.

Another participant filing a separate evaluation was Nichol (1931), who with Goldman was then the most astute biologist in the Southwest. Nichol did not think he or the university should be a signatory to a report containing conflicting recommendations from government agencies. Backing up his conclusions with 34 photos of browse conditions, Nichol considered the overbrowsing on the Coconino-Yavapai refuge tragic and the area in need of better management. He favored opening an antelope season on Anderson Mesa, as he considered the animals numerous enough to hunt even though the range situation was not yet critical. He also disagreed with the committee regarding the elk herd on the Sitgreaves National Forest, considering the summer range there to be in critical condition and the elk population already saturated and causing serious depredation problems. As for the Blue Range, he thought the refuge needed more than hunters to rectify abuse by too many cattle in the past and too many deer at present. Nonetheless, he too was reluctant to let up on lions, lest these predators become out of control.

The governor's response was to have State Game Warden Alfred Mann appoint Joe Prochaska as the department's game expert on November 13, 1931, at a salary of $240 a month. Neither Mann nor Prochaska, a former State Game Warden, were popular with the AGPA. The next month, a reconstituted commission unanimously voted to accept Mann's resignation and terminate Prochaska's position.

As for the Kaibab National Forest supervisor, Walter Mann, he and five deputy wardens conducted another deer survey in January 1932. They estimated 14,700 deer, as opposed to 20,000 in 1931 and between 20,000 and 30,000 in 1930. At least some of the decline in these rough estimates appears to have been due to poor fawn recruitment. Although their reports of a deer decline resulted in demands for a resumption of predator control, it also eased the need for a return to a high deer harvest. As a result, coyote trapping by private parties was encouraged and Goldman softened his stance toward the value of lions as deer-population regulators—a change in attitude perhaps influenced by his disagreements with Vorhies, Rasmussen, and other academics over the desirability of killing predators during times of browse overuse (Young 2002).

In contrast to the National Park Service, which wanted all hunting on the Kaibab to stop, the Forest Service and Game and Fish Department agreed on a compromise hunt that resulted in only 640 deer being killed during the 1932 season. By having the foresight to see past his temporary problems with Hunt and the commission, Mann was able to maintain some semblance of cooperation with all of the committee representatives, including the AGPA, the university, and the Game and Fish Department. Besides, it was now beginning to look as if the problem of too many deer might be lessening.

Commission actions throughout the remainder of 1932 were conservative and uncontroversial. The Forest Service was no longer in a panic over serious range damage and State Game Warden Shelby Lewis made no major changes in the deer season. The

Forest Service personnel conducting a deer hunt check station on the Gila National Forest, ca. 1931. The Forest Service used check stations on the Kaibab and elsewhere to determine the condition of the game and collect hunt data used in making future hunt recommendations. (Arizona Historical Society/Tucson, Fred Winn Collection, #17200, MS0875, Box 9, Folder 84)

same ennui prevented any major boundary changes in the state's refuges. Nor was any new action taken regarding pronghorn, as the commission voted to continue heretofore unsuccessful attempts at trapping excess animals rather than authorize a hunt.

In November 1932, Hunt was voted out of office and the AGPA set about forming a newly constituted commission that would de-politicize the department and assume a more professional role when it came to the Kaibab and other deer management matters. And, the overpopulation crisis appeared to be waning. In 1933, the deer population on the Kaibab was estimated to have shrunk to 16,000 head. The deer management plan authored by the national forest and state Game and Fish Department received support at the regional and Washington levels. For its part, the National Park Service had adopted a policy that closed Grand Canyon National Park to livestock grazing and predator control while going along with the cooperative hunt program outside its borders.

In June 1933, Walter Mann, Shoemaker, Goldman, Shantz, and Nichol again visited the Kaibab with State Game Warden Lewis. They found lower fawn recruitment and milder winters had resulted in a drop in deer numbers and additional browse recovery. The result was a recommendation for continued hunting with no resumption of predator control. The fall harvest was 820 deer, with the deer population in 1934 being estimated at 16,500—a slight increase over the previous year. That the surveys had shown as many deer present as the previous year justified continued hunting. The range still needed relief, despite the progress being made. By now, the national park had abandoned its policy of promoting a "deer spectacle," and the Kaibab was viewed as a cooperative wildlife management success. Supervisor Mann's dedication and patience had paid off.

Progress on Many Fronts

Game conditions elsewhere also appeared to be improving, at least as far as irruptions and the threat of die-offs was concerned. Deer numbers appeared to be stable or increasing without harming the range. In 1933, the commission opened the Blue Range Game Preserve, Copper Basin State Game Refuge, and Coconino-Yavapai Refuge to deer hunting, while keeping the turkey season in these areas closed. Still other refuges were opened to deer hunting in 1934, as white-tailed deer were now considered to be less in need of protection. Turkeys were still a concern, however, and although the Coconino-Yavapai Refuge was opened to turkey hunting in 1934, the bag limit was reduced to one.

The commission's cautious nature was very much evident in 1934, with antelope and elk hunts discussed but no action taken other than the decision that antelope capture efforts should continue. After opening a javelina season for the fall of 1934, the commission rescinded its order and again closed the state to the taking of peccaries. Cooperation and game protection remained the order of the day. That same year, the commission vigorously supported Supervisor Mann's and State Game Warden Lewis's request to oppose an attempt by Utah's governor, Jacob Blood, to have the Forest Service allow 8,000 cattle on the Kaibab. There already were 15,000 deer, 2,400 sheep, and 700 cattle present. In an unprecedented show of unity, this opposition was also vigorously supported by Wid Raudenbaugh and other members of the Flagstaff Game Protective Association.

Meanwhile, the deer range on the Kaibab showed continued improvement, with cliffrose plants coming back nicely. The estimated population in 1935 was upped to 17,000 deer—13,000 on the West Range and 4,000 on the East Range—an increase attributed to another mild winter and good carryover cancelling out low fawn recruitment. The Forest Service had by now adopted a system of winter deer counts and browse survey procedures to be continued each year—a methodology that, when combined with hunter check stations, was increasingly regarded as a prescription for good deer management. Mann's program of joint surveys and cooperative deer hunt regulations was succeeding and would be adopted by the state, if only it could afford such a program.

Finally, after several meetings and much discussion, the commission authorized an elk hunt on September 19, 1935. The hunt took place two months later on Armistice Day and ran through November 15. A principal justification for the hunt was to obtain a more balanced bull:cow ratio, so only bulls would be harvested. Open to both residents who purchased a $15 permit and nonresidents with a $25 permit, the hunt area was south of the Atchison, Topeka and Santa Fe Railway, west of Arizona Highway 77, and east of the Winslow-Long Valley Road, with the Mogollon Rim serving as the southern boundary. Because most of the hunting would be on the Sitgreaves National Forest, the commission directed the department to enter into a cooperative agreement with the regional forester to ensure the Forest Service's cooperation and enforcement assistance.

Other commission actions, increasingly influenced by Commissioner Charles Beach, included closing most of southern Arizona to the taking of bear and band-tailed pigeons. Although opening the mule deer season in southern Arizona was discussed, along with a javelina hunt, the commission again opted for a wait-and-see attitude.

Deer trap on the Kaibab for capturing and translocating surplus deer to areas deemed underpopulated. (AGFD files)

Actions in 1936 included a renewal of a special-permit elk season justified by a continued imbalance of bulls and personal property damage complaints. And although 15 new game refuges comprising 59,047 acres were established, several game preserves on the national forests were abolished. One other, Big Lake, was "re-established" as a 2,600-acre federal waterfowl refuge.

In the meantime, the department continued to trap and transplant deer from the Kaibab and affirm its wildlife management authority. Bull elk permits were issued out of the Phoenix office, and hunters were required to check out at check stations located at Long Valley, Heber, Wallace, or Maine—not all of which were Forest Service ranger stations. The hunt area was expanded to include areas north of Highway 66 east of the Williams-Grand Canyon Highway, but Cabin Draw Refuge remained closed to hunting, along with the San Francisco Peaks, Gentry, and Long Valley refuges.

Frustrated by the Game and Fish Department's inability to field enough personnel for an intensive survey of the bighorn sheep population in the Catalina Mountains, Coronado National Forest Supervisor Fred Winn obtained Works Progress Administration funding to conduct a sheep census using only Forest Service personnel and a Biological Survey trapper named Bee Adkins. Surveying some 185,625 acres of presumed bighorn habitat on foot and horseback, the party classified 81 sheep out of an estimated population of 102. They attributed what they deemed to be a catastrophic reduction from an original population of 1,000 animals to be due to poaching and large numbers of lions and eagles.[4]

Meanwhile, another federal-state game management issue was now developing—this one involving the Biological Survey rather than the Forest Service. In September 1937, the commission directed State Game Warden Lewis to take issue with the Biological Survey's plans to establish mountain sheep refuges in western Arizona and requested that all further surveys and investigations of such areas be conducted with a department

[4]This survey generated a great deal of interest from the Boy Scouts and AGPA and was followed by another bighorn survey in 1941 sponsored by the Audubon Society. Participants included Andrew Nichol, Ted Knipe, Dr. Charles Vorhies, and Phil Welles, who came to pretty much the same conclusions as Winn—the sheep were disappearing as the result of poaching and predation along with competition with feral goats near Thimble Peak.

representative present. Although it went on record as favoring refuges for mountain sheep, the commission wanted all interested parties included before legislative action was taken. Also causing concern was Lewis's transmittal to the commission of correspondence supporting federal legislation establishing several Forest Service refuges and a Boulder Canyon National Wildlife Refuge.

In response, the Game and Fish Commission established Boulder Canyon as a state game refuge in January 1938, a preemptive response to the federal government's increasing role as a protector of desert habitats and wildlife in western Arizona—a role recently affirmed by the creation of Organ Pipe Cactus National Monument by executive order in 1937 and the transfer of its lands to the National Park Service. Also earning strong opposition from the commission was a Forest Service proposal for a federal refuge that would take in portions of the Coconino, Sitgreaves, and Tonto national forests. Another refuge proposal seen as an infringement on states' rights—one that was agreed to out of a desire for state-federal cooperation—was a Bill Williams federal-state refuge south of Williams. The problem was that even though conservationists were increasingly convinced of the need for wildlife protection, the state had neither the resources nor the expertise to manage large parcels of land.

The regional office of the Biological Survey, having worked closely with the state on predator- and rodent-control issues, bolstered that arrangement in 1938 by asking the department to assist in the prosecution of a federal bighorn sheep case against five men, assistance the commission vigorously endorsed. Other cooperative actions were more begrudgingly taken and assisted by the AGPA, which worked with both agencies. The commission initially took no action on an invitation to represent the state's wildlife on the newly formed Taylor Grazing Boards, but later relented and recommended Vorhies and J. B. Edwards as grazing-district representatives for wildlife. Nonetheless, the commission went on record opposing any federal withdrawals of federal game refuges in Yuma and Pima counties as an intrusion into the state's wildlife and land laws—an action similar to a memorial passed by the legislature.

Better Relations

State-federal relations took an enormous turn for the better in March 1939, when the legislature authorized, and the governor signed, Bill 119, making Arizona a cooperating participant in the Pittman-Robertson Act. Agreed to by the commission the same year, the provisions of the Federal Aid in Wildlife Restoration Act ensured that the department would have the financial resources to hire biologists and otherwise participate in big game management programs on a par with federal agencies. No longer would the state have to take a backseat to the Forest Service or other agencies when it came to developing a game management program. Rather, the state would now take the lead as per its constitutional mandate.

Moreover, with the hiring of game experts such as Nichol and Kartchner, the department could now take a proactive stance when it came to big game management. As a result, the commission opened a season on javelina in select counties and rescinded the order closing the season on black-tailed (mule) deer, turkey, and bear south of the

Gila River. The department entered into a new cooperative agreement with the Kaibab National Forest, and State Game Warden William Sawtelle was directed to cooperate with the Forest Service in an antelope survey to determine the feasibility of a short open season. The department was also, if approved by the attorney general, instructed to have all deer hunters purchase an 80-cent deer tag, thereby providing a sampling frame for determining deer harvest numbers for the first time. The two-bird bag limit on turkeys was reinstated and a special three-zone elk hunt was authorized that included the first "any-elk" permits. Special bow and arrow areas were also established for deer, bear, and turkey.

Deer hunting on the Kaibab was now regarded as a sport rather than an instrument for culling. Not only was the browsing crisis over, the winter survey for 1938 had indicated a reduced population of 15,000, as estimated by Forest Service and National Park Service survey crews. The state representative, Deputy Warden Edwards, was even more conservative, stridently insisting that only 12,000 deer were present. Only 692 deer had been harvested that year and it was believed the Kaibab could support more deer. And, despite Jack Butler's having killed 22 lions during the year, the estimated number of deer during the winter of 1938–39 was estimated to be a precise 15,097 head. Another 693 deer were killed in 1939—302 of them antlerless animals.

In March 1940, Kartchner was appointed acting State Game Warden, and at the commission's direction began asserting the department's role as the state's game manager. Kartchner, a 17-year veteran with the Forest Service, and a native Arizonan, was uniquely qualified to assert the state's newfound authority over wildlife matters. That same month, he and the commission had refused to enter into joint management agreements with the Forest Service and newly formed US Fish and Wildlife Service for failing to adequately recognize the state's authority over wildlife on federal lands.

Furthermore, Kartchner demanded the Predator and Rodent Control branch send two coyote trappers and one lion hunter to the Kaibab, as he was convinced there were now no more than 5,000 deer on the plateau. Playing hardball, Kartchner pressed the commission's position in Washington, receiving in response a letter from Secretary of the Interior Harold L. Ickes assuring him that the state's recommendations would not be ignored.

On July 15, 1940, the commission approved a 1,000-permit deer hunt on the Kaibab, the applications to be made to the Forest Service office at Williams along with a $1.50 government fee. Each permit holder would be entitled to one buck and one doe. The season would be from October 25 to November 15, 1940. Both agencies agreed the herd should be increased and that these regulations would allow for more deer. The department and Forest Service also agreed predators were holding the Kaibab deer herd down, and that the Predator and Rodent Control should send lion hunters up there. Finally too, after much prodding and the failure of the Forest Service to capture antelope, the commission ordered that 75 "old" buck antelope be taken during a controlled hunt in April 1941, with the AGPA to be consulted regarding the fee and other details.

Much credit must go to Walter Mann (1941), supervisor of the Kaibab National Forest, who remained confident in state cooperation through even the worst setbacks of the Hunt administration. Mann, encouraged by the role played by the Arizona Game Protective Association and Arizona Game and Fish Commission, continued to cooperate with the state, even to the point of foregoing management plans worked out with his supervisors and the investigative committees he so carefully nurtured. As the instigator of winter deer surveys and cooperative field investigations, Mann continued to believe the state would eventually assume the role of cooperatively managing the Kaibab's deer herd within a jointly determined carrying capacity. This in turn allowed the Forest Service to accomplish its range-management objectives without jeopardizing its status as the Southwest's preeminent federal land management agency.

By the beginning of 1941, the department was well on its way to fulfilling its wildlife management responsibilities. An annual audit had been passed with "flying colors," and the agency's financial health was in the best shape in years, thanks to the Federal-Aid program. Gov. Sidney P. Osborn was appointing commissioners who were more knowledgeable about wildlife while still able to manage a growing budget. Department organization was revised and put on a more professional basis, with all employees, including those in the new Federal-Aid Division, working exclusively under State Game Warden Kartchner. Hunt seasons were expanded and standardized, with a statewide javelina season for both firearm and archery hunters, a 400-permit antelope hunt, and a north- and south-zone deer season. A statewide elk season was approved for bulls only, except on Indian reservations and in the Hualapai Mountains. The cost of an elk permit was reduced to $10 for both residents and nonresidents and no limit was set on the number of hunters. All of these actions increased revenue and provided the increased funding needed to more intensely manage big game populations.

The role of managing deer and other big game species on the national forests was of course played on a bigger stage than Arizona or even the Southwest. Although issues involving range conditions on the national forests would remain of utmost importance in determining whether the state was capable of managing large herbivores, it was now clear Arizona could and would cooperate to a degree that allowed the Forest Service to attain its habitat management objectives.

The Forest Service would continue to conduct surveys, maintain population estimates, and collect harvest figures for several more years, but such statistics would soon be derived almost entirely from Arizona Game and Fish Department biologists. More and more, the department and commission would determine the direction of big game management both off and on the forests. Browse conditions and habitat condition were destined to again become issues, particularly in regards to deer and elk, but there was now no doubt that managing wildlife on the national forests would be a cooperative effort under the purview of the Arizona Game and Fish Commission. Given the many variables, and the imprecise survey data involved, the Kaibab would remain more a political case history than an ecological study. What the Kaibab lesson did was set the stage for a federal-state cooperation strategy for resolving wildlife management problems with the state retaining its constitutional authority over big game populations.

CLEANING UP THE VARMINTS

David E. Brown

By the time the new Arizona Game and Fish Commission took office in 1929, the Predator and Rodent Control Branch of the US Biological Survey was a force to be reckoned with. Victory had been declared over the wolf and the lion. The grizzly had been nearly extirpated from Arizona. Whatever resident jaguars may have been present were thought to have been eliminated. Black bears had been reduced in numbers. The agency's attention was now primarily focused on the coyote and such rodent pests as porcupines, prairie dogs, gophers, and kangaroo rats, along with jackrabbits.

As attention turned to these animals, poisons and other chemical predacides became weapons of choice. That strychnine was not used more for wolves and lions was only due to the objections of lion hunters and other houndsmen. Much progress had been made in the use of poison to eliminate prairie dogs. The black-tailed species (*Cynomys ludovicianus*) was thought to have been completely removed from Cochise, Graham, and Greenlee counties. It was thought to be just a matter of determination, funding, and time until the state became prairie-dog free.

The early PARC administrators at the regional and national levels—Stanley Young, Stokley Ligon, and Mark Musgrave—were competent administrators and accomplished politicians (Brown 1983; Robinson 2005). They and other PARC personnel pushed their agency's agenda at county fairs, stockgrowers conventions, 4-H Club events, and sportsmen's meetings, giving presentations that demonstrated their accomplishments and generated support for their government-funded programs. The most important contacts were one-on-one conversations with individual ranchers, farmers, and government officials about how much money could be saved by eliminating predators and rodents.

With attention turning toward coyotes and rodent pests, chemical compounds developed at the PARC's Denver research laboratory were increasingly intended to replace the trap and the hound—a decision that caused several of the agency's lion hunters to leave the service. In future years, the use of poisons would lead to excesses and the public would decide to rein in the PARC. However, during the 1930s the agency's only enemies were budget-cutting bureaucrats, disgruntled bounty hunters, a few fur trappers, and a handful of academics, people who were beginning to question the rationale of paying mammal-control agents to remove rodents after other agents had removed the predators that preyed upon them.

Sportsmen and the newly created Arizona Game and Fish Commission were also dissatisfied with PARC, but for a different reason. Believing predator control essential to game recovery, the commission wanted the same measure of relief to be provided for game animals as for livestock. The list of PARC cooperators, which included county agricultural agents, the Arizona Agricultural Extension Service, US Forest Service, Indian Service, Farm Bureau, Arizona Woolgrowers Association, Arizona Cattlegrowers Association, irrigation districts, and numerous farmers and ranchers, was continually expanded. Yet neither the Arizona Game Protective Association nor the Arizona Game and Fish

Poison was increasingly used in the 1920s. An early PARC hunter kit consisting of a Number 4 Newhouse trap (left), dies for molding suet cubes, and a lidded can for carrying strychnine-treated baits. The rope and pack frame were used to access remote den sites and other baiting stations. (US Fish and Wildlife Service, from Brown 1983)

Department were major partners at this time, as they had no real money to contribute to a predator-control program designed primarily to increase game animals. Nor did the commission have much interest in rodents and jackrabbits, despite these nuisance animals being resident species under state jurisdiction.

Poisoning prairie dogs, kangaroo rats, porcupines, gophers, and jackrabbits was already well underway. All previous records had been broken during fiscal year 1928, when the PARC's six mammal-control agents and 4,018 cooperators treated 717,861 acres with 119,133 pounds of poisoned bait and distributed 1,894 pounds of poison gas to kill an estimated five million rodents in Arizona—an area 47% greater than the previous year.

The major villain in this "Systematic War on Prairie Dogs and Ground Squirrels" was now the Zuni or Gunnison's prairie dog (*Cynomys gunnisoni*). Some 251,839 acres of prairie-dog towns had been treated on the Apache, Coconino, and Tusayan national forests and the Hualapai Indian Reservation. Appropriations were requested to be doubled so as to treat 321,687 acres of untreated land plus a million acres on Indian reservations, with the hope of eliminating prairie dogs from Gila and Mohave counties within the year. Such an expenditure was justified in that exclosure studies had shown prairie dogs "destroyed" from 50% to 83% of the available grass and caused erosion (cattle-grazed grass not being considered "destroyed" and not contributing to erosion) (Gilchrist 1928). Plans called for dividing the state into three rodent-control districts under Everett Mercer[1]

[1]Everett Mercer had been removing prairie dogs and other rodents in Arizona since 1923 and was destined to become PARC state supervisor after Donald Gilchrist, just as Gilchrist had taken over the reins from Mark Musgrave.

and treating four million acres of prairie-dog towns in Apache, Navajo, Coconino, and Yavapai counties (Gilchrist 1929).

Plans for fiscal year 1929 were even more ambitious, with an accelerated attempt to remove even more prairie dogs, as well as pack rats, cotton rats, and other species—a total treatment involving 643,941 "rodent-infested" acres (Mercer 1929). By year's end, Mohave County had been declared cleaned of prairie dogs, with sizeable areas of Apache, Coconino, and Tusayan national forests treated at a cost of eight cents per acre. The weapons employed were strychnine, thallium, and poison gas, with shooting used to get those animals that learned to avoid the poison bait or escaped gassing (Gilchrist 1929).

With so much progress being made against prairie dogs, pocket gophers were now becoming the primary PARC target, giving rise to the derogatory term "gopher-chokers" ("rat-killers" was another one) for the agency's mammal-control agents. Whatever the term, some 2,189 farm and ranch cooperators signed up for gopher control during fiscal year 1928–29, using 7,992 pounds of poisoned sweet potatoes and 4,292 gopher traps in an effort that involved every county in the state (Gilchrist 1929).

The next year's program was even more ambitious, with 453,079 acres being treated, 72,878 pounds of poison bait distributed, and 11,522 pounds of poison gas used. The number of gopher traps in use climbed to 10,900. Nor were prairie dogs ignored: Some 255,819 acres of prairie-dog towns were poisoned. The program now expanded to the Apache Indian Reservation at the invitation of the Indian Service. All in all, an estimated 3,600,000 rodents were eradicated during 1929–30, with prairie dogs reported removed from 1,831,703 acres of Arizona and jackrabbits from 676,240 acres (Gilchrist 1930).

Cooperators now numbered more than 10,000, and the PARC's agents were hard-pressed to instruct and supervise all of the farmers who had been issued poison. Some of the agents were particularly distressed at the failure of dry-land farmers adjacent to the national forests to pre-bait prairie dogs, as poison grain put out directly often resulted in some of the rodents rejecting the treated grain and refusing to take any more bait (Gilchrist 1930).

In 1929, livestock losses were considered much reduced and big game numbers on the increase, with "overpopulations" of deer in such places as the South Rim of the Grand Canyon, the Sycamore Canyon-Yavapai Game Refuge, and the Pinaleño Mountains. And although academics including Charles Vorhies and Walter Taylor (1933) were beginning to question the relationships between rodent and jackrabbit irruptions, grazing practices, and coyote control, Taylor (1935a) was observing that porcupine "work" tended to be concentrated in areas where lions had been much reduced or eliminated. Few if any Arizonans doubted that predator control was a desirable, even necessary, facet of game management.

Concerned about such game species as antelope and deer, especially mule deer on the Kaibab, the newly formed Arizona Game and Fish Commission was very much in favor of predator control. Despite the department's limited budget, the commission ordered State Game Warden Robert Bayless to employ seven men recommended by former PARC supervisor Musgrave to engage in predatory-animal control work as state cooperators.

Bear trap in Arizona's Blue Wilderness. Government hunters were not the only enemies of grizzly and black bears in Arizona during the 1920s and 1930s. Homesteaders and ranchers used homemade bear traps such as this one to remove bears, whether they actually had killed stock or not. (From Brown 1985, provided by Jim Brooks and John Snyder, Arizona Game and Fish Department)

Hence, the Bayless (1930) administration set about actively cooperating with the PARC, the Forest Service, and the AGPA in a nascent program by which seven trappers were paid $1,045 to take 58 predators, including 11 mountain lions, during the summer of 1930. This effort abruptly ceased the following year, when Gov. George Hunt dismissed Bayless and removed two of the three commissioners, during which time the department was subject to severe personnel cuts and a greatly reduced budget.

Although the new game code treated both species of bears as game animals and provided them with a closed season, it was by now almost too late for the grizzly, and black bears had already disappeared from some of the more marginal mountain ranges such as the Baboquivaris and the Bradshaws. The Forest Service estimated only 10 grizzlies remained in Arizona's national forests. Musgrave (1928) thought this number too optimistic, claiming to know of only one—an animal ranging from the New Mexico line around Blue, Arizona, over into the White Mountains south and east of McNary. Nonetheless, pressure to manage bears, not just kill them, increased, and only six bears were taken by the PARC in Arizona during fiscal year 1928–29.

Moreover, the PARC appeared to have done an about-face in regards to the district's attitude toward bears. In an article in the September 1930 issue of *Wildlife Sportsman*, Arizona district Supervisor Donald Gilchrist stated:

> The Biological Survey finds that very few bear are stock killers, and are doing all that is possible to discourage the killing of them. Only bear that are known

> to be killers are taken, the hunter taking them being required to have an affidavit signed by three stockmen that know of the particular bear in question. Hunters are given no credit for taking even a stock killing bear, and when such a killer is apprehended, he must be taken in accordance with the provisions found in the State Game Code.

Many rank-and-file PARC hunters disagreed with Gilchrist's stated position when it came to bears, and there was general dissatisfaction among them with the law requiring a depredation permit to take one. Not surprisingly, this same attitude was reflected in the ranchers. "There is an undercurrent of feeling among stockmen that bear should be taken off the protected list, due to their resentment of being forced to first secure a permit from the State Game and Fish Department" (Gatlin 1934). Given their allegiance to the stock-raisers, and the commission's only recent and tepid involvement in predator control, the PARC began to underreport the number of bears taken, if not by their men, then by their stockmen cooperators. Only five bears were reportedly taken by the PARC in Arizona in 1929–30. The PARC reported only that bears were on the increase in the early 1930s (Brown 1985).

In his September 1930 statement in *Wildlife Sportsman*, Gilchrist went on to say the PARC would henceforth use strychnine only in country where sheep and goats were pastured or "where it is not possible to stop severe losses of livestock, game or game birds, rapidly enough by means of traps. Strychnine would not be placed in mountainous countries where lion dogs or fur bearers would be endangered." Such a ban did not of course apply to rodent control, which was considered a separate division within the Arizona district of PARC.

Despite the stated limits on strychnine use, the war against wolves, lions, coyotes, and bobcats continued. Wolves proved to be both persistent and frustrating. Gilchrist reported no fewer than 17 lobos being taken in Arizona in fiscal year 1929–30, 13 by PARC hunters and one by a state hunter, with another three claimed to have been killed with poison but irretrievable (Gilchrist 1930). Of the 14 wolf carcasses accounted for, 12 were poisoned and two were caught in steel traps. All of the wolves taken but one, which was not verified as a wolf, were killed within 50 miles of the border, with William Knibbe catching five in one night. Although none was caught, a pack of wolves was also reported to be working the Black River portion of the San Carlos Indian Reservation (Gilchrist 1930).

The annual report for 1931 lists the taking of "a few stray wolves … from Mexico" and an animal finally trapped in the Black River area (Foster 1931). Funding was becoming a problem, as the Depression years impacted congressional appropriations. Not all of the areas reporting significant losses could be visited and not all requests for assistance answered. Nonetheless, the "border patrol" was kept intact and eight wolves were killed in fiscal year 1931–32, despite the fact that only $33,043 was available for salaries. Losses claimed due to wolves included 43 calves, 4 deer, 4 steers, and 2 chickens (Foster 1932).

And so it went, with four wolves taken in 1932–33 and three in 1933–34 (Foster 1933a, 1934). State hunters under PARC supervision now accounted for some of the kills. The Arizona district could now field only three hunters in any given month, despite the losses due to wolves in 1932–33 being estimated at $222,510, of which $45,836 was due to losses of cattle. With total operating costs reduced to less than $21,000 per year, of which $17,469 went for salaries, predatory-animal work in Arizona faced its most crucial period in the history of the PARC, with the result that, "Due to the shortage of funds ... we could not maintain the air-tight patrol [against wolves] which we formerly kept on the border" (Foster 1934).

It is a testimony to changing times that this photograph of dead prairie dogs was used to illustrate the PARC's annual reports on rodent control activities during the late 1920s and early 1930s. (US Biological Survey)

Rodent control also suffered during the early Depression years. Congress appropriated only $37,500 in 1931 for rodent control in Arizona—an amount somewhat alleviated by the Arizona State Legislature's appropriation of $15,000 for fiscal years 1931–32 and 1932–33 to the University of Arizona Extension Service, to be used to eradicate injurious rodents in cooperation with the Biological Survey on a dollar-for-dollar basis. The legislature made similar appropriations of $15,000 a year to the Livestock Sanitary Board to be cooperatively used for the destruction of predatory animals. These combined appropriations allowed the PARC to distribute 59,664 pounds of poison on 267,504 acres in 1931, increasing the acreage to 428,715 acres in 1932 and then having to cut back to 372,590 acres in 1933 (Gilchrist 1931, 1932, 1933). Animals killed ranged from coyotes and prairie dogs to porcupines to chipmunks.

In 1933, federal funding dropped to $9,885.30, and the PARC was able to treat only 193,050 acres with 11,414 pounds of poison. The major emphasis was now on pocket gophers, rabbits, and kangaroo rats, with most of the porcupines killed by tracking in snow rather than poison. Only three mammal-control agents were kept on the payroll. The men were stationed in Mesa, Sulphur Springs Valley, and Yuma. An interesting aside was the ocelot's being added to the state's list of predatory animals in 1933 on the basis of one of these animals having been trapped by one of the PARC's agents (Foster 1933a).

Additional funding and help was realized in 1934 as money continued to become available to PARC from the states and emergency funds. These additional appropriations allowed the PARC to poison rodents on 761,696 acres—a new record. Some 337,564 acres of this total were federal lands, mostly national forests, with the remainder being Indian reservations belonging to the Navajo, Hualapai, and San Carlos Apache peoples. As a result of this additional funding, PARC agents now supervised 82 people, including Indian and non-Indian personnel of the Civilian Conservation Corps. Although prairie dogs and other rodents received the most attention in 1934–35, some 8,997 tree stations were treated with poison to kill porcupines, with another 966 of these animals trailed down and shot (Foster 1935).

Rodent-control measures again expanded in fiscal year 1935–36. PARC foremen were paid by both state and federal funds to supervise crews of the Works Progress Administration and Civilian Conservation Corps. As before, much of the emphasis was on removing prairie dogs and porcupines from the Coconino, Kaibab, and Prescott national forests. The Papago and Salt River Indian reservations joined the list of cooperators. Poisoning rodents was nonetheless proving unpopular with some Native Americans. Certain Navajos and Apaches resisted the use of rodenticides to kill prairie dogs. PARC personnel now also recommended that jackrabbits be controlled through shooting and organized drives, due to exposed baits poisoning livestock, birds, etc. (Foster 1936). Concerns for furbearers also resulted in the commission's closing the season on river otters in 1936 for an indefinite period.

For whatever reason, expenditures for rodent control decreased to $22,751.67 in 1936–37, with more land treated for gophers than for any other species. No longer was the total eradication of prairie dogs expected in Coconino, Navajo, and Apache counties. The policy now was to locate remnant towns and poison those areas reported by stockmen who wanted them removed (Foster 1937).

This policy of treating areas on a complaint basis continued on into 1937–38, when the PARC budget again increased, this time to $28,111, for the treatment of 384,289 acres. Of these, 180,271 acres were occupied by kangaroo rats—now the featured species. Less than 95,000 acres were treated for prairie dogs, mostly remnant towns of *gunnisoni* in Apache, Coconino, Yavapai, and Navajo counties. Field activities now concentrated on dry farms within and adjacent to the national forests, the PARC having always maintained that its prime responsibility was the removal of noxious pests from federal land. An additional 1,000 acres of Forest Service land were also poisoned in a further effort to prevent porcupines from damaging ponderosa pine trees (Mercer 1938).

Although men working for the Works Progress Administration and Civilian Conservation Corps did not take predatory animals, their employment as rodent killers and the appropriation of emergency monies freed up funds for additional predator control. In 1935, the PARC put four men in the field each month and supervised 10 state hunters, with the result that seven wolves were caught that year, including five by state trappers and one by a private trapper. Coyotes and bobcats continued to constitute the majority of the carnivores taken. There remained some fussing over bears: The Arizona Game and Fish Commission was reluctant to give stockmen and the PARC carte blanche when it came to perceived stock killers, as both species of bear were protected in the state's game code. Nonetheless, the commission issued permits to four Clifton men to take stock-killing bears within the Blue Range Game Preserve in the spring of 1934.

A state appropriation bill passed in 1935 allocated $10,500 and $10,000 respectively for the next two fiscal years to be spent by the PARC in Arizona, provided the Biological Survey matched these monies with a like amount. One consequence of the PARC hunters' cavalier attitude toward bears and the commission's allowing for the taking of stock-killers was an increase in the number of bears taken. The most notorious of these was a two- to three-year-old grizzly taken in Strayhorse Canyon by PARC hunter Richard R. Miller on September 13, 1935. Although this animal was later photographed and verified as a grizzly by veteran hunter Bill "Kitt" Casto, and Miller had reported seeing sign of another young grizzly and an adult female, no mention was made of the event in PARC's annual report for 1935–36, Miller's grizzly being only one of 12 generic bears reported killed in Arizona that year.

Operating funds returned to more normal levels in 1936 with the continued help of state sources, allowing 10 federal and 10 state hunters to take to the field. Five wolves were taken that year and five the next, all Mexican lobos caught in steel traps along traditional wolf runs in Cochise and Santa Cruz counties. Prompt action on the part of the "border patrol" resulted in damage from wolves crossing the border being held to a minimum (Foster 1936; Mercer 1937). In 1938, PARC hunters took 2,344 predators of all kinds, and unsupervised cooperators took another 397 bobcats and coyotes. Three wolves were taken, including one along Black River in Greenlee County (Mercer 1938).

In the meantime, predator and rodent control continued to be primarily a PARC responsibility, with eight wolves taken in 1939 and complaints of "border-jumpers" on the rise:

> Wolves frequently entered the state from Mexico and were responsible for serious depredation on cattle … on one occasion it is known that eight of the animals were operating in Santa Cruz and Pima counties at the same time.

Reports indicated that these wolves "killed more than fifty head of cattle. During the fourth quarter, a single pair of wolves … in Santa Cruz county … killed 18 head of cattle and seriously injured 14 more before they were trapped" (Mercer 1939).

Nor was putting Arizona's last grizzly to rest an easy task. Although Miller's grizzly would be regarded as Arizona's "last grizzly" (Housholder 1966), my research disclosed others. While poring through old Federal-Aid reports, I found this startling entry by contract turkey biologist Lynn L. Hargrave: "One grizzly bear, an immature, was killed by Polk on the northwest slope of Mount Baldy, White Mountains, Fort Apache Indian Reservation during the summer of 1939."

Hargrave's (1939) report went on to state he had heard of other grizzlies having been run by dogs and seen that year, both on the reservation and in the adjacent Blue Range. The PARC trapper working on the reservation, B. B. Polk, had been credited with taking 103 black bears between May 5 and November 25, 1939, but the Biological Survey's state report for that year makes no mention of grizzlies on the reservation. Polk, who had been a state supervisor for the PARC in New Mexico, was intimately familiar with both bear species, and it appears Hargrave was calling attention to a situation he knew would not be formally reported by the PARC. This obscure report by a state biologist was therefore meant to become the historical record of Arizona's "final grizzly."

In July 1940, the Biological Survey became the US Fish and Wildlife Service. Fearful of other bureaucratic realignments and changes, State Game Warden Kenner Kartchner notified Arizona's congressional delegation that the National Park Service was attempting to wrest the north Kaibab away from the Forest Service and that, if successful, the Park Service would prohibit any predator-control work being done on the Kaibab. As it was, predator control on the Kaibab from 1930 to 1940 had been limited to private trappers and lion hunters. Kartchner wanted the Forest Service to retain the Kaibab as a multiple-use forest and invite PARC up there, as the estimated number of deer had dropped from 30,000 in 1930 to between 5,000 and 6,000 in 1940.

On signing onto the Pittman-Robertson Act, the Arizona Game and Fish Commission acquired its own federal money and began taking what we would today call a more "proactive" interest in predator control. Although predator control was considered eligible for Federal-Aid matching monies in 1939, the commission insisted that any funds so spent be used to benefit game species, the Kaibab deer herd then being a prime consideration. This action was in response to the Arizona Woolgrowers Association's passage of a resolution in 1938, requesting that an increase in the state's predator and rodent control appropriation be funded by a portion of hunting and fishing license revenue.

In taking this action, the commission noted it had contributed more money since January 1, 1938, for predator control than for the entire period from the beginning of 1932 to the end of 1937 and that all that could be afforded was being spent. Wanting more, commission chairman George Wrench directed all deputy wardens at the close of the hunting seasons to run trap lines in their respective districts as a means of controlling predators (an order that was rescinded on September 19, 1940).

The commission was now anxious to get into the forefront of predator control. Also in 1939, the commission ordered the Game and Fish Department to pay bounties to Junior Wildlife Federation members of $1 per coyote, bobcat, or fox, with bronze badges or pins going to those boys bagging the first 25 coyotes, 25 bobcats, or 25 foxes, the total amount not to exceed $500. State Game Warden William Sawtelle was also to give silver buttons or pins to the first 10 boys who took five predators each.

In a more practical order passed in 1939, the commission directed the State Game Warden to enter into cooperative agreements with various federal agencies regarding benefits to wildlife without jeopardizing the state's rights in any way. The legislature also passed a memorial requesting Congress to increase the annual appropriation for the PARC program from between $480,000 and $600,000 a year to a million dollars.

That same year, the legislature approved an arrangement by which the department would cooperate with the Biological Survey on Pittman-Robertson wildlife restoration projects, without specifically mentioning predator control as a permissible expense. Given the department's budget problems, and its reduction in the field force to eight men as of January 1, 1940, commission chairman Charles Beach directed the department to hire additional trappers only as funds permitted and allow the trappers to keep the hides.

In the summer of 1940, the department and Forest Service agreed that deer numbers on the Kaibab were below their potential due to lack of predator control. As a result, the PARC sent lion hunters and coyote trappers to the Kaibab to supplement the number of animals taken by lion guides and regular fur trappers. The agency took one lion, 113 coyotes, and 11 bobcats in one month (*Arizona Republic*, September 17, 1940, "Kaibab trapping resumed"). Whatever the reason, the estimated number of deer on the Kaibab the following spring was said to be 8,000 (*Arizona Republic*, April 3, 1941).

Forgoing its earlier attitude toward bears, and fearful of the stockmen's influence with the state legislature, the commission also opened a 30-day stock-killing bear season in 1940 at the request of the Arizona Cattlegrowers Association.

In the spring of 1941, Kartchner wanted the commission to sign a cooperative agreement with the Fish and Wildlife Service by which predatory-animal hunters and trappers would be employed on a one-to-one basis between the state and federal government, thus doubling the predator-control effort. The legislature's appropriations bill for 1941 prescribed that the state would spend $10,000 per year for predatory animal control and $10,000 per year for rodent control, with the assumption that at least some of the money would come out of the department's Pittman-Robertson fund.

Original label: "Lobo wolf killed with cyanide shell at Santa Rita in June 1947. This is the first lobo caught in many years, and the first ever caught by the (unnamed) Fish and Wildlife trapper in picture. Photo by Culley." (Data sets were provided by the Santa Rita Experimental Range Digital Database. Funding for the digitization of these data was provided by USDA Forest Service Rocky Mountain Research Station and the University of Arizona.)

By the onset of World War II, the PARC was faced with increasing scrutiny from academics and sportsmen regarding its actions both on and off the reservations. Native American tribes were complaining about the poisoning and killing of such game animals as prairie dogs and jackrabbits and opting out as cooperators. Fielding good agents had always been a problem, and with other work available, PARC district supervisors were now complaining about the difficulty of keeping qualified field men with proven reliability. Unlike the political situation in 1929, when the PARC was intent only on justifying and selling its control programs, the political issue in the 1940s was how to redirect and maintain an effective program (Mercer 1938–50).

Determined to take an active stance in managing more of the state's wildlife, the Arizona Game and Fish Department embarked on a Federal-Aid project to control depredating beavers. It hired trappers to trap and translocate these animals from irrigation canals and other problem areas, so as to maintain populations at acceptable levels. The pelts were turned in to the Phoenix office for public auction and the revenues went to the Game and Fish Fund. To oversee this program and other trapping projects, the department hired B. C. "Bobby" Fox as a fur conservation biologist in 1942, a position elevated to division status in 1944.

In the meantime, the PARC's arch-nemesis, the wolf, continued to show up. Wolves continued to enter the state from Mexico along traditional wolf runs between the Huachuca and Baboquivari mountain corridors, requiring two or three hunters to be kept in the border country to catch these invaders (Mercer 1940).

A single wolf was reported taken during 1941 near Green's Peak in Apache County. That, coupled with a two-year-old wolf trapped the succeeding year some 40 miles southwest of Winslow, suggested a small pack might still be holding out somewhere on the Apache Indian reservations. Seven wolves were also taken in southern Arizona that year, including a male and a litter of pups taken by the PARC's Bill Casto on Fort Huachuca (the female escaped back into Mexico). These were said to be the last native wolves whelped in Arizona (Mercer 1942). Nonetheless, five more wolves were caught in 1944 (Mercer 1944) and another five in 1945, including one on the Apache Indian Reservation, where a number of calves had been killed (Mercer 1945).

Only three wolves were taken in 1947, in addition to 5,846 other "major predators." The brunt of PARC's attention was now focused on coyotes, despite 46 bears also being trapped and 58 caught by dog packs, along with 46 mountain lions (Mercer 1947). Wolves also continued to be taken in southeastern Arizona each year in numbers of up to a dozen when bounty hunters and other cooperators again got into the game (Brown 1983). A mile-marker in wolf history was reached in 1950, when, "The fiscal year has passed without a single wolf being recorded by the cooperative hunting force. This has never happened before" (Mercer 1950). Although wolves would continue to infiltrate into Arizona from Mexico in ones and twos for another decade or so, and another one or two remained on the Apache Indian reservations, the day of the wolf in Arizona was finally over (Brown 1983).

Predator and rodent control continued to be a focal issue for both the PARC and the department after World War II. The trend toward using poisons and chemical predacides continued to accelerate due to a perceived increase in coyote numbers and dropping fur prices. So concerned was the department with coyotes and their impact on pronghorn antelope that the agency entered into an intensive cooperative effort with the Arizona Livestock Sanitary Board and Fish and Wildlife Service in 1945 to obtain maximum results at coyote control, the commission contributing more than $24,000 a year in Pittman-Robertson matching monies for use by the PARC:

With control emphasis now focused on coyotes and a bounty authorized on lions and wolves in 1947, the department's concerns regarding predator control centered on black bears and beavers, both of which were now thought to be making a comeback (Arizona Game and Fish Commission 1949). As for predator and rodent control, the PARC's interest was to continue to meet the needs of its ranching and farming constituencies using whatever means was most effective, with chemical control measures increasingly favored. The next chapter would begin in 1947 when the use of Compound 1080 become operational, the lion bounty was instituted, and coyotes were reported to be practically eliminated in several areas.

Mountain Lions, Bobcats, Wolves, and Coyotes Taken by Government Hunters
Source: PARC Annual Reports, 1942–46

	1942[a]	1943	1944	1945	1946
Lions	71	73	60	35	46
Bobcats	663	1,010	823	489	356
Wolves	5	5	5	4	3
Coyotes	4,357	6,390	6,080	6,647	5,340
Appropriated	$7,752.00	$8,600.48	$13,974.07	$19,100.14	$24,281.02

[a]Federal-Aid monies were not always appropriated during war years, when most of the $6,000 or so allocated to the states each year was spent on predator control. Surplus Pittman-Robertson monies became available after 1946.

JACK O'CONNOR AND THE ANTELOPE CRISIS ON ANDERSON MESA

David E. Brown

Pronghorn in Hermit Basin within Grand Canyon National Park, ca. 1929. Although it persisted for a number of years, this translocated population eventually dwindled away and disappeared. (National Park Service)

By the early 1920s, commercial hunters, subsistence hunting, and settlement had reduced Arizona's once-diverse pronghorn populations to a few remnants. Estimates made in 1922 by US Biological Survey predator hunters and biologists, along with those of the state's deputy wardens and other knowledgeable outdoorsmen, showed fewer than two-dozen populations remaining in Arizona. These were thought to total less than 700 animals (Nelson 1925).

Although this estimate was almost certainly too conservative, remaining antelope occupied only a fraction of their former habitat. Even rehabilitated rangelands remained unpopulated, as restocking vacant areas with pronghorn was thought to be difficult if not impossible. The skittish animals did poorly in confinement, and the first attempts to trap and hold adult antelope wound up maiming or killing the animals.

Early restocking efforts in Oregon and Nevada concentrated on kidnapping newborn fawns, raising the "kids" to adulthood, then releasing the captives in penned enclosures. One of these early transplant attempts included the shipment in 1924 of a dozen pen-reared fawns from northern Nevada to an enclosure in Hermit Basin, about halfway down into Arizona's Grand Canyon. The reasons for choosing this remote and rather unpromising-looking site, while difficult to understand today, were the lack of protected areas elsewhere and the fact that the Grand Canyon National Park was regularly patrolled and closed to livestock grazing.

Whatever the rationale, this attempt, like all early pen-raised pronghorn efforts (including one on the CCC Ranch in Avra Valley west of Tucson), resulted in failure. Captive-raised pronghorn not only succumbed to spells of inclement weather, but also proved susceptible to predators and accidents. Even after their release, half-tame pronghorn could be seen hanging around their former pens seeking handouts.

Although some other Western states continued to lose pronghorn populations during the 1920s, Arizona's remnant herds actually increased. As early as 1930, the newly created Arizona Game and Fish Commission was directing the Arizona Game and Fish

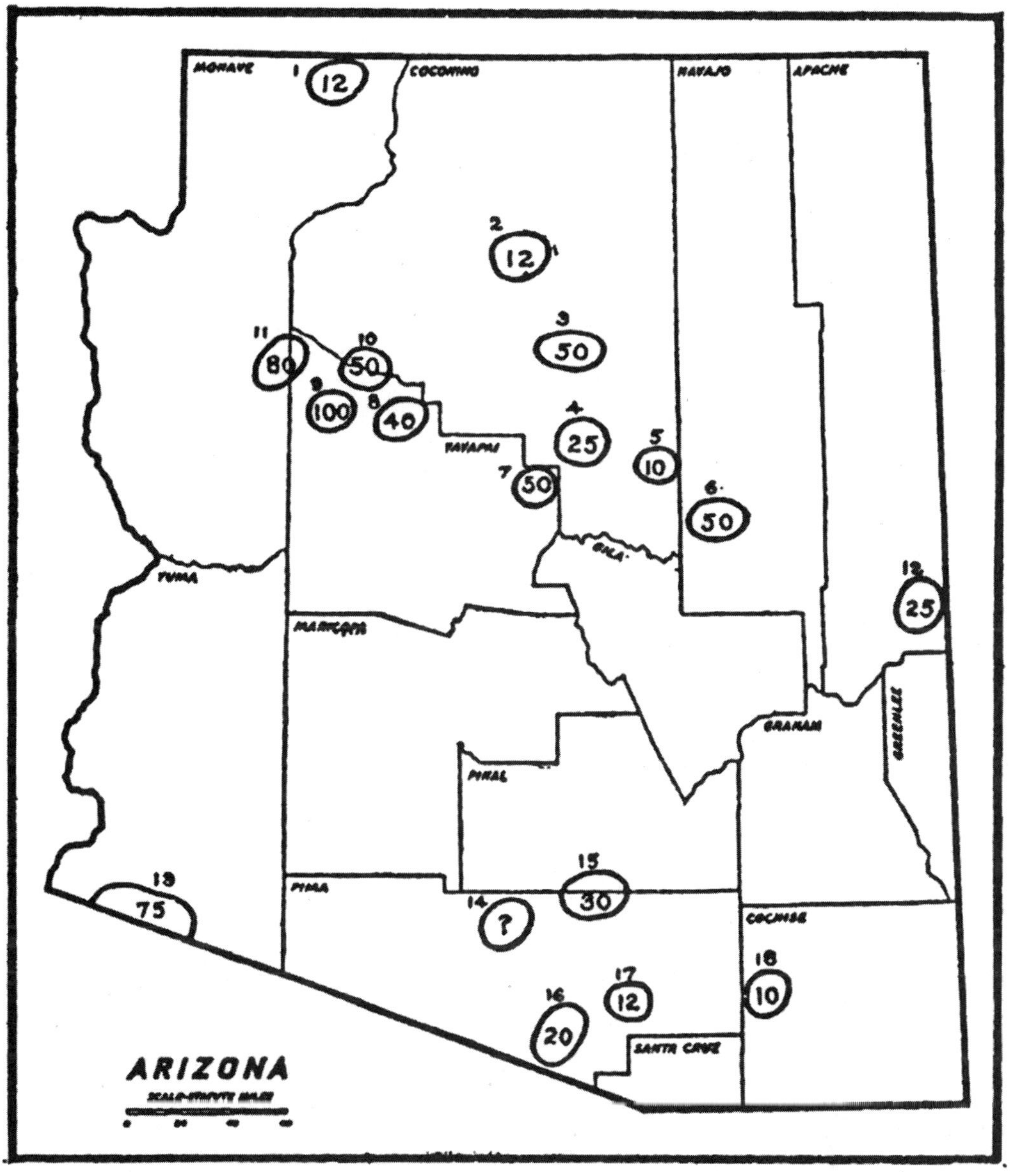

Distribution of antelope in Arizona in 1925, according to Dr. Edward Nelson's survey for the Biological Survey. The estimate of 651 animals in 18 areas, while undoubtedly conservative, reflects the pronghorn's dire status at a time when several states lost their antelope populations entirely. (Nelson 1925)

Department to investigate the feasibility of moving pronghorn from Anderson Mesa southeast of Flagstaff to restock other areas of the state.

For reasons never fully understood, the pronghorn population on Anderson Mesa had bounced back from an estimated low of a hundred or so animals in the summer of 1920 to a number in 1930 that threatened to deplete their food supply (Goldman 1931a). That year, Coconino National Forest Supervisor Edward G. Miller proudly estimated the antelope population on the national forest to number 3,300, including 1,500 to 2,000 on Anderson Mesa (Brown 2008). Stomach samples indicated the pronghorn's diet was

Anderson Mesa had high-lined junipers with a grass understory in 1931. The reason for this overpopulation of pronghorn remains enigmatic, as the animals never again attained the numbers estimated to be present in the early 1930s. Photo attributed to Mark Musgrave. (Governor's Files, Arizona State Library, Archives and Public Records, History and Archives Division)

about equally divided between such plants as snakeweed and juniper—species deemed low in nutritional value. Indeed, photographs taken at the time show an open grassy prairie punctuated by high-lined junipers devoid of foliage below the level reached by antelope (Nichol 1931).

Concerned over forage conditions, the US Forest Service recommended either a hunt or a trapping program to reduce the pronghorn's numbers (Goldman 1931c). But the commission was reluctant to open a season on an animal so recently deemed in need of total protection. Instead, it opted to initiate a trapping program that would move excess animals to areas in Arizona where pronghorn were lacking. This effort was to be supervised by Mark Musgrave, the state director of the Biological Survey's Predator and Rodent Control branch. The project's budget was $300—a not inconsiderable cost at that time. Plans called for a corral trap to be constructed at Chavez Pass, along with a smaller one near Soldier Lake to be built by the Forest Service.

The following year, 1931, Jack O'Connor moved to Flagstaff with his wife Eleanor to teach English at Arizona State Teachers College (now Northern Arizona University). O'Connor, who was destined to become Arizona's most prominent sportsman and outdoor writer, took an immediate interest in Anderson Mesa's pronghorn—a population now estimated to have doubled to more than 4,000 head. Whatever their numbers, and whatever the reason for their increase, the mesa's pronghorn were now being touted as the Arizona conservation success story, so much so that the Arizona Game Protective Association adopted a buck antelope as its logo. Not one to take a backseat when it came to the conservation of game animals, O'Connor wanted in on the action.

O'Connor spent a good part of the next three years visiting what he came to call "Magic Mesa" to observe the pronghorns' physical characteristics, behavior, and numbers.

Not only did he help census antelope, he helped search for dead fawns, finding plenty of both. On some days he reported seeing hundreds of animals and he feared for the mesa's ability to support them. His concern deepened when his friend Andrew Nichol, then a game specialist for the National Park Service, collected a male pronghorn on Anderson Mesa and another south of Williams in June 1933 to compare the two animals' relative body condition and diet. By this time the pronghorn on Anderson Mesa were showing signs of being in poor condition, and O'Connor fretted over the "high-lined cedars" and lack of nutritious browse plants. But most of all, he was intrigued by the phenomenal horn lengths of the bucks, which he considered longer than those in any other pronghorn population in North America (Brown 2005).

In the meantime, capturing adult antelope continued to prove difficult. Losses from trapping and shipping were unsustainably high, with all but two of the animals dying. By 1933, with only two antelope released in Chino Valley, Musgrave had despaired of capturing any animals suitable for transplant. He told the Arizona Game Protective Association the only hope for transplants appeared to be with bottle-fed fawns (Brown and Ockenfels 2007). The Arizona Game and Fish Commission, conservative by nature and believing that a hunt would be unacceptable to the public, directed the department to persevere in its trapping efforts. Any animals lost during trapping would only succumb to drought and starvation anyway.

In May 1934, the year he left Flagstaff to teach at the University of Arizona, O'Connor (1934) wrote his first conservation piece for *Outdoor Life* magazine, "Arizona's Pronghorn Problem." In this article, as in several subsequent ones, he recommended a controlled hunting season to reduce pronghorn numbers and the pressure on their range. Money raised from the sale of hunt permits, he argued, should be used to transplant young pronghorn to Arizona's unoccupied habitats. Efforts to trap adult pronghorn the previous year had again been disastrous, with only three of 30 trapped animals living long enough to be released, and O'Connor doubted whether even these would survive, as "experience has repeatedly proved that the mature animals cannot be shipped."

O'Connor had also developed other ideas about pronghorn, and by his own admission, he never "wrote anything about antelope that someone didn't call me on." Although some of his conclusions were later shown to be in error, others were right on the money. Still others could never be proved one way or the other. For example, it was O'Connor who first opined that a pronghorn's eyesight was equivalent to a person peering through eight-power binoculars (Brown and Ockenfels 2007). He also thought bucks were 20 mph slower than does, because the bucks were always in the rear of a running herd. He postulated that pronghorn in northern Arizona were in the process of adapting to living in pine forest—an observation made years earlier in the same general area by both Edgar A. Mearns and Dr. Edward Nelson. But mostly he was impressed with the fine heads of the bucks on Anderson Mesa, thinking incorrectly that the old, "over-the-hill" fellows made the best trophies.

Although O'Connor (1939) described Anderson Mesa as the "most thickly populated" pronghorn range in North America, he could never decide just what factors had been responsible for the turnaround in the animal's numbers. The general consensus at the time, one stated by future State Game Warden Kenner Kartchner (1931) and initially echoed by O'Connor through the 1930s, was that the increase in the 1920s had been due to a reduction in illegal killing; improving range conditions; and the removal of wolves, coyotes, and lions by ranchers and predator hunters. Years later, O'Connor (1961) would write that the decline in pronghorn on Anderson Mesa after 1940 was due to too much land being closed to livestock and that overgrazing by cattle had been good for pronghorn.

Outdoor writer and hunter Jack O'Connor with a pronghorn buck taken on a museum collecting permit in 1936. O'Connor's efforts to allow hunting and management of antelope were unceasing. (Jack O'Connor Hunting Heritage and Education Center)

One thing was sure: The citizens of Coconino County wanted to protect their pronghorn. This desire was expressed in a September 23, 1927, article in the *Coconino Sun*:

> The antelope is one of the rarest animals in Arizona. Everyone here is inclined to protect the antelope and because of it the number is rapidly increasing. Possession of a dead antelope carries a minimum penalty of $100 fine.

As for the reasons for the pronghorn's recovery during the 1920s, Kartchner probably had it about right. The Forest Service's program delaying the entry of livestock on the pronghorn's summer range until later in the year, and the cessation of dual cattle and sheep use in the 1920s, undoubtedly had beneficial effects. Other factors may also have been at work. According to the *Coconino Sun*, hundreds of fires occurred on the Coconino National Forest between June 1923 and the early summer of 1929; several of these, including at least one larger than 1,000 acres, occurred on or near Anderson Mesa (Brown 2008).

O'Connor, now an active member of the Tucson Game Protective Association, continued to maintain his interest in Anderson Mesa and its pronghorn, although the area was now far from home. When Gordon Baldwin asked O'Connor to collect a pair of pronghorn for the Arizona State Museum in Tucson, O'Connor jumped at the chance. With his hunting companion John McGregor, O'Connor set out in October 1936 for the Hay Lake area on Anderson Mesa where McGregor, an archeologist, had collected a 16-inch buck for the Museum of Northern Arizona the previous year.

O'Connor, describing this hunt in a 1937 article, confessed to having a bad case of "buck fever." He missed a trophy male, the horns of which he thought would measure between 22 and 23 inches long, and failed to get a shot at another that he judged to be even larger. After several more difficulties, he finally collected a pair of antelope, the buck having a reported horn length of 16 inches (actually 15.125 inches). This buck, along with an even larger one collected by McGregor in 1935, was included in the Boone and Crockett Club's first record book (O'Connor 1939).[1]

Like residents of several other western states, who were also experiencing a resurgence in pronghorn populations, Arizonans would have had an antelope-hunting season in the 1930s had the Arizona Game and Fish Commission not been so cautious. Despite a continued rise in the Anderson Mesa antelope herd to an estimated 4,600 animals in 1933, the commission thought it best to hold off on a hunt in the hope that the animals would continue to increase and overflow into other areas. Besides, it was argued, surplus animals were still needed for restocking elsewhere if a suitable trapping and transplanting technique could be developed.

Instead, many of the mesa's pronghorn succumbed to drought and a lack of forage. Hundreds more were said to have died during the severe winter of 1936–37. O'Connor (1940), never at a loss for words, let the commission have it:

> Bad winters killed the animals by the hundred and coyotes flocked in from all over northern Arizona to feast on the weakened and dead animals. They stayed to kill the fawns every spring. To my notion, the Anderson Mesa situation is as good a lesson in how not to manage game as the Kaibab once was. Nine years ago we had 5,000 antelope. With good management the herd should have increased 30 percent annually. The increase between 1930 and 1939 should have been 13,500 animals. Instead, we have today around 2,000 antelope. In other words we have wasted about 15,000 antelope! All you Arizonans did with your antelope, Dr. H. L. Shantz, head of the game management division of the US Forest Service,[2] told me recently, was to furnish a free lunch for the coyotes!

O'Connor, using his position as editor of the AGPA's *Arizona Wild Life Sportsman* magazine, continued to press for an antelope season to take advantage of the mesa's superior trophies and to harvest what he thought were excess, over-mature bucks. Finally, in 1940, when pronghorn surveys again showed a decline in numbers, and as many or more bucks as does, he got his way. Antelope being polygamous, the large number of bucks was deemed excessive, and the Arizona Game and Fish Commission approved a buck-only season for April 1940. This was prior to the breeding season, when the animals' pelage was at its prime and before the horn sheaths had been damaged from jousting. Later, despite O'Connor's objections, the commission changed the season to a split hunt to take place between September 20 and October 5, 1941. A total of 400 permits were issued at a cost of $5 each.

---

[1] That these animals were all taken prior to an open season attests to the frequent complaints then voiced that certain individuals could obtain "scientific collecting" permits from the State Game Warden and/or commission.

[2] Dr. Homer Shantz was actually with the University of Arizona and a senior range advisor to the Forest Service.

O'Connor had not only gotten the hunt he had advocated for so long, he and Eleanor had obtained permits. In the May 1945 issue of *Outdoor Life*, O'Connor told how he and Eleanor teamed up with their Tucson friends Carroll Lemon and Al and Marion Ronstadt to camp near Hay Lake with about 25 other lucky hunters. At the crack of dawn on opening morning, Eleanor shot a nice trophy buck—the first hunter to take a legal antelope in Arizona without a special permit since 1908 (N. L. Lewis 2000). As an indication of how many pronghorn were then present, all of the 30 or so hunters camped near Hay Lake filled their tags on opening day.

Although the hunt did not widen the buck:doe ratio to the degree anticipated, hunters succeeded in harvesting 287 buck antelope for a 73% success rate. The fall season had proven highly popular after all, and was the subject of favorable articles by O'Connor (1943, 1945) in *Outdoor Life*.

In 1942, the Arizona Game and Fish Department, now bolstered by Federal-Aid monies, conducted an extensive survey of pronghorn throughout much of Arizona and recommended that the number of permits be nearly doubled. Still, the ratio of bucks to does after the hunt remained close to one to one. The next year, 1943, aerial surveys were initiated and the commission opened most of northern Arizona to antelope hunting. To alleviate crowding, the more than 1,000 authorized permits were spread between two hunting seasons—the first hunt from September 30 through October 4, and the other from October 7 through October 11. The large number of hunters, and the reduction in department personnel brought on by World War II, resulted in much misbehavior, and the hunt became known as the "dirty hunt of 1943," with many animals left in the field and a number of does killed (Brown and Ockenfels 2007).

That same year, the commission authorized the department to purchase the 20,320-acre Raymond Ranch below Anderson Mesa as a pronghorn wintering area. This purchase marked the department's first large habitat acquisition, a purchase made possible by the commission's acceptance of the Federal Aid in Wildlife Restoration Act—commonly called the Pittman-Robertson Act. A principal reason for the purchase was to capture adult pronghorn for release in southern Arizona, as Paul Russell (1964) had by then developed successful pronghorn capturing and shipping techniques in New Mexico that he demonstrated in other states, including Arizona.

Although Arizona's antelope biologist, Ted Knipe (1944), recommended considering pronghorn from the Dugas and other sub-Mogollon populations to restock southern Arizona, Anderson Mesa continued to be the home of Arizona's largest antelope population and the most practical choice to restock Arizona's former rangelands. A permanent wing trap was therefore built along a drift fence on Anderson Mesa that led to a series of three progressively smaller corrals, each made of wire fencing. The last corral was of such proportions that the antelope, on reaching it, could be forced into an adjacent truck.

After a difficult beginning, the trapping and transplanting crew's efforts at Raymond Ranch eventually succeeded, and in 1943 the first transplant of 22 antelope was made on the mesa southwest of the Winchester Mountains in Cochise County (Niehuis 1943). By

An unusually large number of pronghorn being segregated and captured prior to translocation to Bonito Prairie on the Fort Apache Indian Reservation. (AGFD files)

1945, more than 100 pronghorn had been released in four locations in southern Arizona. Additional translocation efforts, coupled with the imposition of gas rationing and other restrictions brought on by World War II, resulted in no hunts being authorized in 1944 and 1945 (Niehuis 1944).

Wildlife-agency personnel as well as sportsmen were more conservative in the 1940s than today. The department, then under the direction of Tom Kimball, was reluctant to recommend an antelope hunt unless it could be convincingly demonstrated a hunt was needed to harvest surplus animals. Kimball believed in order to sustain hunting, pronghorn had to have an annual fawn recruitment rate of at least 50 fawns per 100 does. In 1944, the department's aerial surveys showed only 25 fawns per 100 does, and in 1945, the fawn:doe ratio was 37:100. While not unusual by today's standards, these ratios were then considered nothing short of disastrous. Even in 1946, when surveys showed a statewide fawn recruitment rate of 62:100, and a ratio of one buck for every two does, the department recommendation was to not have a hunt.

Department biologists thought the reason for the pronghorn's generally poor reproductive performance was a combination of inadequate summer precipitation and fawn predation by coyotes. An intensive coyote-trapping program was therefore begun on Anderson Mesa and in other fawning areas, with mixed results. Although department personnel were convinced the trapping efforts had been beneficial, the fawn to doe ratio in the summer of 1947 was below the hoped-for 50:100. Again, for the fourth year in a row, no hunt was recommended.

Historical Arizona Pronghorn Antelope Translocations, 1924–61
Source: Amber Munig, AGFD, in Brown and Ockenfels 2009

Date	Capture Site	Release Site	Number Captured	Number Released	Age & Sex	Outcome
1924	Northern Nevada	Hermit Basin, Grand Cyn. Natl. Park	12	12	Pen-reared fawns	Eventually failed
1932	Chavez Pass, e. of Anderson Mesa	South of Ash Fork, GMU 19B	10	2	2M	High mortality
1939	Anderson, Mesa, GMU 5	CCC Ranch, Avra Valley	11	7	Fawns	Pen-reared; unsuccessful
6/10–11/1941	Anderson, Mesa, GMU 5	Ellsworth Rn., Whitlock Valley, GMU 28	4	2	Fawns	Pen-reared, both died in corral within 3 weeks
1/22–24/1943	Raymond Rn., GMU 5	G-Ranch, Upper Sulphur Springs Valley, GMU 32	24	22	6M:16F	Successful
2/8/1943	Raymond Rn., GMU 5	Patterson Rn. near Oracle Jctn., GMU 37	6	4	4M	Unsuccessful
1/19/1944	Raymond Rn., GMU 5	Box Springs, Upper Sulphur Springs Valley, GMU 32	3	3	1M:2F	Successful
3/9/1944	Raymond Rn., GMU 5	Box Springs, Upper Sulphur Springs Valley, GMU 32	3	3	3M	Supplemental; successful?
1/6–31/1945	Raymond Rn., GMU 5	Upper Sulphur Springs Valley, GMU 32	40	40	18M:22F	Supplemental; successful
2/9/1945	Raymond Rn., GMU 5	Double Tank, Altar Valley, GMU 36	18	18	5M:13F	Eventually failed
2/11/1945	Raymond Rn., GMU 5	Ashburn Ranch, San Rafael Valley, GMU 35	9	9	4M:5F	Successful
3/8/1945	Raymond Rn., GMU 5	Ashburn Ranch, San Rafael Valley, GMU 35	4	4	2M:2F	Supplemental; successful

(continued . . .)

Then, during the winter of 1947–48, an intensive coyote “reduction program” using the new and lethal predacide Compound 1080 was instituted throughout most of northern Arizona. Perhaps because of the use of 1080, or its use in combination with favorable weather conditions, the percentage of does with fawns in 1948 jumped to nearly 80%. But again no antelope hunt was authorized by the commission. Game wardens patrolling the last hunt in 1943 had reported seeing many wounded antelope and finding a large number of dead does. People within and outside the department continued to question whether Arizona’s antelope could ever sustain a hunt regardless of how many fawns were produced.

Fawn recruitment in 1949 was 67 fawns per 100 does, and after much deliberation and a little persuasion by O’Connor and the hunting community, the department recommended an antelope season if the hunt could be held under stringent controls designed to prevent “flock-shooting” and to protect the does. The commission agreed, and approved the issuance of 606 antelope license-tags in four stratified hunts, each opening at noon.

Historical Arizona Pronghorn Antelope Translocations, 1924–61

Date	Capture Site	Release Site	Number Captured	Number Released	Age & Sex	Outcome
3/12/1945	Raymond Rn., GMU 5	T-W Tank near Oracle, GMU 37	15	15	6M:9F	Supplemental; failed
12/19/1949	Antelope Pass, n. Grapevine Cyn., GMU 5	Fort Huachuca Wildlife Area, GMU 35	72	72	?	Limited success
1/15/1951	Antelope Pass, n. Grapevine Cyn., GMU 5	Fort Huachuca Wildlife Area, GMU 35	28	18	9M:9F	8 escaped; limited success
2/1–6/1951	Antelope Pass, n. Grapevine Cyn., GMU 5	Fence Canyon, House Rock Valley, GMU 12	47	42	20M:22F	Eventually failed
2/1–6/1951	Antelope Pass, n. Grapevine Cyn., GMU 5	San Rafael Valley, GMU 35	68	57	22M:35F	Successful
1959	GMU 5	San Simon Valley, GMU 28	12	12	?	No record; failed?
9/21–22/1959	Raymond Rn., GMU 5	Bonito Prairie, Fort Apache I.R., GMU 25	60	34	2M:18F:14 fawns	16 released at capture site; translocations successful
12/7/1960	Raymond Rn., GMU 5	Bonito Prairie, Fort Apache I.R., GMU 25	57	37	10M:16F: 11 fawns	Supplemental; 19 released at capture site; translocation successful
10/30/1961	Raymond Rn., GMU 5	June Tank, Arizona Strip, GMU 13	125	34	6 M:28F	84 released at capture site; translocation successful

Note: GMU=Game management unit; M=Male; F=Female; Rn.=Ranch; I.R.=Indian Reservation; Cyn.=Canyon; e.=east; n.=north

In addition to placing numerous restrictions on the use of vehicles, the commission encouraged sportsmanlike behavior by instituting a "Sportsman's Award" program. Points were given for the taking of bucks having 12-inch or better horns, with additional points awarded for each additional inch. Killing an antelope with one or two bullets allowed a hunter to accrue another 20 to 25 points. Points could also be earned by taking proper care of the carcass, and a hunter with a perfect score was awarded 100 points (Brown and Ockenfels 2007).

The 1949 hunt was a huge success. Not only was the hunters' behavior exemplary, 437 hunters bagged a pronghorn for a 76% success rate. Thirty-six animals had horn lengths longer than 16 inches, and 7 bucks exceeded 17 inches. Four measured 18 inches. One hundred and eighteen hunters earned Sportsman's Awards for achieving 80 or more points, 45 earned more than 90 points, and 4 had a perfect score of 100.

Although most Arizonans agreed a pronghorn season should now be an annual event, O'Connor was not to be heard from. In 1948, he and his family had moved to Lewiston, Idaho. Arizona, experiencing a postwar boom in human population, was now too crowded for him. Although he would return to hunt small game a time or two, O'Connor would never again hunt pronghorn in the state he had shown to hold more trophies than any other (Carmony 2003).

The trapping and transplanting program was meanwhile now up and running. In 1949, Harold Heddings, the department's antelope trapper, shipped 72 pronghorn from Anderson Mesa to the newly acquired Fort Huachuca Wildlife Refuge—the largest single release to date. In 1951, another 60 pronghorn were translocated to Fort Huachuca, or as it was now called, the Charles T. Vorhies Range Research Area. In 1952, another 57 were released in San Rafael Valley. When the trapping and transplanting operations on Anderson Mesa ceased in 1961, nearly 650 pronghorn had been captured, 433 of them being released at 12 sites in Arizona, the remainder participating in mark-and-release studies. A release in Sulphur Springs Valley was so successful that the commission was later coerced into authorizing a depredation hunt there. All but two of these locations have pronghorn antelope today.

EARLY WILDLIFE STUDIES WITH THE UNIVERSITY OF ARIZONA AND ITS COOPERATORS

David E. Brown

Even before statehood, the University of Arizona was promulgating bulletins reflecting the opinions and findings of its agriculture school faculty and the technicians working on its experimental farm. Most of these articles were less than scientific, and some, such as those promoting "dry-land farming," could be highly misleading. "Boosterism," in those days, appears to have been a greater virtue than peer review.

Over time, the bulletins improved in content and scope. Some of the articles, such as Charles Vorhies's *Poisonous Animals of the Desert* (1917), were factual and highly informative given the knowledge then available.

One reason for the increasing relevance and usefulness of these bulletins in the 1920s was that the university's agriculture and biology departments teamed up with the US Biological Survey and other governmental entities to conduct needed research on select species of wildlife. This interest was due to the economic impacts attributed to various animals on Arizona's resources, especially croplands and the vegetation required by livestock. As methods to solve these wildlife "problems" came under closer scrutiny, the university and government agencies strove to demonstrate the usefulness of their institutions to rural Arizonans. Bulletins, especially scientific ones, served to communicate informed opinions and the results of early studies to other workers and cooperators.

Before Arizona became a cooperator with the federal government under the Pittman-Robertson Act in 1939, nearly all wildlife research conducted in Arizona was the result of a partnership between the Biological Survey and the University of Arizona—the university also being eager to cooperate in various studies with such partners as the US Forest Service and National Audubon Society. Being a state institution, the university also offered its services to the newly formed Arizona Game and Fish Commission in 1929.

The Arizona Game and Fish Department had little money for such collaborations, and wildlife research projects were invariably headed by a university faculty member. Some professors, like Walter Taylor and Andrew Nichol, might be jointly employed by both the university and the Biological Survey or another government agency. Much of this research took place at the university's agricultural experiment station, with only a modicum of support from the Game and Fish Department.

The 41,600-acre Santa Rita Experiment Range and its Research Station south of Tucson was a natural location for field studies in that it was jointly managed by the university and Forest Service to solve livestock management problems, including those caused by wildlife. Created in 1910, this experimental range was an excellent study area for both range management and wildlife studies, as the property was subject to grazing controls. In its heyday prior to World War II, it possessed a staff of up to a dozen technicians. Rain gauges, holding pens, and other facilities for conducting animal-related research were available. The results of studies done there were published in either the university's Agricultural Experiment Station or Biological Sciences bulletins.

Most of these studies and the resulting publications dealt with the life histories, ecology, and food habits of potential competitors with livestock, such as banner-tailed kangaroo rats (Vorhies and Taylor 1922), leaf-cutter ants (Nichol 1931), and jackrabbits. An especially important study relating to hares was Vorhies and Taylor's (1933) *The Life Histories and Ecology of Jack Rabbits,* Lepus alleni *and* Lepus californicus *spp., in Relation to Grazing in Arizona.*

Dr. Charles T. Vorhies was Arizona's first nongame biologist and an influential founder of the Tucson Natural History Society and Arizona Game Protective Association. (UA BioFile, Vorhies; University of Arizona Libraries, Special Collections)

This investigation represented the first and most complete natural history study of an endemic Sonoran Desert wildlife species, the antelope jackrabbit. Not only did this study attempt to determine why both species of jackrabbits were more abundant on grazed rangelands than in ungrazed areas, it investigated some ecological problems that have never been resolved, such as what factors caused jackrabbit populations to increase to spectacular numbers in some years, only to decline to a level of relative scarcity in others.

The first study of an important game species having a positive economic value was one done by David M. Gorsuch (1934) on Gambel's quail. This three-year study was begun in 1930 and sponsored by the Sporting Arms and Ammunition Manufacturers Institute, which under the direction of Aldo Leopold provided most of the funding. Other cooperators were the Biological Survey, the Forest Service, and the Arizona Game and Fish Commission.

Essentially a natural-history study that took place mostly on the Santa Rita Experimental Range, Gorsuch's work was undertaken for the simple reason that the Gambel's quail was the most important bird to Arizona residents, tourists, and hunters. Hunters then enjoyed a 60-day season to pursue their favorite game bird. Gorsuch's principal management objective was to propose methodologies by which maximum numbers of this bird might be realized.

Concentrating on the bird's daily routine, the study followed the movements of Gambel's quail throughout the year and documented the "winter shuffle" as the time when pair bonds were formed and the breeding season commenced. Using field observations and banded birds, Gorsuch showed that most of the "whistling" or calling males were unmated birds and that the species did not "double-clutch"—multiple broods of uneven-aged birds being adopted rather than the result of a "second hatch." A careful examination of the bird's diet and cover requirements showed the most important plants were mesquite, hackberry, and spring annuals such as filaree (*Erodium* spp.)

Gorsuch recognized the relationship between the abundance of winter annuals and quail population levels and noted that summer rains were relatively unimportant to brood production and survival. Soft winter vegetation, high in vitamins, triggered the onset of breeding activity. And, although the birds readily took salt, they were perfectly capable of surviving without drinking water, the latter being more important as a producer of green feed, insects, and other dietary items than as a source of moisture per se. He also found out that quail did not migrate or travel long distances.

Gorsuch pondered the rationale for a possible imbalance in the sex ratio, as 50.7% of his trapped birds were males. He speculated that such an inequality, if it did occur, might serve to provide some survival or breeding advantage.[1] Banded birds showed that the home range of un-hunted birds was small and that covey members typically ranged less than a quarter mile from their nighttime roost, which was the center of the birds' universe.

Important predators on quail and quail nests were cotton rats, gray foxes, round-tailed ground squirrels and Cooper's hawks—the numbers of all of which he recommended be controlled insofar as possible. Gorsuch's study absolved roadrunners and Gila monsters as serious predators, and recommended that the roadrunner be protected, as the bird did more good than harm. Disease, he concluded, was a relatively unimportant cause of quail mortality in Arizona.

Gorsuch did not study the bird's population dynamics and made few management recommendations regarding hunting season or bag limits. He considered hunting losses to be generally unimportant, provided that hunters displayed ethical behavior and did not shoot birds on the ground, kill excessive numbers of quail, or overshoot coveys. He addressed the then-problem of quail depredating farm crops by noting quail fed mostly on wild foods during the critical planting months of May and June. Gorsuch deplored the practice of "clean-farming," stressing the importance of maintaining maximum numbers of birds through habitat quality. He considered overgrazing a serious obstacle to quail abundance and cautioned that the bird's most serious enemy was soil loss due to the erosion associated with this practice.

A summary of Gorsuch's management recommendations showed he stressed habitat protection as the foremost requirement for good quail populations, along with control of the bird's natural enemies, better sportsmanship, and more enforcement of the game laws. He also recommended the hiring of a quail specialist to conduct research and keep the bird under constant attention lest any changes in numbers require management action.[2] Practical efforts to improve quail numbers included his suggestion for the establishment of fenced livestock-free mini-refuges, constructed in prime quail habitat and comprising half an acre or more.

---

[1]It does. Having surplus males assures sexual selection takes place by all females (Brown and Gutiérrez 1980).

[2]Although he had also participated in a successful collecting trip to Sonora for masked bobwhite in 1931, Gorsuch no longer worked with quail in Arizona. The last reference I have found as to his wildlife activities was his appointment in the 1940s as refuge manager for the short-lived Bill Williams Wildlife Refuge, operated jointly by the Forest Service and Arizona Game and Fish Department.

Walter Taylor in Arizona's high country—probably when he was working on porcupines. Photo by Daniel W. Lay. (Courtesy of Harley Shaw)

Another important early life-history study was Walter Taylor's (1935) *Ecology and Life History of the Porcupine* (Erethizon epixanthum) *As Related to the Forests of Arizona and the Southwestern States*, published as Biological Sciences Bulletin No. 3. A federal biologist with the Biological Survey, Taylor had also taken a post as professor of economic zoology at the University of Arizona in 1922. Taylor's investigation remains the one and only study of this animal in Arizona.

Although his study was originally intended to evaluate and alleviate the damage done by porcupines to Arizona's ponderosa pine forests, Taylor also investigated the animal's behavior, and its ecological relationships with its forest home. He began by sending out questionnaires to all offices of the Forest Service and to personnel with the Biological Survey in Arizona and New Mexico, inquiring as to the recipient's porcupine observations and comments. The respondents reported porcupines to be numerous and widely distributed, with most sightings in ponderosa pine forests. In Arizona, the animals were considered especially abundant on the Coconino and Tusayan (now included within the Kaibab) national forests. Here porcupines were considered to frequent cutover forests and to favor ridges, rock piles, crevices, and meadows—the latter being especially important as summer feeding areas, as the animals subsisted at that time mostly on forbs found in forest openings. At other times the porcupines fed on inner bark, mistletoe, pine needles, and fungi.

Taylor followed up his preliminary survey with three years of field study in the vicinity of Fort Valley, near Flagstaff, beginning in June 1924. The trees most vulnerable to "porcupine work" were sapling and pole-sized ponderosas. Some trees were hit repeatedly. The principal damage was caused by girdling the trunks of smaller trees, causing them to develop a spike-top or "stag-head" appearance. Although the study objective was to find a management solution rather than merely justify what was turning into an extermination campaign, Taylor concluded the animal had become so plentiful that no less than 500,000 acres of the Southwest's forests were in danger.

A serious effort to poison porcupines in the Flagstaff area began in 1922, and by the 1930s a coordinated control program was resulting in the enrollment of predator-control agents, foresters, Civilian Conservation Corps crews, and the general public in an attempt to destroy these large rodents. This persecution of porcupines continued through the 1950s and 1960s, when observations of damage waned. The species was protected in 1972 (Brown and Babb 2009).

Even though Taylor never came up with a definite answer as to why porcupines were so numerous during his study, he realized their abundance reflected abnormal conditions. Of the possible reasons suggested for the excessive numbers of porcupines, Taylor considered reduced mountain lion numbers to possibly be the most significant—an observation shared by Ben Lilly and other early lion hunters. But even though reduced mountain lion numbers were suspected of causing an increase in porcupine damage, Taylor and his colleagues did not recommend a let-up in lion control. Like most biologists at the time, Taylor believed that removing porcupines was a better solution to ecological problems than allowing lion predation on deer and livestock to return to former levels.

Other technical studies resulting in bulletins during the 1930s and 1940s included a classification and map of Arizona's natural vegetation (Nichol 1937), a study of deer diet preferences obtained through the experimental feeding of captive animals (Nichol 1938), and another paper on jackrabbit food habits (J. F. Arnold 1942). These publications were in turn followed by such seminal publications as *The Grasshoppers and Other Orthoptera of Arizona* (Ball et al. 1942), *Arizona Range Resources and Their Utilization, Vol. I. Cochise County* (Darrow 1944), and an important and especially relevant paper on the water requirements of desert animals, showing that a number of herbivores met most or all of their water needs through the ingestion of plant material (Vorhies 1945).

It was also during this time that the university and federal government teamed up to publish some of the more popular biological science bulletins, including *The Cacti of Arizona* (Benson and Thornber 1940), *A Manual of Southwestern Trees and Shrubs* (Benson and Darrow 1944), and *Grasses of Southwestern United States* (Gould 1951). These publications would prove so useful that all would be reprinted—some more than once.

The University of Arizona continued to publish range bulletins through the 1950s, including a series of forage evaluation booklets and vegetation maps for several Arizona counties authored by range ecologist Robert R. Humphrey (1950, 1953, 1955, and 1960). Humphrey (1958) was also the first range ecologist to suggest correctly that fire was essential for "desert grassland" to maintain its open character and grass-based forage value, lest it be invaded by noxious shrubs and woody vegetation.

After Arizona became a state cooperator in the Pittman-Robertson program in 1939, the Game and Fish Department assumed the role of primary

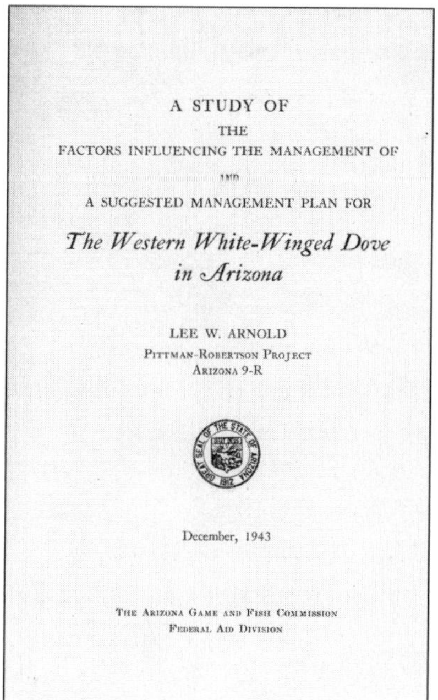
A STUDY OF
THE
FACTORS INFLUENCING THE MANAGEMENT OF
AND
A SUGGESTED MANAGEMENT PLAN FOR
The Western White-Winged Dove in Arizona

LEE W. ARNOLD
PITTMAN-ROBERTSON PROJECT
ARIZONA 9-R

December, 1943

THE ARIZONA GAME AND FISH COMMISSION
FEDERAL AID DIVISION

After Arizona became a state cooperator in the Pittman-Robertson program in 1939, the Game and Fish Commission became the primary publisher of wildlife bulletins authored by Federal-Aid biologists. The first was Lee Arnold's (1943) A Study of the Factors Influencing the Management of and a Suggested Management Plan for the Western White-Winged Dove in Arizona. *(AGFD files)*

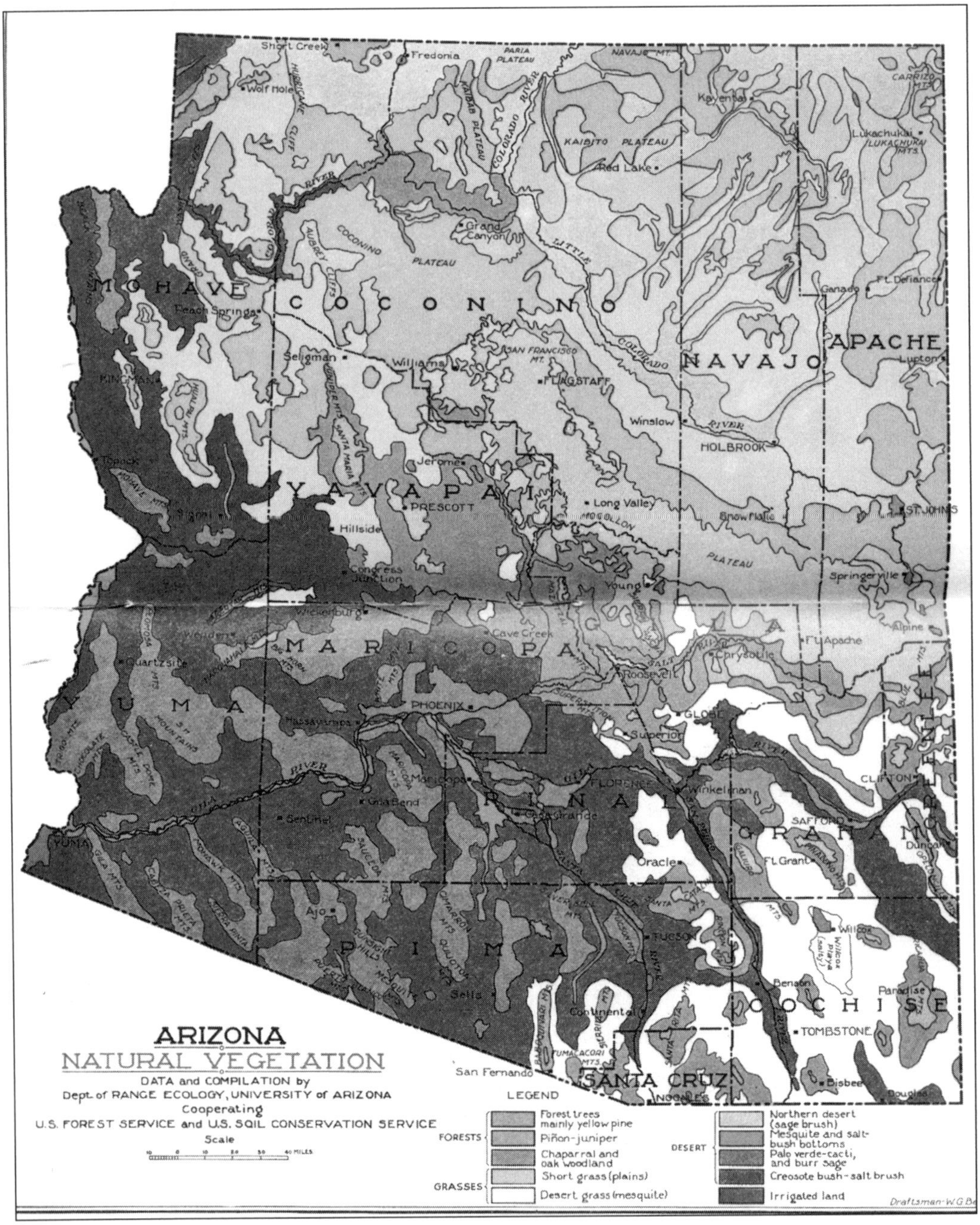

Andrew Nichol's 1937 classification and map of Arizona's natural vegetation was published as a technical bulletin. (Nichol 1937c; AGFD files)

publisher of wildlife bulletins authored by its Federal-Aid biologists. The first of these green-covered department publications was Lee Arnold's (1943) *A Study of the Factors Influencing the Management of and a Suggested Management Plan for the Western White-Winged Dove in Arizona*, closely followed by Ted Knipe's (1944) *The Status of the Antelope Herds of Northern Arizona*. These were in turn followed by such works as James T. Wright's (1959) *Desert Wildlife* and John P. Russo's (1956) *The Desert Bighorn Sheep in Arizona*.

After years of effort by Taylor and Vorhies, Congress finally approved $9,000 for a Cooperative Wildlife Research Unit for Arizona in 1949. Dr. Ira B. Judd at the University of Arizona was chosen unit leader (Vorhies, the logical choice, no longer being available). This appointment caused some consternation on the part of Dr. Herbert Stahnke. He thought Arizona State College would make a better choice, as Tempe was more centrally located and Dr. Hugh Hansen was said to have a wildlife program already in place.[3] Stahnke even offered to have the legislature make Arizona State College a land grant college, if that would help.

The University of Arizona's relationship with the Arizona Game and Fish Commission was longstanding, and Dr. Lyle K. Sowls was appointed leader of the Cooperative Wildlife Research Unit in 1951. Sowls, a graduate student under Aldo Leopold, would undertake a series of research projects with the Arizona Game and Fish Department, including the use of browse plants by deer, an investigation of javelina life history and population dynamics, the use of water by game animals, and a series of investigations into the population dynamics of Gambel's quail, scaled quail, mourning and white-winged doves, tassel-eared squirrels, and cottontail rabbits.

Although the majority of the research unit's program would consist of training wildlife students who produced short-term graduate theses, one undertaking included a book on the early history of wildlife in Arizona (Davis 1982). Other, more extensive natural history publications reflected the work of a new cadre of biological sciences faculty hired by the University of Arizona in the 1950s. These included Lendell Cockrum's (1960) *The Recent Mammals of Arizona*; Phillips, Marshall, and Monson's (1964) *Birds of Arizona*; and most important, Charles H. Lowe's (1964) *Vertebrates of Arizona*. All of these major ecological works were published by the University of Arizona Press, which arrived on campus in 1959.

[3] This was an exaggeration; Dr. Hansen was an ecologist with little or no experience in wildlife studies.

SECTION III

WILDLIFE MANAGEMENT COMES OF AGE

1939–53

LEAN YEARS FOR THE ARIZONA GAME PROTECTIVE ASSOCIATION

David E. Brown, Joseph Monfeli, and Melanie Tluczek

John Phillips, Arizona's "conservationist governor," was replaced in the election of 1930 by George Hunt, who rode in on the wave of pro-Democrat sentiment attendant with the onset of the Great Depression. And Governor Hunt did not like what the Arizona Game Protective Association had done. Irked at the AGPA's support of Phillips, and contemptuous of the commission form of government, Hunt set about abolishing the new game code almost as soon as he took office in January 1931.

The Tumultuous Thirties, 1930–38

Hunt had Representative H. J. Valentine draft a bill, HB165, nullifying the new game code and dissolving the Arizona Game and Fish Commission. This the AGPA could not allow, so President Fred Gibson requested a special hearing before Representative M. V. Decker, chairman of the House Fish and Game Committee. On February 24, 1931, the commission, Gibson, and several AGPA delegates met with the committee and pleaded their case for retaining the existing game code. Among the proponents of HB165 were Alfred Mann (the Capitol custodian and Hunt's choice for State Game Warden) and former State Game Warden Joe Prochaska. After three hours of testimony, HB165 was quashed.

Rebuffed, the vindictive governor now accused the commission and Arizona Game and Fish Department of corruption and nepotism and called for a criminal investigation. Unable to have his charges filed in the courts, Hunt took his case to Decker and his Legislation Committee in the House of Representatives. A summary of the charges included:

1. All of the 1929 license books had been destroyed and been made unavailable by order of the commission, and the department's bookkeeping was below par.
2. License commissions paid to vendors had been excessive and complimentary licenses had been issued contrary to law.
3. The department had not spent all of the money budgeted for stocking fish and had spent too much on the Pinetop hatchery.
4. State Game Warden Robert Bayless was guilty of nepotism and other charges, having had the department hire his minor son, his sister, and his brother.

Charles Flinn of Mesa headed the AGPA contingent. He was joined by several other affiliate delegates, including Tom McCullough, whose term as commissioner had just expired. Again, Mann, Prochaska, and a man named Roy Griswold represented the governor. A key witness would be W. W. Brookner, the state auditor. The commission's response as presented by McCullough noted:

1. The 1929 license books had been removed by State Game Warden Dwight Pettis *prior* to Bayless's assuming office, and the state examiner had complained of poorly kept books not during Bayless's administration but previous ones.

2. The vendor commission was set by legislative law at 15% and was now 10%. A complimentary license had not been issued to Zane Grey's hunting guide as charged, but only to pioneers over 70 years of age with 30 years' residency as provided by law.

3. The federal hatchery providing the fish to be stocked had no more fish available and the department had supplied all that could be produced at both the federal government's and its own hatchery.

4. The nepotism charges were untrue; Bayless did not even have a sister, and his minor son had only a summer job in a fish hatchery that he obtained on his own from the hatchery supervisor.

After a lengthy legislative hearing, the charges were found to be bogus. Although the committee and the legislature were generally supportive of the AGPA, Hunt replaced the two presiding commissioners as was his prerogative. Bayless resigned, Mann was appointed State Game Warden, and Prochaska was given the position of "state game expert." Even Hunt's partial victory proved short-lived; both Mann and Prochaska were replaced within a year. Mann's replacement, William Joyner, a former state senator from Tucson, while not the AGPA's choice, had hunting and fishing experience and a reputation for evenhanded dealings.

The confrontation hurt Hunt more than the AGPA. He failed to win the 1932 Democratic primary despite a full-page ad in the AGPA magazine, *Arizona Wild Life*. In contrast, the AGPA gained in stature, and the sportsmen it represented were now recognized as a force in Arizona politics. It lacked the clout of the livestock industry in "Arizona's cowboy legislature," but the AGPA's annual conventions were now attended by representatives of the Arizona Cattlegrowers Association, Arizona Woolgrowers Association, Arizona Farm Bureau, the Biological Survey's Predator and Rodent Control branch, and the US Forest Service.

No other conservation organization had as much influence on Arizona politics or legislation. The AGPA greatly overshadowed such sometime allies as the Izaak Walton League and Audubon Society, the only other entities having a significant state presence. Power generates friends, and the fracas had strengthened both the AGPA's close relationship with the cattle industry and its status with the legislature. In 1932, Gov. Benjamin Mouer appointed two commissioners friendly to both the AGPA and the ranching industry, Dan Francis of Flagstaff and Charles Beach of Vail.

On the political front, the AGPA now could take on a growing number of issues, usually voting on three to 10 resolutions at its conventions each year. Many were perennial reiterations: more appropriations for predator control, more enforcement of the game laws, and less political interference with the Game and Fish Department. Other favorites included repeated requests to Carl Hayden and Isabella Greenway for a federal fish hatchery in Arizona and a wildlife experiment station similar to the livestock industry's Santa Rita Experimental Range. Other resolutions opposed any more federal land withdrawals or national park expansions.

Still other resolutions spoke to more minor issues, such as changing the bag limits, season dates, and firearm limitations on certain game species. More far-reaching concerns addressed the national decline in waterfowl populations then taking place, prompting strong support for duck stamps and other federal legislation. Some of the more thoughtful resolutions called for an evaluation of the effectiveness of game refuges and game farms in restoring game numbers, and a better home for Arizona's bison. One particularly germane resolution revisited the intent to manage native game species over imports, while contrary resolutions submitted by other affiliates called for more pheasant and chukar releases. Restricting hunting and fishing was more often called for than resolutions expanding hunting opportunities. The AGPA asked at various times for regulations reducing or eliminating the season on band-tailed pigeons and white-winged doves. The most important resolution pertaining to fishing supported a failed federal bill that was a precursor to the Dingell-Johnson Act passed in 1950.

Worsening economic times during the 1930s took a toll on the AGPA's finances. Although new affiliates were organized in Saint Johns and in "North Phoenix" (Glendale), and the number of affiliates rose from 16 in 1934 to 21 in 1937, actual membership remained stalled at between 1,200 and 1,500 paid members. Moreover, the strength of local affiliates varied considerably, ranging in 1938 from only a dozen or so members in some clubs to more than 250 in Flagstaff and 138 in Gila Valley.

More problematic were differences in the attitudes and objectives of the affiliates. Officers of the local affiliates were reluctant to relinquish any decision-making power to a state executive committee. Some of the affiliates' delegates even questioned the need for a parent organization. More interested in hunting and fishing than politics, most of the affiliates were inclined to handle local issues at the local level. While realizing that certain occasions demanded that the AGPA have executive or legislative committees, affiliate members were loath to donate a portion of their dues to a Phoenix-based executive body.

In an attempt to be relevant to local issues and retain the loyalty of the members, the editors of *Arizona Wild Life* continually solicited information from the local affiliates for publication in the magazine. They were only partially successful, and much of the magazine's contents had to be pirated from sources not only outside the association but outside the state.

Obtaining sufficient revenue to publish *Arizona Wild Life* was becoming difficult due to declining subscriptions and reduced advertising revenue. Keeping an editor and supplying sufficient copy constituted a challenge, as only 50 cents from each member went to the state organization. Ben Avery had taken over the editorship from Jim Diffin and Ida Persons of Springerville in September 1931, but resigned in April 1932 for financial reasons. His absence, and the lack of revenue, meant that volunteer associate editors McCullough and Gibson had to scale the magazine down to a newspaper format with no photos and no advertisements—a downsizing that would continue into February 1934, when Gibson was forced to publish the magazine as a bimonthly. Then, after skipping the June 1935 issue, *Arizona Wild Life* appeared as a monthly feature in the January 1936 issue

Hoofs and Horns *was a western range publication catering to the rodeo circuit. For a while, the Arizona Game Protective Association published its magazine in these pages. (Arizona State Library, Archives and Public Records, History and Archives Division)*

of *Hoofs and Horns*.[1] There it remained until June 1937, when it was again published as a monthly in its own right.

Reading the issues of *Arizona Wild Life* published during the 1930s, it becomes apparent a schism had developed between certain affiliates and the state organization. Walter Taylor and Charles Vorhies often chide the locals for their ennui and reluctance to contribute to the state organization. In response, some local officers write their own editorials on such disparate conservation issues as the need to work with Arizona ranchers and the lack of a youth education program.

In time, reports submitted by agency personnel become increasing common, with State Game Warden Shelby Lewis summarizing commission actions and regulation changes. Walter Mann, the national forest supervisor on the north Kaibab, writes about how deer should be given priority on the Kaibab and be managed for the highest number possible within the limitations of their habitat. Ben Foster of the PARC relates the need to step up the campaign against rodents and other varmints, causing Vorhies and other Tucson members to decry the widespread use of poison along with the Yuma affiliate's issuance of bounties on roadrunners as quail predators.

The AGPA's contract with *Hoofs and Horns* called for the inclusion of *Arizona Wild Life* as a regular feature, the AGPA paying 70 cents for four pages of copy every issue. Included with the parent magazine's longhorn on the masthead was the association's antelope logo. Paying for even this modest amount of copy remained a problem. President A. J. Eager and Secretary Vorhies continually badgered the more affluent Tucson and Phoenix affiliates to levy a portion of their membership dues to send to the state organization.

Equally difficult was getting the locals to contribute money to send representatives to attend the North American Wildlife Conference and other out-of-town

[1] *Hoofs and Horns* was in print from July 1931 through the 1940s. Published in Tucson, it sold for 10 to 15 cents a copy (depending on economic conditions) and was read by cattlemen, guest-ranch operators, and rodeo followers. It contained editorial columns, articles, and even poems and covered western history, livestock shows, cattle prices, poisonous plants, weather, obituaries, book reviews, and reminiscences. Writers included John Thornber, Will C. Barnes, Oren Arnold, and Kenner Kartchner. Originally a weekly, it soon became a monthly; other than its partnership with the AGPA, the magazine contained surprisingly little regarding game management and predator-control issues, featuring only the exploits of certain successful hunters.

meetings so the AGPA would be represented on national issues involving duck stamps and other federal legislation. Particularly frustrating to Vorhies was the AGPA's tardiness in becoming an affiliate of the new General Wildlife Federation (later National Wildlife Federation) in Washington, D. C. and in getting behind legislation allowing Arizona to have a Cooperative Wildlife Research Unit—his friend Taylor having been recently appointed leader of the Texas Wildlife Research Unit.

The most intense issue for the locals was predator control. Vorhies and his Tucson Natural History Society cohorts were particularly vocal regarding the PARC's campaign against small mammals and furbearers, and said so at the North American Wildlife Conference. Blanket control programs such as one being proposed for jackrabbits on the Papago Indian reservation were considered particularly offensive. Vorhies and ornithologist Allan Phillips also objected to the use of poison baits, a position bolstered by Deputy Warden Ralph Morrow, who reported instances of songbirds in the Chiricahua Mountains dying from eating treated grain.

Lion hunters and fur trappers were also opposing the use of poison for obvious reasons and finding a voice in the AGPA. Although PARC spokesmen such as Everett Mercer found the AGPA fertile ground to sell his predator and rodent control campaign, he had to tread carefully, lest he offend the sensibilities of certain members who were troubled by federal control efforts such as the killing of 1,100 rattlesnakes in the Tortolita Mountains by wild-cotton eradicators working for the Civilian Conservation Corps.

The AGPA may have had conflicts, but its leaders managed to retain a strong political presence. Although in 1936 the association had less than 2,000 paid members and only $435.11 on hand, both gubernatorial candidates attended the AGPA's convention that year. Nor was the association reticent about expressing its demands. The AGPA expected future governors to confer with the executive committee prior to commission appointments and wanted the department to consult with AGPA prior to making any major changes in the hunt regulations. They would get both.

Finances were in even worse condition by 1937. In the summer of 1936, the AGPA had restricted its contribution to *Hoofs and Horns* to $25 a month for two pages. And even though the AGPA had joined the National Wildlife Federation, sufficient funds could not be raised at 25 cents a head levy to send a delegate to the federation's conference in Saint Louis, Missouri. Dissension among the locals continued. Each local had different objectives, not all of them in line with those of the majority of the executive committee. Some locals even defected, the Phoenix Sportsman's Association disassociating itself from the state organization until 1940.

Nonetheless, AGPA leadership retained the ear of the commission and department, the executive committee being a major architect of the state's annual hunting and fishing regulations. Neither Lewis nor his successor, William Sawtelle, appear to have been particularly strong State Game Wardens. Both usually followed the association's recommendations, which by now had become pretty standard. The local affiliates wanted more varied fish introductions such as smallmouth bass, pickerel, and walleyes (see Appendix E, Table E-1). Many locals continued to submit resolutions for more matching funds for

Bill Beers wearing an AGPA shoulder patch while checking out one of the first legally killed desert bighorn sheep. The AGPA pronghorn logo is shown in black on a red background. (Arizona Wildlife Federation)

PARC, a split duck season, and a shorter quail season. Another perennial request—for a federal fish hatchery on the White Mountain Apache Indian Reservation—finally became a reality due to Diffin's political efforts. So intertwined by now were the activities of AGPA members and the department that a resolution was passed at the 1937 convention requiring the AGPA insignia to be worn in the field by all members to promote better law enforcement—and respect for the association.

Another action of note was the formation of rancher-sportsmen committees to hash out problems with access, the growing elk herd, and vandalism. Issues such as overgrazing and the shortcomings of the Taylor Grazing Act also attracted the notice of the executive committee. An especially interesting political action, given the AGPA's lack of funds, was getting the National Audubon Society to sponsor a three-year study of bighorn sheep in the Catalina Mountains under the direction of Vorhies and Nichol—a funding approach soon superseded by passage of the Pittman-Robertson Act, which financed such projects as game and fish department research. That the winter of 1936–37 had been particularly severe was also a concern, generating a request for Civilian Conservation Corps and Emergency Conservation Work camps at Mayer and Hillside to distribute grain for quail and turkeys. They also anticipated serious antelope and elk losses due to the heavy snow.

A Force in the Making, 1939–45

In 1938, McCullough was once again elected to take the helm of a fractious AGPA. Working with Diffin and other association stalwarts, McCullough attempted to reunify the AGPA and get it back on a course of public service. But even though the number of affiliates held fast, total membership declined, with just under 1,900 members in 1939. Nonetheless, McCullough and his successors—Richard K. Wickstrum, Charles Wilson, and James E. Babbitt—succeeded in bringing the Phoenix Sportsmen back into the fold through a merger with the Arizona Sportsman's Association. And, despite a continuing reluctance to finance a state organization, sufficient funds were raised to field an executive secretary (Vernon Foster) and an editor (James R. Wilson). A new executive committee was formed of four vice presidents, a secretary, and a treasurer. The commission planned to revise the game regulations in 1939, and the AGPA wanted to make sure its input was considered.

Helping to maintain the AGPA's credibility was the 1939 passage of a state bill allowing Arizona to participate in the Pittman-Robertson Act of 1937—an issue dear to Vorhies, Taylor, McCullough, and other AGPA leaders. This legislation was indeed a triumph for wildlife, as it provided a funding mechanism for much-needed game surveys, studies, and research. With game populations beginning to turn the corner, and AGPA members represented in the department and on the commission, interest among affiliates intensified. The number of resolutions passed at the annual convention jumped from 3 in 1938 to 27 in 1939, 25 in 1940, and 30 in 1941.

The AGPA's 17th convention was remarkable in several respects, not the least being that several women were present. Attesting to the AGPA's newfound importance was even stronger attendance by livestock interests and federal agencies. Resolutions included doing for fish what the Pittman-Robertson Act did for game, opposing any more federal land acquisitions (a residue of the Kofa and Cabeza Prieta game range withdrawals), reducing the size of Grand Canyon National Park and Lake Mead National Recreation Area, and extending predator control to national park lands and Indian reservations. More local issues involved opposition to "big buck" contests, the need for merit-based salary raises for the eight to 12 deputy wardens then employed, no increase in hunting or fishing license fees, and numerous regulation changes pertaining to season lengths, bag limits, and drawing procedures. Interestingly, one of the latter included a resolution to change the deer-hunting regulations to allow for either sex to be killed—a resolution strongly opposed by some locals and *not* passed by the commission.

Also of interest was the commission's appointment of Kenner Kartchner as State Game Warden. Kartchner was an AGPA official of long standing and a strong supporter of AGPA policies. Wickstrum was appointed executive secretary in 1941 and assigned to attend all commission meetings (the former executive secretary, Charles C. Niehuis, had joined the Game and Fish Department as its first information and education officer).

The Arizona Game and Fish Department's then-new quail logo on the door panel of Gabby Blaser's department pickup, ca. 1956. (AGFD files)

There were also some disappointments. The Junior Wildlife Federation, an initially promising program strongly advocated by one of the two Tucson affiliates, would be abandoned during the war years. For some reason, youth programs, always an important issue for the AGPA, never seemed to get off the ground, despite attempts to involve the Boy Scouts and other youth groups in beaver transplanting, carp eradication, trout stocking, and other wildlife management activities.

Knowing the magazine was the key communication medium for AGPA members and supporters, McCullough and Diffin set about reviving *Arizona Wild Life*. The magazine briefly re-emerged as a bimonthly in January–February 1938 before dropping some issues to come out as a reorganized *Arizona Wild Life and Sportsman* in January 1939. After skipping November and December 1939, it began again as a monthly in February 1940, with Jack O'Connor assuming the position of editor or associate editor through the end of the year. At this time the commission, at the AGPA's request, agreed to purchase three pages of advertising at $25 per page (an earlier vote was for $50 for two pages) with any additional copy to be published free of charge. To reach people who were not AGPA members, the commission also voted that year to publish its commission orders and a $99 announcement of any changes to the hunting and fishing regulations in the *Arizona Republic*, the department not yet having a publications branch.

Although the name of the magazine was changed to *Arizona Wild Life and Sportsman*, the AGPA continued to retain its antelope-head logo. (It was about this time that the Arizona Game and Fish Department also adopted its Gambel's quail logo.) The masthead slogan, introduced in March 1940, was "Better Hunting and Fishing for Arizona." Each issue carried a monthly summary of all the game and fish regulations, along with game-case arrests. Department technicians, including State Game Warden Kartchner, reported on Federal-Aid projects. O'Connor and Niehuis kept up member's interests with good hunting stories, in addition to the latest reports on the status of elk and antelope. It was also during this time that the first articles critical of grazing appeared; however, the cases illustrated did not pertain to Arizona. That, and the taking on of the livestock industry, was yet to come.

CONGRESS COMES TO THE RESCUE

David E. Brown

The 1930s was a difficult time for both wildlife and the Arizona Game and Fish Department. Little was known about the status of game species, and game numbers were the subject of much speculation. Almost nothing was understood about limiting factors, and with the exception of deer and turkeys, the Arizona Game and Fish Commission authorized new seasons only on species that *needed* to be hunted due to depredation complaints or imbalanced sex ratios. Although game numbers were considered low, nobody really knew, as there was no money to conduct game surveys and no system for determining the numbers of animals bagged. Season closures were the standard remedy for population declines, both real and imagined.

Even the most abundant species were little understood. Quail seasons were adjusted annually to reflect observed population changes, with seasons eventually being closed in Apache, Coconino, and Navajo counties. Even hunt regulations and bag limits on cottontails fluctuated. There was no open season on javelina, elk, antelope, tree squirrels, Mearns' quail, or blue grouse. Deer and turkey harvest numbers were merely guesses. Most biologists and sportsmen believed there was more than one kind of white-tailed deer in Arizona. In 1938, the commission closed the season on ibex, lest it be shown this animal resided in the state without protection.

The impacts of homesteading and livestock grazing continued to lie heavily upon the land. Overgrazing was rampant, and although Arizona was not one of the Dust Bowl states, the drought's effects on migratory waterfowl were felt in Arizona as in the rest of the country. Federal regulations cut the bag limits on ducks from 25 to 15 a day, but still their numbers declined. Deer numbers were thought to be at low levels throughout the state, including on the Kaibab Plateau. Southern Arizona sportsmen reported whitetails to be at an all-time low in 1941. Turkeys, at least in the mountains south of the Gila River, had almost disappeared, and these formerly abundant game birds were now numerous only on the Apache Indian reservations. Quail populations would surge one year, only to decline the next. Even white-winged doves, a species considered by some to be more of a pest than a game bird, were becoming less common. Game management was mostly limited to closing seasons, establishing and abolishing refuges, and conducting an annual buffalo hunt.

As long as the Arizona Game and Fish Department's income was generated solely by sales of hunting and fishing licenses, there was little hope for an improvement in game management. The Game and Fish Fund was constantly impoverished. Department personnel in 1933 consisted of only 18 people, and it was all the agency could do to pay their salaries, enforce the game and fish code, maintain its fish hatcheries, and post game refuges.

And things were getting worse, not better. Hunting license sales declined from 36,945 in 1930 to 32,870 in 1936—an 11% drop (see Appendix D, Table D-1). This lack of money, coupled with political uncertainty, meant deputy wardens had to take side jobs to compensate for periodic layoffs, terminations, and salary cuts. Monthly travel payments were more reliable than salaries, and field personnel were well-advised to have "outside" sources of revenue: selling farm products, dealing in antiques, or even engaging in contraband.

Arizona was not alone in its predicament. With the onset of the Great Depression, most state game departments were hard-pressed to do anything but administer game laws. What was desperately needed was additional revenue—money to conduct game surveys, fund scientific research into the needs of wildlife species, and acquire habitats for specific animals. Without additional sources of revenue, wildlife populations would not, and could not, be restored.

Surprisingly, salvation came not from the states, which were constitutionally responsible for resident game species, but from the also cash-strapped federal government. The solutions, formulated by gun and ammunition manufacturers and promoted by sportsmen-conservationists, were pure genius. That these proposals were actually made law by the US Congress was unprecedented—they became part of the foundation of a uniquely American model of wildlife conservation (Trefethen 1961).

Three major pieces of federal legislation pertaining to wildlife and game management were passed in the 1930s. In 1929, Frederic C. Walcott, a founder of the American Game Protective Association, was elected to the US Senate by Connecticut voters. Shortly after being elected, Walcott introduced a resolution forming a special committee on wildlife headed by Aldo Leopold. A policy developed from this resolution was adopted by the American Game Protective Association and became the "American Game Policy." Adopted in 1934, it called for every state governor to appoint a nonsalaried game and fish commission consisting of from three to six nonpartisan members serving staggered terms in office. These commissions, similar to Arizona's Game and Fish Commission, would give each state's wildlife conservation-agency director full authority over the game and fish affairs of his department, including wildlife laws, regulations, and programs.

In 1931, this same committee had dusted off a proposal for a one-cent tax on shotgun shells, formerly promoted by the American Game Protective Association and the More Game Birds in America Foundation as a means of financing acquisition of wetlands for waterfowl. Although Congress turned down this proposal in 1932 on the basis that upland game hunters should not be taxed to benefit waterfowl hunters, the merit of the idea persisted. The committee opted for the sale of a federal "duck stamp" that would be required of all waterfowl hunters 16 years of age or older. Proceeds from stamps would be earmarked for the purchase, development, and management of wetlands for waterfowl.

Passage of the Migratory Bird Hunting Stamp Act of 1934, commonly known as the "duck stamp" bill, was no shoo-in. It was bitterly fought by wildlife protectionists, who objected to the purchase of wetlands by and for waterfowl hunters and termed the legislation a bill to purchase "duck-slaughtering grounds." Not all of the areas acquired were wetlands or open to shooting. Depending on management objectives, portions of every waterfowl "refuge" so obtained were commonly closed to hunting.

A 1935 migratory bird hunting stamp. The program, still active today, funds the purchase, development, and management of wetlands for waterfowl. (AGFD files)

The US Biological Survey (soon to become the US Fish and Wildlife Service) would eventually purchase and maintain more than 600 national wildlife refuges representing every state in the Union. Although not a major factor in preserving Arizona's few diminishing wetlands, duck-stamp monies would be used to manage refuges along the lower Colorado River beginning in the 1940s. More important to Arizona was the acquisition of refuges north of the state, which would assure nesting areas for ducks, geese, and cranes that visited and wintered in Arizona.

In terms of federal actions taken to assist the states with wildlife management, the most important to Arizona was the Pittman-Robertson Federal Aid in Wildlife Restoration Act, approved by Congress on September 2, 1937. This legislation allowed state game departments to receive a three-to-one match from a fund derived from a 10% tax on all firearms and ammunition sold in the United States. The caveat was that, to participate in the program, each state legislature had to pass an enabling act agreeing the money could be spent only for wildlife management, wildlife research, or habitat acquisition: No money could be spent for law enforcement, or for information and education programs other than publications arising from Federal-Aid projects. Predator control, while not expressly allowed, could be included as part of an approved management or research program. Appropriations to individual states were determined using a formula based 50% on the number of licensed hunters in the state and 50% on the area of the state in relation to the United States. Of the 48 states then existing, 43 signed on the first year. Arizona, always wary of federal money, would take a little longer.

Gov. Robert T. Jones signs the bill authorizing Arizona's participation in federal funding for wildlife restoration under the Pittman-Robertson Act. Standing behind the governor are the Fish and Game Committee legislators, including James E. Babbitt of Flagstaff (far left), State Game Warden William Sawtelle (in dark glasses), Federal-Aid Coordinator Stokley Ligon (second from right), and Arizona Game Protective Association Secretary Vernon Fowler (far right). (Reproduced from Arizona Wild Life *magazine, Arizona Wildlife Federation; Arizona State Library, Archives and Public Records, History and Archives Division)*

Pittman-Robertson funds would allow the states to acquire key habitats, implement research projects, and conduct game surveys, with the proviso that monies derived from hunting and fishing licenses be deposited in a special game and fish fund. The state would then appropriate one-third of the fund as wildlife restoration monies to be matched with federal restoration funds at an original rate of three federal dollars for every state dollar, up to a maximum of $20,000. Any unspent money would revert to the state general fund.

After some debate, on March 10, 1939, the Arizona State Legislature passed HB110 as an emergency measure, empowering the Arizona Game and Fish Commission to cooperate with a Federal-Aid coordinator from the Biological Survey to finance wildlife restoration projects. Because the 10% federal tax on firearms had first been imposed in 1932, sufficient funds had accumulated to begin immediately. In its first year, the excise tax on firearms allocated $2,976,019 to wildlife restoration projects nationwide.

Federal-Aid monies not only provided an important source of revenue for cash-starved game departments, provisions of the act allowed the hiring of college-trained professional biologists, thereby greatly increasing the professional capability of the conservation agencies in those states that agreed to the terms of the act. All of the states, Arizona included, could benefit.

Arizona's commission wasted little time in directing State Game Warden William Sawtelle to enter into an agreement with Federal-Aid Coordinator Stokley Ligon. Arrangements were made to have W. L. "Roy" Gambrell supervise a series of Federal-Aid projects, with Andrew Nichol supervising wildlife investigations in what were called "Project 9-R" studies out of an office at 627 N. Vine in Tucson (Tucson being closer to the

University of Arizona and Santa Rita Experimental Range than Phoenix). Later Federal-Aid project supervisors included Kenner Kartchner and Orville "Pop" Arrington, who would design studies to solve some of the agency's more vexing problems. One of the first projects approved was a white-winged dove nesting study that would determine the percentage of doves nesting prior to September 1 and provide other life-history information.

Including the state's matching monies, Arizona's Federal-Aid allotments for 1939 and 1940 came to $18,611.66 and $29,276.78, respectively. This was an impressive amount of money for a department whose annual budget at the time was only about $100,000.

The year 1940 was a time of transition for the department. State Game Warden Sawtelle resigned and was replaced by Federal-Aid Supervisor Kartchner. With the encouragement of the commission, Kartchner reorganized the department. The agency would now consist of five department heads and their staffs—an office manager, a chief deputy, a director of information, a director of fisheries, and a director of Federal-Aid projects. The Federal-Aid office in Tucson was closed, leaving Gambrell to supervise all Pittman-Robertson–funded projects out of the Phoenix office (Arizona Game and Fish Commission 1942).

Federal-Aid money increased rapidly concomitant with rising license sales. New Pittman-Robertson projects were authorized as earlier ones were completed. These included a tassel-eared squirrel transplanting project approved in late 1940, and two white-winged dove studies (L. Arnold 1941, 1943; Tinkham 1941, 1942) showing that August was a major month for dove production and that habitat conditions were an important limiting factor on the species. Other new projects approved in 1941 included a series of land acquisitions along the lower Gila River between Texas Hill and Yuma, an attempt to restore quail habitats in Cochise County, the purchase of Raymond Ranch below Anderson Mesa as wintering habitat for antelope, and a pipeline to deliver water to the House Rock Buffalo Ranch.

The Federal-Aid director was in charge of several project leaders, each supervising one or more field technicians and/or predator trappers. The hiring of professional biologists gave great impetus to the department's credibility, thereby enabling the commission to initiate an antelope season in 1941, participate more fully in the design of the Kaibab deer hunt, supervise an unlimited elk hunt in 1942, and follow federal guidelines for the hunting of white-winged doves.

Probably the most important Pittman-Robertson innovation consisted of sending mail questionnaires to license purchasers after the 1941 hunting season. For the first time, game harvest estimates were available from both hunter questionnaires and check stations. These initial estimates showed what game was the most popular and approximated how many animals of each species were being harvested. Initial harvest estimates for 1942, undoubtedly low, were:

- 7,009 mule deer,
- 1,829 white-tailed deer,
- 966 javelina,
- 119 bear,

• 2,152 turkeys,
• 494,379 Gambel's quail,
• 25,202 scaled quail,
• 424,486 mourning dove,
• 91,859 waterfowl,
• 219,146 cottontails, and
• 9,140 band-tailed pigeons or "bluerocks."

The statewide game survey recognized three subspecies of mule deer, including the *buro* deer, along with three kinds of white-tailed deer. Although the occurrence and distribution of such species as the blue grouse and Mearns' quail were now officially recognized, pertinent information for other species remained unknown. Examples included the sources of most waterfowl and the wintering ranges of both mourning and white-winged dove.

This lack of knowledge, coupled with the practice of hunting whitewings during the nesting season, resulted in the federal government's disapproving the commission's recommendation for a season opening on this species on August 16 in 1940. It was not until the publication of Arnold's and Tinkham's Pittman-Robertson reports that the commission was convinced an August season was tantamount to leaving young birds to die in the nest. As a result, the commission closed the season on this species in 1941 and 1942—a study by federal biologist Johnson Neff (1940a, 1940b) showing that Arizona's whitewing population had been reduced to only 10% of its former numbers.

In 1942, $70,865.51 in Federal-Aid dollars became available to Arizona—a significant increase over the $63,973.09 available in 1941. Although the war resulted in reduced manpower, and the state's contribution to the Pittman-Robertson fund was frozen at $6,000 per year, the decline in allocated monies was neither severe nor permanent. Arizona's license sales soon rebounded, with corresponding increases in Pittman-Robertson allocations—$60,843 in 1943; $62,925 in 1944; and $73,528 in 1945.[1] At war's height, on July 1, 1943, Arizona had spent some $229,416 on Pittman-Robertson projects, holding some $23,755 in reserve. In 1946, after the end of the war, Arizona's allocation was a whopping $135,520.

The Federal-Aid Division was by now the intellectual force of the department, and it was common practice for project leaders to attend commission meetings. Federal-Aid personnel continued to predominate as policymakers into the postwar years, with Federal-Aid supervisors Fred Merkle and Tom Kimball becoming department directors and Pop Arrington assuming the role of big game supervisor. New projects and new hires added to the department's roster. Fur prices were high then; there was even a Fur Conservation Division under the leadership of the appropriately named Pittman-Robertson biologist B. C. "Bobby" Fox.

If anything, the influence of the Federal-Aid Division increased after the war. Although Congress had failed to make annual appropriations of much of the Federal-Aid

[1] Much of this money was banked because Game and Fish Fund contributions had been frozen at $6,000 per year, despite another $22,000 in state funds being appropriated by the legislature.

Tom Kimball releasing pheasants near Buckeye as part of a Pittman-Robertson project, ca. 1946. (AGFD files)

money allocated during the 1941–46 period, the $15,000,000 that had accumulated was now given to the states. In addition to its regular Pittman-Robertson appropriations, Arizona's legislature was also now appropriating up to $22,000 a year in matching money to be spent on federal predator-control activities (Arizona Game and Fish Commission 1948).

Federal-Aid positions and personnel now included a wildlife development coordinator (Gambrell), a research biologist (James T. "Tommy" Wright), and an ornithologist for upland and migratory game birds (Warren Pulich). Jay Klaus was in charge of game depredation control, and Louis "Buzz" Lawson was the reluctant supervisor of a game bird farm, bequeathed by the Soil Conservation Service and accepted by the department because of public pressure on the commission. The farm raised pheasants, chukars, and mountain quail.

By the end of the 1940s, the department was selling enough licenses and tags to bring in more than half a million dollars a year and receiving more than $250,000 a year in Federal-Aid monies. Federal-Aid monies were so large a proportion of the department's budget that the agency's cash-starved divisions threatened to curtail their services when it came to fisheries and law enforcement.

Prior to 1951, the legislature had appropriated Pittman-Robinson matching money from the general fund. Then, after a ruling by the attorney general, the legislature began appropriating all department funds, allocating the amount needed to obtain the maximum appropriation from a federal fund now based on an 11% excise tax on firearms and ammunition. With increased funding available, the number of Federal-Aid employees increased to 15—more than in any other division, including fisheries and law enforcement (Arizona Game and Fish Commission 1951).

This increased revenue not only allowed aerial antelope surveys and other census procedures to become standard, annual harvest estimates in the state's five game management zones could now be determined from hunter report cards and check stations. As more hunting brought in more Pittman-Robertson money, new projects were authorized and others were retired.

Benefiting from a deer boom then underway, the Federal-Aid Division, now under Arrington's supervision, began employing biologists to study the factors influencing deer numbers and the impacts of high deer numbers on chaparral and other habitats (see e.g., Hanson and McCulloch 1955; Gallizioli 1956; Johnson and Swank 1957). Other studies sought to identify the diseases and parasites affecting game animals (Hanson and McCulloch 1955; Gallizioli 1956; Erling 1956a, 1956b; Johnson and Swank 1957), as it became apparent that enough Federal-Aid money was available to fund research programs as well as ongoing management activities. As a result, the Federal-Aid program was separated into W-78 Research projects and W-53 Management projects, with development, land acquisition, and other Federal-Aid programs contained within other Pittman-Robertson projects.

By 1962, the present Federal Aid in Wildlife Restoration program was essentially in place, and the Arizona Game and Fish Department was well on its way to becoming an established, professional agency for the management of Arizona's wildlife.

TOWARD A MORE PROFESSIONAL GAME AND FISH DEPARTMENT

David E. Brown

Arizona's participation in the Pittman-Robertson program brought in more than much-needed revenue. The hiring of game technicians, as they were called, provided a professional cadre of field men to investigate wildlife problems and provide the commission with biologically sound solutions. Only by so doing could the Arizona Game and Fish Department coordinate with and eventually supplant the expertise of US Biological Survey biologists and US Forest Service range conservationists. Better information also enhanced the department's credibility with the Arizona Game Protective Association and earned the confidence of a diverse public.

These technicians were not political appointees hired by the Arizona Game and Fish Commission; rather, they were vetted through the Federal-Aid coordinator in Albuquerque. This proved especially fortuitous for the Game and Fish Department. Many of the men had some college training and a background with an academic institution or government agency. Few, if any, were selected for their political connections or given responsibilities outside of assigned areas of investigation.

Young, scientifically oriented, and dedicated to doing a good job, this new breed of technicians came to be known as the "milkshake boys" for their preference for soft drinks and ice cream as opposed to the coffee-break beverages preferred by the game wardens (Carr 1994).

A 1942 photo at the Capitol shows some of the first technicans hired after Arizona signed on to the provisions prescribed in the Pittman-Robertson Act. From left to right are Roy Gambrell, Lee Arnold, Orville Arrington, Ted Knipe, Tom Kimball, Kenner Kartchner, and Secretary Dorothy Sparks. (AGFD files, provided by Ted Knipe and John N. Carr)

Kenner Kartchner Takes Control

When the Federal-Aid studies initiated in 1939 and 1940 were completed, the Federal-Aid biologists were required to produce written reports on their findings, reports that included recommendations involving the natural history and limiting factors associated with wild turkeys; use of newly constructed game water catchments; the status of little-known game species such as blue grouse and fool's quail (Montezuma or Mearns' quail); the trapping and restocking of quail, turkeys, pheasants, and beavers (Brown 1989); and a statewide game inventory.

Once their studies were completed, some of the new Federal-Aid hires such as Lynn Hargrave moved on, while other technicians such as Tom Kimball, Roy Gambrell, Ted Knipe, Orville "Pop" Arrington, and Tommy Wright stayed to conduct other studies or assume other positions within the department. Some, including Kimball and Kenner Kartchner, became Pittman-Robertson project supervisors or assumed administrative positions.

In many respects, the department's beginnings as a professional organization can be traced to May 5, 1940, when the commission appointed Kartchner acting State Game Warden. Kartchner was a fortuitous choice.[1] A longtime AGPA member, he was an experienced administrator, having served as supervisor of the Manzano and Cibola national forests in New Mexico. Moreover, recent experience as Federal-Aid project leader had made him deeply familiar with Arizona's game management needs.

Kartchner's relationship with key Forest Service personnel, and his deep roots in the AGPA as a member of the White Mountains Sportsmen, had given him a knowledge of the state's wildlife superior to that of most of the day's "game experts." He had not only published a number of knowledgeable articles about antelope, elk, and other game animals, he had judiciously editorialized on a series of conservation issues, including the lack of game management on the Navajo Indian Reservation. As was the case with many members of the Church of Jesus Christ of Latter-Day Saints, Kartchner also had a penchant for organization.

Contributing to Kartchner's tenure was the appointment of Charles Beach, a rancher from Vail, to the Arizona Game and Fish Commission. Beach, who would serve 18 years on the commission, was highly conservative about hunting regulations and a staunch advocate of predator control. He was nonetheless prone to follow the advice of the technicians, and appears to have had a good working relationship with the AGPA and the state's cattlemen-oriented legislature. Shunning the spotlight, he encouraged the department to follow traditional procedures and embark on new programs with caution. As such, he favored maintaining a traditional May 30 through September 30 trout season, and encouraged public participation at commission meetings by instituting a policy of setting hunt regulations at a single midsummer commission meeting.

---

[1] Kartchner was also a champion fiddler of much renown, presiding at many rural dances. Interestingly, his biography (Shumway and Kartchner 1990) makes little mention of his Forest Service career and almost no mention of his service with the Arizona Game and Fish Department.

Not only were the department's financial matters in disarray, Kartchner's duties as acting State Game Warden were made even more difficult by the resignation of the department's office manager and chief accountant, M. S. Mills. Although Kartchner attempted to continue some of the innovative changes initiated by Sawtelle—including the provision of archery hunts; separate north-zone and south-zone deer seasons; and opening all trout waters to fishing—his influence was tempered by a commission influenced by a very active AGPA and cattlemen's lobby. The AGPA and Arizona Cattlegrowers Association sent delegates to all commission meetings, as did the Forest Service. Complicating any game management agenda was an imprecise knowledge of the status of game animals: Many southern Arizonans believed that mule deer south of the Gila River needed special protection and that white-tailed deer numbers were at an all-time low.

As a commissioner for 18 years, Charles Beach, a rancher from Vail, Arizona, got on well with both the Arizona Game and Fish Department and the Arizona Game Protective Association. (Arizona Wildlife and Sportsman, *Arizona Wildlife Federation; Arizona State Library, Archives and Public Records, History and Archives Division)*

Also inhibiting Kartchner was a somewhat disfunctional commission. Commissioner Thomas Imler of Phoenix often either missed commission meetings or failed to sign commission orders. When Kartchner appointed Herbert Reid as chief of fisheries over Imler's strong opposition, Imler circulated a petition among hatchery workers, objecting to Reid's appointment. Also, Beach and Winslow's George Wrench were prone (at least at first) to looking to the AGPA for guidance as often as, or more than, they looked to Kartchner.

As a result, Kartchner was directed to canvass the local game protective associations as to what duck season to recommend, what to do about Mormon Lake going dry, and which refuges to establish or abolish. Moreover, the AGPA executive committee was now making its own recommendations as to hunting seasons, bag limits, legal weapons, etc. As a consequence, the split north-zone, south-zone deer season was rescinded and the mule deer hunt closure south of the Gila River reinstated. The AGPA was even authorized to check the department's equipment inventory.

On the other hand, relations with federal agencies, particularly the Forest Service, improved. After some serious discussion, both Kartchner and the Forest Service concluded the Kaibab deer herd should be increased, and it was jointly agreed that Everett Mercer of the US Fish and Wildlife Service should send lion hunters and coyote trappers there. Cooperative agreements with the Fish and Wildlife Service and Forest Service also resulted in the department's agreeing to jointly manage the Apache Migratory Waterfowl Refuge in the White Mountains and Bill Williams Wildlife Management Unit south of Williams.

With confidence in Kartchner achieved, the commission appointed him State Game Warden in his own right in August 1940 for a four-year term ending in August 1944 at $300 per month. Feeling the need for an administrative assistant, Kartchner appointed Charles Connally chief deputy game warden early the following year, and in May 1941, Gov. Sidney Osborn appointed William S. Connor of Clarkdale to replace Wrench on the commission. The commission then delegated all budget and operating procedures to Kartchner, who was now in charge of all Game and Fish Department employees—a responsibility formerly assumed by the commission and one later commissions would seek to regain. Perhaps most important from an administrative standpoint, a report by the state auditor for fiscal year 1940–41 showed the department's books to be in a healthy financial condition.

In a vote of confidence, the commission directed Kartchner, not the AGPA, to draw up the 1941 hunt regulations that included a February javelina season. Kartchner was also directed to meet with Nevada personnel regarding the joint management of Lake Mead's fisheries and to arrange for the Fish and Wildlife Service to provide one federal trapper for every state trapper sent into the field, thereby doubling the predator-control effort protecting game animals.

The summer hunt-season–setting commission meeting in 1941 reflected Kartchner's negotiating skills with not only the commission, but the AGPA, the Arizona Cattlegrowers Association, and the Forest Service. A hunt to take 75 "old buck" antelope in the spring of 1941 was replaced with a 400-antelope hunt (bucks only) for the fall of 1941. Depredation complaints notwithstanding—and there were a number of them—the 1942 elk season was limited to bull-only permits, despite Forest Service recommendations for a greater harvest.

Other actions included a return to the split north-zone, south-zone deer season and the opening of a brief mule deer season south of the Gila River. Rather than open a tree squirrel season as requested by the Forest Service, the commission approved a Federal-Aid project for trapping excess squirrels in the Fort Valley area northwest of Flagstaff and transplanting them to ponderosa pine forests where tassel-eared squirrels were absent. It was also decided that no more Pittman-Robertson funds would be expended on chukars—a motion that was later reversed.

In 1942, for the first time, more than 50,000 licenses were sold. The department budget remained small, with only $110,000 being spent—just a little more than in 1941. Nonetheless, Pittman-Robertson funding had greatly increased, and the state's contribution came to $70,865, allowing for a total budget of $229,416.10 for fiscal year 1942–43. Except for land acquisitions, most of these excess Federal-Aid monies were held in abeyance until the end of the war. Exceptions included the purchase of Raymond Ranch in 1942 as winter range for antelope, and the acquisition of 8,000 acres of farmland along the lower Gila River from the federal government for delinquent taxes.

State Game Warden Kenner C. Kartchner in 1942 showing the uniform he designed, with pearl gray Stetson, dark tie, and regulation shirt and trousers. A similar uniform was worn by US Forest Service rangers. The bighorn shoulder patch on Deputy Warden George Peterson may have been optional, as shoulder patches are absent in other photos of department personnel in uniform. (Kartchner photo courtesy of Dale Shumway; Peterson photo AGFD files)

Charles Niehuis was appointed the first director of information in 1942 to handle news releases, negotiate motion picture contracts, and promulgate a department newsletter. The field force of only 12 full-time wardens in 1941 was bolstered that year by 112 part-time deputies, mostly AGPA members. In 1942, a general elk season was opened for all hunters who wanted to obtain meat for the war effort (Arizona Game and Fish Commission 1942).

The AGPA continued to play a major role in department operations. The commission directed that AGPA Executive Director Richard Wickstrum and other AGPA members again oversee the organizational affairs of both the department and commission. Game and fish policies were discussed at length at commission meetings, and it was under AGPA guidance that a department budget was approved and procedures outlined for monthly financial statements. It was also decided the commission would meet more regularly, every six weeks or as needed, with Beach as more-or-less-permanent chairman.

Deputy wardens were directed to wear "standard uniforms" and appear neat and tidy. It was reiterated that all employees were exclusively under the direction of the State Game Warden and not Federal-Aid project leaders, individual commissioners, or AGPA officers. Fleet vehicle purchases went to the lowest bidder, while procedures for license-dealer reporting, equipment purchasing, and inventory taking were tightened and clarified. A $1,000 bond was required of all license dealers and a non-discriminatory rule enforced.

Discussed by the commission, but not acted upon, was Kartchner's proposal that all department buildings, including fish hatcheries, be painted an ivory white with olive-green roofs and trim, similar to Forest Service buildings. In addition to the office at the

Capitol, the department leased a nearby building for $60 a month to house the three division heads and the four permanent employees in the Federal-Aid Division.

Some small game hunt seasons were liberalized. The two-week quail season was expanded to one month in Mohave and Yuma counties, where technicians agreed an "overabundance" of quail existed. The commission was now prone to follow the recommendations of the technicians, which were also quite conservative—a similar extension being denied for Greenlee County on the basis of testimony by technicians Tom Kimball and Andrew Nichol that this county did not have an overabundance of birds. A prototype hunt questionnaire program was also approved as a means to determine game harvests, even though hiring of the game statistician position was postponed, negating the use of comparable hunt survey data until after war's end. An agreement was also reached whereby refuges on national forests would only be established or abolished with the approval of the Forest Service. Also averting a conflict was the commission's approval of an Indian Service request for $10 elk permits on the Fort Apache reservation as long as state licenses and permits were obtained.

Fred Merkle Moves Forward

Now an experienced wildlife administrator, Kartchner, after attending the Seventh North American Conference in Toronto in 1942 and the Western Association of Game and Fish Commissioners in Cheyenne in 1943, left to become the Southwest Federal-Aid coordinator with what was now the Fish and Wildlife Service in Albuquerque.

Connor assumed the commission chairmanship in 1943 and served with Beach and the new appointee, Harry Hamilton. The commission appointed Fred Merkle, Kartchner's assistant, as State Game Warden. A safe if not particularly exciting choice, the veteran Merkle was another Federal-Aid technician and former Forest Service supervisor with experience on the Kaibab, Coconino, and Sitgreaves national forests.

Although license sales continued to increase throughout the war years, and the department's annual budget was now over $135,000, funds were still inadequate to institute much change. The Game and Fish Department did not even have money to cover collision insurance for its fleet of 20 vehicles. As a result, employees had to insure their own cars when used for business.

The commission, realizing that Niehuis was overburdened with plans to publish a hunting pamphlet and other department directives, allowed employees to freelance articles, provided the subject was game, fish, or hunting, and the copy was reviewed by Merkle. To keep the public informed of commission and other regulatory activities, Merkle was directed to advertise in the Phoenix and Tucson newspapers.

Conflicts were bound to occur, particularly between the department, the AGPA, and the Arizona Cattlegrowers Association, and Governor Osborn felt it necessary to appoint a mediator to resolve issues between the three. As a compromise with stockmen, who wanted the bear declared a predator, the bear season was lengthened, and a spring season was authorized with hunting with dogs allowed.

When Hamilton died in office in 1944, Connor remained chairman with Beach as the only other commissioner. Wickstrum was appointed Hamilton's replacement, making the

State Game Warden Fred Merkle was a veteran of long standing with the US Forest Service. He took over from Kartchner as Arizona's wartime State Game Warden. (Arizona State Library, Archives and Public Records, History and Archives Division)

AGPA's influence even stronger. A wartime department staff, coupled with a conservative sportsmen lobby and a strong cattlegrower presence, not only made for more stringent hunt regulations, it fostered a demand for more law enforcement and predator control.

Although the commission continued to deal with beaver, buffalo, and bears as important issues needing attention, it was decided there was "no need" for either an antelope season or an elk season in 1944. Also reducing the department's potential income was closing Yuma County to deer hunting and reducing the quail season to two weeks.

Predator control continued to be a major concern and expenditure, with Arizona sportsmen now contributing 28% of Arizona's predatory-animal control budget through Pittman-Robertson funding and department appropriations. The commission was so eager to escalate the war on predators that it had Merkle appoint one of Arizona's deputy wardens as a member of the Predator Animal Control Committee on the Western Association of Game and Fish Commissioners, and asked the attorney general for an opinion as to whether the state could reinstate a bounty system and conduct predator control on Grand Canyon National Park.

The number of game refuges having ballooned to 81, the commission's goal was now to reduce them to the lowest number conducive to good game management. Research investigations were de-emphasized in favor of stocking and restocking game animals. Other actions included directing Merkle to issue deputy wardens a book of instructions and require them to be in uniform at all times. Merkle was also to supply the commission with quarterly (originally monthly) reports, and division directors, especially Federal-Aid supervisors, were to see to it that employees followed the chain of command. It was agreed that the hiring of another director of information was of the highest importance, Niehuis having left the department to work for the AGPA.

Herbert Reid Takes the Reins

In January 1945, the state game code was opened to revision. One minefield to avoid was conflict with the stockman-friendly legislature when drafting regulations on javelina, bears, jackrabbits, and other potential "predators." Then, in September 1945, Merkle, who had missed the previous commission meeting, abruptly resigned due to ill health. The commission appointed Fisheries Division Chief Reid acting State Game Warden and then director. Originally hired as a deputy warden, Reid had garnered much favor for supervising the construction of the Hunt Bass Hatchery under difficult circumstances. Popular with the commission and sportsmen, Reid was the first career employee to rise to the level of department head. Unlike his two predecessors, the new leader did not have a formal education and had never been a Pittman-Robertson technician.

Because of all the people moving to Arizona, license sales actually increased during the war years. The department budgeted more than $150,000 in 1945 for game management programs, with another $118,320 for fisheries. The commission also approved salary raises. In another action, the commission changed the title of the State Game Warden to State Game and Fish Director, with deputy wardens to be addressed as game rangers and provided with both a dress uniform and field uniform. Rangers were given the responsibility of assisting in the collection of hunt information and helping the game and fish technicians with their duties. In the way of regulations, the commission continued its conservative ways, failing to authorize an elk, antelope, or turkey season due to lower than desired population levels. The season on tree squirrels also remained closed, and the quail season continued to be limited to only two weeks.

Probably due to Connor's influence, the commission directed the department to return to its roots, with the major emphasis to be on hatcheries, predator control, and law enforcement. To emphasize the latter, two rangers-at-large were appointed, Gene Holder in northern Arizona and Reuben McNeill in the south. The director and commission undertook a review of ranger behavior and activities, while giving out a number of personnel raises, mostly to rangers. No new hires were made of men over 45, and an attempt was made to place returning veterans.

In addition to the numerous housekeeping chores brought on by war's end, plans were made to print 20,000 copies of the new game code booklet with no advertising. Otherwise, much of the commission's time was taken up resolving requests for game refuges to protect private property and attempting to draft legislation that would keep hunters away from stock waters. Reid, recognizing his lack of background in game matters, left most such decisions to his game management supervisor, Pop Arrington. Fisheries and law enforcement were Reid's forte and he would stick with them. Meanwhile, Beach began his third successive term as commissioner.

The commission's emphasis on law enforcement posed a conundrum, as a large amount of money was available in backlogged Pittman-Robertson funds at war's end, and a state appropriation of $19,287 could get $57,862.22 in Federal-Aid money. Such funds could not be spent on law enforcement, but could be spent killing predators if it were part of a Pittman-Robertson project. Ranger Jay Klaus was therefore assigned to be the department's representative on predator-control matters, and the commission initiated a short-lived program by which bounties were paid on 50 lions and on 2,343 coyote scalps at a cost of $5,062.89.

Not all the commission's wrath was directed at potential predators. In an effort to forestall the legislature from naming the collared peccary a predatory animal at the request of the livestock industry, the commission agreed to expand the javelina season, while also lobbying to get the bear off the predator list. Other significant actions included hiring a buffalo caretaker, who doubled as a trapper and ranger. In the meantime, Raymond Ranch was stocked with buffalo and a permanent employee was designated to be housed in the facilities at Papago Park.

Several technicians, including Kimball, Gambrell, and Buzz Lawson, returned from the war to be hired back at more pay. Although the commission was again reserving the right to approve hiring and dismissals, it gave Reid permission to hire additional rangers to be stationed in Prescott, Winslow, and Kingman.

It was during this post-war period that the commission and department had the closest ties to the AGPA. Commission actions were not infrequently resolved by polling AGPA members present or referring the issue to Wickstrum's AGPA executive committee. It was also during this period that the commission, in conjunction with the AGPA, began to assert its independence from the Forest Service and other agencies as to who would manage the state's wildlife on national forest lands.

Reflecting the emphasis on law enforcement, the number of game rangers increased from 18 in 1943 to 33 in 1946. Also, in 1945, the department partnered with the Arizona Livestock Sanitary Board in a cooperative predator-control agreement with the Fish and Wildlife Service. With the commission now authorizing an annual predator-control appropriation, Arizona's sportsmen no longer had to rely solely on the stockmen to protect game against wolves, lions, and other predators.

There were also department advances on the public relations front. The agency's *Arizona Wildlife Views* magazine made its debut in the fall of 1947 with an anticipated circulation of 26,000. The magazine was to be printed in-house and published quarterly, with no subscription fee or advertising. Other activities to inform and educate the public included a weekly radio program, movies, lectures, school talks, and the circulation of a department newsletter.

Suffering from ill health, Reid was replaced as director by Kimball, who had just replaced Arrington as game management supervisor. Arrington had just been put in charge of the department's lands and water program. In recognition of his service, Reid was appointed department advisor. As a testament to Reid's frugality, the Fisheries Division, including the hatcheries, continued to have only six persons, under the supervision of A. W. "Dud" Yoder.

Tom Kimball Takes Command

When Kimball took office in February 1948, game management was just coming out of its infancy. Because Congress had failed to appropriate most of the Federal-Aid money during the war years, some $15,000,000 in funds had built up, to be given to the states

Director Herbert Reid passing the reins of office to Tom Kimball. Although the two men came from different backgrounds, Reid in fisheries and Kimball in game, both got along well with Game and Fish commissioners and the Arizona Game Protective Association. Photo by Ben Avery. (Arizona Wildlife and Sportsman, *April 1948, Arizona Wildlife Federation)*

for the 1946–51 period. For fiscal year 1946–47, the commission appropriated $16,016.82 in state funds to receive a total Federal-Aid appropriation of $64,067.28. The first priority was to replace or augment the hunter check-station method of gathering hunt success data with a hunt questionnaire system (see Appendix D).

Federal-Aid projects now proliferated. In addition to turkey, quail, and beaver transplants, numerous windmill and water catchments were funded, including several on newly acquired lands near Texas Hill and on quail habitat study plots in Cochise County. Research studies were initiated on turkeys, deer, javelina, quail, dove, waterfowl, elk, and antelope, with a major effort spent evaluating the relationships between Kaibab deer and livestock. Other studies evaluated the efficacy of desert water developments, and $6,732.65 was spent improving a water delivery system to the buffalo at House Rock. This was also the time when annual game surveys were initiated and hunter report cards used to generate maps showing big game kill locations. The number of refuges had been gradually reduced to 75, and a growing number of elk depredation complaints resulted in the purchase of numerous fencing materials, with 10 electric and five barbed-wire fences being built during 1948.

Meanwhile, other projects were winding down. The fur conservation program was de-emphasized as fur prices declined. The game farm at Pima was closed in 1949 after it was concluded, at a cost of $43,073.90, that ring-necked pheasants were not going to become established. Although the rangers were now equipped with binoculars, and their number increased from 30 in 1947 to 39 in 1949, state funds for law enforcement continued to lag. As a consequence, there was as yet no uniform allowance. Also, publication of the department magazine had to be suspended due to mailing problems and low staffing (there were only two people in the Information and Education Division).

Although the department was flush in Pittman-Robertson money, the allocation of so much money to Federal-Aid projects created a funding problem when it came to other services. Adding to the problem was a continuing annual appropriation by the legislature of $22,000 from the Game and Fish Fund for predator-control projects.

The financial shortage proved short-lived. The years after World War II saw a major upsurge in human immigration to Arizona, which coincided with an increase in deer numbers. By the end of the 1940s, one in six Arizonans was buying a hunting and/or fishing license—double the rate of 10 years earlier. Deer hunt success jumped from 20.5% in 1946 to 28.7% in 1950. More deer, elk, antelope, buffalo, and javelina were being taken than ever before.

In 1950, Congress passed the Dingell-Johnson bill, which assured adequate funding for the state's three trout hatcheries, stocking programs, and fish management surveys. Total license revenues climbed from under $600,000 in fiscal 1950–51, to $715,650 in 1951–52, to $857, 841 in 1952–53. But such funds were no longer to be independently spent by the commission. In 1951, the legislature took it upon itself to appropriate all Game and Fish Fund dollars, not just matching money from the general fund for Federal-Aid projects.

Pittman-Robertson activities in 1951 included the continued collection of survey and hunt data; the restocking of turkey, antelope, and other game species; the evaluation of chukar and other exotic game bird releases; a water development program on the north Kaibab; the construction of housing and other facilities at House Rock; and a series of area investigations, including a special wildlife study on the Tonto National Forest.

Other management activities included a number of waterfowl projects, including a lower Colorado River survey project to determine the status of waterfowl and other wildlife concomitant with changing river conditions. Tommy Wright (1959) conducted an evaluation of water development projects. Also new was a bighorn study by biologist John Russo, adding onto 10 years of data collected on the Kofa and Cabeza Prieta game ranges (Arizona Game and Fish Commission 1954).

Research projects in 1951 included the conversion of Fort Huachuca into the Charles T. Vorhies Research Area, the continuation of the North Kaibab deer-livestock competition study, and an investigation by turkey biologist Robert Reeves of winter range conditions to determine the reasons for depressed turkey numbers. Another new research expenditure included an annual contribution of $6,000 to help fund the Cooperative Wildlife Research Unit at the University of Arizona in Tucson.

Director Kimball proved to be a good negotiator and was able to rein in much of the excess minutiae promoted by the AGPA, while working with the commission to negotiate agreements with the Forest Service and other agencies. Although it helped that Kimball was conservative in his hunt recommendations, he was also aided by the appointment of Jack Mantle as a commissioner in 1951. Mantle tended to let the department manage its own affairs as long as it represented the desires of the commissioners. Relations with the legislature also improved during this time, as the department now submitted commission orders to the attorney general for approval and sought better cooperation with legislative committees. In this last regard, the department was greatly helped by outdoor columnist Ben Avery, who prided himself on fostering a working relationship between the AGPA, the department, and the legislature.

Dud Yoder Dials It Up a Notch

When Kimball left for Colorado and the commission appointed Dud Yoder acting director as of April 26, 1952, Arizona and the department were poised to enter an unprecedented period of prosperity. Not only were people moving to Arizona in droves, game animals were now being taken in record numbers.

Only band-tailed pigeons and the wild turkey were species of concern, the season for the former being closed in 1950 and hunting for the big game birds being limited by special permit in 1955. Browse studies, check stations, and hunt questionnaires were increasingly showing too many deer rather than too few. Deer herds from the Tucson Mountains to Black River were beginning to threaten their food supplies. Forage competition with a growing elk herd and arguments over depredation complaints and harvest goals for that species now generated much wrangling. Antelope and elk hunts had by now become annual events and a bighorn sheep hunt would soon be authorized. Hunt regulations became increasingly complex as most refuges were now abolished.

Sadly, an early heavy snowfall in November 1952 caused Arizona's largest hunting tragedy, when six elk hunters died despite day-and-night rescue efforts.

The department's annual budgets now hovered in the neighborhood of one million dollars, and income was rising about 10% a year. Dingell-Johnson appropriations funded an expanding fisheries program that even promised to provide lakes for the hatcheries to stock. By 1956, more money was spent on administration, law enforcement, and fisheries than on game management—the first year this had happened since the legislature approved Federal-Aid funding in 1939.

The growth attendant with the 1950s required a maturing department and commission to rethink a number of social accommodations and philosophical stances. In 1956, it was agreed that the last Friday in October would be the traditional opening of deer season. The following year, a policy was adopted to manage big game on the basis of habitat, with management goals directed toward achieving a maximum sustained harvest attendant with the greatest amount of recreation. The department also determined that "game populations were not as a rule influenced very greatly by predation" —a proclamation not universally accepted (AGFD 1957, 1959). New game and fish codes were drafted and sent to the legislature, and the legislature passed a state boating bill containing regulations the department would soon have to enforce (AGFD 1959).

Law enforcement was still the major field activity within the department, with four ranger captains and 34 game rangers writing nearly 2,000 citations a year during fiscal years 1954–55, 1955–56, and 1956–57. Their patrols not only kept Arizona's sportsmen honest, they provided added revenue of about $45,000 a year in fines and assessments. For its part, the commission continued to mete out license revocations to the fullest extent possible and insist on a strong law enforcement presence. In an effort to modernize the Law Enforcement Division, Cliff Sorrells sent his rangers to training schools at the University of Arizona and equipped their vehicles with two-way radios. To be a game ranger required not only passing an examination and wearing a uniform, but conducting game surveys, stocking fish, and checking water catchments.

The biggest challenges lay in informing the sporting public and keeping them apprised of the fast-changing status of Arizona's wildlife. Merely having an exhibit at the Arizona State Fair no longer sufficed to communicate the department's message. A revamped Information and Education Division not only printed and distributed complex

ARIZONA GAME DEPARTMENT — DIVISION OF FEDERAL AID

TABULATED INFORMATION — ARIZONA GAME

COMPILED BY STATE-WIDE GAME SURVEY PROJECT

	BREEDING, YOUNG, ETC.								DISTRIBUTION, FOOD, ETC.									
SPECIES	NORMAL BREEDING PERIOD	GESTATION INCUBATION PERIOD	YOUNG APPEAR	AVERAGE NUMBER YOUNG	LITTERS PER YEAR	SEX RATIO *	BREED AGE	ANTLERS SHED	DISTRIBUTION	HABITAT	FOOD PREFERENCES: SPRING	SUMMER	FALL	WINTER	SIZE INDIVIDUAL RANGE	LIVE WEIGHT	PREDATORS OR ENEMIES	AUTHORITY
WHITETAIL DEER	Jan.	200 days	August	2 1-1st year 3 - rare	1	1-3	M-17 mo. F-29 mo.	April, May	4-10,000 ft. Sou'h & east Arizona mts.	Oak-grass, chaparral, y. pine	weeds,	shrubs, summer weeds	mast, shrubs	grass, mistletoe, cacti fruits	4 sq. mi.	M-125 lbs. F-80 lbs.	mt. lion bobcat eagle coyote	Knipe Nichol
MULE DEER (Kaibab)	Nov. 15 to Dec. 15	195 to 205 days	June 15 to July 15	2 1-1st year 3-occas.	1	1-3	M-17 mo. F-17 mo.	Febr.	6-10,000 ft. Kaibab Plateau	Cliffrose, juniper, pine-fir, mt. meadow	aspen weeds	aspen weeds mushrooms	aspen, oak	Cliffrose sage, juniper	20-50 sq. mi.	M-225 lbs. F-125 lbs.	coyote mt. lion	USFS Knipe Nichol
MULE DEER (Northern highlands)		About two to three weeks later than Kaibab Mule Deer							5-10,000 ft. forest areas N. Arizona	Pinon-juniper pine, aspen-fir	As above				10-50 sq. mi.	M-200 lbs. F-110 lbs.	mt. lion coyote	USFS Nichol Knipe
MULE DEER (Desert)	December	200 days	July & August	2 1-1st year 3-occas.	1			March	90-4,000 ft. desert areas S. & W. Arizona	desert shrub mesquite, grassland	winter weeds palo verde	weeds, yucca flrs. shrubs palo verde	mesquite beans, shrubs janusia	coffee-berry, cacti fruit filaree	30-50 sq. mi.	M-200 lbs. F-110 lbs. (?)	coyote eagle mt. lion	O'Connor Knipe Nichol
ANTELOPE (pronghorn)	Aug. 20 to Sept. 30	240 to 250 days	May 10 to June 1	2 1-1st year 3-frequent	1	1-5 to 1-10 or more	M - ? F-16 mos.?	Nov. Dec.	5-8,000 ft. grasslands N. Arizona	open grass forest parks	grasses weeds	grasses weeds	cacti weeds juniper	winterfat chamiso juniper	20-40 sq. mi.	M-110 lbs. F-75 lbs.		Miller Knipe Nichol
ELK (Wapiti)	October	250 to 260 days		1 2-occas. 3-very rare	1	1-6	M-29 mo. ? F-?	April	7-10,000 ft. fir-pine forest N. Arizona	fir-aspen, pine-juniper	weeds, grasses, sedges	grass, shrubs, willow	trees, shrubs, grasses	shrubs, trees	20-30 sq. mi.	M-900 lbs. F-500 lbs.	mt. lion coyote	Rush
JAVELINA (peccary)	year long	112 to 116 days	year long	2	1-?	1-1			1-6,000 ft. desert mts., mostly south of Gila River	cacti, mesquite, oak-grass	cacti, insects	cacti, insects, fruits, seeds	cacti, insects, fruits, seeds	cacti, seeds	4 sq. mi.	M-65 lbs. F-50 lbs.	coyote	Azara Knipe Nichol
DESERT BIGHORN (mountain sheep)	Sept. to November	150 days ?	March, April or later	1-2	1	1-2 or 4		No shedding	90-4,500 ft. desert ranges S. & W. Ariz.	desert scrub ledges, grassy basins	fluff grass, catsclaw ocotillo spurges	buckwheat, mescal, janusia, slim triodia, catsclaw	catsclaw buckwheat, janusia	Indian wheat, filaree, weeds		M-250 lbs. F-140 lbs.	eagle coyote bobcat fox	Nichol
BLACK BEAR	early July	220 days	Jan. in hibernation	2 (1-4)	1/2: breed alternate years	1-1	48 mos.		5-10,000 ft. forest areas throughout Arizona	timber	OMNIVOROUS berries, roots, fish, honey, insects, carrion, occasionally livestock					M-350 lbs. F-300 lbs.		Seton et al
COTTONTAIL (all species)	year long	28 days	year long	3-7	3-5 ?				90-9,000 ft. throughout Arizona	cacti, shrub growth	grasses, weed, cacti, bark, cultivated crops, legume shrubs, etc.				160 acres		snakes, coyotes, foxes, hawks, owls, Gila Monst.	Seton Griner Knipe
GAMBEL QUAIL	April, May, June	23-24 days	May, June, July	9-15 (15-top)	1	1-1	9-12 mos.		90-5,500 ft. S. & W. Ariz.	mesquite-grass, desert shrub	tree & shrub buds green weeds, insects	weeds, seeds, insects	mesquite beans, mustards miscel. seeds	mesquite beans, seeds cacti fruit	60-160 acres	5-7 ozs.	sharp-shinned hawk, foxes, ants, Cooper hawk, house cat, skunks, rodents, snakes	Ligon Gorsuch Griner
SCALED QUAIL (blue)	May, June, July, Aug.	23-24 days	June, July, Aug., Sept.	7-14	1	1-1	9-12 mos.		3-6,000 ft. SE. Arizona	mesquite grass, catclaw	As above				60-160 acres	6-8 ozs.	As above Prairie Falcon	Ligon Griner
TURKEYS (Merriam's)	Late April, May	28 days	June	9	1	1-2 or 3	24 mos.		5-9,000 ft. Mogollon Pt. White Mts.	pine forests	green weeds insects, juniper berries, acorns	green weeds, insects, grass seed	mast, pine seed, grass seed	mast, juniper berries	5-30 sq. mi.	M-15-30 lbs. F-8-12 lbs.	bobcats, coyotes, foxes, eagles, horned owl	Ligon
MOURNING DOVE	Feb. 1 to Sept. 15	15-17 days	Feb. to Sept.	1 or 2, 3-rare	2-4 5 ?	1-1			90-9,000 ft. throughout Arizona	open thickets, farms, desert	Weeds and grain seeds				migratory	3-4 ozs.	hawks, owls, snakes, scaly lizard	Knipe Griner Nichol
WHITEWING DOVE	May 1 to July 2	17-20 days	May, June, August	2	2	1-1			90-5,000 ft. S. Arizona	mesquite cactic, mt. canyons	As above — especially seeds of sahuaro fruit				migratory	4-5 ozs.	As above	Neff Knipe Griner
BANDTAIL PIGEON (blue rock)	April to August	18-20 days	June to Sept.	1	1-4	1-1			4-10,000 ft. throughout	mountain	seeds and mast				migratory	6-7	falcon, Cooper's	Bent

Tabular results of the statewide game survey. A product of the first Federal-Aid project, this factual summary of Arizona's game species greatly improved the public's general knowledge of Arizona's game animals. (AGFD files) hunting and fishing regulations, but published a bimonthly magazine *(Wildlife Views)*, wildlife bulletins and newsletters, and booklets on topics ranging from common reptiles and game fishes to summaries of Federal-Aid studies on waterfowl, javelina, mule deer, and desert bighorn sheep. It was also at this time that wildlife illustrations by artists such as Bill Freeman and Larry Toschik began showing up in department publications. Other department publications dealt with water developments, caring for game meat, and a new lake program, while a film library accumulated movies on subjects ranging from building water developments to hunter safety. Additional activities included producing radio and television programs and developing a firearms safety program complete with a curriculum, instructors, 10,000 graduating students, and a full complement of facilities at Black Canyon Shooting Range.

As the 1950s drew to a close, the Arizona Game and Fish Department had become a professional organization. Some 274,040 people now held hunting and fishing licenses. Annual income from hunting and fishing licenses exceeded \$1.5 million, and the department's operating budget exceeded \$2,000,000, with nearly \$650,000 coming in annually in Federal-Aid funds (AGFD 1962). Appointing a director for political reasons no longer sufficed. The department now needed directors who were trained as technicians and who had a vision for the future.

FEDERAL WILDLIFE REFUGES IN ARIZONA

Bill Broyles and David E. Brown

When Arizona attained statehood in 1912, it had eleven national forests, six national monuments, millions of acres of undedicated government lands, and two federal game refuges—Grand Cañon National Game Preserve, created in 1906, and the Salt River Bird Refuge, established in 1909. By 1962, the federal government was managing two huge national game ranges (today's Kofa and Cabeza Prieta national wildlife refuges) and two national wildlife refuges (Imperial and Havasu national wildlife refuges along the lower Colorado River). But few people know the complex history behind the establishment of these wildlife preserves, or of the federal refuges that came and went during the intervening 50 years.

Two Early Arizona Refuges

During his presidency (1901–9), Theodore Roosevelt proclaimed 50 federal bird reservations and three game preserves in addition to Arizona's Salt River (Roosevelt Lake) and Grand Cañon National Game Preserve. Both of the Arizona areas initially were managed by the US Forest Service. The management focus for both preserves was on restricting the taking of game and keeping these lands from passing into private ownership.

The Salt River Bird Refuge encompassed those lands below the high-water mark of Roosevelt Lake on the Tonto National Forest. This refuge was established by presidential proclamation on February 25, 1909, in conjunction with the construction of Roosevelt Dam, which was dedicated in 1911. The refuge comprised 21,120 acres of Roosevelt Lake shore and surface, with the goal of protecting native and migratory birds. Although the lake was regarded as an important resting area for migrating waterfowl, herons, ospreys, and grebes, it was not a significant nesting area because of its low elevation and fluctuating water levels (US Congress 1937). Management was therefore confined primarily to regulating hunting and restricting access during the waterfowl season, with little done to improve habitat.

In 1959, its management was transferred from the Fish and Wildlife Service to the Tonto National Forest. Then the area was managed jointly by the national forest, the Arizona Game and Fish Department, and the Salt River Project under the name Roosevelt Lake Wildlife Area (Brown 1985a). There is no documentation that fishing was ever restricted, and Roosevelt Lake was stocked with a variety of exotic fishes as soon as the lake was formed.

Meanwhile, the Grand Cañon Game Preserve was fulfilling its purpose as a refugium for mule deer, Uncle Jimmy Owens's buffalo having drifted away into House Rock Valley. Later, in the early 1920s, after the preserve was absorbed into the Kaibab National Forest and Grand Canyon National Park, Goldman (1923) proposed the establishment of an antelope refuge on the Tonto Plateau within Grand Canyon National Park. Sixteen captive-raised pronghorn were released here, but a plan to remove burros and more intensely manage for pronghorn failed to sustain the antelope's numbers, and Arizona remained without a designated refuge for this species.

Impetus for Federal Refuges

The wildlife refuge concept evolved from several strands of the conservation ethic and was considered an important aspect to wildlife recovery at the state and federal levels. The demise of the passenger pigeon and the decimation of bison herds had alerted the nation, especially sportsmen, to the dangers of unrestricted hunting. Advocates for game and nongame species alike feared that threats to habitat (draining of wetlands, forest cutting, plowing of prairies, settlement), uncontrolled shooting for sport and trade (millinery feathers, commercial hunting, indiscriminate shooting), and competition from domestic animals (grazing, mutual diseases, control of waters) would reduce not only waterfowl and large game animals, but also songbirds and small mammals.

Although the nation's first wildlife refuge was reportedly created by the state of California in 1870 at Lake Merritt in Oakland, that event was little noted nationally (Gabrielson 1943). The formative moment for national wildlife refuges came during a speech by President Roosevelt in 1887. Speaking before an audience of hunters and outdoorsmen in New York, Roosevelt challenged his audience to halt the destruction of America's wildlife heritage (G. B. Grinnell 1904; Brown 2009). A year later, the Boone and Crockett Club was founded, and other wildlife organizations such as the National Audubon Society soon followed. The early leaders of this movement, which had ties to New York and Washington, D.C., included such national figures as President Roosevelt, John Burroughs, George Bird Grinnell, and William Hornaday. These men were soon joined by conservationists like Charles Sheldon and John C. Phillips, who, while working at the national level, had an important impact on Arizona and the Southwest.

Refuges Within National Forests

In 1916, the Arizona State Legislature began enacting bills to create game refuges on national forest lands administrated by the US Department of Agriculture. One fervent national supporter of these efforts was Hornaday (1913), who proclaimed, "As conditions are today, it is impossible to have too many game reserves! There is everything to gain and nothing to lose by making every national forest and forest reserve on the whole continent of North America a game preserve in the strictest sense."

Examples of state game refuges created on national forests in Arizona are described in chapter three, "State Refuges Are the First Step to Game Recovery." They included large portions of the Coronado, Crook, and Tusayan national forests, reserved in an effort to protect white-tailed deer, mule deer, antelope, and turkeys (Goldman 1931a; Hart et al. 1931a, b).

The Forest Service had no objections to the legislature's creating preserves on the national forests, and indeed supported such measures as a recognition of a state's right to manage big game animals while maintaining the national forest's mandate to conserve game (USDA Forest Service 1915). Indeed, all of the refuges created prior to 1928 were entirely contained within national forests—in some cases, such as with the Patagonia-Huachuca refuge, comprising the entire forest reserve. As often as not, it was the Forest Service that initiated the refuge designation.

Not included in the state refuge system was a "Sitgreaves Elk Range" on the western border of the Sitgreaves National Forest—a preserve supposedly agreed to by Dr. Edward Nelson and Gov. George Hunt to protect the elk introduced there in 1913 from Yellowstone National Park. This "failure" of the part of the Arizona legislature to designate an elk refuge was due to opposition from local homesteaders and generated consternation in the US Biological Survey's Nelson and Edward Goldman, as well as Charles Sheldon of the Boone and Crockett Club. Hunt had led them to believe a state refuge would be forthcoming (Letter from Sheldon to Governor Hunt, Governor's Files, 1923–33, Box 3, Arizona State Library, Archives and Public Records). Intended to contain about 300,000 acres along the Mogollon Rim east of East Clear Creek, this "refuge" continued to be managed by the Forest Service for multiple use until the Arizona Game and Fish Commission established Cabin Draw State Game Refuge in 1929.

In July 1920, the Sitgreaves National Forest supervisor invited Forest Service Grazing Examiner Milford W. Talbot and Goldman to come over from Albuquerque to evaluate the forest's suitability as an elk refuge. After an extensive two-week inspection of the major elk range, Goldman (1920) concluded the elk then ranged in widely scattered bands as far west as Baker Butte and as far south as the Tonto Rim. He conferred with Aldo Leopold and other Forest Service personnel, then concluded that a refuge holding about 750 head should be established on the elk's summer range, thereby allowing for a statewide population goal of 1,000 elk. The surplus would be removed by hunters outside the yet-to-be-determined refuge's boundaries. Goldman did not recommend that the state open a season at that time unless the Arizona Game and Fish Department could properly patrol such a hunt. The state remained nonresponsive, however, as per the wishes of its legislature.

Like all of the state refuges on national forests, Cabin Draw State Game Refuge remained open to grazing and predator control after its creation in 1929. Elk numbers were judged to have exceeded the range's carrying capacity by 1930, which was then thought to be about 1,000 head. The high use caused Goldman (1931) to proclaim the elk's browsing had become destructive to the willows and other shrubs, which was resulting in conflict with ranchers, and that it was urgent that the elk herd be reduced. Nonetheless, the refuge remained closed to elk hunting when the first elk season was authorized in 1935.

Also by 1930, a Hay Lake Antelope Refuge had been designated on Anderson Mesa, apparently by administrative action by the Forest Service rather than by state action. As such, this refuge was not recognized by the state and was open to antelope hunting in 1941 during the first authorized season for this animal. A more legitimate refuge designation was the short-lived Apache (Big Lake) Refuge. The 2,674-acre refuge, the only federal waterfowl refuge established in Arizona in the 1930s, was jointly administered as a waterfowl area by the Apache National Forest, Biological Survey, and Arizona Game and Fish Department in the late 1930s and 1940s before the lake's transformation into a fishery (S. L. Lewis 1936).

Politics of Federal Refuge Creation

With passage of the Migratory Bird Treaty Act in 1916, the US Biological Survey initiated a series of evaluations of potential bird refuges for migratory waterfowl—big game animals now being generally recognized as a state responsibility. Wetland restoration became a national mission involving organizations ranging from the Boone and Crockett Club and American Farm Bureau Federation to the National Grange and Audubon Society. This impetus to create waterfowl refuges and preserve wetlands had little impact in Arizona, however, other than the Biological Survey's conducting some basic inventories.

Unlike most states, Arizona saw almost no federal bird refuges created as a result of the "Duck Stamp Bill" (Federal Migratory Bird Hunting and Conservation Stamp Act), passed in 1934. Congress, influenced by Biological Survey Chief Jay Norwood "Ding" Darling, was increasingly amenable to the refuge concept, and often piggybacked refuges on reclamation projects, such as making wildlife refuges of the reservoirs resulting from its dams. The only refuges established in Arizona principally for migratory birds before World War II, other than Big Lake, were two federal withdrawals along the lower Colorado River (Imperial and Havasu national wildlife refuges). These were created by executive order as mitigation for the dams being built below what was now called Boulder Dam.

Big Game Refuges

Although many of the state's sportsmen supported them, the concept of establishing federal refuges for big game animals was anathema in Arizona. Any further withdrawals from the public domain would come at the expense of homesteaders and lessees, and thereby hinder development. It had been for such reasons that the Arizona Territorial Legislature and federal government passed on Nelson's suggestion to turn a decommissioned Fort Grant into a preserve for pronghorn antelope and other game in 1904, the rationale being that such valuable grazing land was too important for livestock to be made into a wildlife refuge (Brown 2009). When the federal government released 12 pronghorn fawns to Hermit Basin in Grand Canyon National Park in 1922, it was because this location on the Tonto Platform was the only refuge area then receiving protection from hunting and livestock grazing.

Although State Game Warden George Willard attended the Washington Conference on the Conservation of the Pronghorn in 1925, Nelson and Will C. Barnes's suggestions for a federal antelope refuge on Forest Service land failed to generate a single recommendation for an Arizona site. The only serious proposals for federal antelope refuges were in Nevada and Oregon—proposals that eventually resulted in the establishment of Charles Sheldon and Hart Mountain national antelope refuges.

The National Wildlife Refuge Proposal That Failed

One big game animal Arizona politicians did deem worthy of a federal refuge was the state's bison. Intended to be included within the original Grand Cañon National Game Preserve, what was to become the state's bison herd instead drifted east, where they took up residence in House Rock Valley. Here these animals resided mostly on the public domain, where they had to compete with livestock for the scanty water and forage available.

Realizing that the bison needed a home of their own, the Arizona legislature's Committee on Wild Life Restoration petitioned the federal government to cede most of House Rock Valley to the state as a game refuge for buffalo and pronghorn beginning in 1931. Governor Hunt even telegraphed Interior Secretary Harold L. Ickes expressing his support for the withdrawal as a state buffalo refuge, stating that "this area undoubtedly is the finest for such purpose that can be acquired any place in the United States and ultimately the State desires to secure title to these lands and improve them for wildlife purposes" (McGinnies 1934; Morgan 1934).

Congress did not favorably act on the state's request: The influence of the Grand Canyon Cattle Company and other Utah cattlemen was just too strong. By 1934, the situation facing Arizona's buffalo was desperate. There was simply no rangeland available, and what forage and water there was had to be subleased or otherwise arranged for with the Grand Canyon Cattle Company. That company not only owned Kane Springs and most of the waters, it held the lease to most of the government land. The bison's caretaker, Charles Lewis, worked for both the department and the cattle company. Even worse, homesteaders and local stockmen were running an estimated 8,000 cattle, 2,000 horses, 1,000 sheep, and 4,000 yearling goats largely on what was supposed to be Grand Canyon's rangeland (McGinnies 1934; Walter Mann to McGinnies November 23, 1934 *in* Taylor 1935b).

Unwilling to forgo what many considered a national treasure, University of Arizona president Homer Shantz requested federal assistance. As a result, a committee composed of Walter Taylor (1934a), Charles E. Gillham of the Arizona Game and Fish Department, and two national park service representatives, Dr. M. S. Johnson and Dr. William B. McDougall, were sent to reconnoiter House Rock Valley, photograph the habitats involved, and provide a map of a proposed refuge boundary (Taylor 1935b).

Upon inspection of the area, the committee decided to expand an earlier proposal to include Lees Ferry, the Vermilion Cliffs, and the Paria Plateau. Originally skeptical of the area's stated values, the committee became enthusiastic supporters of a "national wildlife area" after conferring with State Game Warden Shelby Lewis and learning the state would concede its 135 bison to the federal government if such action were needed to save the animals. That Russell K. Grater and Miner Tillotson of Grand Canyon National Park, and Frank Pinkley (director of Southwestern national monuments), had no interest in including the area in a national park also contributed to the area's feasibility as a big game refuge.

The committee envisioned the refuge as a great tourist attraction with bison, pronghorn antelope, and bighorn sheep as attractions. The pronghorn would have to be brought in from somewhere else, but the bison and bighorn were already there, the committee being told the latter species still resided in the Vermilion Cliffs. The livestock would of course have to be removed to give the bison exclusive use, and the "pinto" buffalo removed. Waters would have to be purchased and Grand Canyon Cattle Company compensated. It was believed that this could be worked out through John H. Page and Co., Public Land Specialists. Brokers specializing in land acquisitions and trades, Page and Co. also suggested elk might be introduced.

House Rock Valley buffalo herd about 1935, showing "pinto" animals and lack of forage. (Arizona Historical Society/ Tucson, Fred Winn Collection, #16982, MS0875, Folder 85)

The opposition by Utah-based cattlemen was intense, and by 1935, the area of the proposed refuge had been reduced by half (Executive Order Draft 1935). Taylor (1935c) then filed a supportive report that noted the refuge would also include bighorn sheep in Marble Canyon, Paria Creek, and the Vermilion Cliffs, while admitting the Paria Plateau was not needed as habitat for bison and pronghorn. Although an executive order establishing House Rock Valley Wildlife Refuge under the jurisdiction of the US Department of Agriculture was drafted on March 5, 1935, the order was never enacted.

Even though a proposed refuge on the Utah-Arizona border continued to appear on a congressional map of Arizona as late as 1937, neither a federal refuge nor a federally ceded state refuge was ever authorized. Arrangements were made to provide the bison a Forest Service allotment and House Rock Valley remained with the Grazing Service, the forerunner of the Bureau of Land Management. Eventually, a small portion of the area became House Rock Valley State Wildlife Area (US Congress 1937).

The Search for a Bighorn Sheep Refuge

One animal that had always caught the imaginations of Arizonans and generated concern was the desert bighorn sheep. Early in the twentieth century, outdoorsmen noticed that desert bighorn herds were dwindling and that bighorn sheep could no longer be found in some of the mountain ranges close to towns. Government biologists agreed, and there was genuine concern the state might lose this species as part of its native fauna. Edgar Mearns (1907) reported, "The opinion is general among the white settlers along the Mexican border that the bighorn sheep is doomed to extinction at an early period."

Impetus for a bighorn refuge was also generated in books about Arizona's desert wildlife, notably Hornaday's *Camp-fires on Desert and Lava* (1908), Carl Lumholtz's *New Trails in Mexico* (1912), and Kermit Roosevelt's *Happy Hunting Grounds* (1920, chapter 3). These authors wrote enthusiastically about desert bighorn sheep, deer, and pronghorn. Sheldon

(1993), who hunted bighorn in the Tinajas Altas Mountains in 1913 and 1916, also shared his concerns with his influential colleagues in the East. But it was John C. (Charles) Phillips[1] who was one of the most instrumental forces behind the recovery of America's desert bighorn sheep.

Phillips, a Bostonian, was trained as a physician but never practiced, and he used his inherited wealth to initiate and support conservation movements as an independent public servant. He served as the president or chairman of numerous organizations that worked to protect vanishing species, and often took on projects beyond the reach of local and state agencies. In 1926, he wrote the classic four-volume tome *A Natural History of Ducks*, which had wide influence toward protecting waterfowl and flyway habitats. He actively supported open space and game ranges, and even donated several tracts of land to enhance and expand nature reserves.

Phillips lived in Tucson during the winter of 1930–31. During that time, he made short trips to the desert mountain ranges of southern Arizona and Sonora, Mexico, to survey and estimate bighorn sheep numbers. Motivated by fear that this uniquely adapted animal might become extinct, he wrote a report describing how the welfare of bighorn in northeastern Sonora was related to the scarcity or absence of water, just as a man on horseback or burro was limited in his travels (J. C. Phillips 1931). Phillips was much concerned about trophy hunters wiping out this species, as motor cars allowed hunters to be self-sufficient when it came to water. He thought ranch hands and prospectors were particular threats as the latter, especially, respected no game laws.

He personally inspected bighorn conditions in the Catalina, Tucson, Growler, Tule, Tuseral, and Tinajas Altas mountains in southern Arizona. His estimates of bighorn numbers in these and other ranges are of interest, as they appear to be reasonable estimates of what these ranges can support. Phillips estimated 300–500 bighorn in northwest Sonora, where as yet no cattle roamed. The exception was the Pinacate Mountains, which were heavily visited by trophy hunters and where he thought bighorn were in danger of being eliminated.

Phillips (1931) summarized his ideas in a paper titled, "Necessity for Special Protection for Mountain Sheep in Arizona," in which he proposed the use of federal lands for game refuges. He argued the bighorn in southern Arizona and northern Mexico was a unique race in danger of extinction due to the region's becoming increasingly "accessible [to hunters] by properly equipped motor transport or by aeroplane." After traveling the region himself and speaking with hunters, guides, ranchers, and local citizens, he noted that bighorn already had been extirpated from some mountain ranges and were threatened in others by meat-hunting prospectors, diseases and parasites from domestic livestock, opportunistic ranch hands, and misidentification by deer hunters. Noting that deer and javelina likely needed protection for the same reasons, he proposed a series of

---

[1] John Charles Phillips is not to be confused with two other John Phillips, who also actively supported game refuges during this period. John M. Phillips was a steel-industry executive in Pittsburgh and the Pennsylvania game commissioner who accompanied Hornaday (1909) to Arizona on the trip chronicled in *Camp-fires on Desert and Lava*. John Calhoun Phillips was governor of Arizona (1929–31) and appointed the first Arizona Game Commission. In a quirk of fate that summarizes their lifestyles, both men named John C. Phillips died of natural causes while outdoors: "Boston" John while hunting in New Hampshire in 1938, and "Arizona" John while fishing at Lake Mary near Flagstaff, Arizona, in 1943.

"nature monuments," administered, staffed, posted, and regulated by the Biological Survey. Because of his contacts in government and his prestige as a leader in the birding and hunting communities, his words caught the attention of important people.

As for Arizona, Phillips estimated 35 bighorn in the Muggins Mountains, 15 in the Gilas, 25 in the Chocolates, 40 in the Eagletails, 25 in the Harquahala Mountains, only 20 in the SH (now Kofa) Mountains, 25 in the Ajo Mountains, 9 to 10 in the Quijatoas, 20 in the Santa Rosas, 5 in the Estrellas, 15 in the Mesquite mountains, 6 in the Bolos Blancos, 8 in the Coyotes, and 5 to 6 in the Tucsons—at that time a waterless range except for one well that also supported a small herd of desert mule deer. He estimated 30 or more bighorn in the Catalina Mountains, a population he considered not to be in good health, with some animals reportedly found dead. He himself killed two lions in this range in 1930 and another two in 1931. He thought sheep had already been extirpated from Black Mountain near Casa Grande, the Artesian Mountains southeast of Indian Oasis (Sells), and the Grand Wash Mountains in northwest Arizona. He believed sheep never were particularly common in historic times in southern Arizona, as old-timers told him most of the game legally sold in the Tucson markets was antelope. He thought the low density of bighorn he observed was also due to lung infections obtained from livestock, especially domestic sheep, but also cattle. He thought the Catalinas were atypical sheep range in that they might be "too wet" for this species.

Phillips's 1931 report on bighorn laid a foundation for arguments supporting a series of small bighorn refuges in Yuma and western Pima counties, and he recommended that a federal agent from the Biological Survey come out and study the situation. He thought a bighorn sanctuary might prove feasible given adequate signing and patrolling, and suggested that trapping coyotes and building dams might do some good. He realized the newly created Game and Fish Commission did not have the funds to manage a large sheep refuge, and suggested instead the creation of several small "nature monuments" in the Growler Mountains and other ranges under federal supervision.

Phillips was not the only one visiting southwestern Arizona in the early 1930s in search of sanctuaries. Eager to expand the list of parks and monuments, National Park Service leaders Roger Toll, Frank Pinkley, and Edwin D. McKee canvassed the West in search of new parklands. In a memo to his boss on April 18, 1931, National Park Service naturalist McKee outlined some particular entities he deemed worthy as candidates for inclusion in new national monuments. He recommended the organ pipe cactus, saguaro cactus, and Joshua tree as three plant species of national interest, and the Tinajas Altas and California's Picacho Peak as special landscape features (Eden 1956). Desert bighorn sheep and native palms were considered candidate species in need of protection.

The deserts of western Arizona were a logical place to be looking for refuges and monuments in the early 1930s. For one thing, the federal government had extensive holdings there—more than 10 million acres of public lands in southwestern Arizona. These Sonoran Desert lands were of little value for grazing or farming because of their aridity and were sporadically mined, though hundreds of prospectors had scoured the landscape in search of gold, silver, copper, and other minerals. Homesteads, while available, had only a few takers due to the lack of water. Nonetheless, the forces of preservation would have to contend with more than a little opposition, as the state's governor and business community wanted to keep those lands open for future development, mining, grazing, and settlement. And mixed into any discussion involving a change in land status were issues about which state or federal agency would control the grazing, whether the state or federal government would regulate wildlife, and what tactics were needed to obtain water rights for control and use.

In February 1932, Yellowstone National Park Superintendent Toll made a trip to southwestern Arizona to evaluate a prospective national monument designed to ensure the preservation of the organ pipe cactus and provide a game refuge to save the bighorn. He filed a favorable report for the area with the National Park Service director on March 31, 1932. Early the next year, Toll (1933) made a second reconnaissance, after which he recommended the establishment of Organ Pipe Cactus National Monument, as well as a Saguaro National Monument east of Tucson. Buoyed by Toll's report, Arizona monument supporters were joined by Pinkley, Arno B. Cammerer (director of the National Park Service), and Interior Secretary Ickes. On November 19, 1934, Ickes hosted a meeting of Park Service superintendents, leaders, and staff in Washington, D.C., and issued them a challenge: "I want as much wilderness, as much nature preserved and maintained as possible" (Watkins 1990).

The first plan for creating national monuments in southwestern Arizona was to use the Antiquities Act of 1906 to create an enormous desert national monument encompassing four to five million acres. It would have included most of the public land between State Highway 85 and the Colorado River south of the Southern Pacific railroad to the Mexican border. Key features to be incorporated included four of the five plant and animal species (desert bighorn, saguaro cactus, organ pipe cactus, and desert [Washington] fan palm), as well as McKee's Tinajas Altas.

Resistance came early from Arizona's governor, Hunt, who called the proposal an attempt to create "a damned billy goat pasture" out of most of Arizona. The Arizona Small Mine Owners Association, Arizona Woolgrowers Association, and Arizona Cattlegrowers Association, as well as the Yuma County Board of Supervisors, Yuma Valley Rod and Gun Club, and the Soil Conservation Service, also railed against the plan (Demaray 1936; Hayden 1936). Some political leaders were afraid such a monument or refuge would jeopardize proposed irrigation projects along the Colorado and Gila rivers, though no clear threat or connection was made.

Even so, the Interior Department whittled down the proposal. The Yuma Chamber of Commerce eventually supported the concept of the establishment of a Kofa National Wildlife Refuge (Dunbar 1935), while the Tucson Chamber of Commerce supported Organ Pipe Cactus National Monument (Mackenzie 1935). Complicating the issue was the ongoing creation of the Papago Indian Reservation, to be administered by the Indian Service. These lands contained a number of non-Indian mines and ranches, and threats to such properties went down hard in certain quarters.

Support for the monuments was bolstered by the recent creation of a refuge specifically designated for bighorn sheep. In 1933, the Bureau of Reclamation withdrew the 658,497-acre Boulder Canyon National Wildlife Refuge (in Arizona and Nevada), which would contain Lake Mead once Hoover Dam was finished. This federal refuge was short-lived. It became part of Lake Mead National Recreation Area in 1936, and was scheduled to be managed by the National Park Service and included within the state of Arizona's Boulder Canyon Refuge. A few years later, the state designation was "decommissioned" and the refuge included in the recreation area, the Bureau of Reclamation preferring to let sibling Interior Department agencies manage recreation on reclamation lake–sites.

The Biological Survey's Ding Darling and J. Clark Salyer II wanted refuges, not recreation areas, and in 1936 they oversaw the dedication of Hart Mountain National Wildlife Refuge for pronghorn (Oregon) and the Desert Game Range for bighorn (Nevada). Also that year, the Charles Sheldon Antelope Range in Nevada was expanded after being created for pronghorn in 1931.

Nonetheless, the need for more federal refuges in the West was still thought to be acute, as the newest refuges only "constitute the beginning of the reservoirs needed for our resident game species" and "immense additions" must be made "to attain the objectives of the Federal Government's program of even a minimum sanctuary area." (US Congress 1937). Such proclamations, while cheering to conservationists, were opposed by states like Arizona, which regarded the management and protection of big game species as a states' rights prerogative.

Biological Survey biologists as well as administrators supported the survey's goals, if not the National Park Service's. Nelson, Biological Survey chief (1916–27) and senior biologist (1927–29), had worked in the Southwest and was undoubtedly the most knowledgeable person when it came to Arizona game issues and wildlife in general. He corresponded extensively with Hornaday, Sheldon, John Burnham, George Grinnell, and John C. Phillips (Smithsonian Institution Archives, US Fish and Wildlife Service Collection, 1860–1961 Field Reports, Series 1, Record Unit 7364) in support of refuges, both state and federal. His protégé Goldman, too, had worked extensively in the Southwest, most recently as Biological Survey biologist in charge of game and bird reservations (1925–28) and senior biologist (1928–35). Goldman also supported the creation of refuges as an important measure to ensure game restoration.

And so it was that the Biological Survey commissioned Senior Biologist Walter Taylor to conduct a reconnaissance of southwestern Arizona to evaluate areas suitable for an organ pipe cactus preserve and a desert bighorn refuge. Having previously visited the area with Dr. Charles Vorhies in April 1924, Taylor conducted his reconnaissance over several months and was accompanied at various times on his field trips by Vorhies, Forrest Shreve, Andrew Nichol, Gilbert Sykes, and Randolph Jenks. They represented the University of Arizona, National Park Service, and Arizona Game and Fish Department, in addition to the Biological Survey.

Taylor toured the borderland from Lukeville to Tinajas Altas, and his report supported the creation of an organ pipe cactus monument as large as could be desired, with any remaining bighorn lands to "be set up as a wildlife preserve. It is felt by every man of us in the field that the preservation of the wildlife is the first consideration, and that the departments should cooperate to the fullest extent in bringing this about" (Taylor 1935d). He also urged that Mexico establish a game refuge corresponding to an American monument and wildlife refuge in the Pinacate region of Sonora between the border and the Gulf of California. Interestingly, while Taylor's (1935) report provided an otherwise good description of the proposed refuges' flora and fauna, it makes no mention of desert antelope on either side of the border.

Evaluating the Refuges

Following the establishment of the 330,689-acre Organ Pipe Cactus National Monument by an executive order of President Roosevelt on April 13, 1937, and its transfer to the National Park Service, Nichol was selected to survey the monument's plant life. An inveterate note-taker and cartographer, Nichol made detailed descriptions of the forage and water conditions he encountered and mapped the distributions of cacti and other signature plants. Nichol then surveyed western Arizona's game ranges with Goldman for the Arizona Game and Fish Commission and National Association of Audubon Societies.

As a result of these surveys, Weese (1941) was able to state that Organ Pipe Cactus National Monument contained bighorn, deer of three or more kinds, desert antelope, and javelina. Weese recommended the grazing leases not be renewed after expiring, the area be fenced from feral livestock and kept closed to prospecting and mining, and the monument's present size retained. He also recommended that the area's waters be freed up for wildlife and that the monument be managed as a biotic community and not a recreation area—recommendations thwarted by the Grey family, who continued to graze and water their stock on the monument for nearly 40 more years (Pinto 2010).

Nichol's (1937a) and Goldman's next assignment, to conduct a comprehensive survey of bighorn sheep in Arizona, was complicated, in that although Nichol had recently been on assignment for the National Park Service, he was now working for the Arizona Game and Fish Department and paid by the Audubon Society. During an extended trip that lasted from June through November, Nichol, Edward Goldman and Goldman's son Luther visited nearly every desert mountain range in the state from the Mexican border to the Arizona Strip north of the Grand Canyon. Presenting their findings in a typewritten report that included a range map of the five ungulate species of big game present, Nichol (1938) estimated the number of bighorn in each desert range, and concluded that poaching by prospectors and meat hunters remained the animal's biggest threat. Of particular interest was the sighting of six bands of 40 pronghorn south of Ajo—four of these groups east of where this animal now occurs.

Nichol pointed out the values of the Kofa, Castle Dome, Cabeza Prieta, and Eagletail mountains as refuges, reporting the presence of 145 fan palms and noting that bands of up to 50 to 75 bighorn formerly occurred in the Kofas and Castle Domes, with "Nelson's antelope," caracaras, and black vultures found in the Cabeza Prieta area. He described the Cabeza Prieta as overrun with feral burros and thought refuge status would facilitate water development and eliminate poaching at waters. Noting the situation on Organ

Pipe Cactus National Monument, where the Grey family's grazing leases continued to frustrate the Park Service's aspirations, he recommended that livestock be excluded from future game refuges. Recognizing that railroads and fences were barriers to both bighorn and pronghorn, Nichol was fearful of interfering with the relationship between animals and water, believing bighorn and other game species made mass movements in response to seasonal changes in forage and water availability. Goldman disagreed with this supposition, and, while acknowledging Nichol's ecological and botanical expertise, said so in a December 31, 1937, letter (Smithsonian Institution Archives, US Fish and Wildlife Service, 1860–1961 Field Reports, Series 1, Box 28, Folder 6). But both agreed that large refuges were needed, rather than mini-monuments.

In January 1938, the Arizona Game and Fish Commission established Boulder Canyon State Game Refuge in response to the federal government's increasing role as a protector of big game habitat. Also reflecting this concern was the commission's strong opposition to a Forest Service proposal for an 1,800-square-mile refuge containing portions of the Coconino, Sitgreaves, and Tonto national forests. Another refuge arrangement—a Bill Williams joint Forest Service–state "management area" south of Williams—was also viewed with suspicion as another infringement on states' rights. The problem was that even though the commission was increasingly convinced of the need for wildlife protection, the state lacked the resources to manage large parcels of land.

Establishment of the Kofa and Cabeza Prieta Game Ranges

Proposals to determine the fate of refuges involved politics as well as biological evaluation. In the early 1930s, Congress, the Interior Department, and the Government Land Office were working on plans to assign and administer about 80,000,000 acres of public domain, primarily in the West. The Taylor Grazing Act of 1934 transferring federal lands from the Government Land Office to the Department of Interior was only one major transaction that grew out of this process.

Also taking place in Arizona at this time was the planned transfer of some 5.5 million acres to the Indian Service as the Papago Indian Reservation (now Tohono O'odham Nation; McIntyre 2008). West of the proposed reservation were another five million acres of public land deemed of little economic importance for grazing, mining, homesteading, or settlement. The mines at Fortuna and Castle Dome had played out; the few brave homesteaders present had gone broke; grazing was seasonal and unprofitable. Uncle Sam was the logical custodian of most of southwestern Arizona.

Designating additional parks, monuments, preserves, and Indian reservations made good sense when one considered the conservation and social values of such withdrawals. Or so it seemed. The sparsely distributed stockmen and miners in those parts of Pima and Yuma counties thought otherwise.

The Interior Department suggested two wildlife refuges, one encompassing a 1.5-million-acre area centered in the Castle Dome and SH (Kofa) mountains and extending from the Eagletail Mountains west nearly to the Colorado River, and the other encompassing nearly two million acres approximating today's Cabeza Prieta National Wildlife Refuge. A jurisdictional dispute as to which agency would manage the refuges complicated the issue. Although Interior's Park Service and Grazing Service wanted to be the land management agencies, the Department of Agriculture's Biological Survey was the logical choice for an area dedicated to desert bighorn sheep.

Not only did sheep and cattle growers, small miners, and citizens in Yuma County feel threatened by any withdrawals, the sheer size of the proposals caused even conservationists to blink. Opposition rhetoric of that time echoes objections heard to this day:

> I protest against the proposed withdrawal from entry . . . of two large areas of land in Southwestern Arizona comprising 3,400,000 acres for use and propagation of mountain sheep and goats [sic] and as game refuge. . . . Even hilly land adjacent to farming areas should be left open to entry for settlers thereon for grazing stock. Suitable rougher areas can be found for game, but game protection gets out of its natural and integrated sphere and is ruinous to conservation of water and soil resources and economy and social values and rights if used as a pretext to destroy Arizona and proper watershed development and nation's agriculture on which people fundamentally subsist. (Gibbons 1937; see also Arizona Colorado River Commission 1937)

As for the state, the Arizona Game and Fish Department had expressed a more than casual interest in the matter in September 1937, when the Arizona Game and Fish Commission directed State Game Warden Lewis to take issue with the Biological Survey's intention of establishing bighorn sheep refuges in western Arizona and requested that all further surveys and investigations of such areas be conducted with a department representative present (Nichol). Although going on record as favoring refuges for mountain sheep, the commission wanted all interested parties included in any arrangements made before legislative action was taken. Also causing concern was Lewis's transmittal to the commission of correspondence and national legislation proposals that referenced the creation of several Forest Service refuges and a change in the status of Boulder Canyon Wildlife Refuge.

Despite Nichol's and Goldman's support, the commission continued to balk at the idea of the government's establishing two huge federal game refuges after creating Organ Pipe Cactus National Monument for the National Park Service. The commission's opposition continued to be based on states' rights grounds, the biggest objection being the possibility of ownership of resident game animals being transferred to either the National Park Service or the Grazing Service. That issue was alleviated but not resolved when management authority was decided in favor of the Biological Survey, a federal agency with which the commission and department had enjoyed a longtime working arrangement and with which the state had cooperative agreements.

Nonetheless, the Interior Department continued to be involved, with the Grazing Service given dual management authority with the Biological Survey. As a result, the commission, while formally opposing any federal withdrawals of game refuges in Yuma and Pima counties as an intrusion on the state's wildlife and land laws, begrudgingly acquiesced to the arrangement—an action similar to that expressed in a memorial passed by the legislature. That the state's opposition remained somewhat muted was no doubt due to the department's wanting to protect bighorn sheep, but not having the funds in 1938 to supply the manpower to manage game refuges of such size.

The Arizona Game Protective Association was not so bound by state politics. At its 1937 convention, AGPA member Vorhies resolved to mount a publicity campaign to support the creation of a Kofa and a Cabeza Prieta game range. To this purpose he enlisted Frederick R. Burnham and the Boy Scouts of America as refuge advocates. Burnham (1928), who had a keen interest in saving the desert bighorn, had been a close friend of General Robert Baden-Powell, founder of the Boy Scout movement, and continued to maintain his affiliation with scouting. As a means of fostering refuge support, Burnham asked George F. Miller, Scout executive in Phoenix, to adopt the proposed refuges as a conservation project. An organizational meeting was held February 3, 1938 (Simms 1938), after which a year's publicity on the behalf of 10,000 Boy Scouts helped align public opinion in favor of the refuge proposals despite the continued opposition of small-scale miners and cattlemen. Arizona's congressional delegation, led by Senator Carl Hayden, now gave their support to the Roosevelt administration in its effort to establish both bighorn refuges (Saxton 1978), making a few concessions in the wording to placate the opposition. Both the Kofa and Cabeza Prieta were proclaimed national game ranges by Executive Order 8039 on January 25, 1939.

A list of the speakers at Kofa's dedication gives an indication of who was being credited for the refuge's establishment: Burnham, representing the Boy Scouts of America; William Sawtelle, State Game Warden; Major Shepard Hiscox, president of the Roosevelt Council of Boy Scouts; E. C. Blankenagel of the Division of Grazing; Roscoe G. Willson, former Forest Service supervisor; Everett Mercer, Arizona district supervisor of the Biological Survey; Lee Kirby, Forest Service; and Richard Wickstrum, president of the Arizona Game Protective Association.

Kofa (King of Arizona) National Wildlife Refuge

The 665,400-acre Kofa Game Range, now Kofa National Wildlife Refuge, was jointly managed by the Fish and Wildlife Service (Biological Survey prior to 1940) and the Grazing Service (Bureau of Land Management after 1946) until the Fish and Wildlife Service assumed sole management authority in 1976 (Public Law 94-223). Although the refuge's management emphasis was on desert bighorn sheep, "antelopes" and peccaries were also included as species to be protected.

During the refuge's early management years, Kofa supervisors such as Arthur M. Halloran sought to identify what resources the refuge contained. Of particular interest were its water sources, the springs, tinajas, cattle tanks, and wells—a number of which were enhanced, while others were constructed (Barclay 1947).

Because of the area's mining heritage, which included the King of Arizona Mine, feral burros were a major problem, competing with wildlife for forage and water. In one of the first reports, the manager complained, "Wild burros range over this territory and from the reports of the laborer-patrolmen it is believed their population will have to be

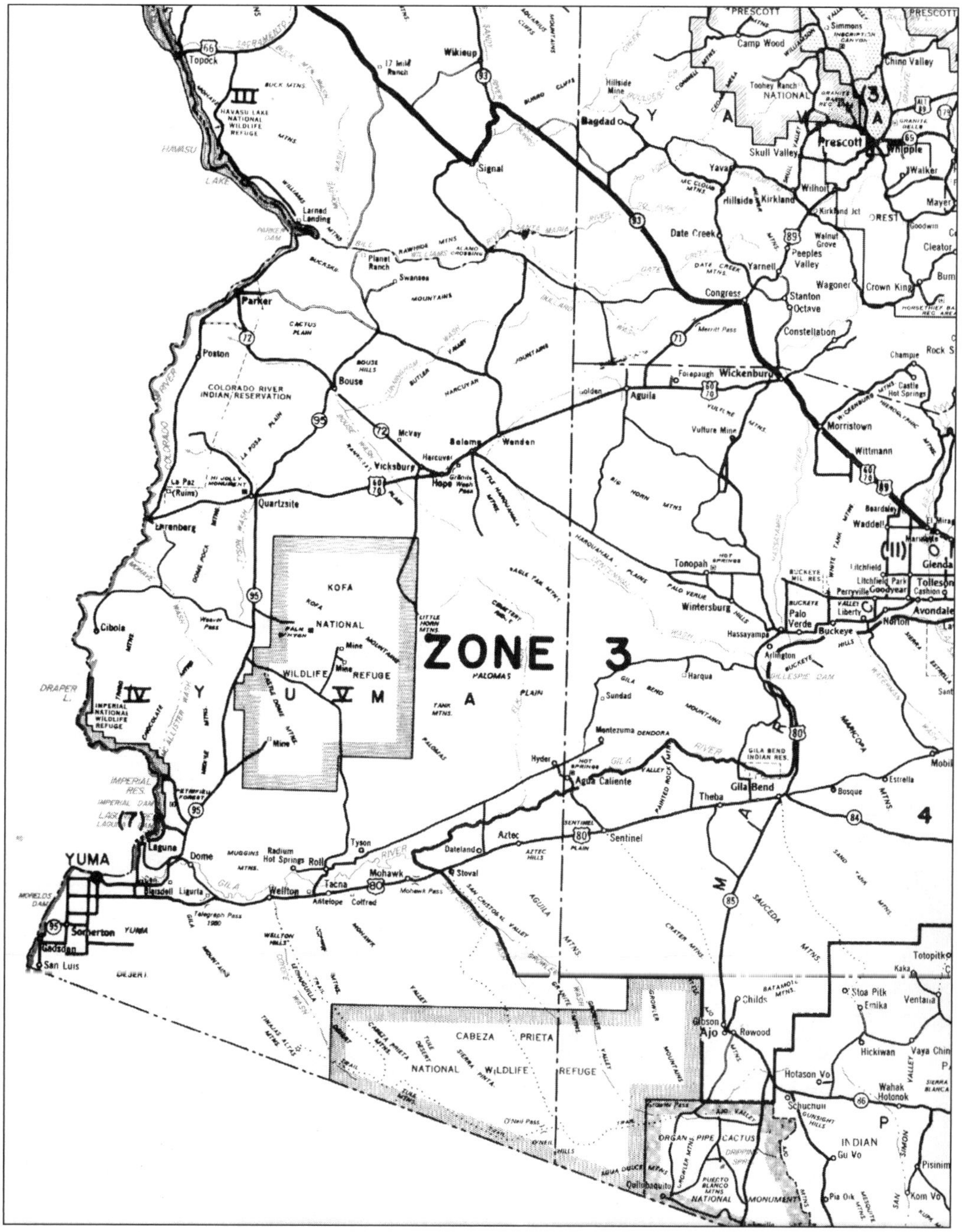

A 1955 map shows the extent of the large federal refuges in southwestern Arizona. (AGFD files)

reduced. No less than 50 wild burros are visiting Thumb Butte tanks daily and quite large numbers of these animals are watering at New Well, Jasper Springs, Alamo Springs, and at many other tanks" (Allison 1939).

To increase bighorn numbers, managers sought to eliminate both burros and predators, and in 1956 the Kofa was opened to deer hunting. Bighorn hunts began in 1960 in cooperation with the Arizona Game and Fish Department, but it was not until 1972 that domestic cattle were officially removed from the refuge.

Early refuge managers tried to survey the many mines in the refuge and determine the number of "pick-nickers" using Baker and Horse tanks, as no information regarding the number of people using the refuge area was available. One of the first projects was a transplant of about 100 Gambel's quail from east of Roll, Arizona, to the Horse Tank area. Refuge managers such as Gale Monson conducted periodic wildlife surveys and later supervised waterhole counts for desert bighorn (Monson and Sumner 1996). A bighorn research project was first conducted during 1953–54 as a joint project between the refuge and the department, during which one bighorn and one deer were taken each month over a 12-month span. Animals were closely examined for diseases, parasites, abnormalities, and general body condition. Measurements were collected, and food preferences recorded (Russo 1956a).

Cabeza Prieta National Wildlife Refuge

The stated purpose of the Cabeza Prieta Game Range (now a national wildlife refuge) was "for the conservation and development of natural wildlife resources, and for the protection and improvement of public grazing lands and natural forage resources" (Executive Order 8038), but desert bighorn were both the implicit emphasis of the refuge and its rallying symbol. Covering an area of 860,010 acres of Sonoran Desert, the refuge's terrain is punctuated by steep, linear mountain ranges and broad alluvial valleys.

In its beginning, the Cabeza Prieta had a staff of one, who reported to a manager in Yuma responsible for both the Cabeza and the Kofa. As was to be expected, one of the first chores was to learn what wildlife inhabited the refuge and what habitats were occupied by what animals. Early reports tell of counting birds and mammals at waterholes, mapping roads and trails, and searching for waterholes and sites where wells or water could be found or impounded. The first work order requested three jobs: constructing 25 permanent watering tanks, building low-class truck trails for refuge vehicles, and erecting ten miles of barbed-wire fence "so that the refuge can be easily patrolled" (Catlin 1939). One worry that dragged on for several years was a herd of over 200 Angora goats in the Growler Mountains near Charlie Bell Well, prime bighorn habitat, and it was not until the early 1970s that the last head of domestic stock was removed from the refuge.

One of the first projects was cleaning out Tule Well and setting up a windmill. As in the Kofas, a predator-control program was initiated in the Cabeza Prieta in the 1940s. Since then, refuge personnel have concentrated on management programs designed to maximize bighorn numbers and preserve Sonoran pronghorn. Bighorn herds were sufficiently stable by 1968 to allow bighorn hunting with permits issued by the Arizona Game and Fish Department.

Waterfowl Refuges along the Colorado River

The flurry of migratory waterfowl refuges acquired in the 1930s had little impact in arid Arizona. The only federal refuge created for waterfowl other than the Apache National Wildlife Refuge was the Safford National Wildlife Refuge, obtained through a Soil Conservation Service program by which tax-delinquent properties were made into national conservation areas. The refuge's artesian ponds were of limited value to waterfowl, and no refuge manager was appointed, only a caretaker. After a series of negotiations between the Fish and Wildlife Service and the Game and Fish Department, Safford National Wildlife Refuge was turned over to the state in 1945 to be operated as a bird farm.

Arizona's first real waterfowl refuges were declared by executive order and included as water reclamation projects resulting from Colorado River dams. These dams had been constructed to provide electric power, flood control, and irrigation water for lands along the lower Colorado River and for southern California. With the taming of the Colorado River by Hoover Dam in 1936, followed closely by the completion of Parker and Imperial dams in 1938, the Colorado River's flood plain was rapidly being converted to agriculture and recreation, necessitating some form of mitigation measures if any semblance of the river's original wildlife heritage was to remain. Accordingly, Imperial and Havasu national wildlife refuges were established in 1941.

Imperial National Wildlife Refuge (Arizona and California) was designated to provide habitat for migratory birds and other wildlife displaced elsewhere on the Colorado River. The refuge's original size was 25,768 acres, but by 1943 it had been expanded to 47,841 acres, primarily on Bureau of Reclamation lands. In an effort to manage waterfowl, mostly geese, and alleviate crop depredations, upstream bottomlands were cleared and farmlands planted in grain. Although waterfowl enjoyed seasonal protection during the winter, and sport fishing was allowed, commercial fishing was prohibited.

Havasu Lake National Wildlife Refuge (Arizona and California) was a more traditional federal refuge, in that it originally involved a riverine environment, waterfowl, and wetland refugia for other migratory birds. The water behind Davis Dam was first called Parker Dam Reservoir and later rechristened Lake Havasu, in honor of the Havasupai Indians. The main purpose of Parker Dam is to divert water through the Colorado River Aqueduct to Southern California, removing 1,212,000 million acre-feet annually from the lower original refuge (which, while later enlarged, only comprised 37,370 acres).

The intention behind Lake Havasu refuge was to preserve waterfowl habitat on the Colorado River flyway, but it also provided recreational opportunities, including hunting and fishing. Management activities between 1941 and 1962 consisted mainly of controlling hunting, with mesquites and saltcedar being removed to farm millet, corn, and other grains for migrating birds. Early refuge managers such as Monson inventoried the refuge's wildlife populations, to better understand the impact of the river's changed ecology and cope with the dam's effects on the age-old cycles of flood, nutrient enrichment, seedling rejuvenation, and water quality. Waterfowl were hunted in season and sport fishing was allowed, but commercial fishing was prohibited. The mountains adjacent to Topock Gorge and other portions of the refuge support desert bighorn sheep, and these were protected in order to allow bighorn numbers to increase until a limited number of hunting permits could be issued.

As with many refuges, not all of the land on Havasu National Wildlife Refuge was federal property, the remainder being acquired from private inholdings with funds from duck stamps. At one time it comprised four units: Topock Gorge, Topock Marsh, the Needles Wilderness, and Bill Williams River, which became a separate refuge in 1992.

A third federal refuge on the Colorado River, Cibola, was created in 1964 as mitigation for the channelizing and lowering of the river between Blythe and the Imperial National Wildlife Refuge. This action, while mandated by law, constituted neither a mitigation, nor a preservation measure, as most of the refuge's lands were formerly included in the Arizona Game and Fish Department's Cibola Wildlife Area, which along with Martinez Lake downstream constituted the two main state refuges on the Colorado River.

Arizona's National Wildlife Refuges, 1912–62

Refuge	Acres	Date Created
Grand Canyon National Game Preserve	612,736	1906
Salt River Bird Refuge (Roosevelt Lake National Game Preserve)	21,129	1909
Boulder Canyon (Lake Mead NRA, including Nevada)	622,000	1933
Apache Migratory Waterfowl Refuge (on Apache National Forest)	2,674	1937
Cabeza Prieta National Wildlife Refuge	860,000	1939
Kofa National Wildlife Refuge	665,400	1939
Havasu Lake National Wildlife Refuge (including California)	37,370	1941
Imperial National Wildlife Refuge (including California)	25,625	1941

Note: NRA=National Recreation Area

FISH MANAGEMENT EXPANDS IN INTENSITY

David E. Brown and Larry Riley

By the early 1940s, fishing opportunities in Arizona were as good as they had ever been. Dams built by the Salt River Project on the Verde and Salt rivers provided an extensive but fluctuating warm-water fishery dominated by the popular largemouth bass–bluegill combination. Also available were other warm-water reservoirs, including San Carlos Reservoir behind the federal government's Coolidge Dam, and Gillespie Dam and Reservoir downstream on the Gila River. Closer to home for most residents of Phoenix was Lake Carl Pleasant on the Agua Fria River, with Frog Tanks just below the dam.[1] Lake Mead was filling, and management plans for the lower Colorado River promised fishing possibilities that beggared the imagination.

The War Years, 1941–45

During the war years, the seven ponds of the Hunt Bass Hatchery in Papago Park operated at full capacity. Working with out-of-state hatcheries, hatchery supervisor Herbert Reid could provide all the largemouth bass and bluegill brood stock needed for new reservoirs as well as for restocking existing ones. Crappie and catfish could be seined from natural populations and transported when needed.

In 1941, some 606,687 warm-water fishes were planted. About half were largemouth bass. By way of contrast, stocking records for the war year 1942 showed only 68,999 largemouth bass, 41,700 smallmouth bass, and 157,060 bluegills planted, with another 20,150 fish coming from US Fish and Wildlife Service hatcheries outside the state. Most of the largemouths that year went to Canyon Lake, which was now filling.

Good trout fishing was also to be had, fueled to some degree by the insatiable demand for more hatchery fish in summer vacation towns in the White Mountains and below the Mogollon Rim. Helping to meet this demand, at least partially, were the Arizona Game and Fish Department's hatcheries at Pinetop, Tonto, and Page Springs. Supplemented by stock from the federal government, nearly 2,000,000 trout were planted on the national forests in 1942, versus only 306,083 in 1941. Most of these fish were fry and fingerling rainbows and browns, with a few grayling and brook trout thrown in.

The nearly threefold increase in trout production in 1942 over 1941 coincided with a major change in trout-stocking policy. Studies had shown only 10%–15% of fingerling trout planted during the summer months survived until spring. The mortality rate for fry was even worse—it was estimated to be 95%–99%. As a result, stocking strategies changed to increase the supply of creel-sized fish (those from seven to nine inches long). These were to be raised in rearing ponds located at the hatcheries. This last action resulted from sportsmen volunteers having failed to look after fish in the more remote rearing ponds on the East Verde River and at Government Springs, as well as an egregious fish-poaching case that made headlines and earned the perpetrator a five-year license revocation.

---

[1] See table next page, and Mueller and Marsh 2002.

Forest Service Estimate of Trout Distribution, 1942
Source: US Forest Service Annual Wildlife Report, 1942, Table 9, "Fish Distribution - Trout, Region 3 - Arizona"

Forest	Species	Fry 1" or less	Fingerlings 1" and up to 5"	Yearlings and Adults over 5"
Apache	Rainbow	--	264,456	176,120
	Brown	--	9,450	--
	Yellowstone Cutthroat	440,000	176,238	--
	Grayling	490,000	--	--
	Totals by Size Classes	**930,000**	**450,144**	**176,120**
Coconino	Rainbow	--	30,500	3,500
	Brown	--	16,800	124,718
	Totals by Size Classes		**47,300**	**128,218**
Coronado	Rainbow	--	--	11,847
	Totals by Size Classes			**11,847**
Crook	Rainbow	--	--	8,011
	Totals by Size Classes			**8,011**
Prescott	Rainbow		2,000	26,200
	Totals by Size Classes		**2,000**	**26,200**
Sitgreaves	Rainbow	--	--	6,794
	Brown	--	3,000	--
	Totals by Size Classes			**6,794**
Tonto	Rainbow	--	194,574	50,540
	Brown	--	--	14
	E. Brook	--	--	46,543
	Totals by Size Classes		**194,574**	**97,097**
Total Arizona		**930,000**	**697,018**	**454,287**

Original Note: "All trout furnished by Arizona State Game Commission except 122,576 Yellowstone cutthroat fingerlings furnished by Federal Hatchery."

Stocking nearly two million trout required more than a strictly "put and take" policy of planting only "catchables." Planting creel-sized fish created its own problems, not the least of which was the time required and higher costs involved. Disease, mortality, and predation all took a toll, which (with losses incurred during planting) could significantly cut the number of fish actually released. Nearly all of the state's fish eggs still came from the federal government or were purchased from private hatcheries, which compounded the problem. Nonetheless, the numbers of creel-sized trout stocked in the succeeding war years was impressive: 286,513 catchables out of 1.5 million released in 1943; 244,359 in 1944; and 286,796 in 1945 (Arizona Game and Fish Commission 1948).

That the Game and Fish Department was now doing most of the trout stocking was the result of considerable effort and cause for celebration. Reid, director of the Fisheries Division, had a reputation as a competent hatchery supervisor and administrator. Having successfully worked through a series of problems with Arizona's trout hatcheries, Reid had just supervised a recent planting of 10,000 rainbow trout in the cold waters of the Colorado River below Boulder Dam; otherwise, most of the trout stocked in the state were now "home-grown."

The major operating expenses for hatcheries were fish food and transportation. The Maricopa Tallow Works was a major supplier of fish food, selling the department 2,000 pounds of horsemeat in 1941 at 3.5 cents per pound. Should the horse be delivered directly, Dud Yoder or another hatchery worker would dispatch the animal with a "horse pistol" maintained for that purpose (Carr 1994). Fish trucks constituted another major expense, but the cost was sometimes allayed by a local game protective association, which provided a vehicle to ensure the delivery of fish to their primary areas of interest.[2]

The major fisheries milestone achieved during the war years was undoubtedly the completion of Williams Creek Hatchery in 1943. Conceived as early as 1934 as a cooperative venture between the Arizona Game and Fish Department and the federal government, this hatchery resulted from much lobbying by the Arizona Game Protective Association and Arizona's congressional delegation.

Located at a spring at the headwaters of Williams Creek on the Fort Apache Indian Reservation, the hatchery was soon producing trout on a cooperative basis, with the state providing three hatchery workers and receiving a third of the fish. The federal share of the production was planted primarily on the reservation and in a few military waters; the state's trout were stocked in the White Mountains. This arrangement, never satisfactory to all parties, failed to meet expectations. As a result, the cooperative agreement eventually would be terminated, and the federal government would take over all production.

Nonetheless, the demand for more hatchery fish remained, especially since the department's Indian Gardens hatchery was failing due to inadequate water and difficulties with the water right. As a consequence, Reid was directed to close portions of Oak Creek to fishing in 1945 and try to purchase the adjacent private hatchery at Page Springs, provided the cost did not exceed $50,000.

Fishing regulations had been much simplified in 1940. A standard trout season was set from May 30 to September 30, with legal fishing hours later extended to between 4 a.m. and 10 p.m. Nonetheless, adjustments continued to be made in the trout bag limit to reduce or increase fishing pressure in certain areas. Variations included changing the limit in Graham County (other than in Frye Mesa Reservoir) from 10 to 15 trout and establishing a bag limit within Grand Canyon National Park of 10 trout per day with 20 in possession.

Other trout-fishing regulations enacted during the war years required the release of all fish less than seven inches long and allowed fishing in Grand Canyon National Park all

[2]The US Forest Service began stocking trout in tributaries flowing off the Kaibab Plateau in 1919, a program the National Park Service picked up the following year. Superintendent reports show Bright Angel Creek, Tapeats Creek, Clear Creek, Shinumo Creek, and Garden Creek being stocked between 1920 and the mid-1960s with the assistance of the US Bureau of Fisheries and personnel from the Arizona and Utah game and fish departments. The species of fish planted varied, but brown trout appear to have been favored early on in Shinumo, Garden, and Bright Angel creeks, the latter probably providing a source for additional plantings. The trout planted below Boulder Dam were also courtesy of the federal government.

year. A portion of Big Lake was closed to reduce the opportunity of snagging cutthroat planted there. At the direction of the Arizona Game and Fish Commission, department personnel met with their Nevada counterparts to discuss how to regulate fishing in Lake Mead—a situation that would bedevil both state commissions for years to come.

Regulations governing warm-water fishes were also relaxed. Bag limits on crappies, bluegill, yellow perch, and channel catfish were eliminated either statewide or in designated waters due to overcrowding. The minimum length of channel catfish was reduced from 12 to 10 inches in 1941, with the length limit abolished on the Colorado River. The minimum length for bass was nine inches. By 1945, bass and all other warm-water game fish could be taken all year, with bag limits on black bass, channel cats, crappies, bluegill, bream, striped (yellow) bass, and bullhead (20). No limits were imposed on the Salt River lakes or Lake Mary.

Rules on the taking of nongame fish (called "rough" or "trash" fish) were also relaxed to allow seining, spearing, clubs, and other devices, with live bait restricted only in Big, Crescent, and Luna lakes. No fewer than four types of seining permits were available, depending on the fisherman's purpose and intended volume. Nor was there any limit on carp, suckers, ring perch, or bonytails. After October 1945, however, rough fish could only be seined for commercial purposes under special permit.

All waters save trout waters remained open to fishing throughout the year, with various fishing lakes and streams subject to particular season openings and closures in an attempt to conserve fish and increase fishing quality. As an example, after Roosevelt and Apache lakes were drained and closed to fishing in 1941, fishing was allowed to resume after the 1942 spawning season when the lakes had been refilled and restocked. Oak Creek was open to fishing yearlong except for trout, but Long Lake near Show Low was closed to all fishing to protect slow-growing populations of bass and bluegills there. San Carlos too was partially closed to fishing, in an attempt to protect spawning bass.

Stunting and the overstocking of certain species, including rough fish, were now recognized as problems (Arizona Game and Fish Commission 1942). By 1944, there were so many carp in Lake Mead that these fish threatened the blue-ribbon bass fishery. Buffalofish, apparently planted by the federal government, had become so numerous in Roosevelt Lake that the commission issued seining permits to commercial fishermen for their removal, with 10% of the receipts going to the Arizona Game and Fish Department.

An open season on bullfrogs (which also included the red-legged frog in California) was first authorized in 1942 for the Colorado River from March 20 to November 30. This season, which originally allowed the use of firearms, was later shortened to run from June 1 to November 30 and made statewide. The bag limit was six bullfrogs per day except on the Colorado River, where the limit was 12. These later restrictions called for the method of take to be with gigs and spears and allowed bullfrogs to be taken at night.

Reid's Postwar Fisheries, 1946–49

Having supervised a successful fisheries program with a good economic record, Reid was a popular choice for director when Fred Merkle retired in November 1945. Intent on

Albert W. "Dud" Yoder, longtime hatchery supervisor and later influential chief of the Fisheries Branch. (AGFD files)

keeping his fisheries program in place, Reid appointed veteran hatchery supervisor Dud Yoder to direct a six-man Fisheries Division, a decision acceptable to Commissioners Charles Beach, George Wrench, and E. G. Dentzer. The only commissioner appearing to have a definite fishing agenda was Wrench's replacement, William Connor, whose pet project was a hatchery below the newly constructed Davis Dam on the Colorado River. With this exception, the postwar hatchery program consisted mostly of acquiring the private hatchery at Page Springs and improving Tonto and Pinetop hatcheries.

As shown in the license table in Appendix D, postwar fishing-license sales displayed a major trajectory upward, rising from 73,528 in 1945 to 111,802 in 1948 and bringing in nearly half a million dollars (Arizona Game and Fish Commission 1949). To encourage an even greater increase in license sales, the commission authorized Information and Education Officer Dan Gish to make a color film with sound on sport fishing in Arizona, in conjunction with the South Bend Bait Company.

The AGPA and the commission soon resumed their demand for more hatchery fish, however, and while Reid was negotiating for Page Springs and the site for a rearing pond below Davis Dam, the AGPA was pushing for more production at Williams Creek, even offering to provide the fish-food. A proposal for a federal warm-water hatchery and fish biologist to take over Papago Park was nonetheless rejected in favor of a hatchery at Peck's Lake in the Verde Valley. Capital outlay continued to be a problem despite increased license revenue, and the commission requested that the Arizona State Legislature fund any new hatchery construction. In 1949, the federal government successfully negotiated a lease for what Commissioner Connor hoped would be a hatchery below Davis Dam.

Meanwhile, studies by George J. Eicher and other fish biologists showed the best carryover of trout fingerlings and fry to be in lakes rather than streams. Another change in fish-planting strategy now followed, with smaller trout again being released in quantity. The result was a great increase in the number of trout stocked, including additional plantings by the Arizona Game and Fish Department and the Fish and Wildlife Service below Boulder Dam—the total number rising from 2,097,467 in 1947 (387,403 catchables) to 2,875,492 in 1949 (342,292 catchables). Most fish stocked were rainbows, with substantial numbers of cutthroats and browns. Less than 10% were graylings and brook trout. Although complaints about the high cost of raising trout continued, generating much discussion over bag limits and other regulations, the commission followed the department's advice and made few or no changes in the fishing regulations.

No formal studies had been conducted, but Reid and Eicher realized warm-water hatcheries were no longer a priority, as natural conditions and natural reproduction in the reservoirs took care of most management needs. Operations at Hunt Bass Hatchery, which had been proposed as a site for a zoo as early as 1945, were put on a standby basis in 1947. Thereafter the hatchery was used mainly for experimental introductions through the late 1950s, while also serving as a regional headquarters. Nonetheless, largemouth bass and bluegill plantings in the state continued, increasing slightly from 227,566 fish at the height of the war in 1943 to 240,090 in 1947, when 22,880 channel cats were also planted.

Fishery biologists of the time considered overcrowding and competition with rough fish to constitute the most serious problems facing game fish, and a renovation program at Ashurst and Kinnikinick lakes poisoned a number of fish, to the consternation of some onlookers. Less controversial was a permit issued to seine carp and rough fish in Lake Mead.

Other serious concerns were die-offs of trout at Big Lake during the summer of 1948 and again the subsequent winter, and the Bureau of Reclamation's dredging and draining of Topock Marsh. Investigating and remedying these situations was difficult, however, as standard operations such as maintaining hatcheries and running a weed cutter took up all of the money budgeted.

Proposals for new regulations nonetheless abounded. A number of recommendations came from the AGPA, by now a major voice at the spring commission meetings where fishing regulations were set. Some proposals acted upon were impractical. Others were innovative and ahead of their time, such as a proposal to allocate certain streams to fly-fishing and a recommendation by commissioner and White Mountain sportsman Dentzer to close five stream sites along the Little Colorado River to fish stocking and fishing to prevent the extinction of native trout. As a compromise, Reid recommended closing only the East Fork of the Little Colorado River, as stream waters were so scarce. The outcome was that the commission recommended a survey be undertaken and the trout plantings continue.

The trout season continued to open on the weekend closest to May 30, with a bag limit of 10 per day, 10 pounds, or 60 per week with certain exceptions. The size limit remained seven inches or better with fishing hours from 4 a.m. to 10 p.m.

Bass fishing was open all year with a 10-fish limit or 15 pounds plus one fish and a 10-inch minimum length. Fishing for bluegills was also open all year with no limit except on the Colorado River. There was also no closed season on channel cats, which were subject to a limit of 10 fish or 15 pounds plus one. All other species were subject to a yearlong season and no bag limit.

One of the bigger changes in fishing regulations occurred in 1949, when the commission required fishermen to have a separate trout-fishing license when fishing in trout waters, fishermen in all other waters having a valid "warm water" license. Trout waters were defined and, along with other selected sites, closed to fishing with "live bait." Streams 100 yards below reservoirs were also closed to fishing and live bait except during trout season.

Fishing closures remained a viable management strategy, often being enacted after plantings and in anticipation of spawning activity. In 1949, Cataract Lake was closed to fishing, as were the now-filling Roosevelt Lake, Mormon Lake, and Lower Lake Mary. The year being one of high water, spawning areas leading into Saguaro and Apache lakes were also temporarily closed. It was therefore a major achievement when the Salt River Project agreed to control water levels to protect spawning bass in 1950.

Establishing regulations governing the seining of baitfish proved to be surprisingly difficult. In 1946, the law prohibited seining, netting, and trapping of fish of any kind, and all fish not wanted (except carp and suckers) had to be returned to the water in good condition. These regulations were soon changed to disallow the use of gill and trammel nets but to allow four types of seining permits to properly licensed fishermen. Then, in 1949, most waters were again closed to seining to prevent the exploitation of native minnows, which were thought to be decreasing. This prohibition, too, failed to last, the regulations being changed again in 1950 at Yoder's request to disallow minnow seining only in trout waters. Several seining permits were then issued, and bluegills and redear sunfish were declared nongame fish.

By 1947, it was becoming apparent that competition for space on Arizona's waterways was increasing, so regulations governing the use of outboard motors were drafted as a means to manage recreation use. Another concern was the incompatibility between fishermen and nesting waterfowl, resulting in motorboats being prohibited at Big and Crescent lakes.

Due to Ben Avery's concerns that bullfrogs were being decimated, the season was shortened to August 1 through September 30, 1948, except for the Colorado River. Plans were made to distribute these amphibians to all warm waters where feasible. A hunting license was required to pursue bullfrogs despite spears and gigs being the only legal method of take. The bag limit was 12 per day or in possession.

Fishermen and ranger complaints regarding inconsistencies in fishing regulations along the Arizona-Nevada border on Lake Mead intensified after the war, resulting in a demand for reciprocal laws between the two states. Initially, the commission opted for joint use along the Colorado River. As the difference between the states in the number of nonresident fishermen became apparent, the decision was made to use the state boundary as a dividing line, each state enforcing its own regulations within its area of jurisdiction.

The problem was that the midline of the water body was not always the boundary, and no one knew where it was. After polling the AGPA on the issue, the commission opted for a $5 Colorado River nonresident license for Nevada and California residents fishing in Arizona. This proved unsatisfactory for the same reasons, and squabbles over the need for a three-state agreement would carry over into 1950 and for years afterward.

Dingell-Johnson Changes Everything, 1950–55

It is hard to overestimate the impact of Congress's passage of the Dingell-Johnson Act on August 9, 1950, on Arizona's fishery program. This bill, which took effect in 1951 after years of effort, essentially did for fish managers what the Pittman-Robertson Act did for game; i.e., provide a federal excise tax of 10% on fishing equipment to be made available to the states for the management and restoration of fish "having material value in connection with sport or recreation in the marine and/or fresh waters of the United States."

Pinetop Hatchery (date unknown). (AGFD files)

Given that the stated goal of the Fisheries Division had recently been declared, "to produce the largest number of desirable fish for the greatest number of anglers at the least possible cost," this meant hatcheries, fish stockings and introductions, rough-fish control, and especially lake building and acquisition would all greatly accelerate.

Reid took a leave of absence for health reasons in March 1948 and was given a light-duty assignment for six months as chief of operations, leaving Tom Kimball to serve out his term as director. With the department's license revenue growing from a little over two-thirds of a million dollars in 1951–52 to nearly $1,000,000 in 1954–55, Yoder's Fisheries Division would have plenty of opportunity for expansion.

With the door to major fishery developments opening, the problem was which projects to prioritize. Helpful in this regard was a recent survey by a Tri-State Fisheries Management Committee of fisheries biologists to develop a comprehensive fish management plan for the lower Colorado River from Hoover Dam to Mexico. For the immediate future, however, Arizona's emphasis would be on formulating a "lake development program."

The department had already been eyeing Luna and Big lakes as fisheries that could be increased in size if money was available. Raising the dam height for Luna Lake began in 1951, increasing its surface area to 175 acres. Attempts to enlarge Big, Crescent, Ashurst, and Kinnikinick lakes followed. Enlargements were justified by creel census surveys showing increased fishing use and success. Other construction work therefore continued on Big Lake, Peña Blanca Lake, Cluff Ranch Ponds, Rose Canyon Lake, and Fool Hollow Lake. The early 1950s also witnessed the end of a long drought. All of the state's lakes save San Carlos and the recently deepened Luna Lake filled.

Studies under Fisheries Division Chief Jack Hemphill included the possibility of establishing additional fisheries on Anderson Mesa and introducing new warm-water forage fishes—57,000 red shiners and threadfin shad were distributed throughout the Colorado and Agua Fria river systems. A biologist in charge of rough-fish control was hired, as renovation programs showed increased fish size in the Salt River lakes, Verde River, San Carlos Lake, Mittry Lake, Lake Pleasant, and other Arizona waters from which these fish were removed.

In 1951, three trout hatcheries and one multipurpose hatchery were in operation. Page Springs Hatchery near Cornville, the largest and most recent acquisition, was only suitable for rearing juvenile trout, as its 68-degree water was too warm for hatching trout eggs. Pinetop Hatchery produced most of the trout eggs, as well as raising about 125,000 catchable trout annually. Pinetop Hatchery faced an insurmountable problem, as its spring-water supply was rapidly diminishing. The hatchery had produced 3,359,000 fry, fingerling, and catchable trout (733,668). Tonto Creek Hatchery hatched and reared trout to stock streams under the Mogollon Rim and supplied fry to be reared at Page Springs. The department also helped manage Williams Creek Hatchery, supplying three hatchery workers and a third of the fish food. All of these hatcheries had by now evolved from "single pass" earthen ponds to intensive raceways made of concrete.

In 1952, Yoder and the department recommended passing on what had come to be called the W. Connor hatchery site below Davis Dam, leaving further hatchery production to Uncle Sam. The National Park Service had taken on the responsibility of providing a hatchery on the Colorado River, and would later establish its Willow Beach Hatchery at the upper end of Lake Mohave below Boulder Dam. And although the commission had recently agreed to renew its 10-year agreement to assist in managing Williams Creek Hatchery, it now opted to instead use the department's $30,000 contribution to the federal facility to purchase catchable trout from the private fish farm at Silver Creek for about $1 a pound. With this action, the department formally withdrew its agreement with what was by then the largest fish-producing station in the Southwest—a fish-producing facility once centermost in the political aspirations of the AGPA.

In 1954, a 157-acre parcel of land adjacent to Page Springs, along with the water rights for Bubbling Pond Springs on the west side of Oak Creek, were purchased from Edgar Page at Pop Arrington's insistence for $90,000. Although attempts to raise trout continued here, water temperatures were unsuitable and the hatchery was prone to diseases and fish kills. Eventually, the hatchery was converted to catfish production and later used as a refugium for native fishes.

Drought and lack of water was a general problem in 1955, resulting in a decline in hatchery plantings. Pinetop Hatchery soon failed completely, and unlike in 1951 when trout stockings totaled some 2.5 million trout, plantings in 1955 dropped to about two million trout, of which only about 500,000 were catchables.

The last hatchery of the 1912–62 period was Porter Springs. Constructed in 1955 following failure of the water supply at Pinetop, it consisted of three rearing ponds. Although about 40,000 catchables were produced here, this water source too proved inadequate. The hatchery closed after only one year of operation.

Fish management procedures were also changing. The use of electroshockers was now supplementing creel census gathering as a survey technique, and planting schedules underwent a number of modifications. When it came to stocking new lakes, catchables were no longer favored over fry. Plantings of legal-sized trout were restricted to the initial stocking, the expectation being that the new lake would allow fingerlings and fry to mature on their own. Another strategy was to accelerate attempts to increase carryover by reducing competition from suckers and other rough fish. Reducing or eliminating these fish would also increase the growth rate of game fishes, or so it was hoped. Also benefiting trout fishermen was a decision by the Safford Water Department to open Fry Mesa to fishing.

For the first time, serious discussion was taking place on the need to propagate native trout (*Salmo apache*), as these fish were becoming scarce. Fisheries Chief Yoder was directed to investigate high-elevation streams in the White Mountains and determine if the remaining holdouts could be perpetuated. Coupled with the decision that year to open the season yearlong for all fish species including trout, this made 1952 a landmark year for fish management in Arizona.

The retirement of Hunt Bass Hatchery, coupled with the policy of easing back on warm-water fish introductions, caused outdoor writer Avery to complain about the lack of a warm-water fishery program. Only 98,000 largemouth bass had been released in 1951 (mostly in Canyon, Apache, and San Carlos lakes) compared with 286,678 in 1950. This concern was heightened by the small number of bluegill, red-ear sunfish, smallmouth bass, and "sunperch" released (783). Selling the department's new, more science-based fisheries program was not going to be easy.

Big (Marsh) and Crescent lakes were shallow and marshy, as were all of Arizona's natural lakes, so these lakes were subject to periodic fish kills whenever excessive weed growth or ice and snow cover resulted in a depleted oxygen supply. Along with greater emphasis on these lakes as trout fisheries came a desire to increase their depth, and thus the amount of water and dissolved oxygen present. The height of Luna Lake's dam was therefore raised. Plans were made to do the same for Big Lake while increasing its water supply via a 10-foot channel from Crescent Lake. To further reduce the incidence of winter kill, an air line was used to pump oxygen into the deeper parts of the lake. An evaluation of the lakes on Anderson Mesa showed similar problems, and plans were made to raise the levels of Ashurst and Kinnikinick lakes to make them yearlong trout fisheries.

Another serious problem impacting warm-water fisheries was the stunting of black bass and other desired game fish by overpopulations of carp and so-called "trash" fish. By the summer of 1951, carp removal and rough-fish poisoning were underway in certain lakes, with yearlong seasons set on such fish as yellow bass, crappies, bluegill, and bullheads—all of which had no possession limits and could legally be used for bait. Some waters were of course impacted more than others: Some 300 tons of carp were removed from Roosevelt Lake through the use of fish traps.

Other problem areas included Mittry Lake, Roosevelt Lake, Kinnikinick Lake, Lake Mary, Lyman Reservoir, and all of the ponds along Show Low Creek. The poison of choice was toxaphene—a treatment that proved thorough if controversial. The city of Flagstaff objected to its use in Lake Mary. By 1953, however, rough-fish poisoning with

Illustrator Larry Toschik produced fine art for various wildlife publications. An example is this portrait of the Gila trout, published in Game Fishes of Arizona *by Mulch (1954). (AGFD files)*

toxaphene had become a routine management strategy. Carp, crappie, and other rough fish were removed from San Carlos Lake along with thousands of striped (yellow) bass.

The red shiner (*Notropis lutrensis*) was being widely introduced as a forage fish. The first releases came from Texas in 1950 and were planted in the Cibola area of the Colorado River, where channels were even blasted into backwater sloughs to create better spawning areas. This introduction was so successful that red shiners were soon being planted in Roosevelt Lake, while another forage fish, threadfin shad, was being raised for introduction into San Carlos and Roosevelt lakes.

The early 1950s saw recommendations by sportsmen to plant muskellunge or northern pike in Ashurst Lake, eliciting a "not good" response from fishery biologist Dick Wagner. The AGPA expressed an interest in packing trout to remote waters. The introduction with the most impact, however, and one that continues to the present day, resulted from Commissioner Homer B. Thacker's suggestion at a September 1953 commission meeting that crawdads be seined from Yuma canals and introduced to the Colorado River and other waters—which the commission directed the Fisheries Division to do.

Commission meetings setting fishing regulations continued to draw a crowd, partially due to the department's proposals to simplify open seasons and big limits. The biggest shocker was an experiment proposed by Fisheries Division Chief Hemphill in 1952 to have a yearlong season on all species including trout, in that closed seasons had not been shown to result in better fishing. Although a yearlong trout season was questioned by many fishermen, especially George Crosby and the White Mountains Sportsman's Association, most sportsmen and administrators, including those representing the Indians, favored the recommendation. The commission agreed by a three-to-two vote, with Thacker and Dentzer voting no.

Other regulations continued to be simplified. The only game fish now were trout, black bass, and channel catfish, with a bag limit of 10 fish per day on each (except for channel catfish in the Colorado River). Grayling were added later. Fish that died would be considered part of the creel. More contentious was the removal of size or weight limits and the decision to restrict fishing to just the heads of dams. As a consequence, only spawning areas were closed to fishing, with the exception that fishing in Lake Carl Pleasant was prohibited in 1951 to protect a planting of white bass there. Another policy change resulted in areas recently stocked with fish no longer being so posted.

That the introduction of live bait posed problems was now recognized, and baitfish continued to be prohibited in redefined trout waters. Live bait also could not be imported into Arizona or purchased within the state unless obtained from licensed dealers. A rule was enacted requiring a permit or license to seine, ranging in cost from $10 for seining nongame minnows for one's own use up to $100 for commercial operations on the Colorado River. Other issues pertaining to live bait, while discussed every year, were never fully resolved. In 1956, the AGPA voted not to restrict "unnatural" baits such as corn, but persuaded the commission to prohibit "chumming" or pre-baiting.

Live-bait regulations were tightened even further in 1956 when the only permissible species were those already occupying the waters involved, and no species deemed a "trash fish" could be imported. As before, species classified as game fish could not be used for bait and no live bait could be used in trout waters. Meanwhile, the war against rough fish intensified, with contracts approved for the commercial taking of carp, which could be seined along with buffalofish, suckers, and bonytails. However, the state attorney general ruled the commission did not have the authority to regulate the taking and movement of waterdogs.

Fishing-license requirements continued to be revamped. The separate cold-water and warm-water license requirements were dropped in favor of a trout stamp to fish in trout waters. The minimum age to have a license, after going through several variations, settled at age 16, with non-licensed children only eligible to take half limits (AGFD 1956).

Joint fishing regulation agreements with Nevada and California for the Colorado River, after much in-house squabbling and several false starts, finally came close to being resolved. The solution, at least for the time being, was to make any of the three states' licenses valid on the Colorado River and its banks, provided a $2 special-use stamp was affixed to the license. Income from stamp sales would be proportionally divided between the states.

A major benefit to Arizona's fishermen was the department's publication of *Game Fishes of Arizona* by Ernest E. Mulch and William C. Gamble in 1954. Partially illustrated with color paintings by Larry Toschik, this booklet and its companion, *Common Reptiles of Arizona*, provided the public with much-needed information and served as a guide to the state's game fishes, replete with maps showing the state's trout and warm-water fishing waters. Toschik's portrait of the native Arizona trout is simply superb.

Fisheries Management Intensifies, 1956–58

Fiscal year 1956–57 marked the first year the department's total operating budget exceeded a million dollars, with about $500,000 coming in Federal Aid. With 32% of the budget allocated to the Fisheries Division, it was time to solidify gains and institute some organizational changes.

Four fishery districts had been formed in 1956, the positions staffed with fisheries biologists Dave Foster (White Mountains), Howard M. "Bud" Bassett (northern Arizona),

Bill Melander (Colorado River), and Roger Gruenwald (central and southern Arizona). The following year there was enough money to hire Bill McConnell as a fisheries professor with the Arizona Cooperative Wildlife Research Unit. The commission and AGPA agreed: It was up to Director John M. Hall to sell a new fishery program. Fisheries management now called for "fishing to not be managed on a sustained yield or monitored basis" but on a "production basis" (AGFD 1956).

In truth, more fishing waters were available than ever before, with the opening of Riggs Flat and Woods Canyon lakes. Most other high-elevation lakes had been deepened and "rehabilitated." Other advances included the Salt River Project's agreeing to schedule major discharges after the bass spawn, thus improving bass reproduction in the Salt River lakes. Fish planting was on a prescribed schedule. Creel surveys and fish studies were now considered more important to fish restoration than stocking.

There were some serious habitat losses, as the years after World War II had not been kind to the Colorado River. The Bureau of Reclamation had channelized 30 miles of the river near Needles and the dredges were moving downstream to Cibola Valley. Dredging, levees, and river-bed scour had straightened and deepened the river, making it a water delivery canal to the agricultural fields near Blythe, Yuma, and the Imperial and Coachella valleys. Topock Marsh had been dewatered and drained to salvage 60,000 acre-feet of water per year (Oliver 1965) and speed up water delivery from Lake Mead. The "Gila" dredged out swampy places between Imperial and Laguna dams, "saving" another 190,000 acre feet and impacting 240 miles of river. All of these actions might bode well for commerce, but their effect on the river as a fishery was great.

Trout planting accelerated due to purchases from Silver Springs and the acquisition of Page Springs. The state was still providing three hatchery workers at Williams Creek and getting one-third of the fish. Altogether, some 208,947 catchable trout were distributed in 1956, a substantial increase over the 120,000 stocked just three years earlier. Figures for 1957 were even higher: 224,000 catchables, 16 tons of which were purchased from the private hatchery at Silver Creek alone. In 1958, trout stockings hit an all-time high with 3.25 million trout planted on the national forests, 338,000 or nearly 250,000 pounds of them seven inches or longer. And this did not even count trout released below Hoover Dam.

Warm-water fish stocking continued but at reduced levels and with new planting schedules. In 1958, the department released 45,179 warm-water game fish, mostly largemouth bass (13,859) and bluegill (29,814). Conscious now of the need for forage fish, the department stocked 33,200 threadfin shad and 5,000 red shiners. Threadfin shad releases into Lake Mead had been deemed a success in that its game fish showed increased growth rates, stimulating plans for more threadfins in other fluctuating reservoirs.

The "Gismatron," or fish shocker, developed in the 1950s, was being used to sample fish densities and size, while Rotenone was the piscicide of choice to remove rough fish from both lakes and streams. Vegetation control was underway at Big Lake and other places, where the weeds were treated with sodium arsenate. Such intense management measures caused conflicts between waterfowl supporters and fishermen. Fishermen were now also increasingly in conflict with recreationists using the Salt River lakes and other

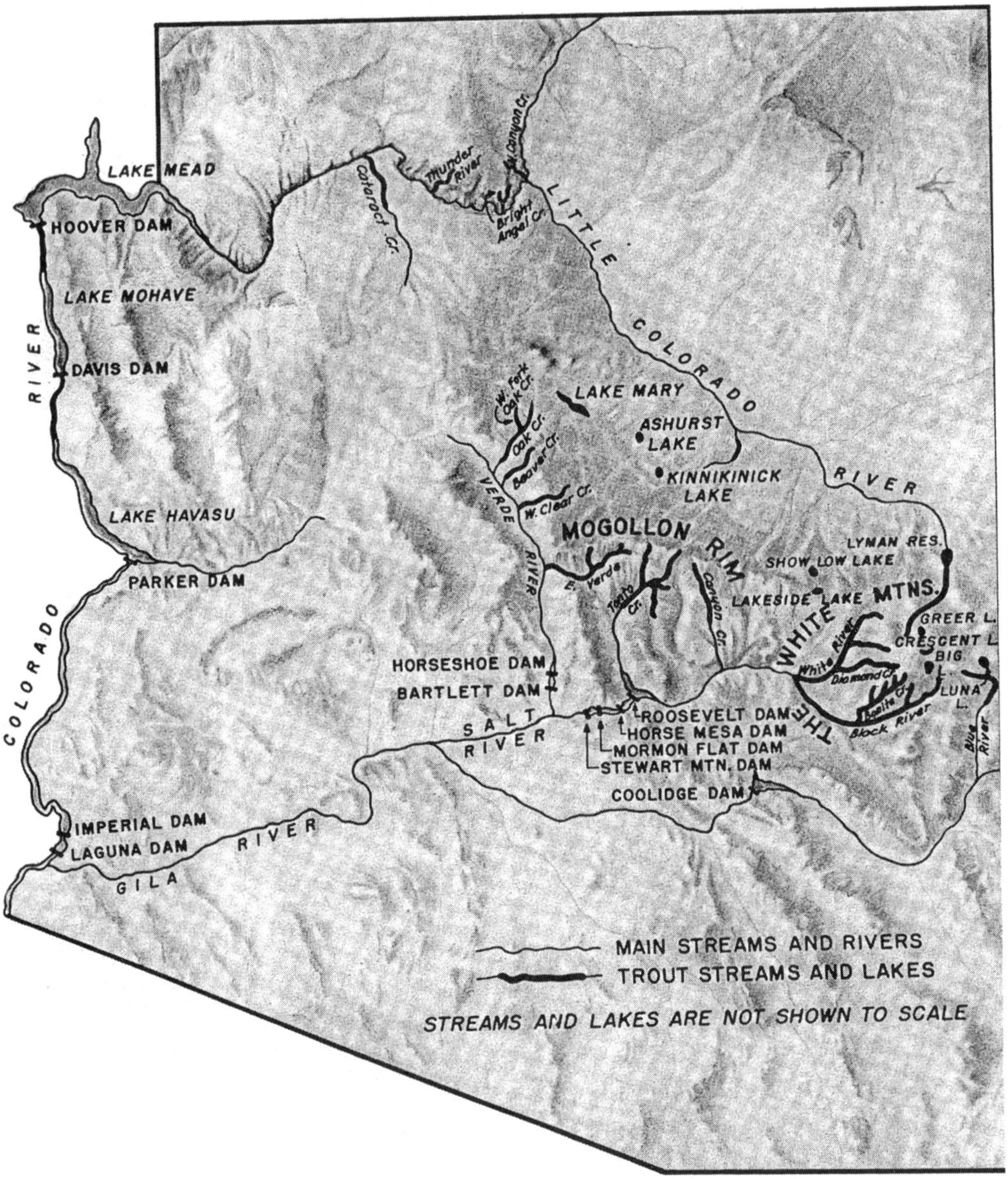

A map of the state's trout fishing waters, published in Game Fishes of Arizona *by Mulch (1954). (AGFD files)*

popular waters. All of this caused some to suggest zoning regulations. Although fishing regulations had been made more serviceable, a new state boating bill meant new restrictions for many fishermen.

The search for new species to introduce continued. A half-million walleye were introduced into Canyon Lake as fry in May 1957. An experimental stocking of "splakes" (a cross between Eastern brook trout and lake trout) was conducted in newly constructed Woods Canyon Lake. More mundane stockings included 62,000 immature bass, 118,000 bluegill, and 2,214 channel cats. (See Appendix E, Table E-1 for a list of species introductions.)

Fisheries and the Reorganization, 1959–62

While the Fisheries Division remained a sideshow in the department reorganization of the late 1950s and early 1960s, its role under Fisheries Chief Yoder was subject to several changes. With wildlife managers available to conduct creel census surveys, and five regional Fisheries District biologists[3] being increased to a fishery biologist for each of the seven regions, there was more opportunity for introductions and experimentation.

Also contributing to the expansion of fisheries investigations were Federal-Aid F-7R studies conducted by the department's Research Division and work being done by McConnell at the University of Arizona's Cooperative Wildlife Research Unit. Meanwhile, more intense monitoring procedures, including electro-shocking and the collection of creel census data, showed that fishing was improving due to increased production brought about by water release agreements with dam operators.

There were some organizational changes within the Fisheries Division. In 1958, hatcheries and fish management became two sections, with $3 out of every $5 from trout-license revenue going to hatchery programs and another $1 to the trout lake program. The rationale for this latter allocation came from studies supporting the importance of lakes and showing that streams, even when improved, could not produce sufficient numbers of trout to meet the increasing demand for fish (AGFD 1960).

Arizona's angler population was exploding, with one out of seven Arizonans fishing and 274,040 licensed sportsmen providing a Dingell-Johnson budget of $122,803.66. The trout program had shifted into high gear with the expansion of Page Springs in 1957, making this hatchery one of the largest fish-suppliers in the world. It produced a quarter-million pounds of trout annually. This hatchery was also unique in that acquisition of the 225-acre facilities and the water rights did not involve any federal money, the two purchases in 1949 and 1955 being accomplished solely with license revenue. The Page Springs and Tonto hatcheries, when operating at full capacity, resulted in the release of nearly 2,000,000 trout. More than a third of these were "catchables," necessitating the purchase of two new fish trucks. Fortunately, the development of new commercial fish foods reduced the cost of feeding the fish by 33 cents a pound (AGFD 1961, 1962, 1963).

---

[3]Jim Bruce, District I: eastcentral Arizona; Bud Bassett, District II: northcentral Arizona; Bill Melander, District III: upper Colorado River; Robert Ringo, District III: lower Colorado River; and Roger Gruenwald, District IV: southcentral and southeastern Arizona.

The Tonto Creek Hatchery in 1956, when operating at full capacity. (Published in Wildlife Views *1956 [Summer]; AGFD files)*

Additional trout were also being purchased from the private hatchery at Silver Springs at 80 cents a pound, a cost only slightly higher than that of trout produced in the department's hatcheries. The department would later purchase Silver Springs after terminating its agreement with the federal hatchery on Williams Creek in 1961, with trout continuing to be raised at both facilities. Also to be considered was the new federal hatchery at Willow Beach at the upper end of Lake Mohave, where 275,473 rainbow trout were produced in 1960, and another 280,679 in 1961. Streamlined stocking techniques and new control measures at all of these hatcheries meant that between 2.3 and 2.7 million rainbows, brown trout, and kokanee salmon (in Luna Lake) were now being stocked in Arizona, between 650,000 and 680,000 of them catchables.

Plans now called for the department's properties at Papago Park to be turned into a zoo and its limited warm-water fish production transferred to Page Springs. In the interim, an experimental stocking program raised tilapia, a tropical fish, in Papago Park's ponds to be released in the dirt-lined Gillespie Canal near Gila Bend. This fish proved to be an outstanding success—until the onset of freezing temperatures decimated populations, and water salvage measures lined the canal in concrete.

Other warm-water fish management efforts included aquatic weed control and the continued stocking of largemouth bass, bluegill, channel catfish, and a few black crappies, with white bass again being stocked in Lake Pleasant. Partially in response to an AGPA resolution calling for more rough-fish control and greater fishing opportunity, the department introduced walleye to Kinnikinick and Lake Mary, in the hope this new species would eat the undesirable species rather than the trout. More beneficial was the planting of some 13,600 forage fish—mostly threadfin shad, but also 5,000 red shiners (AGFD 1962).

By now a number of lake developments were coming to fruition. Five lakes were managed by the Game and Fish Department under agreement with the Coconino National Forest, including Ashurst and Kinnikinick. The 2,240-acre Mittry Lake on the Colorado River was managed by the department in an agreement with the Bureau of Reclamation. National forest special-use permits also governed the use of Pinetop, Tonto, and Sterling Springs hatcheries, with permits from the Coronado National Forest in place for the construction and stocking of Rose Canyon, Peña Blanca, and Rucker Canyon lakes. Rose Canyon and Peña Blanca were opened to fishing in 1960. A Coronado National Forest permit also governed Cave Creek, which needed to be cleaned before stocking.

One interesting study initiated in 1957 was closing Ashurst Lake to fishing during the winter months (September 8, 1957 to May 29, 1958) to see if fishing improved the following summer. By way of a control area, Kinnikinick remained open all year. Both lakes were stocked only with fry and fingerling trout. Creel census surveys and other comparisons showed that Ashurst benefited little from the winter closure.

Other research included a life-history study of threadfin shad and a food-chain study in Papago Park. The dissemination of imported threadfin shad in the lower Colorado River in 1957 was followed by introductions throughout the state from Lake Mead to Peña Blanca Lake when early studies showed their presence coincided with increased growth in largemouth bass and other game fish, as well as in the number of fish caught. The same was claimed for crappies in Roosevelt Lake.

Some fish problems just kept reoccurring. Concerns arose over declining bass sizes and fishing in the lower Colorado River. Winter kills continued at Big and Crescent lakes. Aquatic vegetation remained a problem at Peck's Lake, with weed control also planned for Stehr and Granite Basin lakes. Trout growth in the newly completed Woods Canyon Lake was also disappointing. Threadfin shad were introduced there in the hope that the remedy was a better food supply. Siltation was a problem in certain waters, including the lower Colorado, as were high salt content and summer temperatures.

The most treatable problem was competition with rough fish. The use of toxaphene, the one weapon in the fishery arsenal that had proven effective, was planned for renovation programs at Kaibab, Stehr, Santa Fe, and Cataract lakes, St. John's Reservoir, Lyman Reservoir, Dagg's Reservoir, and Silver Creek, as well as portions of the lower Colorado River.

As the 1960s began, the standard fish-management techniques continued to be gathering creel census data, conducting limnological surveys, and controlling trash fish and aquatic vegetation. By then it was also recognized that the introduction of certain bait and forage fishes was undesirable: golden shiner, fathead minnow, and the formerly much-touted red shiner, not to mention carp and goldfish. Still, new introductions abounded, some intentional, some accidental; some results good, others not so good. The reception to other exotics was mixed. An increase in goldeneye ducks observed on the Colorado River was attributed to the proliferation of a small clam of the genus *Corbicula*.

Fear of unwanted introductions did not apply to game fish, and the department introduced white bass to Lake Pleasant and kokanee salmon in Luna Lake. The search was also on for walleye eggs for Lake Mary, and Yoder reported a source of flatheads, catfish, and paddlefish for the Lake Havasu area, to be taken up with the technical committee of the Colorado River Wildlife Management Committee.[4] Tilapia appeared worthy of further study, and black crappie were recommended for introduction to Bartlett Lake. Flathead catfish were later released in the lower Colorado River. Other plantings included more tilapia in the Gillespie Canal, channel cats, largemouth bass, and bluegills. Despite disappointment in previous stockings, smallmouth bass were again released in the Verde River and an introduction of striped bass, another fish predator, was recommended for the Colorado River as soon as stock could be obtained.

The early 1960s also heralded the first attempts to reintroduce Arizona's native trouts. The existing fish population in Grant Creek and other drainages in the Pinaleño Mountains were renovated[5] and stocked with Apache trout, while searches continued for additional brood stock in the headwaters of the Little Colorado River and Eagle Creek in the White Mountains and on the Fort Apache Indian Reservation.

Attendance at the commission's annual fisheries meetings remained substantial, with 80 or more fishermen often present. As a result, some additional restrictions, most of them temporary, crept into the regulations. A 10-inch limit on bass was reimposed despite stunting problems in many waters, as was a 10-fish limit for kokanee salmon and a 16-inch minimum length requirement for the striped bass recently released into the Colorado River. Attempts to further regulate baitfish and waterdogs were generally unsuccessful, an attempt to restrict the use of waterdogs being tabled by the commission in 1961. Other failed recommendations, including one to have bluegills classified as bait and another to legalize trot lines, came mostly from such organizations as the Yuma Rod and Gun Club.

More successful, and progressive, were recommendations to make Frye Mesa Reservoir a lure-only fishery and open Canyon Creek to fly-fishing only. The emphasis was now less on regulations and introductions, and more on how to continue the lake program and make the resulting lakes—Woods Canyon, Riggs Flat, Fool's Hollow, Rose Canyon, and Peña Blanca—more productive. All of these but Peña Blanca were catchable-trout fisheries and even that lake, which had begun as a bass fishery, became a dual fishing lake, with warm-water species available all year and catchable trout planted during the winter months.

[4]Flatheads were introduced to the lower Colorado River and elsewhere, paddlefish not.

[5]Interest in native trout restoration in Arizona began in the mid-1950s, but it was not until 1963 that Apache trout originating from an Ord Creek-Crooked Creek-North Fork lineage were moved to Sterling Springs Hatchery to be maintained as brood stock by department biologist Minnie McFarland. This effort resulted in the planting of adult Apache trout in a renovated North Canyon Creek on the north Kaibab Plateau in 1963 and as fry and fingerlings in 1965. Other stockings were made in Gap Creek and other non-historic sites, but the fish survived only in North Canyon (Levi Packard, Arizona Game and Fish Department, pers. comm. 1963; Louis Carufel, Arizona Game and Fish Department, pers. comm., 1964). Those populations introduced to Upper Ash Creek and Grant Creek in the Pinaleños persisted in hybridized form before being removed in 2009 to make way for the restoration of Arizona's other native salmonid, the Gila trout.

ARIZONA'S DEER TRANSLOCATIONS

Jim Heffelfinger and Paul Webb

Shooting deer was neither popular nor suggested as the initial solution to the overpopulation of deer on the north Kaibab Plateau in the early 1920s. Much more acceptable to Gov. George Hunt, National Park Service personnel, and many Arizonans was the idea of capturing excess deer and releasing them in areas where deer had been "killed out" or were scarce.

The major problem with this concept was that translocating deer had never before been attempted in Arizona, and the capture, transport, and release of live deer miles from their capture sites was considered a problematic undertaking, the outcome of which was as much in doubt as George McCormick's ill-fated deer drive of 1924. Indeed, if it had not been for the conundrums presented by overpopulations of Rocky Mountain mule deer on the Kaibab Plateau, programs to capture and release large numbers of deer would never have been attempted in Arizona.

As it was, there were two such episodes. Both resulted from overpopulations of deer, which threatened their food supplies, and from not wanting to kill animals in protected areas such as game refuges and national parks. The first attempt was in the 1920s and early 1930s, and the second was from the early 1950s through the early 1960s, when the National Park Service wanted to translocate nuisance mule deer from the South Rim of Grand Canyon National Park to several locations on the Navajo Indian Reservation in the northeastern part of the state. There are no records of either desert mule deer or white-tailed deer ever being translocated, although individual fawns were moved (or taken home) from time to time.

The Early Kaibab Deer Irruption, 1924–32

The history of the deer population on the Kaibab Plateau (1918–24) is covered in chapter seven, "The Kaibab Deer Controversy," along with the early efforts to trap, drive, and shoot deer in an attempt to lower their numbers to a level within the carrying capacity of the winter range. Ironically, this irruption occurred at a time when deer numbers were low in most of Arizona, as deer herds in many areas had been reduced to levels below the carrying capacity of the land to support them. To those dealing with the Kaibab's surplus deer, it just made sense to capture deer from this overabundant population and move them to areas where they were scarce. How best to do that had to be figured out, of course—this was the very beginning of deer management in North America.

The solution developed by the US Forest Service starting in 1924 took a two-pronged approach. First, bucks, does, and fawns would be trapped in large corral traps in fall and winter and transported directly to release areas. Second, fawns would be snatched from the field in June and July, raised with bottled milk on local dairy farms until weaned, and then shipped to release areas in October. Most efforts to restore low deer populations elsewhere in the country had been done with grown animals captured in traps. The fawns from the "fawn farms" were mostly purchased by individuals for private and public parks and zoos. There were probably exceptions, as private individuals also purchased deer to release in the wild on their ranches.

As can be expected, the records of exact numbers of deer captured and released do not always match, and the release records are inconsistent. Because of this, the records of deer captured and released are described here as presented in historical documents, but these may not exactly coincide.

The first step in removing deer from the Kaibab and supplementing deer ranges to the south was to construct a trap. The Big Springs Ranger Station was selected as a trap site because it was a favorite watering place for deer and was in the path of the fall migration (Mann and Park 1933). Trapping efforts began in 1924, with 18 deer trapped in a four-foot by eight-foot pen constructed of two-inch plank lumber using water and/or alfalfa as bait. Ten of these 18 deer were released or escaped, seven died, and the one surviving doe was shipped to Clark, Nebraska, where she died shortly after arrival. This relatively small trap was not capable of capturing the large number of deer desired and was abandoned in favor of larger pens.

In 1925, a larger trap was constructed at Big Springs. This pen, containing two acres of meadow and brush, was surrounded by a woven wire fence eight feet high. It had spring-loaded gates held open with wires that could be released by an observer hidden in a blind nearby. In it, 125 deer were trapped in 1926, but 40 of those were released or died during capture (see table at end of chapter). Of the remaining 85 deer that were shipped off the plateau, 23 died in transit (Russo 1964). In an attempt to minimize such losses, antlered bucks were roped and their antlers were sawed off with a miter-box saw to reduce injury to the other deer in confinement.

Only 37 deer were captured in 1927. Ten died and three were released at the capture site. Of the 24 deer shipped that year, three died in transit. At least four others went to H. G. Bush, a lumber dealer who had the largest private zoo in Arizona on his ranch near Mesa.

Efforts in 1928 were more successful, with 96 deer captured (although only 65 were released). In 1929, an additional two-acre pen was added to the Big Springs trap to be used as a holding pen, while 40 acres of the ranger station's pasture was fenced to serve as an additional trapping pen (Mann and Park 1933). These improvements allowed for the capture of 403 mule deer, 298 of which were released in new areas. Because losses had been so high, capture and transporting techniques were adjusted at every opportunity in an attempt to increase the trapping operation's efficiency.

In the summer of 1931, a second trap was constructed around Slide Tank, consisting of a two-acre holding pen and a one-and-a-half-acre capture pen on one side. The advantage of this site was that it was on the winter range and could be used later in the year. Some 159 deer were trapped that fall (1931) at both Slide Tank and Big Springs. Many of these deer were released at the capture site because the demand for Kaibab deer had waned and the market was satiated (Mann 1932). All translocations ceased by 1932 because the deer population had dropped. Hunting seasons were deemed effective, and deer habitat on the plateau had measurably improved.

Captured deer were transferred from holding pens to shipping crates by running them into a chute with an empty crate on the end. Deer were driven, and sometimes shoved, into the shipping crate and the rear door closed behind them. All deer transported were marked with an aluminum ear tag by a person who reached through a sliding door in the shipping crate. A strip of burlap was tied loosely over the eyes of buck deer during transport. This kept bucks from fighting with one another during the initial shipping stages, but was loose enough for the deer to rub off before arriving at the release site. Through 1928, deer were transported by railroad express from Marysvale, Utah (AGPA 1927a). Mortality via this method was very high, so deer were transported to release locations by truck between 1929 and 1931.

Up to 1928, those wanting Kaibab mule deer had to pay $35 to an established cooperative fund for each deer crated and delivered to a railroad point (Mann and Park 1933). This money funded additional capture efforts. After 1928, applicants paid only $5–$7 per live deer, but they had to provide the transportation and prepare the trucks for transporting deer. The actual cost of capture, feeding, handling, and loading was estimated at $3–$5 per deer.

Many deer translocation destinations are undocumented, but there are vague references to "truck loads to Arizona ranges . . . truck loads to California . . . 11 deer to Colorado." The list of locations deer were shipped to include Oklahoma; Denver, Colorado; Beverly, Massachusetts; the National Zoological Park in Washington, D.C.; London, England; Ontario, Canada; Detroit, Michigan; and San Pedro, California (see table at end of chapter). McCulloch (1968) reported that "at least 383 deer went outside of Arizona to 34 other states and Canada." We will never know the full extent to which Kaibab deer have been spread across the continent and beyond.

While direct trapping of deer was occurring at Slide Tank and Big Springs, an effort to capture fawns was also underway. Applications for deer were sent to the Forest Service and men hired to ride the plateau's fawning areas and search for fawns. The fawns were brought to one of four former dairy farms on the mountain and hand-reared on cow's milk until weaned (Russo 1964). Those fawns that did not die soon after capture were weaned and released into larger pastures, then shipped to places in and outside Arizona (see table at end of chapter).

Crews worked full-time throughout the early summer fawning season, attempting to capture as many fawns as possible. The best method, it was found, was to cruise on horseback along open ridgelines, accompanied by a dog that would seize and hold any fawn seen or jumped (fawns have no scent). Some of the fawn-nappers used Cracker Jack whistles or "fibs" that were supposed to imitate a deer bleat.

In 1926, rangers caught 178 fawns, but only 68 were shipped. The next year, the milk-farm concept was abandoned due to high fawn mortality, and the fawns instead sent to 24 local residents in Fredonia, Arizona, and Kanab, Utah, who were authorized to capture and care for them according to Forest Service specifications. That year (1927), authorized residents captured 355 fawns, but mortality rates were again high, with more than 50% of fawns dying within a month of their capture. That year, only 110 were shipped from the railroad point at Marysvale, Utah.

Kaibab mule deer being "coaxed" into a crate for transportation elsewhere, 1929–30. (US Forest Service, courtesy of Mikele Painter)

In 1928, some 34 locals participated in fawn rearing, catching 403 fawns but only delivering 38% for shipment (Russo 1964). Permits were issued the next year (1930) to 49 fawn raisers, but 10 participants did not catch any fawns (Putnam 1930). One team of two men and a dog caught 14 fawns in one day (Park 1930). Of the 371 fawns captured that year, only 130 were delivered (Blanche Mackelprang keeping one buck fawn for a pet). Those raising fawns were paid $27 for every one delivered alive on October 1. The fawn capture program was abandoned as impractical in 1930.

In the early years of game management, it was thought that a number of small, scattered refuges would act as areas of propagation where deer populations could build up and overflow into surrounding areas. In the 1920s, these refuges received many Kaibab mule deer (Arizona Game and Fish Commission 1930). Little or no monitoring was done after the releases, so we are left with only occasional comments concerning the fate of these deer. The commission report for 1929–30 states that 218 (1929) and 57 (1930) deer where trucked from the Kaibab Plateau, tagged, and released on "the refuges." The report mentions deer being released into the San Francisco Peaks, Munds Park, and Mormon Lake refuges, and includes a photo of the Mormon Lake release. This report indicated the deer were "apparently doing well," but no real monitoring was done.

Of the 25 Kaibab deer released in 1929 on the Granite Basin Refuge near Prescott, three were found dead "but it is believed the balance are doing well" (apparently because they were not found dead). Three does from the truckload of deer liberated on the Tuscumbia Refuge (Bradshaw Mountains) were also found dead, but there was optimism for two truckloads of deer released on Mingus Mountain, where deer sign was plentiful and the forage was in good shape (Arizona Game and Fish Commission 1930). No update was provided that year for the 64 Kaibab deer released in the Pinal Mountains south of Globe, but their photo was published in *Arizona Wild Life* in 1932. It is likely the photo was taken at the original release three years previously.

In an effort to "establish a tame deer herd for the enjoyment of visitors" on the South Rim of the Grand Canyon (Grand Canyon Village), the National Park Service imported bottle-raised fawns from the Kaibab Plateau from 1926 to 1929 (Blaisdell 1961). The first Kaibab deer translocated to the South Rim was a single fawn brought across Lees Ferry by "Mrs. Fred Johnson" in her car in 1926. The next year, 10 more fawns were brought to Grand Canyon Village and given to residents to raise. These deer matured and eventually escaped their pens to take up a semi-domesticated existence in the village.

In 1928, Charles Heaton captured fawns on his ranch west of Kanab Creek and sold 10 of them to the Forest Service for $25–$30 each to supplement those already in Grand Canyon Village. The most elaborate deer translocation in Arizona occurred in 1929, when eight fawns captured on the North Rim were flown in a Ford trimotor airplane 95 miles to Red Butte Airfield south of the park entrance (Russo 1964). These deer were then trucked north and added to those on the South Rim (Blaisdell 1961).

It was not long until the deer in and around Grand Canyon Village became a nuisance and multiplied to exceed what the habitat could support. Good water distribution and absence of grazing cattle in the park proved attractive to both released and native deer, making it necessary for the National Park Service to plan what to do with too much of a good thing.

The two children of Annie Judd of Kanab, Utah, with Kaibab fawns in 1930. Fawns were held until weaned in large, fenced enclosures before being placed in crates and translocated off the Kaibab Plateau. (US Forest Service, courtesy of Mikele Painter)

A few of the 64 Kaibab mule deer released in the Pinal Mountain Refuge in 1929. (Nelson 1932)

Some deer captured in 1930 were released on Santa Rosa Island off the coast of California. This island, 83 square miles in size, is one of the Channel Islands northwest of Los Angeles. Records show that 30 Kaibab mule deer (15 males and 15 females) were released there by the Vail family, who then owned the entire island. The first 4 fawns (3 males and 1 female) were simply loaded into the back of a padded and covered Ford pickup to arrive in Temecula, California, 17 hours later. On October 8, 1929, 46 fawns were loaded on a Vail Company truck that left Kanab, Utah, at 6 p.m. and was driven straight through to the dock in San Diego, where they arrived the next afternoon. From there, some of the youngsters were loaded on a boat and shipped to Santa Rosa Island (Putnam 1930).

As many as 4,000 to 6,000 mule deer have inhabited the island ever since, with no other additions to the gene pool. Thus, this island contains only descendants of the 30 Kaibab deer released 80 years ago.

This population of deer is currently the center of a controversial depopulation effort. Vail & Vickers, which purchased the island in 1901, and imported the deer, sold the island to the federal government for $30 million in 1986. It is now part of Channel Islands National Park. One of the stipulations of the original sale was that all non-indigenous Kaibab mule deer and Roosevelt's elk were to be removed by the end of 2011. Since 1998, the deer herd has been capped at 425 deer and the goal was to reduce the population by 25% each year starting in 2008, with all deer removed by the end of 2011.

In the 1930s, research on deer diets and other aspects of deer ecology were being conducted with captive deer housed at the Florida Canyon Work Center on the north end of the Santa Rita Mountains. Nine Kaibab mule deer were placed in this facility along with a few white-tailed deer. Subsequent reproduction in the pens resulted in 38 of these deer being present at the conclusion of the study in 1938: a mixture of whitetails (9), Kaibab mule deer (19), desert mule deer (1), and some partial whitetail–mule deer hybrids (9) consisting of varying back-cross generations (Nichol 1938). Six of these deer were taken to Onion Saddle on the north end of the Chiricahua Mountains and released there, while another 10 or so were released directly from the pens into Florida Canyon. The records are not clear as to which of the captive deer were released where, but it appears Kaibab deer were released at Onion Saddle (McCulloch 1968; Ted Knipe, retired from Arizona Game and Fish Department, pers. comm., 1979).

The Kaibab Irrupts Again, 1950–54

By the 1950s, the Kaibab Plateau's deer population was high enough once again to require a reduction in numbers to protect the winter range from overuse. Doe hunts through the 1950s and 1960s were used to help control deer numbers, with deer trapping and translocations beginning anew. In the fall of 1950, a large corral trap was built surrounding Slide Tank on the west side's winter range. This was an area of high winter use and the tank provided the only permanent water in several hundred square miles. The trap consisted of aspen poles and eight-foot by 12-foot wood planks with a crowding pen and chute that enabled biologists to run the deer into a squeeze chute for handling and loading into crates.

This was a water trap, so the deer had to be trapped at night as they watered. The corral had a gate that could be closed on a rope-and-pulley system with a large rock acting as a counterweight. The trapper sat in a blind nearby holding a string that pulled a pin that allowed the rock to drop and quickly pull the gate closed.

Despite some early trapping difficulties, 113 deer were captured at Slide Tank in December 1950, with 85 deer going to the Three Bar Wildlife Area and 12 to the Douglas Ranch on the east side of the Santa Rita Mountains (Cosper 1952). All deer trapped on the Kaibab Plateau during this period were ear-tagged and had three inches of their left ear cropped for later identification in the field. In the winter of 1952–53, floodwaters damaged the trap. Combined with early snows, the damage resulted in only eight deer being sent to an enclosure on the Three Bar (Noell 1953).

While plans were being made to again trap deer on the Kaibab Plateau, the department received a request from the National Park Service for assistance in trapping some "nuisance" deer out of Grand Canyon Village. A trapping crew did not arrive until April 1951, however. By that time, storms had scattered the deer and there were as yet no facilities to hold any deer trapped for shipping. Despite these shortcomings, four deer were trapped that year; a buck and two does went to the Douglas Ranch in the Santa Rita Mountains to join 12 from the Kaibab that had just been released there (Cosper 1952).

More nuisance deer needed to be removed. Trapping efforts were intensified the next year, with several methods employed. A portable corral trap was set up and baited with "alfalfa hay, garbage picked up daily from grocery stores and bakeries at the village" (Earl 1952). This trap was useful in capturing some deer during the winter of 1951–52. Another four deer were captured by hand after being fed bait containing the barbiturate Nembutal (Pentobarbital) and becoming unconscious.

Ted Knipe with some of the Kaibab mule deer used for feeding research in the 1930s at the Santa Rita Experimental Range, Santa Rita Mountains, GMU 34. (Nichol 1938)

It was becoming apparent that the most efficient way to capture deer in the village was to lure them onto a noose laid on the ground with food and snare them as they stepped inside. The rope was jerked to snare a foot, then played out until the deer could be thrown to the ground and subdued. That year, Ted Knipe released 39 deer in the Santa Rita Mountains. Henceforth, all subsequent captures in Grand Canyon Village were done with this method. In 1952–53, another 48 deer were released in the Santa Rita Mountains and two bucks were shipped to Robbins Butte Wildlife Area near Buckeye (Noell 1953). In 1954, 20 more South Rim mule deer were added to the east side of the Santa Ritas.

After the mid-1950s, the National Park Service took a lead role in capturing deer from Grand Canyon Village and shipping them to various areas. Nuisance deer captured around Grand Canyon Village were initially taken to areas outside the park (28 deer in 1956–57). Some deer were simply moved about 30 miles to the west (Pasture Wash), and 27 miles to the south (Red Butte). One of the does moved to Red Butte was trapped again the next year in Grand Canyon Village.

For the next five years, the vast majority of the deer trapped in the village went to the Navajo Nation (see table at end of chapter). From 1958 through March 1962, 286 mule deer were released in the following areas: Tall Mountain, Paiute Mesa (Arizona-New Mexico), Nakai Canyon (New Mexico), Mexican Springs (aka Nakaibeto; New Mexico), Bowl Canyon (New Mexico), Tohatchi (Lookout) Tower (New Mexico), Big Mountain (now on the Hopi Nation), Nazlini Canyon, and Fuzzy Mountain (Coffin 1961, 1962; Webb and Robeck 1963). There was no research involving deer at this time and no natural resources personnel for the Navajo Nation, so little information has survived in terms of post-release records.

Other Translocations

When an overpopulation occurred in the Tucson Mountains in 1950–51, original plans were to trap deer, but delays and difficulties encountered in trapping deer in the northern part of the state interfered. The next year a desire to trap deer from this location was mentioned in the department's Federal-Aid reports, but there is no other record that an attempt to do so ever occurred.

In December 1950, 85 deer from the Kaibab Plateau were released on the Three Bar Wildlife Area, where deer research was occurring and biologists were on-site observing deer throughout the year. Since all released deer were ear-tagged and had a cropped ear, these animals were easily differentiated from resident deer. These observations provide some insight into the status and fate of deer released there.

Shortly after the release, department personnel reported about 15 deer had moved eastward across the dry bed of Roosevelt Lake to a 15-square-mile area between the lake and the Sierra Ancha (Ferguson 1951). Some deer moved eight miles to the northeast to near Cactus Butte, and one tagged doe was even seen near Buzzard Roost, 25 miles northeast of the release site. The skull of a marked buck was also found near Greenback Peak, some 16 miles north of the release site (McCulloch 1955a). Three marked does were seen in a group watering at the Gila County highway camp a half mile from their release site and three more tagged deer were seen near Roosevelt Dam eight miles to the southeast.

Observations of Kaibab deer on the Three Bar declined greatly the following year. Of 497 deer observed throughout 1953, only 18 (less than 4%) were marked animals.

The Slide Tank deer trap. Deer are standing at the entrance of the squeeze corral (in the center of the picture) where animals were ear-tagged and loaded onto trucks. (Cosper 1952)

Deer in Slide Tank squeeze corral. Animals were moved individually into the squeeze chute, where the bucks were de-antlered and the deer ear-tagged and loaded for shipping. (Cosper 1952)

Although McCulloch (1954a) noted a number of mature does and bucks that might have been Kaibab deer progeny, two fawning seasons had elapsed since the release, so deer having a Kaibab parent would have been unmarked.

Eight deer were added to the Three Bar's 17-acre enclosure in March 1953 to study the releases more intensively (McCulloch 1955b). Only two of these deer remained in the pen after the first 10 months: two escaped, two died in accidents, and four were lost to apparent starvation/malnutrition. Between the first release in 1950 and August 1955, department personnel only observed two marked bucks and 22 marked does in 1,380 deer observations within five miles of the Three Bar (McCulloch 1968). None of the Kaibab bucks released was ever observed on the Three Bar (McCulloch 1955a), and the last marked animal recorded was a doe harvested in 1959, 13 miles northeast of the release site.

Not counting the handful of deer released in 1938 from the research pens in Florida Canyon, 122 Rocky Mountain mule deer were released in the Santa Rita Mountains between 1950 and 1954. The 12 released in 1950 were the only ones from the Kaibab Plateau, the rest being from the South Rim of the Grand Canyon (Earl 1952; P. M. Webb 1953, 1954). Another buck and two does from Grand Canyon Village were released in 1951, followed by 107 more deer between 1952 and 1954. All 122 deer were released on the Douglas Ranch in Gardner Canyon on the east side of the mountains four miles north of Sonoita.

After the first sizable release of 39 mule deer in January 1952, the liberated deer were observed daily for a month by a man hired for the purpose. Department personnel conducted week-long field trips over the next two months, attempting to locate deer and interviewing local ranchers within a 10-mile radius of the release site (Earl 1952). Results

National Park Service rangers ear-tagging and ageing a deer for translocation to the Navajo Nation. Desert View Subdistrict, Grand Canyon National Park, December 20, 1961. (Andrew C. Wolfe)

were not encouraging, with observations of small groups of deer decreasing over time. These groups stayed mostly within two to three miles of the release site, but gradually ranged farther, some eventually being seen in the Empire-Cienega Valley, Greaterville, and north of Mount Fagan, but mostly in nearby Fish, Hog, and Gardner canyons. Some deer were reported to have traveled as far as 26 miles to the south and east toward the Whetstone and Huachuca mountains. One doe was found dead on the Kinsley Ranch near Continental on the other side of the mountain and another south of the Santa Ritas along Sonoita Creek.

Hunters removed eight Rocky Mountain mule deer bucks and one doe from the Gardner Canyon area during the 1953 hunting season (P. M. Webb 1954). One of these animals had been released almost two years previously and six deer had been released the prior year (1952).

In the winter of 1988–89, the state of Utah had recurring problems with mule deer depredations in fields near New Castle, Utah. The Utah Division of Wildlife therefore captured about 100 of the animals for the Arizona Game and Fish Department to release on the "Arizona Strip" near Mount Trumbull. This release was done to reduce crop depredation and in an attempt to bolster the population near Mt. Trumbull. All deer were ear-tagged and a few were seen near the release site for a couple of years thereafter (Tom Finley, Arizona Game and Fish Department, pers. comm., 2009).

There was also a need to remove a few "tame" deer in the mid-1990s from the North and South rims of Grand Canyon National Park. In these cases, individual deer became aggressive toward tourists and insisted on being fed. A buck was removed from the North Rim in 1993 after knocking a young girl to the ground in the hotel parking lot. It was released near Heaton Knolls on the Arizona Strip (game management unit 13A). Four more deer were removed from the vicinity of El Tovar Hotel and the railroad station on the South Rim in 1995 for creating a similar nuisance. These latter deer were released on the east side of Game Management Unit 9 near Peterson Flat (Tom Britt, retired from Arizona Game and Fish Department, pers. comm., 2009; Elaine Leslie, National Park Service, pers. comm., 2009).

Effects of Translocations on Native Deer Herds

A conservative accounting of the available records shows more than 1,500 deer have been translocated from their native range in Arizona since 1924. There are undoubtedly other movements of deer that were not recorded or that were not found.

The normal reasons for transplanting deer were to reduce an overabundance in the source population or restore deer populations in an underpopulated area—oftentimes both. Translocations can result in positive, negative, or no changes in the areas involved. Nonetheless, if no barriers are preventing existing populations from occupying vacant habitats that appear suitable for supporting a population, one has to wonder why deer are not living there. The absence of a population is often an indication the area in question may not be suitable for sustaining a deer population.

One potential negative consequence of translocating deer to new areas is disease. We now know from other states and provinces that many deer populations testing positive for chronic wasting disease previously received deer from infected areas (Belay et al. 2004).

Another potentially long-lasting impact may be a genetic change in the receiving population. The assemblage of genetic traits a local population acquires through time has been honed by natural selection to accommodate local conditions. Moving animals from distant points to "improve" the gene pool that evolved in an area obviously can be fraught with problems. If a translocation is successful, the genetic makeup of the receiving population will change, and the chance of these changes being positive for the animals' long-term survival is unlikely. Genetic research illustrates how deer translocations can leave a genetic signature in the future population (Latch et al. 2009).

The timing of the breeding season is an important life-history characteristic that is genetically programmed, but triggered by changing day length. Deer on the Kaibab rut about a month earlier than desert mule deer in southern Arizona (Heffelfinger 2006). Rocky Mountain mule deer does translocated to central and southern Arizona went into estrus a month before the resident does (McCulloch 1955c). Bucks from the Kaibab also develop and shed antlers earlier than desert mule deer. Nonetheless, all bucks are ready for breeding over a wider time period than does. This was illustrated by a 4x2 desert mule deer buck, which broke into the Three Bar pen to successfully breed with Kaibab does.

Differences in rut timing did not prohibit the breeding of the two races of mule deer, but it may have reduced the overall integration of Rocky Mountain mule deer genes into the desert deer population. Such changes in chronology and gene flow show the kind of situations created by translocating animals from distinct populations. Also, breeding a male of a larger subspecies with a female from a smaller one can result in a fetus that is too large for the birth canal (dystocia) and cause mortality of the doe and the fawn, as was found in Coues' whitetails.

Probably the most significant problem with translocating deer populations from a restoration standpoint is the dietary changes experienced by the deer. When the department released eight Kaibab deer into a 17-acre pen of native Three Bar vegetation, the result was "disastrous," with almost all the released deer dying before the year's end (McCulloch 1954b). The number of deer released in the pen was above normal carrying capacity, but it was curious that three of the four deer that died of malnutrition had stomachs full of deer food items common to the Three Bar (McCulloch 1955b).

Deer normally have microbes specifically suited to digest the types of plants regularly eaten. Switching a ruminant's diet drastically can result in the rumen bacteria not being able to digest the new type of food. McCulloch (1954b) felt this change of diet contributed to the deaths. It is not easy to extrapolate forage relationships from a pen study to the wild, but similar difficulties may have occurred with all the other Rocky Mountain mule deer released onto desert ranges. This would obviously reduce survival and reduce the contribution of the genes from transported deer into local desert mule deer populations. The releases into the Santa Rita Mountains in Gardner Canyon were monitored by Game Ranger George Peterson, and he remarked that all the animals he saw in the Santa Ritas during 1953 were in poor shape (P. M. Webb 1953).

From a strictly population-enhancement perspective, the benefit of translocations depends on the proportion of subsequent fawn crops that are the offspring of translocated animals. Obviously, if 50% of the next fawn crop has at least one parent that was translocated, then that is an important contribution and effect on the native herds. If only 3% of the next fawn crop is from translocated parents, then there is little to no effect. The Three Bar Wildlife Area appeared to have a robust desert mule deer population at the time the Kaibab deer were released, based on subsequent observations (McCulloch 1968). Although the Santa Ritas may not have had as many native desert deer at the time of the releases, subsequent observations were not monitored to the same degree. Neither area was reported to have a major increase or decrease in deer numbers.

Translocations of ungulates typically result in released animals ranging widely after release and having a high mortality. Mann and Park (1933) reported that two and three years after the initial releases of deer in the 1920s to 1930s, a few ear-tagged bucks were being harvested by hunters, so it is known that at least some deer survived for a while. Deer were reported to scatter widely after release on both the Three Bar and in the Santa Ritas. McCulloch (1968) reported that less than 2% (23 of 1,380) of the deer sightings during the 1952–55 period on the Three Bar were Kaibab deer. Some deer probably lost their markings and some fawns may have been northern offspring, but there is no evidence Kaibab deer contributed much to the local gene pool.

The removal of deer from the Kaibab Plateau was not in itself significant enough to aid in reducing the population, but removals from the Grand Canyon Village seemed to reduce nuisance problems there, thus accomplishing that goal. As for the resulting effect on the deer populations at the receiving end of these translocations, it will never be known how many Rocky Mountain mule deer genes were infused into the desert mule

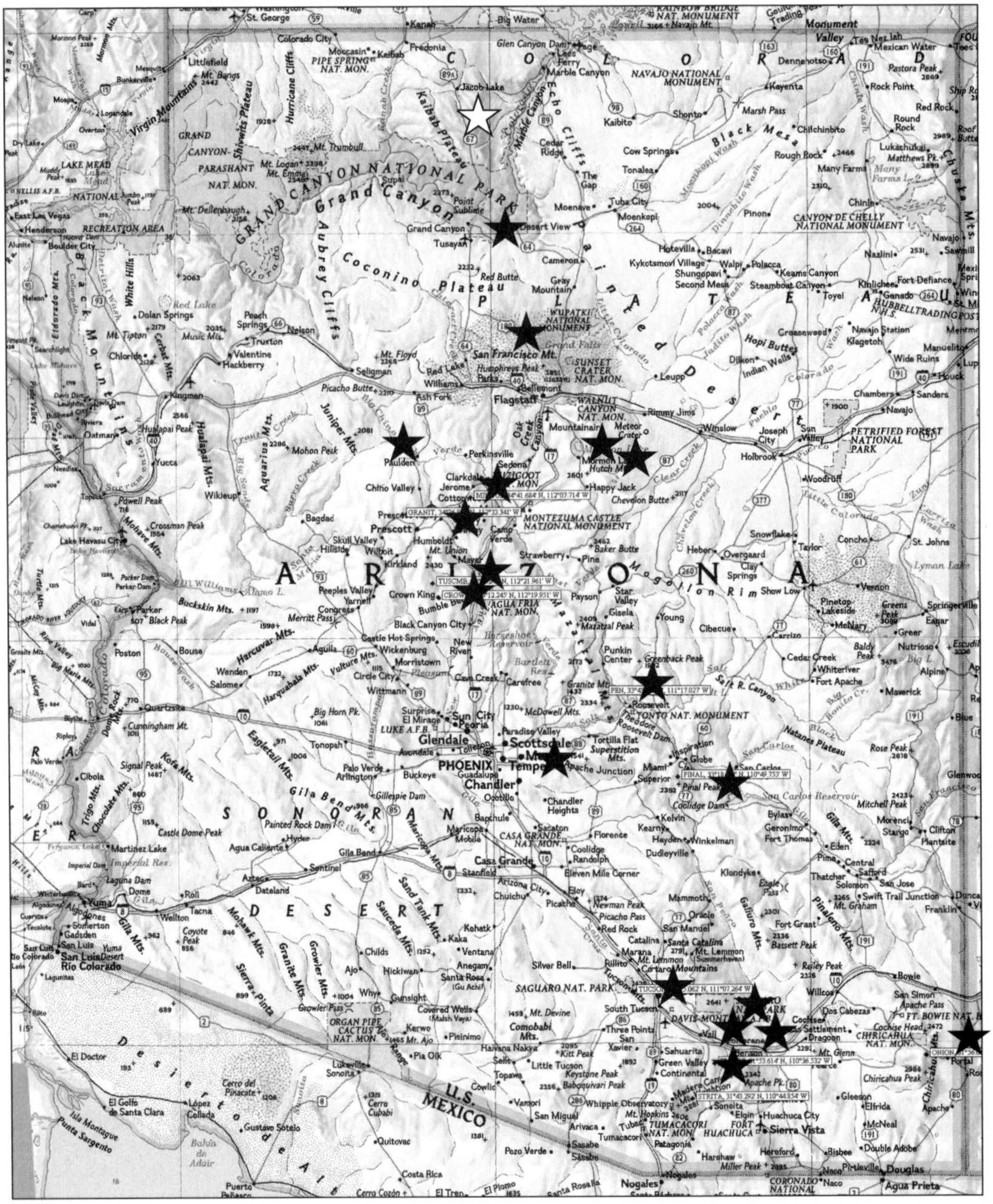

Mule deer trapped on the Kaibab Plateau (open star) have been released at many locations in Arizona (solid stars). (AGFD files)

deer population, but evidence suggests that any contribution was slight due to the high mortality, wide dispersal, breeding season differences, dystocia, and high mortality of the donor population.

Clay McCulloch (1955b) may have said it best when he laconically stated, "[S]uccessful transplanting sometimes requires more than just trapping and transportation of deer."

Historical Arizona Deer Translocations, 1924 to the Present

Capture Date	Capture Site	Release Site	Number Captured[a]	Number Mortalities[a]	Number Released[a]	Source
Fall 1924	Big Springs, Kaibab Plateau (GMU 12A)	Clark, Nebraska	18	7	1	Mann and Park 1933
Summer 1926	Kaibab Plateau (fawn captures)	Oklahoma; Denver, CO; Beverly, MA; National Zoological Park, Washington DC; London; Ontario, Canada; Detroit, MI; San Pedro, CA; AZ	178	110	68 (30:38)	AGPA 1927a; Blaisdell 1961; Russo 1964
Fall 1926	Big Springs, Kaibab Plateau		125	63	62	Mann and Park 1933; Russo 1964
Summer 1927	Kaibab Plateau (fawn captures)	Incomplete records	355	245	110 (49:61)	Russo 1964
Fall 1927	Big Springs, Kaibab Plateau	Incomplete records	37	13	21	Mann and Park 1933; Russo 1964
1927	Kaibab Plateau	H. G. Bush Private Zoo, Mesa			4	AGPA 1927b
1927	Kaibab Plateau	South Rim Grand Canyon			10	Blaisdell 1961
Summer 1928	Kaibab Plateau (fawn captures)	Incomplete records	403	249	154 (68:86)	Russo 1964
1928	Heaton Ranch, west of Kanab Creek (GMU 13A)	South Rim Grand Canyon			10	Blaisdell 1961
Fall 1928	Big Springs, Kaibab Plateau	Incomplete records	96	11	65	Mann and Park 1933
1929	Big Springs, Kaibab Plateau	Incomplete records	403	23	298	Mann and Park 1933
Summer 1929	Kaibab Plateau (fawn captures)	South Rim Grand Canyon			8	Blaisdell 1961
1929	Big Springs, Kaibab Plateau	Tucson Mountains (GMU 38M)	17	2	15	Taylor 1933; Ted Knipe, AGFD, Pers. Comm. 1979[b]; Park 1930
1929	Kaibab Plateau	Jones Mountain, San Francisco Mountain refuges			33	AGPA 1930; AGFC 1930
1929	Big Springs, Kaibab Plateau	Mormon Lake Refuge (GMU 6A)			18	AGPA 1930; AGFC 1930; McCulloch 1968
1929	Kaibab Plateau	Munds Park (GMU 6A)			12	AGFC 1930; AGPA 1930
1929	Kaibab Plateau	Beaver Creek Enclosure			4	AGPA 1930
1929	Kaibab Plateau	Mingus Mountain, Walnut and Crown King refuges (GMU 20A, 6A)			49	AGPA 1930; AGFC 1930
1929	Kaibab Plateau	South of Tuscumbia Refuge, Bradshaw Mountains (GMU 20A)			"a load"	AGFC 1930

(continued . . .)

Historical Arizona Deer Translocations, 1924 to the Present

Capture Date	Capture Site	Release Site	Number Captured[a]	Number Mortalities[a]	Number Released[a]	Source
1929	Kaibab Plateau	Granite Basin Refuge (GMU 17B)			25	AGFC 1930
1929	Kaibab Plateau	Refuge south of Winslow			8	AGFC 1930
1929	Kaibab Plateau	Pinal Refuge (GMU 24A)			64	AGFC 1930
Fall 1930	Big Springs, Kaibab Plateau	Incomplete records	66	5	61	Mann and Park 1933
1930	Kaibab Plateau	Santa Rosa Island, CA	30 (15:15)		30 (15:15)	Putnam 1930
1930	Kaibab Plateau	Empire Mountains, (GMU 34B) by Ed Hilton, Rancher	10		9	Ted Knipe, AGFD, Pers. Comm., 1979[b]
Fall 1931	Big Springs/Slide Tank, Kaibab Plateau	Incomplete records	159	28	37	Mann and Park 1933
Summer 1931	Kaibab Plateau (fawn captures)	Incomplete records			78	Mann 1932
1933	Kaibab Plateau	Near Pantano, Rincon Mountains, (GMU 33)			~12	Ted Knipe, AGFD, Rers. Comm., 1979[b]
1938	Kaibab Plateau	Florida Canyon, Santa Rita Mountains (GMU 34A)[c]			2:8?	Ted Knipe, AGFD, Pers. Comm., 1979[b]
1938	Kaibab Plateau	Onion Saddle, Chiricahua Mountains, (GMU 29)[c]			6	Ted Knipe, AGFD, Pers. Comm., 1979[b]
Dec-50	Slide Tank, Kaibab Plateau	Douglas Ranch, Gardner Canyon, Santa Rita Mountains (GMU 34A)	14 (4:10)	2 (1:1)	12 (3:9)	Cosper 1952
Dec-50	Slide Tank, Kaibab Plateau	Three Bar Wildlife Area (GMU 22)	99	14	85 (28:57)	Cosper 1952
Apr-51	Grand Canyon Village (GMU 9)	Douglas Ranch, Santa Rita Mountains	4	1	3 (1:2)	Cosper 1952
Jan-52	Grand Canyon Village	Douglas Ranch, Santa Rita Mountains	44 (20:24)	5 (2:3)	39 (18:21)	Earl 1952
Nov 1952–Feb 1953	Slide Tank, Kaibab Plateau[d]	Three Bar Wildlife Area 17-acre enclosure	14 (6 released on site)		8 (3:5)	McCulloch 1955b, 1968; Noell 1953
Dec 1952–Jan 1953	Grand Canyon Village	Douglas Ranch, Santa Rita Mountains	53	5 (2:3)	48 (15:33)	Noell 1953
Dec 1952–Jan 1953	Grand Canyon Village	Robbins Butte (GMU 39)	2		2 (2:0)	Noell 1953
Jan-54	Grand Canyon Village	Douglas Ranch, Santa Rita Mountains	23	3 (0:3)	20 (8:12)	Webb and Webb 1954
1955	Grand Canyon Village	Red Butte[e] (GMU 9)			1	Webb 1956
Feb–Mar 1956	Grand Canyon Village[f]	Pasture Wash, 30 miles west of Grand Canyon Village	46		10 (3:7)	Webb 1956

(continued . . .)

Historical Arizona Deer Translocations, 1924 to the Present

Capture Date	Capture Site	Release Site	Number Captured[a]	Number Mortalities[a]	Number Released[a]	Source
Jan–Feb 1957	South Rim Grand Canyon[f]	"outside" Grand Canyon National Park	80		18: (6:12)	Bendt 1957
1958–60	South Rim Grand Canyon	Tall Mountain and Paiute Mesa (AZ), Navajo Nation			110	Webb and Robeck 1963
1960–62	South Rim Grand Canyon	Nakai Canyon, Navajo Nation (NM)			52	Webb and Robeck 1963
1960	South Rim Grand Canyon	Mexican Springs, Navajo Nation (NM)			24	Webb and Robeck 1963
1960	South Rim Grand Canyon	Bowl Canyon, Navajo Nation (NM)			31	Webb and Robeck 1963
1960	South Rim Grand Canyon	Tohatchi Tower, Navajo Nation (NM)			8	Webb and Robeck 1963
Dec 1961–Mar 1962	South Rim Grand Canyon	Big Mountain (AZ), Hopi Nation	33	2	31	Coffin 1961, 1962; Webb and Robeck 1963
Dec 1961–Mar 1962	South Rim Grand Canyon	Nazlini Canyon near Chinle, AZ, Navajo Nation			23	Coffin 1962, Webb and Robeck 1963
Dec 1961–Mar 1962	South Rim Grand Canyon	Fuzzy Mountain, Navajo Nation			7	Coffin 1962, Webb and Robeck 1963
Jan-89	1.5 miles southwest of New Castle, UT	Mt. Trumbull (GMU 13A)	~100		~100	Tom Britt, AGFD, and Douglas Messerly, Utah Div. of Wildlife Resources, Pers. Comm., 2009
Aug-93	Kaibab Plateau, North Rim Grand Canyon	Heaton Knolls (GMU 13A)	1		1 (1:0)	Tom Finley, AGFD, Pers. Comm., 2009
1995–96	South Rim Grand Canyon	Peterson Flat (GMU 9)	4	1	3	Elaine Leslie, National Park Service, and Tom Britt, AGFD, Pers. Comm., 2009

[a]Sex of released deer indicated by number of (Males:Females)

[b]On September 26, 1979, Ted Knipe provided a short table of deer translocations prior to 1940 to the best of his recollection. In some cases, this is the only information that survived.

[c]Deer escaped (Florida Canyon) or were released (Onion Saddle) after the conclusion of a feeding study at the Florida Canyon Work.

[d]Traps were also operated at Jumpup Divide, the road to Jumpup Point, and at Tablerock Tank, but a few deer captured at these sites either escaped, were injured, or were killed fighting one another.

[e]It is not clear how many were released here this year; there is simply a mention of a doe returning to be caught at the Grand Canyon Village the following year.

[f]The remaining deer were killed during this time to alleviate nuisance deer problems around Grand Canyon Village. Most deer carcasses were donated to the Williams Hospital, Phoenix Children's Home, and the Navajo or Havasupai nations.

Notes: AGFC=Arizona Game and Fish Commission; GMU=game management unit. The number of deer captured and those released at various locations do not always match, so all available details are reported here. This results in redundancy in "Numbers Released" column.

AREA INVESTIGATIONS

David E. Brown

Despite the success of C. Hart Merriam's biological survey of the San Francisco Peaks and Dr. Joseph Grinnell's (1914) biological inventory of the lower Colorado River, additional attempts to inventory the biotic resources of sizeable portions of Arizona were few. Such comprehensive surveys were expensive and largely beyond the capacity of individual biologists. That any had been accomplished at all was only due to the funding resources of the US Biological Survey and a university endowment by a wealthy patron.

Hence, the relatively few studies that followed were of a more modest nature and restricted to the inventory of a particular area's rangelands (e.g., Darrow 1944), certain vegetation communities (Merkle 1952), particular biota (e.g., Hoffmeister 1956), or select species in particular areas (e.g., Vorhies and Taylor 1933; Welles 1943). As a result, statewide biological inventories were late in coming in Arizona as opposed to neighboring states. New Mexico preceded Arizona in having statewide compendia of its game animals (Ligon 1927), birds (F. M. Bailey 1928), mammals (V. Bailey 1931), fishes (Koster 1957), and amphibians and reptiles (Degenhardt, Painter, and Price 1996).

Biotic Communities of Kaibab Plateau

An exception was D. Irwin Rasmussen's (1941) *Biotic Communities of Kaibab Plateau, Arizona*. Although this comprehensive investigation was not published as an ecological monograph until 1941, most of the field work was conducted between 1929 and 1931 during the Kaibab deer controversy. This novel, ambitious project is summarized as a published version of Rasmussen's doctoral dissertation, completed under the tutelage of Dr. Victor Shelford at the University of Illinois.

The investigation's purpose was not only to describe the physical environment and climate of the 1,152-square-mile Kaibab Plateau, but to demonstrate the changing relationships between the various plant and animal species in the four major biotic communities present: a spruce-fir-chickaree association, a ponderosa pine–Kaibab squirrel association, a pinyon-juniper-woodrat association, and a needlegrass sedge–pocket gopher association. Elevations ranged from about 3,200 feet to 9,200 feet, with mean annual precipitation ranging from nine to 27 inches. No other area of such size in Arizona had been investigated and analyzed so thoroughly, not even San Francisco Mountain, the subject of Merriam and Stejneger's (1890) "life-zone" study.

To identify the biota present and demonstrate the effects of the more important species or "influents" on other species, Rasmussen had not only to locate and describe each of the plateau's principal plants and animals (including 83 species of invertebrates), he had to determine their biotic affinities and measure their relative densities. Doing so required an accurate map of the plateau's contours and vegetation showing the elevation range not only of the four major associations but also of smaller adjacent areas of shortgrass grassland, Great Basin sagebrush, Canyon (Mohave) desertscrub, and small, discontinuous areas of Petran or Great Basin montane scrub. The only water sources were a

Dr. D. Irwin Rasmussen's Biotic Communities of Kaibab Plateau, Arizona *(1941) remains the most comprehensive ecological investigation ever conducted in Arizona. Rasmussen had a distinguished career with the US Forest Service and studied Kaibab squirrels in his retirement. (Courtesy of the Rasmussen family)*

relatively few springs and periodic "lakes," as live streams were absent on the plateau. National park and forest boundaries were also delineated.

At least a part of Rasmussen's study appears to have been fueled by an interest in the reduction and removal of the plateau's two largest carnivores and the resulting increase in Rocky Mountain mule deer. By 1929, the deer herd was in decline due to insufficient forage, and Shelford, a critic of the Biological Survey's Predator and Rodent Control branch, wanted Rasmussen to show how the increase or decrease in numbers of certain species influenced populations of other plants and animals.

Hence, the study was designed to measure not only the seasonal abundance of various forms of wildlife, but also to estimate populations of such animals as mule deer (45–60 deer per section on the winter range), mountain lions, Kaibab squirrels (seven per section in ponderosa pine forest), goshawks (one per five sections), porcupines (three to five per section), and even grasshoppers. That the forest was then populated by a virgin stand of ponderosa pines and other trees was also of more than casual interest, as were the effects of the deer herd on the vegetation.

One factor that made this study uniquely valuable was the attempt to recreate the plateau's human history from the time of the native Kaibabits clan of Indians on Buckskin Mountain, through the arrival of the first Mormons in the late 1850s, to the area's massive exploitation by livestock operators between 1887 and 1889. These impacts were followed by the designation of large portions of the area as a national game preserve in 1906, and the reassignment of areas into national park status in 1919 and 1927.

From 1906 to 1931, a total of 816 mountain lions were removed from the plateau, along with 30 wolves, 7,388 coyotes, and 863 bobcats. During this same period, Rasmussen reported the estimated deer population grew from about 4,000 animals in 1906 to a number said to approach 100,000 in 1924. Then, between 1924 and 1926, a massive die-off took out 60% of the population, until only 20,000 deer were estimated to be present in 1931. From the time of the first hunt in 1924 until government hunters removed 1,124 deer in 1928, only about 1,000 deer a year were removed from the plateau, after which annual harvests climbed to 4,400 in 1929 and 5,033 in 1930. At this time, Rasmussen reported the range as still severely damaged, with large areas of such species as cliffrose and aspen either dead or decadent, and at least two plant species, a raspberry and a willow, reduced to the point of extirpation.

Other refuge areas would provide potential study areas of almost equal interest, but the investment in manpower and resources attendant with Rasmussen's study was greater than could be undertaken by a cash-strapped game department, and the scope of such studies was beyond the capabilities of most professors, much less graduate students. Nor was the federal government any longer of much help. In the years succeeding World War I, the Biological Survey's attention was directed largely toward predator and rodent control, and/or migratory game birds. Such large federal wildlife refuges as the Kofa and Cabeza Prieta were established without intensive inventories by federal or state biologists.

Financial restrictions were somewhat alleviated with the department's participation in the Federal Aid in Wildlife Restoration Act in 1939, and by wildlife students who began attending the University of Arizona's Cooperative Wildlife Research Unit after World War II under the GI Bill. With a cadre of college-educated wildlife biologists, the state now had the personnel not only to inventory a particular area's plant and animal resources, but to develop a management plan for the area, as well.

Three Bar Wildlife Area

An example of a collaborative effort was the biological inventories of the 38,897-acre Three Bar Wildlife Area. Here, investigators assessed the area's geology (mostly granite), vegetation (mostly chaparral), water resources, plants, and wildlife (Ferguson 1951; Dickerman 1954; McCullough 1955a,b).

Ranging in elevation from about 2,200 feet at the high-water mark of Roosevelt Lake to 7,691 feet atop Four Peaks, the Three Bar represented a mini-San Francisco Peaks when it came to biological assessment. Vegetation types present ranged from Sonoran desertscrub at the lowest elevations, through desert grassland and chaparral, to a montane conifer forest of ponderosa pines, Douglas-firs and Gambel oaks. Deciduous forests of sycamores, ash, cottonwoods, and other deciduous trees grew along Rock Creek and in other riparian areas. Mean annual precipitation ranged from 17.22 inches at Roosevelt Lake to 24 inches on Four Peaks.

After repeated incidents involving the overstocking of livestock, the Tonto National Forest had retired the Three Bar allotment, which was transferred to the Arizona Game and Fish Department in 1949 for use as a research area, with Gambel's quail the featured species. The department also wanted an area where it could investigate the relationships between predators and game populations, as well as the use of water by wildlife.

An initial survey into the status of the game species present was less promising than had been hoped. In 1951, the numbers of both species of deer were described as negligible, despite a rather intensive survey effort. Only 35 to 50 deer were thought to be present in 25 square miles of white-tailed deer habitat and 41 square miles of mule deer country.

A low deer population was also suggested by harvest figures, as hunter report cards only indicated a harvest of about three deer a year for 1946–49. Although it was postulated that this low deer population may have resulted from illegal hunt pressure from GIs during the war years when the landing at Roosevelt was a recreation area, neither

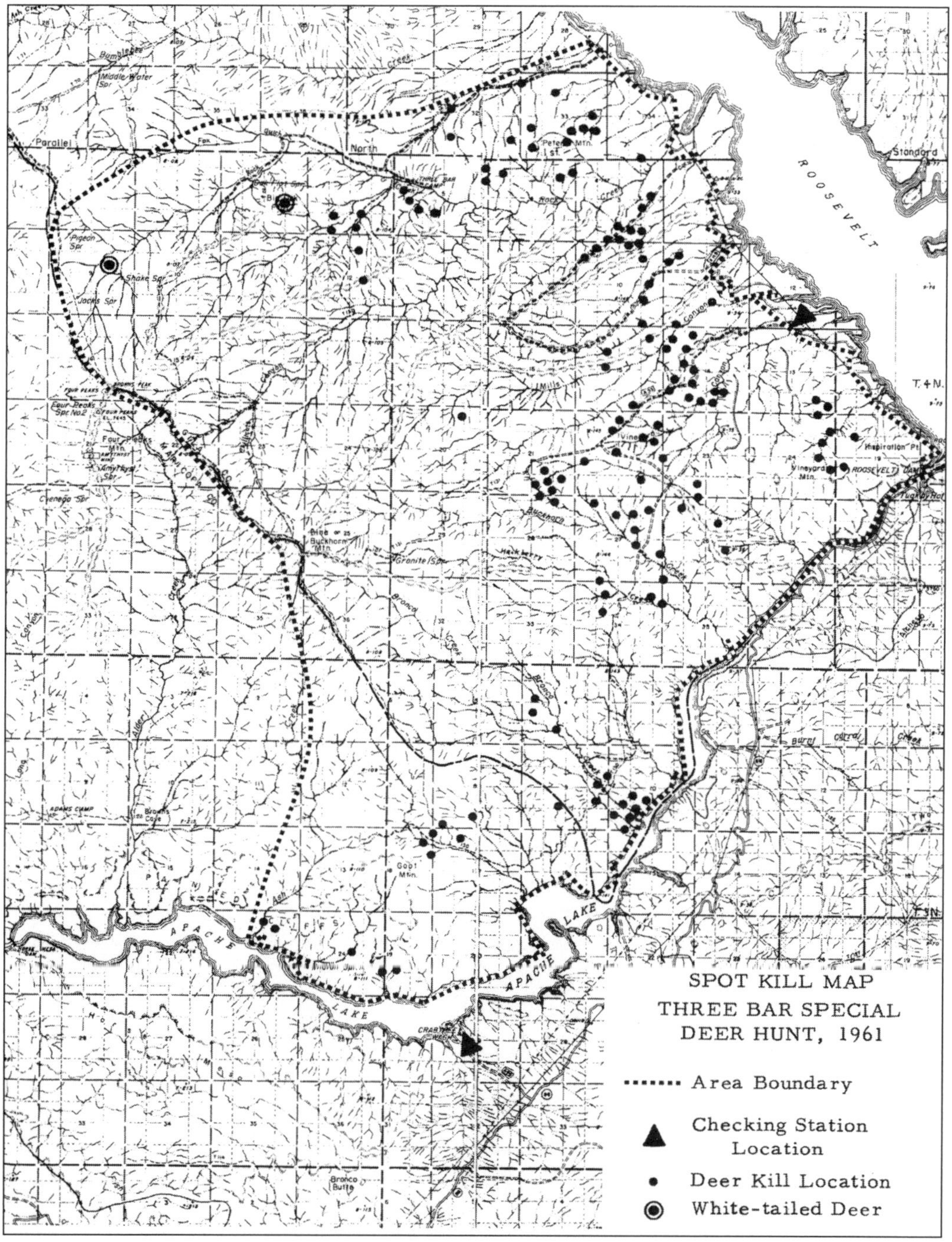

The Three Bar Wildlife Area represented a mini-San Francisco Peaks when it came to biological assessment, and has been the subject of many research projects in the past five decades. This spot kill map is from a 1961 research report. (AGFD files)

this explanation nor depredations by predators appeared plausible for explaining low deer numbers. Also confounding the issue was the introduction of 89 Rocky Mountain mule deer from the Kaibab during the assessment period. It nonetheless appeared that most of these animals left the area soon after being released, and that by 1954 the Three Bar's deer density had increased to about 10 deer per section—a figure similar to deer densities in other chaparral habitats at the time (Swank 1958).

Burns and several years of rest improved range conditions in the Three Bar, and the other game species, especially Gambel's quail and javelina, were judged common to abundant. A recommendation to someday release bighorn sheep in historical habitat on Goat Mountain proved prescient, but no reports mentioned bears—a species that would be studied intensively on the Three Bar in later years (see e.g., LeCount 1977b).

Management improvements included the construction of 16 miles of jeep roads, a cattle guard, and several lengths of fence to keep out trespassing stock. Waters were mapped and nine springs and seeps were developed, with another 18 located. "Permanent" survey routes were selected and mapped, and it was recommended that the area be closed to hunting pending further study.

An intensive predator-control program was also instituted during the winter of 1949–50 that included the establishment of four poison stations using thallium and Compound 1080. These treatments were repeated in 1950–51, along with trap lines using steel traps and cyanide coyote-getters. The results were not particularly impressive, with only 24 coyotes, 87 gray foxes, 3 bobcats, 5 skunks, 3 badgers, 3 ringtails, and 1 raccoon reportedly taken. No sign of lions was found, a situation possibly due to the recent removal of seven of these big cats by houndsmen.

Within a few years, the Three Bar was living up to all of its research expectations and more. Several important mule deer forage and recruitment studies were instituted, as deer populations rose to unprecedented heights and then fell again to levels rivaling those reported in 1951. Other important research studies delved into the population dynamics of Gambel's quail, javelina, and bear. Although studies to determine the relationship of deer to water had to be abandoned due to the area's abundant water sources, a predator-proof enclosure would later facilitate predator studies that would continue on through the turn of the century, the results of which have yet to be analyzed.

Fort Huachuca Wildlife Area

A slightly different approach was taken to conduct a comprehensive analysis of the biotic resources of the 35,000-acre Fort Huachuca Wildlife Area, acquired by the Arizona Game and Fish Department from the US Army in early 1949 (Wallmo 1949–51). This acquisition was deemed a great boon for both range and wildlife management studies, as the area had been owned by the Army since 1887, and except for a short period after World War II, the area had been subject to less intense grazing pressures than the surrounding countryside. It was designated as the Charles T. Vorhies Game Habitat Research Project by the department's recently formed Research Division.

Project Leader Charles O. Wallmo inventoried the wildlife area's range, game, and predator resources through a series of Federal-Aid projects. These studies initially included a number of range transects to determine plant composition and condition, preparation of a detailed range and vegetation map, and an inventory and distribution analysis of the area's wildlife species. Because it was intended to be an active research area, livestock were removed in 1949 and replaced with 132 bison, 90 pronghorn, and 60 Merriam's wild turkeys, along with mountain quail (*Oreortyx pictus*) and chukar. A predator-control program was instituted, with the Rodent and Predator Control branch of the US Fish and Wildlife Service removing the few remaining black-tailed prairie dogs (*Cynomys ludovicianus*) at about the same time (Brown, Todd, and Levy 1974).

The second year of the program at the former military installation saw more range and wildlife evaluations, including the state's first white-tailed deer population and habitat investigation, an antelope range preference analysis, and a buffalo forage evaluation. Introductions consisted of two pronghorn releases totaling 72 animals (18 direct and 72 held in a holding pen) and three bison releases—two from Raymond Ranch and one from House Rock Valley, which, counting calves, resulted in the presence of nearly 400 head of buffalo by 1950. To top off the list of transplants, 46 Benson's quail and 15 masked bobwhite were released on the fort in 1950, despite neither of these birds having been documented as historically present. All the quail releases were deemed failures, as no reproduction was ever noted and the birds disappeared within a year or so of release.

These efforts resulted in several detailed range and vegetation maps, including elevation parameters and range distributions, along with a good presentation of the plant species present and survey data on white-tailed deer, black-tailed jackrabbits, cotton-tailed rabbits, Merriam's turkey, Mearns' quail, band-tailed pigeons, mourning doves, and white-winged doves. The predator-control program, which included the application of Compound 1080, killed 7 lions, 13 bobcats, 75 coyotes, 40 gray foxes, 30 coatis, 27 skunks of two species, 5 badgers, and 4 ringtails. This report, the first detailed account of coatis in Arizona, states that the species was thought to have been first found on the fort in 1924. Compound 1080 was considered so effective it was thought coyotes had been largely eliminated from the wildlife-research area. Only a very few bears were thought to remain in the Huachuca Mountains, and full protection for this species was recommended. Two wolves were said to have been removed from the nearby Canelo Hills. There is no mention of jaguars or other tropical cats ever being present.

Unfortunately for the ongoing research studies, the fort was reactivated in 1951 and the Army subsequently insisted that all bison be removed. Although the fort remained ungrazed by livestock, the expansion of facilities and other activities resulted in fewer pronghorn present in 1952 than in 1950. On the other hand, populations of bears, coatis, and wild turkeys of the *mexicana* subspecies have greatly increased since that time.

The hiring of professional biologists in the early 1950s and their assignment to particular regions of the state and/or game species facilitated a number of Game and Fish Department "area investigations" reminiscent of the old Biological Survey area studies. These were bundled together under Work Plan 5 within the Federal Aid in Wildlife Restoration Project W-53. They included a number of special area investigations, ranging from Mittry Lake on the lower Colorado River to the Arizona Strip (see e.g., Day 1955a,

1955b, 1956; L. E. Powell 1953a, 1953b, 1954a, 1954b, 1955, 1956; Reed 1958, 1959a, 1959b; Russo 1954, 1956b).

Designed to gather information on the distributions, densities, and population composition of game species; predator densities; range conditions; and habitat deficiencies within the areas of interest, these evaluations provided information for further studies that yielded data needed to formulate management plans for an area. Efforts ranged from intensive (e.g., Diem 1954 on the Kaibab) to cursory, the better examples including species accounts and maps on an area's geography and vegetation (Gallizioli 1953b, 1954b).

Mount Graham and Galiuro Mountains

The best example of an area investigation by a single department biologist is undoubtedly Steve Gallizioli's (1953b) 16-page report on the game resources of the 200,000-acre Mount Graham portion of the Crook National Forest and his subsequent investigation of the Galiuro Mountains portion of the same forest (Gallizioli 1954b). Both reports contain vegetation maps and the elevations involved, as well as plant species summaries. The vegetation types are detailed and descriptive, and for the Graham (Pinaleño) Mountains include a desert and desert grassland category, mountain meadows, a spruce zone, a Douglas-fir zone, a ponderosa pine zone, and an oak woodland that is further described as consisting of oak woodland, oak-pine woodland, and chaparral subdivisions. Another map shows the 15 range allotments present and the location of permanent streams and other waters, including water developments. Range conditions are described as generally abused to ungrazed above 5,500-foot elevation.

As with the Three Bar and Fort Huachuca assessments, the various species of game animals are prominently featured and their history and status described. Of these, the white-tailed deer is regarded as the most important, despite this deer's being at a low population level in 1952, with only about 900 estimated on the mountain. This is in sharp contrast to the years 1929–34, when US Forest Service estimates placed the white-tailed deer population at a peak of about "10,000" individuals. This decline was borne out by both survey and hunt data, with annual totals of only 22–26 deer seen from 1951 to 1953 and harvests of 38–55 deer reported from 1946 to 1951. Because no fresh lion sign was seen in 1952 and more water was available to game than at any time in the past 20 years, the investigator suggested the whitetail population had yet to recover from a reported deer "die-off" in the early 1930s attributed to overpopulation and disease.

Desert mule deer and javelina, while found in limited numbers at the lower elevations, were thought to be increasing, in contrast to Merriam's turkeys, which were thought to be decreasing. Wild turkey, having disappeared from the range sometime prior to 1900, were reintroduced in 1926. This original plant of 26 birds was thought to have increased to 250 birds in 1933–34, when the population again declined. The Forest Service estimated only 30 turkeys were present in 1938. Despite additional releases of wild turkeys in the early 1940s, and an estimated population of 1,200 birds in 1947, this species again went into decline. Such indeed has been the history of turkeys in this mountain range. The birds again disappeared during the 1960s, with no birds thought to be present in the Grahams in the 1970s and 1980s.

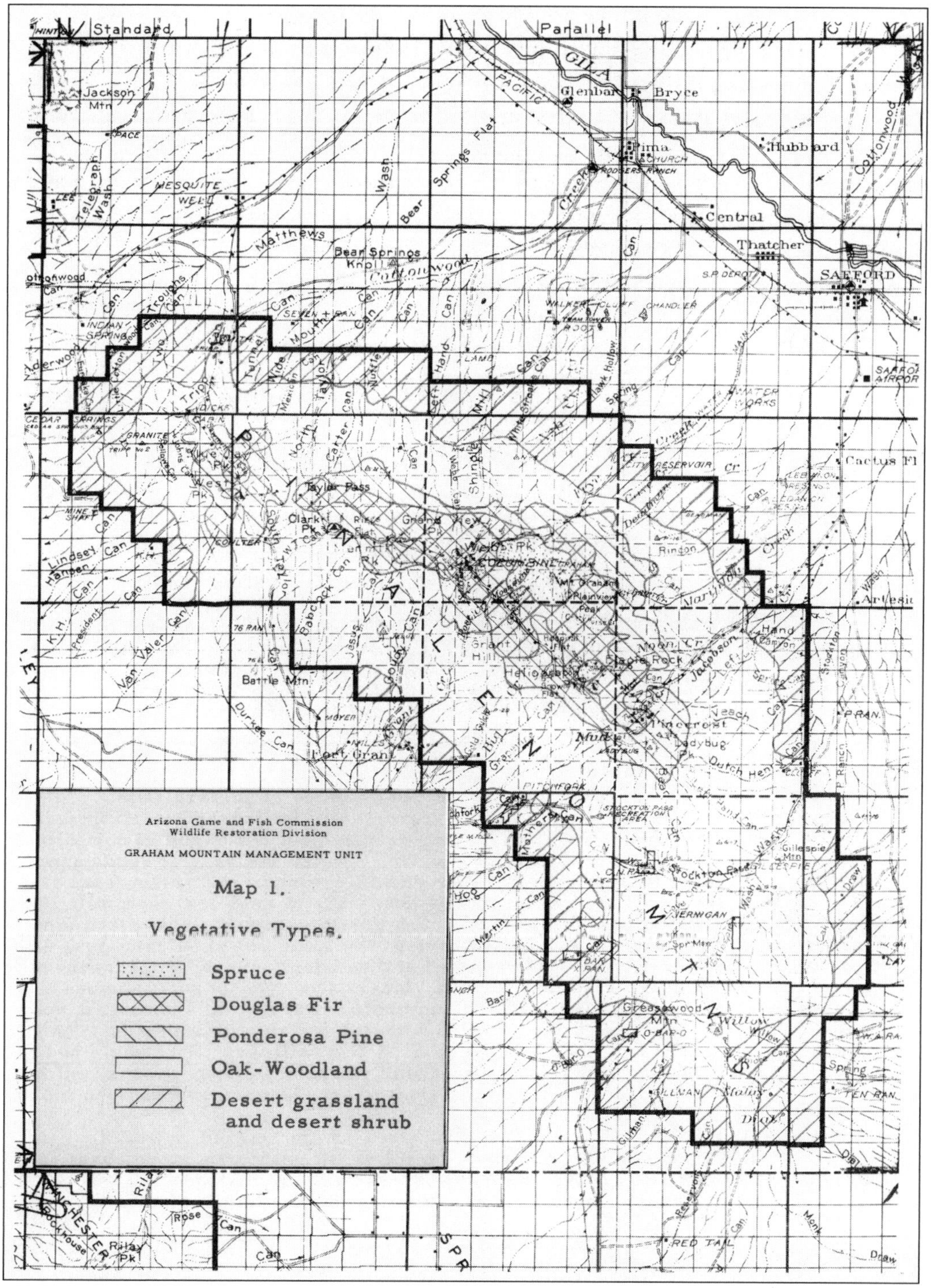

Vegetation map of Mount Graham and vicinity, developed by Steve Gallizioli as part of his study of the Pinaleño Mountains southwest of Safford (Gallizioli 1953). Such ecological investigations were an important aspect of the Federal-Aid program between 1951 and 1958. (AGFD files)

The only game species thought to be abundant during the investigation was the introduced Abert's or tassel-eared squirrel, which as the result of a release of 49 squirrels in 1941 and another 20 in 1943 was now ubiquitous. Curiously, no mention is made of the Graham Mountain spruce squirrel or, for that matter, coatis or Mearns' quail. Bears, although recognized as present, were deemed unimportant as game animals. Gambel's and scaled quail, while present, were mostly below the national forest boundary, and the occurrences of band-tailed pigeons were considered too erratic to be included in a management plan. The status of chukars, released in the Grahams in 1949, was said to be in doubt, despite several reports of what might have been this species.

All in all, the principal management recommendation was to emphasize the mountain's white-tailed deer, with the caveat that the Pinaleño Mountains not be included as a special management unit because the range's geographic isolation was such that further identification and management restrictions were unnecessary.

Such investigations ceased in the 1950s as the state became biologically better known and biologists concentrated on particular species or classes of animals living within particular areas or habitats (e.g., Hoffmeister and Goodpaster 1954; Hoffmeister 1956; Marshall 1957). The only areas remaining in need of biological inventories were some of the Indian reservations, and these were under the administrative purview of the US Bureau of Indian Affairs, which contracted its wildlife work almost exclusively with the Predator and Rodent Control branch of the Biological Survey, and later, the Fish and Wildlife Service.

ARIZONA'S DRYLAND MOUNTAIN LION HUNTERS

Harley Shaw

The dryland[1] lion and bear hunters of the American Southwest had a significant impact on large carnivores during the 1912–62 period. They developed their skills during a time when efforts were being made throughout the West to eliminate all large carnivores—grizzlies, black bears, wolves, mountain lions, jaguars, coyotes, even bobcats. Few in the Southwest questioned this goal. These carnivores were considered enemies of ranchmen and big game hunters alike.

While the thrill of the chase was certainly a motivating force among houndsmen, nearly all hunted for government or private bounty and most spent a part of their life working for the Predator and Rodent Control branch of the US Biological Survey. Fearing for their dogs, most houndsmen resisted the survey's use of poisons, and some resigned when predacides became the agency's weapon of choice.

Houndsmen tended to be specialists. They had little to do with the extirpation of the wolf in the Southwest—that feat was accomplished with traps and poison. Although they undoubtedly contributed to the grizzly's demise, its loss was due more to traps, poison, and the ongoing general warfare against bears than to the use of hounds. Similarly, traps and poison were preferred over hounds in efforts to eliminate coyotes, bobcats, and black bears.

Though traps effectively removed mountain lions from some areas, and poison may have played more of a role in the early reduction of these cats than previously realized, it was houndsmen who kept lions in check during the time frame of this book. Dale Lee, of the famous Lee brothers, said he had too much respect for the lion to hang steel on its foot. I suspect this represents the attitude of most early houndsmen.

The trailing of mountain lions through the rugged mountains of the American Southwest began only slightly before the beginning of the period encompassed here. These trailing and treeing hound breeds had evolved through at least three centuries of crossing English foxhound bloodlines with other canines: French scent hounds, mastiffs, Spanish beagle-like breeds, and bloodhounds, as well as others unknown.

We do not know when trail hounds arrived in the Southwest, and we know little of early efforts to develop the cold-nosed dryland strains. Streever (1948) suggests Spanish or Cuban bloodhounds may have bred into American hound bloodlines in the southeastern United States or possibly into Texas, New Mexico, and Arizona. However, these Latin breeds were known for their savagery and were originally used as war dogs or for recapturing escaped slaves, traits more useful for fighting bears on the ground than putting raccoons or cats in trees. I've found no strong evidence of a hound hunting tradition

[1]Dryland or "slow-trailing" is hunting with hounds trailing a faint scent on dry ground where tracks are faint or invisible until game is jumped and treed, as opposed to hunting on snow or soft, moist ground where tracks are visible and scent is strong. Hunters and hounds hunting on snow or on wet ground can see or smell at least portions of a track and move rapidly due to the moisture, which holds scent longer.

Mountain lion hunter Ben Lilly demonstrated horses weren't necessary to catch lions and bears, even in the dry, rugged Southwest. He covered the country on foot and slept out with his dryland lion-hunting dogs night after night. Detail of photo by J. E. Hawley. (US Biological Survey)

in Latin America that preceded adventuresome houndsmen from the United States who took dog packs south of the border to hunt.

I've found little evidence that mountain lion hunting with hounds became a specialized tradition in the eastern United States. Prior to the Civil War, running foxes and bears was a common sport. Hounds also were used to recapture runaway slaves. None of these pursuits required the cold-nosed dryland dogs now used by lion hunters in the western United States. Untangling the breeding and developmental history of today's specialized dogs would take a more dedicated scholar than I. Here I speculate rather boldly on the dogs' more recent history, hoping someday my ideas will be tested against a full review of primary sources.

In some instances, the dryland mountain lion hunting we know may have evolved from bear hunting, possibly as a result of incidental catches of lions during hunts where bears were the primary prey. This appears to have been the case with Montague Stevens (1943), for example, whose *Meet Mr. Grizzly* tells tales of catching bears with hounds in New Mexico's Gila Wilderness in the 1880s. Stevens hardly mentions lions in his book, and one gets the sense perhaps that the dogs, incidentally catching cats, may have trained Stevens, rather than the reverse.

Hounds were brought westward gradually by settlers through the 1700s and 1800s. The scent-hound tradition was sustained mostly by "Scotch-Irish" seeking open space. Bil Gilbert in *Westering Man* presents the Scotch-Irish as the only culture independent and ornery enough to out-Indian the Indians. According to Gilbert, they didn't like other European cultures and actually didn't care for each other all that much, so they tended to spread over the land in single-family units and settle large areas. Hounds fit well into their need for protection from renegade humans and other large predators.

Another small but possibly significant group of early houndsmen was African American hunters in the southeastern United States. While slaves generally weren't allowed to own dogs, some plantation owners would allow trusted individuals to handle their hounds and to guide guests. African American dog handlers were even more prominent after the Civil War. Theodore Roosevelt hunted with Holt Collier, whose skills he considered better than those of the famous Ben Lilly. Interestingly, both Collier and Lilly had ties to the Confederate general Nathan Bedford Forrest, himself an accomplished houndsman. William Faulkner apparently modeled his guide in *The Bear* after Collier. New Mexico

Giles Goswick, George Goswick, Dorsey Buckley, Bill Goswick, and Frank C. Hibben, about 1936 (left to right). Hibben relied on professional houndsmen while gathering data on mountain lions for his 1937 master's thesis. George Goswick said the best lion hound is "One that will catch a lion." In 1972, he became the principal hunter for the Arizona Game and Fish Department's mountain lion study northwest of Prescott. (Maxwell Museum of Anthropology, University of New Mexico, Frank Hibben Collection)

houndsman Orvel Fletcher, now 86 years old and still hunting, acquired one of his earliest dogs from an African American who claimed his dogs descended from Lilly's pack.

Hound hunting in eastern Texas was therefore an extension of hound hunting in the southeastern United States. Bears or smaller varmints were the usual prey, with lion catches being incidental. Development of the dryland lion hound happened first in the more arid Trans-Pecos Texas, in the Davis Mountains, Big Bend country, and on the eastern slopes of the Llano Estacado. These hound strains were refined through the past century into the present-day dogs with their complex set of abilities.

Insofar as I can determine, only three families who brought hounds with them into the arid Southwest developed a multi-generation tradition of dryland lion hunting and bred strains of dogs associated with their names: the Evans, Lees, and Goswicks.

We know that dryland hound bloodlines persisting in Arizona to this day were developed by these families, as well as by Uncle Jimmy Owens, Buffalo Jones, Babe Haught, and Frank Colcord, augmented possibly by Ben Lilly. Although Stevens preceded these hunters in New Mexico, his dogs died suddenly and tragically as a result of poison. If he produced pups for other hunters, their lineage probably cannot be traced.

I once asked George Goswick what he thought made the best lion hound, hoping he'd tell me his favorite breed. "One that will catch a lion," was his typically brief answer. Will Evans (1950) summed it up: "Having been raised in a 'long-eared dog country,' and knowing the 'cold nose' of the old 'pot-licker' for what he is; the best trailer for beasts of prey of any dog on earth, I don't hesitate to back the old long-ears against any short-eared dog in the world."

Dale Lee and one of his brothers, with mountain lion and dogs. (Arizona Historical Society/Tucson, #2109, MS939, Folder 10-N)

The Evans family hunted little in Arizona, but their dog strains were definitely bred to hounds used by Arizona hunters, including the Lees. Most hound-swapping and cross-breeding went on without serious documentation—the goal being to produce "a hound that would catch a lion."

Jimmy Owens knew the Lees before they moved from Palo Duro Canyon in Texas, and may well have mixed his hound bloodlines with theirs. And genes of Owens's and Buffalo Jones's hounds no doubt exist today in packs used by hunters north of the Grand Canyon. Owens and Jones mentored other hunters, such as Jack Butler and Bob Vaughn, but neither left descendents to continue a family tradition of hunting.

The Lee and Evans families incorporated bloodlines of each other's dogs into their packs, blending two of the best strains. The roots of Goswick dogs are more difficult to trace, but they undoubtedly also incorporated other successful hunting strains into their lineages. According to Rink Goswick, his grandfather, Giles, once bred a hound to a "bird dog," and some of those pups made excellent lion dogs. I find no record of Lilly actively raising pups, but at least one family of hunters near Glenwood, New Mexico, traces the lineage of some of their hounds back to Lilly (Dobie 1950; Carmony 1998). Over the years, many other strains of hounds, as well as Airedale and other non-hound breeds, have been imported and blended with these founding bloodlines.

The Lee brothers, Ernest, Dale, and Clell—more, perhaps, than most houndsmen—were sensitive to bloodlines. Because the old American Kennel Club refused to recognize various hound breeds, listing only the black and tan coonhound as a distinct breed, the

Lees helped form the United Kennel Club, maintaining a registry for six hound breeds. However, Southwestern lion and bear hunters have on the whole been more concerned with dog performance than color, voice, or canine genealogy.

Only the Evans, Lees, Haughts, and Goswicks remain as founding families sustaining family hunting traditions associated with family hound bloodlines, and only the latter three were Arizonans. At this writing, Brian Goswick, a nephew of George, still has a pack of hounds and hunts the Bradshaw Mountains. George's son, Rink, a capable hunter in his own right, joins in when ranch business allows. I know of no direct descendent of the Lees who runs hounds. The Evans tradition is carried on in Texas and New Mexico by members of the Evans-Means family. Kenny Wayne Haught carries on the Haught family tradition.

Dub Evans (1951) stated that his father developed the Evans hound strain from American foxhounds, suggesting perhaps that he began with the southeastern Trigg, Birdsong, and Walker breeds. For Evans, the "short-eared" hounds were the fast-running descendents of English foxhounds such as the July and Walker strains (Trigg 1890). On the whole, the Evans hounds were not papered dogs, but rather animals that proved their mettle in the field. I'm inclined to think George Goswick's definition of a good lion dog remains the best.

While each dog differs, and hunter preferences vary, a "perfect" dryland lion hound is normally smaller and lighter than most eastern bear and coon hounds, thereby possessing greater speed and endurance in rough and rocky terrain. It smells a cold track that is two days old, sometimes older, even on hot, bare ground. It has the intelligence and persistence to stubbornly search for scent when the track grows cold. It knows which other dogs in the pack to honor and goes to them when a strike is made. It learns the characteristics of the terrain and vegetation where scent is retained and focuses its efforts in such places. It adjusts its speed of trailing to the quality of the scent, rather than continuing to slowly cold-trail a fresh track (although one or two such slow trailers in a pack can help move difficult tracks). Once the lion is jumped, the hound shifts from tracking to running the scent in the air, thereby pushing the prey to bay or tree.

Through all of this, it gives voice so the hunter can find it in brushy terrain. It is honest in giving voice, knowing that lion and bear are the only prey and not breaking on deer, javelina, elk, or other herbivores. It will not chase coyotes or wolves. Once on a track, be it lion or bear, the dog does not switch to other game. For lions, it checks trees once the scent disappears. It can determine the lion's location even when the tree is too dense or the cat is too far up the tree to be seen. It stays at the tree, barking, for long periods, sometimes days, until the hunter can catch up. And it has the brains to eventually find its way back to camp or the point of departure if the hunt goes sour and the hunter fails to show. At least two hunters I've known also used their hounds for trailing and stopping cattle on rough, brushy ranges, seemingly without impairing their "straightness" when lion hunting was the order of the day.

While top-quality dryland hounds are necessary for consistently treeing lions in Arizona, one cannot separate the hounds from the houndsmen. They evolved together and their skills complement each other. I therefore suggest that a unique breed of houndsman—the dryland hunter—evolved concurrently with the hounds, mainly between about 1894 and 1960 in southwest Texas, Arizona, and New Mexico. With few exceptions, most current hunters and their dogs can be linked backward to Ben Lilly and the elder Lees, Evans, and Goswicks—the dogs by breeding and training, the hunters through mentoring, thereby inheriting both their predecessors' traditions and skills. Dryland hunting knowledge has now descended through three, perhaps four, generations of southwestern hunters who came from families with a long tradition of hunting with hounds in the Southeast. It is no accident that all of these families save Lilly were homesteading ranchers and stockmen—a background shared by nearly all successful early houndsmen.

As with the hounds, we might envision a "perfect" hunter. I say this with some temerity, because the hunters of today, unlike the hounds, can read my words, argue the point, and even take offense. Each has his own style and none fits a mold. Nonetheless, having had the privilege of hunting with Clell and Dale Lee, George and Rink Goswick, Ollie Barney, Bill Workman, Irving West, Bill Murphy, John Klump, Orvel Fletcher, and Mike Root, I've formed my own notion of the skills that lead to consistent success. My experience has been entirely with hunters of lions. For hunters of dryland lions, I would put extreme patience as the most essential necessary trait. This includes patience with horses, dogs, and, if you guide, people.

Lilly demonstrated horses weren't necessary to catch lions and bears, even in the rugged and dry Southwest. Few people, however, care to cover the country he did on foot and to sleep out with the dogs night after night. I would reverse the concept and say that the primitive lifestyle of Lilly isn't required of a top houndsman. It is possible to return to a good camp at night (although sometimes fairly late), sleep in a warm bed, and eat fairly regular meals while at the same time treeing lions. Good horses or mules make this possible.

To do this requires the ability to select or train dependable equines that will negotiate the roughest terrain. Implicit in this is the hunter's ability to read the landscape and guide his mount through it with minimum strain and risk to hunter, horse and, if guiding, the client. Very often, you cannot go where the dogs and lion have gone and must bypass excessively rough canyons, find suitable stream crossings, and find your way through or around fences. Impatience and poor judgment in any of these can lead to injuries of horses, riders, or both. This can be disastrous if novice riders are involved.

In addition to skill and patience in getting around the country, locating and following tracks requires special abilities. Until the dogs are started on a track, the houndsman is the lead dog, as it were, taking the animals to places where quarry will most likely be found. Here, knowledge of the habits of prey is critical. Familiarity with the country also helps, but an experienced houndsman can read strange terrain and focus on the most likely places to start a track.

Tracking ability is essential. Although the dogs most often locate a scent on their own, the hunter nonetheless must have his eye on the ground constantly and be able to identify even a fragment of a lion footprint. Often, he needs to call the dogs to tracks they have not found. When the dogs find a track first, the houndsman must inspect it as quickly as possible and, especially with lions, ascertain its direction of travel. Nothing is more frustrating than to have a good pack of dogs take a fresh track backwards and run it for a mile or two before the hunter can catch up and turn them around. Such loss of time can mean failure on a short winter day or during the cool hours of a summer morning when mid-morning heat will burn away scent. I've met hunters who claim their dogs won't take a back track, and I've seen a few top hounds that seem to understand the difference, but in general it is up to the hunter to be sure the dogs are lined out in the right direction.

Once the dogs are trailing, the hunter's patience and skill must blend with his knowledge of the dogs to keep them moving. The dogs should be given ample opportunity to trail on their own, with the hunter staying behind to watch them work. Only after the dogs have exhausted every possible route and failed to pick up a scent should the hunter intercede. When the hunter moves out in front, a danger exists of reversing the pack on the track. In such cases the dogs, having already been over the trail, may move much faster along the back track than when going forward.

If the pack needs help, the houndsman must move quietly among the dogs. If he loops on ahead, calm and silence are essential. His goal is to find the track where the hounds have not yet checked and call the dogs to it. Because of the possibility of confusing the dogs, the less often this is done, the better. In this, a team made up of a top houndsman and a mature, experienced pack of dogs becomes pure pleasure to watch. A level of man-dog communication occurs that is rarely seen in other human-animal endeavors.

Even after the quarry is jumped, patience remains essential. Temptation exists here to try to stay with the racing hounds—an act that can get hunter and horses in serious trouble. The hounds must be left to tree the lion; the hunter's job is to try to stay within earshot and interpret the sounds of the dogs. Again, an understanding between man and dog is the key. If a hunter knows his dogs and trusts them to do their work, he need not place himself, his horses, or his clients in serious danger. If the dogs get out of earshot, he may need to put his tracking skills to work, checking the ground to see where the chase has gone.

For a guide, a workable combination is a houndsman with a pack of dogs, accompanied by a "dude wrangler" who understands the hunt and can trail. This arrangement allows the houndsman to stay with the pack, knowing the wrangler will follow more slowly behind, choosing the most suitable route to get the client to the tree. A dude wrangler who can remain calm during heated chases, stay with the clients rather than chase the hounds, explain the nuances of the hunt, and get neophyte riders safely to the tree makes the life of a houndsman infinitely easier.

Although there are accounts of ranchers in Arizona Territory hiring houndsmen to relieve them of lion depredation as early as the 1890s (Brown 2009), the dryland lion hunter of the Southwest is generally a twentieth-century phenomenon. The dogs and the hunter skills began to develop in the 1880s and 1890s, but a founding tradition wasn't in place until the first two decades of the 1900s (Van Dyke 1889; Holder 1906).

Although Murphy (1879) describes pursuing cougars with dogs in California and the Cascade Mountains by the 1870s, he does not describe the dogs, and the hunts are relatively short, with animals mainly being chased from kills. Montague Stevens had hunted big game in parts of the West since 1880, but he first hunted bear in New Mexico with dogs in 1889. He notes the only hounds available were those that had been trained to track trapped animals. He used experienced trap hounds to train younger hounds to trail bears. (As noted earlier, Stevens barely mentions lions in the Gila wilderness, nor does J. H. Cook, who managed the W. S. Ranch near Alma, New Mexico, from 1882 to 1887 [Cook 1923].)

But by the time Stevens was running grizzlies in New Mexico with his mixed pack of dogs, George Evans had been hunting black bears and "panthers" with hounds for at least five years in the Davis Mountains of Texas. Evans had hunted with hounds since his boyhood along the Nueces and Frio rivers (G. W. Evans 1951), killing a jaguar bayed by his hounds when he was 10 years old (W. F. Evans 1950). This must have been in the late 1860s or early 1870s. It was not until 1916 that brothers Joe and Dub Evans, along with in-laws in the Means family, brought hounds with them to Harry Martin's ranch west of Silver City, New Mexico, and assumed the "Slash" brand. In 1917, they bought part of the V Cross T Ranch with headquarters at Beaverhead, New Mexico. This became the famous Slash Ranch, which still exists. Hunting bears and mountain lions was part of their ranching operation (G. W. Evans 1951).

The best-known dryland houndsman of them all, Ben Lilly, arrived in New Mexico about 1911 and had been chasing bears and lions in the Gila country for five years before the Evans family arrived (Carmony 1998). Born in Alabama in 1856, Lilly had drifted westward through Mississippi, Louisiana, and Texas and was well-known, experienced, and 55 years of age by the time he reached New Mexico. Stevens, Lilly, and the Evans brothers ranged into eastern Arizona during some of their hunts, but they mainly hunted in the upper Gila River watersheds of western New Mexico.

In 1910, a year before Lilly arrived in New Mexico, the Lee family had moved from Palo Duro Canyon in Texas to Paradise, Arizona, also bringing hounds with them. The family already had eight sons, and three of these, Ernest, Clell, and Dale, teamed up to become the most influential hunting and guiding force in Arizona for much of the twentieth century (Carmony 1998). Like the Evans family, they developed their own line of hunting hounds, incorporating other bloodlines (such as the Evans's), thereby improving their pack and avoiding inbreeding. More than any other family, the Lees ran their guiding operation as a business, developing a famous line of blueticks. After World War II, they even set up a school for training veterans to hunt lions and bears using GI Bill funds, and were fundamental in developing and testing some of the earliest shock collars for training hounds. At least one of their graduates, Wiley Carroll, became well-known in Nevada and wrote an entertaining, if strangely edited, lion hunting book of his own (Carroll 1983).

The Goswick family arrived in the Southwest in 1894 from Arkansas (by way of Lamar County, Texas). By this time, the family had owned hounds for at least three generations. They spent their first winter near Luna, New Mexico, then settled briefly at Grapevine Spring, near the site of the present-day Roosevelt Dam. They quickly became involved in bounty hunting for ranchers in the area (Branstetter 1976). From there, they drifted northward, joining the Haught family under the Mogollon Rim, then buying a small ranch in Harris Park on top of the rim. From there, Giles Goswick moved to the

Marvin Glenn was a third-generation Arizonan who lived his entire life on the J-A Ranch in Hunt Canyon. He bought his first hound and started hunting mountain lions in 1936, and guided clients until 1990. (Courtesy of the Glenn family)

Verde Valley and ran a freight business until he acquired a ranch of his own. He parlayed this property into a larger holding near Big Bug Mesa in the rugged Bradshaw Mountains. In general, the Goswicks hunted predators mostly to protect their livestock and that of their neighbors. Guiding was incidental to their efforts to control lion numbers.

Babe and John Haught settled under the Mogollon Rim northeast of Payson in 1897. By this time, Jack Payson had already established a ranch and mercantile store supporting the growing numbers of homesteaders in the area. He gave Babe Haught an old hound named Troop, which became the core of a pack of hounds used to hunt bears and lions that threatened the Haught's livestock. That same year, bounty hunter J. W. Goswick visited their ranch with a pack of hounds and left them a started but younger dog named Payson. Payson soon contributed two pups to the pack, and the Haughts went on to early fame by guiding writer Zane Grey.

Other families started hunting later but retained the tradition of training lion dogs. Josiah Jefferson Glenn and his wife brought his family of 11 children with them in covered wagons from near Kerrville, Texas, in 1898. They settled in the south end of the Chiricahua Mountains in High Lonesome Canyon, and the sons homesteaded five different places. One, Ira, homesteaded in Hunt Canyon in 1919. His son, Marvin, was born in Douglas and lived his entire life on the J-A Ranch in Hunt Canyon. Warner Glenn was raised there and lived there until 1963, when he and his wife, Wendy, and their two children moved to the Malpai Ranch in the San Bernardino Valley east of Douglas, on the Mexican border. They still own and operate the J-A Ranch in Hunt Canyon as well.

The Glenn family brought no hounds with them when they moved to Arizona. In 1936, the year Warner was born, Marvin bought his first hound, a two-year-old redbone named Jack, from Martin Williams of Elfrida, Arizona, who owned a Lee Brothers' strain of hounds. Marvin started hunting lions to protect his calves and colts and slowly built a pack of eight hounds made up of bluetick, redbone, and black and tans. He hunted with all these breeds until 1958, when he bought two UKC-registered Walker hounds—a male out of Houses Bawley and a female out of Findley River Chief. Marvin's son, Warner, later replaced the other breeds, and most of the Glenns' hounds now go back to those Walker hounds.

The Glenns are a typical dryland lion-hunting family. Marvin started hunting lions in 1936, took his first paying client in 1948, and guided clients until 1990. Warner started hunting with Marvin at six years of age and, except for school and a 13-month military hitch, has hunted steadily ever since. His daughter, Kelly Glenn Kimbro, is a regular hunting partner to Warner, has been in on almost every hunt, and is a master houndsman in her own right. The Glenns have also mentored younger hunters, including Tommy Todd from the Willcox area and David and Richard Moore from Animas, New Mexico.

Another hunter who attained renown in the first half of the twentieth century was Frank Colcord. Colcord's father settled in the Tonto Basin country around 1885, bringing hounds with him (McLemore 1941). Frank Colcord was born in 1899 in Payson and ultimately worked as a government hunter throughout much of Arizona. Colcord also successfully hunted jaguars in Mexico. I find no evidence that the Colcord family hunting tradition carried on after Frank's death in 1969.

One more family with a tradition of hounds and hunting was the Kane family. Jim Kane came into southern Arizona from Arkansas in 1883 and married Mary Gardner of Sonoita, Arizona (Wood 2007). Jim's son, Robert, was born in 1899 and became a well-known lion hunter, as did Robert's nephew Grover, born in 1923. Grover's son Ross continued the family tradition for some time. Exactly when the Kanes began running hounds is uncertain, but Robert and Grover were accomplished dryland hunters in the 1940s. Robert mentored Sewell Goodwin, who went on to become a prominent houndsman and the only Arizonan to legally take both a jaguar and an ocelot within Arizona, in addition to a large number of lions.

Through the twentieth century, a goodly number of other top-notch hunters developed in Arizona: Ted Ferguson; Ollie Barney; Bill Workman; Bill Martin; Bill Murphy; Irving West; John Hunt and John Hunt Jr.; Larry Hendricks; Steve Smith; John Klump; and at least two generations of Lackners—I'm sure there are those I've missed. Even though some of these men attained fame as guides, others went virtually unknown, mainly because they hunted on their own ranches to protect livestock. Although they might take friends and acquaintances along and allow them to shoot a treed lion, they would not attain the reputation of those houndsmen who regularly guided sportsmen.

While most of these houndsmen were also stockmen who hunted to protect their livestock or to guide sport hunters, several went on to become associated with mountain lion research (Hibben 1937; Shaw 1990). Initial efforts to study southwestern lions would have been nearly impossible without the assistance of houndsmen such as Giles Goswick, Frank Colcord, George Goswick, Bill Workman, Ollie Barney, Clell Lee, Dale Lee, and Bill Murphy. Even Ben Lilly contributed specimens to the Biological Survey for use in early taxonomy studies.

The tradition of dryland lion hunting is only three, or in a few instances, four, generations deep. It was developed by stock-raisers who morphed their predator-hunting skills into a supplemental income through guiding, and, finally, developed lion trailing into a sport of its own wherein skilled hunters with top hounds guide independently of ranching operations.

Bill Workman, ca. 1976. Workman became a well-known houndsman and guide during the 1950s. As shown here, he was one of several hunters who later assisted the Arizona Game and Fish Department in mountain lion research. Photo by Harley Shaw. (AGFD files)

The mountain lion, for its part, proved amazingly resilient in the face of persistent hunting, just as it did with the earlier trapping and poisoning campaign carried out against it. In recent years, many houndsmen have supported increased regulation of their sport due to a concern that overharvesting these big cats will augment losses to civilization and habitat fragmentation. As has so often been the case, those who hunted the animal have come to be the ones who advocate management practices that both regulate and sustain the species.

That 50 years of effort failed to eliminate mountain lions and black bears is due in part to the changing values of houndsmen. While the protection of livestock and big game animals was, and remains, a motive for hunting the former, the thrill of the chase and the economic returns from guiding sportsmen gradually changed the way lions were perceived. By the late 1960s, several houndsmen would join the general public in supporting reclassification of lions and bears to big game status, thus opting to manage these species for sport hunting rather than continue efforts to eliminate them.

FEDERAL AND STATE CONFLICTS OVER BIG GAME NUMBERS—ROUND TWO

David E. Brown

President Franklin Roosevelt and his Democratic Congress and cabinet greatly expanded the federal government's leadership role during his "New Deal" of the 1930s and 1940s, and wildlife legislation was no exception. Nonetheless, the extension of the federal government's role into the realm of game and fish management dealt mostly with laws and funding increases for traditional federal programs such as those dealing with migratory birds, national wildlife refuges, and predator and rodent control (which now included programs primarily intended to protect big game animals).

States' rights advocates also made wildlife management gains during the period, and some important federal legislation, such as the Pittman-Robertson Act, actually strengthened state management authority. Such legislation not only provided the states with technical personnel and expertise, it provided the funding to conduct studies needed for proper management decisions.

The US Forest Service, long a player in state game-management issues, was also eager to expand its involvement with wildlife on the national forests, especially at the regional level, where big game specialists continued to budget game-management programs and estimate big game harvest and population numbers (see tables at end of chapter). The Forest Service's Southwestern District 3 had long been interested in natural vegetation and wildlife habitat, having prepared a vegetation map of Arizona and New Mexico in 1923.

Indeed, the Forest Service's role in wildlife management and restoration might have been much larger if Secretary Harold Ickes' five-year effort to have the Forest Service transferred from the Department of Agriculture to his Interior Department had not fallen short in Congress by a single vote in 1940 (Trefethen 1961).

In 1940, before America's entrance into the war, the Arizona Game and Fish Department and Forest Service had jointly entered into a cooperative agreement on a deer hunt on the Kaibab. Although the issuance of an 80-cent deer tag had led to some misunderstandings as to what constituted a legally taken deer, a single-season deer hunt limited to 1,000 deer of any kind (or "hunter choice" permits) proved to be a generally satisfactory arrangement to both parties through 1945. The only federal-state concerns mentioned by the Arizona Game and Fish Commission during the war years involved Indians. The commission was on record as opposing any attempt to allow hunting on the reservations without a state license and denied any Indian living on a reservation a complimentary pioneer hunting and fishing license regardless of how long he had lived in Arizona.

Kaibab Deer

A major conflict regarding the Kaibab Plateau was brewing, however. In 1945, only 704 of the authorized 1,004 hunters had checked in. Poor weather conditions prevailed during the early portions of the hunt, and hunt success declined to 56.6% (Russo 1964). Many hunters thought deer numbers were low and demanded the hunt be either elimi-

Arizona portion of a 1923 Forest Service map showing vegetation zones in Arizona and New Mexico. (US Forest Service)

nated or greatly curtailed. With accusations of mismanagement proliferating, the Forest Service and Game and Fish Department presented two different views at the May 1946 commission meeting.

The Kaibab National Forest's opinion was represented by Forest Service game specialist Fred Johnson, and the state's by Tommy Wright. Wright (1947), a technician who was conducting a study on the Kaibab (some of it surreptitiously), contended the Kaibab deer herd had been declining since 1930 and even longtime foresters such as Walter Mann wanted the season closed. Wright wanted a new Kaibab agreement, one that would only call for permit hunts in alternate years and require hunters to pay a $5 government fee that would be spent on deer management projects. Johnson, on the other hand, claimed the deer herd was increasing, and wanted antlerless hunting to continue. In a quandary, the commission approved a 500-permit buck-only hunt for 1946 with large areas closed to hunting—the most restrictive hunt ever authorized on the Kaibab.

The Forest Service was accused of exaggerating the size of the deer herd, favoring cattle over deer, and blaming the latter for damaging the deer browse (Russo 1964). A cooperative study on the relationship between deer and livestock was therefore initiated, during which two cattle and four deer were collected per month in select vegetation types. This study, involving some 33 cattle and 115 deer, became extremely controversial, as it blamed cattle for the excess forage use on the summer and winter ranges, despite the study's conclusion that sufficient range existed for both species at present levels (Wright 1947, 1950). Both sides concluded on the basis of the study that deer numbers were increasing, and in August 1947 Wright presented the commission with a signed cooperative agreement with the Forest Service calling for an increase in buck permits on the Kaibab to 1,000. For its part, the commission acknowledged that Johnson had been right and the commission in error regarding deer conditions.

Controversy as to the status of the deer herd continued nonetheless, with the status of livestock remaining unresolved. Interest in the Kaibab was therefore high when technician Alfred C. Edwards recommended again doubling the number of buck permits to 2,000 at the August 1948 commission meeting. Instead, the department's game management supervisor, Pop Arrington, conducted a follow-up study that, like Wright's, was considered by the Forest Service to be biased in favor of deer (Arrington 1950). The findings of competing studies by a Forest Service range specialist (Bostick 1949, 1950) were considered biased in favor of cattle. A composite report containing just the facts was therefore prepared by high-level administrators in both agencies to cool matters down (Kimball and Watkins 1951).

Attendance was even greater at the 1949 commission meeting, when Arrington sought a doe hunt on the Kaibab that Commissioner Fred Faver opposed. Although it was thought there might be too many deer on the north Kaibab, it was also argued there were too many cattle, a point denied by Forest Service biologist E. A. "Art" Schilling. He claimed it was deer that were causing the range to go downhill, and requested a closed commission meeting between the two agencies.

The result was a hot exchange with a representative of the Arizona Game Protective Association, George Richard (who wanted fewer deer permits), as to who owned the deer. Taken to a floor vote, the department's recommendation for 4,000 buck-only permits passed by a vote of 22 to 20, the minority wanting only 3,000 permits. Although the hunt was divided into two seasons to avoid crowding, there was still insufficient public sentiment to make does legal game and reduce the herd.

Buck-only hunting continued. The number of permits increased to 4,500 in 1950, although only 2,552 hunters actually hunted in 1949. Hunt success was a low 54.4%, yet deer population estimates increased during this period from an estimated 21,000 in 1945 to 57,000 in 1949 (Kimball and Watkins 1951). When technician Ken Diem was assigned

A mule deer with antlers in velvet. 1948 photo by R. H. Lewis. (US Forest Service, Southwestern Region, Kaibab National Forest)

to the Kaibab as its first resident deer biologist in 1951, he attributed most overuse of browse plants to deer and concluded that ominous signs were pointing to a repeat of the 1924–25 irruption. Although Diem would only work on the Kaibab for three years, he would see his conclusion verified.

The two-season hunt was again approved in 1950, with hunting for antlerless deer finally reinstated on the winter range during the late hunt. Deer numbers continued to increase, despite this two-hunt strategy and an increasing number of permits (5,099 in 1951; 6,989 in 1952; 10,000 in 1953; and 12,000 in 1954). Then, during the winter of 1954–55, history repeated itself. A major die-off occurred. Biologist Wendell Swank estimated a loss of 18,000 dead deer on the Kaibab. The drawing for the 10,000 deer permits authorized for the 1954 hunt was immediately halted and a cap put on the 4,717 permits already issued.

Although the debates continued, the commission was now more prone to listen to the technicians. Even Ben Avery, an AGPA critic who wrote an outdoor column for the *Arizona Republic* and who led the charge for a discussion of the "Kaibab situation," came to support the Arizona Game and Fish Department's position, believing that more hunts would lead to hunters being less crowded. And although the AGPA continued to want more deer and to pressure the Forest Service to reduce cattle numbers, even Joe Dora, the AGPA representative, realized that the need for fewer cattle was because the range could not support more deer.

Although hunter numbers were reduced in 1955 due to a "low fawn crop," deer numbers were soon rising again. Many any-deer permits were issued in 1956, but just 6,000 of these were on the Kaibab—a number that increased to 10,000 by 1958, when hunters were allowed two deer and successful hunters could obtain an additional bonus permit at the check station. A separate bow hunt was also approved that year, during which archers attained a whopping 20.4% hunt success.

The summer range nonetheless still showed signs of overuse, and biologists were determined to maintain control of the deer herd now that cattle numbers were set at 2,200 head. The hunters had done the job. Only 4,500 any-deer permits were issued in 1960, and by 1961 there was only one hunt in effect. The general agreement was that the Kaibab herd was under control—a monument to mutual cooperation between the two agencies with no need for outside interference from the courts or legislature.

One major benefit of the increasing number of deer permits was an increase in the cooperative agreement budget, by which the Forest Service and Arizona Game and Fish Commission jointly funded deer-management projects on the Kaibab. These funds, only 10% of which could be spent on administrative costs, not only provided sufficient money to hire technicians, check-station operators, and deputies to supervise the hunt, they had financed more than 80 water developments and other habitat improvements on the north Kaibab. Sufficient money was available in 1952 that the commission and Forest Service even agreed to fund recreation facilities at Big Lake on the Apache National Forest—an appropriation objected to by Avery and other Kaibab watchers.

Spending funds off of the Kaibab was a one-time anomaly. Most of the annual appropriations from 1953 on, which generally ranged between $30,000 and $60,000, were spent on Kaibab hunt supervision, range studies, and road construction and maintenance. In 1957 and after, increasing amounts were dedicated to pinyon-juniper eradication in a much-needed attempt to stimulate cliffrose regeneration on the winter range.

Predator Control

As in the previous irruption in the 1920s, predator control both preceded and remained in effect during the rise in deer numbers. But unlike the earlier situation, sportsmen, as represented by the AGPA and Arizona Game and Fish Commission, were the principal supporters of predator control. As with other areas of the state, the primary objective of predator control on the north Kaibab was no longer to reduce livestock losses but to benefit game animals. And here, money was no problem.

When Everett Mercer, supervisor of the Predator and Rodent Control branch of the US Biological Survey, went before the commission in December 1946, he was already assured of an annual appropriation of $10,000 from the department, with more funding said to be possible. And, he did want more. Explaining he was having problems meeting the demand for the PARC's expanded poison campaign, he asked the commission for another $34,000. This was on top of a $30,000 federal appropriation, with an additional $15,000 from the Arizona State Legislature, $10,000 from the department (and another $5,000 in Federal-Aid money), $1,950 from the Grazing Service's Arizona Strip district, $2,600 from the San Carlos tribe, and $3,400 from the Fort Apache Indian reservation.[1]

[1]The PARC had just removed some 12,000 to 15,000 wild horses from the reservation the year before.

In response, the commission told him to contact Director Herbert Reid and the money would be made available. Some on the commission also wanted bounties reinstated, and it was agreed after a lengthy discussion that the Game and Fish Department would pay $50 for each lion taken on the Kaibab and hire two lion hunters on a trial basis.

Commissioners Charles Beach and William Connor were so in favor of predator control that they voted in 1947 to double the department's annual contribution to PARC to $20,000. Recognizing that the state bounties initiated that year on wolves and lions resulted from lobbying by stockmen, they were eager to help in the war on predators lest the protection of game be secondary to livestock.[2] When queried for a recommendation, Director Reid adopted a hands-off approach, preferring to leave predator control and bounties up to the AGPA, which was also lobbying for an improved legal status for bears.

As to who could take predators for bounty, Attorney General John L. Sullivan merely ruled that the authority was there to require a hunting license if the commission wanted to open a predator season. Thus, by declaring an open season on predators and jackrabbits, the department was able to obtain license revenue while making every sportsman a potential predator-control agent and bounty hunter.

That these deliberations took place while the Kaibab deer herd was irrupting was not lost on the technicians. Kaibab biologist Diem had recommended a reduction in predator control prior to the 1954 deer die-off, and an extensive predator and rodent survey on the north Kaibab in 1957 had shown neither group of animals to be abundant. Nonetheless, a PARC agent was assigned specifically to work the Kaibab (Russo 1964).

By 1958, predator control included the use of Compound 1080, 29 bait stations containing this lethal predacide having been established on the north Kaibab alone. Once underway, such control programs proved difficult to rein in, and in 1959 PARC initiated a rodent-control program on the Kaibab—probably at the recommendation of the Forest Service, which was concerned about porcupines damaging ponderosa pines. It was not until the winter of 1960 that Kaibab deer biologist John Russo was able to negotiate some let-up in the effort at predator and porcupine control. By that time, surplus deer were no longer a serious problem, and game managers and their supporters were involved in new Kaibab crises, which included the forest's worst fire to date and applications for a plethora of oil drilling leases on the Kaibab Plateau.

Bill Williams Deer Management Area

The north Kaibab Plateau was not the only federal preserve facing a deer crisis in the years following World War II. Serious overbrowsing was also reported on the Bill Williams Wildlife Management Unit south of Williams. On this cooperative "game management unit," the Arizona Game and Fish Department and the Forest Service were attempting to co-manage deer and livestock numbers within the confines of their habitat—in short, applying the north Kaibab model to the south Kaibab.

Although the commission listened to the Forest Service's request for 1,000 antlerless-

[2]Max Layton, the AGPA delegate from Safford, pleaded for a $30,000 contribution to match the amount paid by the livestock industry.

deer permits on the Bill Williams unit in 1946 and 1947, no antlerless-deer hunts were approved. Neither the commission nor the Williams Game Protective Association, which had supported the unit's creation, were in the mood to reduce deer numbers until the Forest Service reduced livestock numbers, despite all parties agreeing that an excess of both groups of animals existed.

Forest Service range experts Johnson and Schilling defended the service's range management program but agreed with the department's assertion that the range was being seriously damaged. Finally, in 1949, the number of cattle was reduced, and a two-hunt strategy was approved in which another 800 hunters would be allowed to hunt the Bill Williams unit after the general deer hunt. This prescription was modified in 1950, when it was agreed that the Bill Williams unit would constitute a separate hunt unit in which 4,000 buck permits and 350 antlerless permits would be issued at $1 each. Hunters would be selected on a first-come, first-served basis, and have to check in and out at one of four check stations.

In 1951, the Bill Williams unit hunt was reduced to 2,500 permits, only 75 of which were for any deer or "hunter's choice." And although local concern continued to justify the retention of the Bill Williams unit as a special management area for deer and turkeys (both David Gorsuch and Lynn Hargrave had conducted turkey studies there), the commission was leery of another Forest Service cooperative management unit for resident game.

Besides, more and more special hunt units were being approved as the department attempted to keep up with a deer irruption that was spreading to various areas of the state. With no need for a special management program to increase deer numbers, and a growing concern that there were now too many deer and elk in a number of locations, there was little desire for another joint agreement. Within a few years, the Bill Williams unit was relegated to just another special hunt unit and the special $1 fee dropped.

Elk Problems

The Forest Service and Arizona Game and Fish Department were also involved in a beef over another animal. At the 1946 season-setting meeting, the Forest Service's Schilling emphatically told the commission that elk were not only the cause of numerous depredation complaints from livestock lessees, but this animal was a serious threat to deer herds. Although an elk season had been opened in four areas of the state with both bull and cow permits being issued, Schilling thought deer hunters on the Sitgreaves and Coconino national forests should be allowed to kill elk instead of deer, as the deer on the Mogollon Rim were in "dire straits."

The Winslow Game Protective Association was of a different mindset, and their request for a "Sitgreaves management unit" was passed despite strong opposition. As originally construed, this Forest Service "refuge" was to be closed to big game hunting for three years at the discretion of the Game and Fish Department director. It was, however, abolished on January 17, 1949, on the advice of department ranger Gene Holder and with the concurrence of the Winslow Game Protective Association.

When it came to elk issues, the commission appeared to side with the Forest Service—at least at first. Resolutions and regulations were passed to keep elk numbers at

1947 levels and not let the species expand west of Sycamore Canyon and the Coconino National Forest. Elk depredations on crops and grass were becoming a thorny issue and a source of conflict between ranchers, the Forest Service, the Game and Fish Department, and the AGPA. When a 60-acre meadow in Long Valley that had been a chronic problem area was put up for sale in 1947 for $14,000, the commission looked into the legality of purchasing livestock grazing permits, though the asking price in this particular case was deemed too high. That same year, an AGPA application to import elk and turkeys to Mingus Mountain was denied due to the potential for more trouble.

In 1948, an "elk management committee" was formed to handle the burgeoning number of elk problems, and the commission directed the executive secretary of the AGPA to poll the local clubs regarding a reasonable elk hunt strategy. This was done, and the department technician's advice for 2,200 permits upheld. Conflicts over elk continued into the 1950s nonetheless, with the commission authorizing bull, antlerless, and any-elk hunts in various areas.

Increasing elk numbers constituted trouble in other ways. Law enforcement personnel were involved in a number of high-profile elk cases during this time. In 1952, a November storm resulted in a number of elk hunters being snowbound. Five people died before they could be rescued. Both commendations and accusations abounded. The next year an early elk hunt was approved, not only to take advantage of milder weather, but to ensure the taking of more bulls than cows.

Elk numbers continued to trend upward and depredation complaints escalated. Stockmen went to their legislators, but Alfred Paul, chair of the Fish and Game Committee in the Arizona House of Representatives, came to the commission meeting to support the department's policy of recommending bull permits in some areas, cow permits in others. Elk proponents within the AGPA also made themselves heard. Many complaints and promises were made relating to elk, but by 1952 the department was no longer removing "trespass" elk or issuing depredation permits to ranchers as in the past.

Things got more complicated in 1953, when the AGPA came out for a policy of more elk in opposition to the Forest Service's Schilling. The politics got hot and heavy, and by 1955 the commission was becoming concerned about sending controversial regulations for deer and elk to the legislature. Even Governor Ernest McFarland came to sit in on what was now a five-man commission's season-setting meeting. What he found was a huge department staff presence represented by Game Management Chief Phil Cosper, and 87 sportsmen supporting the department's recommendation for only 1,725 elk permits, significantly fewer than the 2,955 approved the previous year. All the department's recommendations were approved unanimously—Avery having paved the way with both the cattlemen and their legislators. Although Ernest Chilson of the AGPA's "stockmen-sportsmen" committee may not have liked the lower number of elk permits, his concerns were alleviated by a substantial increase in any-deer hunts.

Even though elk depredation complaints continued to be filed by cattlemen on and adjacent to the national forests, the AGPA and the department were now easing into a situation that allowed for increased elk populations—at least in some areas. In 1956, the AGPA wanted the commission to limit the amount of deer hunting and cease elk hunting entirely, while the commission objected to a Forest Service plan that gave deer a greater priority than elk or livestock. The following year, the AGPA resolved to close the elk season for three years, probably as much in reaction to the "Sagebrush Rebellion" then taking place as a desire for more elk permits in the future.[3] For its part, the commission lambasted the cattlemen and the farmers who planted oats and other crops in the so-called "dry parks" for their intransigence when it came to preventing and alleviating depredation losses, voting to provide fence materials but not labor in such problem areas as Munds Park.

In 1957, the elk hunt recommendation was a conservative 1,125 permits, even though many sportsmen wanted no hunt at all or one limited to an earlier bull-only season. The following year, the commission agreed that no hunt should result in a smaller elk herd, but later rejected a proposal to introduce elk to the Kaibab. What was approved was a motion to purchase 21 sections of the Chilson Ranch on the Mogollon Rim if such could be obtained for not more than $3 per acre.

In 1960, it was agreed to issue more any-elk permits while holding elk numbers to the present level, and in 1961, a two-season elk hunt became a standard recommendation. Although some in the audience at the commission meeting wanted a still-larger elk herd through more litigation, the commission elected a go-easy approach. Jack Mantle, Commissioner Beach's replacement from Pima County, was, like his predecessor, inclined to be more supportive of the department's recommendations than the sportsmen's when a conflict arose. Either way, elk numbers in Arizona were destined to rise.

Furors Over Furbearers

The relationship between the state and US Fish and Wildlife Service was also under some strain in the years immediately after World War II. Fur prices had been high during the war years and trapping could be a lucrative enterprise; so much so that the department had a Fur Conservation Division under the supervision of Bobby Fox.

Beavers, although still protected in Arizona, caused frequent complaints due to their damage to canal banks and fruit trees. Problem animals were trapped and released by department personnel in vacant habitats (Arizona Game and Fish Commission 1942) or, if suitable release sites were lacking, pelted by hired trappers for sale at public auction, with proceeds going to the department. This last procedure became an important source of revenue along the lower Colorado River, as in 1945 the department sold more than 1,000 pelts and 129 pounds of castors from beavers trapped by George Daniels and Don Moon. This sale alone provided the department with $23,361 in income and a profit of $10,247.33. Although Fox's claim that only two out of 170 beaver transplants were unsuccessful was an exaggeration, these animals were considered a valuable asset, a contract having been issued for 200 pair to be trapped at Tule Lake along the California-Oregon border and released at Fort Mohave.

---

[3]The "Sagebrush Rebellion" was a movement by stockmen in the western states to have the Forest Service abolished or the service's range management authorities turned over to the states. It was defeated by a consortium of conservationists, including the AGPA, as a serious threat to wildlife interests.

Concerned the federal government was infringing on the state's prerogatives, the commission opposed a 1946 edict by Refuge Manager Arthur Halloran that the Fish and Wildlife Service would also trap beaver on Imperial and Havasu national wildlife refuges and sell the pelts. The commission notified Director Fred Merkle that he was to inform Fish and Wildlife Service Supervisor John Gatlin in Albuquerque that these were state animals and that the department intended to trap 40 beavers from these refuges for transplant. There then being a boom in nonresident trapping, Merkle was also directed to object to national wildlife refuge personnel issuing muskrat-trapping licenses, a demand that soon became moot, as muskrats were thought to be in danger of disappearing on the Colorado River, and the season was closed there in 1947.

The state continued to press its jurisdiction over beavers and muskrats on the Colorado River in 1948. Commissioners Connor, Beach, and Richard Wickstrum told Director Reid to ask the California Fish and Game Department to join his department in pressuring their legislature for Imperial and Havasu national wildlife refuges to either be abandoned or turned over to the states. The AGPA was more sympathetic to the federal point of view, and objected to the states' directive having the Fish and Wildlife Service cede all authority over resident wildlife to the states. Such disputes were mostly but not entirely resolved in 1951, when agreements were reached between the International Association of Game and Fish Commissioners and most federal agencies as to how resident wildlife would be managed on federal lands.

Despite falling fur prices and an increase in damage claims, the commission continued to protect beavers, disallowing the department's request for a trapping season in 1951 and rejecting a recommendation in 1953 to remove all beavers from the Little Colorado River drainage. Finally, in 1955, the decision was made that no more beavers would be transplanted, and the following year the commission authorized a beaver-trapping season so fur trappers could be directed to problem areas.

Adjustments to the two big national game ranges, the Kofa and Cabeza Prieta, were less contentious. In 1956, the commission approved a 750-permit any-deer hunt on the Kofa to reduce competition with the refuge's featured species, desert bighorn sheep. The following year, another 500 any-deer permits were authorized for the Kofa by both Refuge Manager Gale Monson and the commission, while the legislature voted a $40,000 appropriation of Texas's money for the department to trap bighorn for eventual release in the Lone Star State. All of the deer hunts were approved that year by a unanimous vote of the commission at a meeting attended by 130 sportsmen, who were also delighted to hear that Monson was in favor of a bighorn sheep hunt. Although the Fish and Wildlife Service regional supervisor reneged on the agreement for a bighorn hunt in 1957, five bighorn permits were agreed to for the Kofa in 1958, along with a buck-only deer hunt.

Other Disagreements

In the meantime, the National Park Service continued its policy of banning grazing and hunting from the national parks. By agreement, the department was still in charge of resident wildlife. So when the Park Service complained of an overpopulation of deer on Grand Canyon National Park in 1956, the commission agreed to trap them and move the park's animals to the north Kaibab and the Cinder Hills area north of Flagstaff.

These arrangements were turned down by the Park Service as being akin to "put and take" deer hunting. Instead, an agreement was reached in 1957 for the department to help remove the "beggar deer" frequenting the roads and tourist areas, which constituted the biggest problem. This arrangement proved satisfactory, the department having a depredation specialist, Don Smith, supervise a capture operation. Finally, in 1962, a decision was made to translocate the remaining surplus animals to the Navajo Indian Reservation.

The federal entity causing the most acrimony when it came to wildlife matters was the US Army. The department had been concerned about military personnel poaching deer on the Navajo Ordnance Depot ever since 1945, and the return of Fort Huachuca to the Army in 1951 exacerbated the situation. The attitude of the base commanders was that base property was under military jurisdiction, and that included the game found there. Military brass had the right to set their own regulations and designate whomever they wanted to hunt and fish on base property.

Attitudes reached a boiling point in 1954 over the killing of deer in defiance of state law on both the Navajo Ordnance Depot and Fort Huachuca, where white-tailed deer were especially numerous. The Army's usurpation of state and federal hunting areas was a national issue in the mid-1950s, even more blatant actions having taken place on the Wichita National Wildlife Refuge and other bases. The situations in Arizona therefore became hot-button issues, not only with the commission, but with the AGPA in general and members Max Layton and Jerome Pratt in particular.

A series of lengthy demands and negotiations followed before it was finally agreed that only the commission could authorize hunting seasons on the military reservations, and that these hunts had to be justified by adequate survey and enforcement procedures performed either by department technicians or competent military personnel. The base commander had the right to restrict hunters and other hunt participants to military personnel and to not open military reservations to public hunting. Given these parameters, a cooperative deer hunt structure was approved on Fort Huachuca in 1956, an arrangement with the commission that remains in effect in modified form for military reservations today.

Relations between the commission and Army continued to be less than ideal, due to the public's being denied access to lands withdrawn by this particular branch of the military. This lack of involvement resulted in the commission's opposing (unsuccessfully) the annexation of additional federal land for the Army's Yuma Proving Ground in 1957.

One major Arizona landholder that the commission appeared to make some headway with after World War II was the Indian reservations. This cooperation contrasted with some of the commission's past actions, including the initial denial (in 1950) of a request by the Indian agent for the Fort Apache Indian Reservation to waive the state license requirement for the issuance of special $10 elk permits. At that time, the commission not only insisted that any permit holders buy a state license, it required them to pay the special $10 elk license fee.

But in 1952, the White Mountain Apaches and the commission agreed to authorize a 750-permit elk hunt on Fort Apache even though the San Carlos tribe had closed their elk hunt to non-Indians. That situation changed the following year, when the San Carlos tribe drafted its own game code, and the Navajos requested a game management program. The commission was willing to cooperate with the tribes, and in 1954 issued 500 any-elk permits on Fort Apache and 150 on the San Carlos. The department insisted that some semblance of proper management be adhered to, and the commission refused the San Carlos tribe's request for a 25-elk permit hunt in 1955 due to a lack of any survey data. Livestock interests on both reservations wanted elk numbers reduced and controlled; hence the request for any-elk permits. The San Carlos also wanted to remove all elk from the Mescal Mountains, which was regarded more as rangeland than elk habitat. Nonetheless, the commission approved 400 any-elk permits for Fort Apache that year, and later relented to approve 100 any-elk permits on the San Carlos.

In truth, the Indians and Bureau of Indian Affairs made a good-faith effort to become game managers in the Arizona tradition. Jim Sparks, an AGPA officer, was hired as recreation manager on Fort Apache, and the San Carlos Apaches formed their own three-man game commission and requested Willie Nozie be hired as a game ranger at $100 a month using department funds. But different nations and cultures were involved. Arizona rangers working the reservation hunts reported many problems working with the Indians, and disagreements by no means ceased. In 1955, the San Carlos tribe wanted to extend the javelina season 30 days, declaring in essence that they considered peccaries a pest, as this animal is "no good to us."

Both sides made concessions. The commission and department continued to cooperate with tribal requests in minor ways, donating two quarters of buffalo meat to the Indian BBQ in Phoenix in 1956 and transporting excess deer to the Navajo reservation. For the most part, the Indians continued to clear their hunts through the commission despite some of their requests being denied.

Eventually, bigger issues developed that would separate the tribes from the state. The San Carlos Indians petitioned for and succeeded in getting the "Mineral Strip" north of Aravaipa Canyon returned to them—an action opposed by the commission. Then, after a series of legal rulings in the 1960s stating the tribes were the sole owners of their game and fish resources, and that non-Indians did not have to possess state licenses to remove game and fish from Indian lands, the department and reservations went their separate ways. And so it remains to this day.

Forest Service Estimate of Big Game Populations, 1942
Source: US Forest Service Annual Wildlife Report, 1942, Table 1A, "Estimated Big Game Populations, Region 3 - Arizona"

Forest	Antelope	Black Bear	Rocky Mountain Mule Deer	Southwestern Mule Deer	Desert Mule Deer	Plains White-tailed Deer	Arizona White-tailed Deer	Elk	Bighorn	Peccary	Wild Turkey
Apache	20	100	--	3,300	--	--	3,500	280	--	--	1,600
Coconino	4,000	200	--	5,000	--	--	600	1,400	--	--	2,600
Coronado	10	90	--	--	250	--	12,000	--	70	1,400	600
Crook	--	200	--	1,000	100	--	9,600	70	--	3,000	700
Kaibab	700	20	10,000	2,400	--	--	--	130	30	--	400
Prescott	700	20	--	8,300	--	--	40	10	--	--	500
Santa Rita Exp. Range	--	--	--	--	45	--	--	--	--	--	--
Sitgreaves	60	40	--	1,400	--	--	60	1,860	--	--	1,600
Tonto	10	350	--	4,000	400	--	3,000	350	100	4,000	1,400
Total Arizona	**5,500**	**1,020**	**10,000**	**25,400**	**795**	**0**	**28,800**	**4,100**	**200**	**8,400**	**9,400**

Forest Service Estimate of Populations of Furbearers and Large Predators, 1942
Source: US Forest Service Annual Wildlife Report, 1942, Tables 1B and 1C, "Furbearers and Larger Predators (Estimated), Region 3 - Arizona"

Forest	Badger	Beaver	Fox	Mink	Muskrat	Raccoon	Ringtail	Skunk	Weasel	Bobcat	Coyote	Mountain Lion	Wolf
Apache	200	500	400	30	300	300	200	2,500	100	300	1,100	25	0
Coconino	400	100	2,000	--	300	1,000	100	4,000	1,000	1,500	4,500	30	2
Coronado	400	3	3,000	--	--	400	600	7,000	--	1,500	4,000	60	13
Crook	500	200	4,000	--	--	1,000	2,000	6,000	100	2,000	3,300	100	0
Kaibab	400	4	800	--	--	100	100	1,200	300	800	1,500	40	6
Prescott	500	50	3,000	--	200	2,000	700	4,000	100	1,300	4,000	60	0
Santa Rita Exp. Range	100	0	60	0	0	0	0	100	0	70	200	0	0
Sitgreaves	200	60	600	30	500	500	100	800	100	400	900	20	0
Tonto	500	200	6,000	-	200	3,000	4,000	10,000	1,000	3,000	9,000	120	0
Total Arizona	**3,200**	**1,117**	**19,860**	**60**	**1,500**	**8,300**	**7,800**	**35,600**	**2,700**	**10,870**	**28,500**	**455**	**21**

The estimated number of coyotes in the Coconino National Forest was raised from 2,800 in the 1941 report "at 1:3 ration bobcats to coyotes"

Forest Service Estimate of Big Game Harvest, 1942
Source: US Forest Service Annual Wildlife Report, 1942, Table 2, "Estimated Hunter Take of Big Game, Region 3 - Arizona"

Forest	Antelope	Black Bear	Rocky Mountain Mule Deer	Southwestern Mule Deer	Desert Mule Deer	Plains White-tailed Deer	Arizona White-tailed Deer	Elk	Peccary	Wild Turkey
Apache	--	7	--	100	--	--	20	20	--	40
Coconino	120	10	--	240	--	--	40	100	--	200
Coronado	--	--	--	--	30	--	400	--	40	--
Crook	--	6	--	40	30	--	160	--	30	20
Kaibab	30	1	564	463	--	--	--	9	--	140
Prescott	10	--	--	810	--	--	--	--	--	--
Santa Rita Exp. Range	--	--	--	--	--	--	--	--	--	--
Sitgreaves	5	2	--	100	--	--	3	140	50	50
Tonto	--	30	--	250	40	--	50	10	--	60
Total Arizona	**165**	**56**	**564**	**2,003**	**100**	**0**	**673**	**279**	**120**	**510**

SECTION IV

WILDLIFE MANAGEMENT'S HAPPY TIMES

1954–62

NEW APPROACHES TO MANAGING BIG AND SMALL GAME

David E. Brown

The average Arizona sportsman in the 1930s and 1940s was not an ardent big game hunter. He was most likely a shopkeeper or businessman, a laborer in a mine, or a utility company employee. A trip to the high country or a familiar mountain range during deer season constituted his annual big game hunt, and he most likely knew the rancher or forest ranger on lands where he hunted. Day trips to local areas to shoot doves, quail, or ducks comprised his small game hunting. Most of his fishing took place at the nearest reservoir or during a summer vacation in the White Mountains trout country. Hunting for antelope, elk, or bear was dreamed about more than participated in. Guides or outfitters were local men who did so for ready cash and not as a profession.

"Habitat" and "game management" were unfamiliar words. The factors impacting game numbers were assumed to be hunting and predators. Only a few hunters were experienced enough to be expected to get "their deer" every year. Does were brood stock and protected from hunting to leave enough game for "seed." Closed seasons and refuges prevented overkill. Such species as blue grouse, "fool quail" (Montezuma or Mearns' quail), and tree squirrels were either too rare or too "pretty" to hunt. Nongame animals, if considered at all, were divided into "beneficial species" and "varmints." From the ranks of such men came most members of the Arizona Game Protective Association, game wardens, game and fish commissioners, and even many of the early "technicians," as Pittman-Robertson biologists were called.

Federal-Aid projects initiated in the 1940s stressed life-history studies coupled with investigations into the impacts of range conditions and water developments. Species of concern, in rough order of importance, included turkey, deer, quail, doves, antelope, elk, waterfowl, and beaver. Trapping and transplanting programs for the above species assumed a high priority, but there were also specific studies such as the one determining the relationship between livestock and deer on the Kaibab. Such life-history studies often provided baseline data used to set hunt seasons and determine harvest numbers—important information for measuring the status of big game populations.[1]

Around World War II, a rapidly increasing human population fueled massive growth in the Federal-Aid funding system. Ensuing studies saw the development of survey techniques for indexing both big and small game populations, which in conjunction with data from check stations and hunt questionnaires, monitored the status of just about every game species in the state. As game populations were inventoried more carefully, more

[1]The first game harvest estimates in 1941 resulted from data obtained from hunt questionnaires and check stations (Arizona Game and Fish Commission 1942). Although undoubtedly conservative, these harvest estimates of 7,009 mule deer; 1,829 white-tailed deer; 2,152 wild turkeys; 966 javelina; 119 black bears; 494,379 Gambel's quail; 25,202 scaled quail; 219,146 cottontails; 424,486 mourning doves; 9,140 band-tailed pigeons; and 91,859 ducks and geese provided baseline data for more statistically sound data in later years and replaced US Forest Service estimates, which were merely guesses.

Steve Gallizioli with five drake pintails or sprig taken along the Gila River during the 1959–60 waterfowl season. Many department technicians were ardent hunters and fishermen who could be counted on to advocate more hunting and fishing, not less. (Courtesy of Wendell Swank)

complex hunt regulations dividing the state into zones, units, and management areas permitted more targeted harvest objectives.

By the late 1940s, survey techniques had been developed for most game species, with checking stations and hunter report cards from big game tags providing reasonably sound harvest data for big game animals. Money was available for land acquisition for such game animals as pronghorn antelope, and grazing boards were striving for a more equitable allocation of range resources (Arizona Game and Fish Commission 1951).

Other Federal-Aid studies provided predator-control money for studied animals, but not always an evaluation of the control itself. The refuge program, the major conservation strategy through the 1940s, was by the late 1940s being increasingly debunked, except in the case of waterfowl. Forage utilization studies in key areas were increasingly important, with much of the biologists' time spent on range surveys and plant evaluations. Area investigations produced a working knowledge of game habitats throughout the state, and cooperative agreements with the US Forest Service resulted in improved range conditions, with 60,000 acres of federal lands temporarily removed from stock grazing. Water developments for both big and small game continued to be constructed and assessed.

Attitudes about how to manage wildlife began to change in the 1950s, when the Arizona Game and Fish Department began hiring college graduates as game managers and the state experienced a resurgence in game numbers. Regulatory problems now often centered on the issue of having too many animals, rather than too few. Meetings of the Arizona Game and Fish Commission were increasingly taken up with technicians presenting slide shows of fence-line contrasts and overbrowsed range plants. Conflicts with stockmen intensified as range conditions assumed the role of being a primary limiting factor, replacing hunting and predators.

Not only were many of the new technicians such as John Russo, Wendell Swank, and Steve Gallizioli ardent hunters and fishermen, these "college boys" could always be counted on to advocate more hunting and fishing, not less. Their studies showed that weather and habitat conditions were the factors most often governing game and fish populations, and they tended to discount the importance of refuges and predators.

Such attitudes and conclusions were hard to accept for resident Arizona hunters who had grown up during times of scarcity. The new dictum appeared to be, "The more you harvest, the more you have," and it was not an easy sell. Some meetings of the Arizona Game and Fish Commission were attended by as many as 100 people and became so contentious they threatened to get out of control. Also present at these commission meetings were department staff, technicians, and AGPA members. Although the now five-man commission actively sought public comment, and an increasing number of "any-deer" hunts generated considerable controversy, the commission approved most department recommendations.

By 1960, management work plans and publications were available for nearly every game species. The state had been divided into seven regions and some 50 game management units. While the rangers had always participated in such management activities as stocking fish and conducting game surveys, a growing cadre of college-educated "wildlife managers" was now making the hunt recommendations for their respective districts. To justify these recommendations, wildlife managers took browse measurements, conducted game surveys, and relied on the advice of technicians in the Game Management Division. Annual Federal-Aid completion reports were written by wildlife managers rather than personnel in the Phoenix office. In 1960, the introduction to the department's 50-year progress report boldly claimed that, "These are the good old days."

Research biologists had also made their mark. The Cooperative Wildlife Research Unit, after getting off to a rocky start with the commission, began conducting wildlife studies in the early 1950s with the guidance of the Arizona Game and Fish Department, University of Arizona, US Fish and Wildlife Service, and Wildlife Management Institute. Even more important, the unit was graduating entry-level wildlife biologists and training graduate students.

Unit research included investigations into the use of browse plants and water developments as part of life-history studies to determine the limiting factors on desert mule deer, white-tailed deer, elk, javelina, wild turkeys, Gambel's quail, scaled quail, tassel-eared squirrels, cottontails, and mourning and white-winged doves. As a result, the most important forage plants were identified. Fenced exclosures enabled researchers to demonstrate overuse by excess numbers of deer as well as cattle. Some of the most important and practical findings concluded that quail reproduction and population dynamics were determined by seasonal rains and the vitamin content in green feed during the breeding season. Hunting was shown to have virtually no impact on quail population densities, a conclusion also reached for cottontail rabbits and other small game species. The investigations showed that breeding season, recruitment rate, and population dynamics depended almost entirely on nutritional levels. No small game species were demonstrated to benefit from water developments.

The department's own Research Division, created in 1958 and funded under Federal-Aid Project W-78-R, made additional contributions. By 1959, 15 different studies were in place, including evaluations of survey techniques that included call counts as a means of indexing quail numbers prior to setting hunting seasons. Other studies investigated methodologies used to estimate deer and elk numbers and measure population trends for turkeys. The effects of hunting on desert mule deer and other game species were studied and evaluated, resulting in more generous hunt regulations. Also investigated were the impacts of disease on collared peccaries, and it was found that the cause of blindness in elk was *Elaeophora*, a parasite transmitted by the green-headed horse fly.

After 1960, research efforts concentrated more on habitat issues than on life histories. Attempts were made to determine the impacts of the pinyon-juniper removal programs then in vogue with the Forest Service. Other watershed treatment projects being conducted by the Salt River Project and Forest Service on Beaver Creek were also evaluated, including a delayed study on the use of herbicides to control chaparral. Toward the end of the 1950s, biologists began research on the use of immobilization drugs for capturing and marking various species of animals—studies that would revolutionize the wildlife management profession by allowing the capture, radio-tracking, and monitoring of marked animals.

The following sections note advances and changes in the management of major game species.

Deer

No game species were as important to Arizona sportsmen as mule deer and white-tailed deer. Yet, the factors controlling deer numbers were little understood in the 1940s, as was the status of the animals themselves. Not only were three species of mule deer recognized as occurring in Arizona (Rocky Mountain, desert or Crook's, and *buro* deer), many hunters and some biologists believed there was more than one species of white-tailed deer in the state. So prevalent was the belief in a diminutive "Sonora fantail," or *cavito*, that a 25-permit-only white-tailed deer hunt was authorized in a portion of the Baboquivari Mountains to determine if such an animal did indeed exist (it does not). All deer being conservatively managed under buck-only hunt regulations for years, it was therefore a pleasant shock when deer populations rapidly increased after World War II. Estimates using hunter report cards showed deer harvest numbers going from 6,300 bucks in 1946 to more than 33,000 deer in 1958, with hunt success rising from 18% to a high of 40%. Hunter numbers followed the trend, attaining an all-time high of 94,302 deer hunters in 1962, who took nearly 36,000 deer (see Appendix D, Table D-2).

Managing a burgeoning deer herd and protecting habitat were both challenging and controversial. The state was first split into north and south zones and then subdivided

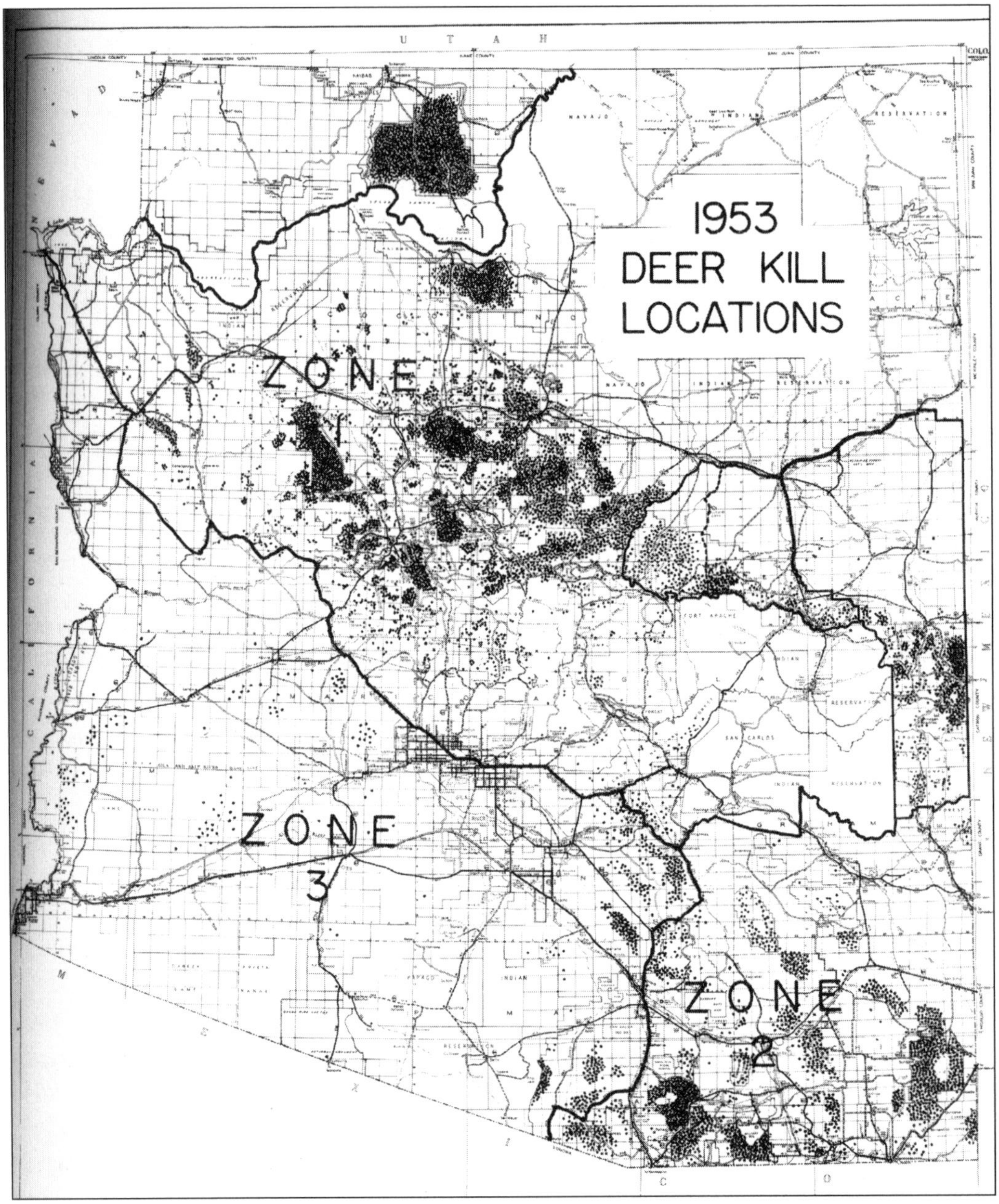

Deer harvest location map derived from hunt questionnaires sent out after the 1953 season. Plotting big game kills from hunter questionnaire reports was a major program of the Game Management Division during the 1950s. Note also the deer hunt zones then in effect rather than today's game management units. Zones 2 and 3 (white-tailed deer and desert mule deer) were also regarded as the south zone and subject to different season proposals than the north zone. (AGFD files)

into zones, areas, and game management units. When the commission approved 12,000 any-deer or "doe-hunting" permits in 1956, resistance to "modern deer management" was actively demonstrated, particularly in southeastern Arizona. But the technicians persevered, and the commission, under chairman Jack Mantle, stuck by them. Refuges were abolished, deer surveys intensified, deer tags revamped, and dot maps of kill locations promulgated. Department publications such as Swank's 1958 *Mule Deer in Arizona Chaparral* stressed the need for larger deer harvests, while the north Kaibab Plateau deer herd was held at lower levels than desired to allow cliffrose plants to recover. By the time game management was made a separate division in 1958 and the wildlife manager program went into effect in 1960, Arizona's deer herds had been brought under control.

Elk

The progression of the situation with elk is interesting, in that sportsmen and the AGPA were ahead of the department in allowing elk numbers to increase. When elk hunting resumed after World War II, the department's plan, worked out with Forest Service biologists, was to hold elk herds to 1947 levels and keep elk from expanding west of Sycamore Canyon and the Coconino National Forest. The reason for this conservative approach was to reduce livestock-elk competition and alleviate depredations on oats and other dry-farmed crops then raised on homesteads located on "parks" within the national forests. Although a number of elk depredation problems were resolved by the department's fencing the fields with electric and five-strand barbed wire, elk depredations continued to be a major issue, with the department issuing depredation elk permits to some landowners and killing elk as a last resort.

Forest Service agreements and rancher-sportsmen committee resolutions aside, keeping a lid on elk numbers proved difficult from both biological and political standpoints. Although the number of game refuges in elk country was reduced and significant numbers of "any-elk" permits were issued, elk numbers continued to rise until depredation complaints came to dominate the discussion at commission meetings.

Realizing that higher elk numbers came at the price of fewer deer, department biologists opted for an open hunting season in select areas in 1953, selling 6,400 tags and harvesting 1,500 elk in the process. When sportsmen wanted less hunting and more elk in 1957, the public was cautioned that elk hunting might now be the best it would ever be, due to competition with livestock for forage and increased recreational encroachments in the high country. Again, in 1960, elk numbers were said to be at maximum levels. A "no vacancy" sign was put up stating the carrying capacity was believed to have been approached, with the department issuing a warning that "maintaining good elk hunting through the years to come is going to be a difficult task" (AGFD 1962).

Such was not to be the case. A desire for more elk, numerous water developments, and the animal's adaptable nature, all conspired for a future increase in elk numbers.

Pronghorn Antelope

Although pronghorn were once decried as an animal that would probably never support hunting in Arizona, the first pronghorn hunts were held in 1941 and 1942. They were justified as "needed" to reduce intraspecific competition and correct an unbalanced sex ratio. When the hunt in 1943 resulted in the illegal killing of an excessive number of does, the season was closed. Standardized aerial surveys were instituted in 1944, and when fawn recruitment rates were judged sufficiently improved, a more carefully controlled hunt was authorized in 1948.

Hunting, coupled with an aggressive trapping and transplanting program that saw Anderson Mesa pronghorn successfully translocated to such historic Arizona habitats as San Rafael Valley, Sulphur Springs Valley, the Arizona Strip, and Bonita Prairie on the Fort Apache Indian Reservation, produced steady improvement in pronghorn numbers through the 1950s. With populations in some areas appearing to reach maximum carrying capacity, some biologists thought the species to be density-dependent, i.e., responding to higher harvests with increased recruitment rates. As a result, "any-antelope" permits were issued until harvest levels peaked in the late 1950s and early 1960s. In 1962, 1,420 antelope permits were issued, including 130 any-antelope and doe antelope permits with 755 animals harvested (see Appendix D, Table D-3).

Javelina

Collared peccaries represented another management success story. Although these little desert "pigs" were regarded initially as little more than a novelty if not a nuisance by many Arizonans, a life-history study by technician Ted Knipe (1957) showed they were not a threat to Arizona's rangelands, as claimed by certain stockmen. Rather, the javelina was a desirable game animal that could support limited sport hunting. This attitude, coupled with complimentary articles by outdoor writers such as Bob Housholder and Jack O'Connor (1961), resulted in this animal's becoming a valued trophy for both resident and nonresident hunters. Management prescriptions limiting firearms hunting to two weeks in late winter, along with several transplants of javelina north of Wickenburg, resulted in this species gradually expanding its numbers and distribution. By 1962, more than 20,000 javelina hunters were taking some 4,350 javelina, with archery hunters accounting for another 100 or so as this weapon became increasingly popular for hunting javelina.

Bighorn

No animal's status was more improved during this period due to a change in management approach than desert bighorn sheep. Though they were protected in refuges, some dating back to the 1920s, bighorn numbers languished until Russo's study, which took advantage of 10 years of data collected on the Kofa and Cabeza Prieta game ranges. It showed this species was suffering from competition with other ungulates, disease, and neglect more than illegal hunting. Russo (1956a) recommended a controlled hunt both to generate support for an active management program and to build a constituency of hunters dedicated to the animal's welfare.

The result was a limited hunt on aged rams that was expanded each year without any detriment to desert bighorn sheep populations. A bighorn trapping program, initiated in 1956, was also undertaken along with an any-deer hunt in the Kofa Mountains to reduce competition with desert mule deer. Trapping and transplanting sheep proved to be a

John Russo's research on desert bighorn sheep showed the species was suffering more from competition with other ungulates, disease, and neglect than from illegal hunting, and would benefit from a controlled hunt. (AGFD files)

difficult undertaking despite the allocation of a 120-acre holding pen in Aravaipa Canyon. Persistence prevailed, and "direct releases" eventually led to a translocation program that saw this species again occupying most of its historic range in Arizona. By 1962, more than a dozen game management units were open to sheep hunting, with 89 sheep hunters harvesting 27 bighorns.

Wild Turkey

The commission always regarded turkeys as an enigmatic species subject to periodic declines and even disappearances. Believing that bobcat and other predators were impacting numbers, biologists began studying the life history of this species as soon as Federal-Aid funds became available. Restocking vacant habitats was also a priority, and wild birds were trapped and transplanted through the early 1960s (Arizona Game and Fish Commission 1942; AGFD 1956, 1962). When Bob Reeves, Harley Shaw, and other technicians found habitat conditions on the summer and winter ranges to be limiting factors, turkey management shifted to protecting herbaceous vegetation and mast supplies rather than providing refuges and predator control.

As a result, hunting restrictions were relaxed, permit numbers increased, and shotguns made legal weapons. Transplants accelerated, and the successful introduction of wild turkeys to non-historic habitats on the north Kaibab and Mount Trumbull made for even greater hunting opportunity. Other transplants, particularly those to Mount Graham and other southern Arizona mountain ranges, were less successful.

Black Bear

The status of black bears was more tenuous, with these animals declared to be big game, game, and predatory animals at various times for certain localities. No bear studies were initiated during the period, and the animal's welfare was largely left to the black bear's adaptable nature. Closed seasons were always in place, and bear tags were required for their taking after 1958. Gradually, with better range management practices and fewer depredation problems, bear numbers increased. Harvest data were not collected on this species until 1964, when 178 bears were reported taken in the state (AGFD 1988).

Small Game

The importation and release of exotic birds erratically subsided as emphasis was placed on resident game birds. Trapping and transplanting quail ceased as inventory techniques improved, culminating in a hunter report-card system to monitor harvest levels in 1962. Quail were the species of primary concern, and at one time five full-time biologists were studying Gambel's, scaled, and Mearns' quail. As life-history and limiting-factor data accumulated, it was shown that hunting had little or no effect on quail numbers. Population levels of the various species fluctuated with changes in food and grass cover—factors dependent on variations in the weather.

As a result, quail hunt regulations were liberalized, the early December season being split in 1958 into a 15-day early fall season and a 23-day late hunt. When 1960 proved to be an excellent quail year, the season was lengthened to 56 days and the bag limit increased from 10 to 15. Opening weekend check stations showed 5.2 quail per hunter being taken at Oracle Junction in 1960 vs. 2.5 in 1959. Further relaxations in the hunt regulations followed, and in 1960 a two-day Mearns' quail season was authorized, during which 116 hunters killed 47 quail.

After the white-winged dove season was closed in 1941 and 1942, dove hunting steadily improved through the 1950s with the planting of suitable grain crops and a September 1 season in place. Banding studies not only determined the migratory habits of both dove species, band recoveries showed that even in the highest hunter concentration areas only about 5% of the mourning doves and 7% of white-winged doves were being harvested. Hunter success at Arlington was 11 doves per day, compared to a mean of 8.75 for 1954–59. This period was the heyday of Arizona dove-shooting, with the percentage of whitewings in the bag going from 17.8% in 1953 to 40.5% in 1957.

Cottontail hunters were also enjoying banner years. Longer seasons and a standardized bag limit were adopted as studies showed hunting had little influence on rabbit numbers. The same was also true for tree squirrels, a standardized 25-day season and daily bag limit of five squirrels becoming the norm during the 1950s.

Although the federal government closed the season on band-tailed pigeons in the Southwest in 1950 due to a decline in the number of birds, a snipe season was authorized in 1960.

When the first statewide small game questionnaires were mailed out in 1961, responses indicated seasonal bags of 303,980 quail, 613,537 mourning doves, 302,668 whitewings, 185,795 cottontails, and 5,332 tree squirrels.

Waterfowl

Increasing or even maintaining waterfowl numbers was more of a challenge. A series of waterfowl investigations and cooperative studies with federal wildlife agencies included a major survey of waterfowl habitats along the lower Colorado and Gila rivers in 1951. These and other investigations indicated a need to acquire and develop waterfowl habitat in these areas if ducks and geese were not to lose out to the developments then taking place. Not only ducks and geese but all water birds were being displaced by Bureau of Reclamation and other government projects transforming waterfowl wintering habitats along the Colorado and Gila rivers into farms and water delivery systems. Compounding this loss was the fact that nesting ducks were suffering from an increase in recreational developments in the White Mountains and on Anderson Mesa (Arizona Game and Fish Commission 1954).

The result was a department program that would use Pittman-Robertson and other Federal-Aid monies to acquire and develop lands and waters at Mittry Lake, Topock Marsh, and Cibola on the lower Colorado River, and Arlington and Robbins Butte wildlife areas along the middle Gila River (AGFD 1955a). Other potential waterfowl management areas were also investigated in Navajo (Winslow Lake), Cochise (Parks Lake), Pinal (Picacho Reservoir), and Graham (Cluff Ranch) counties.

The main thrust was along the Colorado and Gila rivers, where it was hoped that, in conjunction with the federal refuges being developed at Havasu and Imperial, waterfowl could be managed through the alternate use of refuges and management areas to both "hold" waterfowl in Arizona *and* maintain or expand hunting opportunities. Other species in waterfowl management areas, such as mule deer, quail, and white-winged doves, would of course also benefit, as they would with the federal withdrawal of a 6,896-acre greenbelt of tamarisk and mesquite-infested lands along the Gila River (AGFD 1955b).

The commission had little experience in land management, and wildlife management areas proved difficult to administer. Many obstacles had to be overcome, including evicting squatters, securing restrictive water rights, constructing water delivery systems, supervising farming leases, and cooperating with agencies with different management objectives. Nonetheless, the department persevered in developing five wildlife areas along the Colorado and Gila rivers, including 2,500 acres of patented and state land at Cibola, 500 acres of which was farmland.

Other waterfowl management developments included instituting a standardized system of winter waterfowl surveys in 1956, waterfowl banding programs for both nesting and migrating ducks, the use of check stations, and better coordination with the flyway objectives worked out in cooperation with the Fish and Wildlife Service. The effectiveness of Arizona's refuges at holding waterfowl was attested to in 1958, when 10,000 more ducks and 2,000 more geese were counted on the winter waterfowl survey than in 1957. A stable system of managed waterfowl refuges allowed Arizona to participate in a standard 90-day waterfowl season approved in 1962, when the bag limit on Canada geese was increased attendant with more generous bag limits being approved for the Pacific Flyway to which Arizona belonged.

Furbearers and Nongame Animals

A decline in fur prices after World War II resulted in less attention being paid to furbearers, other than depredating beavers and muskrats. Although the department was still trapping, transplanting, and pelting beavers in the early 1950s, and battling for jurisdiction with Havasu and Imperial national wildlife refuges over muskrats, interest in even these species declined, and the department's Fur Conservation Division was disbanded. When Housholder requested permission to capture and collect two river otters on Black River, his request was denied. Nobody was assigned to verify the animal's occurrence, despite its absence from nearly all of its former habitats.

Interest in predator control on the part of the commission and department remained strong through the early 1950s, and a predator program coordinator (Jay Klaus) was assigned to work with the Fish and Wildlife Service on control-related issues (Arizona

Game and Fish Commission 1949). With Pittman-Robertson monies now available for predator control, the department was soon spending up to $30,000 annually on this effort (Arizona Game and Fish Commission 1951). However, with game numbers increasing, the importance of predator control to the game management program subsided, and the commission would eventually reduce the department budget for such work to $18,000 per year (AGFD 1956).

Although predator control continued to be regarded as an important management procedure by some, the stated opinion within the department was now that "over-all game populations were not as a rule influenced very greatly by predation" (AGFD 1960). As a result, the department ceased its predator-control efforts while continuing to be a partner with the Fish and Wildlife Service and Arizona Livestock Sanitary Board in joint predator-control operations aimed at benefiting select species such as pronghorn. Department participation decreased further when the Livestock Sanitary Board began paying bounties on lions and wolves in 1947. Although the payment of bounties on lions soon became a significant expenditure, the payment of a wolf bounty was now a rare event (see Appendix D, Table D-2).

After 1962, the status of most game species leveled off or began to decline. Elk numbers and harvests continued to rise, and unlimited turkey hunting would again be reinstated, but deer harvests lessened, especially in the case of Rocky Mountain mule deer units on the Mogollon Rim. And although deer harvest figures on the department's Three Bar Wildlife Area were still increasing, fawn recruitment rates were falling. Survey figures also showed antelope fawn recruitment dipping, so any-deer and any-antelope permits were reduced accordingly.

Changing demographics and development pressures meant that future concerns would focus more on land and water management projects than on game management per se. The "good old days" were coming to an end.

THE HEYDAY OF THE ARIZONA GAME PROTECTIVE ASSOCIATION

David E. Brown, Joseph Monfeli, and Melanie Tluczek

Despite the loss of manpower attendant with World War II, hunting and fishing license sales doubled between 1941 and 1945 (see Appendix D, Table D-1). Given the lack of other conservation organizations, the Arizona Game Protective Association was uniquely poised to take advantage of this new pool of potential members. And it did.

With money now available, Bill Misak was hired to edit the October 1944 issue of the AGPA's magazine, *Arizona Wildlife and Sportsman*. Arizona Game and Fish Commission news remained a regular feature, with "Hunting and Fishing Regulations" providing an up-to-date rundown on any changes in the game and fish laws. Contributing authors Charles Niehuis and Jack O'Connor continued to submit provocative editorials on such management issues as what to do with desert bighorn sheep, the need to issue deer tags, and strategies for more effective predator control. An "Arms and Ammunition" column reported on the pros and cons of select firearms and provided ballistic information for the growing number of gun enthusiasts.

A Growing Influence, 1946–50

By war's end the AGPA was an affiliate-driven organization within a responsive state organization presided over by former local officers such as James A. Beaman and Max Layton. It was closely aligned with the commission and Arizona Game and Fish Department. The AGPA's influence with the latter was greatly enhanced by the appointment of Tom Kimball as department director in March 1948, the association now acting as one leg of a three-legged stool determining hunting and fishing regulations and policy. Not only did the AGPA dominate commission meetings, with local delegates sitting as a block to vote on agenda items, the resolutions passed at the AGPA's annual convention were acted upon by the commission as if they were department recommendations.

Governors and legislators on the Fish and Game Committee attended both commission meetings and annual AGPA conventions, a fitting tribute to a politically active and influential organization. Also present at these convocations were the Arizona Cattlegrowers Association, Arizona Woolgrowers Association, and representatives of the US Forest Service, Arizona Farm Bureau, and Everett Mercer of the US Biological Survey. To formulate or address impending regulations and legislative matters, the AGPA maintained an executive director and standing committees regulating changes in the game code, sportsman-stockman relations, and other issues of concern.

Increasingly adding to the AGPA's political clout was Ben Avery, who now covered all commission meetings for the *Arizona Republic* as did Dick Lee for the *Phoenix Gazette*. Avery, an outspoken AGPA member of long standing, had a history of commenting on a wide range of issues, from the posting of state lands to the protection of bullfrogs and the promulgation of minutiae on firearm regulations. He now not only had the ear of the AGPA's executive committee and the Arizona Game and Fish Commission, his column gave him cachet with both the general public and a number of influential government figures. His opinion (and column) therefore served as a sounding board on all sorts of environmental issues. He was indeed becoming "Mr. Outdoor Arizona," as he would one day be known (Smith 2000).

Ben Avery, ca. 1960, when he was on the staff at the Arizona Republic. *(Courtesy of the* Arizona Republic)

The executive director and editor were the AGPA's only paid positions, as the association's total membership still hovered around just 3,000 members. Because the AGPA remained an activist organization driven by issues of interest to its affiliates, the president and director had to focus on local as well as state issues, and there was much infighting as to which causes to support. Executive sessions became increasingly common, and there were several internal reorganizations.

The one issue that was sure to result in consistent if heavily debated support was a demand for increased predator control. Fueled by PARC Supervisor Mercer, Director Kimball, and commissioners such as Charles Beach, AGPA Executive Director Layton's commitment to predator control was absolute. Nor did this dedication go unrewarded. In 1949, the commission voted to match the livestock owners' contribution of $30,000 to the state predator-control fund. Potentially controversial items such as the expanded use of strychnine, cyanide, and Compound 1080 were wholeheartedly supported, save a few objections from individual members such as Charles Vorhies and Allan Phillips, who pointed out that the sportsmen's monies were also being spent on jackrabbit, rodent, and grasshopper control.

There were other issues generating interest. The Kaibab was developing into an AGPA *cause célèbre* with a plethora of recommendations by everyone from Jack O'Connor to former national forest supervisor Walter Mann on how to best manage the growing deer herd there. Nor could any hunt recommendations regarding turkey, deer, or elk be passed without polling delegates from the AGPA's affiliates and getting their input—members even participated in the game surveys used as a basis for the recommendations. The commission even solicited the AGPA's recommendations as to whether game refuges should be retained or retired.

Resolutions included propositions wanting bears removed from the list of predators and an equitable solution to the angler licensing problems attendant with the states of California and Nevada sharing the Colorado River. Support for the beaver transplanting program remained popular, and the development of Long Lake near Show Low as a fishing and waterfowl area nearly became an AGPA crusade. Increasing the number of available game fish fueled resolutions to expand Williams Creek hatchery on the Fort Apache Indian Reservation and build a warm-water hatchery below Davis Dam on the Colorado River.

Other resolutions of note during this period included proposals to raise license fees and Game and Fish Department salaries—issues again reflecting the closeness of the two organizations. Still other AGPA recommendations and resolutions reflected minor if not frivolous concerns. These included banning .22s and shotguns for taking turkeys; prohibiting turkey trapping in the White Mountains for translocation to California; and adjusting season dates, bag limits, and other hunt regulations to take advantage of holidays and work schedules.

Not all issues were resolved to the AGPA's satisfaction, nor were all of its actions successful. The Winslow affiliate's desire for a Sitgreaves management area similar to the Kaibab got a cold shoulder from the commission. A more substantial letdown after World War II involved the AGPA's longstanding touch-and-go relationship with the Arizona State Legislature. Despite a well-reasoned argument in "An Ear to the Earth" column in *Arizona Wildlife and Sportsman*, calling on the locals to get more active with the legislature and oppose the Wimberly Bill moving the game and fish budget to the general fund, the bill passed in 1949.

Once again, the legislature had control over the department's budget when it came to appropriating Pittman-Robertson monies. Although the new appointees to the House Fish and Game Committee had been regarded as friends of the AGPA and department, both were soon decrying the legislature's earmarking appropriations that kept department salaries low. More successful was a combined effort of the AGPA and National Rifle Association to defeat a firearms registration bill—an alliance of forces that persists into present times.

The hiring of Bill Sage as editor in November 1944 resulted in *Arizona Wildlife and Sportsman* taking on a more professional appearance and publishing schedule. Also, under the editors who followed, especially Niehuis, there was an attempt to better inform the membership. With articles on subjects as diverse as the status of the black-footed ferret and the native fishes of the Colorado River, the magazine attempted to fill a natural-history niche ignored by the popular press. Game species were naturally most often featured, and the editorial content in such columns as "Editor's Notebook," "Count and Classify," "Hitting the High Spots," and "Tom Kimball Talks" served both to promote the policies then taking shape within the AGPA and Arizona Game and Fish Department and to ventilate some of the conflicts involved.

Columns of special interest to sportsmen included Carroll Lemon's "Calling the Shots," which replaced O'Connor's earlier "Arms and Ammunition" column. Profiles of Game and Fish Department and AGPA personalities became regular features, as did obituaries of past members. By 1949, the AGPA was producing a newsletter in addition to a regularly appearing magazine. Nonetheless, costs remained a concern, and one affiliate, Cochise County Sportsmen, formally moved that the department take over what was now *Arizona Wildlife Sportsman*—a proposal rejected if for no other reason than that the department was now interested in publishing its own magazine.

Not all of the editorials, especially those written by Director J. Charles McWilliams and Niehuis, kept to safe subjects such as hunting and fishing stories. Niehuis not

Charles Niehuis was an AGPA member of long standing whose contributions to Arizona Wildlife and Sportsman *covered the gamut from hunting and fishing tips to controversial conservation issues. (Courtesy of* Arizona Highways *and the Niehuis estate)*

only covered the various sides of the Kaibab issue, he wrote a column defending federal refuges against the state's jurisdictional complaints and explored several other difficult issues, including the then-evolving "Sagebrush Rebellion," destined to become the definitive land-management issue of the 1950s.

In this same vein, the AGPA came out firmly for retaining the public domain, even going so far as to call for a revision of the laws governing the use of state lands (Title 37) to manage such lands on a sustainable basis and make them available for multiple use. Risking an always tenuous alliance with the livestock industry and "Arizona's cowboy legislature," Niehuis opposed any attempt to transfer national forests and other public lands to the state, describing the state's land as chronically overgrazed. Although Niehuis and the executive committee received much blowback from such editorials, the AGPA stuck to its guns, appointing special committees to determine the ramifications of any proposed land use legislation.

Niehuis and other contributors also aired a debate over refinements in fishing policy and the need to protect Forest Service watersheds as trout producers. Originating with the White Mountains sportsman's club, a movement to replace fish hatchery quantity with wild-raised "quality" had become a point of contention in fisheries management. A guest editorial by Les Quen argued that by restricting certain streams to fly-fishing only, and limiting fishermen to only one or two fish, Arizona's fishing ethic would be more in line with natural recruitment and less dependent on artificial propagation. This proposition was rebutted by Avery and the department's fish biologists, the hatchery program only recently having acquired Page Springs and Williams Creek hatcheries.

Time to Reload, 1950–52

Local influences, no matter how strong, did not always translate into power at the state level. Although new affiliates continued to be charted, total membership levels declined by nearly 1,000 in 1949 and the AGPA's roster again dropped to about 3,000 members, where it stagnated. Being a locally oriented organization, while a source of strength when promoting regional concerns, could be a handicap when it came to settling state and national issues. The result was again much infighting and a reluctance to send money to the state organization. So great was the acrimony that in 1950 Alfred Paul, chair of the House Fish and Game Committee, chastised the AGPA in a two-hour off-the-record discussion on how the local affiliates were crippling the political power of the organization. With local affiliates reluctant to share their dues with the AGPA headquarters in Phoenix, it was all the executive board could do to continue to field an executive director and publish the magazine.

A chronic shortage of funds prohibited the AGPA from sending delegates to national conventions and participating in out-of-state meetings with other conservation organizations. As such, the AGPA, despite being accepted as the Arizona affiliate of the National Wildlife Federation, was destined to remain a state force with little impact on federal legislation. Nor was there much opportunity to participate in joint conservation efforts with other organizations in the Southwest, as there were few organizations to meet with even if travel money had been available. Lack of funds meant little ability to support special studies or projects. Even recruitment programs and youth projects, favorite causes of both the locals and the state organization, languished for lack of financial support. Because of failures in funding and follow-through, the AGPA eventually would stop sponsoring local scout troops, cease its efforts to form a Junior Arizona Game Protective Association, and only half-heartedly support the national Junior Wildlife Federation program.

The one juvenile recruitment effort that attained a modicum of success was preparation of a conservation education manual for teachers to use in the state's school system. Persistently pushed by AGPA presidents Layton, Joe Dora, and others, this was one program that both the state organization and local affiliates could support. Nonetheless, despite some minor allocations of less than $2,500, and the manual's being accepted in a few schools, this program too would eventually fall by the wayside.

Not that there wasn't plenty of controversy. With deer, elk, and antelope numbers rising, numerous opinions arose as to how to best maintain the gains so recently won. As often as not, the AGPA challenged at least some part of the recommendations made by the Game and Fish Department's technicians, so commission meetings generated lively debates, with local affiliates lobbying to form voting coalitions. Several of the "newer" fish and game management procedures such as antlerless-deer hunting and fish poisoning remained controversial, as they conflicted with long-standing sensibilities. Even regulations about whether or not to have a closed season on roadrunners generated controversy and a lot of ink—the bird at different times being considered a protected species or a predator.

The biggest hullabaloo to stimulate the AGPA came about as a reaction to a movement by the stockmen. The Sagebrush Rebellion was gathering steam throughout the West, and Arizona was included in a proposal to transfer federal lands, including the national forests, to the states. Nothing generated AGPA opposition more than a proposal to take away a member's place to hunt and fish, and this was one issue that all of the locals could agree on. The lands administrated by the Arizona State Land Department, besides being overgrazed, had a long history of access problems. Transferring such places as Big Lake and the north Kaibab to the state was unthinkable. The AGPA's Land Committee

Report came out strongly in favor of Forest Service ownership—at least until legislation was passed that provided better protection and husbandry for state lands under a multiple-use mandate.

Egregious actions by a handful of ranchers had also set the stage for a battle royal. Niehuis, Avery, and Lee Kirby had all written editorials on the costs of range degradation to Arizona's wildlife, and there was an escalating conflict over elk depredations in the Flagstaff area, where at least one rancher had killed elk to protect his crops. Adding fuel to the fire was a full-page letter in *Arizona Wildlife Sportsman* by a New Mexico rancher taking the AGPA to task for being cowards and not supporting their state over the federal government. These were fighting words that solidified AGPA support for the Forest Service and opposition to any transfer of national forest or Taylor Grazing Act land either to the state or to private ownership.

One result of the Sagebrush Rebellion was a fraying of the AGPA's relationship with Gov. Howard Pyle, who resented the implication that the state's land management was inferior to the federal government's. This action also offended some members of the legislature, the AGPA's relationship with that body having recently soured when the Arizona State Senate assumed the right to confirm or veto commission appointments.

Nonetheless, the AGPA stuck by its guns, publishing several in-depth editorials and articles by Niehuis and Avery supporting the association's position. These articles did not take on the livestock industry per se; instead, they opposed any legislation that would result in fewer places to hunt and fish. For the most part, these were not fiery rebuttals but carefully worded essays pointing out the generally good relations between Arizona ranchers, the Forest Service, and the AGPA and emphasizing how all could continue to work together. As for the elk killings, readers were advised not to avenge past actions by committing acts of vandalism, but to work with the sportsman-stockman committee and the Game and Fish Department to prevent, or at least alleviate, future depredations.

Other letters and editorials in the magazine reflected the AGPA's increasing endorsement of wilderness areas, detailed some stormy sessions with the commission (which wanted to hold elk numbers to present levels), and expressed a desire to have Arrington replaced as chief of game management. It was also proudly pointed out that the commission had appropriated $29,153.42 in 1952 for predator control as opposed to the Livestock Sanitary Board's $15,000, more than paying for any additional damage done to ranchers due to elk. Further issues of importance included a demand for more pay for the Game and Fish Department director and the agency's employees and the need for a resolution to the long-standing problem of reciprocal fishing license agreements with California and Nevada on the Colorado River.

The magazine too continued to change. Charles E. "Ernie" Douglas had replaced George Richard as editor in 1950, and was in turn replaced by Niehuis in 1951. Although the magazine continued to include the "Conservation Pledge" on its masthead, the byline was now changed from "Official Publication of the AGPA" to "The Voice of Arizona Outdoorsmen." The magazine also announced a revised mission statement, to wit: Fight for the rights of Arizona's hunters and fishermen and provide a more up-to-date news format. Although Niehuis would only serve as editor for a few months before being replaced by Chuck Maybery, he wrote much of the copy during his tenure, which saw a doubling of circulation. As he had before being editor, Niehuis continued to write after his departure, his more substantial material appearing in *Arizona Wildlife Sportsman* with general-interest articles written by Grits Gresham, Ernie Mulch, and other contributors.

The early 1950s also saw Avery become the AGPA's chief spokesperson, his newspaper columns broadcasting the organization's actions and calming concerns within the legislature and governor's office. His work on the sportsman-stockman committee resulted in a compromise on bear regulations and the approval of standard signs regarding public access. Avery also worked with the department to resolve differences between it, the commission, and the AGPA over deer and elk hunt recommendations (the AGPA wanted fewer elk and deer taken than the department). Avery's principal complaint with the department was that it had grown complacent and needed a more modern approach to warm-water fish management—without stating just what improvements he deemed needed.

The department was not the only organization accused of clinging to the past. A major debate now took place within the AGPA over the claim that some members were reluctant to accept modern game and fish management techniques and were hindering the commission's goal of modernizing the department. Improved game and fish numbers came with a price, as department technicians claimed there were now too many "rough" and small fish. What may have been worse, game technicians were now proposing any-deer hunts to reduce deer numbers. Conservative by nature, the sensibilities of many AGPA members were also offended by the widespread use of Compound 1080 to kill predators and toxaphene to kill nongame fish. Other evolving controversies concerned what to do about an increasing deer herd on the Kaibab and reports of the military hunting deer on Fort Huachuca and the Navajo Ordinance Depot outside the parameters of state seasons.

Controversy being good for recruitment, the AGPA had risen to the occasion.

Glory Years, 1953–55

The mid-1950s was a time for growth and rebuilding. Presidents included Lee Hover, Chuck Morgan, and L. C. Dingess—two-year terms having become regular with the re-election of Hover in 1954. Layton was executive director and Maybery editor of a smaller, color-cover version of *Arizona Wildlife Sportsman*. The AGPA's bylaws had been redone in 1951, and in 1953 a new logo showing the head of a bighorn sheep ram replaced the former antelope buck. Jack Mantle of Tucson, an AGPA stalwart, was appointed to what was now a five-man commission, where he would serve for an even longer time than Beach. The AGPA and commission were now on such friendly terms that the latter took action on all 17 resolutions passed at the 1952 convention—a time-consuming exercise

The AGPA retired its pronghorn logo in 1953 in favor of a desert bighorn sheep, this species then being available to hunters for the first time. The bighorn continued to represent the association through its name change to "Arizona Wildlife Federation" in 1968, which reflected its affiliation with the National Wildlife Federation. (Arizona Wildlife Federation)

C. J. "Jack" Mantle, manager of the Santa Rita Bottling Plant in Tucson, was Arizona's longest-serving commissioner. Working by telephone behind the scenes in addition to presiding at meetings, he was instrumental in allowing the department's directors to professionalize the agency. (AGFD files)

that would be greatly curtailed or dismissed in subsequent years.

The major political battle involved a still-miffed Governor Pyle nominating Andy Wolf for commissioner. The AGPA had not approved Wolf's candidacy, so his nomination was considered a major breach of etiquette. Relations with the legislature were such that Wolf's nomination was rejected by the senate. Then, whether due to his directing a raid on polygamists in Short Creek, or to his antagonism with the state's sportsmen, Pyle lost out to Ernest McFarland, a longtime ally of the AGPA, in the election of 1954.

A particularly vexing issue for the AGPA, one that Layton and Jerome Pratt took all the way to Congress and the Department of Defense, was the military's insistence that its personnel could be the sole managers of the game on Fort Huachuca and the Navajo Ordinance Depot—even to the point of having their own harvest strategies. Prompted by a post-only hunt to remove surplus deer on Fort Huachuca, the AGPA succeeded in getting such hunts canceled and approved only after going through the normal hunt proclamation process followed by the Arizona Game and Fish Department and commission. The importance of this victory was blunted by a ruling that only authorized military personnel might participate in the resulting hunts—not the public.

Conflicts with the department's technicians over deer and elk hunts also appear to have lessened, both the AGPA and commission now relying more on the game technicians' recommendations than on outside advice when it came to hunt recommendations, refuges, the number of Kaibab deer permits, and other game management issues. The main concern on this front—an apparent decline in elk numbers—had by now been shown by joint department and AGPA surveys to be just the reverse. Elk numbers and distribution were actually increasing.

Relations with the livestock industry and its representatives in the legislature also improved, in no small part due to the soothing efforts of Avery and other AGPA mediators. A good example was a column Avery wrote on "Why Fight," detailing the commonality of purpose between stockmen and sportsmen, even as he exposed another attempted grab of national forest land in his "Legislation Report." Although elk numbers and grazing remained hot issues, and continued to be featured regularly in *Arizona Wildlife Sportsman*, most conflicts were resolved through negotiations with stockman-sportsman committees.

Both sides also agreed to endorse the use of Compound 1080 as a means to destroy predators where the use of coyote getters and other control methods were impractical.

These were the years when the magazine had the highest production values and most relevant content. Maybery, and later Bill Minette, proved competent and resourceful, producing a magazine with a mix of natural history articles, personnel portraits, obituaries, editorials, and hunting and fishing stories by such authors as Avery, Niehuis, Arthur Halloran, Chuck Morgan, and Weldon Heald. Despite increasing memberships, money continued to be a problem, and in a choice between sending representatives to meetings and conferences and publishing the magazine, the executive committee agreed in 1955 to reorganize the AGPA and sell its remaining stock in Arizona Wildlife Sportsman, Inc.

Reaping the Bounty, 1956–58

By 1956, the AGPA could feel secure in its role as the preeminent wildlife conservation organization in Arizona. Other organizations such as the Izaak Walton League and Audubon Society might take political positions and even foster projects in Arizona, but only the AGPA commanded the attention of the governor, the legislature, and most important, the Arizona Game and Fish Commission it had created. Having achieved this position of prominence, it was again deemed time to reorganize the AGPA and run the association more like a business—a program that began when Jim Sparks undertook the presidency on January 1, 1956.

The most serious problems were, as always, how to organize the locals and how to fund a state office. In truth, many local affiliates did not want a strong state organization with a president or executive secretary speaking for them at commission meetings or in the legislature. Of more concern to the locals was the issue of proportional representation, i.e., whether the number of delegates on voting issues would be based on the number of club members or a set number per club. Nor did they want to send an increased portion of their dues or additional money to Phoenix. As a result, the AGPA was understaffed. The underfunded executive secretary only received $3,000 per annum, and even these payments were often late. This resulted in high turnover; when Layton resigned as executive secretary, the position was taken by Vincent L. Fitzgerald, who resigned in July 1956. The situation with the magazine was equally precarious.

Also contributing to the difficulty of forming a strong state organization was a major tiff fomented by Avery, who pitted AGPA President Dingess and Layton against the department and commission for the latter's having *ex parte* communications in Bisbee regarding AGPA resolutions, which it acted upon without public notice or input. Disparaging remarks about certain department leaders were also reported to have been said, and there was much dissatisfaction with the "professionalism" of the department, now under an acting director, Dud Yoder. Of particular concern was the Fisheries Division, from which several biologists had recently resigned for better pay and working conditions elsewhere. The consensus, according to Avery, was that both the department and AGPA could benefit from more scientific management practices.

In the meantime, the magazine continued to function under Minette with the traditional "Over the Embers" and "Out of Doors" columns and contributors. Finding a

Local Affiliates of the Arizona Game Protective Association, 1957, 1958
Source: *AGPA Outdoor News* 3 (September)

Club	1957 Membership	1958 Membership
Arizona Trail Hounds Association	9	8
Bellco Rod & Gun Club	69	51
Blue Range Sportsmen's Club	55	72
Blue Ridge Sportsmen's Club	11	8
Calapco Rod & Gun Club		12
Casa Grande Rod & Gun Club	32	28
Chandler GPA	200	109
Cochise Sportsmen's Club	71	34
Coconino Sportsmen	339	248
Colorado River Rod & Gun Club		13
Copper Cities Hunting and Fishing Club	46	27
Coronado Trail Sportsmen	105	83
Desert Sportsmen's Club	88	76
Gila Bend Sportsmen's Club	46	37
Douglas Wildlife Sportsmen	18	30
Glendale GPA	22	45
Globe Rod and Gun Club	38	43
Mesa Outdoor Sportsmen		7
Mt. Graham Sportsmen	51	41
Oak Creek Sportsmen's Club	18	18
Peoria Rod & Gun Club	102	159
Phoenix Sportsmen's Association	369	341
Powder Horn Clan		13
Prescott Archers		5
Prescott Sportsmen's Club	229	220
Scottsdale Sportsmen's Club	25	39
Seligman GPA	20	14
Show Low Sportsmen's Club	29	16
Sportsman's Rod & Gun Club	58	120
Sun Valley Bowhunters	6	8
Superior GPA	31	13
Superstition GPA	22	24
Tucson Rod & Gun Club	318	854
Western Sportsmen		9
White Mountain Sportsmen	67	58
Wickenburg Sportsmen's Club	105	38
Winslow GPA	41	33
Yarnell Sportsmen's Club	5	6
Yuma Bowmen		7
Yuma Valley Rod and Gun Club	21	136
Total	**2,666**	**3,103**

Note: GPA=Game Protective Association

buyer who would also include AGPA news in a game and fish format was proving difficult. In 1956, the AGPA asked the department to underwrite a newspaper version of *Arizona Wildlife Sportsman* and secure an editor, but was turned down. Nonetheless, the magazine continued to produce a mix of AGPA and department news interlaced with natural history features on wolves, antelope jackrabbits, and the fact that deer numbers were so high that 200 were being killed each month on highways in the Prescott area alone.

Reorganization plans aside, the AGPA was destined to remain what it was—an association of local clubs. Influence would be limited to resolutions generated by local affiliates and unfunded actions by an executive committee. Issues of interest, such as a hunter safety education program and a state hunting and fishing survey, would be handed off to the Game and Fish Department and University of Arizona to be conducted with Federal-Aid money. With no money available for lawsuits or lobbyists, requests for land withdrawals such as those at Cibola and Topock would be passed on directly to the governor or friendly legislators.

Commission meetings would continue to be the principal venue for action when it came to hunting concerns, including deer permits in the Chiricahua Mountains, efforts to limit deer hunting on the Kaibab, and the need to protect elk on the Mogollon Rim. The same was true for fishing, except that Show Low's desire for Long Lake was fueling a demand to step up the department's nascent lake program. As a result, attendance at commission meetings remained high, some 130 sportsmen attending the 1958 season-setting meeting despite all of the department's recommendations being approved unanimously. In line with the AGPA's role as a cooperative player, the association was invited to submit suggestions for a new Title 17 game code, with a committee composed of one AGPA representative and one department representative to meet with the Legislative Council.

As for resolutions, certain members continued to call attention to such issues as the ecological ramifications of the Barr Report, the disposition of the so-called "Aztec Lands," and other concerns regarding federal and state land policy. Other, less informed or more provincial members voiced more mundane concerns, expressing their desires for a year-long fishing season, more rough-fish control, or a three-year closed season on elk. Most of these resolutions, like the AGPA's hunt recommendations, continued to be heard by the commission, if not always acted upon. Despite the state's burgeoning population, the AGPA, while continuing to acquire affiliates, remained stalled out at just over 3,000 members in 1958.

A Mature AGPA, 1958–62

The late 1950s and early 1960s saw the development of a more mature AGPA. Commission season-setting meetings no longer drew an attendance that exceeded 100 sportsmen, as the issues were less contentious and most often ended with the commission's adopting the department's recommendation. Those present might be asked to vote on whether they preferred metal deer tags to paper ones, but voting on regulations was no longer requested. Both the AGPA and the Game and Fish Department now had a better understanding of their respective roles. In 1958, department Director Robert Smith forbade department personnel from holding office in the AGPA, while encouraging them

Recognizing the importance of the Kaibab National Forest and its deer herd to the history of the Arizona Game Protective Association, the AGPA erected this memorial to President Theodore Roosevelt, commemorating establishment of the Grand Canyon National Game Reserve in 1906. Photo by George Andrejko. (AGFD files)

to maintain a membership in the association. It was enough that Fred Faver, Jack Mantle, Gordon Evans, Bill Beers, and other commissioners belonged to the AGPA.

A better if not closer relationship between the three entities now ensued. Sparks became recreation supervisor for the Fort Apache Indian Reservation, and presidents-elect Evans and Robert Spillman went on to become commissioners (see Appendices B, C). The association and department now worked in tandem, with the Game and Fish Department funding the AGPA's recommendation for a hunting and fishing survey through the University of Arizona, and Jim Levy of the AGPA lobbying for and obtaining a permit-only deer hunt on the Santa Rita Experimental Range.

On May 21, 1960, commission meeting attendees were invited to attend an AGPA executive meeting to discuss proposed bylaw changes. The commission's closed executive sessions now occurred more often with the department than with the AGPA. Issues such as hunter education and vandalism continued to be addressed, as were federal land issues: Both the AGPA and Game and Fish Department approved of the Forest Service wilderness bill. On August 11, 1962, the two entities honored Tom McCullough with a memorial, and the AGPA made the McCullough Award its highest conservation achievement.

Arizona Wildlife Sportsman magazine, edited by Bob Housholder since 1958, was now owned by John Akers. It still covered major department happenings, but contained little AGPA news. Nonetheless, an AGPA membership still bought you a subscription to the magazine. Events such as Pop Arrington's getting the 1962 American Motors Conservation award continued to make the pages of what was now a full-color magazine with illustrations by artists such as Bill Freeman and Larry Toschik and lots of advertising.

Guiding, travel, and resorts were now the main emphasis. The magazine would soon change its name to *Arizona Wildlife Travelogue,* while continuing to carry outdoor news such as warning hunters of poison stations for coyotes. Most articles consisted of vignettes of such species as antelope and bighorn sheep or historical articles on wolves, jaguars, and grizzlies. As befit its travelogue mission, the magazine was often divided into regional sections or featured a particular portion of the state—a format that would continue in future issues. As for the Game and Fish Department, it now had its own publication, *Arizona Wildlife Views* magazine.

Past presidents and officers of the AGPA in 1972, after the organization's name had changed to Arizona Wildlife Federation. Top row left to right: Bill Winter (president 1966, 1967), Gene Tolle (president 1968, 1969), Bill Beers (president 1958, 1959), Jim Levy (president 1972), Tom Sullivan (executive director). Bottom row left to right: Lee Hover (president 1953, 1954), Bob Spillman (president 1961, 1962), Fred Weiler (Bureau of Land Management), Gordon Evans (president 1960). Photo by Seymour Levy. (Arizona Wildlife Federation)

It was not only a more mature AGPA that entered the 1960s, it was a more boardroom-type operation, led by urban professionals such as Spillman and Phil Clemons. Indeed, the organization had pretty well accomplished all it had set out to do. Arizonans did enjoy better hunting and fishing, and a professional game and fish department was in place and relatively free of overt political influences from both the legislature and governor. And, the AGPA's political reach remained a formidable force. No commissioner would be approved without AGPA endorsement—a situation that would last until 1968, when the AGPA became the Arizona Wildlife Federation and Bruce E. Babbitt was governor.

The concerns of the AGPA had shifted and increased in scope. Haggling over the number of deer permits and where to stock fish had been replaced by strategies on how to keep the Bureau of Reclamation, US Army Corps of Engineers, and other bureaucracies from destroying the habitats the AGPA had fought so long to protect.

Even so, several wildlife-oriented battles lay ahead. The use of Compound 1080 eventually led to some nasty confrontations with the US Fish and Wildlife Service, as the AGPA and Game and Fish Department had softened their predator-control stance after the deer boom of the 1950s. A number of worthy causes also claimed AGPA political support, such as the US Department of Agriculture's program to eradicate screwworms, passage of wilderness bills, and the perennial need to address access problems. Environmental education, while continuing to be a concern, never generated enough money or political support to fund such a program. The AGPA was by now increasingly forced into taking defensive positions, defending their prerogative to vet commissioner appointments, protecting department actions and protecting public lands from encroachments. Unfortunately, the need to continually assume a defensive posture neither attracted new members nor generated new affiliates.

WATER FOR WILDLIFE

David E. Brown

Probably no management action has proven as popular with conservation organizations and agencies as providing water for wildlife. As game numbers began to improve through the 1940s, water developments were increasingly viewed as a way to benefit game populations. As a result, the construction of rainwater catchments, dams, windmills, and other water developments became a wildlife-restoration measure for species ranging in size from birds to desert bighorn sheep. So commonplace have these developments become that few today realize that programs authorizing and evaluating their construction are essentially limited to the years following World War II.

Efforts to manipulate and increase water supplies for humans have of course been going on in the Southwest since Holocene times. But by the 1880s, wells and windmills were being built in Arizona on a massive scale—a building boom that burgeoned through the droughts of the 1890s and the early years of the twentieth century. Later, these efforts were supplemented, and then overwhelmed, by the construction of *charcos*—dams used to block small drainages, created at first using wooden *fresno* scrapers drawn by mules, and later, by pushing earth into place with bulldozers. The construction of windmills and stock tanks designed to distribute and maintain livestock accelerated greatly during the 1930s, with the most active period of stock-tank building occurring after World War II, when large-scale earthmoving equipment became widely available, and reaching a crescendo in Arizona about 1958 (Jody Latimer, Arizona State Land Department, pers. comm., 2008).

Water developments constructed solely for the benefit of wildlife were later in coming. The first record of a water being improved or developed solely for the use of a big game animal in Arizona was the report by Walter Taylor that State Game Warden George Willard had modified a natural tank or *tinaja* in the Tank Mountains of Yuma County in 1917 so bighorn sheep could drink without falling in and drowning (Halloran 1964).

Despite this long-standing interest in improving and restoring wildlife habitat, until the Pittman-Robertson Act and other federal legislation passed in the late 1930s, there was neither the money nor the means to provide water for wild animals. For example, with no actual water development program in place and with so few personnel available in the late 1930s, it was all the Arizona Game Protective Association and Arizona Game and Fish Commission could do to erect two windmills to water mule deer in Tucson Mountain Park, even though the actual wells were already in place.

Federal Water Developments Begin

It was not until the federal Kofa and Cabeza Prieta game ranges were established in 1939 that a government agency had sufficient money and manpower to invest in permanent waters solely for desert bighorn sheep and other wildlife. At that time, the only available year-round or permanent waters on the Kofa Game Range were Budweiser Springs,

New Samson windmill erected by the Ligon Brothers, ca. 1912. The windmiller at work may be Stokley Ligon's brother Ed, probably on Jornada del Muerto. (Ligon Collection, Denver Public Library)

Tunnel Mine Springs, Horse Tank, and Alamo Springs, which was used principally by deer (Barclay 1947). These waters were also available to livestock, and bighorn were sometimes reluctant to use them (Russo 1956a).

With the Kofa and Cabeza Prieta game ranges under government control, a program was undertaken in 1940 to provide a safe and permanent water source every five miles within the refuges, with intermittent waters no more than two miles apart. In an effort to make some former waters permanent, plans were made to construct large retention dams, enlarge and deepen natural potholes, and develop seeps and springs. Steps were also taken to reduce or eliminate livestock numbers to ensure that water would be available for wildlife during drought periods.

Work on the refuges continued through the war years, despite a lack of manpower and equipment and the military's use of both refuges. Bighorn waters completed on the Kofa included one large dam 35 feet high with a silt retention barrier (Four Peaks), four spring developments, and nine retention tanks or potholes from 10 to 30 feet deep. Accomplishments on the Cabeza Prieta were more modest and limited to the renovation of Tule Well.

Although most of these waters were also available to cattle, their locations and modifications were such that separate access was made available to wildlife. When Refuge

Manager Arthur Halloran, his assistant John A. Kempton, and Fish and Wildlife Service Assistant Regional Director Kenner Kartchner visited these developments in February 1947, water was present in all of them. The program was declared a success, with few additional developments still needed (Barclay 1947). So important did Halloran consider these water developments that he initiated summer waterhole counts in 1949 as the refuge's primary census method for desert bighorn sheep.

Access to water on parts of the federal refuges remained a problem, however, especially on the Cabeza Prieta, as the only developments available in the Ajo area were waters used by livestock—Charlie Bell, Juan Tank, Quitobaquito Springs, and the Civilian Conservation Corps' newly constructed Charo Tank, just outside the refuge boundary. These waters, while usually open to deer and antelope, were also unavailable at critical times due to periodic droughts and the presence and trapping of livestock. Accordingly, plans were made to expand the number and capacity of waters on both refuges, with the intent of separating use by bighorn, deer, and livestock (Russo 1956a).

State Programs Start Up

When federal matching dollars became available to the Arizona Game and Fish Department in 1940, wildlife water developments were high on the list of programs to be developed. Statewide Research Project W-9-R authorized a study of the state's wildlife populations, their habitat requirements, and the need, if any, for restoration measures. Despite questions from biologists such as Andrew Nichol and Charles Vorhies about how best to water desert-adapted wildlife, water developments were deemed an important game-restoration measure provided food and shelter were adequate (Wright 1959).

Department biologists had concluded water was the limiting factor for several wildlife species, and recommended the development of permanent water sources in western Arizona where existing waters (springs, tanks, and wells) were few and too often closed to wildlife. Indeed, the chief investigator, Tommy Wright, concluded there was less permanent water now available to wildlife in desert mountain ranges than in historic times due to many waters having dried up or been fenced and used as cattle traps. Also, despite claims by stockmen that they were the only ones supplying water for wildlife (which they oftentimes were), livestock waters were often allowed to dry up during droughts or when livestock were not on the range. Only in the wetter portions of northern and eastern Arizona was enough water thought to be available to supply the needs of both stock and game.

Once it was concluded that developing permanent waters exclusively for wildlife was a practical means of improving game numbers in those areas able to support additional animals, a series of water-related projects were undertaken under Federal-Aid Project W-52-D. These included the construction of rainwater catchments, wells, windmills, and retention dams; the improvement of natural tanks; and the installation of a long-needed water pipeline for buffalo. Earthen reservoirs were deemed impractical as game waters, as these structures were accessible to livestock and tended to go dry at critical times. A series of windmills and pipelines was also constructed to bring water to eight parcels of land along the lower Gila River in Yuma County as well as to Raymond Ranch. These water development projects, begun in 1942, accelerated after the war, when several game waters

Stock tank or charco, *ca. 1958, blocking a small drainage on state land near Oracle Junction, used for watering livestock. Most of these structures, which are also used by wildlife, were constructed by ranchers. While serving the purpose of better distributing stock and game, such sites also promote heavy grazing, resulting in major vegetation changes over time. (AGFD files)*

were also developed in desert areas. These latter developments were dubbed "gallinaceous guzzlers" and were built in some of the county's better quail habitats.

By 1950 or so, the department had more than 100 water developments in place, including a number of 1,000-gallon rainwater catchments, constructed in groups of one to 11 units located not more than two miles apart. In addition to these "guzzlers," intended to benefit small game, eleven 2,000-gallon catchments up to five miles apart were built on the Moqui District of the Kaibab National Forest, for the purpose of increasing the numbers of deer and antelope in the arid "cinder pile" area north of Flagstaff. Other rainwater catchments were constructed southeast of Ajo, in the Sand Tank and Tank Mountains, and in other arid mountain ranges. Wildlife was now drinking from troughs at the Mesquite Springs and State Well windmills north of Gila Bend and from several wells drilled on the Texas Hill properties along the lower Gila River. A retention dam and artificial springs had also been developed in the Eagletail Mountains and natural *tinajas* in the Tank Mountains had been improved for bighorn sheep (Wright 1959).

Initially, the habitat improvement program concentrated on small game water developments under Project Leader Tommy Wright, with additional developments and watershed work for general wildlife use to receive emphasis in the future. Accordingly, the most numerous and widespread developments were rainwater catchments in the foothills of the Superstition Mountains, in the Sacramento Valley west of Kingman, in the Tanque area of Graham County, near the towns of Congress and Aguila, around the 96 Ranch area

Tom Kimball demonstrates a new game water catchment on state land at the base of the Superstition Mountains, ca. 1946. The asphalt apron of these "gallinaceous guzzlers" allowed water to flow into a concrete cistern accessible to both big and small game animals. The fenced perimeter is to keep livestock from drinking the catchment dry. (AGFD files)

off the Florence Highway, in the Page-Trowbridge exclosure near Oracle Junction, in the Owlhead Buttes, in Paradise Valley and the McDowell Mountains, near New River, and on the Three Bar Wildlife Area. In addition to the windmills previously mentioned, two others were added in the Silverbell Mountains and in Butler Valley.

Other structures included a siphon in Alta Mine, a retention dam in the Castle Dome Mountains, two dams in the Trigo Mountains, and catchments in such arid ranges as the Harquahala and Eagletail mountains. Also of interest were eight quail-restoration plots in Cochise County—range exclosures constructed upslope from water developments. Except for the cinder-pile catchments north of Flagstaff, all these developments were in semidesert grassland or desert vegetation, where the presence of water was thought to govern the range and distribution of game species (Wright 1959).

Studying the Results of Wildlife Water Developments

The construction of so many water developments required some sort of evaluation as to whether these structures were accomplishing the objective of increasing game numbers and distributions. Accordingly, a water development evaluation project was approved on May 1, 1951 under Federal-Aid in Wildlife Restoration Project W-62-R (Wright 1952).

Under the terms of this project, water development areas were visited and evaluated in order to make recommendations as to their habitat improvement value. The objective was not only to see if water developments improved game numbers, but to check for structural failures and recommend design improvements. Recognizing that determining the value

Tom Kimball displays a "coyote drinking guard" (Kimball 1945). The contraption's purpose was to deny coyotes and other predators access to the department's early water developments. It consisted of two planks set too close together for a coyote to squeeze its nose through, but not so close that quail couldn't reach the water. (AGFD files)

of water developments to wildlife could be subjective and subject to interpretations based on weather and other variables, the evaluation was scheduled to take five years and not be completed until 1957. The major species of concern were the desert-inhabiting game species: Gambel's quail, the two species of doves, desert mule deer, and desert bighorn sheep.

The evaluation project proved to be inconclusive and posed more questions than answers (Wright 1952, 1953; Wright and Schadle 1954; Wright and Webb 1955, 1956, 1957). The responses of quail to the 32 rainwater catchments was somewhat disappointing, in that populations at the end of the study period were judged to be lower than at the beginning even though quail had been released in the vicinity of several units. Wright and the other investigators concluded only that quail populations declined during dry years, with the catchments having an undetermined effect on population numbers. Water availability did influence the birds' distribution by concentrating quail use. Although catchments were thought to have contributed to an increase in quail in the Congress and Paradise Valley areas between 1941 and 1956, Wright and his colleagues had to conclude most fluctuations in quail numbers were in response to variations in food supplies rather than the presence of catchments. On the plus side, they also noted little loss of quail to predators, despite the fact that catchments attracted coyotes, badgers, and other small carnivores as well as game animals. Nor did hunting in the vicinity of water sources appear to have any impact on quail populations, the principal wildlife use being during the arid, hot season of May through July.

The concept of "gallinaceous guzzlers"—rainwater catchments designed especially for quail—remained extremely popular in the Southwest through the 1940s and 1950s (see e.g., Glading 1943), and Arizona was no exception. It was also recognized that habitat quality played an important role in quail numbers. Hence, an overt attempt was made in the 1940s to ensure adequate nesting and protective cover for both scaled and Gambel's quail by constructing 10- to 160-acre livestock-free exclosures upstream from water catchments in Cochise County (Kimball 1945). These exclosures eventually had to be abandoned, due to maintenance difficulties and the observation that quail populations fluctuated more in response to precipitation changes than to the presence or absence of grazing. Although the abandonment of these exclosures may have been premature—most of the 34 test plots showed an increase in ground cover that might have resulted in long-term population benefits—these structures, like the rainwater catchments, failed to show free water could increase quail numbers (Brown 1989).

The tendency of Gambel's quail to visit watering sites once a day (Gorsuch 1934) nonetheless led many observers to conclude that water was essential to the quail's welfare. These daily visits continued to be used to justify the construction of guzzlers through the 1950s, despite convincing arguments from other investigators that water was not necessary for Gambel's quail survival and its provision did not contribute to larger populations (Vorhies 1928; Gorsuch 1934; Lowe 1955). Moreover, Hungerford (1960b) and others were now showing that the availability of succulent green foods, not water, was the natural limiting factor for quail population size (Smith and Gallizioli 1963).

These later evaluations also resulted in a number of observations on the status of quail where water was and was not present. Water utilization by quail declined when green feed was available, even in the dry spring months. It was also noted that the release of quail in areas where catchments were being built made little difference in the number of birds seen in subsequent years. With the knowledge that green feed, not water, was the determining factor for quail abundance, the recommendation was made that no more quail would be released in areas where these birds were not present. It was also noted that quail would come some distance and cross sparsely covered ground when coming to water, resulting in the conclusion that providing water in the better habitats would reduce quail mortality and increase quail numbers by not exposing them to travel in poor habitats. An interesting aside was the observation that the ratio of scaled quail seen drinking at the Page-Trowbridge catchments near Oracle Junction was 72 to 31 Gambel's quail—the latter quail presently being nearly the only species occurring in this area (Brown 1989).

The evaluators considered the quail catchments in the Superstition Mountains, McDowell Mountains, near New River, and in the 96 Hills to have met their objective of improving habitat for wildlife, particularly quail. The judgment was that rainwater catchments in the Tanque area of Graham County and in the Camp Creek area of the Tonto National Forest were not successful. Once it was realized that quail numbers only improved around catchments in those years when food and cover increased, the experiment to protect quail habitats in Cochise County from grazing was reluctantly abandoned (Kimball 1945). What was particularly disappointing was that Cochise Plot No. 36 proved an outstanding success in range rehabilitation, and showed that 14 years of

White-winged doves perched around Mesquite Springs in the Sand Tank Mountains, ca. 1960. The concentration of doves watering at this early development declined as other waters were developed in the vicinity. (AGFD files)

protection from grazing had resulted in the area's having outstanding grass cover. Nonetheless, scaled quail numbers continued to decline in dry years, and maintaining the restoration plots proved problematical. Cooperative agreements with ranch lessees were difficult to enforce: Cattle were let into the pastures and drank the water. The bottom line was that quail numbers of both species were more influenced in the short term by weather than by the presence of catchments: Quail numbers had peaked in 1952 and declined thereafter, despite water being available yearlong.

Findings regarding other small game species were more definitive. Rainwater catchments had no apparent effect on cottontail populations, and numbers of dove using some of the waters actually declined as new water sources were developed. Food and space were apparently more important as limiting factors than water: Mourning and white-winged doves merely traveled a shorter distance to drink when additional waters were developed. Maintaining the windmills and catchments along the lower Gila River near Texas Hill was also becoming increasingly difficult to justify, due not only to the propensity of doves to use other waters, but to habitat degradation near the acquired lands as a result of farming and ranching activities. The mesquite forest adjacent to the river deteriorated as the study progressed, and what little values the developments had for wildlife were compromised by the difficulty of maintaining the windmills and keeping them in working order.

The Federal-Aid evaluation also concluded that the data were not sufficient to make a final judgment regarding the value of water developments intended for big game. Some

Water development shared by livestock and wildlife, ca. 1960. Note the mesh wire fence and other obstructions used to trap cattle. At such times these waters might be made unavailable to deer and other big game. (AGFD files)

wildlife developments benefited livestock more than deer, and many former waters of importance to big game animals dried up due to exploitation or mismanagement. Oftentimes, these losses were due to game populations being forced to share waters with domestic or feral stock. Nor could any significant improvements be documented in the distribution or numbers of deer or antelope in the cinder hills, either due to the catchments going dry at critical times or to lack of sufficient forage. All in all, it was noted that deer observations increased in some areas where catchments were built (e.g., in the Tank Mountains), but not in others.

The impact of water developments on desert bighorn sheep, while also open to interpretation, was viewed as more positive. A dam constructed to provide water for deer and bighorn in the Castle Dome-Kofa area in 1949 showed little use by either, a situation judged to be due to the vegetation's inability to sustain these ungulates. On the other hand, Wright noted bighorn using an improved natural tank and a rainwater catchment in the Eagletail Mountains and a well, windmill, and rainwater catchment in the Sand Tank Mountains. Bighorn, deer, and antelope were using three catchments in the Black Mountain area southeast of Ajo, but two retention dams in the Trigo Mountains held insufficient water to supply the yearlong water needs of bighorn.

Many of the recommendations coming out of the inspections and evaluation involved improvements in the design, locations, and carrying capacities for the catchments, wells, and tanks. Ramps to give quail and other birds access to water were emphasized, as was the need to keep livestock and game waters separate to reduce competition and disease.

The major conclusion was that water developments to improve habitat conditions in west-central Arizona were desirable and feasible as long as sufficient food and shelter were available to support larger game populations.

How this was to be determined was not given, but particular recommendations called for developing waters on the Cabeza Prieta Game Range for antelope and constructing experimental waters in the Gila Bend area to assess the area's game potential. In summary, it was decided that providing water in desert habitats was a good thing. Every area from Vekol Valley in Pinal County westward to Standard Wash in Mohave County (now La Paz County) was recommended to be evaluated as to its potential for water development. In addition to the perceived need for water, it was also suggested that an investigation be made into the value of improving salt distribution.

A Popular Program

In truth, an expanded water development program was already well underway, having proven to be one of the most popular Federal-Aid wildlife restoration measures, and found favor not only with biologists but also the public, the Arizona Game and Fish Commission, and government administrators. A series of wildlife water projects were approved in 1953, with $75,000 a year allocated for their construction. Five years later, in 1957, there were more than 200 water developments throughout Arizona, the vast majority consisting of 1,000- and 2,500-gallon rainwater catchments.

Given the huge expense involved and the inconclusiveness of the evaluation, further investigation was called for, as it was still uncertain if providing water would increase game numbers. Accordingly, a research project was begun under Federal-Aid Project W-78-R to determine the impact of wildlife water catchments on the numbers of quail and deer—the two species of most importance (E. L. Webb 1960).

Unfortunately, the deer portion of this evaluation was scheduled to take place on the Three Bar Wildlife Area. Heavy rains and an adjacent fire had so replenished natural water sources that the value of the study area was compromised. Deer population estimates on the Three Bar had grown from 14 deer per section before the fire in April 1959, to 26 deer per section in December 1959 following the fire, due to an increased amount of forage and predator control. An attempt to study the importance of water developments to deer was thwarted when trapping efforts failed to capture any deer at water sources due to the abundant forage and natural salt supplies found elsewhere. More important, the presence of a large number of heretofore unknown springs and the abundance of permanent water meant it was impossible to find a waterless control area on the Three Bar, and the big game aspect of the evaluation had to be abandoned. As a result, an objective evaluation of the effects of water catchments on deer populations based on scientifically gathered data remains lacking to this day.

The practical aspects of water developments on quail populations were resolved by a department study in the Paradise Valley-Pinnacle Peak area north of Phoenix that began in 1958 and concluded in 1962. Nine rainwater catchments were sealed off in the study area from January 1961 through the end of the 1962 quail season, effectively drying up 200,000 acres of quail habitat with the exception of one intermittent stock tank. Despite the fact that 1961 was a drier than average year, quail call-counts and hunt success during both the 1961 and 1962 seasons was slightly higher in the study area than in the adjacent control area where several rainwater catchments supplied quail with water throughout the spring and summer. It thus appeared that, although water developments served to concentrate birds within certain portions of a covey's range, water developments had little effect on quail numbers and overall distribution (Gallizioli 1961; Webb and Gallizioli 1963; Brown 1989).

Bighorn sheep were thought to be another story. Russo (1956a) favored water developments for desert bighorn sheep provided that the structures were large enough to hold water during droughts and located in bighorn terrain not shared by deer or livestock. Russo recommended a widespread water development program in bighorn habitat that would reduce competition with ungulates downslope and thereby reduce mortality caused by travel and disease. Bighorn numbers rose accordingly, and soon no management effort was more universally embraced than the provision and enhancement of waters in desert bighorn habitat. Such developments not only evolved into the primary management tool employed by bighorn managers, these activities provide a *raison d'être* for bighorn organizations composed of citizen volunteers who invested untold hours in the creation, enhancement, and maintenance of bighorn waters. These organizations developed into a formidable political lobby seeking to promote the welfare of their totem animal.

The department's water development program has not only been accepted as a legitimate big game management measure, it has continued to expand as a management effort to benefit a multitude of species, becoming an integral part of the agency's operations and budget. Providing waters for desert mule deer and bighorn sheep remains a management objective despite the effectiveness of these developments at producing more game having never been demonstrated through scientific study. By 1962, as a matter of policy, such studies were declared no longer necessary. Desert bighorn sheep, desert mule deer, and javelina had all increased in numbers during the 1950s and water developments received much of the credit. Game managers, sportsmen, and ranchers agreed that water developments benefited desert wildlife and no further investigations were needed.

THE DEER IRRUPTION OF 1956–62

David E. Brown

Today's hunters find it difficult to imagine how many deer there were in Arizona during the latter half of the 1950s and early 1960s. The phenomenon had to be experienced to be believed. The only skill a hunter needed for success was the ability to shoot. A three-hour hike through reasonable deer habitat might result in the sighting of a dozen bucks. And, although deer numbers peaked in different parts of the state at different times, the irruption[1] in numbers was essentially statewide. Nor was it confined to either white-tailed deer or mule deer. While whitetail numbers were slower to increase, Rocky Mountain mule deer, desert mule deer, and white-tailed deer all participated in the boom.

Deer irruptions were nothing new in Arizona or the rest of the country, of course. In addition to the famous irruption on the Kaibab Plateau between 1918 and 1924, deer population numbers were high enough in the Graham and Catalina mountain refuges in the late 1920s to concern range managers. Other irruptions took place at about the same time on the South Rim of the Grand Canyon and on the Gila National Forest in New Mexico. By the late 1940s, deer irruptions had become so widespread in North America that Leopold, Sowls, and Spencer (1947) published a paper documenting their occurrences and postulating opinions as to their origin and remedy.

Some irruptions had proven to be relatively short, while others were chronic. Few subsided before having a negative impact on the environment. This was especially so in those parts of Arizona where high deer numbers persisted for several years, resulting in game managers including a slide show of overbrowsed deer ranges at nearly every commission meeting where deer hunt regulations were set. That department personnel continued to press for "any-deer" hunts and doe seasons to reduce deer populations became a cause for much debate, much anger, and bitter recriminations—recriminations that echo to this day. Those times remain, to a dwindling few who remember, the "good old days" of deer management in Arizona.

From Scarcity to Abundance

The situation began slowly and appears to have had its beginning in the late 1930s and early 1940s when deer populations were thought to be slowly increasing. With reliable survey and harvest information difficult to come by, sportsmen and department wardens could only present their impressions. Populations were judged sufficiently high in 1939 that the Arizona Game and Fish Commission opened the season on desert mule deer south of the Gila River and directed State Game Warden William Sawtelle to investigate the feasibility of making "any deer" a legal deer. The problem was that nobody knew how many deer were actually being killed, with harvest data then only haphazardly gathered at check stations. It was not until the years immediately after World War II that a standardized questionnaire was used to collect comparable statewide deer-hunt estimates.

---

[1]We use this imperfect term as did Leopold, Sowls, and Spencer (1947), realizing that such phenomena are subject to periodicities and are not cyclic.

Check stations on the north Kaibab Plateau were busy during the deer irruption of the 1950s. (AGFD files)

What is known is that in 1946, deer hunters reported harvesting 5,724 deer for a hunt success of 20.5%. One in five hunters got a deer—not an unusual success rate. The makeup of the harvest, according to dot maps plotted from the hunt reports, showed 69.9% of the harvest to be Rocky Mountain mule deer, 12.8% desert mule deer, and 17.3% Coues' white-tailed deer (Arizona Game and Fish Commission 1949).[2]

Fawn recruitment after World War II was high by today's standards, fawn:doe ratios averaging just under 50 fawns per 100 does for both species between 1948 and 1953. As a result, deer harvests and hunt success steadily climbed in the late 1940s, with more than 10,000 deer being harvested in 1950 at a success rate of 28.7%. Deer hunting was becoming increasingly popular, with a sixth of all Arizonans now buying a hunting and fishing license—double the number of only 10 years earlier.

Realizing the importance of these increases, the Arizona Game and Fish Department initiated a number of Federal-Aid projects designed to monitor the "deer situation," including standardized game surveys conducted by five regional biologists, the use of both checking stations and hunter report cards to gather harvest data, and forage utilization studies to measure the impacts of deer in key areas (Arizona Game and Fish Commission 1951, 1954).

Things only got better. Tag sales, harvests, and hunt success continued to climb annually through 1955, when 63,141 tags were sold to 53,791 hunters who harvested 22,492 deer (a figure greater than the total number of hunters in 1930). Hunt success that year was a whopping 41.8%, meaning that an average of two of five hunters in a deer camp had

[2]See Appendix D, Table D-2. Also see chapter seven, "The Kaibab Deer Controversy," for a table titled "Estimated Deer, Precipitation, Hunt Information, and Livestock Numbers Reported for North Kaibab, 1906–62."

a deer hanging. Most of the rise was due to an increase in Rocky Mountain mule deer, the Kaibab and Mogollon Rim zones contributing then more than 80% of the deer harvest; desert mule deer composed another 10.8%, and whitetails only 8%. Does were now a significant part of the harvest, and had been since 1952. By 1955, some 5,783 antlerless animals were being taken, including 300 whitetail does in the Chiricahua Mountains (AGFD 1955a, 1955b, 1988).

Hunter and harvest numbers continued to increase until 1957, when only 12,000 any-deer permits were issued, public outcry having convinced the commission to temporarily "lighten up" on the amount of antlerless deer hunting (AGFD 1957). The next year saw another record harvest, with a record-breaking 77,189 hunters taking 33,000 deer for an all-time high hunt success of 42.9%. More than 11,500 of these deer were does and fawns, 1,700 of which were whitetails, this species now constituting more than 15% of the statewide harvest. Archery hunters were starting to make their presence known, with 2,181 bowhunters reporting taking 400 deer in 1958 (AGFD 1959, 1988).

Hunter and harvest numbers continued to increase through 1961, when an all-time high of nearly 36,000 deer were taken by 92,941 hunters during the rifle season for a 38.9% success rate. But although hunter numbers peaked in 1962, with 98,407 tags sold and hunting license sales in excess of $1 million, the number of deer taken dropped to less than 30,000.

What followed was a gradual decline in both hunter numbers and deer harvests. Hunting success fell below 30% in 1963 and continued downward until it dropped below 20% in 1965. The deer boom was over, and although hunter and harvest numbers would continue to fluctuate, hunter and harvest figures would never again equal those attained in the early 1960s.[3]

Possible Explanations for the Irruption

It is said that success has many claimants and failure none. A number of explanations have been postulated as to the reason for Arizona's deer irruption, several of which coincide with the increase in deer numbers and appear reasonable on first examination.

Protection: All the deer herds involved had received some degree of protection prior to the buildup in numbers. Some of the largest increases were in former game refuges. During the 1930s and 1940s, all deer hunting had been subject to lengthy closed seasons and "buck-only" regulations. Moreover, many of Arizona's rural residents had moved to town, if not during the difficult years of the 1930s, then during the prosperous years of World War II, when the great infusion of military bases provided numerous war-related jobs. Nor did these people return to their former lifestyle at war's end. One result of this emigration was a great decrease if not a halt in subsistence hunting in postwar Arizona.

---

[3]Although archery hunters and the percentage of white-tailed deer harvested would continue to increase for several more years, overall hunter numbers, harvests, and hunt success continued to decrease until 1970, when declining deer numbers and a drought caused hunt success to drop to 16.3%. This prompted the Arizona State Legislature to demand that the department either close the deer season or institute permit-only deer hunting.

James B. Hamblin and James C. Wilson with deer at the first section Kaibab check station in 1958. Photo by John Russo. (AGFD files)

Predator Control: It has also been pointed out that all of Arizona's deer-hunting range had been subject to predator-control measures—particularly after the 1930s, when the Arizona Game and Fish Department became a "cooperator" with the Predator and Rodent Control branch of the US Fish and Wildlife Service (see e.g., Leopold, Sowls, and Spencer 1947). PARC hunters had eliminated the wolf and made serious inroads on mountain lions prior to the deer irruption, and the widespread use of poisons, especially Compound 1080 after World War II, was credited with greatly reducing the number of coyotes and smaller predators. It should also be noted that a generous bounty law had come into effect in Arizona in 1947, the $75 bounty on mountain lions making the hunting and taking of the deer's chief predator worthwhile for those ranchmen inclined to protect their stock while running hounds or guiding sportsmen.

Range Improvements: Other explanations also make sense, at least initially. Most range managers agree the passage of the Taylor Grazing Act in 1935 heralded a time of improving range conditions on federal lands. The national forests, which provided most of the deer range, were regarded as having generally improved since the 1920s (Rowley 1989), the US Forest Service having made serious attempts to protect and improve rangelands for game ever since the days of the Kaibab controversy. The Forest Service's attempt to control wildfires and protect rangelands from heavy grazing after fires has also been suggested as benefiting deer (Mule Deer Working Group 2006).

Game Waters: Finally, there was the proliferation of water developments. Begun by stockmen in the last century, the provision of windmills and stock tanks by ranchers and land management agencies reached a crescendo in the mid-1950s (Jody Latimer, Arizona State Land Department, pers. comm., 2008). That the Arizona Game and Fish Department embarked on a major program to construct water catchments for big game in 1950 also coincided with the deer irruption and was used to justify this Federal-Aid program as a self-evident success (AGFD 1955b, 1959).

Weather: The one factor that has not been suggested is weather, and for good reason. Unlike the Kaibab irruption of the early 1920s and the other increases in deer numbers on the refuges in the late 1920s that were preceded by several years of above-average precipitation, the 1940s and early 1950s were mostly deficient in both winter and summer rainfall in Arizona. Indeed, the year 1954 marked the end of a long drought (Turner et al. 2003; Arizona Game and Fish Commission 1954). The consistently high recruitment rate experienced by mule deer and white-tailed deer populations during the late 1940s and early 1950s was therefore unusual and cause for further examination.

Fawn recruitment is known to be tied to the vagaries of Arizona's climate. Deer population increases have been correlated with high fawn recruitment into the adult population, and mule deer fawn recruitment rates have correlated with previous winter precipitation amounts (LeCount 1977a; Smith and LeCount 1979; McKinney 2003). White-tailed deer fawn recruitment is less variable, but declines occur during periods of drought, with annual recruitment rates correlating with regional Palmer Drought Severity Indices—measurements of how wet or dry conditions are based on rainfall, temperatures, and evaporation rates (Brown and Henry 1981; Brown 1984b).

It is therefore interesting that even though the late 1940s was a time of high mule deer fawn recruitment (and population increases), winter precipitation during most of this time was less than average. Similarly, neither winter rainfall amounts, Palmer Drought Severity Indices, nor fawn recruitment rates were particularly high during the 1950s. The 35–50 fawn:100 doe ratio during this period was sufficient only for herd maintenance, under normal circumstances (AGFD 1988; Heffelfinger 2006).

Causes of the Irruption

A better rationale than above-average precipitation to explain the increase in fawn recruitment is therefore needed to determine the causes of the deer irruption. Fortunately, we now have a 50-year perspective to review this irruption and subsequent variations in deer populations to help us understand what actually happened.

When the numbers of both mule deer and white-tailed deer took a decided upswing during the wet years of the early and mid-1980s, this increase was rightfully attributed to above-average precipitation and high fawn recruitment. When winter precipitation amounts returned to average or below-average amounts in the 1990s, fawn recruitment returned to lower levels, as did population levels. Current deer populations (2012) are therefore low by historic standards and attributable to below-average precipitation.

Since the 1980s, the rise and fall of deer populations have occurred both in areas subject to deer hunting and in areas closed to deer hunting (e.g., national parks). Such was also the case during the deer irruption under discussion, when deer numbers were also high in areas not subject to deer hunting with firearms (e.g., Tucson Mountain Wildlife Area and Saguaro National Monument West). Nonetheless, protection from deer hunting did not prevent deer numbers from declining when populations were subjected to lower fawn recruitment rates in the 1970s and 1990s. Protection from hunting cannot therefore explain the 1950s deer boom, as populations rose and fell in areas closed to hunting as well as open to hunting.

A similar argument can be made for improved range conditions, the occurrences of fire, and water developments:

- Livestock grazing pressure has declined in many areas of Arizona and at the present time a number of ungrazed or lightly grazed pastures are in the best condition within memory.
- A number of major range fires have also occurred since the 1950s. However, the hoped-for improvement in deer numbers in these burned areas has not materialized. Fires in the Bradshaw Mountains, Catalina Mountains, and below and above the Mogollon Rim have greatly improved the range for deer, but fawn recruitment rates and deer numbers have not responded as they did after similar phenomena in the 1950s.
- The same can be said for water developments. Although water is now available to deer in every mountain range and most every pasture, deer numbers remain far below those enjoyed in the 1950s and early 1960s. This is especially so in the desert ranges, where most game water developments were constructed. Providing water, it appears, neither results in improved fawn recruitment nor higher deer numbers in the absence of winter precipitation and nutritious forage.

Despite the statement that "game populations were not as a rule influenced very greatly by predation" (AGFD 1961), all the available information suggests predator control was the principal factor responsible for the deer irruption of the 1950s and early 1960s. When the department became a cooperating partner with the PARC in 1945, predator control expanded to include previously untreated game country. By fiscal year 1954, the state was appropriating $40,000 to the Livestock Sanitary Board for predator control, with an additional $27,000 coming from an Arizona Game and Fish Protection Fund that allocated $8,500 for predator control from Pittman-Robertson projects. Much of this money was spent distributing lethal predacides including Compound 1080, with the objective of reducing predation on game animals—a program that those involved agreed was highly effective if not particularly discriminatory (Mercer 1960). That the legislature had authorized a new bounty system in 1947, by which the Livestock Sanitary Board was paying bounties of $75 on mountain lions and wolves, also played a role in removing predators from formerly untreated game country, including the Indian reservations.

How else but through the application of predator control could one explain how deer numbers increased on the Three Bar Wildlife Area and elsewhere when winter precipitation was below par and fawn recruitment low (AGFD 1964)?[4] One is forced to conclude that the first Game and Fish Commission's statement that the "control of predators contributed more than any one feature to the increase of game" was probably correct.

So the question remains, why then did the irruption cease in the mid-1960s and why did deer numbers continue to decline to their present state? The reason, it appears, is the letting-up of predator control in the late 1950s and a gradual increase in predators thereafter. Faced with the problem of too many deer in the late 1950s and early 1960s, the department backed off from recommending predator control in deer habitat. Similarly too, the PARC, having come under increasing fire for its use of Compound 1080 and "coyote getters," scaled back its predator-control operations to an "as-needed" basis and concentrated instead on rodents and nuisance wildlife (see e.g., Mercer 1960).

Moreover, with lion bounties in effect, sport-hunting of lions gaining in popularity, and the Arizona Varmint Callers and other organizations demanding an end to lethal predacides, there was now a demand for less predator control generally. And, true to its history, the PARC had no problem altering its programs when subjected to public pressures.

This trend toward decreased control and increasing predator numbers has continued through to the present time. Also favoring an increase in the number of mountain lions has been the removal of the bounty system in 1971 and the designation of the mountain lion as a big game animal in 1972. The aging and retirement of professional houndsmen has undoubtedly been another factor in increasing lion numbers, as was the abolishment of leg-hold traps on public lands in Arizona in 1994. Also of likely importance to an increase in lion numbers and distribution has been the proliferation of water developments: Lions were almost unheard-of in desert ranges in the 1950s (Russo 1956a); now, these cats appear to be nearly everywhere (Brown and Babb 2009).

And while it is tempting to think that a return to the good old days of the 1950s might be good management, such thinking would be short-sighted. The irruption of deer taking place in the 1950s was an overpopulation event and an aberration. Department biologists were right to be concerned with range conditions and the welfare of browse plants. One shared feature of all deer irruptions is that once overuse becomes apparent, and browse plants are damaged, a full recovery of the plants and the deer herd is nearly impossible. Remedial measures to remove excess deer invariably come too late or are inadequate to prevent a decline in deer numbers caused by a reduction in nutritious forage. The result is a reduced carrying capacity that, once lost, is never fully regained (Leopold, Sowls, and Spencer 1947).

[4]Further evidence of the impact of predator control was a recent study on the Three Bar Wildlife Area in which the number of deer in a 600-acre predator-proof enclosure was maintained at ca. 90 deer per section vs. three deer per section found on the remainder of the Three Bar.

THE REORGANIZATION OF 1960 AND THE WILDLIFE MANAGER CONCEPT

David E. Brown

The promotion of Pittman-Robertson technicians to higher positions as department directors and staff during the 1940s and early 1950s came with a cost. The Arizona Game and Fish Department was primarily a wildlife law-enforcement agency, so the advancement of newer and often younger men who had never worn a badge to leadership roles was cause for a certain amount of resentment.

As a result, disputes within the department did not always follow the chain of command. Certain game rangers were prone to going directly to their local commissioner, senator, or representative to inform him of what was "really going on." In this way, internal differences of opinion regarding deer management and other department actions made their way to the Arizona State Legislature and the Arizona Game and Fish Commission. Of particular concern to some game rangers were game technicians recommending the killing of does, along with other measures designed to increase game harvests. Was it not, the rangers claimed, enforcement of the existing game code and conservative hunt regulations that allowed game populations to recover?

Commissioners tended to agree with this argument, as attested to by the large number of license revocations brought before them in the 1950s, nearly all involving the taking of big game out of season. Although the two most recent directors, Herbert Reid and Tom Kimball, had come up through the ranks, they had never been game rangers. This led to commissioners and legislators going to local field personnel for information and to hear the opinions of the "man on the ground" as to what should be done.

Commission leaders such as Charles Beach, Jack Mantle, and Gordon Evans were well aware of these potential conflicts and usually followed the technicians' recommendations. But commissioners were also sensitive to any in-house dissatisfaction and recognized that the rangers were the mainstay of the department. To bolster ranger morale, the commission directed Kimball to hire several new deputies in 1948, and to adjust the ranger's salaries upward whenever the budget allowed. And, in an effort to professionalize the department, Kimball asked the commission to appoint four ranger supervisors to oversee a staff of 24 full-time rangers. These supervisors were located in four districts: northern (Glen Hunter), central (Reuben McNeill) southern (Ralph Morrow), and a "ranger at large" (John Carl Jones) who went where needed.

As a further professionalization measure, the commission, at Kimball's recommendation, withdrew the cards and badges of all nonsalaried deputies. Rangers were also directed to make management recommendations at commission meetings, assist in the drafting of new regulations, and recommend whether to retain or retire specific refuges.

All of this led to administrative problems. In 1949, a ranger was accused of political campaigning—an illegal activity. Knowing some disciplinary action was required, the commission interceded by backing Ranger Morrow's transfer of the man over local objections. Angry that certain game rangers were going behind his back, Director Kimball had Rudy Switzer of the California Fish and Game Department take over as chief executive officer of the Law Enforcement Division and fire three district supervisors—Hunter, McNeill, and Morrow[1] (Ben Avery, *Arizona Republic*, May 9, 1950). Additional administrative actions resulted in hiring seven new rangers, initiating a law enforcement training school, and tightening the *per diem* regulations for out-of-town reimbursements. To improve morale, the commission set the salary of district supervisors at $230 a month—then considered to be good wages.

Cliff Sorrells, influential chief of the Law Enforcement Branch of the Arizona Game and Fish Department in the 1950s. (AGFD files)

In the first of several reorganizations, the department was organized into five divisions in 1950: auditing (under John Boland), fisheries (Dud Yoder), law enforcement (Rudy Switzer), information and education (Dan Gish), and game management (Pop Arrington). Kimball, the first director with a college degree (having graduated from Brigham Young University in Utah), touted the fact the department had 10 college men. All the college men were technicians, however, and conflicts with certain game rangers continued. More than one or two executive sessions of the Game and Fish Commission produced minutes "off the record," some continuing for hours.

Kimball's attempts at professionalization continued in 1951 when a five-man commission went into effect. Cliff Sorrells had meanwhile been appointed law enforcement chief, a position for which he was admirably suited. He soon became the department's spokesman on legal issues—not only in staff meetings, but at commission meetings, in conferences with the attorney general, and in the legislature. An exam was now given to all game rangers, and policies on annual leave, sick leave, and paid holidays were established. Commission regulations were re-codified and divided into Permanent (P) Orders and Temporary (T) orders. The following year, Sorrells demonstrated a new dress uniform for the rangers and saw to the provision of a uniform allowance. As a vote of confidence, Sorrells and his rangers were put in charge of the buffalo hunts in 1953—an operation formerly supervised by the Game Management Division.

When Kimball announced he was becoming director of Colorado's fish and game agency in 1952, the commission appointed Yoder as acting director. Yoder was a fisheries supervisor of long standing with a clean record, his tenure going back to 1928, when he

[1]Morrow, who had served as a game warden in southeastern Arizona for many years, was later reinstated and eventually became a commissioner himself.

In 1953, Cliff Sorrells and the department's rangers were put in charge of the buffalo hunts, an operation formerly supervised by the Game Management Division. Left to right: Clyde Sellers, Jack Bennett (assistant chief of law enforcement), Pat Kelly, Cliff Sorrells (chief of law enforcement), Ralph Morrow, Harold Heddings, and Don Smith. (AGFD files)

supervised South Fork Hatchery. The commission, at an impasse as to whom to appoint as director, kept him in office for the better part of a year.

Then, in October 1953, the commission named John M. Hall director. Although he had been hired as a regional biologist from the Springerville area, Hall came from a ranching background. While working as the biologist for northern Arizona, he had distinguished himself by successfully negotiating such loaded issues as resolving elk depredation complaints and promulgating turkey hunt recommendations that were acceptable to both local and visiting sportsmen.

Hall, with the support of commissioners Mantle and Evans, continued Kimball's attempt to professionalize the department while supporting the game rangers and the important role they played in addition to their law enforcement duties. This was no easy task. William P. "Blue" Tharp, one of the department's most prominent officers, had recently pleaded *nolo contendere* to smuggling gold for illegal sale, and Hall was soon faced with another game ranger appealing his firing to the commission. He also had to call an executive session of the commission to negotiate a conflict between District Supervisor Morrow and Game Management Chief Arrington.

In May 1955, Hall presented the commission with a list of qualifications for new game ranger hires that required candidates to have two years of college or related wildlife work, be between 21 and 40 years of age, be at least 5 feet 9 inches tall, and weigh a minimum of 150 pounds. Transfers from other agencies were acceptable, but all applicants had to pass a competitive exam and be interviewed by a board. This was not as radical as some complained, as graduates from the University of Arizona's Cooperative Wildlife Research Unit and other land grant colleges were now becoming available. At this

John Hall, a Federal-Aid biologist specializing in elk management, came from a ranching background. As Director, he initiated the early phases of the department's reorganization. (AGFD files)

time, the department had 16 people in administration, 10 in fisheries, 5 in information and education, and 40 in law enforcement including the district rangers.

Still, administrative problems continued. A minor squabble occurred over whether the Law Enforcement Division or the state would administer the game ranger exam, and Jack Hemphill, popular fishery supervisor, resigned and went to another agency for more pay. Hall was also forced to address complaints by *Arizona Republic* columnist Ben Avery, sportsmen, and rangers that he and the commission had met secretly in Bisbee and approved 2,000 "any-deer" permits for the Chiricahua Mountains. That department staff failed to heed the public's requests to limit deer hunting and eliminate elk hunting was more than just a communications problem.

In June 1956, Hall announced that more harmony was needed in the department, and that he was planning a reorganization. In a terse statement to the commission, he promised an expansion of the rangers' law enforcement role in which they would also participate in other department duties, including conducting game surveys and stocking fish. He advised the commission that the Fisheries Division was in need of improvement and required closer supervision from Yoder so the department could benefit from his experience. To better accomplish these tasks, he requested an assistant director be appointed. The commission, generally supportive of recommendations from the director and his staff, agreed.

Changes began in 1957. Yoder was moved to chief of the Fisheries Division and Robert Smith from the Development Branch was made assistant director. Smith, drawing on recommendations from the just-released Gabrielson Report, was assigned to designing a "conservation-type organization plan" to be implemented the following year. This plan was to divide the state into six conservation districts or regions, each supervised by a regional supervisor who would oversee the activities of the rangers and integrate their activities in the department. These men would be chosen after an examination and selected on the basis of their knowledge of public relations, law enforcement, fish and game management, and other facets of department work. All interested parties were invited to compete, with up to four men a year to be chosen. After some discussion, the commission voted to put the plan in motion. Just two months later, Hall resigned to take a job with the Forest Service and Smith was appointed director.

Original caption: "Fisheries biologist Bud Bassett (without hat) explains creel census procedures to rangers Jack Bennett, Buck Wallace and Pat Kelly. Future wildlife managers will be performing this type of fishery activity." (Arizona Wildlife Views, *July 1960; AGFD files)*

Smith continued his and Hall's reorganization plans under commission chairman Evans and commissioners Mantle and Marcell N. Forman. A draft plan was presented by which the regions were divided into 40 game management units, each of which might also serve as a working district. The commission then appointed Smith to complete Hall's term of office, with biologist Wendell Swank as assistant director.

Commission meetings were now more formal, with division chiefs presenting agenda items relating to their divisions. Sorrells, working with the state attorney general and the legislature, handled all law enforcement items, and Larry Powell made the game management recommendations. That same year, 1958, an in-service training school was instituted and area (regional) supervisors were elevated to division-chief level with a new salary schedule.

The men selected to be regional supervisors were equally divided between those having law enforcement backgrounds and those with wildlife management experience. Five, and then seven, regional offices were to be located in the Phoenix-Mesa area, Tucson, Globe, Flagstaff, Pinetop, Kingman, and later Yuma. The new supervisors were northern Arizona game biologist Bob White (Region I, Pinetop), northwest game biologist George Welsh (Region III, Kingman) and southern game biologist Ted Knipe (Region VI, Tucson); game rangers who became supervisors included Bill Farrow (Region V, Papago Park), Levi Packard (Region II, Flagstaff), and Pat Kelly (Region VII, Globe and later Cluff Ranch). Don Smith, the department's depredation control officer, was chosen to manage the Yuma region (IV), and Don Wingfield, a fish hatchery supervisor, replaced Welsh when his wife's passing required him to take time off.

Bob White

Levi Packard

George Welsh

Don Smith

Bill Farrow

Ted Knipe

Pat Kelly

Portraits of the first regional supervisors: Bob White (I), Levi Packard (II), George Welsh (III), Don Smith (IV), Bill Farrow (V), Ted Knipe (VI), and Pat Kelly (VII). Bob White had a master's degree and Ted Knipe had attended college; Packard, Farrow, and Kelly were game rangers; and Don Smith was a biologist in charge of depredations. (AGFD files)

Forty-four game management units were in place by 1959, each delineated by highways, rivers, jurisdictional boundaries, or other prominent features. As originally intended, all or portions of these units would be managed by a wildlife manager, who would be responsible for all department activities within his "district." Duties included, in addition to law enforcement patrols: conducting game surveys, assisting with creel checks, servicing the area's license dealers, and attending sportsmen club meetings. In essence, the wildlife manager was to be the department's local representative in his district. The wildlife manager would also make the initial hunt recommendations for his game management unit to his regional supervisor.

Rangers and biologists who qualified would be grandfathered in as wildlife managers without an examination, while the four fisheries biologists would continue on as regional specialists. Experienced rangers who were unwilling to become wildlife managers were assigned as rangers-at-large within the Law Enforcement Division. Smith was ready to take his plan to the commission in the spring of 1960, with a proposed implementation date set for fiscal year 1961–62.

With all the regional supervisors selected, and the region and unit maps amended to reflect needed boundary changes, Smith set about implementing his reorganization in the spring of 1960. The first series of wildlife managers had been selected and a second series

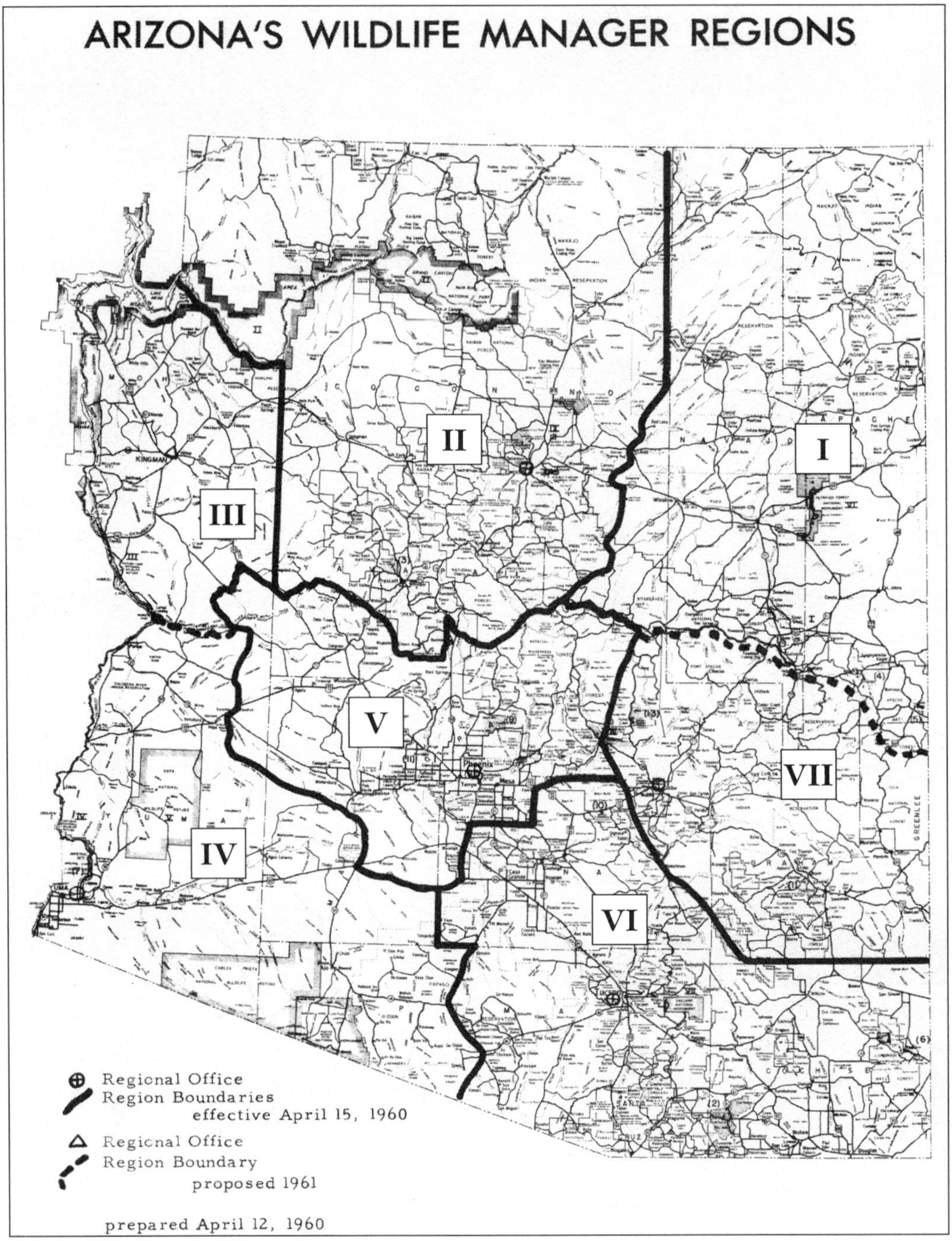

The original seven regions established after the reorganization of 1960, with offices in Pinetop (I), Flagstaff (II), Kingman (III), Yuma (IV), Phoenix (Papago Park; V), Tucson (VI), and Globe VII (later Pima). (Arizona Wildlife Views, *April 1960; AGFD files)*

of wildlife manager "trainees" was in the process of being recruited, all but one with a wildlife management or equivalent degree from a college or university.[2] That only two of them came from the University of Arizona was intentional, in that Swank wanted a variety of major professors and institutions represented in what he hoped would become a new cadre of leaders for the department.

The commission was now fully committed to the reorganization, and in December 1962 directed the director to hire, appoint, and dismiss employees, and to set salaries accordingly. The commission would retain responsibility for classifying or reclassifying various department positions, setting performance standards, and establishing salary structures.

Director Robert J. Smith presided over the reorganization of 1960 and upgraded the professional abilities of the department by hiring college graduates in wildlife management from all over the West. (AGFD files)

Swank had each wildlife manager trainee exposed to a six-month training program, during which time he worked with department employees in different regions in the state. This extended training period, coupled with a summer law enforcement school, enabled new wildlife managers to become familiar with the state's varied personnel, resources, and programs. Later, as the wildlife managers matriculated, they would become regional supervisors, division chiefs, department staff, and directors.

So successful was Smith's reorganization that it remains in effect today, in modified and expanded form, with wildlife managers the basic law enforcement/biologist entry-level position within the department.

Dr. Wendell Swank from Texas A&M was Smith's assistant director and later the acting director in charge of implementing the wildlife manager program. (AGFD files)

Perhaps the strongest aspect of Smith's reorganization was that it retained the department's basic law enforcement structure at a district level while also allowing for science-based wildlife management recommendations. Specialists would continue to be hired for certain positions, allowing the department to conduct investigative stud-

[2]Roger Baker (Colorado State College), David Brown (San Jose State College), John Carr (University of Arizona), Wes Martin (Humboldt State College), Dave Mitchell (Missouri University), and Mike Yeager (University of Arizona). Another trainee, Paul Miller, had been promoted from creel clerk to wildlife manager.

ies to answer particular biological questions while continuing its basic mission to design, present, and enforce wildlife regulations.

There were of course some unforeseen consequences to what was in essence an experiment in the decentralization of responsibilities. Regional supervisors tended to have strong personalities, and their actions might result in the development of a regional "persona." For example, elk hunt recommendations for several years tended to be more liberal in Region I than in Region II, with virtually no cow or any-elk permits in the latter. Similar variations also occurred on a smaller scale in wildlife manager districts. Nonetheless, such variations often reflected local sentiments as well and made the system more responsive to local change and mores, thereby leading to greater public acceptance and stability.

By 1962, the department was a major business venture as well as Arizona's foremost resource management agency. The annual income from hunting and fishing licenses sold was more than $1.5 million, and its operating budget was in excess of $2,000,000, with nearly $650,000 coming in annually in Federal-Aid funds. The total number of employees was just over 170, more than half of whom worked in the regions and in the field.

POP ARRINGTON'S LAKES PROGRAM

David E. Brown

By the late 1940s, the difficulties inherent in managing Arizona's waters for both fish and game were increasingly apparent. Unlike the lands occupied by resident game species, the best habitats of which were on the national forests, Arizona's water bodies were subject to claims by farmers, ranchers, irrigation districts, mining companies, and other entities, both public and private. How these waters were allocated involved a complex legal code based on beneficial prior use. Managing such waters to benefit wildlife could be not only exceedingly difficult, it might be against the law.

Because Arizona has few natural lakes, and these, such as Mormon Lake, periodically go dry, most fishing was confined to man-made impoundments. The problem with such water bodies was that water levels and content were typically under the jurisdiction of irrigation districts, municipal water companies, or a government agency contracted to provide water for irrigation projects, municipal development, or hydroelectric power. Fish spawning and fishing opportunity were always of lesser concern. Fishermen, game and fish commissioners, and local governments agreed that Arizona needed more lakes—lakes that could be managed primarily for fishing and recreation.

Lakes and reservoirs, while not native trout habitats, were desirable as destinations for hatchery-raised trout, if for no other reason than that most of the trout streams were on national forests or Indian reservations and subject to livestock grazing and other multiple-use activities. Stocking streams with fingerlings or fry during the late summer and fall had been shown to result in poor survival rates—a situation that improved when the fish were stocked in one of Arizona's high-country lakes.

Hence, beginning in 1942, the Arizona Game and Fish Department elected to emphasize planting "catchable-sized" trout during the spring months in such waters as Big Lake, Ashurst Lake, and Lake Mary. Lakes and reservoirs not only proved to be better "holding ponds" than streams, fish stocked in lentic sites showed greater growth and a better "recovery rate" (percentage of trout taken by fishermen) than fish planted in streams (Arizona Game and Fish Commission 1948). The planting of fingerling trout now concentrated on remote Forest Service streams where trout either no longer occurred in desired numbers or never did occur.

Fishery studies had also demonstrated that lakes, not streams, supplied Arizona's fishermen with most of the trout and other game fish. Not only were lakes the water bodies most likely to sustain a viable fishery, lake managers could, at least theoretically, manipulate water levels, discharges, and even water temperatures to produce and hold more and bigger fish. The seven lakes at the Hunt Bass Hatchery were proof of that.

A fishing-lake development program was therefore a logical progression in the state's wildlife management curriculum, provided cooperative agreements could be worked out with the water users—as was the case with Granite Basin and Frye lakes, which were water sources for the municipalities of Prescott and Safford. Another more limited option was to block the outflow and raise the level of one of Arizona's natural lakes, which otherwise tended to be shallow and marshy. Or, do as the Bisbee Sportsmen did in 1947: Get the US Forest Service and Game and Fish Department to help them build Rucker Canyon Lake in the Chiricahua Mountains.

The problem was that prior to World War II, little money was available for fishing lakes or other habitat purchases. Although the department had initiated a land acquisition program using Pittman-Robertson money in 1942, few lands had been purchased, much less water rights. This changed on December 11, 1946, when Big Game Supervisor Orville N. Arrington was put in charge of all Federal-Aid acquisitions.

Arrington's Initial Accomplishments and the Challenge of Long Lake

Arrington, better known as "Pop," was admirably suited for the role of department real-estate expert. Energetic, loquacious, and knowledgeable, Arrington made presentations to the Arizona Game and Fish Commission that were both informative and entertaining. A commission favorite, he soon became the department's top authority on land and water projects.

Energetic, loquacious, and knowledgeable, Orville "Pop" Arrington became a real-estate expert and helped the Arizona Game and Fish Commission build lakes and acquire wildlife habitat throughout the state. (AGFD files)

Although details concerning water rights, engineering studies, and legal opinions would eventually become his special forte, his initial accomplishments were arranging land purchases and selling the commission on complex construction projects. As Federal-Aid supervisor, Arrington was intimately familiar with Pittman-Robertson funding mechanisms and had access to duck-stamp funds and other monies. Given his new assignment, it was only a matter of time before he became familiar with other funding sources, including the new pot of Dingell-Johnson money that became available in 1950. Arrington also learned how to work with the Arizona State Legislature, that body having been given final say on all department appropriations in 1949.

When Congress passed the Dingell-Johnson Act, the law established a 10% tax on all fishing tackle to provide assistance to the "states for the management and restoration of fish having material value in connection with sport or recreation in the marine and/or fresh waters of the United States." To department technicians, that meant money for fish studies and hatcheries. To Arrington, that meant money for an ambitious land-and-water-acquisition agenda, with a "lake development program" as a top priority (AGFD 1960).

The least expensive and most forthright method of acquiring a fishing lake in 1951 was to improve existing lakes. Early projects involved raising Luna Lake Dam and using Dingell-Johnson money to raise the heights of Big and Crescent lakes to provide more surface water and alleviate winter-kill problems. Other promising possibilities included deepening natural lakes on Anderson Mesa to make them more permanent. These and other "improvements" increased the size of Luna Lake to 175 surface acres, and enlarged Big, Crescent, Ashurst, and Kinnikinick lakes in the five years that followed.

Although winter-kill problems continued to bedevil the high-elevation Big Lake, all these enlargements could be deemed a success for fishermen, creel census surveys showing an increase in fishing use (AGFD 1960). The biggest project being proposed, however, was the development of Long Lake on Show Low Creek, some $800,000 in both Dingell-Johnson and Pittman-Robertson monies having been appropriated for that purpose in 1950.

Originally intended to be a waterfowl area as well as a fishing lake, Long Lake was a difficult proposition from the beginning. First there was a series of water-rights disputes, initially with the Show Low Irrigation District and later with Phelps Dodge Corporation, the Arizona State Land Department, and the state attorney general. Questions also arose as to the propriety of using Federal-Aid monies, given the tenuous benefits to fish and waterfowl in what was clearly intended to be a recreation lake. As a result, the commission deferred funding pending more information, despite a strong push for action by the Show Low Chamber of Commerce. In lieu of Long Lake, the commission voted to purchase the water rights to Willow Lake Dam near Prescott for $72,000 from the Chino Valley Irrigation District—a purchase that was approved by the Federal-Aid coordinator in Albuquerque.

Long Lake's backers proved to be determined lobbyists. One of the commissioners, E. G. Dentzer of Greer, represented the White Mountains, and in 1951 the commission approved an agreement with Phelps Dodge by which the department would build a dam on Long Lake at a cost not to exceed $225,000, in exchange for certain water rights—an agreement not approved by the Arizona State Land Department or attorney general.

There were other legal difficulties, and the Long Lake project was put on hold until the following year, when a delegation from Show Low came to the April 1952 commission meeting pressing for favorable action. Considerable disappointment therefore ensued when an engineering report showed the site was undesirable for both waterfowl and fish, due to a high water-loss potential and expected high turbidity.

The citizens of Show Low were not easily dissuaded, and the commission decided to proceed with the construction of Long Lake under a new agreement. Money already paid to Phelps Dodge for construction costs would be recouped and the department's 1,200 acre-feet of water diverted to other uses. Nonetheless, the legalities of the arrangements with Phelps Dodge were questioned, and the squabbling continued for over a year, with private landholders adjacent to the proposed lake wanting the Arizona Game and Fish Department to have only shoreline-to-shoreline ownership.

As other lake options appeared more promising, the commission reviewed Long Lake's history and cost estimates (a minimum of $210,000) at an Armistice Day meeting in 1953. The crux of the discussion was the biological report showing that the lake was unsuitable for either waterfowl or fishing and that it would be dry three years out of 10. Although certain members of the Arizona Game Protective Association continued to push for Long Lake, Arrington deflected the local demand for a lake by having the Soil Conservation Service lead the commission on a tour of other potential lake sites in the White Mountains.

The department had been involved with a number of important projects during the preceding two years, and Arrington had spearheaded them. Combination projects at Mittry Lake on the Colorado River and Luna Lake in the White Mountains were designed to benefit both fishing and waterfowl. Silt had been removed from lower Sabino Dam near Tucson, and a pipeline and water-rights arrangement worked out to use water from the newly acquired Cluff Ranch ponds near Pima to also irrigate crops for wildlife. Using $5,000 of Kaibab Coop money, campground facilities had been developed at a newly raised Big Lake, and Lyman Reservoir had been renovated, drained, and refilled. As 1952 got underway, plans were made to raise the dam at Luna Lake 12 feet, at a cost of between $15,000 and $20,000 in Dingell-Johnson monies. And Arrington was just getting started.

The New Lands Division

It was creating new lakes that most stimulated Arrington's talents—a passion shared and approved by the commission. Having a fishing lake in their county was a project a commissioner could brag about to his constituents with the ardor formerly reserved for hatcheries. The controversies and setbacks attendant with Long Lake had not dimmed Arrington's enthusiasm for projects. On the contrary, Arrington's "Lands" was now made a full division within the Arizona Game and Fish Department, equivalent to Enforcement, Fisheries, and Game. Arrington and his complex projects would continue to dominate commission meetings for years to come. Arrington would soon be regarded by many as the single most important person in the department.

As the 1950s progressed, recommendations for new lake sites came not only from the AGPA but from the general public and the commissioners themselves. Game and Fish Department Director Tom Kimball solicited submissions from game technicians, fish hatchery supervisors, and deputy wardens. John Hall in the Game Management Division recommended two dam sites in Rose Canyon in the Catalina Mountains and another in Peña Blanca Canyon northwest of Nogales. Dick Wagner, a fisheries technician, suggested a survey of Woods Canyon on the Mogollon Rim.

Engineering studies showed these lake sites to be feasible and a program to develop fishing lakes in both northern and southern Arizona proved highly popular with the commission. The legislature thought so too and quickly approved use of the Game and Fish Fund, including Federal-Aid monies, for lake construction. Other sites being evaluated at this time included Canyon and Heber lakes on the Mogollon Rim, a 200-acre lake site in Whitewater Draw near Douglas, and another site in a major wash near Ajo. Not wanting to be left out, Prescott residents explored the possibility of a cooperative agreement to manage Goldwater Lake in the Bradshaw Mountains. To secure Pittman-Robertson and duck stamp monies, Arrington directed that the investigations consider waterfowl as well as the lake's fishery potential.

Enhancing existing structures continued to receive high priority. To further reduce winter-kill caused by oxygen depletion, the commission approved a proposal to dig a 10-foot channel from Crescent Lake to Big Lake. Another project planned to raise Ashurst and Kinnikinick lakes to improve them as trout fisheries.

By fiscal year 1954–55, the commission had earmarked $1,700,000 to evaluate prospective lake sites. Not all of the investigations panned out. Engineering studies nixed a number of proposals, such as Ruby Lake near Arivaca. Other studies showed an insufficient precipitation amount and watershed for the proposed lake near Ajo, and the costs of maintaining sufficient water in Whitewater Draw were deemed prohibitive due to soil conditions. Preliminary work on alternative lake sites to Long Lake, termed Fool Hollow and Turkey Track, also showed potential problems—problems that had to be worked out to the satisfaction of the state attorney general, who had to approve all land purchases.

The community deemed most in need of a lake was Prescott. In 1953, the Prescott Game Protective Association leased land on Lynx Creek with the idea of building a dam and trout fishery there. Another community eager for a lake was Winslow, which wanted a 550-surface-acre duck-feeding area that would use water from Clear Creek Dam, to which the city would retain the water rights. The commission was sympathetic to both proposals, especially the Lynx Lake site with its 18-square-mile watershed. Although an engineering study recommended that the original dam site selected be moved, location was not the most serious obstacle. The biggest barrier, one that kept Lynx Lake from being built for years, was water-rights protests, particularly those filed by the Fain Ranch downstream.

No problem was so complex that Arrington would not try to find a solution, and the mid-1950s saw Arrington and the department involved in a plethora of lake projects. In 1956, the commission approved Rose Canyon and allocated $75,000 for building Peña Blanca. The most satisfying progress was being made with Woods Canyon, where construction was underway using department development crews rather than contractors.

Always in search of projects, Arrington was also investigating other lake sites and considering whether to recommend the purchase of Tusayan Dam near Williams. The city of Winslow's waterfowl project was also revised to include fishing. An offer to purchase Lee Valley and Mexican Hay lakes in the White Mountains for $45,000 using development and maintenance money was under discussion. And, Rucker Canyon Lake leaked and the Cochise County sportsmen wanted the department to seal it.

Big projects meant big problems, and there were some dandies. Any work on Lynx Lake was tied up with injunctions, and contract disputes slowed Peña Blanca's progress. The most serious difficulties were associated with Fool Hollow—critics deeming the lake's name prophetic. The dam site had to be changed due to engineering problems. Rights to the water, which came from Jacques Lake, were disputed, delaying the onset of construction. Phelps Dodge demanded $225,000 for the transfer of water rights. Phelps Dodge also wanted $40,000 for the engineering investigations and to pay only $184,995 of the construction costs. Complicating the issue further was the presence of private land that required property-owner agreements. There was also the issue of a concessionaire agreement to consider once the lake was completed.

Lynx Lake, despite its legal problems, was still judged the most feasible of the Prescott-area lake sites from a construction standpoint. After an engineering survey, Arrington reported the dam could be built for $85,000 using earth rather than cement. Bill Beers, a prominent Prescott Game Protective Association member and future commissioner, was delegated to politic the city of Prescott for the water rights, 11 protests having been filed as of September 2, 1956. The department had already paid $700 for a legal assessment and spent $3,000 on quitclaim deeds to resolve mining claims along Lynx Creek, paying up to $500 for each claim. Water-rights issues remained unresolved, however, even after construction bids went out in January 1958. Indeed, such issues continued to plague Lynx Lake even after an initial agreement was signed in 1959. Litigation was still ongoing when bids were rejected in 1961 as being too far above the estimated cost of $132,000.

Arrington's Program Comes of Age

Not all of the lake projects were so problematic. On July 27, 1957, the commission was informed that Woods Canyon had been completed with a minimum of difficulty and was now filling after being planted with fingerling trout. A year later, Woods Canyon and a reconstituted Ashurst Lake were open to fishing. Indeed, Woods Canyon was so successful it was selected as the site of a commission meeting and ballyhooed as just the first in a string of Mogollon Rim lakes—which it was. Supplementing the planned complex of lakes on the Rim was the completion by Phelps Dodge of Blue Ridge Reservoir and an agreement to share jurisdiction with the department. An added incentive to a Rim lakes program was the growing realization that conflicts were inherent between certain wildlife species, fishermen, and recreationists. Arrington was emphatic that the time to build lakes primarily for fishermen was now.

Peña Blanca Lake was also being touted as a success, although one that had been a long time coming. After construction began in 1956, disputes with the contractor caused delays lasting more than a year. Problems with the rebidding process resulted in additional time lost, the commission finally approving a bid that exceeded estimated cost. Finally, in May 1959, the lake was filled, fish were planted, and the lake was officially opened.

The history of Rose Canyon Lake in the Catalina Mountains paralleled that of Peña Blanca in several ways. Begun with an initial appropriation of $31,000 in 1956, the dam eventually cost $73,000, with $53,000 of the total being Dingell-Johnson money and additional money coming out of the Game and Fish Fund. Even these funding sources proved insufficient, and Arrington tapped other Federal-Aid monies, which if unspent in this way, would be spent on migratory birds instead. In 1957, the commission voted to call for new bids and appropriate the additional funds after the Pima County Parks Board agreed to ante up another $20,000. Given the financial and political fallout attendant with abandoning the project, the commission approved the revised costs and Rose Canyon was completed, stocked with fish, and opened to fishing in May 1960.

After the dam site had to be changed due to engineering problems and the water rights disputes were settled, construction finally began on Fool Hollow Lake in the 1950s. (AGFD files)

When Woods Canyon Lake was nearing completion, the commission was faced with the desirability of having concessionaires and recreational facilities at its lakes. Pressing this issue was Max Layton's request that the AGPA bid for a concession at Fool Hollow, the renewed building of which was now being funded by Federal-Aid money. Although the commission agreed in 1957 to build access roads to its lakes and develop specifications for concessionaires, neither the department nor the Forest Service was eager to get into the lake recreation business. The commission had approved a boat-concession agreement with a lessee for a cooperatively managed Show Low Lake in 1957, and was already involved in too many legal agreements. It was therefore decided that concessionaire leases and agreements would be the responsibility of the landowner; for example, the concessionaire for Peña Blanca was under the jurisdiction of the Coronado National Forest.

In the interim, other projects accumulated. In 1956, it was agreed that $35,000 in Dingell-Johnson funds would be used to construct Riggs Flat Dam in the Graham Mountains, and an application for 11.2 surface acres of water rights was filed. Bids were accepted and work began that same year. Unlike other southern Arizona lake projects, on Riggs Flat the work went relatively smoothly and the citizens of Safford soon had a trout-fishing lake to call their own.

Much easier than building a lake and applying for water rights was purchasing an existing lake and its water rights. In 1956, the department asked the commission to purchase water rights to Lee Valley and Mexican Hay lakes and other lower Colorado River

Mexican Hay Lake under construction. (AGFD files)

reservoirs—a request that came to fruition in December 1959. More timely was the purchase of Nelson Reservoir and its dam, which had been designed by the Soil Conservation Service and rebuilt in 1950. Acquired through a land exchange with the Forest Service and a lease-purchase agreement, the 120-acre reservoir was paid for in full in 1961 with a last payment of $10,000. That same year an offer was made for the department to buy or lease Becker Lake near Springerville using $32,000 in Dingell-Johnson money and $110,000 in Pittman-Robertson funds—a blue-ribbon fishery purchase that would also eventually be consummated.

Other lake investigations never materialized into projects. A request to purchase Hulsey Lake in 1956 was turned down as too expensive and that same year the Arizona State Land Department denied the commission the water rights for a proposed Escudilla Lake, a denial the commission originally wanted to take to superior court. Another proposal rejected despite commission approval was a 70-foot-deep, 150-acre lake in Cottonwood Wash. No fewer than seven lake sites were investigated in the Bisbee-Douglas area; only one, Leslie Canyon, proved potentially feasible, even though it came with an estimated price tag of $150,000 and a host of legal problems. An attempt to acquire and rehabilitate Silver Springs Hatchery required adding $50,000 to the preliminary investigation and engineering budget. The cost of these preliminary commitments caused Commissioner Milton Evans to remark that too much money was being spent evaluating dam sites with too little result and Lee Hover of the AGPA to suggest that, when possible, water rights be obtained prior to proceeding further on all future projects.

Water rights were indeed the crux of most of Arrington's lake-project troubles. Ironically, it was an attempt to raise the small dam enlarging Kinnikinick Lake 10.5 feet that initiated a protest that showed just how complicated water rights issues could be. When a downstream rancher objected to the department's interfering with stream flow, no matter how small, the implications were obvious. Stock tanks, stock use, and stream access all came with an implied water right. As a result, Arrington was directed to apply for and clear the water rights on all Arizona Game and Fish Department projects—an action that not only complicated the agency's lake program, but future water projects throughout the state, both public and private.

It was also at this time that the Barr Report came out. Commissioned by the legislature, this 1956 report by the University of Arizona suggested effective precipitation on the Salt River Project watershed could be increased by manipulating the vegetation—in essence reducing transpiration rates by using herbicides and mechanical means to replace trees and other woody plants with grasses. The report's impact on water rights was open to interpretation and the cause of much consternation, resulting in an executive session between the Arizona Game and Fish Commission, the US Forest Service, and other government entities.

Not only would all of the national forest's watersheds be affected, every wildlife species using chaparral, pinyon-juniper woodland, and riparian vegetation was now in jeopardy. Hence, the Barr Report was vigorously opposed by the AGPA on both wildlife conservation and scientific grounds. So great were its ramifications that in 1958 the department hired a full-time person to work on watershed projects, and several research studies were set up to evaluate the effects of various vegetation treatments on wildlife species. Another consequence, perhaps one less intended, was to put existing water-right amounts in jeopardy and cause the Arizona Game and Fish Department and other parties to file for water rights on nearly every anticipated activity. Rather than have the cattle-growers fight with the department over water rights, the commission recommended that ranchers file claims on their stock waters, leaving the department to object to claims by downstream users.

Managing lakes was not as simple as some had hoped. Despite pumping the top 10 feet of Crescent Lake to deepen Big Lake, trout die-offs from winter kill were still occurring at both lakes. Weedy vegetation plagued Kinnikinick Lake as well as lower non-department lakes such as Peck's, Stehr, and Granite Basin. Plants of kokanee salmon in Luna Lake failed to result in better fishing, and several lakes had to be renovated because of competition with stunted nongame fish populations. The worst news from Arrington's perspective was that Fool Hollow was leaking and creel surveys showed that trout in Woods Canyon Lake exhibited poor growth rates. Unlike Peña Blanca, where warm-water fish were showing phenomenal growth, measures would have to be taken to increase the productivity of the Rim Lakes.

An Empire of Lakes

Not one to be deterred, Arrington continued to undertake a steady stream of new projects. In 1960, he announced plans for Parker Canyon, Tusayan, and Martinez lakes, as well as for a hatchery at Sterling Springs on Oak Creek costing between $10,000 and $14,000. The most impressive of these proposals was Parker Canyon, a complicated three-way deal involving 93 acres of George Parker's land, the Coronado National Forest, and the Game and Fish Department. Approved the following year using Pittman-Robertson and duck-stamp money, Parker Canyon was about to join Lynx Lake as the department's primary construction project, with seven Rim lakes also in the hopper and a dam at Red Rock in the Patagonia Mountains in the exploration phase (AGFD 1962).

By 1962, Arrington's lake program was reaching its zenith. The Rim lakes complex was well underway, with Woods Canyon completed and construction for Knoll Lake approved. Rim, Bear, Black Canyon, Chevelon, Pinedale, and Willow Creek reservoirs were in the planning stage. In southern Arizona, Riggs, Rucker, Fry Mesa, Peña Blanca, and Rose Canyon lakes were in place, with Parker Canyon underway and a lake at Red Rock in the planning stage (AGFD 1963). A $75,000 emergency appropriation finally assured the construction of Lynx Lake. Other projects in the hopper but never built, or done by others, included lakes at Patagonia, Pinedale, Cottonwood, Weimer, and Golder Dam, the latter a real-estate venture near the town of Catalina. Arrington even continued to push for the revised Hole in Ground Lake, after engineering studies showed the site was unsuitable for a lake of the size envisioned. Never one to think small, Arrington and his staff began filing applications with the Bureau of Reclamation for Colorado River water for a series of recreational lakes to be part of the Central Arizona Project (AGFD 1964).

Although the commission's fervor for lake-building remained intense, and a few more lakes, such as Arivaca near the town of that name, would be completed, a lack of

Measured in terms of hours of recreational pleasure, Pop Arrington's lake-development program has to be deemed a success. Here, anglers show off stringers of rainbow trout. (AGFD files)

suitable sites, legal complexities and skyrocketing construction costs now limited the number of projects under consideration. And, despite some lakes such as Peña Blanca initially showing amazing productivity, such benefits proved short-lived, as was the case with most lakes. The values of other lakes were compromised by mineral contamination or structural problems. That most of the Rim lakes exhibited low fertility and their fish had lower growth rates than had been initially hoped was disappointing. Moreover, visitation surveys showed campers, picnickers, and other recreationists to greatly outnumber fishermen on most lakes. The time for Arrington's lake-building efforts was coming to a close, to be replaced by newer programs with a higher cost:benefit ratio. One of these, the highly popular "Urban Fishing Program," which involves cooperative ventures between the department and cities and towns, is a direct descendent of Arrington's lake program.

Even though Arrington's lakes may not have realized the full fishing potential that was planned, his lake program has to be viewed as one of the Arizona Game and Fish Commission's greatest successes. Not only do many of these lakes continue to provide fishing for thousands of Arizona residents, their construction enabled fishing-license sales to steadily increase during the 1950s and 1960s and continue at a high level, thereby funding additional fishing ventures (see Appendix D, Table D-1). And even though some of these, such as the Urban Fishing Program, may be more cost-effective when it comes to putting fish in the creel, Arrington's lakes continue to supply both urban and rural residents of the state with the outdoor recreation promised 50 years ago. All of which makes for a legacy to remember.

FORMATION OF THE ARIZONA COOPERATIVE WILDLIFE RESEARCH UNIT

David E. Brown

The Pittman-Robertson Act was not the only Depression-era measure that led to a better understanding and management of Arizona's wildlife. Also in the 1930s, a committee of wildlife conservationists and academics, including Aldo Leopold and Walter Taylor, realized there would soon be a need for land-grant colleges to train state and federal conservation agencies in the new field of wildlife management.

Working through the American Wildlife Institute, an amalgam of national conservation organizations and firearms and ammunition manufacturers, the committee developed a plan: The institute and the US Biological Survey would contribute two-thirds of the cost of an advanced training program, and the remainder would be funded by colleges and state fish and wildlife agencies. The first of these Cooperative Wildlife Research Units was formed in the Midwest in 1935; by 1937, 10 other land-grant colleges had signed on, along with their respective state wildlife conservation departments (Trefethen 1961).

Each unit was supervised by a biologist with the Biological Survey. Universities and state conservation agencies each contributed $6,000 in funds, services, or equipment to match an equal contribution from what would soon be called the Wildlife Management Institute. Directors of the various "Coop Units," as they came to be called, not only conducted long-range research and trained graduate students, but oversaw a curriculum that made undergraduates eligible for professional wildlife positions.

Formation of Arizona's Coop Unit

Although Arizona was slow getting on board, the growing pressures on fish and game resources after World War II made such a program increasingly necessary, there then being only some 500 wildlife professionals in the entire United States to implement the game investigations funded by the Pittman-Robertson Act (Trefethen 1961). With passage of the GI Bill in 1944, loans became available to veterans from working class, farming, and ranching backgrounds to provide them with a college education in game and fish biology and wildlife management.

Prior to World War II, most Arizona Game and Fish Department personnel came up through the ranks as self-taught game wardens or biologists. Only a few, such as Kenner Kartchner, transferred into the Game and Fish Department from the US Forest Service or another natural resources agency. Biological training was at a premium, as little was known of the natural history of most game animals, including their limiting factors. No one was even certain how many species of deer were found in Arizona. The only college-trained biologists available were found largely outside the department, and consisted mostly of academics at the University of Arizona or biologists with the Biological Survey or Forest Service.

Arizona needed a state wildlife curriculum and a professional cadre of Game and Fish Department biologists and wildlife managers. In 1950, at the urging of Taylor and the

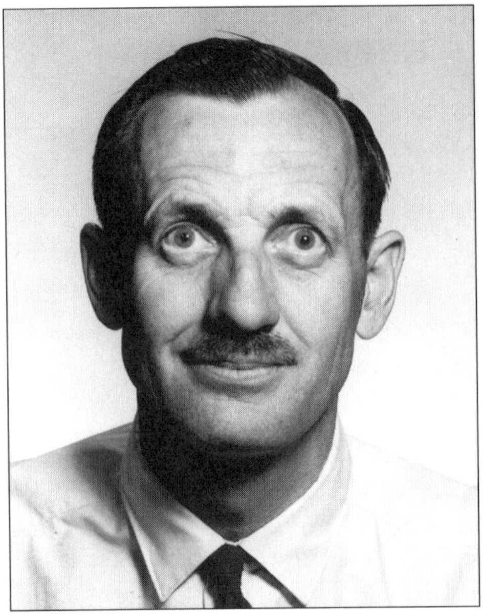

Lyle K. Sowls served as the Cooperative Wildlife Research Unit leader at the University of Arizona for more than 20 years. Sowls and his students investigated the population dynamics of just about every game species in Arizona, but were especially involved with the study of the collared peccary (javelina). (UA Biofile, Sowls; University of Arizona Libraries, Special Collections)

Roger Hungerford was assistant leader of the Cooperative Wildlife Research Unit and earned a PhD studying the factors determining reproductive success in Gambel's quail. While Dr. Sowls concerned himself mostly with graduate students, Hungerford was a mentor to both undergraduates and graduates. (UA Biofile, Hungerford; University of Arizona Libraries, Special Collections)

Arizona Game Protective Association, the Arizona Game and Fish Commission voted to appropriate $6,000 for the department's share of a fund to establish a Cooperative Wildlife Research Unit at the University of Arizona in Tucson—making Arizona the sixteenth state to enroll in this program.

The Arizona Cooperative Wildlife Research Unit went into service in 1951. As per the usual arrangement, the Coop Unit was a partnership between the US Fish and Wildlife Service (formerly the Biological Survey), the Game and Fish Department, the University of Arizona, and the Wildlife Management Institute. The Coop Unit's purpose from the start was not only to train wildlife biologists, but to have graduate students conduct studies on wildlife species of particular interest to the partners.

Dr. Lyle Sowls, a former graduate student of Aldo Leopold's who had earned his doctorate working with waterfowl on the Delta Marsh in Manitoba and authored the award-winning book *Prairie Ducks*, was chosen Arizona's director and unit leader. Sowls wasted little time on arriving in Arizona, beginning a new study that expanded on David Gorsuch's Gambel's quail investigations (1934) and Ted Knipe's work on collared peccaries (1955) while also studying the reproductive potential of desert cottontails.

One student, C. Roger Hungerford, after investigating incidences of avian malaria in quail, went on to become assistant leader of the unit and earn a PhD studying factors determining reproductive success in Gambel's quail (Hungerford 1955, 1960a). In this capacity, Hungerford became leader of the undergraduate program, building a mentoring relationship with students that they would remember long after his premature passing from an aneurism in 1982.

Productive from the Beginning

The Coop Unit's early years were highly productive. In addition to conducting basic research into the food and water requirements of Gambel's quail (Hungerford 1960b, 1962), the unit researched the use of desert and chaparral browse plants by big game; water hole use by desert mule deer and collared peccaries; and life-history information on scaled quail, mourning and white-winged doves, white-tailed deer, and Abert's squirrels. Much of this work was in the field and involved students identifying important forage plants, developing a method to determine the age of javelina, collecting tree squirrels to analyze their diet, and performing other basic natural-history investigations.

In the meantime, Dr. Sowls's (1957) studies determined the breeding season, litter size, and population dynamics of desert cottontails, while he immersed himself in a banding study of Gambel's quail (Sowls 1960). Much of the success of this early work was due to the close cooperation between the Coop Unit and the Arizona Game and Fish Department, including joint participation in such management-related activities as operating javelina check stations (Sowls 1961b) and trapping and releasing wild javelina north of Wickenburg (Neal 1957, 1959a, 1959b; AGFD 1956).

In 1956, the Coop Unit initiated a turkey production study in the Graham Mountains, while Dr. Sowls and his students intensified their study of collared peccaries, investigating the animal's diet (Eddy 1959, 1961; Schweinsburg 1969), home-range size (Bigler 1964, 1974; Minnamon 1962), tooth irruption patterns (Neal and Kirkpatrick 1957; Kirkpatrick and Sowls 1962), and reproductive cycle (Sowls 1961a, 1961b). So fascinated did Sowls become with peccaries that he continued working on them throughout his life, and became a recognized authority on this family of animals (Sowls 1984).

Other Coop Unit activities in 1956 included building a fenced white-tailed deer exclosure in the Chiricahua Mountains to measure the effects of deer browsing on key food plants, moving into offices in the Biological Sciences East building on the University of Arizona campus, and acquiring space for wildlife pens at the university's farm on Campbell Avenue. The following year, the unit's horizons expanded even further as students attempted to evaluate the impacts of pinyon-juniper removal and other land-use projects then being conducted by the Forest Service (AGFD 1957).

Forays into Fisheries

The Coop Unit's research concern with only game animals changed in 1958, when a fisheries training and research component were added under Dr. Bill McConnell and a fisheries curriculum was instituted. The unit's staff increased to four—the director or unit leader, two associate professors, and a secretary. As prescribed in the enabling legislation, all were employees of the Fish and Wildlife Service and University of Arizona, with operating funds provided by the Wildlife Management Institute. The Game and Fish Department continued to pay $6,000 annually to support paid assistantships for graduate students.

Fisheries assistant leader McConnell's investigations began with the exploration of the food chain in the newly created Peña Blanca Lake, where he attempted to determine why the productivity of reservoirs declined over time. As part of this study, McConnell and his students analyzed the relationship between winter precipitation and plankton availability, and the influences of these phenomena and the introduction of threadfin shad on bass growth.

The Peña Blanca Lake studies also showed the complexity of the role played by forage fish in small impoundments and the problems associated with too many predatory fish. Channel catfish did well in this reservoir for three years, and the crappie population increased as well. These initially high production rates were attributed to a rise in primary plant forage during the lake's early years, coupled with heavy fishing pressure that reduced intra-species competition. For this reason, the introduction of threadfin shad as forage fish was not as important for black bass in Peña Blanca as in some of the larger reservoirs. This was due to lower temperatures and a tendency for young bass in Peña Blanca to be more prone to predation by larger bass than the shad. Creel census data also showed that most of the lake's use was by non-anglers, despite the Game and Fish Department's having borne most of the construction costs.

Another of McConnell's investigations involved tilapia, a tropical freshwater fish then new to the United States. Tank trials showed tilapia growth rates to be better than those of carnivorous fish when plant forage was adequate, both fish groups being dependent on reservoir fertility for growth. At this time, hybrid tilapia showed the most promise as a sport fishery. Prevented from overpopulating, these fish were released in the earth-lined Gillespie Canal near Gila Bend with considerable success.

On Their Way

By 1960, the unit was off and running. Ongoing studies included research into Abert's squirrel food habits near Flagstaff (Keith 1965), an investigation into the disappearance of Merriam's turkeys from the Graham Mountains, and deer watering requirements in the Tucson Mountains. Other studies morphed into an investigation of white-tailed deer food habits in the Santa Rita, Canelo, and Chiricahua mountains (Day 1960), deer use and distribution within the Three Bar Wildlife Area near Roosevelt Lake (McCulloch 1955a–d), and a more intensive investigation of the reproductive biology, nutritional needs, and population dynamics of Gambel's quail (Sowls 1960).

In addition to continuing his work on javelina, Sowls also finalized his study of reproduction in desert cottontails (Sowls 1960 in AGFD 1960). Other Coop Unit activities initiated in the late 1950s and early 1960s included an examination of the history of wildlife in Arizona (Davis 1982) and participation in in-service training schools for Game and Fish Department personnel.

Later studies continued to add to the knowledge bank on javelina behavior, reproduction, and disease. Many of these findings had management application (e.g., Sowls and Minnamon 1963). Check stations, for example, showed that about 25% of the javelina harvest normally consisted of juvenile animals, but that annual reproductive success was much influenced by drought (Day 1985). Other studies noted that quail populations fluctuated greatly due to variations in the amount of green feed. A direct correlation was found between the amount of winter rainfall and the occurrence of vitamin A in the quail's liver, egg production, and hatching success (Hungerford 1964). Less successful were experiments using hormones as an inducement to get fish to spawn, and increasing hatching success by supplying quail with vitamin A supplements (AGFD 1960, 1961, 1962).

The Three Bar Wildlife Area has been the subject of numerous studies, including this one involving the use of browse plants by deer in the early 1950s. (AGFD files)

In the meantime, Coop Unit personnel had determined that white-tailed deer in southern mountains were not migratory and that this species was responsible for the damage done to browse plants in the Chiricahua Mountains (Day 1964). Relationships between the Coop Unit and department personnel continued to be productive, and the commission not only continued funding the Coop Unit's graduate students, department personnel actively assisted in the unit's Gambel's quail and collared peccary studies (AGFD 1961). Using penned animals, biologists learned much about javelina physiology and age structure, while noting that these animals could live up to five months without drinking water, the animals subsisting entirely on prickly-pear cactus. Nonetheless, as with other animals, the peccary's annual reproductive success was limited by diet and drought (Day 1985).

Two other studies done in conjunction with the department involved an analysis of deer population dynamics on the Three Bar (McMichael 1967) and the effects of land treatment practices on national forests and other public lands (McCulloch 1961, 1972). It was also learned that mule deer on the Kaibab Plateau's summer range fed intensively on grasses and other herbaceous vegetation that had been released by fire, logging, or other disturbances (see e.g., Diem and Illige 1952). Less conclusive were studies into the population decline of wild turkeys in the Grahams and the status of coatis in the Chiricahuas—the birds in the former study mysteriously disappearing, and coatis being significantly reduced in numbers due to a distemper epidemic in 1961 (AGFD 1962).

The Coop Unit in 1962

By 1962, the Coop Unit was undertaking studies farther afield and looking into the movements of bighorn sheep in an attempt to determine the reasons for poor lamb survival in this species. The effects of feral burros on bighorn sheep were also being investigated, and unit personnel were learning that forage competition was more of a problem than competition for water. Although javelina check stations and marking studies continued in the Tortolita Mountains (Bigler 1964), the emphasis was now shifting to other species and other problems, including:

- a determination of the limiting factors constituting the habitat requirements of Mearns' quail;
- an evaluation of the effects of land treatment practices on mule deer and other big game;
- means to alleviate the problems associated with raising masked bobwhite in captivity; and
- an investigation into the relative contributions of breeding and wintering mourning doves to the Arizona dove harvest (e.g., R. L. Brown 1967).

Experiments into uses of tilapia for sport fishing ended about this time. Despite these hybrid populations being saline-tolerant, good eating, and catchable, tilapia were limited to waters with temperatures above 70°F, a situation rarely found in most winters in Arizona waters (AGFD 1964; Minckley 1973).

The Cooperative Wildlife Research Unit accomplished much in its first dozen years at the University of Arizona. Not only did it contribute greatly to our knowledge of desert cottontails, Gambel's quail, and collared peccaries, it graduated hundreds of wildlife students and bestowed 14 graduate degrees. Many of these students became wildlife managers and research biologists for the Arizona Game and Fish Department. Some became regional supervisors or branch or division chiefs, and one became a director.[1] Others became refuge managers or regional biologists for the Fish and Wildlife Service, while still others found employment with the Forest Service or Bureau of Land Management.

Solving wildlife management problems proved more difficult after 1962, as investigative assignments became increasingly involved with environmental impact and mitigation studies. The limits of studies by graduate student has also become increasingly apparent: Many wildlife phenomena cannot be understood, much less acted upon, in the two to four years graduate students have to complete their schoolwork—a conundrum not then fully appreciated by either the university or the Game and Fish Department.

Sensing these limitations, the Arizona Game and Fish Commission wisely allowed the department to retain its own Research Branch, contrary to a recommendation in the Wildlife Management Institute's Gabrielson Report that all wildlife research in Arizona be conducted by the Coop Unit. The causes of population changes in wildlife species are complex, particularly those related to the vagaries of climate and other natural phenomena, and often require decades to decipher if they can indeed be determined at all.

[1]This number would have been higher had not Director Robert Smith and Assistant Director Wendell Swank encouraged recruitment from other colleges and universities to open the department to a greater variety of experiences and philosophies.

THE ARIZONA GAME AND FISH DEPARTMENT BECOMES A LAND MANAGEMENT AGENCY

David E. Brown

With most of Arizona's big game and trout residing on national forests and much of the state designated either public domain or State Trust land, there was little incentive to acquire public hunting grounds in Arizona. Indeed, most of Arizona was considered public land, and the concept of another government agency acquiring more land was a hard sell at best. Nor was habitat protection deemed a problem, in that the US Forest Service was considered to be doing as good a job of land husbandry as conditions allowed, and most ranchers were regarded as the friends of game rather than its enemies. The only big game that needed better land husbandry, and therefore habitat acquisition, were such grassland species as bison and pronghorn.

Grasslands for Pronghorn (and Bison)

Hence, when the Arizona Game and Fish Commission decided to use Federal-Aid funds in 1942 to acquire pronghorn winter range, it was with the utmost caution, lest the Arizona State Legislature disapprove of the action and forbid any future purchases.

The purchase of Raymond Ranch was only possible due to the successful arguments of Orville "Pop" Arrington, then the Arizona Game and Fish Department's big game supervisor. The pronghorns' summer range on Anderson Mesa was on Forest Service land, but the winter range was another story. If sufficient winter forage was to be provided, and the commission-directed trapping and transplanting program to succeed, the Arizona Game and Fish Department would need an area where the management effort was focused on pronghorn.

Negotiations to acquire Raymond Ranch were complicated, involving the Forest Service and Arizona State Land Department, in addition to private land. Thanks to Arrington, the purchase was completed at a favorable price in a reasonable time, and a subsequent land trade was negotiated with the Forest Service. The commission was so pleased that it publicly commended Arrington for his good work and put him in charge of all Federal-Aid land acquisitions as of December 11, 1946—just in time for him to negotiate the transfer of most of the House Rock buffalo herd to Raymond Ranch.

Other than Raymond Ranch, the department's few land acquisitions up to 1949 came from a program by which the federal government transferred tax-delinquent lands to the state for conservation use. This was how the department gained title in 1947 to eight parcels of land along the lower Gila River, and in 1949 to Cluff Ranch on Ash Creek south of Pima.

Then in 1949, over several other competing interests, the department gained title to 35,000 acres of Fort Huachuca—another great coup for Arrington and his Lands Division. The department now had its own experimental wildlife area, dubbed the Charles T. Vorhies Research Project Area—a longtime goal of the commission and Arizona Game

Hunter with a bag of waterfowl taken along the lower Colorado River. Waterfowl hunting was relatively more important in Arizona prior to 1962 than later. (Arizona Historical Society/Yuma)

Protective Association. Together with Raymond Ranch's 20,320 acres and some lands along the lower Gila River, the commission had made the department a serious land management agency.

Wetlands for Waterfowl

Besides pronghorn and bison, one other class of wildlife having limited habitat in the state was waterfowl. Although most of Arizona's waterfowl nesting occurred on the national forests, the number of home-raised ducks was limited and hunters mostly took migrating or wintering birds from out of state. With natural wetlands in short supply, and man-made waters limited, resting and feeding sites for wintering ducks, geese, and shorebirds were at a premium. No wetlands were managed with waterfowl in mind, and the relatively few areas along the lower Colorado and Gila rivers that regularly hosted good populations of wintering birds were subject to water compacts and other agreements that made their water levels dependent on downstream demands rather than the needs of ducks and duck hunters. Even such important duck-hunting locales as Picacho Reservoir suffered from management limitations due to conflicting water rights, irrigation demands, and other competing uses. Because duck hunting provided a greater proportion of hunting activity in the 1940s and 1950s than today, there was much demand that something be done for the ducks.

In the late 1940s, the state made a number of attempts to acquire waterfowl resting and shooting areas. Particularly attractive to Arrington were such projects as Mittry Lake on the Colorado River and Luna Lake in the White Mountains. Such efforts were thought to benefit both fishermen and waterfowlers. Nor were other small game species ignored. Water developments in the form of windmills and guzzlers were constructed near Texas Hill and other lands along the lower Gila River, and in 1949 a pipeline and water-rights arrangement was worked out for the newly acquired Cluff Ranch, with the water to irrigate crops for wildlife.

Like many biologists in the 1950s, Wes Fleming was a World War II veteran who got his education through the GI Bill. He pioneered the development of Mittry Lake, Arlington, Robbins Butte, and Cibola wildlife areas. (AGFD files)

Working with biologist Wes Fleming, Arrington committed the department to obtaining wetland habitats that would attract and hold migrating waterfowl in southern Arizona. Wetland opportunities for migrating ducks and geese existed throughout the state, but appeared especially promising along the middle Gila River and on the lower Colorado River. By 1952, Fleming and Arrington were developing wildlife area plans for the middle Gila near Arlington and at Robbins Butte, and at Topock Marsh and Mittry Lake on the lower Colorado.

Meanwhile, efforts to acquire and develop waterfowl habitats in other areas of the state continued. Areas investigated for purchase and/or management included Picacho Reservoir, Sullivan Lake at the head of the Verde River, Parks Lake in Cochise County, Stoneman Lake, Jacques Lake, and Kingsley's ponds between Tucson and Nogales. Acquiring such areas came with many difficulties, however, ranging from obtaining water rights, to finding suitable lessees willing to farm croplands, to ejecting squatters.

The Bureau of Reclamation proved particularly difficult, and it was only due to legal action that the bureau finally dredged a channel to rehabilitate 39,000 acres of Topock Marsh. Arrington and Fleming persisted, nonetheless. Political pressures eventually resulted in lands at Mittry Lake and Arlington being leased for the benefit of waterfowl hunters. The commission had little influence on the bureau, so it asked the AGPA to ask the governor to withdraw federal lands along the lower Colorado River near Topock and Cibola so selected parcels could be purchased or leased for wildlife.

Elsewhere, the purchase of Tusayan Lake Dam was still being considered. The evaluation of Parks Lake in San Simon Valley resulted in a recommendation for a waterfowl management area that would include a dam, two artesian wells, and a pipeline to direct water onto Hospital Flat for only $5,000. To arrest erosion and prevent further arroyo-

It was only due to legal action that the Bureau of Reclamation finally dredged a channel to rehabilitate 39,000 acres of Topock Marsh in 1957. (AGFD files)

cutting along the San Simon River, the department helped forge an agreement with ranchers and the Bureau of Land Management that created a waterfowl area and closed 320 acres to grazing—an agreement similar to others the bureau had made for upper Centennial Wash near Salome. Unfortunately, none of these efforts succeeded, and erosion and floods took out all of the structures.

Although a blow from a game management perspective, the department's need to dispose of its Wellton-Mohawk Project lands along the lower Gila River came with financial benefits. Unable to pay the project's annual assessments on what was "only" wildlife habitat, the commission elected to sell and/or trade these lands to farmers. Only one of the 11 parcels originally put up for sale was sold at auction, but that sale brought in $32,000, which was now available for other Lands Division projects. And although disposing of the remaining lands proved to be a lengthy proposition, and some parcels sold for below appraised value, these lands enabled the department to pick up 160 acres of land at Cibola through trade, and eventually bring in $164,598 before the last sale was completed in 1962.

As should have been envisioned, developing wildlife areas for waterfowl proved even more contentious than building fishing lakes. The Parks Lake project was abandoned due to erosion problems. Fleming and his staff were hard-put to have the farming lessees at Arlington, Robbins Butte, and Cibola fulfill their cropland quotas and meet other agreements. Squatters and thieves were a source of numerous difficulties at Cibola and greatly handicapped the planting of wildlife foods there.

After several false starts, the Bureau of Reclamation finally agreed to an arrangement by which the department would secure the water rights to acquire 320 acres of Topock Marsh at $130 per acre. It was small compensation for the huge disappointment when Arizona's congressional delegation returned Fort Huachuca to the US Army Signal Corps. The AGPA, Game and Fish Commission, and department had always wanted a wildlife experiment station and had invested heavily in the research area during the brief time it was under department management. Not only did the department now have to remove its

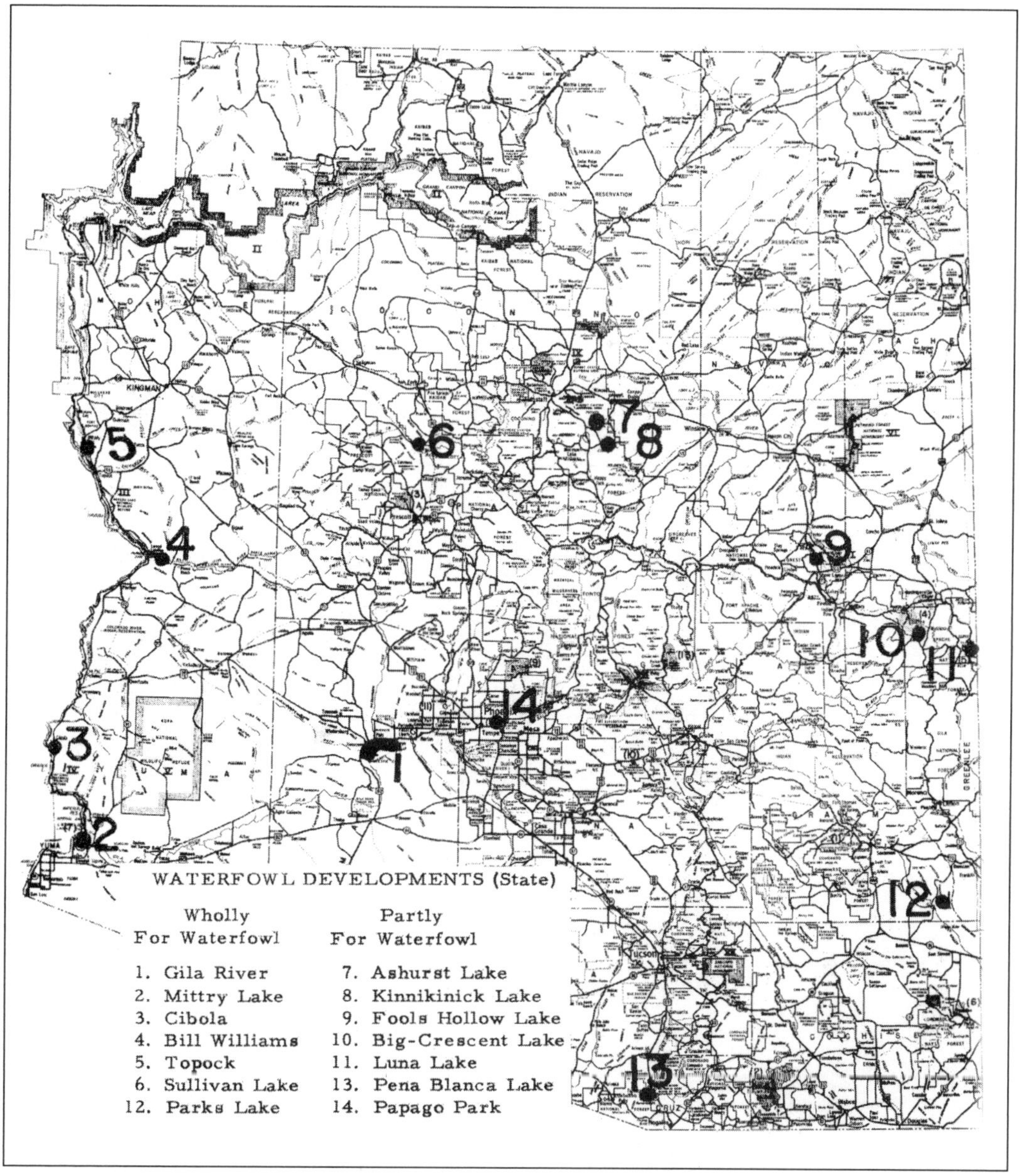

A map showing developments wholly or partially for waterfowl. Under Pop Arrington's guidance, the Arizona Game and Fish Commission developed and improved lakes for wildlife and fishing throughout the state. (AGFD files)

largest buffalo herd, this Korean War–era action put the quietus on wildlife watershed studies involving everything from Mearns' quail to deer, antelope, and turkeys (see e.g., Wallmo 1951).

Difficulties and delays aside, Mittry Lake, Topock Marsh, Arlington, Robbins Butte, and Cibola wildlife areas were all in operation and open to waterfowl hunting by 1958—a major feat given the logistical and legal complexities with the agencies and personnel involved. Also that same year, supervisors were hired for each of the wildlife areas and given salaries commensurate with their responsibilities.

Overview of Three Fingers Lake on the Colorado River, ca. 1959. Overflow areas and oxbow lakes made the lower Colorado River an important waterfowl and small game area before the Bureau of Reclamation lowered and channelized the river in the 1960s. (AGFD files)

The Lands Program Expands

The maintenance of wildlife areas posed its own problems. In 1958, the US Army Corps of Engineers proposed to clear the Gila River channel of vegetation, which would degrade the value of Robbins Butte and Arlington wildlife areas as dove-nesting habitat. Although the commission successfully opposed this particular proposal after consultation with the US Fish and Wildlife Service and Bureau of Land Management, other difficulties continued to crop up. Siltation was an ongoing problem at Cibola, Topock, and Mittry lakes, requiring further coordination with the Bureau of Reclamation and agreements for what would be more-or-less continuous dredge work.

A more positive development, at least initially, was the Army Corps of Engineers flood-control project on the lower Gila that resulted in a 200-acre lake forming in the borrow pit below the newly constructed Painted Rock Dam. Never one to let an opportunity lie idle, Arrington arranged to lease the 33,000 acres of federal land in the Gila River flood plain above the dam, as well as the downstream lake, as part of a Painted Rock Wildlife Area. Three thousand of these acres were then subleased and either reserved as mesquite forest or put into cropland for the benefit of wildlife before waters from the dam inundated the wildlife area in 1979.

The Black Canyon Shooting Range, ca. 1961. The property turned out to be one of the Game and Fish Commission's wisest investments. (AGFD files)

One project that was neither a lake nor a waterfowl area was a 1957 recommendation by AGPA member Ben Avery to build a rifle range near Adobe Mountain on Highway 69. This proposal, which morphed into an Arizona Game and Fish Department request for 1,700 acres of Bureau of Land Management and State Trust land north of Biscuit Flat, was facilitated by Governor Ernest McFarland. He informed the state land commissioner that no money need be spent acquiring State Trust land for a shooting range.

Using the need for firearms safety instruction as justification, the commission eventually applied for, and received, 1,200 acres of state land and 191 acres of federal land for what was initially called the Black Canyon Shooting Range. Easing the acquisition was the department's drilling a well to compensate the grazing lessee, the Lockett Sheep Ranch, for the loss of forage during and after construction. Eventually the department acquired 500 acres from the Bureau of Land Management under the Recreation and Public Purposes Act for what is today the Ben Avery Shooting Facility.

Arrington's land projects, while continuing to focus on lake building and waterfowl developments, expanded in scope after 1960. The major land development project was now the Chevelon waterfowl area at the junction of Chevelon Creek and the Little Colorado River, where the department would obtain water rights and buy 114 acres of private land. In 1961, Arrington was also involved with land exchanges around Fool Hollow, Pinetop (22 acres), Bubbling Ponds near Page Springs (30 acres), Clay Springs, and on the north Kaibab Plateau.

Frustrated in his dealings with the Arizona State Land Department, Arrington wanted the commission to authorize institutional "takings" measures to acquire state land near Martinez Lake for recreation and wildlife purposes. Of the more than 1 million dollars spent by the department in fiscal year 1961–62, Dingell-Johnson expenditures accounted for $122,803.66 and Pittman-Robertson monies, $448,924.20—most of the Federal-Aid money going to development projects (AGFD 1962).

The goals for the waterfowl areas Arrington and Fleming envisioned have been modified with time. Although Pittman-Robertson and duck-stamp funds were used in their construction, none of the lakes materially benefited waterfowl or waterfowl hunters or compensated for the loss of natural wetland habitats.[1] Topock Marsh and Cibola wildlife areas, once so demanding of Fleming's time and expertise, were eventually absorbed into the National Wildlife Refuge system as mitigation for the Bureau of Reclamation's channeling and lowering of the Colorado River.

On the other hand, Arlington and Robbins Butte, while never attaining their planned waterfowl potential, have provided increasingly important habitats for white-winged doves, mourning doves, Gambel's quail, and cottontail rabbits. These areas, and other lands adjacent to the Gila River greenbelt, are now of immense value as open space. Their croplands host annual junior dove hunts and other hunting-oriented activities—the worth of which cannot be denied.

That Ben Avery Shooting Facility was one of the department's wisest investments in capital outlay will also never be open to question, and the shooting facility remains a monument to its venerable namesake.

[1] Unlike fishing licenses, federal duck-stamp sales in Arizona declined or remained relatively constant during the 1950s and 1960s (see Appendix D, Table D-1).

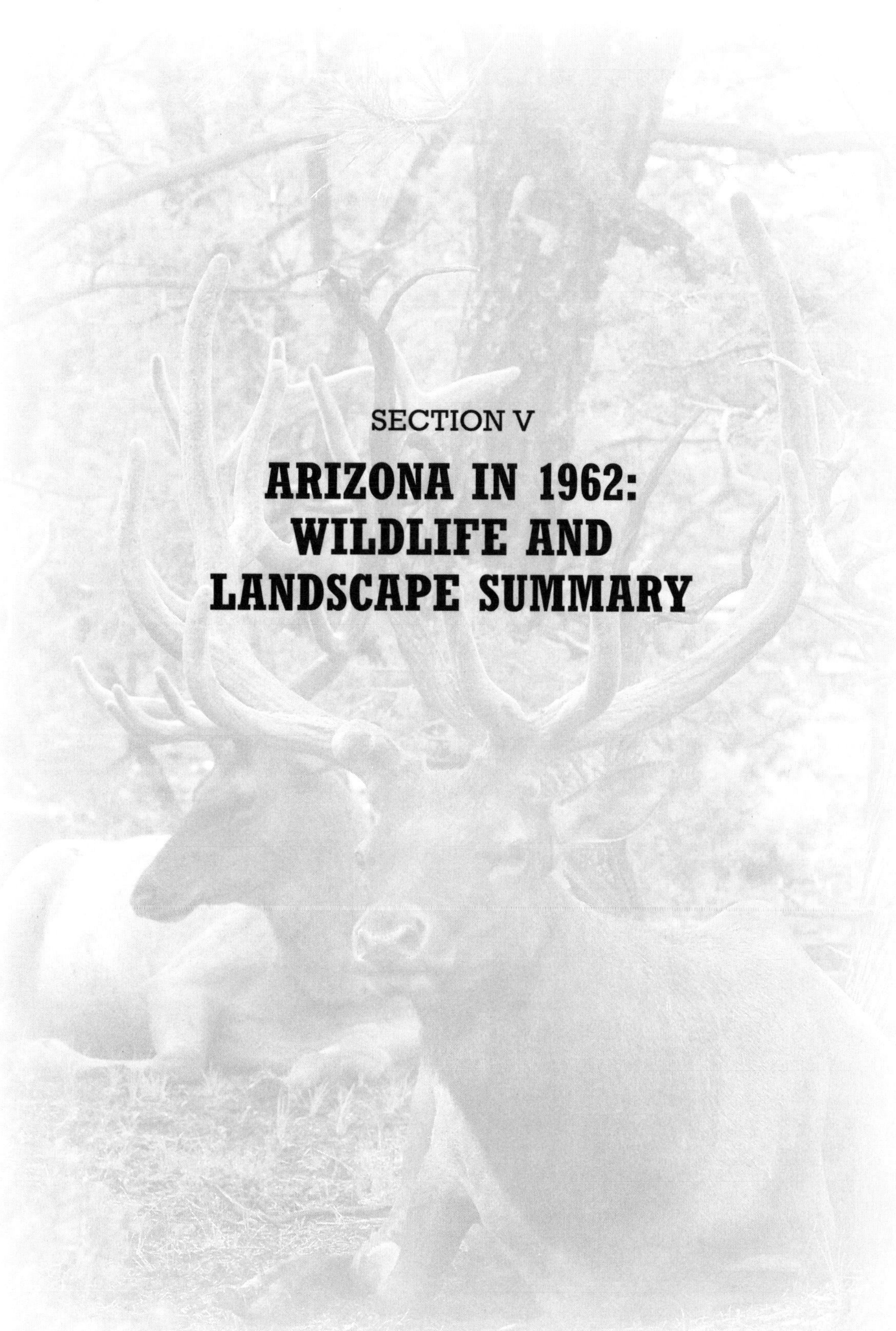

SECTION V

ARIZONA IN 1962: WILDLIFE AND LANDSCAPE SUMMARY

STATUS OF WILDLIFE SPECIES IN 1962

David E. Brown

By the early 1960s, Arizona sportsmen were seeing the benefits of 50 years of effort. Harvests of white-tailed deer and mule deer were at the highest levels since harvest estimates were initiated in 1946 (see Appendix D, Table D-2). This was especially remarkable given that populations of Coues' white-tailed deer had been described as reaching an all-time low in the late 1930s when the season on desert mule deer was closed south of the Gila River. Even the Kaibab, the home of the state's premier deer herd, had been judged to be at such a low level during the 1930s and early 1940s that only 500 buck-only permits were issued and 251 deer killed there in 1946. Now, in 1962, estimated harvests were a whopping 19,064 Rocky Mountain mule deer, 5,427 desert mule deer, and 4,213 whitetails, with nearly a third of the harvest being "excess" antlerless deer (AGFD 1988).

Elk numbers had also improved dramatically by 1962. After more than 20 years of slow population growth and conflict with dryland homesteaders, an elk season was finally authorized in 1935 to alleviate crop damage and correct an "imbalance" in the sex ratio. That year, 266 hunters took 145 bull elk. Now, 27 years later, 2,759 hunters harvested 871 elk, consisting of 435 bulls and 317 cows and calves. But sportsmen had not seen anything yet. Despite biologists' admonishment that hunters had best enjoy what were then thought to be maximum elk numbers, elk numbers and harvests would continue to increase.

The situation with pronghorn antelope was even more serendipitous. Once deemed Arizona's most difficult big game species to restore, the state's pronghorn population was only thought to total 618 animals in 1925. Even after a hunt was initiated on what was regarded as a local overpopulation in 1941, many inside and outside the Arizona Game

Bill Sizer packing out a deer on horseback on the north Kaibab (Tater Canyon), ca. November 1957. (AGFD files)

A busy check station on the Kaibab Plateau in 1961 attests to the area's abundant deer herd. (AGFD files)

and Fish Department thought pronghorn would never be a huntable species in Arizona, and the season was again closed from 1944 through 1947. Imagine the surprise of earlier biologists and sportsmen when 5,000 of these animals were censused in 1963 and 729 tagged by hunters—39 of them legally taken does.

The story of the collared peccary or javelina in Arizona is equally remarkable. The javelina was not even considered a game animal until the game code of 1929, and the season was closed from 1932 to 1938 because of a reported scarcity of animals (Day 1985). When the season was again tentatively authorized in 1939 for 15 days, only four counties were open to hunting. Even by 1950, when a standardized early spring season became the norm, the harvest was only 1,344 animals. Yet by 1962, more than 20,000 hunters were hunting "desert pigs" and taking a then-record 4,343 javelina for a 21% hunt success rate.

The status of desert bighorn sheep had dramatically improved from an animal whose fate was once described as sealed to that of Arizona's premier trophy animal. After three major mountain sheep refuges were established and two investigations into reasons for the animal's decline ended inconclusively, a study begun by John Russo in 1950 determined that active management measures, including hunting, were necessary to obtain the support needed for bighorn to recover. As a measure of this approach's success, two initial hunting seasons in 1953, in which 37 hunters took 10 rams, were expanded in following years, until 90 special permits were issued in 1962 with 27 rams taken. More important, interest in this species grew so high that plans to transplant bighorn were begun and special organizations such as the Desert Bighorn Council and Arizona Desert Bighorn Sheep Society were formed to champion the animal's continuing welfare.

Bison numbers, despite the elimination of the Fort Huachuca herd, were also at high levels by 1962. The department now prescribed harvests of about 100 animals a year, alternating between the two remaining herds at House Rock and Raymond Ranch. This was a sizeable increase over the number of animals annually killed at House Rock during the 1930s and 1940s. Unfortunately, even this modest number could not be sustained, given the small amount of arid rangeland allocated to these animals. Even the 400–500 or so animals present in the early 1960s would be reduced eventually, to protect range resources that were supposed to be shared with pronghorn.

No game animal had been subject to more management efforts than the wild turkey. Attempts to restock depleted areas with wild and pen-reared birds dated back to at least 1919. Yet, despite some notable achievements including the establishment of Merriam's turkeys in nonhistoric habitat on the north Kaibab Plateau, turkey numbers continued to wax and wane. Populations were thought to have reached an all-time low in the mid-1930s (Ligon 1946), resulting in the implementation of additional game refuges, establishment of game waters, enactment of more restrictive hunting restrictions, and an acceleration in trapping and transplanting programs.

Although some turkey populations did respond, others, such as those in the Pinaleño and Galiuro mountains, remained at low levels or disappeared. Then, with the initiation of Pittman-Robertson studies in the 1940s, biologists realized turkey numbers were related to weather and habitat quality on both the birds' summer and winter ranges. With a gradual improvement in herbaceous vegetation, turkey numbers grew erratically. Season length and the number of hunt permits were therefore gradually increased, from less than 1,000 permits in 1949 to 8,550 in 1960. In 1963, a general turkey season was again authorized, and 15,939 hunters took 1,472 turkeys.

The recovery of bear populations was more problematic. The grizzly bear had been extirpated in Arizona, the last of this species being killed on the Apache Indian reservations by US Biological Survey predator-control agents in the late 1930s. Black bears too were killed as depredation animals, and in 1945 the Arizona State Legislature removed the black bear from the list of big game animals. The species proved resilient, however, with black bears only eliminated from some of the more marginal ranges such as the Bradshaw, Baboquivari, and Atascosa mountains. As depredation pressures gradually subsided, bear numbers increased. Full game status was reinstated in 1964, as were more protective hunt regulations. That year's sport harvest of 178 bears heralded a time when black bears would continue to increase in numbers and distribution.

Mountain lions, then classified as predators, were considered under control in the early 1960s, with an average of 240 bountied annually—a figure slightly lower than the mean of today's sport harvests. Estimates regarding the status of other predators in the early 1960s are difficult to derive, despite the annual tallies then maintained by the US Fish and Wildlife Service's Predator and Rodent Control branch. Coyotes, while remaining ubiquitous, had entirely replaced wolves by 1962, the last breeding wolves in the state having been removed from Fort Huachuca in 1944 (Brown 1983).

Furbearer numbers in the early 1960s are also difficult to estimate, as these species were subject to decreasing trapping pressures after World War II due to the decline in fur prices. What is known is that the black-footed ferret and river otter were extirpated during the 1950s attendant with the widespread use of Compound 1080 and other poisons.

Changes in small game populations are hard to gauge before the advent of hunter report cards in the 1960s. The numbers of Arizona's most popular resident game bird, the Gambel's quail, fluctuated as they do now, as indicated by the great changes in season lengths that accompanied observed permutations—ranging from four months long to closed seasons. By 1962, investigations were showing that fall numbers of Gambel's quail were mostly determined by the success of the hatch, which in turn was determined by the amount of winter rain and the vitamin content in the birds' food.

Another factor impacting quail management was reduction in the brush-bordered grain fields that had generated numerous crop-depredation complaints during the first half of the twentieth century. With populations fluctuating primarily on the basis of weather conditions, hunting seasons were lengthened and bag limits standardized—measures facilitated by generally robust quail numbers during the early 1960s. From 1961 to 1968, the daily bag on quail averaged 4.3 birds per hunter. That both hunt questionnaires and check station data indicate quail numbers that were measurably higher in the early 1960s than now remains unexplainable and is probably due to environmental factors not yet understood.

Dove hunting was also good in the early 1960s. White-winged dove numbers were especially robust with an ideal combination of grain crops and river-bordered thickets present. With season dates having been worked out with the Fish and Wildlife Service, hunters from all over the country were drawn to Arizona by the 25-whitewing bag limit. The September 1 opening day was a gala event for sportsmen's families, movie stars, and professional sports figures. And the numbers of birds taken was large, the daily bag of white-winged doves and mourning doves averaging 4.0 and 5.6 birds per hunter, respectively. Such days, unfortunately, were not to last, as reclamation projects and changing agricultural practices began whittling away the favorable combination of woodlands and cropland that had made Arizona a dove-hunting mecca since statehood.

Waterfowl hunting was one sport that did not materially gain from changes wrought during the first 50 years of statehood. Increasing consumptive pressures and managed water levels gradually reduced the numbers of birds produced on the small wetlands in northern Arizona, while migration and wintering stopovers in southern Arizona were continually altered and/or reduced in size. Development of the lower Colorado River, impoundment of the state's rivers, and a management emphasis on fishing and other water uses conspired to limit or concentrate migrating waterfowl in Arizona. One notable exception is the numerous stock tanks or *charcos* that were constructed mainly from 1930 through the 1950s. Formerly one of the most popular of outdoor sports, duck shooting over decoys was destined to become increasingly limited. As a result, the numbers of duck hunters, waterfowl hunting days, and daily bags had plateaued and eventually would decline (see Appendix D, Table D-3).

Fifty years after statehood, Arizona's warm-water reservoirs were producing healthy numbers of sport fish. Game and Fish Department information chief Bill Sizer with black bass in April 1955. (AGFD files)

Rabbit and hare populations, while difficult to quantify, also appear to have declined. Although jackrabbit drives and other responses to large rabbit populations largely ceased after 1950 (Brown 2009), jackrabbit and cottontail numbers were probably higher in 1962 than at present. Mean cottontail-hunt success 1966–69 was 1.85 rabbits per hunter day—twice the rate of 0.8 rabbits per hunter day in 1998–2005 (AGFD 2009). One has to wonder if factors other than weather were in play and if predator control was a factor in the numbers of rabbits and certain rodents, as it appears to have been for deer and porcupines (Brown and Babb 2009).

Tree squirrel hunting, subject to closed seasons for many years, was reopened in the 1950s. Based on the increasing numbers of hunters, this sport was just becoming popular in 1962. The number of squirrels present then appears to have been high. At least the 2.0 mean number of squirrels per hunter day taken between 1966 and 1969 was greater than the average 1.5 squirrels claimed per hunter day 1998–2005 (AGFD 2009).

With a preponderance of data showing hunting to have little effect on small game populations, and numbers of most game animals thought to be increasing, seasons were opened on species that had been protected in the game codes of 1912, 1916, 1929, 1939, and 1958. An experimental season on Mearns' or Montezuma quail was opened in 1960, and in 1964 a hunting season was initiated on blue grouse. Other hunting seasons would follow on band-tailed pigeons and sandhill cranes—the season on the former being closed in 1950 due to too few birds being available.

Not all wildlife species benefited from the changes wrought during the state's first half-century. Some nongame grassland species suffered greatly (Brown and Davis 1994). Scaled quail experienced measurable restrictions in distribution and numbers, while other grass-affiliated birds such as the rufous-winged and five-striped sparrow nearly disappeared (Phillips, Marshall, and Monson 1964). At least two grassland raptors, the aplomado falcon and white-tailed hawk, no longer nested in Arizona (Brown and Glinski 2009). The by-now almost mythical masked bobwhite was believed to be extinct in both Arizona and Sonora, Mexico, despite heroic efforts by Stokley Ligon and his colleagues to trap birds in Sonora and reintroduce them back into Arizona. The problem was that the bird's historical habitat in Arizona was imperfectly known and probably unavailable.

Like hunters, fishermen too had cause to rejoice. For one thing, there were a lot more places to fish. Reservoirs, both large and small, had proliferated. The big dams along the Salt, Verde, Agua Fria, and Colorado rivers provided abundant new fishing sites, all now inhabited by largemouth bass, black and white crappie, channel catfish, and bluegill. Smallmouth bass and channel catfish inhabited the state's larger streams. More localized successes included walleyed pike in the Salt River reservoirs and white bass in Lake Pleasant. Wanting bigger game fish, the department was now, or would soon be, involved in the introduction of such major predators as the flathead catfish, northern pike, and striped bass—species that would later prove problematic to both game and nongame fishes alike. This had been the case with the early introduction of such hoped-for commercial species as carp and buffalofish (fish of the genus *Ictiobus*). Introductions of yellow perch, green

With the hatcheries at Page Springs and Tonto running at full capacity, trout anglers reeled in sizeable catches in the late 1950s and early 1960s. (AGFD files)

sunfish, and yellow and black bullheads resulted in stunted populations, while bullfrog and crayfish releases succeeded wildly in nearly every spring, stock tank, and reservoir.

Trout fishermen also benefited. The department's hatcheries at Page Springs and Tonto were operating at full capacity, producing an average of up to 2 million trout annually, with as many as 500,000 of these being "catchables" seven inches or more in length. The long-awaited and lobbied-for federal hatchery had come to fruition with the dedication of Williams Creek Hatchery in 1944, and a new federal hatchery at Willow Beach was providing catchable trout above and below Davis Dam. Studies having shown the difficulty of raising fry fish to adulthood, some 10,000 more pounds of catchable trout were stocked in 1962 than the previous year. By way of comparison, some 1,261,347 trout (mostly rainbows) and 232,700 warm-water fishes were planted in 1936 (S. L. Lewis 1936). Best of all, trout fishermen could now enjoy many new or newly improved trout lakes, with more on the way.

Unfortunately, the successful establishment of game fishes, along with altered stream flows, had decimated the state's native fishes. The big-river fishes such as the Colorado salmon (now pikeminnow), razorback sucker, and humpbacked chub were by now functionally extirpated from the state or soon would be, due to altered stream flows and competition with introduced game fishes (Minckley 1973). One once-ubiquitous endemic, the

Gila topminnow, had been almost totally replaced by the similar adapted but nonnative mosquitofish. That the state's chubs, suckers, and native minnows were under siege due to competition from introduced baitfish and predation from game fish was as yet imperfectly recognized. No longer considered food or game fishes, the native fishes were as yet little missed and their absence was considered merely the price paid for the proliferation of reservoirs. That these same waters now provided an abundance of predatory game fishes was a beneficial trade-off that met with objections from almost no one.

Help for Arizona's native trout was on the way, however. With the demand for hatchery-produced trout finally met, an active program would soon start propagating the state's native trouts—species we know today as Apache and Gila trout. Searches were initiated in 1963 to locate Apache trout brood stock in the White Mountains for the department's Sterling Springs hatchery (AGFD 1963), while New Mexico was already actively working to recover the Gila trout.

All in all, the changes to wildlife populations in the first 50 years of Arizona statehood had been much more beneficial than negative. And although these gains were real, and due in part to a better understanding of the state's biota and improved game laws, it can also be said that these mostly game species benefited from the application of sound game and fish management practices. But it is also true that the sociological and cultural changes brought about by Arizona's unique history of land tenure were also at work—changes that, as the next chapter explains, had more impact on wildlife numbers than laws, regulations, and more enlightened management practices.

LAND TENURE AND LAND USES IMPACTING WILDLIFE

Harley G. Shaw and David E. Brown

Arizona's history of land ownership and management is complex and to some extent unique. Arizona has one of the lowest percentages of private land of any state, with most of the land area being in government ownership—only 18% of Arizona land is privately owned. Almost all of Arizona historically was wildlife habitat, but the human impacts on habitat, including impacts to habitat on "government lands," have been profound.

Indeed, land uses or "tenure," principally water development, ranching, irrigated farming, and urbanization, have resulted in a massive alteration of landscapes that is now difficult to appreciate. Foremost among these changes has been soil erosion—both surface soil loss through wind and water removal and arroyo-cutting caused by flooding (Cooke and Reeves 1976; McAuliffe 1994). Less apparent to the inexperienced eye are the twin effects of grazing and fire suppression—the invasion and thickening of woody and noxious plants at the expense of herbaceous species, the desertification and replacement of former grasslands by scrublands, and the total loss of certain deep-soil grass-weed habitats (Turner et al. 2003; Arrington 1942b; Brown and Glinski 2009).

How this all came about remains poorly understood but is worth exploring, as it is inextricably tied to land ownership and land husbandry. Part of the difficulty is that different lands have different histories depending on land status, access, water availability, and land law. In the following pages, we explore the histories of the various land classifications, the impacts of settlement, and the laws that determined their use.

The period under consideration here, 1912–61, witnessed major modifications in land tenure, some beneficial to wildlife, a lesser number devastating. While some settled holdings were grandfathered in as private land when Arizona became a state, most of Arizona remained the property of the US government at statehood. As such, it was public domain, and early use was barely regulated, if at all.

Disposing of the Public Domain

Except for lands administered by the US Forest Service, most of which had been withdrawn prior to statehood (Brown 2009), Arizona's land tenure history involves an incremental conversion of public domain to private lands or a reclassification of government lands through a sequence of federal legislation. Early on, the effects of such legislation were small, but they set in motion growing cumulative effects on wildlife habitat, most of which remain in place today.

Initially, all public-domain lands were intended to be converted to private ownership as quickly as possible, thereby encouraging the settlement of an underpopulated state. Wildlife's role, to the extent it was recognized, was to provide food and other necessities until the land was domesticated. In his annual message to the legislature, John N. Goodwin, Arizona's first territorial governor, stated the attitude clearly on September 30,

Homestead Acres Entered in Arizona and New Mexico, 1868–1961

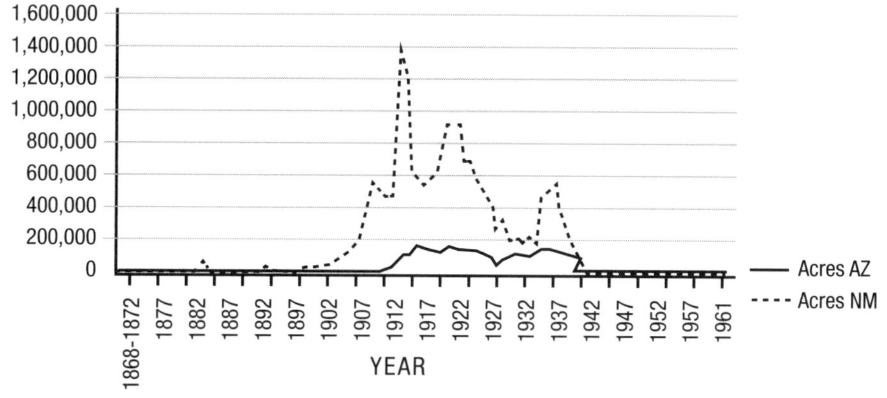

Number of Homestead Entries in Arizona and New Mexico, 1868–1961

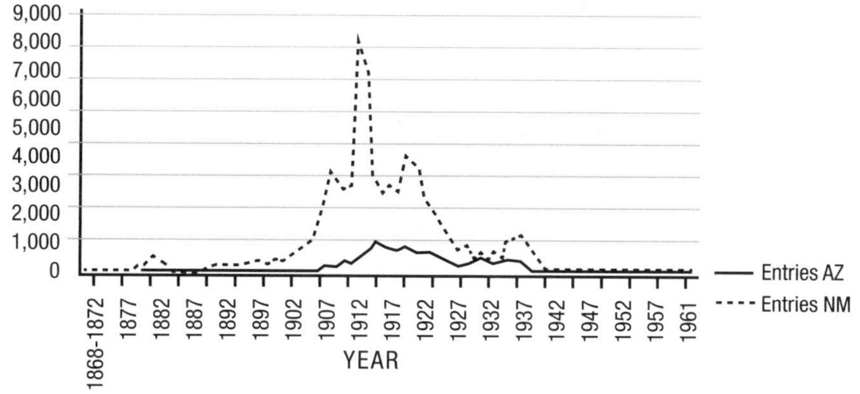

1864, when he said, "[T]he Indian and the antelope must disappear together before the Anglo-Saxon race" (Lamar 1966).

Hostile Indians, aridity, and the distance from population centers nonetheless slowed the process of settlement to the extent that Arizona was the last conterminous state admitted to the Union. By this time many settlers had come to believe much of the state was unsuitable for domestication. Agriculture was thought to be forever limited by the amount and distribution of water, and most Arizona landscapes were considered suitable only for ranching and mining.

The state's waters outside of the Colorado River had already been allocated if not adjudicated. Even before the first federal Homestead Act in 1862, certain agricultural lands along the middle Gila and lower Salt rivers had been claimed by Pima and Tohono O'odham tribes, Hispanic settlers, and Anglo homesteaders. Minuscule acreages had also been farmed for centuries by Moqui Pueblos in northern Arizona, but most of the private farmland was in the southern half of the state south of the Gila River, the United States government having recognized the private and communal grants within the Territory of New Mexico carried over from Spanish and Mexican rule.

In 1891, the US government established the Court of Private Land Claims to adjudicate land grant claims in New Mexico and Arizona. As a result, some 200,000 additional acres in Arizona were allocated to satisfy the legal claims of persons who held Spanish land grants in New Mexico and had lost their holdings when their lands were claimed illegally by United States citizens (Lamar 1966). Most private holdings during Arizona's territorial period were obtained by non-Arizonans filing homesteads, with only a few Native Americans and early settlers acquiring ownership of property in this manner. As for Native Americans, the federal government recognized their communal sense of property by creating tribal reservations that ultimately encompassed some 26% of Arizona's land area (see table below).

By the time of statehood, federal legislation encouraging settlement included the 1862 Homestead Act and the Desert Lands Act of 1877. These would soon be bolstered by the Stock Raising Homestead Act of 1916 and other homestead laws (Stein 1990).

Disposition of the public domain was also fostered through enabling legislation granting lands to the state as an incentive to obtain money to develop schools and other public institutions. Large land grants to railroad companies encouraged the construction of railroads. In some cases, public land, including even forest reserves, was sold outright as a means to stimulate development (Greever 1954). Even so, at statehood, less than two percent of Arizona was in private hands (see table below). Of those lands remaining, some 12.4 million acres had been withdrawn for the national forests, leaving 51,749,566 acres as undesignated public domain available for disposal. Another 8,065,209 had been granted to Arizona as State Trust Lands, the income from which was intended to be used to support public institutions, especially schools.

Land Tenure in Arizona in 1912 and 1961 (Acres)

Land Ownership	1912	1961
Public Domain/Railroad (Bureau of Land Management)	51,749,566	12,200,000
National Forests	12,400,000	9,503,000
National Parks	None	2,962,853
Federal Wildlife Refuges	700,000	1,738,104
Federal Total[a]	**64,849,566**	**30,717,777**
Indian Lands	Most reservations in place by 1912	20,138,019
State Trust Lands	8,065,209	9,266,407
Arizona Game and Fish Dept. Lands[b]	None	39,883
Homesteads and Other Deeded Lands[c]	549,074	3,000,000
Total Private[d]	749,074	12,841,636
Total Arizona Acreage	**72,963,840**	**72,963,840**

[a]Includes Bureau of Reclamation, military, and other withdrawals

[b]Not including wildlife areas managed but not owned by the Arizona Game and Fish Department (Angie Lohse, Arizona Game and Fish Department, pers. comm., 2009)

[c]Peaked at 4,748,000 acres, but nearly 2,000,000 were returned to government ownership

[d]Includes state, county, and some small federal parcels.

The biggest constraint thwarting the conversion of public land to private land was lack of rainfall and permanent water. This limitation did not always apply to seasonal use, and livestock grazing was soon destined to become Arizona's most widespread form of land use. Historical accounts vary in details, but where water was available or had been developed, virtually all of Arizona was at or above livestock carrying capacity by the time of statehood (Brown 2009). In 1912, livestock pressures had penetrated to encompass even the most remote timbered and mountainous areas.

Early Impacts of Livestock

Not only were there pressures from range livestock but also from domestic and feral horses and burros. For more than 70 years, heavy grazing reduced vegetative ground cover; as a result, there were no fine fuels to carry surface fires. Grazing, which reduced competition from herbaceous species, allowed rapid growth of pinyon, juniper, and oaks in adjacent communities (Nabi 1978).

The numbers of range cattle and sheep in the Southwest peaked during or shortly after World War I. Before declining after 1920, range cattle numbers in Arizona reached about 1.6 million head. Currently, by way of comparison, there are about half a million head of cattle in Arizona. Sheep numbers have experienced an even steadier and more dramatic decline.

Getting control and maintaining sound range management procedures were the most difficult resource management problems facing the Forest Service during the first five to six decades of the agency's existence. As a result, ecosystems grazed by domestic livestock, and to a lesser extent browsed by wildlife, suffered significant damage during this period. Only a substantial investment and total protection could save some plant communities, and it was not until the early 1960s that the Forest Service began to gain some control over its most damaged rangelands.

Since then, with livestock numbers continuing to shrink, and more intensive management systems initiated, grazing allotments have regained productivity. Annual grazing reports document the decreases in permitted numbers of cattle, horses, and sheep in Arizona: All livestock classes have declined by more than half from their peak numbers in 1919. Sheep and goats are a small fraction of their 1919 levels, both in Arizona and nationwide. These rapid declines were due to the Forest Service's generally favoring cattle leases over those for sheep, as well as the post-1940 decline in both exports of mohair to Europe and its domestic use for automobile upholstery.

Fewer Cows, More Deer and Elk

At the same time that livestock numbers decreased, populations of wild ungulates have increased. Mule deer populations and range grew with the development of stock tanks and increases of woody vegetation (Heffelfinger 2006; this volume). After elk were reintroduced from 1913 to 1928, their numbers increased until the annual elk harvest in Arizona in 1963 exceeded 1,000 animals. In some areas, such as the Apache and Gila national forests, livestock numbers had to be adjusted in response to resource use by elk as these animals moved into areas and their numbers grew.

Cattle in Arizona 1910–61, Thousands

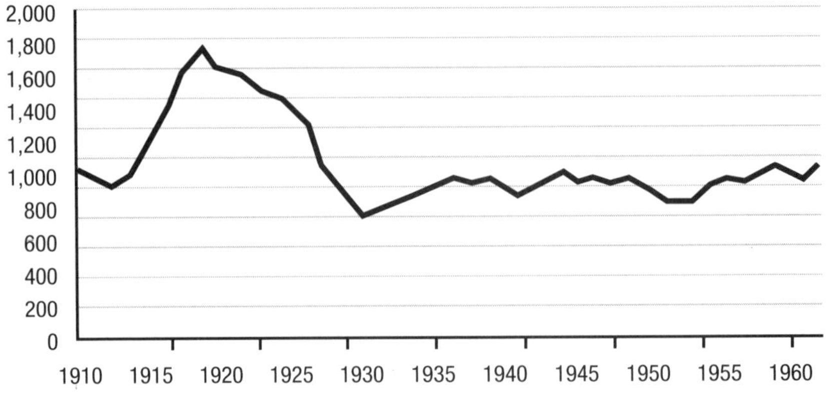

Sheep in Arizona 1920–61, Thousands

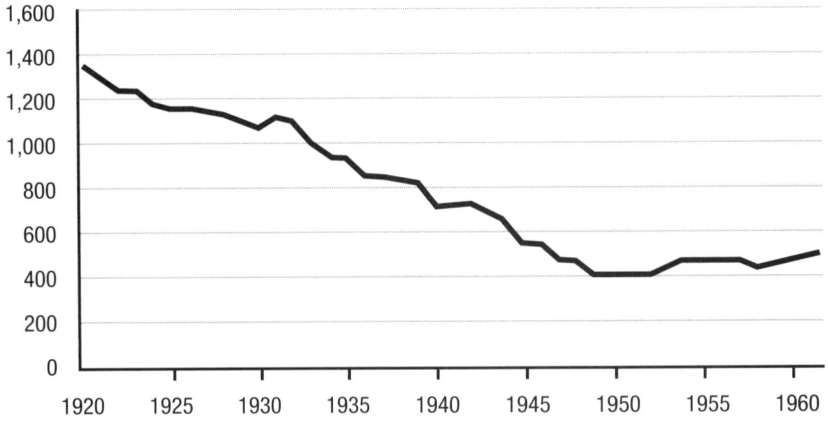

Mohair, Thousands of Goats Clipped, 1921–61

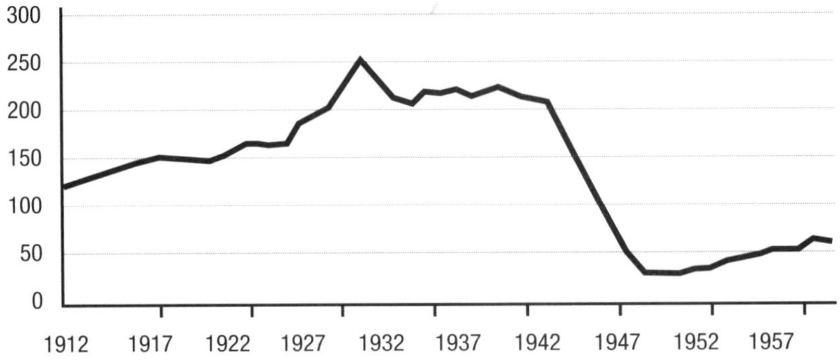

As grazing and browsing pressures in the Southwest intensified, rangeland ecosystems were impacted directly and indirectly. Forest, woodland, grassland, and to a lesser extent, desert ecosystems, have gone from no or light grazing prior to 1865, through severe pressures during the last decade of the nineteenth century and first several decades of the twentieth, to levels that attempted to balance livestock numbers with capacity—at least on the national forests.

This has not been the case on many Bureau of Land Management, state, and private lands, where annual productivity is such that sustained grazing cannot be managed effectively, these lands being subject to "ephemeral" or seasonal grazing leases—often in addition to lower base allotment numbers. The result of this grazing history has been to reduce the amount and diversity of Arizona's rangeland soils and vegetation, thereby altering plant compositions to the point that these lands cannot absorb water or carry fires to the degree they formerly did.

Such intense use was reduced on the national forests, particularly after World War I, when the Forest Service worked with the larger cattle companies to bring livestock numbers more in line with carrying capacity. The Forest Service also negotiated a gradual but steady reduction in sheep numbers in favor of cows. Overstocking, especially during drought years, remained a problem, nonetheless, and water development and erosion control continued to be priority management remedies on federal lands through the 1950s. The result was that few if any of Arizona's rangelands had not been grazed by 1962, by which time virtually no rangelands went ungrazed, including those in wilderness areas.

This ubiquitous presence of livestock was due to water development, as ranchers attempted to expand livestock range and numbers. Prior to the region's acquisition by the United States, Mexican and Indian ranchmen developed wells, cisterns, and *tinajas* for their animals along with the construction of *represos* and *charcos* using *fresno* scrapers drawn by horses or mules. These efforts greatly accelerated with the arrival of Anglo-Americans and the advent of large-scale ranching operations in the 1880s. Windmills and stock tanks designed to distribute and maintain livestock were continually added. Large-scale earth-moving equipment became available after World War II, and the most active period of stock-tank construction occurred about 1958 (Jody Latimer, Arizona State Land Department, pers. comm., 2008). Although wildlife may have benefited from these structures initially, the end result was too often overstocking of livestock with subsequent surface soil erosion, channel cutting, and desertification (McAuliffe 1994).

Homestead Lands

Of the 749,074 acres of land patented by statehood, about 550,000 acres had been obtained through 3,577 claims filed under the various homestead acts. "Preemption laws" also recognized the presence of "squatters" or "nesters" already on the land, allowing them to purchase or patent their holdings if certain residency requirements were met and other procedures were followed. Oftentimes these early holdings were irregularly shaped, and nearly all were located along streams or near natural springs, thereby having a disproportionately large impact on wildlife. The preemption process, and the legal recognition of such lands, would become one of the primary methods by which the federal government ceded lands to settlers. Oftentimes, such holdings provided the base properties and waters for livestock operations, which then grazed the surrounding public domain (Waggoner 1952).

Between 1868 and 1962, 20,268 homestead entries were made in Arizona, encompassing 4,134,356 acres. Homestead entries increased after passage of the Enabling Act in 1910 and greatly accelerated after statehood in 1912. The highest number of successful homestead entries recorded in Arizona took place in 1916 and 1917. By 1920, homesteading filings were declining, although another surge occurred in the Depression years between 1930 and 1936.

Major factors affecting homesteading were the Stock Raising Homestead Act of 1916; World War I, which created a booming demand for meat and produce; and the Depression, which brought immigrants from the Midwest to Arizona lured by free land. From 1912 to 1961, 3,621,420 acres were withdrawn from the public domain via 16,691 homestead entries, the filings occurring in virtually every township in the state (Hage 1989; Stein 1990).

Homesteading in the arid Southwest was not a successful enterprise. The earliest act, allowing filing on 160 acres, set many hopeful pioneers up for failure. This small acreage was barely large enough to support a hardworking family in the more fertile habitats of the Great Plains and Midwest, much less the non-forested, dry portions of Arizona. In the state's deserts, grasslands, and woodlands, attempts to survive solely on the products of such meager acreage were usually doomed, as not enough water was available to irrigate much more than a garden, or to produce enough forage for a livestock sufficient to make ends meet. Later versions of the Homestead Act attempted to correct the problem, increasing the allowed land areas to 640 acres. But even in these cases, such areas proved too small and/or infertile, and rainfall too variable, to support families. The only way to survive was to use the homestead as base property and graze livestock on the adjacent public domain.

Land fraud also thwarted the purpose of the acts. As early as 1887, Arizona's surveyor general reported that: "Speculators of all degrees have now turned their attention to the facilities offered by the desert land law. . . . Parties have obtained 4,000 or 5,000 acres under this law by illegal methods. . . . The desert land law as it stands fosters a wild spirit of speculation." More than half of those filing desert claims, claims covering 400,000 acres in the aggregate, were from outside Arizona: men in Chicago, St. Louis, and other eastern cities who were holding the land for speculation (Hibbard 1965). Much of this land was eventually patented, but it would be an exaggeration to describe its ownership as "settlement."

By 1912, the only areas remaining ungrazed, on and off the national forests, were those much more than a mile from water. With the lands within range of water increasingly impacted by grazing, ranchers and homesteaders sought to develop additional waters—the former to expand usable grazing land and establish tenure, so that they might continue to lease range from the government; the latter so that they might obtain patents and grazing access to surrounding government acres.

The smaller homestead ranches were ultimately unable to compete with the larger, established cattle ranches, which were given preference for federal and state grazing leases on which they owned the water rights. It was only a matter of time before the larger cattle operations absorbed the smaller outfits. "Shane" and other popular films notwithstanding, the larger cattlemen bested the homesteaders in the arid Southwest.

While the extent of homestead acreages relative to the total land area of Arizona was small, the potential impact on wildlife habitat was disproportionately large due to the tendencies of homesteads to include springs and live streams, and to take in the best grasslands. In addition, the conversion of homesteads up to 640 acres into patented land, even when incorporated into larger ranch holdings, set the stage for their future sale and residential development. In general, homesteading would therefore have its greatest impact in those lands close to larger towns, with less rapid effects in such remote areas as Anderson Mesa and Doney Park in Coconino County (Rice 1959), and in the vicinities of small towns in southeastern Arizona such as Willcox.

Impacts of Homesteading and Private Land Ownership

As previously noted, homesteading land around a water source allowed a rancher to graze his livestock on not only his private land but on surrounding expanses of public domain. Lack of fences meant that livestock belonging to several ranches might graze the same extensive areas concurrently. The result was overgrazing of the commons, which reduced the forage available to domestic and wild animals.

In addition to this, wildlife was relatively unprotected and subject to being poached. The actual impacts of homesteaders shooting wildlife around their holdings is difficult to assess. The number of game wardens present during most of the homestead period was so small that game laws were effectively unenforceable. Some ranchers, with government encouragement, considered eliminating wild ungulates, jackrabbits, and rodents good policy, seeing these animals as competitors for forage. Poorer homesteaders, trying to eke out a living on overused land, sequestered their water sources for exclusive use by their livestock, and took wildlife to supplement a meager income. Oftentimes the larger ranchers (and many sportsmen) viewed these settlers or "nesters" as undesirable neighbors, and conflicts between these groups sometimes led to violence.

Over time, most homesteads were absorbed by the larger outfits. Such abdications, along with more intensive management of national forest lands and the beginnings of protection for other federal lands, led to slowly improving conditions for most wildlife after 1920. As ranching became the primary use of federal and state lands and the larger private holdings, the number of people on the land declined. Although overgrazing and erosion remained a problem, the negative impacts on wildlife were slowly ameliorated after the mid-1920s (Ligon 1927).

In all, more than 4,748,000 acres in Arizona passed from public to private ownership through homesteading (Stein 1990). By the end of the 1930s, however, some of these lands were reverting to government ownership. More than 1,000,000 acres of former homestead lands were eventually repurchased by the government through the Bankhead-Jones Farm Tenant Act, a New Deal program designed to correct maladjustments in land use, control soil erosion, favor reforestation, preserve natural resources, and protect fish and wildlife habitat. Beginning in the 1930s and ceasing in the early 1940s, a number of refuges and hatchery sites were transferred to government ownership under authority of this act, including the Cluff Ranch Game Farm near Pima, Arizona. The years after World War II saw an improvement of conditions for wildlife on many publicly owned lands, as federal and state agencies incorporated wildlife habitat management programs into their mandates. The State Land Department, financially starved by a parsimonious legislature, and with conflicting management mandates, was less able to partake in wildlife recovery efforts.

While wildlife habitat on private lands usually received little protection, many large private holdings in the state's grasslands were closed to the public. In such cases, hunting was prohibited or severely restricted, even though the range might be improving. The net result was sometimes beneficial to certain wild species such as pronghorn, and detrimental to others such as prairie dogs.

By the 1960s, a new era of land occupation was underway. With improving economic conditions and a growing human population, land values in Arizona rose. Ranchers or their heirs found they could realize more income by subdividing their ranges than by raising livestock. In areas having a benign climate or a nearby population center, splitting a single square mile of private land could set a family up for life. This contrasted with the hard labor and climatic and market uncertainties attendant with raising livestock. In addition, ranchers who had developed homesteads during the 1910s through the 1950s were aging, and their descendants were often not interested in assuming the risks and hard work that raising livestock entailed. Developing and subdividing acreages made more economic sense, and people once again began to occupy former homesteads, this time bringing with them electricity, drilled wells, roads, fencing, and higher rates of disturbance.

Railroad Grants

During the American settlement era, land was viewed as capital. To encourage building of railroads through New Mexico and Arizona, the Atlantic and Pacific (later Santa Fe) Railroad was granted 640-acre sections of land alternating with public lands along the proposed right-of-way (Greever 1954). In Arizona, these donated bands of land reached 40 miles out from the railway on each side, roughly centered along the 35th parallel. The intent was for the railroads to convert these lands into capital through sales, thereby raising the funds needed to construct the tracks and at the same time encouraging the expansion of human settlements within reach of the railroad. These railroad grants were not without strings, and provisions for them to revert to public ownership should the railroads fail to use them within a given time were written into most acts. This seldom happened, and railroad grants set the stage for a series of long-term impacts on wildlife habitats, especially grasslands.

While seemingly straightforward, the railroad grant program, even in late-settled areas such as northern Arizona, ran into an array of complications, not the least of which were settlers and homesteaders already present on the allocated sections. Other problems included the prior allocation of lands for Indian reservations and forest reserves. One especially important railroad grant fiasco involved the subsequent sale of Santa Fe Railroad land to the Aztec Land and Cattle Company—best known for its Hashknife brand. This sale resulted in a checkerboard pattern of private lands being located within a 40-mile stretch of forest reserve and government lands south of the railroad tracks from Holbrook to Flagstaff.

A second sizeable sale of railroad grant lands went to Dr. E. B. Perrin, a sheepman and land speculator, who purchased almost 260,000 acres of railroad land around Flagstaff. Additional large sales went to the Arizona Cattle Company (121,491 acres), S. G. Little Company (75,749 acres), Cebolla Cattle Company (41,592 acres), and Charles Zeiger (11,528 acres). The Atlantic and Pacific thus sold about 1,511,633 acres of its ceded lands for grazing and land speculation. An additional 3,492,685 acres went to its parent companies to satisfy debts, converting some 5,004,318 acres of the Southwest to private land. Exactly what portion of this was in Arizona is uncertain, as much of this land was never surveyed or deeded. The railroad also rented grazing rights and sold timber on some of its own land. As far as game and fish values were concerned, these lands were the same as other private lands, hence managed with little thought to conservation or multiple use.

Although railroad lands changed owners over the years, the checkerboard pattern prevailed southward from the Navajo and Hopi reservations to the Mogollon Rim. In the grasslands of northern Arizona, this checkerboard pattern of private and public lands reached across the width of the state, and over time became interspersed with State Trust lands, national forest lands, and private homesteads, as well as the large ORO Ranch, which was created as a means to compensate the Baca family heirs for the loss of a portion of their land grant in southern Arizona.

Many private landholders who found their properties designated as railroad lands, forest reserves, or Indian lands were allowed to deed their property to the federal government and select land in the public domain of equal value. While not necessarily designed to benefit the railroads per se, this policy opened the way for companies to gain ownership of lands outside of the designated 80-mile-wide band along the railroad right-of-way and amalgamate some of their alternating sections into continuous swaths.

From the standpoint of wildlife, the impact of the railroad grants was not immediate and has not, even now, been fully realized or evaluated. While particular habitats were not consciously targeted, the route selected for the railroad was necessarily influenced by terrain. Large acreages of grasslands, juniper woodlands, and timberlands were among those landscapes converted to private ownership, setting the stage for future battles over public access, unrestricted grazing, and unregulated timber harvest. This pattern of alternating private and public land sections, including State Trust lands, would complicate the management of Arizona's lands for years to come.

State Trust Lands

The history of State Trust lands for the United States is too long and complex to be summarized here. It has been covered in detail by Souder and Fairfax (1996), and the following historical overview is taken from that source and from the Arizona State Land Department (www.land.state.az.us/history.htm).

The Territory of Arizona was established on February 24, 1863, by an act of Congress. This act reserved sections 16 and 36 of each township for the benefit of the "Common Schools." The State Enabling Act of 1910 that prepared the Territory of Arizona for statehood added sections 2 and 3 of each township to the previously designated school sections. Congress also considered the needs of other public institutions, and through the Enabling Act, more than two million additional acres were allocated to the state of Arizona. An 1881 act had already granted the Territory of Arizona about 60,000 acres for the University of Arizona Trust and a 1929 act authorized an additional 50,000 acres, the income from which was to be used for the Miners' Hospital Trust. All in all, about 10,900,000 acres were ceded to the state. Today, monies from State Trust lands are apportioned out among 14 schools, charities, and penal institutions.

In 1912, the first Arizona State Legislature created a three-member State Land Commission to formulate rules for the administration and management of the state's holdings. This commission concluded Arizona should not sell its State Trust land outright as other states had done. Instead, it should put the lands to their "highest and best use."

The commission recommended the creation of a permanent State Land Department "[I]n order that the multitudinous detail attached to the State's varied land interests may have constant attention and to prevent irretrievable loss." The State Land Department and the system by which State Trust lands were to be managed were established in 1915 by a special session of the legislature that also established a State Land Code. In compliance with the Enabling Act and the State Constitution, the State Land Code gave the State Land Department authority over all Trust lands and their natural products.

As the federal government completed land surveys, title to four school sections in each township—2, 16, 32, and 36—automatically passed to the state. When school section lands were not available to the state (because they had been previously claimed by homesteaders or miners or because they fell within a federal reservation, national forest, or park, or on an Indian reservation) the state was given the right to select an equal acreage of federal public domain land as indemnity in lieu of lands it would have received.

The State Land Department's mission was therefore to maximize the revenues from its lands for its beneficiaries. All uses of the land must benefit the Trust, a legal requirement that distinguishes State Trust lands from the way federal lands are managed. While public use of State Trust land is not prohibited, attorneys general have ruled such use must be regulated to ensure protection of the land and reimburse its beneficiaries.

After acquiring title, the state traded certain Trust lands for other federal or private lands of equal value in order to relocate and block up its holdings in select areas. These choices were made by the State Selection Board, which consisted of the governor, state attorney general, and state land commissioner. In recent years, the land commissioner has been replaced on the board by the state treasurer. Most of the land selections were made in the 1915–60 era, under the leadership of Obed Lassen, state land commissioner, with in-lieu selections not being completed until 1982.

Because the state was precluded by federal laws from acquiring mineral lands, and because homesteaders had already acquired much of the potential agricultural land, the state focused on choosing the best grazing lands. Most of the acreage chosen during the

1915–60 era was therefore in grasslands and former grasslands in central and southeastern Arizona (e.g., around Congress Junction, Oracle Junction, in Sulphur Springs Valley, and in the checkerboard land areas along the railroad routes across north-central Arizona). As agriculture developed in Arizona, later selections were made in areas irrigated by government-sponsored irrigation projects such as in the lower Gila River valley, Casa Grande-Coolidge area, Harquahala Valley, and other level sites. The final selections, made after 1962, would concentrate on commercial and agricultural lands along the Colorado River and those serviced by the Central Arizona Project.

Most Arizona Trust lands are currently leased for livestock grazing and irrigated agriculture; another several hundred thousand acres of mostly seasonal grazing lands have become urban lands within the city limits of Phoenix, Tucson, and other expanding cities. The University of Arizona Trust benefits from a significant amount of timbered land in the Flagstaff area, which is managed by the State Land Department's Forestry Division. The State Land Department also performs an extension role on agricultural lands near Yuma and on certain private lands.

Since statehood, the state has disposed of, or exchanged, about 1,628,100 acres of Trust lands. Some 9,228,787 acres remain. Almost all of these lands are under one or more leases for natural resource use and/or commercial development. Public access to these lands, a contentious issue since statehood, was finally resolved by disallowing grazing leaseholders to ban trespassing by holders of a state hunting license.

Because State Trust lands are managed to provide maximum income for their beneficiaries, game management has never been a management priority. That there has been a tendency for the legislature to withhold funds for the monitoring and restoration of state lands has also been a problem for wildlife. Moreover, the State Land Department has always been severely underfunded and understaffed, with no real range management or other resource allocation authority. Nonetheless, as a result of the early in-lieu selections and exchanges, many State Trust lands were, and in part remain, extremely important habitat for pronghorn and other grassland species. Although the sale of the state's grasslands to private parties had only begun by 1961, such transfers would become more extensive as the years progressed.

Other Government and Indian Lands

National forests occupied roughly only 17% of the state at statehood. During the next 50 years, other government categories protected additional lands, including those administered by the National Park Service, US Fish and Wildlife Service, and Department of Defense, along with later withdrawals for the Bureau of Reclamation and Army Corps of Engineers. After 1940, additional large blocks of land, particularly in southwestern Arizona, were withdrawn as military reservations.

With the establishment of the Colorado River Indian Reservation and the finalization of the Papago Indian Reservation in 1939, Indian lands took up some 20,138,019 acres or 28% of the state's area. Although the wildlife value on some Indian lands was high, ownership of the game on these so-called "reservations" increasingly passed from state jurisdiction to the tribes after 1946.

Also in 1946, the state's remaining public domain was placed under the Bureau of Land Management when that office was created by combining the General Land Office and the Grazing Service. Since then, these federal "grazing" lands have been managed principally for "multiple use," their dispersal to private owners no longer a priority since passage of the Taylor Grazing Act in 1935.

In general, federal lands in Arizona have been increasingly managed in favor of wildlife. All the national forests have wildlife management programs, and all federal and state land management agencies claim a wildlife habitat responsibility. The decline in national forest acreage from approximately 12,400,000 in 1912 to 9,503,000 acres in 1961 was largely due to converting forest reserves to national parks, which now take up 2,962,853 acres of Arizona. For its part, the Bureau of Land Management would eventually administer some 12,200,000 acres of the public domain.

The trend for federal land management agencies between 1912 and 1961 has generally been one of increasing recognition of wildlife for its recreational values. Some public lands have fared better than others when it comes to grazing history and land use, depending on regional climate, cultural values, and jurisdictional history. The large acreages held and managed by such agencies and the inclusion of wildlife in their management plans has resulted in a change of trends in wildlife numbers, from a status of near-depletion in 1912 to a restoration of most species in 1962—notable exceptions being the grizzly, wolf, Gunnison's and black-tailed prairie dogs, black-footed ferret, and river otter. It should nonetheless be also noted that the high-water mark in the harvests of such big game animals as mule deer, white-tailed deer, and pronghorn antelope, as well as several small game species, was also just prior to or about 1962.

Farming and Irrigation Districts

Also impacting wildlife to a large degree was the nature and amount of Arizona agriculture. Initially confined to Native Americans and homesteaders dry-farming wheat or oats on relatively few acres in Arizona's high country, or farmers irrigating small plots of land along the state's limited supply of live streams, the cultivation of crops did not benefit wildlife to the degree that it could have. Although irrigated cropland might support greater numbers of quail, doves, and other birds, irrigation ditches often formed death traps to native fishes moving upstream and the fields themselves could attract birds and other animals to slaughter. Both dry farms and irrigated fields were prone to crop depredations by animals ranging from jackrabbits to elk, and their presence may have resulted in the loss of as much game as was gained.

Whatever impacts small-time agriculture had on small game and other animals paled when compared to the changes wrought by the formation of the Salt River Water Users Project in 1903 and construction of Roosevelt Dam in 1911. Encompassing the Salt and Verde rivers and their Forest Service watersheds, the resulting irrigation bonanza soon made Maricopa County the dove-hunting capital of the nation. So successful was the Salt River Project at reallocating water that it became the model by which private farmers and corporations contracted with the government for water delivery elsewhere. Having only 185,396 acres of irrigated farmland in 1900, the project's acreage nearly doubled to

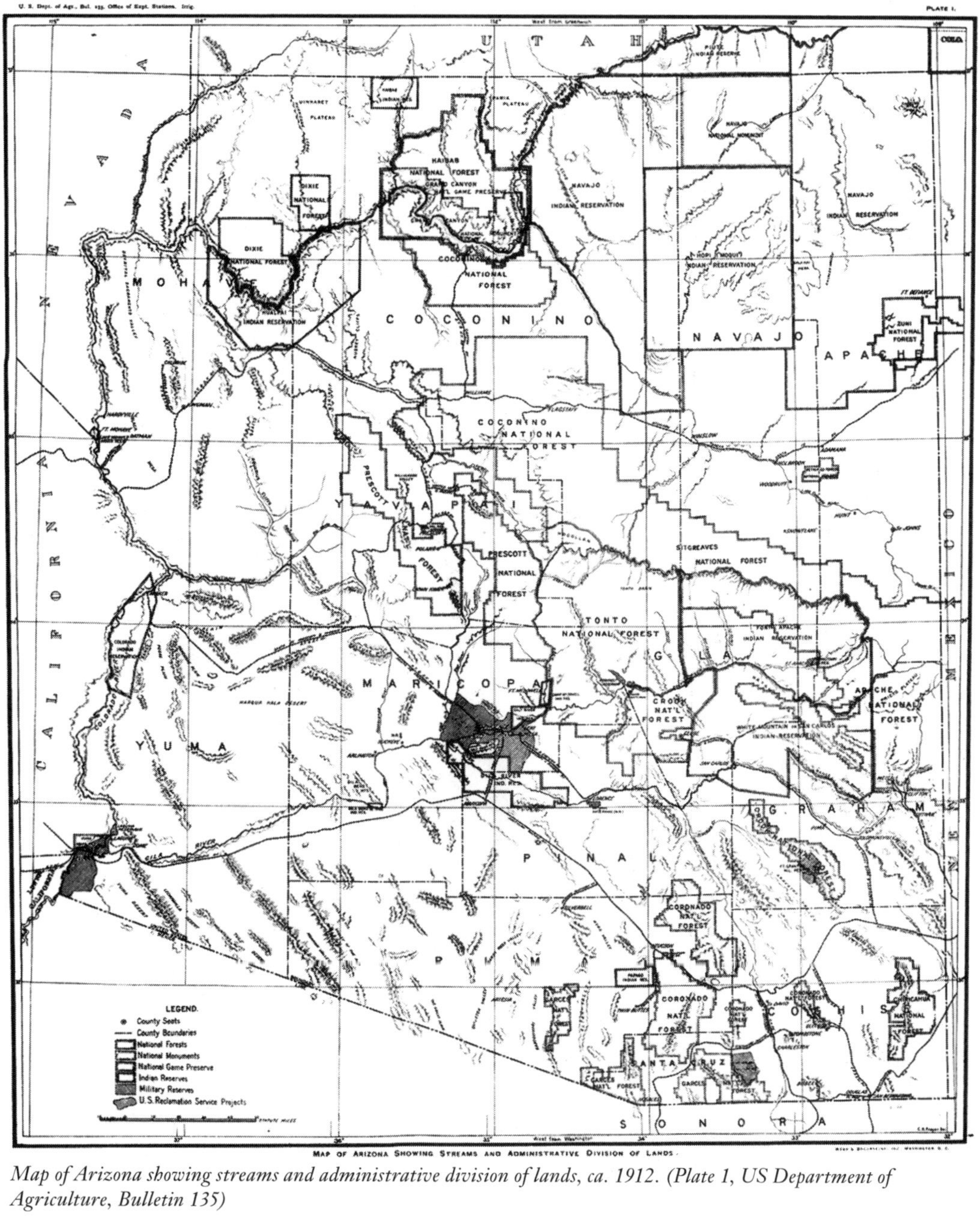

Map of Arizona showing streams and administrative division of lands, ca. 1912. (Plate 1, US Department of Agriculture, Bulletin 135)

320,000 acres in 1910. Eventually, with the formation of the Agua Fria (Roosevelt) Irrigation District in 1923, the San Carlos Irrigation District in 1926, the Wellton-Mohawk Irrigation District in 1951, and other irrigation districts, nearly all of Arizona's surface waters were allocated (or over-allocated) to irrigate 1,125,396 acres of farmland in 1964. By this time, too, Arizona's groundwater was also being depleted with the advent of powerful diesel pumps after World War II.

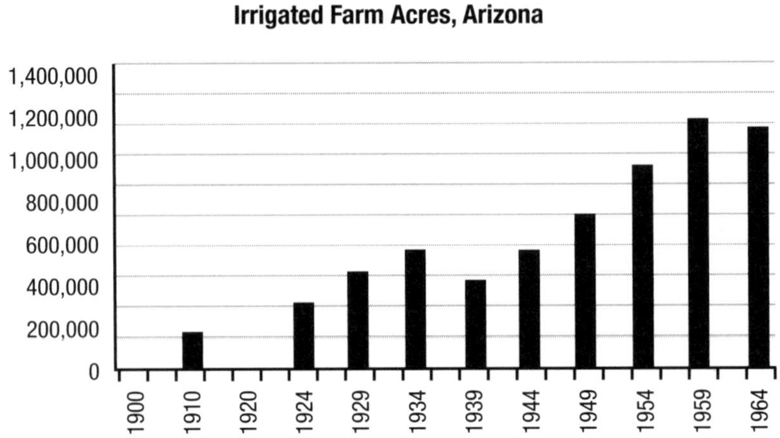

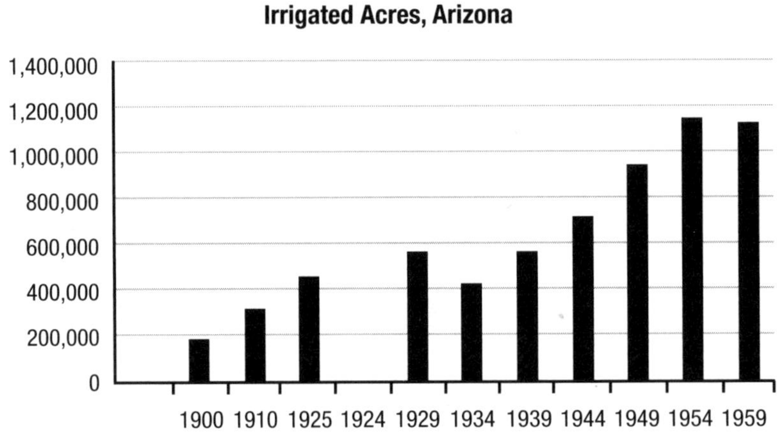

Not all irrigation attempts succeeded. Individuals attempting to farm former government land might fail, and dry farming, which depends only upon the amount of rain that falls, was attempted in such disparate places as Anderson Mesa, Sulphur Springs Valley, and even such harsh desert sites as Mobile. Without external sources of water, most of these farms were attempted after good years and abandoned during the drought years that always succeeded them. For this reason, the numbers of farms peaked (at about 14,000) around 1930 and the number of acres under cultivation topped out in 1956. By 1964, the only agricultural districts retaining maximum size were confined to the Salt River Project area, lands irrigated by the lower Colorado River Projects, and along the Gila and San Pedro rivers.

The crops raised in these irrigation districts were initially a great boon to wildlife—not only such species as white-winged doves and Gambel's quail, but mourning doves, cottontail rabbits, and even waterfowl in certain instances. Indeed, the rise and fall of white-winged doves in the statewide harvest was reportedly tied to the types of crops raised (the crash in cotton prices during the early 1920s being good for bird hunting).

Number of Farms in Arizona, 1910–60

Year	Number of Farms
1910	9,200
1911	9,300
1912	9,400
1913	9,500
1914	9,500
1915	9,600
1916	9,600
1917	9,700
1918	9,800
1919	9,800
1920	10,000
1921	10,000
1922	10,200
1923	10,500
1924	10,600
1925	10,800
1926	11,500
1927	12,200
1928	13,000
1929	13,600
1930	14,200
1931	14,200
1932	14,200
1933	14,300
1934	14,300
1935	14,300
1936	14,200
1937	14,100
1938	14,000
1939	13,800
1940	13,700
1941	13,600
1942	13,500
1943	13,500
1944	13,500
1945	13,500
1946	13,200
1947	12,900
1948	12,500
1949	12,000
1950	11,400
1951	11,000
1952	10,700
1953	10,300
1954	10,000
1955	9,700
1956	9,400
1957	9,100
1958	8,800
1959	8,500
1960	8,200

Gradually, as more acres came under cultivation and the allocations of water became more efficient, benefits to wildlife declined. Dirt canals lined with mesquites and other desert vegetation gave way to cement conduits. Vegetation at the edges of farm fields was scraped clean and fence rows were eliminated to reduce boll weevils and other insect pests. Particularly damaging were dredging, realignment, and dewatering operations along the lower Colorado, which transformed significant portions of Arizona's once-powerful river wilderness to a farm-lined canal punctuated by reservoirs.

By 1962, the advantages to wildlife created by the formation of irrigation districts were often being nullified by new farming protocols using cement-lined canals, "clean farming" practices, and high concentrations of pesticides. Worse yet, groundwater pumping was lowering the water table, which killed the roosting trees that supported the dove and other wildlife populations fed by the crops. Earth cracks appeared and, in combination with the canals, intersected drainages, interrupting runoff needed to support vegetation used by quail, cottontails, and other wildlife. Finally, reclamation projects and

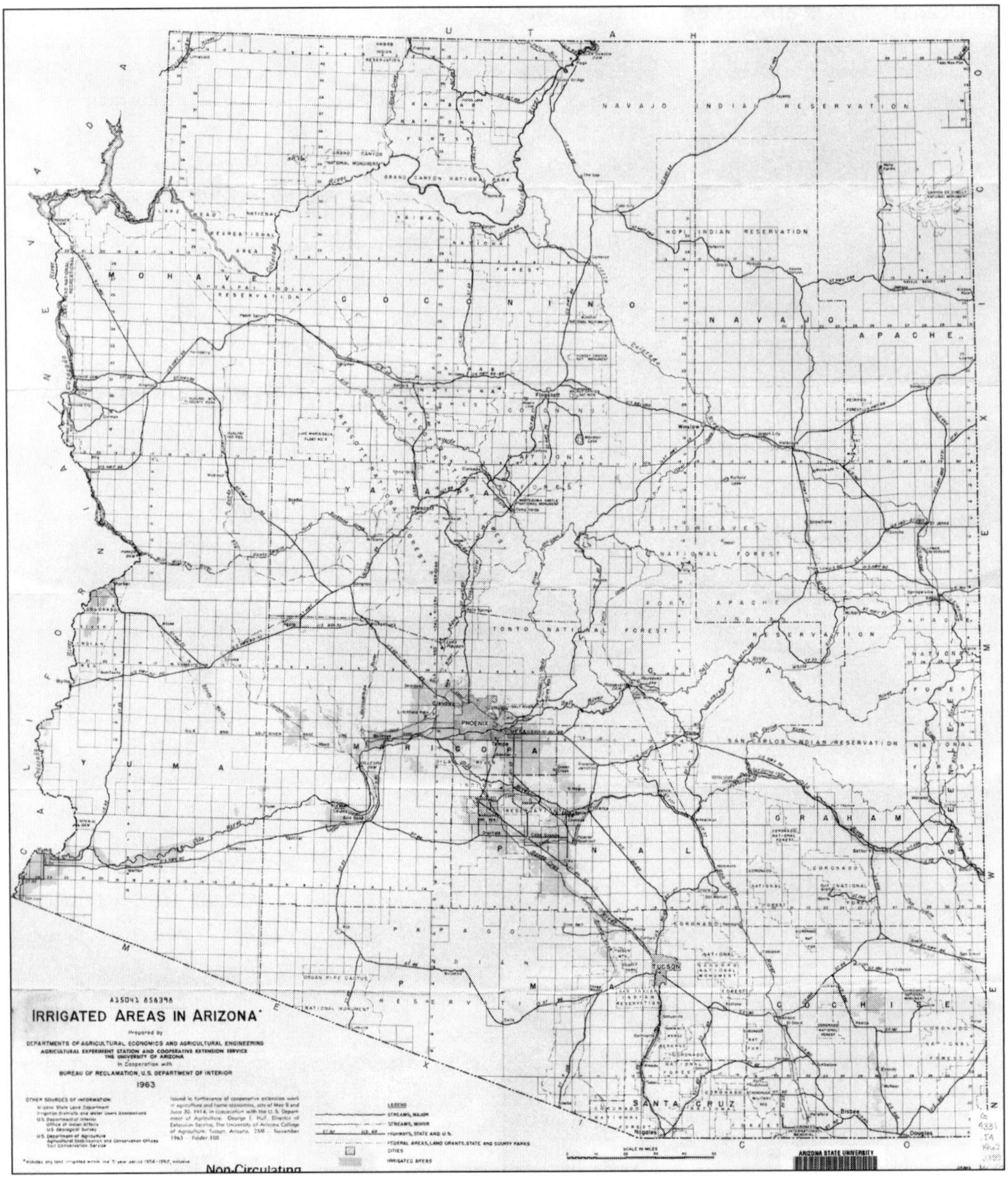

Irrigated areas in Arizona, ca. 1963. With projects such as the Salt River Project and numerous irrigation districts in place, by the mid-1960s nearly all of Arizona's surface waters were allocated to irrigate some 1.1 million acres of farmland, shown in gray on this map. (University of Arizona Agricultural Experiment Station and Extension Office)

flood-control districts were beginning to attack the riparian communities increasingly suffering from interrupted, restricted, or unnaturally swift water flows. As flooding became more and more a thing of the past, waterfowl was confined to narrowing stream channels and stock tanks. Arizona's agricultural boom was coming to an end—at least as far as benefit to waterfowl, white-winged doves, and small game species were concerned.

Other Influences

There were of course numerous other land ownership and tenure factors impacting wildlife during the 1912–62 period, not to mention urban expansion and highways (see maps on following pages). It must be remembered that it was road construction and Arizona's explosive population growth, particularly after World War II, which permitted its citizens to harvest the improved game populations they had come to expect. Access was therefore an essential part of the equation.

Paved highways, absent in 1912, would eventually connect nearly every town in the state as "new roads committees" sought to connect population centers, markets, and recreation areas. Nor were the federal government and state highway department the only agencies building roads. The Forest Service, counties, and even individual ranches and mines were bent on providing access. Even the Arizona Game and Fish Department, fearful that surplus deer would go to waste, embarked on a road-building program in the 1950s (Swank 1958).

So powerful was the demand, and so pervasive the remedy, that the Forest Service saw fit in the 1930s to protect some of its roughest country such as the Superstition and Mazatzal mountains as Primitive and Wilderness areas, lest there be no place left solely for horsemen and hikers. Once primary travel methods shifted from horse or horse-and-buggy to motorized vehicles, the major factor affecting the taking of wildlife became the automobile and pickup truck. The use of four-wheel-drive vehicles greatly increased after World War II, until one had to search for a place to hunt where no one with a vehicle could go. Although Arizona's miles of paved highways increased greatly through 1962, the big impacts of freeways had not yet occurred, and many rights of way remained unfenced. What was not yet realized was that this expansion of paved highways would increasingly fragment the habitat of wildlife species ranging from pronghorn to desert tortoises.

Arizona Wildlife in 1962

In summary, wildlife habitat conditions generally improved between 1912 and 1962, particularly on national forests and in national parks. National refuges and military withdrawals created other wildlife havens as grazing pressures and other land uses became less intense or ceased. A similar but more modest recovery also took place on lands managed by the Bureau of Land Management. Conditions continued to deteriorate on most state lands, while range conditions generally improved on many private lands.

Nonetheless, the original productivity of most of Arizona's lands, while much recovered by 1962, can never be fully recaptured, mostly due to surface soil loss and other, more insidious causes such as the invasion of woody plants and noxious weeds (Bahre 1991; Turner et al. 2003). As a result of these changes, and perhaps other factors yet to be appreciated, the potential carrying capacities of many of the state's habitats was realized by 1962, and have since declined or reached an equilibrium less than their potential. Grasslands, especially those at lower elevations, have been especially impacted, and attempts to restore certain habitats that formerly existed below an elevation of 3,500 or so feet elevation may now be futile. Future wildlife managers would have to make do with less.

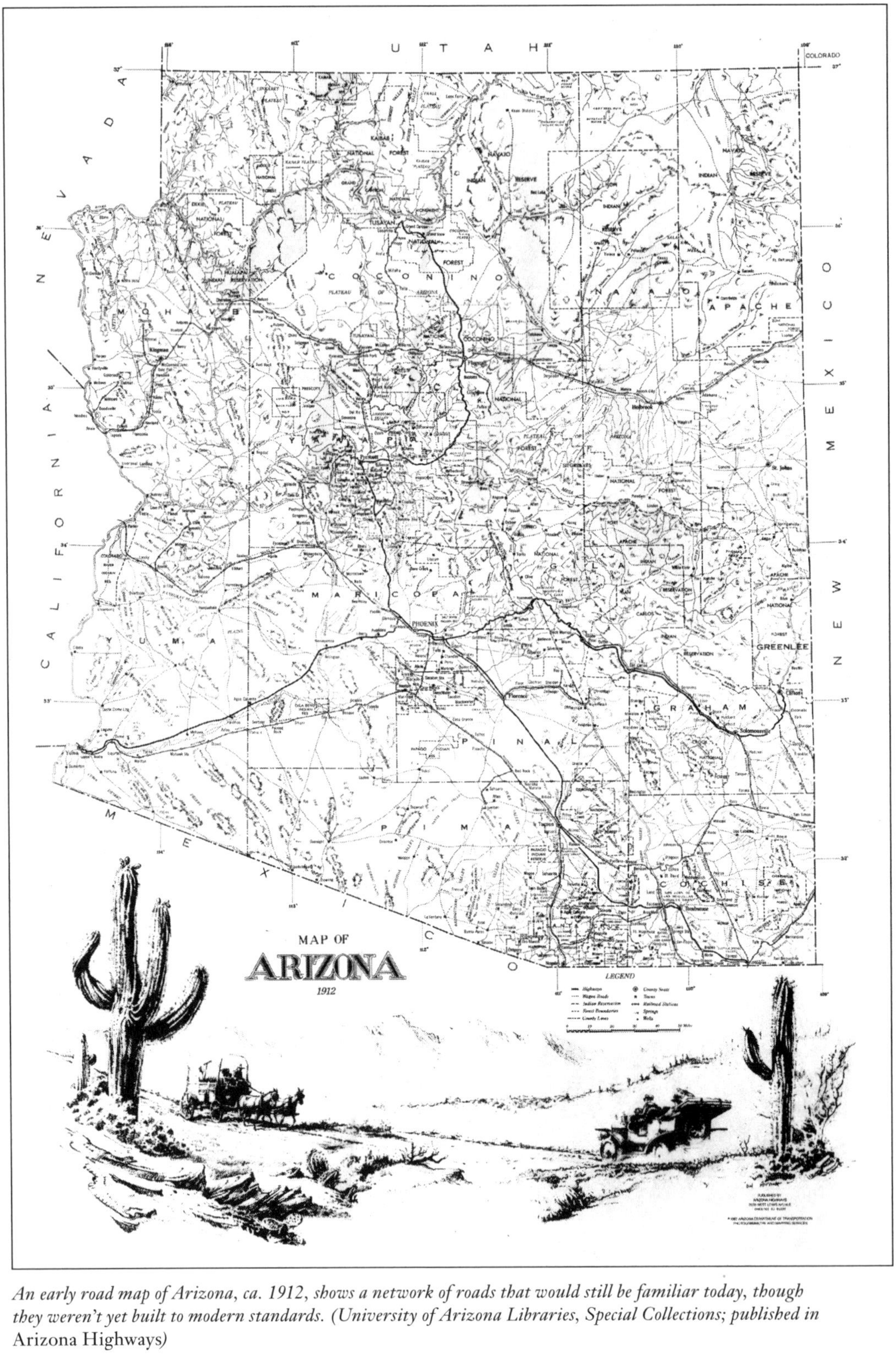

An early road map of Arizona, ca. 1912, shows a network of roads that would still be familiar today, though they weren't yet built to modern standards. (University of Arizona Libraries, Special Collections; published in Arizona Highways*)*

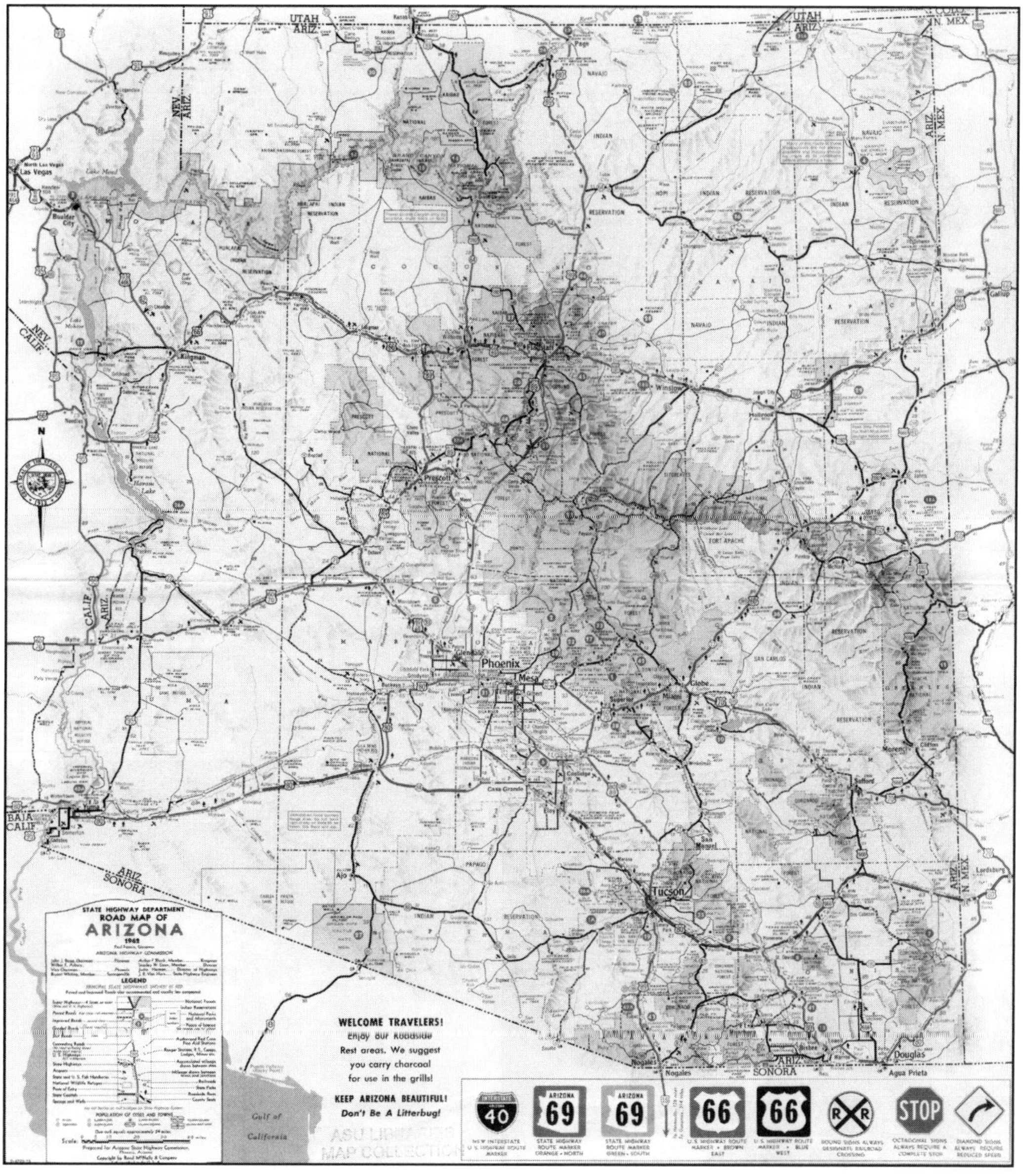

A road map of Arizona in 1962, 40 years later, shows a more extensive web of roads in many parts of the state. (AGFD files)

APPENDICES
REFERENCES
INDEX

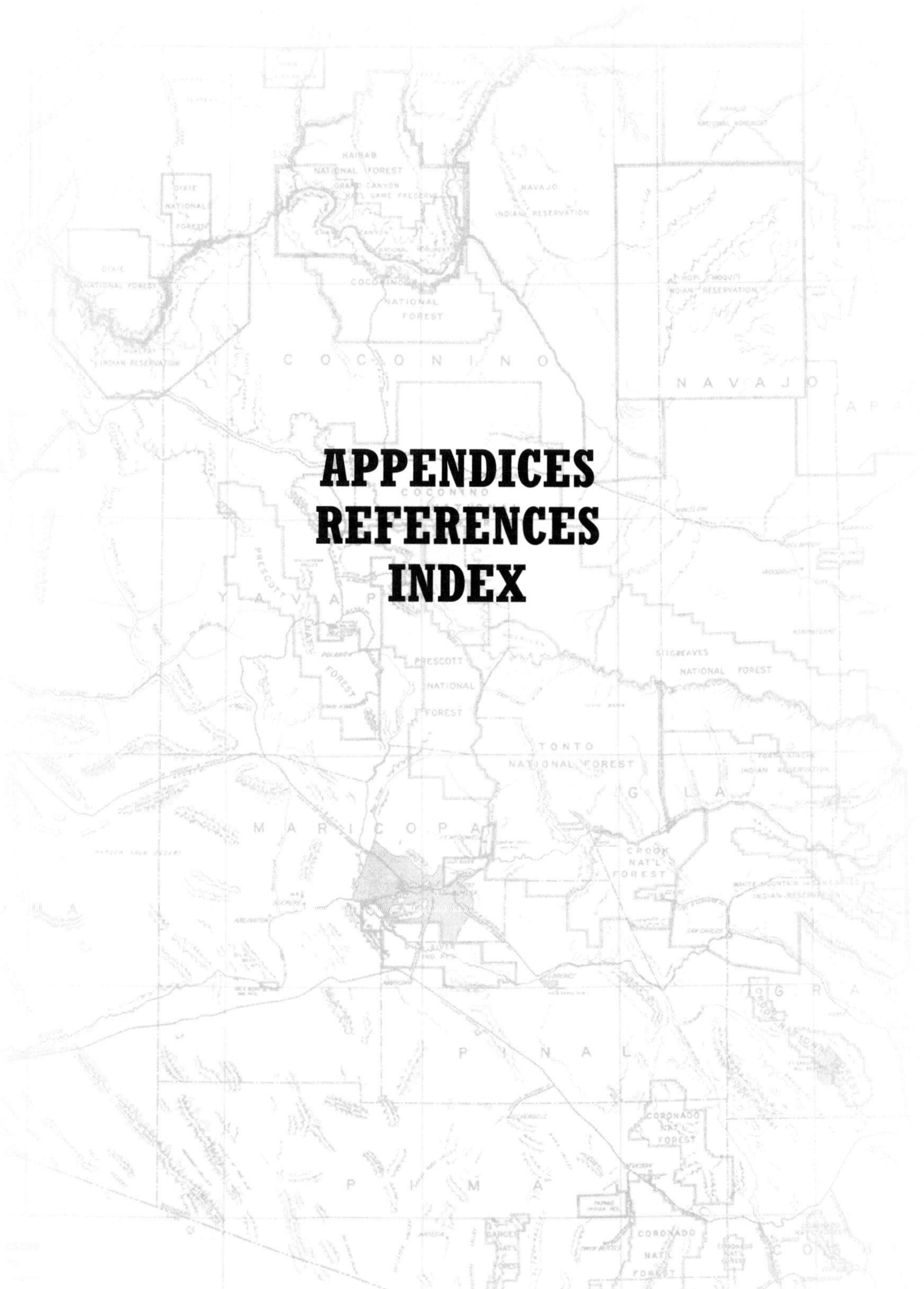

APPENDIX A: State Game Wardens and Arizona Game and Fish Department Directors, 1913–62

Year	State Game Warden/Director	Governor	Notes
1911		Richard Sloan	W. L. Pinney (Phoenix) and T. T. Swift (Safford) are appointed Territorial fish and game commissioners
1912		George W. P. Hunt	Hunt appoints A. W. Snyder, Chas. M. Bledsoe, and T. T. Cull as fish and game commissioners May 10, 1912
1913	Frank W. Rogers	Hunt	Hunt appoints Rogers State Game Warden Jan. 28, 1913 in accordance with new game law; three commissioners are retired
1914	George M. Willard	Hunt	Rogers dies June 10, 1914; Hunt appoints Willard June 11, 1914
1915	Willard	Hunt	
1916	Willard	Hunt	
1917	Joseph V. Prochaska	Tom Campbell	Prochaska appointed May 10, 1917; a recount returns Governor Hunt to office in December 1917
1918	Willard	Hunt	Willard appointed Jan. 1, 1918
1919	Prochaska	Campbell	Willard resigns; Prochaska appointed Jan. 6, 1919
1920	Prochaska	Campbell	
1921	Prochaska	Campbell	
1922	Prochaska	Hunt	
1923	Prochaska/ E. C. Castleberry/ C. E. Golding	Hunt	Prochaska resigns Jan. 6. 1923; Castleberry is replaced by Golding Feb. 15, 1923; Willard reappointed June 14, 1923
1924	Willard	Hunt	
1925	Willard	Hunt	Willard reappointed Jan. 5, 1925; 10 field deputies.
1926	Willard/Dwight E. Pettis	Hunt	Willard dies; Pettis appointed April 12, 1926
1927	Pettis	Hunt	Pettis reappointed Jan. 3, 1927
1928	Pettis	John C. Phillips	
1929	Robert L. Bayless	Phillips	Bayless appointed Jan. 7, 1929; Commission to appoint future State Game Wardens
1930	Bayless	Hunt	
1931	Bayless/Alfred E. Mann	Hunt	Bayless resigns Aug. 8, 1931; Mann appointed but resigns Dec. 22, 1931
1932	William C. Joyner	Benjamin B. Moeur	Joyner appointed Jan. 1, 1932
1933	Joyner/Shelby L. Lewis	Moeur	Joyner reappointed April 24, 1933 but resigns; Lewis appointed May 15, 1933
1934	Lewis	Moeur	
1935	Lewis	Moeur	
1936	Lewis	Rawghlie C. Stanford	
1937	Lewis/ William H. Sawtelle	Stanford	Lewis reappointed May 19, 1937; Sawtelle appointed Nov. 21, 1937 after Lewis resigns

(continued . . .)

APPENDIX A continued: State Game Wardens and Arizona Game and Fish Department Directors, 1913–62

Year	State Game Warden/Director	Governor	Notes
1938	Sawtelle	Robert T. Jones	
1939	Sawtelle	Jones	
1940	Sawtelle/Kenner C. Kartchner	Sidney P. Osborn	Sawtelle resigns March 20, 1940; Kartchner becomes acting State Game Warden April 16, 1940 and State Game Warden Sept. 17, 1940
1941	Kartchner	Osborn	
1942	Kartchner	Osborn	
1943	Kartchner/Fred Merkle	Osborn	Kartchner resigns Oct. 28, 1943; Merkle appointed Nov. 1, 1943
1944	Merkle	Osborn	
1945	Merkle/Herbert L. Reid	Osborn	Merkle resigns Sept. 14, 1945; Fisheries Chief Reid becomes acting Director and Director; no more State Game Wardens
1946	Reid	Osborn	
1947	Reid	Osborn	
1948	Reid/Tom Kimball	Dan E. Garvey	Reid resigns March 21, 1948; Kimball appointed March 31, 1948
1949	Kimball	Garvey	
1950	Kimball	Howard Pyle	
1951	Kimball	Pyle	Kimball reappointed July 1951
1952	Kimball/A. W. Yoder (acting)	Pyle	Kimball resigns May 15, 1952; Yoder becomes acting Director
1953	Yoder (acting)/John M. Hall	Pyle	Hall appointed Director Nov. 1, 1953
1954	Hall	Ernest McFarland	
1955	Hall	McFarland	
1956	Hall	McFarland	
1957	Hall	McFarland	Hall resigns Dec. 16, 1957, effective Feb. 13, 1958
1958	Robert J. Smith	Paul Fannin	Smith becomes acting Director Jan. 15, 1958, and Director April 19, 1958
1959	Smith	Fannin	
1960	Smith	Fannin	
1961	Smith	Fannin	
1962	Smith	Fannin	

APPENDIX B: Progression of Arizona Game and Fish Commissioners, 1929–62

Arizona Game and Fish Commissioners by County, 1929–62	
Apache County	
E. G. Dentzer	1951–53
Ernest J. Becker	1956–61
Cochise County	
Harry A. Clark	1931–33
Ralph Morrow	1964–67
Coconino County	
Tom McCullough	1929–31
Gordon Evans	1955–58
Milton Evans	1964–69, 1969–74
Greenlee County	
O. M. Sizer	1961–66
Maricopa County	
Albert F. Jones	1929–30
John B. Sloane	1930–35
Dan W. Francis	1931–35
Lynn Lockhart	1931–37
Thomas Imler	1937–41
Harry Hamilton	1941–43
Richard K. Wickstrum	1944–47
Fred Faver	1947–49, 1949–55, 1955–60
Lee Hover	1960–65

(continued . . .)

Arizona Game and Fish Commissioners by County, 1929–62	
Mohave County	
Dr. W. J. Richards	1948–53
Navajo County	
George Wrench	1935–41
Pima County	
Les B. Hart	1929–33
Charles P. Beach	1933–39, 1939–45, 1945–51
C. J. "Jack" Mantle	1951–57, 1957–62, 1962–64
Pinal County	
B. Van Voorhis	1951–56
Yavapai County	
William S. Connor	1941–47, 1947–48
Harry Funk	1959–64
Yuma County	
Homer B. Thacker	1953–58
Marcell N. Forman	1958–63
Gila, Graham, and Santa Cruz County Not Represented	

APPENDIX C: AGPA Presidents and Annual Convention Sites, 1923–62

Year	President	Convention Location	Notes	No. of Resolutions Acted On	Magazine Editor/s
1923	Tom McCullough (Flagstaff)	Flagstaff	AGPA formed with 4 affiliates		
1924	Tom McCullough (Flagstaff)	Prescott			
1925	Tom McCullough (Flagstaff)	Springerville?	10 affiliates; 891 members		
1926	F. E. A. Kimball acting president for Fred L. Benham	Santa Rita Hotel, Tucson	10 affiliates; address by J. Stokley Ligon	4	
1927	Fred L. Benham	Adams Hotel, Phoenix	10 affiliates		
1928	Fred Sutter	Adams Hotel, Phoenix	19 affiliates; 11 at convention	3	F. O. Krohn, Walter P. Taylor, James Diffin, Tom McCullough, Presky (first name not known)
1929	James A. Diffin (Bisbee)	Adams Hotel, Phoenix		8	Diffin et al.
1930	James A. Diffin	Adams Hotel, Phoenix	Tom McCullough and Robert L. Bayless present	6	Diffin and Glenn W. Persons
1931	Fred Gibson	Superior Court Room, Globe	Ben Avery becomes an active member	4	Diffin and Ben Avery
1932	William H. Heger	El Portal Hotel, Mesa	Robert L. Bayless present	12	Avery and Fred Gibson
1933	James A. Diffin	Santa Rita Hotel, Tucson	Senator George McFarland present	10	Gibson
1934	Glenn W. Persons	The Armory in Safford	16 affiliates	9	Diffin
1935	Glenn W. Persons	American Legion, Tempe		5	Diffin/McCullough
1936	A. J. Eager	Westward Ho, Phoenix		4	James A. Wilson
1937	A. J. Eager/Tom McCullough	Flagstaff	21 affiliates	8	Diffin
1938	Tom McCullough	Safford		3	McCullough
1939	Richard K. Wickstrum	Prescott		27	Wilson
1940	Charles Wilson			25	Wilson and Jack O'Connor
1941	James E. Babbitt	Kingman		30	James A. Wilson
1942	James E. Babbitt	Globe		12	Roland Cochrane
1943	Harry Funk	Prescott		23	Cochrane and Fred P. Misak

(continued . . .)

APPENDIX C continued: AGPA Presidents and Annual Convention Sites, 1923–62

Year	President	Convention Location	Notes	No. of Resolutions Acted On	Magazine Editor/s
1944	Dr. L. S. Hoopes	Phoenix		15	Fred P. Misak/Bill Sage
1945	M. H. Baldwin			7	Bill Sage
1946	James A. Beaman	Prescott		14	Bill Sage/Charles C. Niehuis
1947	James A. Beaman	Willow Beach		10	Charles C. Niehuis
1948	Max Layton	Flagstaff		20	Charles C. Niehuis/George Richard
1949	Max Layton	Douglas	Arizona Cattlegrowers Association present		George Richard
1950	Joe Dora	Globe	Tom Kimball present	16	George Richard/Charles Ernest Douglas
1951	Joe Dora	Springerville	Tom Kimball, Everett Mercer present	12	Charles E. "Earnie" Douglas/Charles C. Niehuis
1952	Ray Moore	Winslow	Everett Mercer, Arizona Cattlegrowers Association present	17	Charles C. Niehuis/Chuck Maybery
1953	Lee Hover	Chandler	Everett Mercer, Arizona Cattlegrowers Association present	13	Chuck Maybery
1954	Lee Hover	Prescott	Arizona Cattlegrowers Association	19	Chuck Maybery/Bill Minette
1955	L. C. Dingess	Bisbee	Alfred Paul, House Fish and Game Committee present	11	Bill Minette
1956	James Sparks	Flagstaff		16	Bill Minette
1957	James Sparks		33 affiliates		Bill Minette/Clarence Powell
1958	Bill Beers	Yuma	40 affiliates; Everett Mercer present		Clarence Powell/Bob Housholder
1959	Bill Beers	Springerville	Gov. Paul Fannin present; also two state congressmen		Bob Housholder
1960	Gordon Evans	Scottsdale	19 affiliates		Bob Housholder
1961	Robert Spillman	Ramada Inn, Phoenix	Tom McCullough present	7	Bob Housholder
1962	Robert Spillman	Sedona	Gov. Paul Fannin, Tom Kimball present		Bob Housholder

APPENDIX D: Game Information

Table D–1: Hunting and Fishing Licenses Sold, 1915–62

Year	Licenses sold[a]
1915	20,000
1916	18,000
1917	no data
1918	no data
1919	no data
1920	no data
1921	no data
1922	no data
1923	no data
1924	no data
1925	30,000
1926	30,615
1927	38,765
1928	no data
1929	34,953
1930	36,945
1931	no data
1932	no data
1933	no data
1934	no data
1935	no data
1936	32,870
1937	no data
1938	no data
1939	no data
1940	no data
1941	51,980
1942	57,839
1943	59,427
1944	61,323
1945	71,103
1946	84,366
1947	95,299
1948	104,090
1949	103,143
1950	106,743
1951	116,594
1952	140,400
1953	135,224
1954	142,230
1955	no data
1956	147,009
1957	142,054
1958	169,559
1959	169,448
1960	188,830
1961	194,397
1962	208,944

[a]License sales data up to 1941 are incomplete, but the numbers given do include both hunting and fishing licenses to residents and nonresidents. License sales from 1941 to 1962 include all sales to residents and nonresidents of hunting, fishing, or combination hunting and fishing privileges (the three basic classes of licenses sold at that time). In the years since 1962, the Arizona Game and Fish Department has added additional license classes and stamps to provide for specialized and reciprocal privileges.

Table D–2: Hunting Licenses Sold, Deer Harvested, and Mountain Lions and Wolves Reported Taken by PARC, 1915–62

Year	Hunting Licenses sold[a]	Mule Deer North Zone	Mule Deer South Zone	White-tailed Deer	Total Deer	PARC Lions[b]	PARC Wolves
1915	20,000					?	?
1916	18,000					?	?
1917						?	?
1918						?	27
1919						42	26
1920						79	64
1921						52	37
1922						54	58
1923						77	37
1924						77	22
1925	30,000					127	31
1926	30,615					93	18
1927	38,765					112	16
1928						108	5
1929	34,953					145	43
1930	36,945					146	14
1931						174	3
1932						86	8
1933						80	4
1934						68	3
1935						129	7
1936	32,870					94	5
1937						79	5
1938						55	3
1939						63	8
1940						78	6

(continued . . .)

Table D–2 cont.: Hunting Licenses Sold, Deer Harvested, and Mountain Lions and Wolves Reported Taken by PARC, 1915–62

Year	Hunting Licenses sold[a]	Mule Deer North Zone	Mule Deer South Zone	White-tailed Deer	Total Deer	PARC Lions[b]	PARC Wolves
1941	33,249			1,829	8,838	54	1
1942	35,090					66	8
1943	35,370					71	5
1944	39,223					73	6
1945	45,384					60	5
1946	48,837	4,000	733	991	5,724	35	4
1947	55,509	5,488	932	1,152	7,572	46	3
1948	59,538	6,470	888	1,347	8,705	190	4
1949	47,611	7,116	735	1,203	9,054 (386)	185	1
1950	48,771	8,948 (797)	858	1,175	10,981 (797)	212	0
1951	55,827	9,155 (658)	1,121	1,234	11,510 (658)	181	2
1952	66,836	11,699 (2,707)	1,583	1,490	14,772 (2,707)	198	2
1953	72,333	14,844 (3,948)	1,694	1,791	18,329 (3,948)	200	0
1954	77,995	16,462 (6,421)	1,625 (4)	1,500	19,587 (6,425)	201	0
1955	No data	18,272 (5,471)	2,431 (12)	1,789 (300)	22,492 (5,783)	230	0
1956	85,697	22,946 (8,826)	2,172 (117)	2,423 (357)	27,541 (9,300)	189	0
1957	87,711	17,853 (4,587)	2,313 (272)	2,401(593)	22,567 (17,115)	266	0
1958	10,0474	25,213 (9,010)	2,821 (860)	5,096 (1,702)	33,130 (11,572)	264	3
1959	101,488	23,760 (8,399)	2,018	5,446 (1,902)	31,224 (10,301)	243	0
1960	113,126	23,597 (7,247)	4,253 (1,149)	4,998 (1,111)	32,848 (9,507)	215	3
1961	118,659	26,006 (7,187)	5,111 (1,212)	4,780 (871)	35,897 (9,270)	242	1
1962	123,682	19,064 (6,228)	5,427 (1,458)	4,213 (983)	28,704 (8,669)	231	0

[a]Includes later combination hunting and fishing licenses

[b]Includes bountied animals after 1947.

(= any or antlerless animals)

Note: See also chapter seven, "The Kaibab Deer Controversy," for a table titled "Estimated Deer, Precipitation, Hunt Information, and Livestock Numbers Reported for North Kaibab, 1906–62."

Table D–3: Compendium of Wildlife Harvests, 1927–62

Year	Elk	Pronghorn	Javelina	Turkey	Bighorn	Federal duck stamps sold in Arizona	Notes
1927	No hunt	No hunt		?	No hunt		
1928	No hunt	No hunt		?	No hunt		
1929	No hunt	No hunt		?	No hunt		
1930	No hunt	No hunt		?	No hunt		
1931	No hunt	No hunt		?	No hunt		
1932	No hunt	No hunt		?	No hunt		
1933	No hunt	No hunt		?	No hunt		
1934	No hunt	No hunt		?	No hunt		
1935	145	No hunt		?	No hunt	2,332	First elk hunt; bull permit only
1936	85	No hunt		?	No hunt	1,760	
1937	65	No hunt		?	No hunt	1,736	buffalo hunt postponed due to inclement weather
1938	85	No hunt		?	No hunt	2,383	
1939	110	No hunt		?	No hunt	2,919	
1940	95	No hunt		?	No hunt	3,555	
1941	173	286	966	2152	No hunt	3,951	First antelope hunt
1942	319	487		?	No hunt	4,348	
1943	25	522		?	No hunt	3,535	"Dirty pronghorn hunt"; gas rationing in effect
1944	No hunt	No hunt		?	No hunt	4,145	No hunts due to war
1945	No hunt	No hunt		?	No hunt	5,535	No hunts due to war
1946	116	No hunt	?	526	No hunt	6,203	First antlerless elk taken; turkey hunts by permit
1947	501	No hunt	?	296	No hunt	7,525	
1948	920	No hunt	?	403	No hunt	7,427	
1949	856	437	?	307	No hunt	8,562	1949 bison taken in Dec. 1948; antelope hunt resumes
1950	1,484	382	1,344	365	No hunt	7,443	91 bison to Raymond
1951	1,693	548	1,851	549	No hunt	7,083	70 bison from Raymond; 22 from House Rock
1952	1,189	739	1,762	782	No hunt	8,645	250 to Fort Huachuca
1953	1,558	828	2,510	1216	20	11,982	First bighorn hunt; two seasons
1954	629	1,146	2,661	971	12	9,938	also 20 Fort Huachuca bison to Sonora; elk overharvest concerns
1955	612	578	3,142	887	5	9,125	Fort Huachuca
1956	302	297	2,930	1367	6	10,247	30 bison from Raymond; antlerless elk hunts cease
1957	177	205	2,236	692	6	9251	
1958	251	301	2,511	727	18	10,145	
1959	382	605	3,010	1108	19	9,256	
1960	637	722	3,098	1402	24	7,077	
1961	650	755	4,251	1303	26	7,039	includes 60 archery javelina kills
1962	871	612	4,343	1363	27	7,288	includes 72 archery javelina kills

Note: See also chapter 12, "The Game Department Takes Up Buffalo Ranching," for a table titled "Bison Harvested, 1927–62."

APPENDIX E: Fish Information

Table E–1: Fish Introductions in Arizona, 1878–1962
Source: Bill Silvey and Kirk Young, Arizona Game and Fish Department

Game Fish (In Order by Year of Introduction)	Year Introduced	If No Longer Present, Approximate Year of Initial Disappearance
Catfish (sp.?)	1878	
Carp	1880	
American Shad	1883	1888
Largemouth Bass	1896	
Rock Bass	1896	
Rainbow Trout	1897	
Cutthroat Trout	1899	
Brook Trout	1902	
White Crappie	1902	
Black Crappie	1902	
Channel Catfish	1904	
Bigmouth Buffalo	1917	
Black Buffalo	1917	
Smallmouth Buffalo	1917	
Yellow Perch	1918	
Black Bullhead	1919	
Yellow Bullhead	1919	
Smallmouth Bass	1920	
Mosquitofish	1925	
Goldfish	1925	
Green Sunfish	1925	
Yellow Bass	1929	
Golden Shiner	1929	
Brown Trout	1930	
Bluegill Sunfish	1931	
Brown Bullhead	1935	1937
Rio Grande Killifish	1937	
Warmouth	1939	
Arctic Grayling	1939	
Spotted Bass	1941	
Redear Sunfish	1945	
Flathead Catfish	1940	
Red Shiner	1948	
Redside Shiner	1948	
Pumpkinseed Sunfish	1949	1950
Mexican Tetra	1949	1969
Fathead Minnow	1950	
Sailfin Molly	1951	
White Bass	1951	
Threadfin Shad	1952	
Walleye	1956	
Sockeye Salmon	1957	1964
Striped Bass	1958	
Mozambique Tilapia	1959	
Variable Platyfish	1962	1968

Timeline: Changing Abundance of Arizona's Fishes Through 1962
Source: Bill Silvey and Kirk Young, Arizona Game and Fish Department

Species	up to 1912	As of 1922	As of 1932	As of 1942	As of 1952	As of 1962
Apache Trout*	•	•	•	•	•	•
Beautiful Shiner*	•	•	•	•	•	•
Bluehead Sucker	•	•	•	•	•	•
Bonytail Chub*	•	•	•	•	•	•
Colorado Pikeminnow*	•	•	•	•	•	•
Desert Pupfish*	•	•	•	•		
Desert Sucker	•	•	•	•	•	•
Flannelmouth Sucker*	•	•	•	•	•	•
Gila Chub*	•	•	•	•	•	•
Gila Topminnow*	•	•	•	•	•	•
Gila Trout*	•					
Headwater Chub*	•	•	•	•	•	•
Humpback Chub*	•	•	•	•	•	•
Little Colo. Sucker	•	•	•	•	•	•
Little Colo. Spinedace*	•	•	•	•	•	•
Loach Minnow*	•	•	•	•	•	•
Longfin Dace	•	•	•	•	•	•
Mexican Stoneroller*	•	•	•	•	•	•
Pacific Tenpounder**	•	•	•	•	•	•
Quitobaquito Pupfish*	•	•	•	•	•	•
Razorback Sucker*	•	•	•	•	•	•
Roundtail Chub*	•	•	•	•	•	•
Santa Cruz Pupfish	•	•	•	•	•	•
Sonora Chub*	•	•	•	•	•	•
Sonora Sucker	•	•	•	•	•	•
Speckled Dace	•	•	•	•	•	•
Spikedace*	•	•	•	•	•	•
Striped Mullet**	•	•	•	•	•	•
Virgin Chub*	•	•	•	•	•	•
Virgin Spinedace*	•	•	•	•	•	•
Woundfin*	•	•	•	•	•	•
Yaqui Chub*	•	•	•	•	•	•
Yaqui Sucker	•	•	•	•	•	•
Yaqui Catfish*	•	•	•	•	•	
Yaqui Topminnow*	•	•	•	•	•	•
Zuni Bluehead Sucker*	•	•	•	•	•	•

Footnotes:
• Known to be present up to or as of that year (a blank indicates the species was not known to be present)
* Rare or uncommon by 1962
** Saltwater species dependent upon water connection with Sea of Cortez

REFERENCES CITED AND CONSULTED

AGFD (Arizona Game and Fish Department). 1955a. Annual report, July 1, 1953–June 30, 1954. Phoenix: Arizona Game and Fish Department.

———. 1955b. Annual report, July 1, 1954–June 30, 1955. Phoenix: Arizona Game and Fish Department.

———. 1956. Annual report, July 1, 1955–June 30, 1956. Phoenix: Arizona Game and Fish Department.

———. 1957. Annual report, July 1, 1956–June 30, 1957. Phoenix: Arizona Game and Fish Department.

———. 1959. "Annual Report Issue" (July 1, 1957–June 30, 1958). Special issue, *Wildlife News* 6 (1).

———. 1960. "1957–58: 30 Years of Progress." Special issue, *Wildlife Views* 7 (1).

———. 1961. "Annual Report Issue" (July 1, 1959–June 30, 1960). Special issue, *Wildlife Views* 8 (1).

———. 1962. "Annual Report Issue" (July 1, 1960–June 30, 1961). Special issue, *Wildlife Views* 9 (1).

———. 1963. "Annual Report Issue" (July 1, 1961–June 30, 1962). Special issue, *Wildlife Views* 10 (1).

———. 1964. "Annual Report Issue" (July 1, 1962–June 30, 1963). Special issue, *Wildlife Views* 11 (1).

———. 1988. Arizona Game Survey and Harvest Special Data Summary, Statewide Historical 1919–87 Data. Federal Aid Project W-53-R-38. Phoenix: Arizona Game and Fish Department.

———. 2009. *Hunt Arizona 2009 Edition: Survey, Harvest and Hunt Data for Big and Small Game.* Phoenix: Arizona Game and Fish Department.

AGPA (Arizona Game Protective Association). 1927a. *Arizona Wild Life* 1 (2).

———. 1927b. "To Own His Own Zoo Was Ambition From Boyhood." *Arizona Wild Life* 1 (3).

———. 1929. "Deer Range Survey on the Crook and Coronado National Forests." *Arizona Wild Life* 1 (4): 3, 4, 18, 19, 20, 21.

———. 1930. "Notes on Arizona Game and Fish Commission Activities: Kaibab Deer Herd." *Arizona Wild Life* 4 (9).

Allen, G. M. 1939. "In Memoriam: John C. Phillips, MD." *Auk* 56 (3): 221–26.

Allison, M. N. 1939. Kofa and Cabeza Prieta Refuge report, fiscal year ending June 30, 1939. Ajo, AZ: Fish and Wildlife Service files.

Arizona Colorado River Commission. 1937 (August 4). Night letter to President Franklin D. Roosevelt and others. Arizona State University Library, Hayden Collection.

Arizona Game and Fish Commission. 1930. Biennial report of the Arizona Game and Fish Commission: 1929–30. Phoenix: Arizona Game and Fish Commission.

———. 1942. Report of activities of Arizona Game and Fish Commission, 1941–42. Phoenix: Arizona Game and Fish Commission.

———. 1948. Report of activities of Arizona Game and Fish Commission, January 1, 1943–June 30, 1947. Phoenix: Arizona Game and Fish Commission.

———. 1949. Report of the Arizona Game and Fish Commission for the biennium, July 1, 1947–June 30, 1949. Phoenix: Arizona Game and Fish Commission.

———. 1951. Biennial report, July 1, 1949–June 30, 1951. Phoenix: Arizona Game and Fish Commission.

———. 1954. Biennial report, July 1, 1951–June 30, 1953. Phoenix: Arizona Game and Fish Commission.

Arnold, J. F. 1942. *Forage Consumption and Preferences of Experimentally Fed Arizona and Antelope Jack Rabbits.* Tucson: Univ. of Arizona, Agricultural Experiment Station Technical Bulletin 98:86.

Arnold, L. 1941. "Mesquite Forest and the Whitewing." *Arizona Wildlife Sportsman* 3 (11): 5–6.

———. 1943. "A Study of the Factors Influencing the Management of and a Suggested Management Plan for the Western White-Winged Dove in Arizona." Pittman-Robertson Project 9-R. Phoenix: Arizona Game and Fish Commission.

Arrington, O. N. 1942a. "Pheasant Restocking." Federal Aid Project 11-D. Phoenix: Arizona Game and Fish Commission.

———. 1942b. "A Survey of Possible Refuge Areas for Masked Bobwhite in the Arivaca and Altar Valleys." Federal Aid Project 11-D, Special Report. Phoenix: Arizona Game and Fish Commission.

———. 1943. "Status of Restoration Areas Stocked With Game Species Under Federal Aid in Wildlife Restoration in Arizona." Federal Aid Project 11-D, Completion Report. Phoenix: Arizona Game and Fish Commission.

———. 1950. "The Kaibab North Livestock-Deer Relationship Study." Federal Aid Project W-27-R-3, Completion Report. Phoenix: Arizona Game and Fish Department: 207–23.

———. 1952. "Buffalo Herd Information." Federal Aid Project 53-R-1, Work Plan 2, Job 8, Completion Report. Phoenix: Arizona Game and Fish Commission.

———. 1991. *A Legacy of Change: Historic Human Impact on Vegetation of the Arizona Borderlands.* Tucson: Univ. of Arizona Press.

Bailey, F. M. (with W. W. Cooke). 1928. *The Birds of New Mexico.* Santa Fe: New Mexico Department of Game and Fish.

Bailey, V. 1907. *Wolves in Relation to Stock, Game and the National Forest Reserves.* USDA Forest Service Bulletin 72:1–31.

———. 1908. *Destruction of Wolves and Coyotes—Results Obtained During 1907.* USDA Bureau of Biological Survey Circular 63:1–11.

———. 1909. *Key to Animals on Which Wolf and Coyote Bounties are Often Paid.* USDA Bureau of Biological Survey Circular 69:1–3.

———. 1931. "Mammals of New Mexico." *North American Fauna* 53:413.

Baker, R. D., R. S. Maxwell, V. H. Treat, and H. C. Dethloff. 1988. *Timeless Heritage: A History of the Forest Service in the Southwest.* FS–409. Washington, DC: USDA Forest Service.

Ball, E. D., E. R. Tinkham, R. Flock, and C. T. Vorhies. 1942. *The Grasshoppers and Other Orthoptera of Arizona.* Tucson: Univ. of Arizona, Agricultural Experiment Station Technical Bulletin 93:1–373.

Barclay, G. F. 1947. "Mountain Sheep … Are Coming Back." *Arizona Wildlife-Sportsman* (October): 10–11, 22–23.

Barnes, W. C. 1924. "Know Your Own State: The Tale of a White-Tailed Squirrel." *American Forests and Forest Life.*

———. 1936. "Herds in San Simon Valley." *American Forests* 42 (10): 456–57.

Bassett, B., B. Silvey, and R. Sorensen. 1998. "From Earthen Ponds to Raceways—the History of Arizona's Hatcheries." *Arizona Wildlife Views* 41 (6): 2–7.

Bayless, R. R. 1930. Biennial report of the Arizona Game and Fish Commission: 1929–30. Arizona State Library, Archives and Public Records, Phoenix.

Beach, R. 1917, 1918. "On the Trail of the Cowardly Cougar." *Cosmopolitan* (December, January).

Belay, E. D., R. A. Maddox, E. S. Williams, M. W. Miller, P. Gambetti, and L. B. Schonberger. 2004. "Chronic Wasting Disease of Deer and Elk and the Species Barrier." *Emerging Infectious Diseases* 10 (6). doi:10.3201/eid1006.031082.

Bendt, R. H. 1957. "Report on 1957 Nuisance Deer Control Program." Internal memorandum to superintendent. Grand Canyon, AZ: Grand Canyon National Park files.

Benson, L., and R. A. Darrow. 1944. *A Manual of Southwestern Desert Trees and Shrubs.* Tucson: Univ. of Arizona, Biological Bulletin 6.

Benson, L., and J. J. Thornber. 1940. *The Cacti of Arizona.* Tucson: Univ. of Arizona, Biological Bulletin 5.

Bezy, J., C. F. Hutchinson, and C. J. Bahre. 2007. "Buenos Aires National Wildlife Refuge Arizona." *Desert Plants* 23 (2): 1–44.

Bigler, W. J. 1964. "The Seasonal Movements and Herd Activities of the Collared Peccary *(Pecari tajacu)* in the Tortolita Mountains." Master's thesis, Univ. of Arizona.

———. 1974. "Seasonal Movements and Activity Patterns of the Collared Peccary." *Journal of Mammalogy* 55:851–55.

Blaisdell, J. A. 1961. "Deer Management Plan: Grand Canyon National Park-South Rim." Grand Canyon, AZ: Grand Canyon National Park.

Bostick, V. B. 1949. "North Kaibab Deer-Livestock Forage Relationship Study." Unpublished progress report. Albuquerque: USDA Forest Service files.

———. 1950. "Deer and Livestock Forage Relationships on the Grand Canyon National Game Preserve." Unpublished progress report. Albuquerque: USDA Forest Service files.

Branstetter, M. 1976. *Pioneer Hunters of the Rim.* Mesa, AZ: Norm's Publishing House.

Brown, D.E. 1983. *The Wolf in the Southwest: The Making of an Endangered Species.* Tucson: Univ. of Arizona Press.

———. 1984a. *Arizona's Tree Squirrels.* Phoenix: Arizona Game and Fish Department.

———. 1984b. "The Effects of Drought on White-Tailed Deer Fawn Recruitment in the Southwest." In *Deer in the Southwest: A Workshop,* edited by P. R. Krausman and N. S. Smith, 7–12. Tucson: School of Renewable Natural Resources, Univ. of Arizona Press.

———. 1984c. "Mrs. Bates and the Great Arizona Bison Hunt." *Gray's Sporting Journal* 12 (3): 19, 21–28.

———. 1985a. *Arizona's Wetlands and Waterfowl.* Tucson: Univ. of Arizona Press.

———. 1985b. *The Grizzly in the Southwest.* Norman: Univ. of Oklahoma Press.

———. 1989. *Arizona Game Birds.* Tucson: Univ. of Arizona Press.

———. 1990. "In the Beginning: The Lean Years." *Arizona Wildlife Views* 33 (10): 6–7.

———. 1999. "One Hundred Years of Vicissitude: Changes in Mammal and Bird Distribution Since 1890." *Arizona Wildlife Views* 42 (6): 29–34.

———. 2001a. "Turning on the Worm That Turned." *Arizona Wildlife Views* 44 (3): 12–15.

———. 2001b. "Visiting With Aldo Leopold." *Arizona Wildlife Views* 44 (5): 18–23.

———. 2003. "Alligators in Arizona?" *Arizona Wildlife Views* 46 (2): 14–17.

———. 2004. "Picacho Reservoir—Pinal County's Unnatural Wonder." *Arizona Wildlife Views* 47 (1): 24–28.

———. 2005. "Jack O'Connor and the Pronghorn of Anderson Mesa." *Arizona Wildlife Views* 48 (3): 6–10.

———. 2008. "Historical Assessment of Pronghorn Management on Anderson Mesa: Miscalculations and Remedies." In *The Colorado Plateau III: Integrating Research and Resources Management for Effective Conservation,* edited by C. Van Riper III and M. K. Sogge, 109–40. Tucson: Univ. of Arizona Press.

———, ed. 2009. *Arizona Wildlife: The Territorial Years, 1863–1912.* Phoenix: Arizona Game and Fish Department.

Brown, D. E., and R. A. Babb. 2009. "Status of the Porcupine *(Erethizon dorsatum)* in Arizona, 2000–07." *Journal of the Arizona-Nevada Academy of Science* 41 (2): 36–41.

Brown, D. E., and P. Bosman. 1989. *Arizona Game Birds.* Tucson: Univ. of Arizona Press and Arizona Game and Fish Department.

Brown, D. E., and N. B. Carmony. 1990. *Aldo Leopold's Southwest.* Harrisburg, PA: Stackpole Books.

Brown, D. E., and R. Davis. 1994. "One Hundred Years of Vicissitude: Terrestrial Bird and Mammal Distribution Changes in the American Southwest, 1890–1990." In *Biodiversity and Management of the Madrean Archipelago: The Sky Islands of Southwestern United States and Northwestern Mexico*, 231–44. USDA Forest Service, Rocky Mountain Forest and Range Experment Station General Technical Report RM-GTR-264E.

Brown, D. E., and R. L. Glinski. 2009. "The Status of the White-tailed Hawk in Arizona and Sonora, Mexico." *Journal of the Arizona-Nevada Academy of Science* 4 (3): 8–15.

Brown, D. E., and R. J. Gutiérrez. 1980. "Sex Ratios, Sexual Selection, and Sexual Dimorphism in Quails." *Journal of Wildlife Management* 44:198–202.

Brown, D. E., and R. S. Henry. 1981. "On Relict Occurrences of White-Tailed Deer Within the Sonoran Desert in Arizona." *Southwestern Naturalist* 26:147–52.

Brown, D. E., and C. López-González. 2001. *Borderland Jaguars: Tigres de Frontera*. Salt Lake City: Univ. of Utah Press.

Brown, D. E., and C. H. Lowe Jr. 1994. "Biotic Communities of the Southwest, Map (1: 1,000,000)." Revised and reissued version of USDA Forest Service General Technical Report RM-78. Salt Lake City: Univ. of Utah Press.

Brown, D. E., and R. Ockenfels. 2007. *Arizona's Pronghorn Antelope*. Glendale, AZ: Arizona Antelope Foundation.

Brown, D. E., and D. L. Perkins. 1981. *The Sandhill Crane in Arizona*. Special Publication 11. Phoenix: Arizona Game and Fish Department.

Brown, D. E., R. L. Todd, and S. H. Levy. 1974. "Proposal for the Reintroduction of the Black-Tailed Prairie Dog into Arizona." Arizona Small Game Investigations, 1972, 1973, and 1974. Federal Aid Project W-53-R. Phoenix: Arizona Game and Fish Department.

Brown, H. 1884. "*Ortyx virginianus* in Arizona." *Forest and Stream* 22 (6): 104.

———. 1900. "Conditions Governing Bird Life in Arizona." *Auk* 17:31–34.

Brown, R. L. 1967. "The Extent of Breeding by Immature Mourning Doves *(Zenaidura macroura marginella)* in Southern Arizona." Master's thesis, Univ. of Arizona.

Bryan, K. 1925. "The Papago Country, Arizona, a Geographic, Geologic, and Hydrologic Reconnaissance with a Guide to Watering Places." US Geological Survey Water Supply-Paper 449.

———. 1928. "Change in Plant Associations by Change in Ground Water Level." *Ecology* 9:474–78.

Buffington, R., and M. S. Garrettson (American Bison Society). 1980. "History of the Buffalo With a 1928 Letter by W. J. Anderson's Father to Arizona Senator Henry Fountain Ashurst." *Arizona Wildlife Views* 23 (8): 1, 8–9.

Burnham, F. T. 1928. *Scouting on Two Continents*. Garden City, NY: Doubleday, Doran & Company.

Butcher, R. D. 2003. *America's National Wildlife Refuges: A Complete Guide*. Lanham, MD: Roberts Rinehart Publishers.

California Fish and Game Department. 1923. "Mourning Dove a Migratory Game Bird, Court Decides." *California Fish and Game* 9:34.

Carmony, N. B. 1990. "The Road to Game Restoration." *Arizona Wildlife Views* 33 (10): 8–9.

———. 1998. *Ben Lilly's Tales of Bears, Lions, and Hounds*. Silver City, NM: High-Lonesome Books.

———, ed. 2002. "The Grand Canyon Deer Drive of 1924: The Accounts of Will C. Barnes and Mark E. Musgrave." *Journal of Arizona History* 43 (Spring): 41–64.

———. 2003. "George McCormick and the Great Kaibab Deer Drive." *Arizona Wildlife Views* 46 (6): 20–24.

———. 2005a. "Aldo Leopold and the Arizona Game and Fish Commission." *Arizona Wildlife Views* 48 (4): 23–27.

———. 2005b. "The Changing Mile Revisited." *Arizona Wildlife Views* 48 (1): 18–23.

Carmony, N. B., and D. E. Brown. 1993. "Charles Sheldon's Southwest Legacy." In Sheldon 1993, 193–204.

Carr, J. N. 1960. "Mourning Dove and White-Winged Dove Nest Surveys During the Summer of 1960." Federal Aid Project W-53-R, Supplemental Report. Phoenix: Arizona Game and Fish Department.

———. 1994. *It Was a Rough Road... and Other Arizona Game and Fish Stories.* Phoenix: Heart Track Publications.

———. 1998. *Memories: A Collection of Photos.* Album of photos from the Arizona Game and Fish Department. Wickenburg, AZ: Privately published.

Carroll, W. 1983. *History of American Lion Hunting.* Spearman Publishing and Printing. Reprint, Silver City, NM: High-Lonesome Books.

Catlin, J. C. to Ira Gabrielson. 1939 (June 8). "Cabeza Prieta Work Proposals." Ajo, AZ: Cabeza Prieta National Wildlife Refuge files.

Caughley, G. 1970. "Eruption of Ungulate Populations, With Emphasis on Himalayan Thar in New Zealand." *Ecology* 51 (1): 53–72.

Cockrum, E. L. 1960. *The Recent Mammals of Arizona: Their Taxonomy and Distribution.* Tucson: Univ. of Arizona Press.

Coffin, A. L. 1961. Grand Canyon National Park: December monthly report. Grand Canyon, AZ: Grand Canyon National Park files.

———. 1962. Grand Canyon National Park: Monthly reports (January–March). Grand Canyon, AZ: Grand Canyon National Park files.

Connor, W. S. (chair), H. Hamilton, C. P. Beach, and K. C. Kartchner. 1942. Report of activities of Arizona Game and Fish Commission, 1941–42. Phoenix: Arizona Game and Fish Commission.

Connor, W. S. (chair), C. P. Beach, F. Faver and T. L. Kimball. 1948. Report of activities of Arizona Game and Fish Commission, January 1, 1943–June 30, 1947. Phoenix: Arizona Game and Fish Commission.

Cook, J. H. 1923. *Fifty Years on the Old Frontier as Cowboy, Hunter, Guide, Scout, and Ranchman.* New Haven: Yale Univ. Press.

Cook R. U., and R. W. Reeves. 1976. *Arroyos and Environmental Changes in the American South-West.* Oxford: Clarendon Press.

Cosper, P. M. 1952. "Statewide Trapping and Transplanting Project." Federal Aid Project W-11-D-11. Phoenix: Arizona Game and Fish Department.

Croxen, F. W. 1926. "History of Grazing on Tonto." Presentation by senior forest ranger at the Tonto Grazing Conference, Phoenix, AZ, November 4–5. Typed manuscript.

Cutting, H., T. G. Pearson, T. W. Tomlinson, and J. B. Burnham. 1924. "Report of the Kaibab Deer Investigating Committee." Williams, AZ: Kaibab National Forest files.

Dahms, C. W., B. W. Geils, tech. eds. 1997. "An Assessment of Forest Ecosystem Health in the Southwest." General Technical Report RM-GTR-295. Fort Collins, CO: Rocky Mountain Forest and Range Experiment Station, USDA Forest Service.

Darrow, R. A. 1944. *Arizona Range Resources and their Utilization*, vol. 1: Cochise County. Tucson: Univ. of Arizona, Agricultural Experiment Station Technical Bulletin 103:311–66.

Davis, G. P. Jr. 1982. *Man and Wildlife in Arizona: The American Exploration Period, 1824–1865.* Phoenix: Arizona Game and Fish Department.

Day, G. I. 1955a. "Investigation of Tumacacori Mountains." Federal Aid Project W-53-R-5, Work Plan 5, Job 14. Phoenix: Arizona Game and Fish Department.

———. 1955b. "Investigation of Whetstone Area." Federal Aid Project W-53-R-6, Work Plan 5, Job 18. Phoenix: Arizona Game and Fish Department.

———. 1956. "Investigation of Canelo-Patagonia Mountains." Federal Aid Project W-53-R-6, Work Plan 5, Job 19. Phoenix: Arizona Game and Fish Department.

———. 1960. "Carrying Capacity of Various Vegetation Types for White-Tailed Deer." Federal Aid Project W-78-R-4, Work Plan 5, Job 6. Phoenix: Arizona Game and Fish Department.

———. 1964. "An Investigation of White-Tailed Deer *(Odocoileus virginianus couesi)* Forage Relationships in the Chiricahua Mountains." Master's thesis, Univ. of Arizona.

———. 1985. *Javelina Research and Management in Arizona.* Phoenix: Arizona Game and Fish Department.

Degenhardt, W. G., C. W. Painter, and A. H. Price. 1996. *Amphibians and Reptiles of New Mexico.* Albuquerque: Univ. of New Mexico Press.

Dellenbaugh, F. S. 1908. *A Canyon Voyage: The Narrative of the Second Powell Expedition Down the Green-Colorado River From Wyoming, and the Explorations on Land, in the Years 1871 and 1872.* New York and London: G. P. Putnam's Sons.

Demaray, A. E. to US Senator Carl Hayden. 1936 (September 26). Arizona State University Library, Hayden Collection, Box 505, Folder 1.

Dickerman, R. W. 1954. "An Ecological Survey of the Three-Bar Game Management Unit Located Near Roosevelt Arizona." Master's thesis, Cooperative Wildlife Research Unit, Univ. of Arizona.

Diem, K. L. 1953. "Investigation of Effects of Predation (Kaibab North)." Federal Aid Project W-53-R-3, Completion Report. Phoenix: Arizona Game and Fish Department.

———. 1954. "Investigation of Kaibab North." Federal Aid Project W-53-R-4, Completion Report. Phoenix: Arizona Game and Fish Department.

Diem, K. L., and D. J. Illige. 1952. "Kaibab North Range Utilization Investigations." Federal Aid Project W-53-R-2, Completion Report. Phoenix: Arizona Game and Fish Department.

Dimock, B. 2004. "Jack Fuss and the Great Kaibab Deer Drive." *Boatman's Quarterly Review* 17 (2): 16–23.

Dobie, J. F. 1950. *The Ben Lilly Legend.* Reprinted Austin: Univ. of Texas Press, 1981.

Dutton, C. E. 1882. "The Physical Geology of the Grand Canyon District." Second annual report. US Geological Survey, 1880 and 1881. Washington, DC: Government Printing Office.

Dyson, R. F. 1969. "Nutritional Investigations With the Collared Peccary *(Pecari tajacu).*" Master's thesis, Univ. of Arizona.

Earl, J. C. 1952. "Statewide Trapping and Transplanting Project." Federal Aid Project W-11-D-12. Phoenix: Arizona Game and Fish Department.

Easton, R., and M. Brown. 1961. *Lord of Beasts: The Saga of Buffalo Jones.* Tucson: Univ. of Arizona Press.

Eddy, T. A. 1959. "Foods of the Collared Peccary *Pecari tajacu sonoriensis* (Mearns) in Southern Arizona." Master's thesis, Univ. of Arizona.

———. 1961. "Foods and Feeding Patterns of the Collared Peccary in Southern Arizona." *Journal of Wildlife Management* 25:248–57.

Eden, J. 1956. "A History of Organ Pipe Cactus National Monument." Unpublished manuscript. Organ Pipe Cactus National Monument library.

Erling, H. G. 1956a (January). "Report on a Study of Reproduction in Antelope." Federal Aid Project W-53-R-5, Work Plan 2, Job 1, Special Report. Phoenix: Arizona Game and Fish Commission.

———. 1956b (April). "Report on a Study of Reproduction in Antelope." Federal Aid Project W-53-R-6, Work Plan 2, Job 1, Special Report. Phoenix: Arizona Game and Fish Commission.

Evans, G. W. 1951. *Slash Ranch Hounds.* Albuquerque: Univ. of New Mexico Press.

Evans, W. F. 1950. *Hunting Grizzlys, Black Bear and Lions "Big-Time" on the Old Ranches.* El Paso: McMath Company.

Executive Order Draft. 1935. "Establishing House Rock Valley Wildlife Refuge in Arizona." Revisions of March 5. Smithsonian Institution, US Fish and Wildlife Service Collection, 1860–1961. Field Reports. Series 1, Record Unit 7176, Box 30, Folder 18.

Faver, F., C. P. Beach, W. J. Richards, and T. L. Kimball. 1949. Report of the Arizona Game and Fish Commission for the biennium, July 1, 1947–June 30, 1949. Phoenix: Arizona Game and Fish Commission.

Felger, R. S., W. Broyles, M. Wilson, G. P. Nabhan, and D. S. Turner. 2007. "Six Grand Reserves, One Sonoran Desert." In *Dry Borders: Great Natural Reserves of the Sonoran Desert*, edited by Richard S. Felger and Bill Broyles, 3–26. Salt Lake City: Univ. of Utah Press.

Ferguson, J. W. 1951. "Investigation of the Three Bar Game Management Area." Federal Aid Project W-53-R, Work Plan 5, Job 6. Phoenix: Arizona Game and Fish Department.

Fitzhugh, E. L. 1970. "Literature and Bibliography of the Band-Tailed Pigeons of Arizona, Colorado, New Mexico and Utah." Special Report. Phoenix: Arizona Game and Fish Department.

Fleming, W. B. 1959. *Migratory Waterfowl in Arizona: A Management Study.* Wildlife Bulletin 5. Phoenix: Arizona Game and Fish Department.

———. 1970. "Arizona's Buffalo: A Stranger History You Couldn't Find in Ripley's." *Wildlife Views* 17 (6): 9–11, 13.

Foster, B. E. 1931–1936. Predatory animal control. Arizona District annual reports for 1931–36 inclusive. Phoenix: USDA Bureau of Biological Survey.

———. 1933b. Narrative report of operations in Arizona for controlling rodent pests for the fiscal year ending June 30, 1933 … as conducted by the United States Department of Agriculture Bureau of Biological Survey and the Agricultural Extension Service University of Arizona. Phoenix: USDA Bureau of Biological Survey.

Fox, S. 1981. *The American Conservation Movement: John Muir and His Legacy.* Madison: Univ. of Wisconsin Press.

Fuss, J. 1999. "The Great Kaibab Deer Drive." Transcribed from a 1963 tape of a talk given at the Flagstaff Lions Club. *Arizona Wildlife Views* 42 (6): 18–23.

Gabrielson, I. N. 1943. *Wildlife Refuges.* New York: Macmillan.

Gallizioli, S. 1953a. "Dove Investigations." Federal Aid Project W-53-R. Phoenix: Arizona Game and Fish Department.

———. 1953b. "Investigation of the Mount Graham Area (Zone 2, Unit 12)." Federal Aid Project W-53-R-3, Work Plan 5, Job 1. Phoenix: Arizona Game and Fish Department.

———. 1954a. "Hunting Season Information on the Mourning and White-Winged Doves of Arizona." Special Report. Phoenix: Arizona Game and Fish Department.

———. 1954b. "Investigation of Galiuro Mountains." Federal Aid Project W-53-R-4, Work Plan 5, Job 1, Completion Report. Phoenix: Arizona Game and Fish Department.

———. 1956. "Field Observations of Deer in the Prescott Study Area." Federal Aid Project W-71-R-3, Work Plan 3, Job 2. Phoenix: Arizona Game and Fish Department.

———. 1961. *Water and Gambel Quail.* Wildlife Bulletin. Phoenix: Arizona Game and Fish Department.

———. 2012. "A Short History of the Arizona Wildlife Federation." Arizona Wildlife Federation website, http://www.azwildlife.org.

Gambrell, R. 1940. "Catalina, Chiricahua and Pinaleño Mountain Turkey Restocking Project." Federal Aid Project 2-D. Phoenix: Arizona Game and Fish Commission.

———. 1941. "Trapping and Transplanting." Federal Aid Project 11-D. Phoenix: Arizona Game and Fish Commission.

———.1953 (March). "Buffalo Hunt Information." Federal Aid Project W-53-R-3, Work Plan 2, Job 8, Completion Report.

Gatlin, J. C. 1934. Predatory animal control. New Mexico District annual report. Albuquerque: USDA Bureau of Biological Survey.

Gibbons, J. 1937 (August 5). Telegram to President Franklin D. Roosevelt and others. Arizona State University Library, Hayden Collection.

Gilchrist, D. A. 1928. Report of operations in Arizona for controlling rodent pests during the period July 1, 1927–June 30, 1928 as conducted by the United States Department of Agriculture Bureau of Biological Survey and the Agricultural Extension Service University of Arizona. Phoenix: USDA Bureau of Biological Survey.

———. 1929. Rodent pest control. Arizona District annual report. Phoenix: USDA Bureau of Biological Survey.

———. 1930. Predatory animal control. Arizona District annual report. Phoenix: USDA Bureau of Biological Survey.

———. 1931. Rodent pest control. Arizona District annual report. Phoenix: USDA Bureau of Biological Survey.

———. 1932. Predatory animal control. Arizona District annual report. Phoenix: USDA Bureau of Biological Survey.

———. 1933. Predatory animal control. Arizona District annual report. Phoenix: USDA Bureau of Biological Survey.

Gilman, M. F. 1911. "Doves on the Pima Reservation." *Condor* 13:51–56.

Glading, B. 1943. "A Self-Filling Quail Watering Device." *California Fish and Game* 29:151–64.

Glinski, R. L. 1998. "Golden Eagle." In *Raptors of Arizona*, edited by R. L. Glinski, 112–14. Tucson: Univ. of Arizona Press and Arizona Game and Fish Department.

Goldman, E. A. 1920. "Report of Investigations of Summer Conditions Affecting Elk on Sitgreaves National Forest, Arizona, July 1–15, 1920." Typewritten report. Springerville, AZ: Apache-Sitgreaves National Forest files.

———. 1923. "Report on the Tonto Plateau, Grand Canyon National Park, Arizona, as a Prospective Antelope Refuge, April 8–13, 1923." Smithsonian Institution, US Fish and Wildlife Service Collection, 1860–1961. Series 1, Record Unit 7176, Box 25, Folder 3.

———. 1925a. "Predatory Mammal Problem." *Journal of Mammalogy* 6 (1): 28–33.

———. 1925b. "Report on Conditions Affecting Deer of Kaibab Plateau, Arizona, in June 1925." Typewritten memo, USDA Bureau of Biological Survey. Smithsonian Institution.

———. 1926a. "Breeding Birds of a White Mountain Lake." *Condor* 28:159–64.

———. 1926b. "Surplus Game—A Problem in Administration." *American Game* 15 (1): 28–31.

———. 1931a. "Report of the Committee Investigating Big Game Ranges on Certain National Forests in Arizona, April 7–26, 1931, Inclusive, and Including Auxiliary Reports by the Arizona Game and Fish Commission and E. A. Goldman's Individual Account." Smithsonian Institution, US Fish and Wildlife Service Collection, 1860–1961. Field Reports. Series 1, Record Unit 7176, Box 21, Folder 3.

———. 1931b. "Report on a Survey of Game Refuges in Certain National Forests in Arizona." Smithsonian Institution, US Fish and Wildlife Service Collection, 1860–1961. Field Reports. Series 1, Record Unit 7176, Box 25, Folder 12.

———. 1931c. "Report Supplementing the Report of the Committee Investigating Big Game Ranges on Certain National Forests in Arizona, April 7–26, 1931, Inclusive." Smithsonian Institution, US Fish and Wildlife Service Collection, 1860–1961. Series 1, Record Unit 7176, Box 25, Folder 12.

———. 1932. "Management of our Deer Herds." *Transactions of the 19th American Game Conference* 49:58.

Goldman, E. A., and S. B. Locke. 1922 (October 19). "Report on the Summer and Fall Deer Range Examination: Memorandum Regarding Grand Canyon National Game Preserve." Williams, AZ: Kaibab National Forest files.

———. 1923 (April 19). "Memorandum Regarding Grand Canyon National Game Preserve. Supplement To Memorandum of October 19, 1922, Covering the Same Subject." Smithsonian Institution, US Fish and Wildlife Service Collection, 1860–1961. Series 1, Record Unit 7176, Box 24, Folder 13.

Gorsuch, D. M. 1934. *Life History of the Gambel Quail in Arizona.* Tucson: Univ. of Arizona, Biological Science Bulletin 2:5–89.

Gould, F. W. 1951. *Grasses of Southwestern United States.* Tucson: Univ. of Arizona, Biological Sciences Bulletin 7:7–352.

Governor's Files. 1912–16. Section 8C, Fish and Game, Box 1A, Folder 18. Arizona State Library, Archives and Public Records, Phoenix.

Governor's Files. 1923–33. Deer in Kaibab, 1923–24, Box 2A, Folder 5. Arizona State Library, Archives and Public Records, Phoenix.

Greever, W. S. 1954. *Arid Domain—The Santa Fe Railway and Its Western Land Grant.* Palo Alto: Stanford Univ. Press.

Gresham, G. 1953. "Buffalo in Arizona." *Arizona Wildlife-Sportsman*, January: 24–27.

Grey, Z. 1924a. *Roping Lions in the Grand Canyon.* New York: Grossett and Dunlap.

———. 1924b. "Kaibab Deer Refuse To Herd." *Arizona Republican,* December 19, 1924.

Griner, L. A. 1940a. "Proposed Quail Management Plan for Cochise County, Arizona." Federal Aid Project 9-R. Phoenix: Arizona Game and Fish Commission.

———. 1940b. "Proposed Quail Refuge Area in Pinal County, June 12–17, 1940." Federal Aid Project 4-D. Phoenix: Arizona Game and Fish Commission.

Griner, L. A., and A. A. Nichol. 1940. "Preliminary Report on a Quail Survey of Certain Parts of Mohave County." Federal Aid Project 9-R. Phoenix: Arizona Game and Fish Commission.

Grinnell, G. B. 1904. *American Big Game in its Haunts.* New York: Boone and Crockett Club, Forest and Stream Publishing Co.

Grinnell, J. 1914. *An Account of the Mammals and Birds of the Lower Colorado Valley.* University of California Publications in Zoology 12 (4): 51–294.

———. 1927. "A Critical Factor in the Existence of Southwestern Game Birds." *Science* 65:528–29.

Hage, W. 1989. *Storm Over Rangelands: Private Rights in Federal Lands.* Bellevue, WA: Free Enterprise Press.

Hall, E. R. 1925. "Kaibab Deer." Unpublished memorandum to USDA Bureau of Biological Survey. Williams, AZ: Kaibab National Forest files.

———. 1930. "Predatory Mammal Destruction." *Journal of Mammalogy* 11 (3): 362–69.

Halloran, A. 1964. "Yuma Area Refuge Biological Review." Mimeograph, December. Albuquerque: Fish and Wildlife Service files for Yuma, AZ.

Hanson, W. R., and C. Y. McCulloch. 1955. "Factors Influencing Mule Deer on Arizona Brushlands." *Transactions of the North American Wildlife Conference* 20:568–88.

Hargrave, L. L. 1939. "Reconnaissance Report of Turkey Food on a Portion of the Winter Range of the Wild Turkey in Arizona." Federal Aid Project 3-R. Phoenix: Arizona Game and Fish Commission.

———. 1940. "Data on Grouse and Quail." Federal Aid Project 3-R. Phoenix: Arizona Game and Fish Commission.

Hart, L. B., K. C. Kartchner, H. A. Kinnison, E. A. Goldman, F. Winn, D. A. Shoemaker, E. M. Hornibrook, and M. E. Musgrave. 1931a. "Report of a Committee Investigating Deer Range in the Santa Catalina Mountains, Arizona, April 7–9, 1931. Tucson." Smithsonian Institution, US Fish and Wildlife Service Collection, 1860–1961. Field Reports. Series 1, Record Unit 7176, Box 21, Folder 3.

Hart, L. B., K. C. Kartchner, H. A. Kinnison, E. A. Goldman, F. Winn, D. A. Shoemaker, E. M. Hornibrook, M. E. Musgrave, and Others. 1931b (April 28). "Report of a Committee Investigating Big Game Ranges on Certain National Forests in Arizona." Smithsonian Institution, US Fish and Wildlife Service Collection, 1860–1961. Field Reports. Series 1, Record Unit 7176, Box 21, Folder 3.

Hayden, C. to A. E. Demaray, associate director of the National Park Service. 1936 (September 23). Arizona State University Library, Hayden Collection, Box 505, Folder 1.

Heffelfinger, J. R. 2006. *Deer of the Southwest.* College Station: Texas A&M Univ. Press.

Heffelfinger, J. R., and P. M. Webb. 2010. "The History of Arizona Deer Translocations." In *Arizona Wildlife Trophy Records Book*, 9th ed., edited by R. L. Glinski, D. J. Aubuchon, and B. Keebler, 43–70. Mesa, AZ: Arizona Wildlife Federation.

Hibbard, B. H. 1965. *A History of the Public Land Policies.* Madison: Univ. of Wisconsin Press.

Hibben, F. C. 1937. *A Preliminary Study of the Mountain Lion.* Albuquerque: Univ. of New Mexico Press.

Hoffmeister, D. F. 1956. "Mammals of the Graham [Pinaleño] Mountains, Arizona." *American Midland Naturalist* 35:237–388.

———. 1962. "The Kinds of Deer, *Odocoileus*, in Arizona." *American Midland Naturalist* 67:45–64.

———. 1984. *Mammals of Arizona.* Tucson: Univ. of Arizona Press.

Hoffmeister, D. F., and W. W. Goodpaster. 1954. "The Mammals of the Huachuca Mountains, Southeastern Arizona." *Illinois Biological Society Monograph* 24:1–152.

Holder, C. F. 1906. *Life in the Open—Sport With Rod, Gun, Horse, and Hound in Southern California.* New York: G. P. Putnam's Sons.

Hornaday, W. T. 1908. *Camp-Fires on Desert and Lava.* New York: Charles Scribner's Sons.

———. 1913. *Our Vanishing Wild Life: Its Extermination and Preservation.* New York: New York Zoological Society.

———. 1931. *Thirty Years War for Wildlife.* Stamford, CT: Permanent Wild Life Fund.

Housholder, R. 1966. *The Grizzly Bear in Arizona.* 2nd ed. Phoenix: printed by author.

Humphrey, R. R. 1950. *Arizona Range Resources*, vol. 2: Yavapai County. Tucson: Univ. of Arizona, Agriculture Experiment Station Bulletin 229:1–55.

———. 1953. *Forage Production on Arizona Ranges*, vol. 3: Mohave County. Tucson: Univ. of Arizona, Agriculture Experiment Station Bulletin 244:1–79.

———. 1955. *Forage Production on Arizona Ranges*, vol. 4: Coconino, Navajo, Apache Counties. Tucson: Univ. of Arizona, Agriculture Experiment Station Bulletin 266:1–84.

———. 1958. "The Desert Grassland: A History of Vegetational Change and an Analysis of Causes." *Botanical Review* 24:193–252.

———. 1960. *Forage Production on Arizona Ranges*, vol. 5: Pima, Pinal, Santa Cruz Counties. Tucson: Univ. of Arizona, Agriculture Experiment Station Bulletin 302:1–138.

Hungerford, C. R. 1955. "A Preliminary Evaluation of Quail Malaria in Southern Arizona in Relation to Habitat and Quail Mortality." *Transactions of the North American Wildlife and Natural Resources Conference* 20:209–19.

———. 1960a. "The Factors Affecting the Breeding of Gambel's Quail *Lophortyx gambelii gambelii* in Arizona." PhD dissertation, Univ. of Arizona.

———. 1960b. "Water Requirements of Gambel's Quail." *Transactions of the North American Wildlife and Natural Resources Conference* 25:231–40.

———. 1962. "Adaptations Shown in Selection of Food by Gambel's Quail." *Condor* 64:213–19.

———. 1964. "Vitamin A and Productivity in Gambel's Quail." *Journal of Wildlife Management* 28:141–47.

Ickes, H. L. 1953. *The Secret Diaries of Harold L. Ickes, the First Thousand Days, 1933–1936.* New York: Simon and Schuster.

IUCN (International Union for Conservation of Nature and Natural Resources). 2010. "Notes on Dr. John C. Phillips." http://cmsdata.iucn.org/jcp_background.doc.

Johnson, A., and W. G. Swank. 1955. "Population Dynamics of Arizona's Important Deer Herds." Federal Aid Project W-78-R-1, Work Plan 4, Job 1. Phoenix: Arizona Game and Fish Department.

Kant, C. C. 2000. "Zane Grey." In N. L. Lewis 2000, 32–41. Mesa, AZ: Arizona Wildlife Federation.

Kartchner, K. C. 1931. "Arizona's Pronghorn." *Arizona Wild Life* (September): 11–13.

Keith, J. O. 1965. "The Abert Squirrel and Its Dependence on Ponderosa Pine." *Ecology* 46 (1 and 2): 150–63.

Kimball, T. L. 1940. "Quail Survey of the Congress Junction-Date Creek Area, June 22–30, 1940." Federal Aid Project 9-R: Quail. Phoenix: Arizona Game and Fish Commission.

———. 1945. "Survey of Conditions in Cochise County Quail Areas." Federal Aid Project 9-R. Phoenix: Arizona Game and Fish Commission.

Kimball, T. L., and A. G. Watkins. 1951. "The Kaibab North Cooperative Deer-Livestock Forage Relationship Study." Phoenix: Arizona Game and Fish Commission.

Kirkpatrick, R. D., and L. K. Sowls. 1962. "Age Determination of the Collared Peccary by the Tooth-Replacement Pattern." *Journal of Wildlife Management* 26:214–17.

Knipe, T. 1944. "The Status of the Antelope Herds of Northern Arizona." Pittman-Robertson Project, Arizona 9-R. Phoenix: Arizona Game and Fish Commission.

———. 1955. *Javelina in Arizona: A Research and Management Study.* Wildlife Bulletin 2. Phoenix: Arizona Game and Fish Department.

Koster, W. J. 1957. *Guide to the Fishes of New Mexico.* Albuquerque: Univ. of New Mexico Press.

Lamar, H. R. 1966. *The Far Southwest 1846–1912: A Territorial History.* New Haven: Yale Univ. Press.

Lamb, J. J., R. Pinto, R. Leighninger Jr., P. Booth, M. Smith, and J. Mehulka. 2008. "The New Deal in Arizona: Connections to our Historic Landscape." Map and text. Phoenix: Arizona Humanities Council.

Latch, E. K., J. R. Heffelfinger, J. A. Fike, and O. E. Rhodes Jr. 2009. "Species-Wide Phylogeography of North American Mule Deer: Cryptic Glacial Refugia and Post-Glacial Recolonization." *Molecular Ecology* 18: 1730–45.

Lauver, M. E. 1938. "A History of the Use and Management of the Forested Lands of Arizona, 1862–1936." Master's thesis, Univ. of Arizona.

Lawson, L. L. 1940a. "Investigation of Pheasant Release Area in the South Mountain-Phoenix Region of the Salt River." Federal Aid Special Report. Phoenix: Arizona Game and Fish Commission.

———. 1940b. "Statewide Pheasant Restocking." Federal Aid Project 10-D. Phoenix: Arizona Game and Fish Commission.

———. 1949a. "Chukar Partridge Investigations." Federal Aid Project W-40-R-1. Phoenix: Arizona Game and Fish Commission.

———. 1949b. "Whitewing Dove Study." Federal Aid Project 40-R. Phoenix: Arizona Game and Fish Department.

———. 1951. "Special Investigations on the Status of Pheasant and Chukar Partridge in Arizona." Federal Aid Project W-40-R-2. Phoenix: Arizona Game and Fish Commission.

Laycock, George. 1965. *The Sign of the Flying Goose: A Guide to the National Wildlife Refuges.* Garden City, NJ: Natural History Press.

LeCount, A. 1977a. "Causes of Fawn Mortality." Federal Aid Project W-78-R, Work Plan 2, Job 11. Phoenix: Arizona Game and Fish Department.

———. 1977b. "Some Aspects of Black Bear Ecology in the Arizona Chaparral." *Bear Biology Association Conference* Series 3:175–79.

Lendt, D. L. 1979. *Ding: The Life of Jay Norwood Darling.* Ames: Iowa State Univ. Press.

Leopold, A. 1920. "Determining the Kill Factor for Black-tail Deer in the Southwest." *Journal of Forestry* 18 (2): 131–34.

———. 1933. *Game Management.* New York: Charles Scribner's Sons.

Leopold, A., L. K. Sowls, and D. L. Spencer. 1947. "A Survey of Over-Populated Deer Ranges in the United States." *Journal of Wildlife Management* 11:162–77.

Levy, S. H. 1963. "Bighorns and Papagos." *Transactions of the Desert Bighorn Council* 7:114–19.

Lewis, N. L. 2000. *Arizona Wildlife Trophies*, millennium edition. Mesa: Arizona Wildlife Federation.

Lewis, S. L. 1936. Annual report of the Arizona Game and Fish Commission. Phoenix: Arizona Game and Fish Commission.

Ligon, J. S. 1916. Predatory animal control inspectors annual report. July 1, 1915–June 30, 1916. USDA Bureau of Biological Survey.

———. 1917. Predatory animal control annual report, fiscal year 1917. Arizona and New Mexico, July 1, 1916–June 30, 1917. USDA Bureau of Biological Survey.

———. 1918. Annual report, predatory animal campaign, Arizona-New Mexico. USDA Bureau of Biological Survey.

———. 1919. Predatory animal control. New Mexico and Oklahoma sub-district annual report. USDA Bureau of Biological Survey.

———. 1924. Predatory animal control. Arizona annual report. USDA Bureau of Biological Survey.

———. 1927. *Wild Life of New Mexico: Its Conservation and Management.* Santa Fe: New Mexico Game Commission.

———. 1946. *History and Management of Merriam's Wild Turkey.* Albuquerque: Univ. of New Mexico Press.

Locke, S. B. 1930. "The Study of Big Game Ranges." *Ecology* 11:770.

Lockhart, L. (chair), G. Wrench, C. P. Beach, and S. L. Lewis. 1936 annual report of the Arizona Game and Fish Commission. Phoenix: Arizona Game and Fish Commission.

Looney, R. L. (with commentary by N. B. Carmony). 2003. "How Arizona was Restocked With Elk." *Arizona Wildlife Views* 46 (1): 24–28.

Lowe, C. H. Jr. 1955. "Gambel Quail and Water Supply in Tiburón Island, Sonora, Mexico." *Condor* 57:244.

———, ed. 1964. *The Vertebrates of Arizona.* Tucson: Univ. of Arizona Press.

Lumholtz, C. 1912. *New Trails in Mexico: Travels Among the Papago, Pima and Cocopa Indians.* New York: Charles Scribner's Sons.

Mackenzie, G. 1935 (February 7). Letter from the Pima County Board of Supervisors to US Senator Carl Hayden. Arizona State University Library, Hayden Collection, Box 607, Folder 1.

Mahoney, S. 2007. *Opportunity for All: The Story of the North American Model for Wildlife Conservation.* DVD.

Mann, W. G. 1932. "Kaibab Game Management." *Arizona Wild Life* 6 (1).

———. 1941. "The Kaibab Deer—a Brief History and Recent Management." Unpublished report. Fredonia, AZ: USDA Forest Service files.

Mann, W. G., and S. B. Locke. 1931. "The Kaibab Deer—A Brief History and Recent Developments." Mimeographed report. Williams, AZ: Kaibab National Forest files.

Mann, W. G., and R. H. Park. 1933. "1933 Deer Trapping on the Kaibab National Forest." Williams, AZ: Kaibab National Forest files.

Marshall, J. T. Jr. 1957. "Birds of the Pine-Oak Woodland in Southern Arizona and Adjacent Mexico." Cooper Ornithological Society, *Pacific Coast Avifauna* 32:1–125.

Martinez, C. R. 2011. "Dewitt Clinton Booth." *Eddies: Reflections on Fisheries Conservation* 4 (3): 7.

Maxa, C. 2003. "100 Years of Honoring Wildlife: The National Wildlife Refuge System Celebrates a Centennial." *Arizona Wildlife Views* 46 (2): 18–22.

McAtee, W. L. 1939. "Obituaries (John C. Phillips)." *Journal of Wildlife Management* 3 (2): 144–45.

McAuliffe, J. R. 1994. "Landscape Evolution, Soil Formation, and Ecological Patterns and Processes in Sonoran Desert Bajadas." *Ecological Monographs* 64 (2): 111–48.

———. 1998. "Rangeland Water Developments: Conservation Solution or Illusion?" In *Proceedings of a Symposium on Environment, Economics, and Legal Issues Related to Rangeland Water Developments*, presented by The Center for the Study of Law, Science and Technology, Arizona State Univ., Tempe, November 18–19, 1997: 310–35.

McCormick, Charles. 1924. "Increase Boundary Lines." *Outdoor America* 3 (5): 61–65.

McCulloch, C. Y. 1954a. "Field Observations of Deer in the Three Bar Vicinity." Federal Aid Project W-71-R-1, Work Plan 3, Job 1. Phoenix: Arizona Game and Fish Department.

———. 1954b. "The Investigation of Penned Deer in Chaparral Habitat." Federal Aid Project W-71-R-1, Work Plan 5. Phoenix: Arizona Game and Fish Department.

———. 1955a. "Field Observations of Deer in the Three Bar Vicinity." Arizona Chaparral Deer Study. Federal Aid Project W-71-R-2, Work Plan 3, Job 1. Phoenix: Arizona Game and Fish Department.

———. 1955b (March). "The Investigation of Penned Deer in Chaparral Habitat." Federal Aid Project W-71-R-2, Work Plan 5. Phoenix: Arizona Game and Fish Department.

———. 1955c (August). "The Investigation of Penned Deer in Chaparral Habitat." Federal Aid Project W-71-R-3, Work Plan 5. Phoenix: Arizona Game and Fish Department.

———. 1955d. "Ecological Investigation of Three Bar Study Area." Federal Aid Project W-71-R-2, Completion Report. Phoenix: Arizona Game and Fish Department.

———. 1961. "The Influence on Carrying Capacity of Experimental Water Conservation Measures." Federal Aid Project W-78-R-5, Job 7. Phoenix: Arizona Game and Fish Department.

———. 1968. "Transplanted Mule Deer in Arizona." *Journal of the Arizona Academy of Science* 5:43–44.

———. 1972. "Deer Foods and Brush Control in Southeastern Arizona." *Journal of the Arizona Academy of Science* 7:113–19.

McGinnies, W. G. to W. G. Mann. 1934 (November 14). Smithsonian Institution, US Fish and Wildlife Service Collection, 1860–1961. Field Reports. Series 1, Record Unit 7176, Box 30, Folder 18.

McGuire, E. 1941. "Report on Investigation of Potential Antelope Range in the Safford Area, February 25–27, 1941." Federal Aid Special Report, Arizona 9-R.

McIntyre, A. J., and Arizona Historical Society. 2008. *The Tohono O'odham and Primeria Alta* (Images of America: Arizona). San Francisco: Arcadia Publishing.

McKinney, T. 2003. "Precipitation, Weather, and Mule Deer." In *Mule Deer Conservation: Issues and Management Strategies*, edited by J. C. deVos Jr., M. R. Conover, and N. E. Headrick, 219–37. Logan: Berryman Institute Press, Utah State Univ.

McLemore, M. 1941. *Nevada State Journal.* January 29: 8.

McMichael, T. J. 1967. "Investigation of Factors Influencing Deer Populations." Federal Aid Project W-78-R-11, Work Plan 4, Job 5. Phoenix: Arizona Game and Fish Department.

Mearns, E. A. 1907. *Mammals of the Mexican Boundary of the United States: A Descriptive Catalogue of the Species of Mammals Occurring in That Region; With a General Summary of the Natural History, and a List of Trees.* United States National Museum Bulletin 56. Washington, DC: Smithsonian Institution. Reprint: New York, Arno Press, 1974.

Meine, C. 1988. *Aldo Leopold: His Life and Work*. Madison: Univ. of Wisconsin Press.

Mercer, E. M. 1929–50. Predatory animal and rodent control. Arizona District annual reports for 1929, 1938, 1939, 1940, 1942, 1944, 1945, 1947, and 1950. Phoenix: USDA Bureau of Biological Survey.

———. 1953. Narrative report: Predator and rodent control operations. July 1, 1952–June 30, 1953. Phoenix: Branch of Predator and Rodent Control, Fish and Wildlife Service.

———. 1960. Predatory animal control. Arizona District annual report. Phoenix: Fish and Wildlife Service.

Merkle, J. 1952. "An Analysis of a Pinyon-Juniper Community at Grand Canyon, Arizona." *Ecology* 33:375–84.

Merriam, C. H. 1922. "Map of the Distribution of Grizzly Bear." *Outdoor Life* 12.

Merriam, C. H., and L. Stejneger. 1890. "Results of a Biological Survey of the San Francisco Mountain Region and Desert of the Little Colorado in Arizona." *North America Fauna* 3:1–101.

Miller, R. R. 1972. "Classification of the Native Trouts of Arizona, With the Description of a New Species, *Salmo Apache*." *Copeia:* 401–22.

Miller, W. H. 1916. *The Outdoorsman's Handbook*, 4th ed. New York: Angler's Guide Co.

Minckley, W. L. 1973. *Fishes of Arizona*. Phoenix: Arizona Game and Fish Department.

Minnamon, P. J. 1962. "The Home Range of the Collared Peccary *Pecari tajacu* (Mearns) in the Tucson Mountains." Master's thesis, Univ. of Arizona.

Monson, G., and L. Sumner, eds. 1980. *The Desert Bighorn*. Tucson: Univ. of Arizona Press.

Morgan, D. B. to Homer L. Shantz. 1934 (November 10). Smithsonian Institution, US Fish and Wildlife Service Collection, 1860–1961. Field Reports. Series 1, Record Unit 7176, Box 30, Folder 18.

Mueller, G. A., and P. C. Marsh. 2002. "Lost, a Desert River and Its Native Fishes: A Historical Perspective of the Lower Colorado River." Information and Technology Report USGS/BRD/ITR-2002-0010, US Geological Survey. Denver: Government Printing Office.

Mulch, E. E., and W. C. Gamble. 1954. *Game Fishes of Arizona*. Phoenix: Arizona Game and Fish Department.

Mule Deer Working Group. 2006. "Habitat Guidelines for Mule Deer; Southwest Deserts Ecoregion." Cheyenne, WY: Western Association of Fish and Wildlife Agencies.

Murie, O. J. 1951. *The Elk of North America*. Washington, DC: The Wildlife Management Institute.

Murphy, J. M. 1879. *Sporting Adventures in the Far West*. New York: Harper and Brothers.

Musgrave, M. E. 1919–29. Predatory animal control. Arizona District annual reports. Phoenix: USDA Bureau of Biological Survey.

Nabi, A. A. 1978. "Variation in Successional Status of Pinyon–Juniper Woodlands of the Great Basin." Master's thesis, Utah State Univ. (Logan).

Neal, B. J. 1957. "Techniques of Trapping, Tagging, and Transplanting the Collared Peccary, *Pecari tajacu sonoriensis* (Mearns) in Arizona." Master's thesis, Univ. of Arizona.

———. 1959a. "A Contribution of the Life History of the Collared Peccary in Arizona." *American Midland Naturalist* 61:177–90.

———. 1959b. "Techniques of Trapping and Tagging the Collared Peccary." *Journal of Wildlife Management* 23:11–16.

Neal, B. J., and R. Kirkpatrick. 1957. "Anamalous Canine Tooth Development in an Arizona Peccary." *Journal of Mammalogy* 38:420.

Neff, D. J. n.d. "The Life of a Homesteader." Unpublished manuscript. Phoenix: Research Branch, Arizona Game and Fish Department.

Neff, J. A. 1940a. "Notes on Nesting and Other Habits of the White-Winged Dove in Arizona." *Journal of Wildlife Management* 4:279–90.

———. 1940b. "Range, Population and Game Status of the Western White-Winged Dove in Arizona." *Journal of Wildlife Management* 4:117–27.

———. 1947. "Habits, Food and Economic Status of the Band-Tailed Pigeon." *North America Fauna* 58:1–76.

Nelson, E. W. 1904. "The Black Mesa Forest Reserve of Arizona and Its Availability as a Game Preserve." Report at US National Museum, Smithsonian Institution Archives.

———. 1925. *Status of the Pronghorned Antelope: 1922–24.* USDA Bulletin 1346. Washington, DC: US Department of Agriculture.

———. 1932. "Mule Deer (*Odocoileus* and its Subspecies)." *Arizona Wild Life* 4 (2): 7, 15.

Nichol, A. A. 1931. "Report on a Survey of the Game Refuges in the Tusayan, Coconino, Sitgreaves, Apache and Crook National Forests, April 9 to May 1, 1931." Typewritten report. Arizona State Library, Archives and Public Records, Phoenix.

——— 1936. "Hunters, Conservationists, Game and Cattlemen." *American Cattle Producer* 18 (5): 6–7.

———. 1937a. "Desert Bighorn Sheep Study, June to November, 1937 Inclusive." Mimeograph. Smithsonian Institution, US Fish and Wildlife Service Collection, 1860–1961. Field Reports. Series 1, Record Unit 7176, Box 28, Folder 6.

———. 1937b. Smithsonian Institution, US Fish and Wildlife Service Collection, 1860–1961. Field Reports. Series 1, Record Unit 7176, Box 27, Folder 6.

———. 1937c. *The Natural Vegetation of Arizona.* Tucson: Univ. of Arizona, Agricultural Experiment Station Technical Bulletin 68: 181–222. Reprint, 1943.

———. 1938. *Experimental Feeding of Deer.* Tucson: Univ. of Arizona, Agricultural Experiment Station Technical Bulletin 75:1–39.

———. 1940. "Game Reconnaissance of Southeastern Arizona, South of the Gila River." Federal Aid Special Report 9-R. Phoenix: Arizona Game and Fish Commission.

———. 2006. "Large Game Mammals, From 1936 to Today." Introduced and annotated by Neil Carmony. *Arizona Wildlife Views* 49 (5): 29–32.

Niehuis, C. C. 1943. "Trapping of Antelope: The First Successful Trapping and Transplanting of Antelope in Arizona has been in Cochise County." *Arizona Wildlife and Sportsman* (August): 6.

———. 1944. "Data on Elk and Antelope Hunting." *Arizona Wildlife and Sportsman* (6): 8.

Noell, J. I. 1953. "Deer Restocking." Federal Aid Project W-11-D-13, Work Plan 1, Job 3. Phoenix: Arizona Game and Fish Department.

O'Connor, J. 1939. *Game in the Desert.* New York: Derrydale Press.

———. 1940. "Conversation on Conservation." *Arizona Wild Life and Sportsman* 11 (February): 2, 4–5, 8.

———. 1943. "The Incredible Antelope." *Outdoor Life* (September): 22–23, 64.

———. 1945. "Antelope Aplenty … Pick Your Buck." *Outdoor Life* (May): 28–29, 107–108.

———. 1961. "The Pronghorn." In *Big Game Animals of North America*, 67–76. New York: E. P. Dutton and Co; also published in *Outdoor Life.*

Oliver, P. A. 1965. "Dredging the Braided Colorado: The Reclamation Era." *Bureau of Reclamation* (February): 14–15.

Park, R. H. 1930. Trapping mule deer at Big Springs Ranger Station. Annual report. Williams, AZ: Kaibab National Forest files.

Pettis, D. E. 1928 (September 1). Report of Arizona State Game Department, 1926–27. Arizona Game and Fish Commission report in Arizona State Library, Archives and Public Records, Phoenix.

Phillips, A. R., J. T. Marshall, and G. Monson. 1964. *The Birds of Arizona.* Tucson: Univ. of Arizona Press.

Phillips, J. C. July 1931. "Remarks on the Necessity for Special Protection to Mountain Sheep in Arizona—With Suggestions for Reserves Devoted to This Purpose." Typed manuscript. Smithsonian Institution, US Fish and Wildlife Service Collection, 1860–1961. Field Reports. Series 1, Record Unit 7176, Box 27, Folder 10.

Pinto, R. 2009. "The History of Ranching at Organ Pipe Cactus National Monument, Pima County, Arizona." Tucson: Preservation Studies Program, College of Architecture and Landscape Architecture, University of Arizona.

Powell, J. W. 1925. *The Exploration of the Colorado River of the West and Its Tributaries.* Washington, DC: Government Printing Office.

Powell, L. E. 1953a. "Investigation of the Bradshaw Mountain Area." Federal Aid Project W-53-R-3, Work Plan 5, Job 7, Completion Report. Phoenix: Arizona Game and Fish Department.

———. 1953b. "Investigation of the Moqui-Skinner Ridge Area." Federal Aid Project W-53-R-3, Work Plan 5, Job 6, Performance Report. Phoenix: Arizona Game and Fish Department.

———. 1954a. "Investigation of Bagdad-Kingman Area." Federal Aid Project W-53-R-4, Work Plan 5, Job 11, Performance Report. Phoenix: Arizona Game and Fish Department.

———. 1954b. "Investigation of the Moqui-Skinner Ridge Area." Federal Aid Project W-53-R-4, Work Plan 5, Job 10, Completion Report. Phoenix: Arizona Game and Fish Department.

———. 1955. "Investigation of Bagdad-Kingman Area." Federal Aid Project W-53-R-5, Work Plan 5, Job 11, Completion Report. Phoenix: Arizona Game and Fish Department.

———. 1956. "Investigation of Music Mountain-Grand Wash Area." Federal Aid Project W-53-R-6, Work Plan 5, Job 17. Phoenix: Arizona Game and Fish Department.

Prochaska, J. V. 1921 (received February 21, 1922). State Game Warden reports, 1917–21. Typewritten report. Arizona State Library, Archives and Public Records, Phoenix.

Pulich, W. M. 1947. "Waterfowl Survey of the Salt and Gila Rivers." Federal Aid Project 24-R-1. Phoenix: Arizona Game and Fish Commission.

———. 1948. "White-Winged Dove Survey." Federal Aid Project 24-R-2. Phoenix: Arizona Game and Fish Commission.

———. 1949. "Waterfowl Survey of the Colorado River." Federal Aid Project 24-R-1, Work Plan 1, Job 3. Phoenix: Arizona Game and Fish Commission.

Putnam, H. E. 1930. Report on catching and raising fawns. Annual report 1930. Williams, AZ: Kaibab National Forest files.

Rasmussen, D. I. 1941. "Biotic Communities of Kaibab Plateau, Arizona." *Ecological Monographs* 11:229–75.

Reed, J. J. 1958. "Investigation of Mazatzal Mountains." Federal Aid Project W-53-R-8, Work Plan 5, Job 22. Phoenix: Arizona Game and Fish Department.

———. 1959a. "Investigation of Areas North of the Colorado River." Federal Aid Project W-53-R-9, Work Plan 5, Job 24. Phoenix, Arizona Game and Fish Department.

———. 1959b. "Investigation of the Superstition Mountains." Federal Aid Project W-53-R-9, Work Plan 5, Job 25. Phoenix: Arizona Game and Fish Department.

Rice, I. 1959. *Valley Over the Hill.* San Antonio: Naylor Company.

Roak, J. C. 1920. Annual report. Williams, AZ: Kaibab National Forest files.

Roberts, P. H. 1963. *Hoof Prints on Forest Ranges.* San Antonio: Naylor Company.

Robinson, M. J. 2005. *Predatory Bureaucracy: The Extermination of Wolves and the Transformation of the West.* Boulder: Univ. Press of Colorado.

Roosevelt, K. 1920. *The Happy Hunting Grounds.* New York: Charles Scribner's Sons. Partially reprinted in *Counting Sheep: 20 Ways of Seeing Desert Bighorn,* edited by G. P. Nabhan, 1993. Tucson: Univ. of Arizona Press.

Roosevelt, T. 1908. *Outdoor Pastimes of an American Hunter.* New York: Charles Scribner's Sons.

———. 1913. "A Cougar Hunt on the Rim of the Grand Canyon." *Outlook* (October): 259–66.

Rowley, W. D. 1985. *US Forest Service Grazing and Rangelands: A History.* College Station: Texas A&M Press.

Russell, P. T. 1964. *Antelope of New Mexico.* Bulletin 12. Santa Fe: New Mexico Department of Game and Fish.

Russo, J. P. 1954. "Mittry Lake Investigation." Federal Aid Project W-53-R-4, Work Plan 5, Job 12. Phoenix: Arizona Game and Fish Department.

———. 1956a. "The Desert Bighorn Sheep in Arizona: A Research and Management Study." Federal Aid Project W-55. Phoenix: Arizona Game and Fish Department.

———. 1956b. "Investigation of Ajo Vicinity." Federal Aid Project W-53-R, Work Plan 5, Job 2. Phoenix: Arizona Game and Fish Department.

———. 1964. *The Kaibab North Deer Herd: Its History, Problems and Management.* Wildlife Bulletin 7. Phoenix: Arizona Game and Fish Department.

Saxton, E. H. 1978. "Saving the Desert Bighorn." *Desert Magazine* 41 (3): 16–18.

Schadle, D. 1959. "Water! Nothing is More Valuable to our Wildlife." *Wildlife Views* 6 (4): 17–35.

Schweinsburg, R. E. 1969. "Social Behavior of Collared Peccary (*Pecari tajacu*) in the Tucson Mountains." PhD dissertation, Univ. of Arizona.

Seymour, G. R. 1998. "The Civilian Conservation Corps in Arizona: A Context for Erosion-Control Features." *Kiva* 63 (4): 360–77.

Shaw, H. G. 1961. "Influence of Salt Cedar on White-Winged Doves in the Gila Valley." Federal Aid Project W-3-R, Special Report. Phoenix: Arizona Game and Fish Department.

———. 1990. *Soul Among Lions.* Tucson: Univ. of Arizona Press.

———. 2009. "Rangers, Robins and the Birth of Environmental Ed." *Arizona Wildlife Views* 52 (4): 28–30.

Shaw, H. G., and J. Jett. 1960. "Mourning Dove and White-Winged Dove Nesting in the Gila River Bottom Between Gillespie Dam and the Junction of the Salt and Gila Rivers, Maricopa County, Arizona." Federal Aid Project W-53-R, Special Report. Phoenix: Arizona Game and Fish Department.

Shaw, H. G., and R. H. Smith. 1977. "Habitat Use Patterns of Merriam's Turkey in Arizona." Federal Aid Project W-78-R, Work Plan 4, Job 11, Final Report. Phoenix: Arizona Game and Fish Department.

Shaw, H. G. and M. E. Weisenberger. 2011. *Twelve Hundred Miles by Horse and Burro: J. Stokely Ligon and New Mexico's First Breeding Bird Survey.* Tucson: University of Arizona Press.

Sheldon, C. 1993. *The Wilderness of the Southwest: Charles Sheldon's Quest for Desert Bighorn Sheep and Adventures With the Havasupai and Seri Indians.* Edited by N. B. Carmony and D. E. Brown. Salt Lake City: Univ. of Utah Press.

Shiras, G., III. 1924. "The Mule Deer of the Kaibab National Game Reserve." Unpublished letter in Kaibab National Forest files, cited in Rasmussen 1941.

Shumway, L. V., and K. C. Kartchner. 1990. *Frontier Fiddler: The Life of a Northern Arizona Pioneer.* Tucson: Univ. of Arizona Press.

Simms, W. H. 1938. "Minutes, February 3: Arizona Scout Committee for Preservation of the Bighorn Sheep." Phoenix: Roosevelt Council of Boy Scouts of America.

Smith, D. 2000. "Ben Avery." In N. L. Lewis 2000, 5–11. Mesa: Arizona Wildlife Federation.

Smith, R. H., and S. Gallizioli. 1963. "Gambel Quail Population Trend Techniques." Federal Aid Project W-78-R. Phoenix: Arizona Game and Fish Department.

Smith, R. H., and A. LeCount. 1979. "Some Factors Affecting Survival of Mule Deer Fawns." *Journal of Wildlife Management* 43:657–65.

Souder, J. A., and S. K. Fairfax. 1996. *State Trust Lands—History, Management, and Sustainable Use*. Lawrence: Univ. Press of Kansas.

Sowls, L. K. 1957. "Reproduction in the Audubon Cottontail in Arizona." *Journal of Mammalogy* 38:234–43.

———. 1960. "Results of a Banding Study of Gambel's Quail in Southern Arizona." *Journal of Wildlife Management* 24:185–90.

———. 1961a. "Gestation Period of the Collared Peccary." *Journal of Mammalogy* 42:425–26.

———. 1961b. "Hunter-Checking Stations for Collecting Data on the Collared Peccary *(Pecari tajacu)*." *Transactions of the North American Wildlife Conference* 26:496–505.

———. 1984. *The Peccaries*. Tucson: Univ. of Arizona Press.

Sowls, L. K., and P. S. Minnamon. 1963. "Glass Beads for Marking Home Ranges of Mammals." *Journal of Wildlife Management* 27:299–302.

Sowls, L. K., V. R. Smith, R. Jenness, R. E. Loan, and E. Regehr. 1961. "Chemical Composition and Physical Properties of the Milk of the Collared Peccary." *Journal of Mammalogy* 42:245–51.

Stair, J. 1958. "Dove Hunt Information and Dove Investigations." Federal Aid Project W-53-R-8. Phoenix: Arizona Game and Fish Department.

Streever, F. 1948. *The American Trail Hound*. New York: A. S. Barnes and Co.

Stein, P. H. 1990. "Homesteading in Arizona, 1862 to 1940: A guide to studying, evaluating, and preserving historic homesteads." Phoenix: Arizona State Historic Preservation Office and Arizona State Parks Board.

Stevens, M. 1943. *Meet Mr. Grizzly*. Albuquerque: Univ. of New Mexico Press.

Strode, J. W. 1924 (February 11). "Know Your Own State." Game and Fish Commission File; Governor's Files; Arizona State Library, Archives and Public Records, Phoenix.

Swank, W. G. 1958. *The Mule Deer in Arizona Chaparral and an Analysis of Other Important Deer Herds*. Wildlife Bulletin 3. Phoenix: Arizona Game and Fish Department.

Taylor, W. P. 1933. "Field Notes Filed in the US Biological Survey." Cited in Hoffmeister 1962.

———. 1934 (November 1). [House Rock Valley Wildlife Refuge] "Report to Chief of Biological Survey." Smithsonian Institution, US Fish and Wildlife Service Collection, 1860–1961. Field Reports. Series 1, Record Unit 7176, Box 30, Folder 18.

———. 1935a. *Ecology and Life History of the Porcupine* (Erethizon epixanthum) *as Related to the Forests of Arizona and the Southwestern United States*. Tucson: Univ. of Arizona, Biological Science Bulletin 3.

———. 1935b (January 10). "Memorandum on Proposed Game Preserves in Western Arizona." USDA Biological Survey, Smithsonian Institution, US Fish and Wildlife Service Collection, 1860–1961. Field Reports. Series 1, Record Unit 7176, Box 30, Folder 16.

———. 1935c (January 14). "Report on Proposed Preserves in Western Arizona." Smithsonian Institution, US Fish and Wildlife Service Collection, 1860–1961. Field Reports. Series 1, Record Unit 7176, Box 30, Folder 16.

———. 1935d (November 19). "Report on Proposed Cabeza Prieta Wildlife Refuge, Arizona." Smithsonian Institution, US Fish and Wildlife Service Collection, 1860–1961. Field Reports. Series 1, Record Unit 7176, Box 30, Folder 17.

Taylor, W. P., C. T. Vorhies, and P. B. Lister. 1935. "The Relation of Jack Rabbits to Grazing in Southern Arizona." *Journal of Forestry* 33:490–98.

Tinkham, E. R. 1941. "An Ecological Study of the Western White-Winged Dove *Melopelia asiatica mearnsi* in the Saguaro-Palo Verde, Mesquite and Oak Zones of Pima County in South Central Arizona." Special Report, Federal Aid Division. Phoenix: Arizona Game and Fish Commission.

———. 1942. "White-Winged Dove Investigations in Pima County, Arizona." Federal Aid Project 9-R. Phoenix: Arizona Game and Fish Commission.

Toll, R. W. 1933 (March 7). Letter to National Park Service Director Arno B. Cammerer, with report. Copy at Organ Pipe Cactus National Monument library, James M. Eden Collection, Section IV.

Trefethen, J. B. 1961. *An American Crusade for Wildlife*. New York: Boone and Crockett Club and Winchester Press. Reprinted Montana: Boone & Crockett Club, 1975.

Trigg, H. C. 1890. *The American Fox-Hound—Embracing a History of the Celebrated Trigg, Birdsong, and Maupin Strains*. Published by the author in Glasgow, Kentucky.

Turner, R. M., R. H. Webb, J. E. Bowers, and J. R. Hastings. 2003. *The Changing Mile Revisited*. Tucson: Univ. of Arizona Press.

US Congress. 1937. Senate Special Comm. on Conservation of Wildlife Restoration. *Wildlife and the Land: A Story of Regeneration*. 75th Cong., 1st sess.

USDA (United States Department of Agriculture). 1932. "Directory of Field Activities of the Biological Survey." Miscellaneous Publication 49. Washington, DC: Government Printing Office.

———. 1939. "Directory of Field Activities of the Biological Survey." Miscellaneous Publication 343. Washington, DC: Government Printing Office.

USDA Forest Service. 1915. "Game and Fish Handbook for Officers of the National Forests of Arizona and New Mexico." Albuquerque: District Forester, District 3.

Van Dyke, T. S. 1889. *Rifle, Rod and Gun in California—A Sporting Romance*. New York: Fords, Howard and Hulbert.

Vorhies, C. T. 1928. "Do Southwestern Quail Require Water?" *American Naturalist* 62:446–52.

———. 1935. "The Arizona Specimen of *Euderma maculatum*." *Journal of Mammalogy* 16:224–26.

———. 1945. *Water Requirements of Desert Animals in the Southwest*. Tucson: Univ. of Arizona, Agricultural Experiment Station Technical Bulletin 107:485–525.

Vorhies, C. T., and W. P. Taylor. 1922. *Life Histories of the Kangaroo Rat,* Dipodomys spectabilis spectabilis Merriam. Tucson: Univ. of Arizona, Agricultural Experiment Station Technical Bulletin 1:1–40.

———. 1933. *The Life Histories and Ecology of Jack Rabbits,* Lepus alleni *and* Lepus californicus *spp., in Relation to Grazing in Arizona*. Tucson: Univ. of Arizona, Agricultural Experiment Station Technical Bulletin 49:471–587.

———. 1940. *Life History and Ecology of the White-Throated Wood Rat,* Neotoma albigula albigula Hartley, *in Relation to Grazing in Arizona*. Tucson: Univ. of Arizona, Agricultural Experiment Station Technical Bulletin 86:455–529.

Waggoner, J. J. 1952. *History of the Cattle Industry in Southern Arizona,* 1540–1940. Tucson: Univ. of Arizona, Social Science Bulletin 20.

Wall, Dennis. 1996. *Western National Wildlife Refuges: Thirty-Six Havens From California to Texas*. Santa Fe: Museum of New Mexico Press.

Wallmo, C. O. 1949–51. "Fort Huachuca Wildlife Area Investigations, 1950–51." Charles T. Vorhies Game Habitat Research Projects 46-R1, R2, Completion Report. Phoenix: Arizona Game and Fish Department, Wildlife Restoration Division.

———. 1951. "Buffalo Forage Requirement Study." Federal Aid Project 46-R-2, Job 6, Wildlife Restoration Division, Completion Report. Phoenix: Arizona Game and Fish Commission.

Watkins, T. H. 1990. *Righteous Pilgrim: The Life and Times of Harold L. Ickes, 1874–1952*. New York: Henry Holt.

Watt, B. 2007. "Passing on the Legacy to Secure the Future for All: The North American Model of Wildlife Conservation." *Arizona Wildlife Views* 50 (3): 8–12.

Webb, E. L. 1960. "The Effect of Water Development on the Distribution and Abundance of Quail and Deer." Federal Aid Project W-78-R-4, Work Plan 4, Job 4, Completion Report. Phoenix: Arizona Game and Fish Department.

Webb, E. L., and S. Gallizioli. 1963. Federal Aid Project W-78-R-6, Work Plan 4, Job 4, Completion Report. Phoenix: Arizona Game and Fish Department.

Webb, P. M. 1953. "Statewide Wildlife Restocking Project." Federal Aid Project W-11-D-13. Phoenix: Arizona Game and Fish Department.

———. 1954. "Statewide Wildlife Restocking Project." Federal Aid Project W-11-D-14. Phoenix: Arizona Game and Fish Department.

———. 1955. "Statewide Wildlife Restocking Project." Federal Aid Project W-11-D-15. Phoenix: Arizona Game and Fish Department.

———. 1956. "Statewide Wildlife Restocking Project." Federal Aid Project W-11-D-16. Phoenix: Arizona Game and Fish Department.

Webb, P. M., and R. Robeck. 1963. "Statewide Wildlife Restocking Project." Federal Aid Project W-11-D-23. Phoenix: Arizona Game and Fish Department.

Webb, P. M., and E. L. Webb. 1954. "Deer Restocking." Federal Aid Project W-11-D-14, Work Plan 1, Job 3. Phoenix: Arizona Game and Fish Department.

Weese, A. O. 1941. Letter to National Park Service, Outlining a Trip to Organ-Pipe Cactus National Monument and Recommending Its Continued Status. Smithsonian Institution Archives, US Fish and Wildlife Service, 1860–1961. Field Reports. Series 1, Record Unit 7176, Box 31, Folder 7.

Welles, P. 1943. "Status of the Bighorn Sheep in the Santa Catalina and Tucson Mountain Areas." Unpublished Pittman-Robertson Quarterly Report, June. Phoenix: Arizona Game and Fish Commission.

———. 1944. "Findings of the Bighorn Sheep Study in the Santa Catalina Mountains." Unpublished Pittman-Robertson Project 9-R, Special Report. Phoenix: Arizona Game and Fish Commission.

Wetmore, A. 1920. "Observations on the Habits of White-Winged Doves." *Condor* 22:140–46.

Wigal, D.D. 1973. "A Survey of the Nesting Habits of the White-Winged Dove in Arizona." Special Report 2. Phoenix: Arizona Game and Fish Department.

Willard, G. M. 1914 (December 31). "Report of the State Game Warden of Arizona." Published report to Governor George W. P. Hunt. Arizona State Library, Archives and Public Records, Phoenix.

———. 1916. "Introduction to Proclamation of Bird Day." *Arizona Bird Day Pamphlet*. Arizona State Library, Archives and Public Records, Phoenix.

Willard, G. M. to Governor George Hunt. 1923 (var.). Arizona Game and Fish Department files, Arizona State Library, Archives and Public Records, Phoenix.

Willard Profile. 1916. Profile of George MacDonald Willard, vertical file, Arizona State Library, Archives and Public Records, Phoenix.

Wood, T., and J. K. Wood. 2007. *The Other Side of the Mountain*. Tucson: Tom Wood Books.

Wright, J. T. 1947. "Report on Progress." Federal Aid Project W-27-R, Completion Report. Phoenix: Arizona Game and Fish Department.

———. 1950. "The Cooperative Kaibab North Livestock-Deer Forage Relationship Study." Federal Aid Project W-27-R-1 and W-27-R-2, Completion Report. Phoenix: Arizona Game and Fish Department.

———. 1952. "Investigation and Evaluation of Wildlife Use of Water Developments." Federal Aid Project W-62-R-1, Work Plan 1, Job 1, Completion Report, Jobs 1A–1E. Phoenix: Arizona Game and Fish Department.

———. 1953. "Investigation and Evaluation of Wildlife Use of Water Developments." Federal Aid Project W-62-R-2, Completion Report. Phoenix: Arizona Game and Fish Department.

———. 1959. *Desert Wildlife: A Research Study.* Federal Aid Project W-62-R. Wildlife Bulletin 6. Phoenix: Arizona Game and Fish Department.

Wright, J. T., and D. P. Schadle. 1954 (May). "The Evaluation of Water Developments in Wildlife Habitat Improvement." Federal Aid Project W-62-R-3, Completion Report. Phoenix: Arizona Game and Fish Department.

Wright, J. T., and E. L. Webb. 1955. "The Evaluation of Water Development in Wildlife Habitat Improvement." Federal Aid Project W-62-R-4, Completion Report. Phoenix: Arizona Game and Fish Department.

———. 1956. "The Evaluation of Water Development in Wildlife Habitat Improvement." Federal Aid Project W-62-R-5, Completion Report. Phoenix: Arizona Game and Fish Department.

———. 1957 (June). "The Evaluation of Water Development in Wildlife Habitat Improvement." Federal Aid Project W-62-R-6, Final Report. Phoenix: Arizona Game and Fish Department.

Young, C. C. 2001. *In the Absence of Predators.* Lincoln and London: Univ. of Nebraska Press.

INDEX

Page numbers followed by f indicate figures; t indicates tables; n indicates notes.

ANIMALS

Mammals

Birds

Reptiles, Amphibians and Fish

Invertebrates

PLANTS

PEOPLE

GOVERNMENT AGENCIES, INDIAN TRIBES, NONGOVERNMENTAL ORGANIZATIONS AND OTHER GROUPS

PLACES